SYNTHESIS: LEGAL READING, REASONING, AND WRITING

ASPEN PUBLISHERS

SYNTHESIS

Legal Reading, Reasoning, and Writing

Third Edition

Deborah A. Schmedemann
Professor of Law

Christina L. Kuntz
Professor of Law

both of William Mitchell College of Law

Wolters Kluwer
Law & Business

AUSTIN   BOSTON   CHICAGO   NEW YORK   THE NETHERLANDS

Aspen Publishers
Attn: Permissions Department
76 Ninth Avenue, 7th Floor
New York, NY 10011-5201

To contact Customer Care, e-mail customer.care@aspenpublishers.com,
call 1-800-234-1660, fax 1-800-901-9075, or mail correspondence to:

Aspen Publishers
Attn: Order Department
PO Box 990
Frederick, MD 21705

Printed in the United States of America.

1 2 3 4 5 6 7 8 9 0

ISBN 978-0-7355-6283-7

Library of Congress Cataloging-in-Publication Data

Schmedemann, Deborah A., 1956-
    Synthesis : legal reading, reasoning, and writing/Deborah A. Schmedemann,
Christina L. Kunz. — 3rd ed.
        p. cm.
    Includes bibliographical references and index.
    ISBN 978-0-7355-6283-7
    1. Legal composition.   2. Law—United States—Interpretation and
construction.   3. Forensic oratory.   I. Kunz, Christina L.   II. Title.

    KF250.S36 2007
    808'.06634—dc22

                                                                    2007009695

About Wolters Kluwer Law & Business

Wolters Kluwer Law & Business is a leading provider of research information and workflow solutions in key specialty areas. The strengths of the individual brands of Aspen Publishers, CCH, Kluwer Law International and Loislaw are aligned within Wolters Kluwer Law & Business to provide comprehensive, in-depth solutions and expert-authored content for the legal, professional and education markets.

CCH was founded in 1913 and has served more than four generations of business professionals and their clients. The CCH products in the Wolters Kluwer Law & Business group are highly regarded electronic and print resources for legal, securities, antitrust and trade regulation, government contracting, banking, pension, payroll, employment and labor, and healthcare reimbursement and compliance professionals.

Aspen Publishers is a leading information provider for attorneys, business professionals and law students. Written by preeminent authorities, Aspen products offer analytical and practical information in a range of specialty practice areas from securities law and intellectual property to mergers and acquisitions and pension/ benefits. Aspen's trusted legal education resources provide professors and students with high-quality, up-to-date and effective resources for successful instruction and study in all areas of the law.

Kluwer Law International supplies the global business community with comprehensive English-language international legal information. Legal practitioners, corporate counsel and business executives around the world rely on the Kluwer Law International journals, loose-leafs, books and electronic products for authoritative information in many areas of international legal practice.

Loislaw is a premier provider of digitized legal content to small law firm practitioners of various specializations. Loislaw provides attorneys with the ability to quickly and efficiently find the necessary legal information they need, when and where they need it, by facilitating access to primary law as well as state-specific law, records, forms and treatises.

Wolters Kluwer Law & Business, a unit of Wolters Kluwer, is headquartered in New York and Riverwoods, Illinois. Wolters Kluwer is a leading multinational publisher and information services company.

DEDICATION

We dedicate this book to Professor Ken Kirwin, who has co-coordinated the first-year writing course at William Mitchell with great enthusiasm and creativity; to Darlene Finch, who has administered the course with great skill and dedication; and to the terrific attorneys who take time from the practice of law to teach legal writing at the College.

On a personal note, we dedicate this book to Craig, Mary, Karen, Keith, Anna Mary, Barb, and Joan; and to Rachel, Barbara, Carol, Suzy, Ruth, and Hal.

SUMMARY OF CONTENTS

CONTENTS

CHAPTER 1

INTRODUCTION: THE LAWYER'S ROLES AND THE LEGAL SYSTEM

CHAPTER 2

THE STRUCTURE OF LEGAL RULES

CHAPTER 6

INTERPRETING STATUTES 63

CHAPTER 7

READING COMMENTARY 75

CHAPTER 8

APPLYING A RULE TO FACTS: DEDUCTIVE REASONING 79

CHAPTER 19

ADVOCACY WRITING IN THE APPELLATE SETTING: THE FUNCTION AND FORMAT OF THE APPELLATE BRIEF 201

CHAPTER 20

ADVANCED ADVOCACY 227

APPENDIX III.A

CITATION: *ALWD CITATION MANUAL*   455

APPENDIX III.B

CITATION: *THE BLUEBOOK*   465

Appendix IV

LIST OF EXHIBITS

LIST OF STUDIES
AND ETHICS BOXES

PREFACE

If you are reading this book, you probably have heard the phrase, "thinking like a lawyer." This book is about thinking like a lawyer—thinking that is both structured and open-ended, expansive and precise, rigorous and creative; thinking that is grounded in careful reading of legal texts and insightful understanding of the situations of real people; thinking that is both intellectually rewarding in its own right and critically important to the well-being of clients.

We worked on this book for six years before we came up with the first word in its title: synthesis. We chose "synthesis" as the flagship concept for this book for several reasons. According to the eleventh edition of Merriam Webster's Collegiate Dictionary, "synthesis" means "the composition or combination of parts or elements so as to form a whole." The two chief forms of law, cases and codes, both consist of parts that form the whole. Legal reasoning consists of three processes: deductive reasoning, reasoning by example, and policy analysis. Every legal document you will write has standard components that work together to form the whole. Furthermore, the overall process of legal analysis combines reading, reasoning, and writing to form a whole.

"Synthesis" also means "the dialectic combination of thesis and antithesis into a higher stage of truth." In turn, "dialectic" means, "any systematic reasoning . . . that juxtaposes opposed or contradictory ideas and usually seeks to resolve their conflict." Much of the time, law is about disputes between people, conflicting interests, opposed or contradictory ideas. To resolve conflict in a fair and just way is the purpose of the legal system and the highest calling of a lawyer.

This book is itself a synthesis of elements that, we believe, make for effective learning of the skills discussed here. As you will see, this book:

- describes each skill in general terms, setting out steps to follow, identifying factors to consider, detailing criteria for your work, exploring pertinent ethical principles, and providing insights from studies of legal writing as well as cases discussing unethical legal writing;
- presents many processes and products of legal analysis not only in text but also in drawings or diagrams;
- draws analogies between the skills discussed here and other fields of endeavor, such as architecture;

- demonstrates the skills through the HomeElderCare case file, which documents a case from initial client interview to appellate argument; and
- provides an opportunity for practice in the exercises, which explore an evolving area of tort law.

During each of the fourteen years we have worked on this book or its predecessors, about 300 students have used these materials in the first-year writing course at William Mitchell College of Law. Each year, twenty-five to thirty practicing lawyers, teaching the course as adjunct professors, have taught from these materials. We have learned much from our "co-authors" and are pleased to pass their insights along to you in the following pages.

We hope you are stimulated by the process of learning to think like a lawyer. And we hope you use what you learn from this book to think like a highly competent, creative, and caring lawyer.

Note to professors: For those of you who have read or used the second edition of this text, we hope you will be pleased to discover the following changes:

- We have included a brief preview of deductive reasoning in Chapter 2, so that students better appreciate, right away, why understanding rules is so important.
- We have pulled out IRAC from the chapter on the office memo discussion into its own chapter on rule-driven writing. The new chapter serves as the transition from reasoning to writing. Thus it facilitates assigning a brief IRAC as an early writing exercise and discussing IRAC in the context of a document other than the office memo.
- The discussion of the organization of the office memo is considerably streamlined: in addition to removing the IRAC coverage, we have consolidated the discussion of large- and middle-scale organization.
- To broaden the scope of the book, we have added coverage of deal-oriented practice in the chapters discussing office memos. One of the two memos in the HomeElderCare case and the advice letter are now deal-oriented.
- We have added a chapter on demand letters, which serves as a transition from the advice letter to the motion practice unit. In addition, we have included sample demand letters (a complete letter aimed at a lay reader, a partial letter aimed at the opponent's lawyer) and exercises pertaining to demand letters.
- The postscript to the exercises, which pertain to dram shop liability, notes several significant developments since the previous edition. Those changes can be the basis for further exercises or discussion of the interaction between court and legislature.

We hope you will let us know how this third edition works for you and your students.

Deborah A. Schmedemann
Christina L. Kuntz
St. Paul, Minnesota
April 2007

ACKNOWLEDGMENTS

We had the good fortune to be able to write and revise this book during nearly a decade of classroom use. We were able to revise each chapter many times and to incorporate the valuable suggestions of our students and our legal writing faculty. Also important was the wholehearted and long-term support of this project by Deans James Hogg, Harry Farnsworth, and Allen Easley.

We also had the good fortune of working with talented research assistants, many of whom worked on bits and pieces of the book in the course of their other duties. We note here those who made major contributions: Anthony Massaros and Katie Crosby Lehmann wrote the initial drafts of the HomeElderCare office memos, motion practice memoranda, and appellate briefs; they also delivered the appellate oral argument that appears in transcript form in the HomeElderCare case file. Tony also developed the library for the torts exercises. Lynn Bebeau Psihos, Kerry Cork, Renee Michalow, and Jodi Sharrow worked closely with us to produce this multi-faceted book. We thank them for their excellent work.

Our colleagues generously contributed their insights and feedback on a wide variety of topics: Professor Kenneth Kirwin as a fellow co-coordinator of the first-year writing course, Professor Daniel Kleinberger on rule structure and levels of organization, Professor Russell Pannier on logic, Professors Eric Janus and Robert Oliphant on civil procedure, Professor Phebe Haugen on living wills, and Professor Curtis Stine on legal issues affecting the elderly. Professor Kirwin, Professor Stine, and Professor Denise Roy served as the judges for the appellate oral argument that appears in the transcript in the HomeElderCare case file.

An evolving manuscript of this size and complexity depends on high-quality production work. Cal Bonde contributed superb word processing skills and overall document management for our countless revisions; in recent years she was assisted by Linda Thorstad. Dawn Ives copied and bound each year's manuscript for our students. Early on, Judy Holmes provided excellent administrative support for the first-year course, Legal Research and Writing, as well as this book. More recently, Darlene Finch has done a stellar job of administering the new first-year course, Writing & Representation: Advice & Persuasion, and nurturing the revision of this book. We are grateful to each one of them for every way in which they helped us bring this project to fruition.

The original encouragement for this project came from some of our favorite people at what was then the law division of Little, Brown and Company. Rick Heuser, Carol McGeehan, and Nick Niemeyer each played an important role in moving this book forward. Carol McGeehan has our special gratitude for bridging the contract transition from Little, Brown to Aspen Law and Business. Elizabeth Kenny, Ellen Greenblatt, and Melody Davies on the editorial end of the process, and Karen Quigley and Kathy Porzio in design and production matters, skillfully brought the first edition to press for Aspen Law and Business. With equal skill, the following teams brought the second and third editions, respectively, to press: Curt Berkowitz, Elizabeth Kenny, Barbara Rappaport, Karen Quigley, and Kathy Porzio; Christie Rears, Peter Skagestad, Elizabeth Kenny, Marla Cook, and Melissa Mathlin.

This textbook owes much of its richness to the ideas of colleagues in the field of legal reading, reasoning, and writing across the country. Their presentations, publications, and personal observations over the years have made legal writing a rigorous and vibrant discipline. We deeply appreciate being part of a national community of legal writing teachers with a strong ethic of teaching each other.

Working on this book requires long hours and intense concentration. From the bottom of our hearts, we thank our families, friends, and colleagues for the many ways in which they supported us and worked around us while we worked on this book.

We also would like to acknowledge those publishers who permitted us to reprint copyrighted material in this book:

Illustration 11.6: Lynn B. Squires et al., *Legal Writing in a Nutshell* 95-98 (2d ed. 1996). Reprinted with permission of Thomson West.

"The Road Not Taken," from The Poetry of Robert Frost, edited by Edward Connery Lathem and published by Jonathan Cape. Reprinted by permission of The Random House Group Ltd.

HomeElderCare case file:

Dick Weatherston's Assoc'd Mech. Servs. v. Minn. Mut. Life Ins. Co., 100 N.W.2d 819 (Minn. 1960): Reprinted with permission of Thomson West.

Buckley v. Humason, 52 N.W. 385 (Minn. 1892): Reprinted with permission of Thomson West.

Minn. Stat. § 481.02 (1992): Reprinted with permission of the Revisor of Statutes, State of Minnesota.

Minn. Stat. §§ 145B.0l.-.06 (1992): Reprinted with permission of the Revisor of Statutes, State of Minnesota.

Peterson v. Hovland (In re Peterson's Estate), 42 N.W.2d 59 (Minn. 1950): Reprinted with permission of Thomson West.

Gardner v. Conway, 48 N.W.2d 788 (Minn. 1951): Reprinted with permission of Thomson West.

Annotation, *Activities of Law Clerks as Illegal Practice of Law*, 13 A.L.R.3d 1137 (1967): Reprinted with permission of Thomson West.

8 Dunnell's Minn. Digest Contracts § 3.20 [at 163-64] (4th ed. 1990): Reprinted from *Dunnell's Minnesota Digest* with permission. Copyright 1990 Matthew Bender & Company, Inc., a member of the LexisNexis Group. All rights reserved.

Howard Orenstein, David Bishop & Leigh D. Mathison, *Minnesota's Living Will . . .*, Bench & B. Minn., Aug. 1989, at 21. Reprinted with permission of Howard Orenstein, David Bishop, and Leigh D. Mathison.

Restatement (Second) of Contracts § 181 (1979) (with comments and illustrations): Copyright 1981 by The American Law Institute. Reproduced with permission. All rights reserved.

E. Allan Farnsworth, *Contracts* § 5.6, at 377-79 (2d ed. 1990): Copyright 1990 by E. Allan Farnsworth, McCormack Professor of Law, Columbia University. Reprinted with permission of Patricia Farnsworth, Executrix of Prof. Farnsworth's Estate.

Exercises:

Moore v. Bunk, 228 A.2d 510 (Conn. 1967): Reprinted with permission of Thomson West.

West's Connecticut General Statutes Annotated § 102 (1990): Reprinted with permission of Thomson West.

SYNTHESIS: LEGAL READING, REASONING, AND WRITING

1

INTRODUCTION:

THE LAWYER'S ROLES

AND THE LEGAL SYSTEM

A. Introduction
B. The Lawyer's Roles
C. The Legal System
D. About This Book
E. The HomeElderCare Situation

> Every calling is great when greatly pursued.
> —Oliver Wendell Holmes
> "The Law," *Speeches* (1913)

A. INTRODUCTION

"A lawyer, as a member of the legal profession, is a representative of clients, an officer of the legal system and a public citizen having special responsibility for the quality of justice," according to the Preamble to the Model Rules of Professional Conduct for lawyers, drafted by the American Bar Association. In fulfilling these roles, what do lawyers actually do? And how do legal reasoning and writing fit in?

B. THE LAWYER'S ROLES

1. Representing Clients

Whether law practice is a calling, an art, a science, or a business, practicing law entails helping clients solve their problems. The practice of law encompasses a very wide range of tasks and settings. In broad strokes, most practices can be categorized as transactional practice or litigation.

As a transactional lawyer, a lawyer acts prospectively, counseling the client about the law that governs actions the client may take. The lawyer identifies options, assesses their legal implications, and often executes the option selected by the client. Transactional lawyers draft wills, write employee handbooks, prepare stock prospectuses, and review license applications.

A litigator acts primarily retrospectively, pleading the client's case before a decision-making body so as to obtain a fair and favorable resolution of an existing dispute between the client and the opponent. The lawyer constructs legal arguments based on the facts and the law, then presents them, sometimes orally, sometimes in writing, sometimes both. Litigators prosecute or defend an individual charged with a crime, represent an employer in labor arbitration, present a landowner's argument before a zoning commission, or argue before an appeals court on behalf of a patent-holder.

In many situations, a litigator "bargains in the shadow of the law."[1] That is, the dispute is not actually resolved by someone else's decision, but rather through negotiation. Many minor disputes are resolved by the parties themselves. Major disputes, where much is at stake, the facts are murky, the law is unclear, or the parties are less than congenial, are resolved by lawyers for the opposing parties through negotiation. For example, one side may assert that a jury would award substantial damages; the other may argue that the case would not get to the jury because the judge would quickly dismiss the case. Most likely, the negotiated outcome would be somewhere between the parties' valuations of the case, reflecting not only the parties' legal positions but also many other factors, such as their respective tolerance of or aversion to risk, economic situations, and desires for privacy or publicity.

In all of these instances, one of the lawyer's fundamental contributions is to develop and present a legal analysis of the client's situation. The lawyer places the facts of the client's experience within certain legal rules and assigns to the client's experience the legal significance suggested by the rules.

> [I]n the law: we convert immediate experience into the subject of thought of a particular kind, which has at its center the question of meaning: what this event means, and should mean, in the language of the law; and what that language itself means, as a way in which we articulate our deepest values and attain collective being.[2]

This assignment of legal meaning, or legal analysis, occurs through several steps, as depicted in Exhibit 1.1. Although the exhibit shows the usual order of steps, legal analysis is not entirely linear, as signified by the arrows looping back to earlier steps. Ethical considerations enter in at every step.

---

1. See Robert D. Cooter, Stephen Marks, & Robert Mnookin, *Bargaining in the Shadow of the Law: A Testable Model of Strategic Behavior*, 11 J. Legal Studies 225 (1982).
2. James Boyd White, *Meaning in the Life of the Lawyer*, 26 Cumb. L. Rev. 763, 770 (1996).

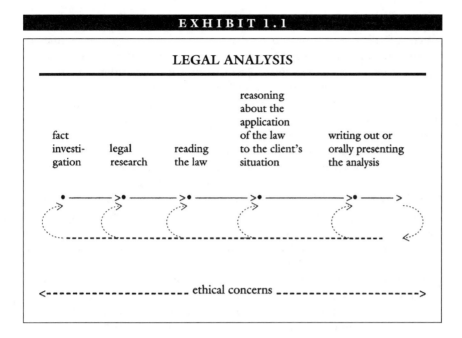

Of course, the client ultimately controls the case, whether it is a deal or a dispute. The client may rely not only on the lawyer's expertise, but also on the counsel of other professionals as well as the client's own experience and values. There is no such thing as a purely "legal problem."

Nor is legal analysis radically different from the types of analysis performed by other professionals. Rather, sound legal analysis resembles other forms of rigorous problem-solving. Legal analysis requires the engineer's precision, the literary critic's close attention to text, the physician's openness to alternatives, and the minister's concern for social good and individual well-being. Thus, no matter what background you bring to the law, your skills will be useful in the study and practice of law.

2. Serving the Legal System and Justice

As lawyers help clients solve problems, they also serve the public. Lawyers act as officers of the legal system and public citizens with a special responsibility for the quality of justice in several ways.

First, a transactional lawyer aids in the implementation of the law. The lawyer advises the client on how to conform its conduct to the law and implements a legally permitted solution. The public benefits from the client's law-abiding conduct.

Second, a litigator, as a gatekeeper into the legal system, screens out frivolous claims and guides real disputes into litigation or less formal and less costly forms of dispute resolution. There, the lawyer fairly depicts the facts and the law. The public benefits from fair and efficient resolution of disputes.

Third, lawyers participate in the law-making process. Law is a reiterative system of client problems and legal rules. Lawmakers create legal rules in response to conflicts brought to their attention—typically by the disputants' lawyers. The new rule then applies to other persons involved in similar situations. When the application of an existing rule proves troublesome, a new conflict arises, and lawmakers may revise the rule—again with the guidance of the disputants' lawyers. Thus, when a lawyer pleads a client's case, the lawyer also influences the direction of the law for the future.

Fulfilling these various roles often entails difficult judgment calls. For example, the lawyer must decide how to protect client confidences, how to present testimony in court, and whether to facilitate transactions that push the boundaries of the law. In making these decisions, a lawyer is guided by his or her own personal values, as well as codes of professional ethics, which set the standards by which lawyers are judged.

In addition to serving clients and the legal system, lawyers are called upon to serve justice. Phrased in the terms of ethics codes, lawyers have a professional responsibility to engage in pro bono publico, which means "for the public good." The ABA's Model Rule 6.1 recognizes that many activities serve the public good. Representing people of limited means for free and representing organizations that aim to serve people of limited means for free are emphasized in the ABA rule and are for many lawyers the essence of pro bono. Other options include working for civil or public rights, representing community organizations, and participating in activities aimed at improving the law or legal system. Failing to perform pro bono will not lead to professional discipline, yet many lawyers perform pro bono and find it very meaningful and deeply rewarding.

3. Some Examples

To provide a glimpse into law practice, we asked practicing attorneys from a range of settings to describe their day-to-day activities. Here are several responses from litigators in private law firms:

> I am on the phone five hours a day talking to clients and other lawyers. I listen sympathetically to everything they say, guide them, and lay the foundation for future calls when bad news may come. Talking to plaintiffs is a matter of providing reassurance, much like in the ministry, but you need to be efficient. I also go to hearings, write briefs, take clients to lunch.

> I write—research and write. I'm usually part of a team. We spend lots of time developing a strategy, constructing arguments, figuring out what will happen down the road. I spend some time in client contact, advising them. Sometimes I go to court (motion practice and appellate work). I take depositions and spend a lot of time working with documents. [Note: A deposition is a pre-trial interview of a witness or a party.]

> Currently I am setting up mediation for a large piece of litigation. [Note: Mediation is a negotiation process aided by a third-party

neutral.] So I talk on the phone with ten other attorneys. I keep in mind what the client wants, what the issues are, what procedures to follow. At the same time, I'm preparing for trial, in case mediation doesn't work: preparing a chronology of the facts, deciding which witnesses to call, analyzing evidentiary issues. I try mediation to avoid the time and expenses of trial for everyone, yet prepare for trial so I know the case well and can anticipate what the other side will do.

Here are two responses from transactional lawyers in private firms.

I talk on the phone a lot of the day. I attend periodic day-long board meetings of my clients. The week before, I prepare opinions on new issues and status reports on pending matters. During the meetings, I advise on matters that were referred earlier, answer questions that come up. When I leave the meeting, I have a list of things to do for the next meeting. I consult with the client's in-house staff often, indeed on a daily basis.

I work for government entities or private individuals that want to build and need funding. I write documents that run over 100 pages to accomplish the deal and draft opinions about the deal. These must be written by an attorney in the "red book," a guild-like system.

Other lawyers work within their clients, such as corporations or the government. Here are excerpts from an in-house corporate lawyer and a state assistant attorney general:

We handle every day-to-day problem that comes in the door. For example, how do we fire an employee, accept service of process on an employee who is hiding from it, draft articles of incorporation, manage litigation, pay off a mortgage, arrange executive compensation, modify an employee handbook? I do whatever I can to comply with the law and get the project off my desk: research, draft a letter or call someone, talk to the other side, talk to the client (the corporation's officers) or employees. I try to see what the problem is and what I can do to fix it, by contract, or phone call, or letter, or getting people to work together to work it out, or by paying a little money.

I do a lot of litigation—courtroom work—and heavy-duty brief writing. I research the applicable law, both sides of it; synthesize the cases; write the brief in support of the client's position. I write it to win, by making all arguments within the bounds of ethical conduct. Then I review it, file it, prepare for oral argument. I also advise the department I work for, when the department wants to do something new. So I research, brainstorm, think about it, give the best opinion as to whether the new action will withstand legal action. When there is a pervasive problem, I advise on initiating legislative action and consider: What is the evil to remedy? What is the solution? How can we write up the solution so it will be understandable to many people?

The following two excerpts are from lawyers on either side of the criminal justice system, a prosecutor and a public defender:

> I review police reports and decide what offense to charge. I advise police officers in ongoing investigations by answering the question on the other end of a ringing phone. I try cases: plan out the presentation of the evidence, meet with witnesses, prepare exhibits. I negotiate out most cases, since ninety-eight percent settle, which entails offering a plea to the defense attorney and agreeing to the sentence. I also research, write, and argue cases on appeal.

> My time is spent in client interviews, brief writing, oral arguments, as well as some trial court hearings. Because our clients have an absolute right to an appeal, we are not bound by professional responsibility rules on frivolous appeals, but we do retain the right to choose issues. It takes creativity to find colorable issues sometimes, although some cases do have real appealable issues.

Finally, the following excerpt describes a lawyer's pro bono representation of an Ethiopian man seeking asylum in the United States, based on his well-founded fear of persecution in his own country:

> At our first meeting—I'll never forget—he said to me, "If you can do this thing for me, you will be my brother." This sticks in your mind and is considerable motivation. I knew very little about the Oromo people. So I did research on the Internet and traditional library research, gathered material from Amnesty International and the State Department, and learned from my client. I came to know his story by sitting with him and talking to him; over six months, we met maybe twenty times for about an hour. We'd just talk about the asylum case—we didn't socialize. I wanted to keep this clinical, so I could remain dispassionate and objective. The first meeting, I got maybe five or ten percent of the story; he didn't open up with gruesome details until the third or fourth or fifth meeting. I needed to get him ready to talk about his situation before the asylum officer—he had to have some sort of interior distance from it.
> So then I wrote a letter, explaining why my client should get asylum and going through the three or four factors in the rule about well-founded fear. And I went with him to the interview with the asylum officer. The lawyer doesn't say anything until the end of the interview when you bring your client back to inconsistencies or other troublesome parts of the interview. Happily, my client was granted asylum.

As these excerpts demonstrate, the day-to-day activities of law practice vary, depending on the lawyer's setting. Yet all lawyers aim to solve problems for their clients by assigning to them a legal meaning, that is, by use of legal processes and by reference to legal rules.

HOW IMPORTANT IS LEGAL WRITING?

In an American Bar Foundation survey of lawyers practicing in various settings, lawyers consistently identified "written communication" and "oral communication" as the two most important skills.[3]

In a similar study, over 95 percent of the lawyers rated the following skills as the most important:

- ability to diagnose and plan solutions for legal problems (97.9%),
- ability in legal analysis and legal reasoning (97.5%),
- written communication (97.2%), and
- oral communication (96.8%).[4]

---

3. Section of Legal Education and Admissions to the Bar, *Lost Words: The Economic, Ethical, and Professional Effects of Bad Legal Writing* 7-14 (1993) (Report by Bryant G. Garth).
4. John Sonsteng & David Camarotto, *Minnesota Lawyers Evaluate Law Schools, Training, and Job Satisfaction*, 26 Wm. Mitchell L. Rev. 327, 337 (2000).

C. THE LEGAL SYSTEM

The American legal system is rather complex, reflecting the intricate structure of American government. Exhibit 1.2 presents the major institutions of our government and the forms of law each creates.

The three *levels* of government are federal, state, and local. The federal government generally occupies the highest position in a hierarchy, with state government in the middle and local government at the lowest position. In some areas of law, the federal government is the primary lawmaker, with state and local governments either supplementing the federal law or being precluded from lawmaking. In other fields, state or local law is the traditional and predominant source of law.

Under our tripartite system of government, the three *branches* of government are the legislature, the judiciary, and the executive. Each has its essential function in the legal system: the legislature making the law, the judiciary interpreting and applying the law to resolve specific disputes, and the executive implementing the law. There is, however, considerable overlap. For example, the judiciary makes law via the common law (cases decided when there is no pertinent statute) and court rules, and the executive branch also may do so by executive order. Administrative agencies in the executive

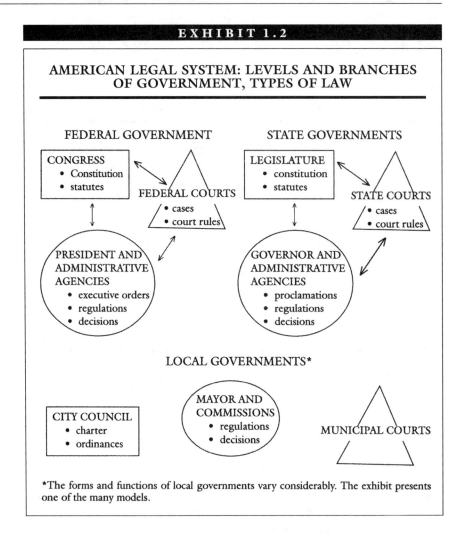

EXHIBIT 1.2

AMERICAN LEGAL SYSTEM: LEVELS AND BRANCHES OF GOVERNMENT, TYPES OF LAW

FEDERAL GOVERNMENT   STATE GOVERNMENTS

CONGRESS
• Constitution
• statutes

FEDERAL COURTS
• cases
• court rules

LEGISLATURE
• constitution
• statutes

STATE COURTS
• cases
• court rules

PRESIDENT AND ADMINISTRATIVE AGENCIES
• executive orders
• regulations
• decisions

GOVERNOR AND ADMINISTRATIVE AGENCIES
• proclamations
• regulations
• decisions

LOCAL GOVERNMENTS*

MAYOR AND COMMISSIONS
• regulations
• decisions

CITY COUNCIL
• charter
• ordinances

MUNICIPAL COURTS

*The forms and functions of local governments vary considerably. The exhibit presents one of the many models.

branch resolve specific disputes much as courts do, although within limited spheres.

The genius of the tripartite system lies not only in the allocation of functions to each branch, but also in the checks and balances among the branches. For example, the judiciary may overturn legislation or agency actions that exceed the legislature's or agency's power. The legislature may overturn decisions of the courts deemed contrary to the public's will.

The three branches and three levels of government engage in a continual process of lawmaking that can yield complex results. Thus, it is not surprising that a substantial body of legal scholarship explains the law and proposes reforms. Legal scholarship, also called "commentary" or "secondary authority" because it is not the law itself, is written by lawyers, law professors, law students, and occasionally lawmakers. Although commentary is not itself law, it can be a helpful aid to legal analysis.

D. About This Book

This book covers three linked processes: reading the law, reasoning about the application of the rules of law to your client's situation, and presenting your legal analysis. Thus, this book has three major units:

- Chapters 2 through 7 cover how to read legal materials: cases, codes, and legal commentary.
- Chapters 8 and 9 cover three forms of legal reasoning: deductive reasoning, reasoning by example, and policy analysis.
- Chapters 10 through 19 cover how to present the analysis of a client's situation, in an internal office memo, letters to the client or opposing counsel, a motion practice memorandum to a trial court, a brief to an appellate court, and oral argument before one or more judges.

Throughout, the book emphasizes four criteria by which to judge all of your work: (1) completeness, (2) correctness, (3) coherence, and (4) comprehensibility. In addition, advisory work is judged by its creativity, and advocacy work is judged by how well it convinces the reader.

Three appendices to this text cover facets of writing that are critical to any document you may write as a lawyer: the writing process (Appendix I); paragraph design, sentence structure, and word usage (Appendix II); and citation (Appendices III.A and III.B). We encourage you to consult them from time to time as you refine your written work. Appendix IV briefly covers the drafting of a contract—an important skill that is both related to but also different from the analytical writing discussed in the rest of the book.

This book offers various presentations of each skill. Each skill is first described in general terms. For many topics, we have included diagrams and analogies.

Each skill is then demonstrated in the context of a representative (although fictional) client problem: the HomeElderCare case. Notes regarding the HomeElderCare situation appear on the next page. The HomeElderCare case file at the end of the book contains some of the legal authorities consulted, notes taken along the way, final written documents, and an oral argument transcript. The facts unfold as the file progresses, as indeed a client's situation unfolds during the course of representation. Note that the file was developed in the early 1990s; please do not rely on it as a statement of current law.

E. The HomeElderCare Situation

Client representation typically begins with a conversation between lawyer and client. Here are notes regarding the two-staged HomeElderCare situation.

1. Consultation Before the Living Will Service Is Created

Meeting with Mary Mahoney, Executive Director of HomeElderCare, Sept. 9, 1992

HomeElderCare (HEC)
not-for-profit corporation
    clients = elderly
    250 clients
    staff = 10 social workers, variable # of volunteers
    social worker duties:
        initial interview to find needs (finances, family concerns, home
            cleaning, etc.)
        set up schedule
        monthly check-in
        liaison to atty or physician is possible
    fee per service, differs for each client
legal concern
    some clients want living wills & help with health care decisions
    has form living will that looks straightforward (gave me copy)
        is it?
        does atty need to do it?
        if not done by atty, will it be valid?
        will HEC's fees be collectible?
    social workers' role (not volunteers)
        need training
        would ask Qs on form & fill in client's answers
        would help get form notarized
        would charge fee for those services
client would save $ by not hiring atty
client already knows social workers, so easier than hiring atty
social workers' background/training
minimum = bachelor's degree in social work, licensed (5 staff)
some have master's degree + second-level licensing (5 staff)
4 possible levels of licensing
some master's degree classes focus on care of elderly
do they need additional 1-2 seminars?

I'll send her opinion letter soon, before her trip, then call re additional Qs.

2. Representation in a Dispute Between HomeElderCare and Client Roger Nelson

- HomeElderCare did create and implement a living will service not involving a lawyer.
- Nelson's living will nominates his medical proxy to be his guardian. This is contrary to his current desires.

THE STRUCTURE

OF LEGAL RULES

> Logical consequences are the scarecrows of fools and the
> beacons of wise men.
> —Thomas H. Huxley
> *Animal Automatism* (1884)

A. INTRODUCTION

The law is formed of rules. A rule of law is "a general statement of what the law permits or requires of classes of persons in classes of circumstances."[1] Rules of law appear in many legal authorities, such as cases, statutes, regulations, and court rules. They all have the same function: to identify the legal consequences that flow from the specified factual conditions.

Rules of law benefit society. They specify predictable legal consequences of particular actions; this predictability allows people and other legal entities (such as corporations, nonprofit organizations, and government agencies) to plan and conduct their activities in reliance on the law. Rules of law also guide disputants and judges as they resolve disputes, so that similarly situated disputants obtain similar outcomes.

How do lawyers draw guidance from a legal rule? In what can feel like a seamless process, the lawyer works through the rule to discern its content and

---

1. Steven J. Burton, *An Introduction to Law and Legal Reasoning* 13 (3d ed. 2007).

structure, then links the rule's clauses to the pertinent facts of the client's situation. This chapter covers the first step, parsing the rule, and previews the second; Chapter 8 covers the second step, deductive reasoning, in more detail.

B. FRAMING RULES IN IF/THEN FORM

Even though legal rules come in various legal authorities, they all can be framed, with a bit of work, in an if/then statement as follows:

IF   the required *factual conditions* exist,

THEN   the specified *legal consequence* follows.

The if-clause contains words or phrases describing a class of situations. Typically the if-clause refers to one or more actors (whether individuals or legal entities such as corporations), one or more actions, and circumstances under which the actions occur.

The then-clause identifies the legal consequence that follows when the factual conditions are met. The consequence may be a benefit to or burden on a specified party, and it may be multi-faceted. Often a benefit flows to one party, and a burden is imposed on another, as when one is ordered to pay monetary damages to the other.

1. Separating Factual Conditions from Legal Consequences

Stating a rule of law in if- and then-clauses is a critical step in legal analysis. If you do not know which factual conditions are required, you might apply an inapplicable rule to your client's facts. Or you might misperceive the legal consequences of your client's situation.

Some rules consist of two clauses. If so, evaluate whether the factual conditions and legal consequences are in separate clauses; the words "where" and "when" often mean "if." If the rule is not so constructed, you will need to identify each concept as a factual condition or legal consequence and group them accordingly.

For example, consider the following rule, which could apply to the HomeElderCare case:

> If a person not admitted or licensed to practice law in this state renders legal advice or counsel to another, the unlicensed practitioner generally shall be guilty of a misdemeanor, upon the charging of a fee, and punished therefor.

This rule has two clauses, suggesting an if/then structure:

IF   a person not admitted or licensed to practice law in this state renders legal advice or counsel to another,

THEN   the unlicensed practitioner generally shall be guilty of a misdemeanor, upon the charging of a fee, and punished therefor.

But the then-clause above contains a factual condition (charging of a fee),
which needs to be moved to the if-clause. The result is as follows:

IF   a person not admitted or licensed to practice law in this state renders legal
advice or counsel to another and charges a fee,

THEN   the unlicensed practitioner generally shall be guilty of a misdemeanor and punished therefor.

Some legal rules are stated in complex and wordy sentences. Thus, the
next step may be to carefully paraphrase the rule, making sure that you do not
remove meaning from the rule, in an effort to make it simpler.[2] A legal dictionary can help you determine which words carry particular legal meanings.

In the example, you could delete "admitted" or "licensed"; you also
could delete "advice" or "counsel." The then-clause refers to both guilt
and punishment; it also uses a legalistic term ("therefor"). One simpler phrasing reads as follows:

IF   a person not licensed to practice law in this state renders legal advice to
another and charges a fee,

THEN   generally the unlicensed practitioner commits a misdemeanor.

2. Dealing with Exceptions

Some rules state not only factual conditions necessary for the legal consequence to follow, but also factual conditions that stave off the legal consequence. These rules take the following form:

IF   some factual conditions exist,

THEN   the specified legal consequences follow,

UNLESS   other factual conditions exist.

The unless-clause contains exceptions to the if-clause. A rule in if/then/
unless form can be restated as follows:

IF   some factual conditions do exist and other factual conditions do *not* exist,

THEN   the specified legal consequences follow.

For example, consider the following sample rule and elaboration:

If a person not admitted or licensed to practice law in this state
renders legal advice or counsel to another, the unlicensed practitioner

---

2. *See generally* Richard Wydick, *Plain English for Lawyers* (4th ed. 1998).

generally shall be guilty of a misdemeanor, upon the charging of a fee, and punished therefor. However, where the legal advice is incidental to another legitimate professional service and addresses only settled legal points, the unlicensed practitioner shall not be guilty of a misdemeanor.

The second sentence introduces an exception; note that the exception clarifies why the first sentence includes the word "generally." Here is a simplified restatement of the more complete rule:

IF   a person not licensed to practice law in this state renders legal advice to another and charges a fee, and the advice is not incidental to another legitimate service and confined to settled points,

THEN   the unlicensed practitioner commits a misdemeanor.

3. Deriving Individual Elements and Consequences

Some if-clauses are complex, stating more than one element. An element is a factual condition that can be analyzed as a unit. Most elements can be stated in a simple clause, and some have sub-elements. Thus, once you have developed your if/then statement, your next goal is to restate the if-clause so that each element (with or without sub-elements) is stated separately.

For example, the if-clause of the rule developed above can be dissected into the following elements and subelements:

IF   (1) a person is not licensed to practice law in this state, and
      (2) that person renders legal advice to another, and
      (3) that person charges a fee, and
      (4) the advice is not
           (a) incidental to another legitimate service and
           (b) confined to settled points

Then-clauses also can be broken into parts if the rule contains more than one legal consequence. For instance, if the rule developed above also indicated that a court could enjoin, or prohibit, the unlicensed practice, the resulting then-clause would look like this:

THEN   (1) that person commits a misdemeanor, and
        (2) the unlicensed practice may be enjoined.

C. ANALYZING THE RULE'S ELEMENTS

The elements in a rule must be connected to each other in some discernible way. Virtually every rule follows one of four patterns—conjunctive, disjunctive, aggregate, balancing—or is a mixture of these. Exhibit 2.1 summarizes the four patterns.

EXHIBIT 2.1

RULE STRUCTURES

Rule Structure	Linguistic Concept	Applicability of Rule	Characteristics
Conjunctive	and	must satisfy all elements	predictable; easy to apply; relative lack of discretion in application
Disjunctive	or	must satisfy only one of multiple elements	predictable; easy to apply; relative lack of discretion in application
Aggregate	some but not all of the listed elements:	depends on weight accorded to various factors	unpredictable; difficult to apply; vests considerable discretion in judge; potentially inconsistent application
Balancing	IF [x] outweighs [y], then. . . . Balance [x] against [y] to determine whether. . . .	depends on weight accorded to each side	unpredictable; difficult to apply; vests considerable discretion in judge; potentially inconsistent application

Some rules have multiple elements connected by the word "and," so all of the elements of the if-clause must exist for the legal consequences of the then-clause to follow. This kind of rule is a *conjunctive rule* ("conjunctive" meaning joining or coming together). Conjunctive rules are fairly simple in structure and relatively predictable in application because courts have relatively little discretion in applying them. The rule discussed in this chapter is a conjunctive rule. Note that the consequence occurs only when all of the following elements are met:

IF (1) a person is not licensed to practice law, *and*
    (2) that person renders legal advice, *and*
    (3) that person charges a fee, *and*
    (4) the advice is not
    (5) (a) incidental to another legitimate service and
        (b) confined to settled points

THEN that person commits a misdemeanor.

A second type of rule contains multiple elements connected by the word "or." The "or" connector tells you that only one of the alternative elements of the if-clause must exist in order for the legal consequences of the then-clause to apply. This kind of rule is a *disjunctive rule* ("disjunctive" meaning separating or presenting alternatives). Disjunctive rules are fairly simple in structure and relatively predictable in application because courts have relatively little discretion in applying them. For example, consider the following rule:

IF   the parties form a contract
      (1) involving fraud in the inducement, *or*
      (2) involving mutual mistake, *or*
      (3) contravening public policy,

THEN   that contract is unenforceable against the disadvantaged party.

Note that the consequence of unenforceability can occur when only one of the disjunctive elements is met.

Few rules are completely disjunctive, but many are conjunctive as to the major elements and disjunctive as to one or more sub-elements. For example, consider the following rule:

IF   (1) a person is not licensed to practice law in this state *and*
    (2) that person
        (a) renders legal advice to another, *or*
        (b) prepares legal documents for another, *or*
        (c) appears in court for another, *and*
    (3) that person charges a fee,

THEN   that person commits a misdemeanor.

The three main elements are conjunctive, and the second element has disjunctive sub-elements. For there to be a misdemeanor, (1) and (3) must occur along with 2(a) or (2)(b) or (2)(c).

The third and fourth types of rules are similar in that they state factors to consider; no specific factor is necessarily critical by itself. An *aggregate rule* requires a determination whether enough of the suggested factors are present, so as to justify the legal consequence. A *balancing rule* requires you to balance factors favoring one outcome and factors favoring the other outcome to determine whether the legal consequence will follow. A rule may be purely aggregate or balancing, or it may be a mix, for example, aggregate and conjunctive.

Aggregate and balancing rules are difficult to apply. Courts may come to different results as they decide cases with similar facts. Parties seeking to order their behavior in reliance on these rules may have a difficult time predicting the rule's impact on their conduct. The advantage of these rules is that courts have discretion to come to results called for by particular circumstances.

For example, consider the following aggregate rule:

IF   (1) a person is not licensed to practice law in this state and
    (2) that person engages in significant legal advising, *as determined by:*
        (a) the difficulty of the legal issue,
        (b) the impact of the advice on the client,

(c) the duration of the relationship, and

(d) the charging of a fee,

THEN   that person commits a misdemeanor.

This rule is aggregate as to element (2). That is, factors (2)(a), (b), (c), and (d) are all to be considered together; the absence or presence of any one is not dispositive. (The rule's overall structure is conjunctive.)

As an example of a balancing rule, consider the following example:

IF   (1) a person is not licensed to practice law in this state, and

(2) that person renders legal advice to another, and

(3) (a) the harm caused by that advice—measured by any cost to the client, other loss suffered by the client, loss suffered by third parties, and fraud perpetrated on the client or others—*outweighs*

(b) the benefits of the advice—measured by any advantage received by the client and the person's interest in practicing a related profession—

THEN   that person commits a misdemeanor.

This rule is balancing as to element (3). That is, the factors in (3)(a) are to be weighed against those in (3)(b) to determine whether element (3) is met. (This rule's overall structure is conjunctive.)

D. ANALYZING THE LEGAL CONSEQUENCES

Just as the if-clause merits careful analysis, so too should the then-clause be carefully analyzed to discern the number and nature of the legal consequence(s). Exhibit 2.2 presents the questions you need to answer.

Many legal rules state one consequence of conduct fitting within the if-clause. Others provide for more than one consequence, so you must discern the relationship between those consequences. Some rules provide for *plural* consequences; both consequences are to occur. For example:

EXHIBIT 2.2

THEN-CLAUSE ANALYSIS

NUMBER OF CONSEQUENCES	How many consequences? If more than one, are they: • plural → client may experience more than one? • alternatives → client will experience only one?
NATURE OF CONSEQUENCES	Is the consequence • the ultimate practical consequence? • the intermediate legal label? If the latter, what additional rule establishes the ultimate practical consequence of conduct fitting the intermediate legal label?

IF   a person engages in unauthorized practice of law

THEN   that person pays a fine *and*
            that person may be imprisoned.

Other rules provide for *alternative* consequences; one or the other consequences are to occur. For example:

IF   a person engages in unauthorized practice of law

THEN   that person pays a fine *or* that person may be imprisoned.[3]

Some legal rules identify the *ultimate practical* consequence of conduct
fitting within the if-clause; that is, they directly state the impact on the people
involved. A rule may provide for a fine or state that damages may be recovered.
For example:

IF   unauthorized practice of law

THEN   fine [ultimate practical consequence].

Other rules identify an *intermediate legal* consequence of conduct fitting
within the if-clause. Such a rule affixes a legal label to the conduct, and you
must consult an additional rule to determine the ultimate practical consequence. For example, if a rule has as its consequence that an individual is
guilty of a misdemeanor, you would need to consult another rule on misdemeanors to discern what practical consequence (such as a fine) flows from that
label. For example:

IF   unauthorized practice of law

THEN   misdemeanor [intermediate legal consequence]

IF   misdemeanor

THEN   fine [ultimate practical consequence]

Careful attention to these dimensions of the then-clause will permit you to
properly identify the significance of a legal rule for your client's situation.

E. DEPICTING A RULE IN VARIOUS WAYS

Rules of law can be depicted various ways. Your choice should be based on the
nature of the rule and your needs in working with the rule. If the rule has a
simple structure, it may be easily understood in sentence or paragraph form.
As shown throughout this chapter, tabulation and enumeration can aid you by
displaying the structure of more complex rules.

---

3. "Or" can be understood various ways: A or B or both. A or B but not both. If not A, then B.
Generally context will aid you in discerning which meaning is intended.

EXHIBIT 2.3

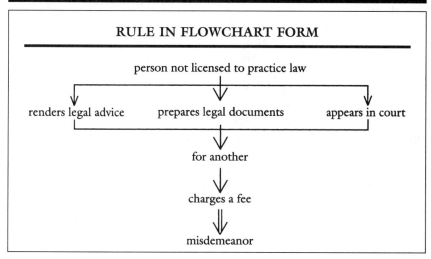

RULE IN FLOWCHART FORM

person not licensed to practice law

renders legal advice   prepares legal documents   appears in court

for another

charges a fee

misdemeanor

For long or complex rules, you may prefer to state the simpler then-clause first and the more complex if-clause second. Although this order inverts the logic of an if/then rule, it may be easier to read because the then-clause sets the context for the upcoming set of phrases.[4] For example:

A person commits the misdemeanor of unauthorized practice of law when:

1. that person is not licensed to practice law in this state, and
2. that person renders legal advice to another, and
3. that person charges a fee, and
4. the advice is not incidental to another legitimate service and confined to settled points.

Another way to depict complex rules is a flowchart. See Exhibit 2.3. Generally the elements precede the consequences. Disjunctive elements are depicted across horizontal lines, while conjunctive elements are depicted along vertical lines. A double arrow can show the transition from the factual conditions to the legal consequences.

F. PREVIEW OF DEDUCTIVE REASONING

Deductive reasoning is fundamental to legal analysis. It entails using a legal rule to predict the outcome of a client's situation. This process builds on a careful analysis of the rule, as discussed in this chapter. Once you have discerned the rule's elements and thus developed the framework of your analysis

---

4. *See generally* Bryan A. Garner, *Legal Writing in Plain English: A Text with Exercises* 100-04 (2001).

of your client's situation, you can match each element to the relevant facts in your client's situation.

The type of rule under consideration is very important. For example, if the rule is conjunctive, all elements must be met for the consequence to follow, and your analysis should reflect this. If the rule is a balancing rule, your analysis would encompass the various factors in a less mechanical way.

One way to approach this task is to identify each element as entailing one or two of the six classic questions journalists ask: who, what, when, where, how, and why. As discussed in more detail in Chapter 8, this process can be very easy or rather difficult, depending on the complexity of both the rule and the client's situation.

For example, consider the HomeElderCare situation in light of the rules presented in this chapter. The "who" element specifies a person not admitted or licensed to practice law in the state; HomeElderCare's social workers clearly fulfill this element. The "what" element specifies rendering of legal advice or counsel; this is much less clear. As discussed in Chapter 9, reasoning by example and policy analysis can complement deductive reasoning and help clarify the match between an element and the client's situation.

G. REVIEW OF CHAPTER 2

This chapter has covered the following analytical steps in stating rules of law as if/then statements with clearly identified elements and consequences:

(1) Frame the rule in an if/then form.
   (a) Segregate the factual conditions and the legal consequences into if- and then-clauses. As needed, carefully paraphrase the rule for ease of use.
   (b) Reword any factual conditions framed as exceptions to read as negative conditions in the if-clause.
   (c) Separate the if-clause into individual elements, and list distinct consequences separately.
(2) Determine whether the rule's elements are conjunctive, disjunctive, aggregate, balancing, or some combination.
(3) Discern the number and nature of the legal consequences.
(4) Depict the rule in a helpful way.

As you will see in the next few chapters, you will draw out of various types of legal authority rules to work with in this way.

3

READING CASES

> The prophecies of what the courts will do in fact, and nothing
> more pretentious, are what I mean by the law.
> —Oliver Wendell Holmes
> *The Path of the Law,* 10 Harv. L. Rev. 457, 461 (1897)

A. INTRODUCTION

This chapter introduces case law, that is, law that emanates from decisions of various tribunals adjudicating specific disputes. In law, the word "case" has several related meanings. Many lawyers use "case" to refer to a client's situation or problem. Once a dispute enters litigation, it becomes a "case" in a more formal sense; it is referred to by the names of the litigants. When a tribunal renders a written decision, that decision also is referred to as a "case." This book uses the word "case" in all of these ways.

This chapter focuses on decisions of courts because they are present in virtually every area of law and constitute the final and weightiest decisions. Nonetheless, keep in mind that other tribunals, such as federal administrative agencies and local commissions, decide cases. In many areas, the parties may choose arbitration, which involves a private decision-maker.

How do lawyers read cases that govern their clients' cases? Keeping in mind how cases operate as law in the United States legal system, they read cases as fables, seeking lessons for their clients. This chapter first covers the operation of cases in the United States legal system; then deconstructs cases so you know how to read them; then presents case briefing, a way to thoroughly and carefully read and take notes on cases.

Along the way, this chapter refers to a specific case, *Dick Weatherston's Associated Mechanical Services v. Minnesota Mutual Life Insurance Co.* This case is a leading authority that a lawyer would use in analyzing the Home-ElderCare case. *Weatherston's* appears in the HomeElderCare case file at page 271; we urge you to read it before reading this chapter.

B. THE UNITED STATES COMMON LAW SYSTEM

To understand how cases work, you must know these elements of the United States legal system: (1) court structures, (2) jurisdiction, (3) stare decisis and precedent, and (4) retroactivity of cases.

1. Court Structures

Although each court system has unique features, all court systems share certain fundamental features and procedures. Exhibit 3.1 illustrates the federal court structure and representative state court structures.

Every court system has trial courts, sometimes called "district courts." Cases enter the legal system at this level, and most conclude there. Many cases settle through negotiations conducted by the parties' lawyers. Some court systems require or encourage litigants to pursue informal means of resolving their disputes, such as mediation (negotiations aided by a neutral) or arbitration (an informal trial leading to a decision by an expert neutral).

If the case remains unresolved, the case enters litigation, and the trial court resolves it, one way or another (although the parties may still settle it themselves as the litigation is underway). The trial court resolves disputes about the facts, applies the law to the facts, and determines an outcome. A jury may decide the case after a trial, by a jury verdict. At trial, witnesses testify, and the decision-maker closely views objects and documents. Alternatively, a case may be resolved by the judge, either after a bench trial (a trial without a jury) or through motions. A motion is a request by one party that the judge take a specified action, which may entail deciding the case without trial.

Every court system also has one or more appellate courts. An appellate court reviews the trial court's work for errors that are significant enough to have led to an improper result. These errors may include misunderstanding the law, failure to conduct the trial according to rules of evidence, failure to handle motions according to the rules of civil or criminal procedure, and coming to a judgment contrary to the facts. An appellate court makes law as well, as described further in section 3 below.

Because the appellate court's function is to review the trial court's work, not re-do it, the appellate court does not conduct trials. Rather, the appellate court reviews the written record created at the trial court and the written and oral arguments of the parties' attorneys.

A two-tier court system has a single appellate court. That court handles all cases coming out of the trial courts, and that court both corrects error and makes law.

EXHIBIT 3.1

COURT STRUCTURES

Federal Court Structure	*Primary Roles*

Federal Court Structure

Supreme Court (1)   lawmaking

Courts of Appeals (13)   error correction

District Courts (over 90)   factfinding and application of law to facts

Three-Tier State Court Structure

supreme court (1)   lawmaking

court of appeals
(1 or several)   error correction

district or trial courts   factfinding and application of law to facts
(numerous)

Two-Tier State Court Structure

supreme court (1)   lawmaking and error correction

district or trial courts   factfinding and application of law to facts
(numerous)

A three-tier court system has two tiers of appellate courts. In these systems, the intermediate court, typically called the "court of appeals," handles virtually all cases coming out of the trial courts and focuses on correction of error. Some systems have multiple intermediate courts, each handling cases coming out of the trial courts in its geographic region. Other systems have a single intermediate court; all cases from around the state are heard by a panel of several judges or the entire court.

The highest court in a three-tier appellate court system, typically called the "supreme court," handles a fairly small percentage of the cases coming out of the intermediate court(s). The supreme court has the power to select most of its cases through grant of certiorari or grant of petition for review. The court selects cases with new or especially difficult legal questions or broad impact, because the supreme court's task is not so much to correct error as to make law. Some supreme courts also are required to handle certain limited categories of cases.

As noted in Exhibit 3.1, the federal court system includes the United States Supreme Court; thirteen intermediate appellate courts, i.e. the courts of appeals, for eleven numbered circuits as well as the Federal and District of Columbia Circuits; and more than ninety federal district trial courts for the fifty states, the District of Columbia, and American territories. Each federal district (trial) court covers either an entire state or a portion of a large state.

The Minnesota state court system,[1] which created the law applicable to the HomeElderCare situation, has resembled both the two-tier and three-tier state-court structures in Exhibit 3.1. Before the court of appeals was created in 1983, Minnesota had a simple court structure, with the Minnesota Supreme Court being the only appellate court. Thus, in the *Weatherston's* case, after the trial court decided the last motions after the jury's verdict, the case went directly to the Minnesota Supreme Court. The Minnesota state court system currently includes the Minnesota Supreme Court; the Minnesota Court of Appeals (a single court with multiple panels); and ten district, or trial, courts.

2. Jurisdiction

Every court has the power to decide only certain classes of cases.[2] A court has jurisdiction over a case when the court is empowered to decide the case and enforce its decision. There are two types of jurisdiction, both necessary for a court to handle a case. First, a court has *personal* jurisdiction over a *party* based on the party's contact with the state, based on such factors as the location of the events and the party's citizenship. Second, a court has *subject matter* jurisdiction over a *dispute* when the subject matter of the litigation is within a category the court has the power to decide. The term "jurisdiction" also is used to describe the geographic range of a particular court.

In terms of subject-matter jurisdiction, most court systems have courts of general jurisdiction and courts of limited jurisdiction. Courts of general jurisdiction handle a wide range of cases not assigned to courts of limited jurisdiction. The latter have very specialized roles. For example, at the federal level, specialized courts handle military matters, bankruptcies, and patent cases. Some state courts use relatively informal procedures to handle relatively small cases, such as residential landlord-tenant disputes.

Some cases are complex from a jurisdictional standpoint because they span the federal and state systems or involve the law of more than one state.[3] In two fairly common situations, the federal courts handle issues of state law. First, where citizens of two different states have a case with an amount in controversy of more than $75,000, the plaintiff may opt to sue in federal court rather than state court; this situation is called "diversity jurisdiction." Second, where the case involves related federal and state claims and is brought in federal court, the federal court will consider the state claims under its supplemental jurisdiction.

Similarly, state courts on occasion address issues of federal law. This situation occurs when the federal Congress has chosen not to deny state courts jurisdiction over a claim arising out of federal law.

---

1. Table T.1 of *The Bluebook* provides basic information about the courts in each state.
2. Jurisdiction is a complex topic. For a more complete explanation, see Charles Alan Wright, Arthur R. Miller et al., *Federal Practice and Procedure* (various editions and publication dates).
3. *See* Wright et al., *supra* note 2.

Finally, from time to time state courts handle issues that are governed by the law of sister states. For example, if a contract involving events taking place in more than one state indicates that the law of one of those states shall govern the contract, that law usually governs a dispute under the contract, even if the litigation occurs in a different state. In other situations, when it is not readily apparent whose law should govern, the court will use choice-of-law principles to resolve the question.

Weatherston's, the sample case, came within the jurisdiction of the Minnesota state courts. They had *personal* jurisdiction because the company sued was a Minnesota company and the case involved a project in Minnesota. The claim was breach of contract, a *subject* governed by state law and commonly handled by state courts of general jurisdiction.

3. Stare Decisis and Precedent

Judges write opinions explaining their decisions for various reasons. In difficult cases, the process of explaining the decision no doubt helps the judge actually come to the decision. In addition, the opinion justifies the result so that the parties (and in some cases the public) will accept it as just. Finally, in the United States common law system, which emanates from the English common law, the opinion operates as law under the doctrine of stare decisis.

"Stare decisis et non quieta movere" means "to stand by precedents and not disturb settled points." The term "precedent" refers to decisions in past cases. Stare decisis is a doctrine based on consistency with the past; a court is to decide the present case in accord with decisions rendered in similar cases in the past.[4]

Stare decisis has several advantages. Litigants perceive that they are treated fairly, because similarly situated persons receive the same results. The doctrine makes for predictability; a lawyer can predict the legal outcome of a present or future situation by examining the outcome in a case involving a similar situation. By eliminating the need to reinvent solutions where one already has been developed, stare decisis preserves scarce judicial resources.

If stare decisis operated inflexibly, however, it would be counterproductive. As circumstances, information, and societal values change, so too should the law. Fortunately, the doctrine of stare decisis permits change. Where the needed change is not dramatic, the courts modify the existing rule, typically by adding a new element or reframing an element of the existing rule. Where the needed change is dramatic, the courts overrule the precedent and create a new rule in the new case.

Stare decisis operates within a court system, according to its internal hierarchy. Courts are bound by decisions of courts higher in the same court structure and are expected to decide cases consistently with their own decisions. Decisions that a court must follow are called "mandatory precedent" or "binding precedent."

By way of illustration, the Minnesota state district courts are bound by the decisions of the Minnesota Court of Appeals and the Minnesota Supreme

---

4. For a more extended discussion, see Oliver Wendell Holmes, *The Common Law* (1881); Edward Levi, *An Introduction to Legal Reasoning* (1949).

Court. The single court of appeals is bound by the decisions of the supreme court and is expected to decide cases consistently with its own decisions. And the supreme court is expected to decide cases consistently with its own prior decisions or explain why it has chosen to chart a new course.

As a second illustration, in the federal system, a federal district court is bound by the decisions of its circuit court of appeals and the United States Supreme Court. Each circuit court of appeals is bound by the decisions of the Supreme Court, is expected to decide cases consistently with its own decisions, but need not align with the other circuits. The Supreme Court is expected to decide cases consistently with its prior decisions or explain why it has chosen to chart a new course.

When one court is applying the law of a different system, it seeks to follow that system's precedent. For example, a federal court deciding a diversity jurisdiction case seeks to follow the cases of the state's highest court on the state law issues in the case.

In some situations, a court may choose to follow a decision it is not bound to follow, such as a decision from the highest court in a neighboring state, i.e., a "persuasive precedent." Courts typically rely on persuasive precedent when there is no binding precedent or when the law is undergoing change in the direction set forth in the persuasive precedent.

Especially when a court is considering persuasive precedent, but also when a court is considering only binding precedent, there may be several applicable precedents from which to choose. Several factors determine the weightiness of various cases.

- Obviously, a binding precedent carries more weight than a persuasive precedent.
- A precedent from the highest court within a system carries more weight than a precedent from a lower court.
- As a general principle, the newer the precedent, the weightier it is, although longstanding precedent followed in recent decisions also carries significant weight.
- Unanimous decisions are weightier than split decisions.
- The more thorough and cogent the court's reasoning is, the weightier the case.
- The greater the factual and legal similarities between the precedent and the client's case, the more useful the precedent.
- Some courts command more respect than others, because the general quality of their research and reasoning is high or because their decisions frequently represent the cutting edge in an area of law.
- Many courts turn to certain courts within the same broad region of the country or with similar orientations toward broad issues of public policy.

Some courts designate some of their decisions for publication and designate other decisions as unpublished decisions. Typically, the court views an unpublished decision as not adding to the common law but rather applying settled law to unremarkable facts in a routine way. Indeed, some courts limit reliance on unpublished decisions. Through various tools of legal research, you will be able to locate unpublished decisions. However, you should be alert to the reduced precedential weight of an unpublished decision.

For example, in reasoning through the *Weatherston's* case, the Minnesota Supreme Court referred to previous decisions of the Minnesota Supreme Court in somewhat similar cases. See, for example, footnote 7 at page 276, where the opinion refers to *Peterson, Minter,* and *Brimhall.* In turn, *Weatherston's* is itself a significant precedent on the topic of contracts to perform professional services without a license. As a Minnesota Supreme Court decision from 1960 with a significant discussion of an aspect of contract law, it is binding precedent for later cases arising in the Minnesota state courts and involving similar contract claims.

4. Retroactive Effect of Cases

As a general rule, judicial decisions are retroactive: they apply to a set of facts that arose in the past.[5] The court applies the rules of law set out in the case to yield an outcome in the present dispute. Furthermore, the case governs the resolution of similar disputes currently in litigation.

The retroactivity of case law can be troublesome when the decision creates a significant shift in the law, most clearly when the court overrules an existing precedent. The difficulty arises because the parties may well have relied on previous law. Despite this reliance, courts generally apply the new precedent retroactively. On rare occasions, courts overrule their precedents prospectively, by declaring a new rule of law effective as of the date of decision, not applying the new rule to the case currently before the court, and not applying the new rule to other cases then in litigation based on disputes that occurred before the new rule was recognized. In making this judgment, courts consider how the law has developed and the equities of the situation.

As for *Weatherston's,* the rule there, which permits enforcement of some contracts for unlicensed professional services where public policy is not violated, did not diverge sharply from pre-existing law. It was used to resolve the case in favor of Mr. Weatherston and his business.

C. READING A CASE

Viewed as literature, judicial opinions can be very complex, and some are quite long. Yet they must be read—and fully understood—if they govern your client's case. How do lawyers read cases efficiently?

1. An Analogy: Cases as Fables

Cases are like fables. Fables consist of two components: the story and its moral, which suggests an outcome for similar stories occurring in the future. Cases, too, contain a story and a moral, or prediction. The story is the real-world narrative. The moral or prediction derives from the court's response; in

---

5. For more detail, see Edgar Bodenheimer et al., *An Introduction to the Anglo-American Legal System* (2d ed. 1988).

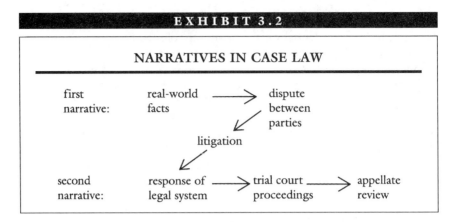

EXHIBIT 3.2

NARRATIVES IN CASE LAW

assigning a legal meaning to the real-world facts, the court thereby sets a precedent for future similar disputes. Both the real-world story and the legal-system story are important to understanding the case, just as a fable needs both story and moral to make its point.

2. Two Narratives

Lawyers realize that a case contains two narratives, as shown in Exhibit 3.2. The first narrative consists of the events prompting the litigation—what lawyers call the "real-world facts." The second narrative consists of the response within the legal system. As to both narratives, it is helpful to ask the six standard questions journalists are trained to ask: Who? What? When? Where? Why? How?

As you read the real-world facts, ask yourself: Who is litigating against whom, and are there other important people? What happened between the parties? When did that happen? Where did that happen? Why did that happen? How have the events between the parties become the basis of litigation?

Ask comparable questions about the second narrative, the legal system's response. There may be more than one response if the case you are reading is an appellate opinion. Because few trial-court decisions are published, most cases you will read will be appellate opinions. So ask yourself: Who—which courts—have considered this case before the court whose opinion I am reading, and what did that court or those courts decide? Who wrote the opinion I am reading now? When did this court rule? Where is this opinion published? What has this court decided—who wins, who loses, or is it unsettled? Why did this court rule this way? How did this court respond to the rulings below?

3. Organization of a Case Report

Most published cases follow a standard organization with the components listed below. The *Weatherston's* case at page 271, reproduced from the North Western Reporter (a commercial publication containing decisions from state courts in Minnesota and nearby states), has these components labeled.

Citation information: Located at the very beginning (it varies from publication to publication), this information identifies where the case is published. Lawyers must provide citations to cases so that readers may locate them.

Case name: This critical information identifies the parties. The most common party designations are as follows:

- Plaintiff: the party that brought the lawsuit
- Defendant: the party sued by the plaintiff
- Appellant or petitioner: the party that brought the appeal (and hence lost in the lower court)
- Appellee or respondent: the party opposing the appeal

The plaintiff generally is listed first, but some courts list the defendant first if it is the appellant. Some party designations are complicated; examples include litigation involving more than two parties and cross-appeals, in which both sides won and lost below and thus seek reversal of their losses.

Court, date, and docket number: This information tells you which court decided the case, when it did so, and what docket number was assigned to the case by the clerk of the court. Some citation forms include docket numbers.

Publisher's editorial matter: The publisher's staff may insert a synopsis of the case and short paragraphs summarizing various points made in the opinion. (In the case of opinions published by West Publishing Company, the short paragraphs are called "headnotes.") This editorial matter plays an important role in researching cases. However, it is not a part of the case, so you should not rely on it.

Court's editorial matter: Some courts provide synopses of their opinions. These synopses may be written by the court's staff or designee, not by the judges themselves. Again, you should not rely on them in lieu of the opinion itself.

Attorneys: Whether the attorneys like it or not, their involvement in the case is noted.

Authoring judge: Immediately before the opinion itself is the name of the author of the opinion. In appellate cases, which involve three or more judges, if the decision was not unanimous, you also will learn which other judges agreed with the lead opinion. Some brief opinions on which the judges were generally in agreement are not attributed to any judge but are labeled "per curiam." As a general rule, the judges of the highest court of a jurisdiction are referred to as "justices," while others are referred to as "judges."

Opinion(s): The lengthiest portion of a case report—and obviously the most important—is the opinion itself. There is no standard format for judicial opinions. However, generally the following appear at the beginning to orient the reader: the procedure in any lower court(s) before the case reached this court, the issue(s) raised by the case, and the outcome(s). Typically, the next segment is a recitation of the real-world facts. The bulk of the opinion is devoted to a discussion of the legal issues raised by the parties and a statement of the court's resolution of those issues. The concluding paragraph indicates the court's ultimate decision: a trial court judge's ruling in favor of one party or the other; an appellate court's decision to affirm, modify, or reverse the decision of the lower court and to remand the case. When a court remands a case, it sends the case back to the trial court with instructions as to how to proceed.

A case decided by an appellate court may yield more than one opinion. The opinion receiving over half the votes is called a "majority opinion."

EXHIBIT 3.3

SAMPLE CASE BRIEF

Dick Weatherston's Associated Mechanical Services v. Minnesota Mutual Life Insurance Co., Minnesota Supreme Court 1960, 100 N.W.2d 819.

FACTS: P is air conditioning contractor in MN. Although P's assignor Dick Weatherston (DW) had B.S. in mechanical engineering, he was not registered as engr in MN. D needed air conditioning for new building & asked P to submit design plans & pricing. DW told D he wasn't licensed & raised concern about conflict w/Ellerbe, D's architects & engrs. Ellerbe agreed to act as consultant. P submitted plans; they were modified after review by Ellerbe & approved. No charge for design or plan was included. P was told to start, but 2 weeks later, P was informed that D had given project to different contractor (also not regd engr).

PROCEDURE: P sued D for damages for breach of K. Jury found offer & acceptance & awarded damages. D moved for new trial or JNOV; denied. D appealed.

*ISSUE: Is K illegal, or can unregd engr recover damages for breach of K, where statute requires regn as engr to practice engrg, work covered by K includes profl engr services, engr has training as engr, services are subject to approval of architect/engr retained by D, & D knows engr isn't regd?

HOLDING: Affirmed & remanded to trial ct w/directions re damages. Unregd engr can recover damages for breach of K including engr services where engr has training, D's engr approves plans, & engr tells D of non-regn.

REASONING: Rule: Ks made in violation of licensing statutes typically are illegal & void. But statute & transaction must be viewed as whole to determine whether legislature intented K to be illegal.

Statute: Minn. Stat. § 326.02 requires that person who practices as profl engr be registered in MN. Statutory purpose is protect public against fraud & incompetence & promote public health & welfare.

Application: Here K should be enforced: Engr work was incidental to & part of entire job. DW had training. Work was approved by regd engrs. D sought out P, & DW told D of unregd status. Case does not raise concerns about incompetence, harm to public welfare, fraud. Nor does P's claim for "designing & preparing drawings" establish P's work was illegal engrg practice.

Policy: Assure that parties who K for engr services are not harmed by fraud or work done by incompetent persons. Safeguard public welfare (through properly engrd buildings presumably).

PERTINENCE: Look into statute re practice of law, training, & oversight of social workers.

*Challenges to jury verdict & damages award are not covered.

A judge "concurs" when he or she agrees with the result but chooses to state reasoning different than the majority's. A judge "dissents" when he or she disagrees with the majority result. On occasion, a court splits so significantly that there is no majority opinion; the opinion drawing the largest number of votes is called the "plurality opinion" and generally is viewed as the most influential of the opinions.

4. Reading Stages

You most likely will find that you must read a case several times before you fully understand it. Scan the case first, without marking it or taking notes, to obtain an overview and general sense of the case. Then read it more carefully, highlighting important points and making marginal notes, such as key phrases or the components of the case brief (illustrated in Exhibit 3.3 and covered in the next part). Be sure to look up terms you do not know in a legal dictionary. Then ponder the case for a few moments, asking yourself the who, what, when, where, why, and how questions suggested above. Once you believe that you have good answers to all of them, you are ready to brief the case.

D. BRIEFING A CASE

A case brief is a structured set of notes on a case; writing one is an excellent way to test, as well as record, your understanding of the case. Because the brief is written for the writer, formats vary from person to person. Many employ the components discussed here. As illustrated in Exhibit 3.4, these components encompass the answers to the six questions about the two narratives described in Part C. At this point, you may want to read the sample *Weatherston's* brief in Exhibit 3.3.

1. Opening Components

The opening components set the context for the core components discussed in section 2 below.

Heading: The heading typically includes the case's name, court, date, and citation (where it is published).

Facts: This component contains the real-world facts. Be sure to answer all of the journalist's questions set forth in Exhibit 3.4.

You should present material that is critical to the court's decision; omit extraneous material. To sift through the facts effectively, first ask yourself which facts you must know to understand the court's reasoning; these relevant facts belong in the case brief. Then ask yourself which other facts provide important context for the relevant facts; these background facts also belong in the case brief. Facts failing these two tests should not be included.

In addition, note as needed any procedural facets of the facts. For example, if the court addresses a challenge to a jury verdict, note the facts in dispute. If it is significant, you may need to cover this in your core components too.

Take care to state the facts in a useful way:

- Some writers prefer to use P and D for plaintiff and defendant, while others prefer proper names or functional labels, such as social worker and client.
- Present the facts in a logical order, which generally is chronological.
- Where timing is critical and intricate, you may want to draw a timeline.

EXHIBIT 3.4

QUESTIONS TO ASK AND CASE BRIEF COMPONENTS

Six Questions	Case Brief Components
First narrative: real-world facts	
• Who are the parties and other important people?	heading; facts
• What happened between the parties?	facts
• When did that happen?	facts
• Where did that happen?	facts
• Why did that happen?	facts
• How have these events become the basis of litigation?	procedure
Second narrative: response of legal system Lower court(s)	
• Which courts considered this case prior to the current court, and what did they decide?	procedure
Appellate court opinion	
• Who wrote this opinion?	heading
• When did this court rule?	heading
• Where is this opinion published?	heading
• What has this court decided: who wins, and who loses?	issue, holding (also rule of law)
• How did this court respond to the lower court's outcome?	holding
• Why did this court rule this way?	reasoning (also rule of law)

- Where the parties and other participants relate to each other in a complicated way, diagram the relationships.
- Condense what can be stated briefly.
- Avoid unnecessary detail. Use abbreviations for a more compact presentation.

In the *Weatherston's* example, the major issue was whether the contract between Weatherston's and MMLIC was illegal because Mr. Weatherston was doing engineering work without a license. Hence it is relevant that Mr. Weatherston did not have a current license to perform engineering work. That the contract involved an air-conditioning project in MMLIC's office building provides useful context. MMLIC's difficulty providing ventilation in a particular area for computing equipment need not be included.

Procedure: This component chronicles the events within the legal system that predate the opinion being briefed. First state who sued whom, on what type of claim, and what remedy was sought. Then, as applicable, state who won in the trial court and how (by motion, judge trial, or jury verdict); then the outcome in the intermediate appellate court, if any; and finally who has brought the current appeal.

As you might expect, litigation takes time. The dealings between Mr. Weatherston and MMLIC occurred in 1956 and 1957; the Minnesota Supreme Court decided the case in 1960.

2. Core Components

The remaining components of the case brief address the most important dimensions of the legal system's response: the decision of the court whose opinion you are reading as well as how and why the court so decided the case. This material constitutes the precedent established by the case.

A case may well involve several distinct topics. For example, the plaintiff may have brought several claims against the defendant, or the defendant may have asserted several defenses, or a case may address both the claims and the remedy. Generally, you will not be concerned with all of the topics in a multi-topic case but instead will focus on topics pertinent to your client's situation. Read through the entire opinion at least once to be sure that a seemingly extraneous discussion really does not pertain to your client's situation.

If your brief covers more than one topic, you have an organizational dilemma to resolve. Should you work through the following components for topic A, then work through them again for topic B? Or should you cover all topics, then all holdings, then all rules? In outline form:

first approach	second approach
issue A	issues A & B
holding A	holdings A & B
rule A	rules A & B
reasoning A	reasoning A & B
issue B	
holding B	
rule B	
reasoning B	

The more distinct the two topics are, the more likely you will choose the first approach; the second works well when the topics are closely connected.

Issue(s): The issue is the question the court had to answer to decide the case. Because the court resolves specific disputes involving real people and real events, and because the court applies the law to these events, the issue refers to both a rule of law and real-world facts. In other words, *issue = law + facts, in question form.*

Issues vary on several dimensions. First, some issues are primarily questions about what the law is or should be, with the real-world facts in a clearly secondary role. Other issues involve the application of settled law to facts, with the law in the secondary role and the facts in the primary role. Others involve evenly balanced interactions between law and facts.

Second, some issues involve primarily substantive legal rules, while others involve primarily procedural legal rules, and others are mixtures of the two. Substantive legal rules govern the conduct of people in the real world, while procedural rules govern the conduct of litigation, that is, events within the legal system.

Third, some issues are quite simple, dealing with a single legal concept. Others are more complex, involving several legal concepts that are so closely related that they raise sub-issues of the main issue.

You can deduce the issue(s) in a case in several ways:

- The court may state the issue (although not necessarily artfully or completely).
- The court may summarize the arguments of the parties; often you can convert a party's argument into an issue.
- Put yourself in the position of the court, and ask yourself what you need to address to decide the case.
- You may want to read the court's syllabus and the publisher's editorial matter to confirm your understanding.

If you were to brief *Weatherston's* so you could advise HomeElderCare, you would focus on MMLIC's argument that Mr. Weatherston contracted illegally when he agreed to perform engineering services without an engineer's license. The sample brief focuses on that topic. Note that the issue in the brief combines legal concepts (recover damages for breach of contract) and real-world facts (unregistered engineer, work includes professional engineering services, etc.); it is balanced between facts and law. It is a substantive (not procedural) issue. The issue in the brief draws on the court's issue statement at page 273.

Holding(s): The holding is the court's answer to the issue. Mirroring the issue, it connects the law to the facts of the case to reveal the legal significance of those facts. In other words, *holding = law + facts, in statement form.* As with issues, some holdings are more legal than factual, or vice versa; some are substantive, while others are procedural; some are simple, while others are complex. If there are several decided issues, there will be several holdings.

A holding answers the issue; it also constitutes precedent. Under stare decisis, the deciding court and lower courts should come to a similar holding on similar facts in the future.

You can discern the holding(s) in a case several ways:

- Determine who won the case. For example, if the lower court's ruling is affirmed, the appellant has lost, and the court has resolved the issue against the appellant. Indeed, you may want to state this procedural outcome at the beginning of the holding.
- Focus on the court's discussion of the real-world facts and how the parties' dispute concludes.
- Of course, if the court states a holding in so many words ("We therefore hold . . ."), this statement merits close attention.

Holdings can be phrased narrowly, broadly, or in-between. A narrow phrasing refers specifically to the facts before the court and thus suggests that the case's impact does not extend much beyond the case before it. A broad phrasing states the facts in more abstract terms, suggesting that the case's reach is expansive. The court may signal the breadth of its holding; if so, this statement commands respect.

In practice, your client's situation will drive how you state a case's holding. If your client's situation is very similar to the facts of the case, a narrowly phrased holding is appropriate. If your client's situation is similar only in a broad sense to the facts of the case, you may need to use a broadly phrased holding to draw out the case's significance for your client's situation.

For strategic reasons, you may be tempted to state a case with an unfavorable outcome narrowly or state a case with a favorable outcome broadly. However, you must be faithful to the decided case and mindful of your client's circumstances. In an advisory context, a neutral or cautious approach is preferable, to provide your client a margin of safety as your client contemplates various possible options. When you are advocating for a client who has already taken action, you are more likely to read an unfavorable precedent narrowly and a favorable precedent broadly to persuade the tribunal to favor your client.

For example, the *Weatherston's* holding could be framed in terms of Mr. Weatherston himself, engineers who lack licenses, or unlicensed professionals generally. The sample case brief takes the middle ground, which most closely reflects the court's approach.

A lawyer advising HomeElderCare should note that the case (which favors HomeElderCare) may not extend to social workers and legal work. A lawyer defending HomeElderCare would argue that the case stands for a broad principle encompassing licensed professionals in general, including social workers.

Rule(s) of law: In reasoning to its holding, a court employs one or more rules of law. A rule of law states the legal consequences that flow from certain broadly stated factual conditions. The court determines how the facts of the case compare to the factual conditions of the rule and thereby deduces what legal outcome to order. The rule of law is similar to the holding; the case stands for the rules of law stated within it. Indeed, a broadly stated holding closely resembles a rule of law.

As with issues and holdings, you can draw rules of law out of a case various ways:

- Look for an important statement of legal consequences paired with a set of factual conditions. The legal consequences may be implied, rather than stated explicitly. The factual conditions will be described in fairly general terms, so as to cover not only the particular case but also other similar cases.
- The court may state an existing rule; in such a case, there ordinarily will be a citation to legal authority, such as a binding precedent.
- The court may create a rule of law in the case you are reading, if the court has not addressed the area before or is turning in a new direction. In these situations, the court may well use a signal such as "we thus rule . . . ."

You may state the rules in a separate component of your case brief. Or you may state the rules—clearly labeled as such—within the reasoning component, discussed next. Either way, the rule is critical to your work on your client's case, so be sure you have presented the rule correctly. You may follow the court's formulation or, as needed, re-work the court's statement into an if/then statement, as discussed in Chapter 2.

For example, the sample *Weatherston's* brief refers to a general rule at the opening of the reasoning component. That rule is a consolidation of sentences at pages 275 and 276, which are supported by footnotes referring to commentary and Minnesota case law. Note that the rule is phrased more broadly (by reference to licensing statutes) than the holding (by reference to engineers).

Reasoning: As just noted, the reasoning component may cover the rules of law stated in the case. It also should synopsize the court's explanation of its holding. The court's reasoning is important because it provides guidance on how narrowly or broadly to read a case and insight into how the court will analyze future cases. Indeed, you will track the court's reasoning in analyzing your client's situation.

The court's reasoning may be quite lengthy. To keep your case reasonably brief and in any event focused on useful material, seek out and include the following material, which you may want to so label in your brief:

- In a more or less thorough and insightful way, the court shows *how the rule applies to the specific facts* of the case before it, connecting the factual conditions of the if-clause to the specific facts of the case before the court.
- In many cases, the court identifies the *competing arguments of the parties* (as to what rule of law is applicable or should be created or how the facts should be analyzed), evaluates those arguments, and then accepts or rejects them.
- The court may *draw a comparison* to an important precedent.
- The court sometimes describes the *public policy* or broad social goals it seeks to serve.
- The court usually cites *the major authorities* it relied upon in reasoning to its holding. If these authorities could also clearly pertain to your client's situation, include them in your case brief.

For example, the *Weatherston's* court was especially concerned about fraud, incompetence, and the public welfare in that case; these concerns are certainly pertinent to HomeElderCare's situation as well. Therefore the sample case brief emphasizes these points. So, too, the brief emphasizes the court's statements of public policy. The sample brief provides fairly little reference to authorities the court relied upon because the court itself did not emphasize them much.

3. Optional, Concluding Components

Some components do not occur in every case brief, but only where needed.

Dictum: On occasion, the court remarks upon matters not essential to the holding(s). When the court does so, no matter how clear and unequivocal the remarks seem to be, the remarks are considered dicta. The plural term "dicta," or the singular "dictum," derives from "obiter dictum," which means "a remark by the way." Dicta are not considered precedent because they are unnecessary to the outcome and perhaps less than fully considered.

Dicta typically arise in two situations. First, the court may rule on one of several issues in a case in such a way that it need not address the remaining issues, yet the court may provide a discussion of the remaining issues. Second, to clarify its reasoning, the court may hypothesize about how it would handle a slightly or even radically different case.

You should note pertinent dicta in your case brief because the statements do emanate from the court. In the future, the dictum may become law, or the court may repudiate the dictum. In the meantime, the dictum does provide some insight into the court's current thinking.

For example, had the *Weatherston's* court concluded that the contacts between Weatherston and MMLIC did not in fact form a contract, any comments on the legality of such a contract would have been dicta.

Concurring and dissenting opinions: If the court has split, you should note briefly who voted differently than the majority and how they would have decided the case. Also note who supported the outcome but would have reasoned differently. Dissents are not precedent. Concurrences only rarely are, in situations where the concurrence adds to a plurality to form a majority. Nonetheless, some of these opinions eventually do inspire the court to change the law in a future case, and all of them show the thinking of some members of the particular court.

In the example, the court ruled unanimously for Weatherston's. A dissenting justice might have written that the contract was illegal because Mr. Weatherston was practicing engineering without a license. A concurring justice might have written that none of Mr. Weatherston's work would have constituted engineering practices.

Questions: Here you may note any questions the court explicitly reserved for a future case—or questions you had as you read the case.

Pertinence: When you are reading a case for a specific client's situation, you likely will draw connections as you go between the two. While it may be inefficient to write out an extended analysis of the client's situation as you read each case, noting some key ideas should help you when you turn to reasoning through your client's situation.

4. Some Drafting Suggestions

It is important to produce case briefs efficiently (as indeed all lawyers' tasks must be performed efficiently). Your goal is to record the information you need to fully understand the case, but no more.

As you practice reading the law, you will build efficiency fairly naturally. In the meantime, you can conserve your time and energy by use of such timesavers as notes in the margin signifying which component is discussed, a standard set of abbreviations for various common terms, and a form tailored to your own preferences. You may find it easier to draft your briefs if you begin with the part of the case you generally understand the most readily.

Be sure to review the draft of your case brief carefully. At least where the case is complicated or central to your analysis of a client's situation, consider skimming the case again after writing the brief, to check the brief against the case. Check the brief against itself, to be sure, for example, that the facts alluded to in the reasoning section are covered in the facts component. As you evaluate your own case briefs, consider the following four criteria of sound legal writing:

- *Completeness:* Is everything present that is needed for a sound understanding?
- *Correctness:* Are all points stated accurately?
- *Coherence:* Do all parts of the brief fit together?
- *Comprehensibility:* Can you readily understand the brief?

E. REVIEW OF CHAPTER 3

Because courts follow precedent created in earlier cases in the particular court system, decided cases have tremendous authority. Decided cases are like fables, with real-world facts constituting the story and the holding constituting the moral. This chapter has set out the following steps for reading, understanding, and briefing cases:

(1) Read the case several times, and look up unfamiliar terms.
(2) Annotate the case, perhaps by labeling the paragraphs according to the components of the case brief.
(3) Ponder the two narratives in the case: Who did what, when, where, why, and how in the real world? Who did what, when, where, why, and how in the legal system?
(4) Write a case brief with the following components:
    - opening: heading, facts, procedure;
    - core: issue, holding, rule of law, reasoning;
    - optional: dictum, dissent, concurrence, questions, pertinence.
(5) Review your brief against the case and itself. Verify that it is complete, correct, coherent, and comprehensible.

Following these steps should yield sound case briefs, permitting you to move on to fusing multiple cases—the topic of Chapter 4.

4

FUSING CASES

A. Introduction
B. Selecting Cases to Fuse
C. Arraying Cases
D. Fusing Cases
E. Recognizing the Limits of Fusion
F. Review of Chapter 4

> [Common law] stands as a monument slowly raised, like a coral reef, from the minute accretions of past individuals, of whom each built upon the relics which his predecessors left, and in his turn left a foundation upon which his successors might work.
> —Learned Hand
> Book Review, 35 Harv. L. Rev. 479, 479 (1922) (reviewing Benjamin N. Cardozo's *The Nature of the Judicial Process*).

A. INTRODUCTION

Despite the enormous output of United States courts, only rarely does a lawyer find a mandatory precedent that so parallels the client's situation that the lawyer need read no further. (The enormous output of the courts, it seems, is well exceeded by the capacity of people to create problems needing judicial intervention.) Much more often, a lawyer reads a good handful or two of more or less pertinent cases.

What, then, does a lawyer do with a pile or file of cases? It may be tempting to count favorable versus unfavorable outcomes and use the score as the basis of analysis, but counting is too blunt a tool. Rather the lawyer processes each case in light of the others, deriving a whole—a case fusion that is greater than the sum of the individual cases.

Case fusion is similar to analysis of multiple incidents that people do outside of the law. Perhaps you have analyzed an employer's response to various employees' work, to discern performance standards, or tracked customer responses to new products, to develop a marketing approach. The goal of the analysis is to discern an overall rule or pattern or underlying policy—or all three. This is also true of legal case fusion.

Occasionally, the fusion process is easy because you can use a recent case or commentary that surveys the case law to date. However, this statement was not written with your client's situation in mind, so be sure to check and adapt it as needed. In the absence of a pre-existing fusion, you will need to fuse the cases yourself by taking three steps: selecting cases to fuse; arraying them; and, finally, fusing them.

The examples in this chapter refer to *Weatherston's* (discussed in detail in Chapter 3) and two additional cases: *Buckley v. Humason* and *Solomon v. Dreschler*. *Buckley* and *Solomon* deal with an issue similar to the illegal contract issue in *Weatherston's*. You should look over the cases and briefs at pages 280-83 before you read further.

B. SELECTING CASES TO FUSE

As you choose cases to fuse, keep several principles of the common law system in mind.

First, cases from the same court system should, by virtue of stare decisis, be consistent with each other and thus amenable to fusion. Thus, cases decided within the same state court system should be incorporated in your fusion. Cases from other court systems need not be consistent with each other and thus should be left out. As you make this call, keep in mind the United States legal system. For example, the federal courts of appeals may, and often do, take different approaches to issues not yet resolved by the United States Supreme Court, so it could be difficult to fuse decisions from various circuits into a single rule. As another example, a federal court may rule on an issue of state law, but this decision does not bind the state courts, so it should be excluded or given less weight than state court cases.

Also keep in mind that, as discussed in Chapter 3, cases from a given court are of varying weights. For example, cases from a higher court are very weighty, as are recent cases. In particular, watch out for older cases that may have been overruled.

Finally, because rules depend on their factual circumstances and legal contexts, be sure that the cases you are fusing pertain to the same legal issue or very nearly the same legal issue. For example, a rule making certain conduct criminal may be quite different from a rule permitting a wronged person to sue the perpetrator for damages.

C. ARRAYING CASES

Fusing cases depends on your full understanding of each case, so be sure you have read and briefed the cases carefully. As you review the cases, follow a logical progression, e.g., oldest to newest (or vice versa) or highest to lowest court. Focus on the relationship of each case to the cases you read before it.

To focus your attention on the relative precedential values of the cases, array them hierarchically, using the triangular court diagram of Exhibit 4.1. If there is more than one case from a particular court, list those cases from top to bottom in reverse chronological order. This hierarchical array is especially useful when you have cases from multiple levels of the same court system.

Array your cases on a timeline from oldest to most recent, placing cases with one result above the line and cases with the other result below the line. For each case, sketch out the key facts and reasoning. Again, see Exhibit 4.1. Start looking for a pattern—what is true of all cases above the line *and* not true of cases below the line?

From the array of HomeElderCare cases in Exhibit 4.1, you can see that two of the three cases, the older ones, came out the same way: the contract was not enforced. But the most recent case came out differently—the contract was enforced—perhaps because the court's approach has shifted after seventy years, or because the facts were more favorable for the unlicensed practitioner, or both.

EXHIBIT 4.1

HIERARCHICAL AND CHRONOLOGICAL ARRAYS OF CASES

Minn.
S.Ct.:

Weatherston's (1960)
Buckley (1892)
Solomon (1860)

Ct. App. (after 1983):

trial cts.:

Solomon (Minn. 1860): Unlicensed liquor dealer's K is invalid, bcz stat policy is to protect public from evils of unrestrained liquor sales

Buckley (Minn. 1892): Unlicensed realty broker's comm'n K is invalid; no discussion of policy

Weatherston's (Minn. 1960): Unlicensed engr's K is valid, bcz incidental part of larger K, public protected agst fraud & incompetence by P's training & D's supervision, public health & safety protect'd

D. FUSING CASES

There are various ways to fuse cases. If the cases all have fully articulated (albeit somewhat different) rules, you can use rule fusion. On the other hand, if the rule is not well articulated, you may want to use the features chart to help you discern patterns in the facts or policies of the cases. For the strongest fusion, you would combine the methods.

1. Focusing on Rules

You may wonder why the statement of a rule is not the same in every case. As the opening quote to this chapter notes, the common law is built by "minute accretions of past" cases, as each case builds upon past cases and adds to the foundation for future cases. Because a court can decide only the controversy presented to it, the court's opinion generally discusses only so much of a rule as is needed for that case. Other cases on the same general topic may entail other aspects of the rule. Another possibility is that the court may adjust the elements stated in previous cases to keep the rule current. Or the court may alter the phrasing of a rule, while not intending to change the meaning.

Rule fusion involves a word-by-word analysis of the similarities and differences in the rules drawn from the fused cases. First, compare each word and phrase of the rules to be fused, and separate the language into four categories: (1) material that is *identical* in all rules, (2) material that is *similar* in all rules, (3) material that *appears in only some* rules, or (4) material that *differs* from rule to rule.

(1) Begin to assemble the fused rule with the material that is *identical* in all rules.

(2) If *similar material* can be rephrased into a single broader term that still adequately describes the original material, use that new term in the fused rule. If it cannot, use one or more of the similar phrasings for this material.

(3) Add material *appearing in only some cases* to the fused rule, one item at a time. Test each new item by asking whether its addition would change the results of cases in which that item does not appear. If not, add the new item to the fused rule. If the addition would change any of the cases, try to adjust the new item by rewording it or by presenting the item as a disjunctive element (alternatives connected by "or").

(4) As for material that *differs,* consider the possibilities covered in Part E below.

In the end, aim for a well crafted if/then rule, perhaps with enumerated elements.

Exhibit 4.2 shows a fusion of the rules from *Weatherston's* and *Buckley.* Many of the words in those rules are identical and appear in the fused rule. Four boldface concepts are phrased in similar but not identical terms. One italicized item is unique to *Weatherston's;* element 3 is a pivotal portion of that

EXHIBIT 4.2

TEXTUAL FUSION OF RULES

italics = appears only in one case
boldface = similar terms

Buckley	*Weatherston's*
IF (1) statute makes particular **business** unlawful for unlicensed person & (2) person not **authorized** in that **business** makes **contract,**	IF (1) statute requires person practicing particular **profession** to obtain license or **certificate**, & (2) person in that profession enters into **agreement** of **professional** character without license or **certificate**, & (3) *circumstances surrounding agreement violate any reason for licensing statute's existence,*
THEN contract is void.	THEN that agreement is **illegal** & void.

Fused Rule

IF (1) a statute requires a person practicing a particular profession or engaging in a particular business to obtain a license, and

(2) a person in that profession or business enters into a business or professional contract without a license, and

(3) the circumstances surrounding the contract violate any reason for the statute's existence,

THEN that contract is void.

---

rule. It is difficult to test its consistency with *Buckley* because the *Buckley* facts are so sparely stated. *Weatherston's* was decided much later than *Buckley*, so the additional element in *Weatherston's* signals the rule's evolution and is included in the fused rule.

As you work with the cases, you no doubt will notice how the rule applied to the facts of the various cases. Furthermore, in most cases, the court will discuss what one or more elements of the rule mean. This information, which exemplifies and elaborates upon the rule, can be very helpful to you as you seek to apply the rule to your client's situation, so you may wish to incorporate it into your statement of the rule.

For example, *Solomon*, *Buckley*, and *Weatherston's* provide three examples of the concept of licensed profession: liquor dealer, realty broker, and engineer. As another example, the *Weatherston's* court focused on the incidental nature of the engineering services, fraud, incompetence, and risks to public safety. Exhibit 4.3, an if/then rule distilled by fusing the three cases, incorporates these points.

2. Focusing on Facts or Policies

Another approach is to look for patterns in the cases' facts, results, and reasoning, including policies. This approach is especially effective where the court has not articulated the rule fully or clearly, perhaps because the area is new for the court or an old rule is losing support. A fusion method well suited to this approach is the features chart.

This chart captures the potentially significant features of the cases. In addition to the case name, court, and year, possible features include the real-world roles of the parties; the claim, also known as "cause of action"; the relief sought, also known as "remedy"; the most salient facts; policies stated by the court; and the holding(s) of each case on the issue(s) being examined. If the court stresses a specific feature, it should appear in your features chart. Be sure to list the cases in a logical order, such as oldest to most recent.

The next step is to look for patterns that explain the holdings:

- Does a particular holding always follow from a particular fact or combination of facts?
- Does a particular policy consideration result in one holding or the other?
- Does one result occur until a certain date, and then another result appears?
- Has one fact or policy become more or less important over time?

EXHIBIT 4.3

IF/THEN PRESENTATION OF FUSED RULE

IF   (1) statute requires licensure of person practicing profession/ business, and

- exs: liquor dealer, realty broker, engineer

(2) person in that profession/business enters into contract without license, and

(3) circumstances violate reason for statute

- such as fraud, incompetence, danger to public safety & health

- not so where engineering task is incidental part of larger contract, professional told client of unlicensed status, unlicensed professional is licensed in another state & supervised by licensed professional,

THEN   contract is void.

These patterns may be cause/effect relationships, or they may be coincidences. A close reading of the cases should tell you which is true.

If you cannot find a pattern that explains the holdings, reread the cases to find additional facts that may not have seemed significant on first reading. If the cases truly conflict, concentrate on the later cases and the cases from the highest court.

Finally, align the findings from your features chart with whatever rule material the court has presented. The aspects you have identified as important should be consistent with the concepts identified by the court.

Exhibit 4.4 is a features chart comparing *Solomon, Buckley,* and *Weatherston's.* The columns to the right of center suggest that the key aspect is violation of the statute's policy. Note, however, that some question remains because this aspect was not analyzed in *Buckley.* On the other hand, this factor is emphasized in the most recent decision of the state's highest court.

3. Checking Your Work

However you perform your case fusion, be sure to check it for compliance with the four criteria of sound legal writing:

- *Completeness:* Are all cases, elements, and consequences included?
- *Correctness:* Have you accurately reflected the cases? Have you attended closely to the courts' language? Have you accurately represented the holdings?

EXHIBIT 4.4

FEATURES CHART

Case Court Year	Parties	Claim	Additional Facts	Purpose of License Statute	Purpose Violated Here?	Contract Valid?
Solomon Minn. 1860	unlicensed liquor dealer and buyer	recover price of liquor delivered	NA	protect public from evils of unrestrained liquor sales	yes	no
Buckley Minn. 1892	unlicensed realty broker and client	recover broker's commission	NA	none stated	NA	no
Weatherston's Minn. 1960	unlicensed engineer and client	recover damages for breach of contract	engineer was competent; no fraud; services were incidental to permitted transaction	protect public from fraud and incompetence; protect public health and safety	no	yes

- *Coherence:* Does the fusion make sense? Are the elements consistent with each other?
- *Comprehensibility:* Can you understand the fusion?

If you have prepared both a rule fusion and a features chart, check the results of each against the other.

E. RECOGNIZING THE LIMITS OF FUSION

On occasion, you may find yourself trying to fuse material that cannot be fused. For instance, your work with the rules might yield an element as to which the cases differ dramatically, in a way that cannot be accommodated by a disjunctive element or a wording change. In other situations, your features chart may not yield a pattern that explains all of the cases' holdings. This typically arises in two situations.

First, the court may not merely modify a rule over time but instead impliedly overrule previous case law, without saying so. It is not possible or desirable to fuse cases that, frankly, are meant to conflict.

Second, you may have an anomalous case (or two) in an otherwise fusible set of cases. Although anomalous cases frustrate lawyers seeking to understand an area of case law, they do not surprise most experienced lawyers. Recall that courts not only make precedent; they also resolve real-world disputes. Some litigants have facts sympathetic enough to persuade a court—despite the legal weaknesses of their cases. If you have discovered a truly anomalous case, consider omitting it from your fusion. This omission is especially justifiable if later cases discount the anomalous case or do not take note of it.

F. REVIEW OF CHAPTER 4

The goal of case fusion is to generate a rule or pattern that encompasses the content of a set of cases. The steps of fusion are as follows:

(1) Select the cases to fuse.
(2) Prepare hierarchical and chronological arrays, to help you to understand the precedential relationships among the cases.
(3) (a) Where possible, fuse the rules stated in the cases and note examples and elaborations.
    (b) Where appropriate and useful, seek a pattern or policy in the cases by constructing a features chart.
(4) Check your fusion for completeness, correctness, coherence, and comprehensibility.

Fusing cases in the way before you apply them to your client's case will strengthen your understanding of the law and your analysis of your client's legal position.

READING STATUTES

A. Introduction
B. Legislative Process and Legislative Intent
C. Reading a Statute
D. Briefing a Statute
E. Review of Chapter 5

> The law is a living growth, not a changeless code.
> —Inscription carved over the entrance to the Yale Law
> School, 1929–1931

A. INTRODUCTION

This chapter introduces codified law—law in the form of a code, that is, a set of rules of general applicability. The discussion focuses on statutes, the codes enacted by legislatures.

There are other types of codified law: legislatures (and voters) create constitutions, administrative agencies create rules and regulations, and courts create rules governing the litigation process. These forms of law stand in a hierarchical relationship: constitutions at the top, statutes and court rules in the middle, administrative regulations at the bottom. Thus, for example, statutes must accord with constitutional requirements, and regulations must accord with statutes.

How do lawyers read codes, which are very different in design than cases? Keeping in mind how statutes are created, a lawyer approaches a statute as one might approach the rules of a game, seeking directions for a specific client situation within the set of interlocking rules.

Along the way, this chapter discusses two specific statutes. When the HomeElderCare Case was created, section 481.02 of the Minnesota Statutes, which governs the unauthorized practice of law, was the major statute. Minnesota's Living Will Act, Minnesota Statutes sections 145B.01-.17, was also relevant. Pertinent portions of both appear at pages 284-93, and you may find it helpful to read them now.

B. LEGISLATIVE PROCESS
AND LEGISLATIVE INTENT

To understand why statutes read as they do and why lawyers approach them as they do, you must know about (1) the legislative process; (2) its corollary, legislative intent; (3) prospectivity of statutes; and (4) the interplay between federal and state statutes.

1. Legislative Process

The legislative process[1] is a highly collaborative and loosely structured process, in which legislators, the executive, and interested members of the public participate. See Exhibit 5.1.

Proposals for new legislation come from many sources: legislators, the executive branch, individual citizens, organizations such as industry associations and public interest groups, and law reform commissions. Ultimately, for a proposal to receive the legislature's official attention, it must become a bill introduced by one or more legislators.

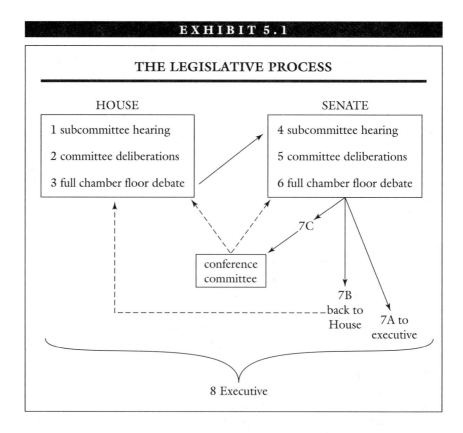

EXHIBIT 5.1

THE LEGISLATIVE PROCESS

HOUSE

1 subcommittee hearing

2 committee deliberations

3 full chamber floor debate

SENATE

4 subcommittee hearing

5 committee deliberations

6 full chamber floor debate

7C

conference committee

7B back to House

7A to executive

8 Executive

---

1. For further detail, see Jack Davies, *Legislative Law and Process in a Nutshell* (2d ed. 1986).

In the United States, most legislatures, including the federal Congress, are bicameral, consisting of both a house of representatives and a senate. For a bill to become law, it must be passed in identical form by both chambers. Sometimes a bill begins in and is passed by one chamber, then proceeds to the second. Other times, companion bills are considered simultaneously by both chambers. Both chambers typically consider bills in several stages:

(1) A subcommittee specializing in the general area of the bill's topic considers the bill. The subcommittee may hold a public hearing and receive testimony from interested individuals and groups. In the later stages, lobbyists may be very involved, informally and very effectively in some situations.

(2) The committee deliberates on the bill, discussing its strengths and weaknesses and honing its language. The committee either reports the bill favorably to the full chamber or tables it, the latter precluding further action on the bill. When a committee reports a bill favorably, it usually generates a report on the bill.

(3) The full chamber debates the bill. When the bill is controversial, the debate may actually be a true airing of competing views involving most members of the chamber. In other situations, the so-called debate entails a series of speeches by the bill's supporters that go unheard by most other legislators. Ultimately, the legislators vote on the bill.

(4)–(6) A similar or abbreviated process occurs in the other chamber.

(7) If both chambers have passed identical bills (7A), that bill goes to the executive (president or governor). If the two chambers considered non-identical bills and the differences are minor (7B), one chamber may accede to the other's changes; then the bill clears the legislature. If the differences are major (7C), a conference committee, with members from both chambers, resolves the differences and reports a consensus bill back to the two chambers, which may then pass the consensus bill.

(8) Once both chambers pass the same bill, it proceeds to the executive for signature. The executive may disagree with the bill and veto it, subject to override by the legislature. On the other hand, if the executive signs it, or in some systems neither signs nor vetoes it, the bill becomes law and is labeled a "statute."

The legislature may amend the statute at a later time for various reasons. The legislature may not be satisfied with the way the statute has worked out and may modify troublesome language to more closely reflect what the legislature intended. Or the legislature may become aware of facts it did not initially have and revise the statute to reflect that new knowledge. Or the legislature may change its collective mind about what the law should be and alter the statute accordingly.

In some respects, the legislative process is similar to the judicial process. For example, both are lawmaking processes, both involve participation by those governed, and both have mechanisms for adjusting the law.

However, the two processes also differ in important ways, as shown in Exhibit 5.2. The courts are reactive, considering only cases brought to their attention by the parties; the legislature acts both reactively and proactively, taking on problems brought forth by the public and also those discerned by the legislators themselves. The courts take the issues as framed by the parties' dispute; the legislature defines its own issues. A small segment of the public participates in judicial lawmaking through litigation, which is a very formal process defined by rules of procedure; a wider segment participates in legislative lawmaking through lobbying, a quite informal and ill-defined process. The judicial process is intended to be non-political; the legislative process is intended to be highly political.

As an example, consider the Minnesota statute on living wills, chapter 145B. For five years, two sides with strongly held views battled: on one side, Minnesota Citizens Concerned for Life (MCCL); on the other, a coalition of senior citizen groups, the state bar association, and medical provider associations. Eventually, the chair of the House committee sought to mediate the conflict, and in 1987 and 1988, the House committee held thirty-five hours of hearings around the state. Then the chief voice for the MCCL lost his seat, and the coalition in favor of the bill enlisted a new chief author in the Senate. Ten more hours of hearings were held. Several changes were made in committee and on the floor, and the bill passed as the Adult Health Care Decisions Act, ch. 3, 1989 Minn.

EXHIBIT 5.2

COMPARISON OF CASES AND STATUTES

	Cases	Statutes
Lawmaking Process	• reactive • parties frame issues • litigation • non-political	• reactive and proactive • legislature frames issues • lobbying • political
Focus	• facts of current litigation • case before the court	• future situations • broad class of situations
Effect	• generally retroactive	• generally prospective
Form	• primarily narrative with embedded rule • narrative in parties' case • fable with story and moral	• primarily rule with implied narrative • narrative in paradigm case • rules of game

Laws 8.[2] The statute was amended in 1991, including a new title, the Minnesota Living Will Act. *See* Act of May 20, 1991, ch. 148, 1991 Minn. Laws 308.[3]

2. Legislative Intent and Word Choice

The ultimate product of the legislative process is a statute: a collection of words chosen to express the will of the legislature. The premise of a statute is that it expresses legislative intent. To a certain extent, "legislative intent" is a legal fiction. In any statutory provision, some legislators probably intended to state one idea, others intended another, and yet others did not think seriously enough about the matter to have a clear intent. Although there may be individual legislators' intentions, rarely is there a single legislative intent. Furthermore, a particular factual situation may pose a question that the legislature never even contemplated.

Nonetheless, the premise of legislative intent is powerful. For whatever reasons, the legislature has enacted the precise language in the statute—each word, each phrase, each punctuation mark—and this language commands respect.

Statutes thus differ from case law. Again, see Exhibit 5.2. Judges write most directly to the parties to the case, explaining the outcome of the litigation for them. However, certain portions of an opinion, chiefly the rules of law and the holding, are also written with an eye toward unknown participants in future disputes, and these portions are quite carefully worded. By comparison, the legislature writes entirely to unknown persons whose future activities fall within the statute's scope. Thus, every word in a statute carries the potential impact of the rule of law and the holding from a case.

3. Prospective Effect of Statutes

Unlike case law, which typically is retroactive, statutes typically have prospective effect. A statute covers conduct occurring on or after the statute's effective date. Some statutes take effect on the date of enactment, which generally is the date of signature by the executive. Others do not take effect until a date specified in the statute, which is usually some months after the date of enactment. Others take effect on the legislature's default effective date for statutes with no stated effective date.

There are some limited exceptions to this general rule of prospectivity. The legislature may provide that the statute is to be applied retroactively. A statute addressing procedures or remedies for a wronged party may be retroactive in the sense that a party whose loss occurred before the statute's enactment would proceed under the new statute if the litigation occurs after the effective date.

---

2. *See* Howard Orenstein, David Bishop & Leigh D. Mathison, *Minnesota's Living Will . . .* , Bench & B. Minn., Aug. 1989, at 21.
3. For an overview of 1998 legislation that substantially altered the living will statute, *see* Barbara J. Blumer, *The New Health Care Directive*, Bench & B. Minn., Sept. 1998, at 25.

Thus, determining which language was effective at the time of the events you are analyzing is critical, especially if a statute has been amended. That version (not necessarily the current version) of the statute governs your client's situation.

4. Federalism

Statutes exist at multiple levels of government. A legal topic may be governed by state statutes, by federal statute, by local ordinance, or by a combination of these. Federal statutes govern matters Congress has perceived to be of national interest, such as air and water pollution, the operation of the securities market, and union-management relations. The Constitution reserves to the states matters of primarily local interest such as property, contract, and tort issues.

Where both federal and state statutes exist, the federal statute typically identifies the permissible role of state law. In some areas, Congress has sought to control a field with federal law, so state statutes cannot also exist. In other areas, Congress has sought to assure minimum standards while permitting the states to provide similar or additional protection. In yet other areas, Congress has created a federal model that the states may opt in or out of; states opting out may be required to enact comparable state statutes.

C. READING A STATUTE

1. An Analogy: Rules of a Game

Statutes resemble the rules of a game. Both are written in fairly abstract terms. Some statutes govern discrete, uncomplicated situations, and the rules are quite simple. Others govern a wider range of complicated situations, and the rules are quite elaborate. In either event, you may find it helpful to imagine that you are seeking certain information about how to play the game:

- What is the name of the game?
- What is its purpose?
- Who can play?
- What kind of conduct is generally encouraged or prohibited?
- Are there any exceptions to these general rules?
- What are the consequences of playing or not playing the game as described?

2. Organization of a Statute

A statute reads like an expansive rule of law. It thus differs from a case, because only a small portion of a case is framed as a rule of law. Although each statute is unique, statutes have some standard components. The following material outlines the components you are likely to find in longer statutes. Shorter statutes do not contain all of these components. The statute regarding the unauthorized practice of law in the HomeElderCare case file at pages 284-87 is labeled according to these components.

Title: Legislatures occasionally name major statutes, and some statutes come to be called by their names, rather than their section numbers. The living will statute's name is the Minnesota Living Will Act, according to section 145B.01.

Preamble, purpose statement: On occasion, the legislature includes a statement of its purpose in enacting the statute: the problems the legislature sought to address, the interests the legislature sought to serve, or the results the legislature desired. Although this language does not itself constitute any portion of the statute's rule, it can provide helpful insight into the legislature's intent. Neither sample statute contains a purpose statement.

Definitions: Many statutes employ particular meanings for terms used in the statute. These statutory terms of art generally are set out in a definition section near the beginning of the statute, or they may appear in the scope section (see below) or elsewhere. Regardless of location, these definitions are critical, because they help to define the factual conditions leading to the statute's legal consequences. For example, the living will statute provides a particular, narrow meaning of "health care" in section 145B.02 subdivision 3.

Scope: Some statutes contain scope provisions, generally found near the beginning of the statute, which state the situations to which the statute does apply and thereby imply which situations are not within the statute's reach. A statute's scope typically has three dimensions: the actors (whether people or entities) covered by the statute, their actions, and the circumstances in which they act. If there is no separate scope provision, you must infer the statute's scope from the definitions and other components. For example, section 145B.03 subdivision 1 of the living will statute indicates that the statute governs living wills regarding health care, entered into by competent adults.

The following three components constitute the operative provisions of the statute. All statutes contain general rules. Most also contain exceptions. Many contain consequences/enforcement provisions; for others, the consequences appear in another statute or case law.

General rule: The core of the statute describes the conduct the legislature has chosen to encourage or prohibit. Many statutes contain multiple general rules, because the legislature has chosen to govern several forms of related conduct in one statute. Section 481.02 subdivision 1 of the unauthorized practice statute is a general rule prohibiting the unauthorized practice of law.

Exceptions: Frequently, the legislature grapples with competing policies in enacting a statute. The legislature may favor one policy in the general rule but seek to accommodate a competing policy by carving out an exception. For example, section 481.02 subdivision 3 of the unauthorized practice statute delineates numerous situations that would have fallen within the general rule prohibiting unauthorized law practice, except that the legislature chose to exempt them.

Consequences and enforcement: The purpose of the general rule is to link the identified conduct to a specific legal consequence. If the conduct is encouraged, the consequence is a legal benefit, such as recognition of a transaction as legally enforceable or exemption from a fee. If the conduct is prohibited, the consequence is a legal penalty, such as a criminal sanction, a civil fine, non-enforcement of the transaction, or payment of damages to a harmed party. These consequences may be stated in the same section as the general rule, or they may be stated in a separate section. The statement of the consequences may refer explicitly to an enforcement mechanism, or the enforcement mechanism may be implied. For example, if a statute indicated that a party is liable for damages, one could infer that the harmed party would bring a lawsuit to obtain damages. In the unauthorized practice statute, section 481.02 subdivision 8 identifies both the consequences of engaging in the unauthorized practice of law and the means by which the statute is enforced.

Severability or saving clause: Some statutes include a provision indicating that, should any specific provisions be deemed unconstitutional, the rest of the statute is intended by the legislature to stand. Neither sample statute includes a severability provision.

Effective date: As noted above, the legislature may specify the effective date of a new law. Neither sample statute has a stated effective date.

3. Reading Stages

You should read a statute several times. The first time through, read the entire statute to discern its overall design and scope. Second, identify which provisions are pertinent to your client's case and which (if any) are not; err on the side of including information that may or may not be pertinent. Third, identify which pertinent material fits into each of the components set forth above.

At first reading, or even second or third, a statute may seem to lack a narrative of specific real-world events, as there always is in a judicial opinion. However, if you think carefully about the statute, you will be able to envision a specific situation that would clearly bring the statute into play, i.e., its paradigm case. You may want to write out that paradigm case, along with the briefs described in the next part; the paradigm case may prove helpful if the statute proves to be ambiguous when you apply it to your client's facts.

D. Briefing a Statute

Statutory briefing is a means of analyzing and taking notes on a statute. You can organize your brief by statutory components or, ideally, by the if/then rule structure introduced in Chapter 2. And you can use various means of depicting the statutory rule. Any brief should be focused on your client's situation; the aim of the brief is to distill the statute into a rule you can apply to your client's facts.

1. Brief Based on Statutory Components

A brief based on statutory components parallels the case brief (discussed in Chapter 3) in that it presents material under component headings. Although you can simply copy the statutory language under each heading, the brief will be more useful if you condense the key ideas and use enumeration or spacing so that the language most pertinent to your client's situation is highlighted. However, in accord with the premise of legislative intent, adhere to the statute's language. You may find it helpful to note the sections or subsections where the information appears.

Exhibit 5.3 is an example of such a brief for section 481.02. Note how the key material in a lengthy statute has been extracted and is presented in a more accessible form.

EXHIBIT 5.3

COMPONENTS-BASED STATUTORY BRIEF

TITLE: Unauthorized practice of law.

DEFINITIONS: None expressly stated, tho atty is member of MN bar admitted & licensed. Subd. 1.

SCOPE: None expressly stated; governs actions of non-attys as stated below. Subd. 1.

GENERAL RULES: Subd. 1 states: Unlawful for non-attys to:

- give legal advice or counsel
  perform for or furnish legal services
  to another
  for fee or consid'n
  OR
- prepare directly or thru another
  for another person, firm, corp
  will, testamentary disp'n, instrument of trust serving purposes
    similar to will
  (for or w/o fee or consid'n)
  OR
- prepare for another person, firm, corp
  any other legal document
  for fee or consid'n.

EXCEPTIONS: Permissible for:

- person to draw will for another
  in emergency if imminence of death leaves insuff time for atty
    superv'n—subd. 3(2).
- person to confer or cooperate with atty of another
  in preparing any legal document
  if atty is not emp'd by non-atty or by person, firm, corp rep'd
    by non-atty—subd. 3(6).
- corp to furnish
  to person lawfully engaged in practice of law
  information or clerical service that is lawful
  provided that atty maintains responsibility to clients for info &
    services—subd. 7.

CONSEQUENCES/ENFORCEMENT: (1) Misdemeanor.
  County attys prosecute; jurisdiction in dist ct. (2) Injunction against
  illegal actions, brought by county atty or atty general. Subd. 8.

2. Brief Based on If/Then Format

Because a statute is an expansive rule statement, it makes sense to brief a statute by creating one or more if/then rule statements. You can derive an if/then brief from the brief based on statutory components, according to the following formula:

IF   the situation (actor/action/circumstances)
      meets the *definitions*, and
      falls within the *scope*, and
      falls within the *general rule*, and
      does not qualify for any of the *exceptions*,

THEN   the *consequences* follow, through the *enforcement* mechanism.

If/then briefs are more useful than components-based briefs. All information related to the factual conditions appears together in the if-clause, although this information may be scattered throughout the statute in definition, scope, general rule, and exception provisions. Similarly, all information related to the legal consequences appears in the then-clause, even though this information may be scattered in the statute among the general rule, consequences, and enforcement provisions.

An if/then statement of a statute can be presented in various ways. Options include a traditional paragraph, a quasi-outline using tabulation or enumeration, and a flowchart. Exhibits 5.4 and 5.5 are examples of if/then briefs for section 481.02, in quasi-outline and flowchart form.

3. Drafting Carefully and Checking Your Work

As you create any statutory brief, you will inevitably reconfigure the statute's structure and language slightly. Make sure that the brief accurately reflects the overall design of the statute; for example, keep the exceptions connected to the general rules to which they pertain.

Guard against a very understandable temptation to paraphrase the statute into language that is easier to work with or more desirable from the client's perspective but does not capture the statute's meaning. Take care not to lose relevant content in the statute when you paraphrase or condense language. More specifically:

- Pay special attention to the grammatical units in the statute's provisions. These units typically are nouns, verbs or verb phrases, and modifiers.
- Attend closely to details. For example, there is a major difference between "and" and "or" in a statute.
- Be sure you know what a modifying phrase modifies.
- Statutory terms of art should be employed as defined throughout the statute, even though a statutorily defined term might have a different meaning in everyday speech.

Finally, insert section and subdivision references, to allow you to easily locate the statutory provisions you have briefed.

EXHIBIT 5.4

IF/THEN STATUTORY BRIEF

IF   any person/ass'n except members of MN bar admitted & licensed
to practice

    A. does 1 OR 2 OR 3 (all in subd. 1)
       1. gives legal advice or counsel
         or performs for or furnishes legal services
         to another
         for fee or consid'n
       2. prepares directly or thru another
         for another person/firm/corp
         any will or testamentary disp'n or instrument of trust serving
          purposes similar to will
         (for or w/o fee or consid'n)
       3. prepares for another person/firm/corp
         any other legal document
         for fee or consid'n

    B. AND NOT person drafting will
      for another
      in emergency leaving insuff time for atty superv'n
      subd. 3(2)

    C. AND NOT person conferring or cooperating
      with licensed atty of another
      in preparing any legal document
      where atty is not emp'd by that person or by person/firm/corp
       rep'd by that person
      subd. 3(6)

    D. AND NOT corp furnishing
      lawful info or clerical services
      to atty
      who maintains responsibility to clients for info & services
      subd. 7

THEN   misdemeanor prosecuted by county atty in dist ct OR
        injunction brought by county atty or atty gen'l—subd. 8.

By way of illustration, all three briefs reflect a careful parsing of section
481.02. Section 481.02 subdivision 1 prohibits five separate activities (three
potentially pertinent to HomeElderCare's situation), all in one massive
paragraph. When the verb phrases ("to appear," "to hold out," etc.) are

EXHIBIT 5.5

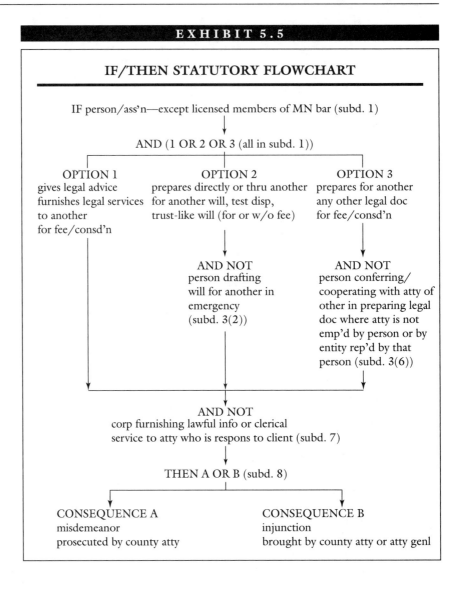

IF/THEN STATUTORY FLOWCHART

IF person/ass'n—except licensed members of MN bar (subd. 1)

AND (1 OR 2 OR 3 (all in subd. 1))

OPTION 1
gives legal advice
furnishes legal services
to another
for fee/consd'n

OPTION 2
prepares directly or thru another
for another will, test disp,
trust-like will (for or w/o fee)

OPTION 3
prepares for another
any other legal doc
for fee/consd'n

AND NOT
person drafting
will for another in
emergency
(subd. 3(2))

AND NOT
person conferring/
cooperating with atty of
other in preparing legal
doc where atty is not
emp'd by person or by
entity rep'd by that
person (subd. 3(6))

AND NOT
corp furnishing lawful info or clerical
service to atty who is respons to client (subd. 7)

THEN A OR B (subd. 8)

CONSEQUENCE A
misdemeanor
prosecuted by county atty

CONSEQUENCE B
injunction
brought by county atty or atty genl

separated from each other (as revealed by the numbers in circles on the copy at page 284), the paragraph is easier to understand. These five major activities are stated in the disjunctive. Note how important it is to link the modifying phrases "for or without a fee or any consideration" and "for a fee or any consideration" to the proper activities. Although the statute has no definition provision, it implies a definition of "attorney" (someone admitted and licensed to practice in Minnesota), which should be carried throughout the statute.

Following these suggestions should enable you to satisfy the four criteria:

- *Completeness:* Are all pertinent provisions included?
- *Correctness:* Have you accurately captured the concepts the legislature meant to convey in the specific words it chose?

- *Coherence:* Do the parts of the brief fit together well? Does the overall point (that the specified legal consequence will follow the specified factual conditions) make sense?
- *Comprehensibility:* Can you understand the brief?

E. REVIEW OF CHAPTER 5

Statutes and other forms of codified law resemble the rules of a game. They state rules of law in broad terms applicable to classes of situations occurring in the future. Your chief focus in reading statutes is on the words chosen by the legislature to express its intended meaning. This chapter has set out the following steps for reading and understanding statutes:

(1) Read the entire statute to discern its overall design and coverage.
(2) Identify the statutory provisions that are pertinent to your client's situation.
(3) Label the pertinent provisions according to the standard statutory components.
(4) Create a brief based on the statutory components.
(5) Create a brief based on the if/then rule stated in the statute—with due care taken to respect the words chosen by the legislature.
(6) Review your brief against the statute to verify that it is complete, correct, coherent, and comprehensible.

Following these steps should provide you with an accurate understanding of the statute and prepare you to explore aids to interpretation of the statute, described in Chapter 6.

INTERPRETING

STATUTES

> Law is merely the expression of the will of the strongest for the time being, and therefore laws have no fixity, but shift from generation to generation.
> —Brooks Adams (American historian)
> *The Law of Civilization and Decay* (1896)

A. INTRODUCTION

Once a lawyer locates a pertinent statute, it may seem that the analysis of the client's situation is nearly done. However, more often than not, ambiguity will arise as the statute is applied to the client's facts.

How do lawyers bring clarity to their understanding of statutes? Mindful of the importance of legislative intent and aware of the reasons that statutes are ambiguous, they employ a variety of statutory interpretation tools.[1] Some tools are more powerful than others. Some involve reasoning from the statute itself; others involve considering other materials. Not infrequently, different tools lead you to different conclusions. Informed judgment and careful thought are critical in statutory interpretation.

---

1. *See generally* Norman J. Singer, *Statutes and Statutory Construction* (5th ed. 1992).

Most examples in this chapter are drawn from the unauthorized practice of law statute, while a few are drawn from the living will statute, both discussed in Chapter 5. The statutes appear at pages 284-93. This chapter introduces a new case, *Peterson v. Hovland;* you may wish to read it and its brief at pages 294-302.

B.   AMBIGUITY IN STATUTORY LANGUAGE

1. Why and How Ambiguity Arises

As a rule of law, a statute provides for certain legal consequences to follow certain actions, undertaken by certain actors, in certain circumstances. Several questions thus arise: Which actors fall within the statute, and which do not? Which actions fall within the statute? Which circumstances matter? Which consequences follow?

Ambiguity in statutory language makes answers to these questions uncertain. Statutory language is ambiguous when more than one meaning is possible. Some statutes are ambiguous because the language is vague or puzzling; others are ambiguous because a point logically related to the statute's topic is omitted.

Statutory ambiguity has several causes. The legislature may have intentionally chosen ambiguous language because legislators were unable to agree on clearer language and were willing to defer to the courts or a later session of the legislature. Or the legislators may have tried but been unable to write less ambiguous language. Or the legislature may not have perceived an ambiguity in its choice of words; one can think of only so much when writing any document. Or new situations may have arisen since the statute's enactment, turning language that once was clear into ambiguous language.

For example, two clauses in section 481.02 subdivision 1 prohibit the drafting of "any will or testamentary disposition or instrument of trust serving purposes similar to those of a will" and the drafting of "any other legal document." Does a living will come within either of these clauses? This ambiguity stems from the use of a puzzling word—"will"—and the use of a vague, undefined term—"any other legal document." Most likely, the legislature did not think about living wills in drafting this language because living wills postdate the statute's enactment.

As a second example, section 481.02 subdivision 8 specifies that someone who violates the statute is subject to prosecution for a misdemeanor or an injunction. But is the transaction void? This latter consequence is simply not addressed in the statute. Perhaps the legislature did not think of this question; perhaps it chose to leave the question for the courts to resolve.

2. An Analogy: Rules of a Game

As noted in Chapter 5, statutes are like the rules of a game. When the rules of a game are unclear, there are several possible means of clarification. You can puzzle through the language. You can seek an authoritative interpretation. You can try to discern the point of the game and interpret the unclear rule accordingly. You can draw on your knowledge of the rules of other similar games.

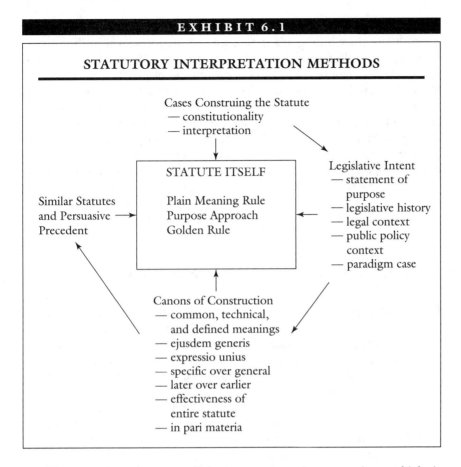

EXHIBIT 6.1

STATUTORY INTERPRETATION METHODS

Cases Construing the Statute
— constitutionality
— interpretation

STATUTE ITSELF

Plain Meaning Rule
Purpose Approach
Golden Rule

Legislative Intent
— statement of
  purpose
— legislative history
— legal context
— public policy
  context
— paradigm case

Similar Statutes
and Persuasive
Precedent

Canons of Construction
— common, technical,
  and defined meanings
— ejusdem generis
— expressio unius
— specific over general
— later over earlier
— effectiveness of
  entire statute
— in pari materia

These options have parallels in statutory interpretation, which is sketched in Exhibit 6.1. Keep in mind that the legislature's words must be respected at all times. These tools help you interpret the statute; they do not supplant it.

C. EMPLOYING THE PLAIN MEANING RULE, PURPOSE APPROACH, AND GOLDEN RULE

Statutory interpretation can be approached in various ways. One is the plain meaning rule. According to this rule, the lawyer's task is to follow the letter of the law, that is, the words chosen by the legislature. When the statute's meaning is plain, one need not use the methods of interpretation discussed in this chapter.

A second is the purpose approach. According to the purpose approach, the lawyer's task is to ascertain and then give meaning to the legislature's purpose in enacting the statute, that is, to respect legislative intent.

In many situations, these two approaches converge because the legislature's purpose is well articulated in the statute's language. But the two approaches diverge when the statutory language leads to a result probably not intended by the legislature. The bridge between the plain meaning rule and the purpose approach is the golden rule. The golden rule instructs lawyers not to honor the wording of a statute when it produces an absurd or unreasonable result, calls for an impossible outcome, or yields an unconstitutional result. The meshing of the purpose approach and plain meaning rule is thus left to the sound discretion of the lawyer interpreting the statute.

For example, imagine that the legislature prohibited the drafting of "any document" by a non-lawyer. According to the plain meaning rule, the statute could prohibit government employees from completing birth certificates and coroners from completing death certificates. By contrast, according to the purpose approach, the statute would not be construed to prohibit these actions because these results would not serve the statute's purpose of precluding non-lawyers from engaging in work requiring legal expertise. The golden rule suggests that the latter interpretation is the better one.

D. RELYING ON CASES INTERPRETING STATUTES

In many situations, the lawyer's choice among various statutory meanings is firmly guided by the decisions of the courts. When a dispute is governed by a statute and the parties are unable to settle the dispute themselves, they bring the dispute to the courts (not the legislature) for resolution. In addition to resolving the dispute for the parties, the court undertakes two very important tasks in relation to the statute.

First, the court assesses whether the legislature acted within constitutional bounds when it enacted the statute. The court will attempt to read the statute to render it constitutional, if possible. If not, the statute is declared unconstitutional in whole or in part, and the unconstitutional portion has no further legal effect.

Second, courts provide authoritative interpretation of a statute and thereby reduce the ambiguity in the legislature's language. The statute provides the rule of law by which the case is decided. The court may elaborate on this rule, give definition to unclear language, or fill gaps left in the statute. It then links the abstract language of the statute to the facts of a specific dispute. The rule of law, holding, and reasoning in the case have precedential effect.

The lawmaking process can also work in the opposite direction. When the court declares a statute unconstitutional, the legislature may enact a revised statute. When the court interprets a statute, the legislature generally accepts the interpretation by not amending the statute. On occasion, however, the legislature registers its objection to the court's interpretation by amending the statute. Where the law consists of an original statute with amendments as well as case law, you must fully understand the dialogue between the legislature and courts; creating a timeline can be helpful. Exhibit 6.2 is an example.

In the HomeElderCare situation, neither the living will statute nor the unauthorized practice statute has been declared unconstitutional. The living will statute does touch upon a patient's constitutional right of privacy to refuse invasive medical treatment, under the Minnesota Constitution.[2]

---

2. *See Jarvis v. Levine*, 418 N.W.2d 139 (Minn. 1988).

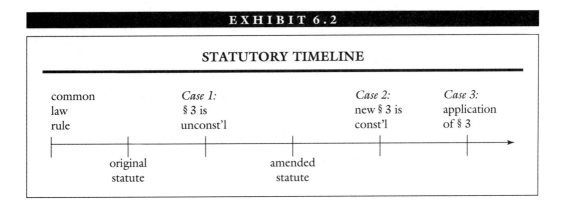

Had the statute impaired, rather than facilitated, the exercise of this right, it may well have been unconstitutional.

An important case interpreting section 481.02 is *Peterson v. Hovland,* a 1950 Minnesota Supreme Court case involving a challenge to a will on the grounds it was drawn by a bank cashier several weeks prior to the testator's death. The court resolved the issue of the effectiveness of a document tainted by the unauthorized practice of law. The court reasoned that the statute focuses on penalizing the incompetent drafter. The testator should not suffer adverse consequences because of the drafter's violation of the statute. Therefore, the will was not void by virtue of the unauthorized practice by the drafter.

Exhibit 6.3 is an expanded version of the brief of section 481.02 with the bulleted items showing the points from this chapter that elaborate on the statute's elements.

E. INCORPORATING LEGISLATIVE INTENT

The touchstone of statutory interpretation is to respect legislative intent. Although the most straightforward indication of legislative intent is a statement of purpose in the statute itself, few statutes contain this statement. Generally, you must rely on a statute's legislative history, legal and public policy context, and paradigm case.

1. Legislative History

A first step, where possible, is to examine the record developed during the legislature's consideration of the bill and enactment of the statute, known as "legislative history." Some legislative history materials are more authoritative than others. For example, the committee report is very authoritative, because it is a formal document prepared by the legislators most involved in the statute's enactment. The comments of legislators during the debates vary in significance, with the sponsor's comments generally viewed as the most authoritative.

EXHIBIT 6.3

EXPANDED IF/THEN STATUTORY BRIEF

IF   any person/ass'n except members of MN bar admitted &
     licensed to practice

    A. does 1 OR 2 OR 3 (all in subd. 1)
       1. gives legal advice or counsel
          or performs for or furnishes legal services
          to another
          for fee or consid'n
       2. prepares directly or thru another
          for another person/firm/corp
          any will or testamentary disp'n or instrument of trust
            serving purposes similar to will
          (for or w/o fee or consid'n)
       3. prepares for another person/firm/corp
          any other legal document
          for fee or consid'n
          • common meaning of "legal" "document": official paper
            relied on as basis or proof, established by law or
            conforming to law
          • in pari materia: § 145B.04 equates living will with "legal
            document"
    B. AND NOT person drafting will
       for another
       in emergency leaving insuff time for atty superv'n
       subd. 3(2)
    C. AND NOT person conferring or cooperating
       with licensed atty of another
       in preparing any legal document
       where atty is not emp'd by that person or by person/firm/
          corp rep'd by that person
       subd. 3(6)
    D. AND NOT corp furnishing
       lawful info or clerical services
       to atty
       who maintains responsibility to clients for info & services
       subd. 7

THEN   misdemeanor prosecuted by county atty in dist ct OR
          injunction brought by county atty or atty genl—subd. 8.
          • *Peterson*: illegally drafted document is *not* void
            —policy of statute is to penalize drafter, not testator
            —expressio unius

In most situations, there are two practical obstacles to using legislative history. First, legislative history is difficult to research, especially for older statutes and state statutes. It may not have been preserved in any form; if it was preserved, it may be fairly inaccessible. Second, there may be nothing pertinent on a given point or conflicting statements by different legislators.

In the HomeElderCare example, the key language in the unauthorized practice statute dates back to 1931.[3] The legislative history of this language would be difficult to research, if indeed it was recorded.

2. Legal Context

Fairly few statutes represent the first law on a topic; most join an existing body of law, of which the legislature presumably is aware. A statute's common law, statutory, and constitutional context can provide helpful background information about the legislature's intent.

Statutes relate to the common law in several ways:

- In some areas, the legislature acts to codify or clarify the common law.
- In other areas, the legislature acts to overturn or substantially modify the common law.
- In yet other areas, the common law and statutory law operate in tandem, each addressing an aspect of the behavior they regulate.

Similarly a new law may affect existing statutory law in several ways:

- The new law may cover a topic not yet addressed by existing statutes.
- Amendments clarify or add to existing statutes.
- Repealers delete existing statutes and thus signify a dramatic change in the law.

When the legislature has revisited an area, it may be possible to make inferences about the legislative intent behind a particular version of the statute by examining its previous or subsequent forms.

Finally, lawyers presume that the legislature acted with knowledge of and in accordance with constitutional provisions. Statutes are interpreted so as to avoid unconstitutional applications.

As an example, the unauthorized practice statute operates in the context of a common law rule: that transactions in violation of licensing statutes typically are void. The unauthorized practice statute also has a rich statutory context, because the legislature has added exceptions to the unauthorized practice statute a number of times since its original enactment in the late 1800s.

3. Public Policy Context

In some situations, there are no clear indications of legislative intent in a purpose statement, legislative history, or legal context. Nonetheless, you

---

3. *See* Act of April 4, 1931, ch. 114, 1931 Minn. Laws 119.

may be able to deduce the legislature's intent from the public policy issues at the time of enactment. Sometimes the statutory language itself suggests what these issues were. In other situations, you may be able to find extrinsic evidence of them.

For example, the *Peterson* court engaged in this type of analysis regarding the unauthorized practice statute. The court observed that the legislature must have been concerned with how testators and survivors were affected by the bungled drafting of wills by non-lawyers. Thus, the court viewed the testator as a person protected by the statute and declined to void the will drafted by the bank cashier.

As a different example, according to an article written by some of the legislators involved in the passage of the living will statute,[4] they were concerned that, without living wills, medical care could be given to persons who have not requested and do not want such care and, when the time comes, are not able to speak for themselves.

4. The Paradigm Case

Although a statute does not state a specific story as a case does, it may imply one or more paradigm cases. A paradigm case is a situation that clearly would bring the statute into play. It entails actors, actions, and circumstances that fall squarely within the statute. You can discern a paradigm case by reading the statute carefully and then asking what situation clearly falls within this language.

One value of a paradigm case is that it permits inferences about legislative intent. If you can assume that the legislature was concerned with the paradigm case, then you can ask what broader concerns underlie that paradigm case. A second value is that you may compare your client's situation to the paradigm case.

For example, a paradigm case implied by the unauthorized practice statute is the drafting by a non-lawyer of a document that is significant primarily in a legal sense and requires a lawyer's expertise to draft correctly, such as divorce settlements or articles of incorporation for a new company. The document would be drafted by someone without legal training or other basis for competent performance; the interests of the client would be imperiled. And the drafter would charge a fee, thus gaining financially from his or her dubious endeavor. This paradigm case reveals the legislature's concern with incompetence, harm to the client and the public, and financial gain by the unauthorized practitioner.

F. APPLYING CANONS OF CONSTRUCTION

Canons of construction are maxims for reading—and writing—statutes. Each is based on a psychological principle of language use. Because some have Latin

---

4. *See* Howard Orenstein, David Bishop & Leigh D. Mathison, *Minnesota's Living Will . . .* , Bench & B. Minn., Aug. 1989, at 21.

names, they appear more mystical than they really are. Seven of the more commonly used canons are:

Defined, common, and technical meanings: Some terms are defined in the statute itself. Otherwise, according to this canon, which reflects the importance of context in word choice, terms should be understood in their everyday sense or, where the context suggests it, in a technical sense.

This canon supports one approach to discerning what "legal document" means in the living will statute—looking up the terms in a legal or general purpose dictionary.

Ejusdem generis: The phrase means "of the same class," and the canon applies where the legislature has created a list and included a general term as a catch-all. The catch-all term then refers to items of the same class as the specific items in the list, as one would expect from standard list-making practice.

For example, assume that the list "will or testamentary disposition or instrument of trust" was followed by "or other legal document." According to this canon, the phrase "other legal document" would be construed to refer to documents similar to those listed, namely will-like documents.

Expressio unius: The full phrase, "expressio unius est exclusio alterius," means "expression of one excludes others." According to this canon, where the legislature created a list with specific items but did not mention others or include a catch-all term, unmentioned items are not included, again, as one would expect.

It was this canon that the *Peterson* court used. The legislature's choice of misdemeanor penalties and injunctions precluded voiding Mr. Peterson's will as an additional consequence of the unlicensed practice of law.

Specific prevails over general: Where there is a conflict between two provisions, the more specific provision should take precedence over the more general provision, since specific information is more salient than general. In essence, all exceptions to general rules rest on this principle.

For example, even if there were no statement in the unauthorized practiced statute making the general rule of subdivision 1 subject to the exceptions of subdivision 3, one would give effect to the exception of wills drafting in an emergency over the general prohibition against will drafting.

Later prevails over earlier: Later enacted provisions prevail over earlier provisions when there is a conflict, because recent information is more reliable and current than older information.

If, for example, the legislature had written two exceptions relating to drafting of a will by a non-lawyer—one permitting it only in emergencies, the other allowing it only by a licensed legal assistant without any limitation as to circumstance—a conflict could arise. The more recent of the two provisions would govern.

Effectiveness of entire statute: This canon assumes that all statutory language is meant to communicate some meaning. Hence, language that could be construed to add nothing should, if possible, be construed to add something.

For example, consider the effect of adding the following statement to the existing penalty provisions of the unauthorized practice statute: "The courts shall consider any action in violation of this statute illegal." Because the existing language already provides for misdemeanor penalties and injunctions, perhaps one could infer an additional consequence from this language, such as voiding the transaction.

In pari materia: This phrase means "of the same matter," and the canon comes into play when two or more statutes relate to the same topic. The statutes must be considered together; consistency is assumed. One application of this canon is that a word should carry over its meaning from one statute to a related statute.

For example, the unauthorized practice statute prohibits drafting of "legal documents." In section 145.B04, the living will statute contains a form living will, which states: "This is an important legal document." This equation of a living will with the category of legal document should carry over to the unauthorized practice statute.

Other canons: Finally, some canons pertain to particular types of statutes. For example, penal (criminal) statutes are to be construed narrowly to avoid criminal sanctions where conduct was not clearly forbidden.

You may well find that different canons of construction point in different directions. If so, consider the application of these canons in the context of the other methods described in this chapter.

G. Looking to Similar Statutes and Persuasive Precedent

When the methods described above do not reduce the ambiguity, a court may rely on the interpretation that a sister court has given a similar or identical statute in the sister jurisdiction, even though that case is not binding precedent. The court will look for an opinion interpreting a similar, if not identical, statute and examine the opinion to determine whether the two statutes rest on the same policy.

Reliance on persuasive precedent for statutory interpretation occurs most regularly in two situations. First, some state statutes are based on a model law promulgated by a law reform organization. Use of persuasive precedent to interpret these statutes is common because the language is (nearly) identical from state to state and the origins of the statutes are the same. Second, some state statutes are based on federal statutes on the same topic. The state court may want to provide for uniformity in state and federal law by following federal precedents.

In the HomeElderCare situation, the courts have not used persuasive precedent much in interpreting unauthorized practice statutes, as they differ from state to state. Minnesota was the fortieth state to pass a living will statute in a fairly short period of time; perhaps state courts will look to each other for guidance as they interpret these statutes.

H. REVIEW OF CHAPTER 6

You can use various methods to reduce ambiguity in statutory language, all aimed at deducing the legislature's intent and giving meaning to the words the legislators chose. This chapter has set out the following methods:

(1) Consider application of the plain meaning rule, purpose approach, and golden rule.
(2) Seek an authoritative interpretation in a case construing the statute.
(3) Seek information about the legislature's intent in the statute's purpose statement, its legislative history, the legal context of the statute, its public policy context, or its paradigm case.
(4) Apply canons of construction to the statute's language.
(5) Seek guidance in cases from other jurisdictions that interpret very similar statutes.

All of these methods require you to exercise judgment to reach an appropriate result. Proper use of these options reduces statutory ambiguity and prepares you for the next stage of analysis.

7

READING COMMENTARY

A. Introduction
B. Types of Commentary
C. Using Commentary to Advance Your Legal Analysis
D. Review of Chapter 7

> Delusive exactness is a source of fallacy throughout the law.
> —Oliver Wendell Holmes
> *Truax v. Corrigan*, 257 U.S. 312, 342 (1921)

A. INTRODUCTION

In many areas, the law is complex, or controversial, or both; furthermore, the law changes over time. It can be hard to understand fully how the law has evolved, what the law is, or what the law should be.

How do lawyers make sense out of a difficult area of law? One option is to read legal commentary. Commentary is written by persons without lawmaking authority (professors, students, attorneys) or persons with lawmaking authority (judges, legislators, agency heads) acting in other than a lawmaking capacity. Commentary, also called "secondary authority," cannot substitute for the law itself (i.e., "primary authority") in your analysis, but it can further your analysis in several ways.

This chapter refers to several examples pertinent to the HomeElderCare problem; they appear at pages 317-33. You should read them before reading further.

B. TYPES OF COMMENTARY

In most situations, you are likely to find commentary that falls into one of these five categories: annotations, encyclopedias, periodicals (law reviews), Restatements, and treatises. Exhibit 7.1 provides brief information about the purpose, authoritativeness, format, and coverage of each.

EXHIBIT 7.1

TYPES OF COMMENTARY

Type	Purpose	Authoritativeness	Authors	Format	Coverage Updating
American Law Reports Annotations	summarize case law, especially splits among jurisdictions	minimal, except to document jurisdictional splits	attorneys and editors	overview; then series of case descriptions, grouped by holdings	selected topics discussed in considerable depth; updated
Encyclopedias	summarize statutory and case law	depends on credibility of particular encyclopedia	attorneys and editors	overview of legal rules supported by footnotes	very wide range of topics described in general terms; updated
Periodical Articles	describe and explain the law; advocate for change	varies, depending on author; highly authoritative if well regarded judge or professor; less so if student	attorneys, judges, legislators, professors, students	essay with extensive supporting footnotes	selected narrow topics discussed in great detail; not updated
Restatements	"restate" the law, although some state what the law should be in the view of the drafters	generally highly authoritative, with some sections adopted by courts	American Law Institute (attorneys, professors)	rule statement followed by explanations (comments) and examples (illustrations)	broad statement of selected general areas of law; some Restatements are infrequently updated; recent cases citing to Restatement are listed
Treatises	primarily describe and explain the law; may also advocate for change	varies according to author's prestige	professor, attorneys	textual discussion supplemented with fairly extensive footnotes	each covers discrete broad or narrow topic in fair depth; may or may not be updated

C. Using Commentary to Advance Your Legal Analysis

As you research a client's case, commentary can assist you in locating the law. In the analysis stage, although commentary cannot substitute for the law, it does have several important roles.

First, and most commonly, you may use commentary to solidify your understanding of the law. Commentary may provide clarification where the law is murky, complex, or fragmented. Most commentary distills out details and presents general principles on a legal topic; this broad perspective often is helpful when you have been, by necessity, focusing on the fine points of each case or statute. However, keep in mind that the author did not have your client's situation in mind and thus may not have discussed a pertinent nuance. So you may use commentary to solidify, but not supplant, your own understanding of the law.

Second, commentary may provide background information not stated in the primary authorities. The most common type of insight afforded by commentary is historical; commentary may provide information about the background of a case or line of cases or the history of a statute. Or commentary may document a trend in the law, so that you can better predict upcoming changes. Again, this information generally is helpful, but it does not, of course, replace the rule as it now stands.

Third, commentary presents perspectives on the law, from such diverse intellectual schools as feminist jurisprudence and law and economics, which may strengthen your understanding of public policy. You are most likely to look to the discussion of public policy in commentary in several situations: when you must make a close call in advising a client, when you need additional support for the argument you are making on a client's behalf in an advocacy setting, or when you are seeking to change the law.

Although you have little discretion in selecting which cases, statutes, and other primary authorities to analyze, you do have considerable discretion in choosing commentary. Obviously, the more pertinent the commentary the better. Additional factors weighing in favor of a particular source are its credibility (in turn, a function of the author and publisher), comprehensiveness, and quality of analysis. Also important is how current the commentary is; be sure to consult any updating materials in addition to the original publication.

The materials in the HomeElderCare case file are all commentary you might consult in analyzing that case. The *American Law Reports* annotation discusses the unauthorized practice of law, but the fact settings are rather different from the HomeElderCare situation. The encyclopedia provides a summary of the law in Minnesota on the same topic; it is a good way to confirm your reading of the cases. The periodical article provides insight into the legislative purpose of the Minnesota Living Will Act; that information may help you clarify the statute's ambiguous provisions. The Restatement section comes from a very credible source and underscores the common law rule on contracts for unlicensed work. The excerpt from a highly influential contracts treatise provides both a potentially useful statement of general legal principles on that topic as well as a statement of the modern trend.

D. Review of Chapter 7

Although much of the commentary you read will seem more familiar in form than the law, it is not the law. Thus, you should use commentary not to supplant but rather to supplement your own analysis. Look for material that is pertinent to your situation, comes from a credible source, is current, and presents a comprehensive and cogent discussion.

8

APPLYING A RULE

TO FACTS:

DEDUCTIVE REASONING

A. Introduction
B. What Is Deductive Reasoning?
C. Linking Elements and Client Facts
D. Depicting Deductive Reasoning
E. Cautions About the Negative of the Rule
F. Review of Chapter 8

> Reasoning is an ancient subject but an everyday practice.
> —David A. Conway and Ronald Munson
> *The Elements of Reasoning* (1990)

A. INTRODUCTION

Lawyers read the law and legal commentary not only because it is interesting but also, primarily, because they seek to derive the legal meaning of a client's situation. How does a lawyer connect a legal rule to a specific client's situation?

Lawyers engage in legal reasoning, which is structured but not mechanical, technically demanding yet creative. Legal reasoning requires considerable judgment. This chapter and Chapter 9 cover three forms of legal reasoning:

- In *deductive reasoning*, you apply elements of a rule from case law, codified law, or both to the facts of a client's situation, in order to reach a preliminary conclusion. Deductive reasoning is a necessary step in legal reasoning.
- In *reasoning by example*, you compare the facts of a client's situation, which has no known legal result, to the facts of a decided case, which

has a known legal result. Reasoning by example is frequently helpful but not necessary.

- In *policy analysis*, you consider the purposes of the law and discern how various outcomes would or would not serve those purposes. Policy analysis is frequently helpful but not necessary.

This chapter and Chapter 9 draw on the rules, cases, and statutes referred to in the previous chapters. In addition, this chapter draws on a new case, *Gardner v. Conway*, beginning on page 303 and briefed at page 314. You should review that brief and the HomeElderCare facts at pages 267-78 before reading further.

B. WHAT IS DEDUCTIVE REASONING?

Deductive reasoning, which involves using known general principles to solve a specific unknown situation, is very common outside the law. For instance, a mathematician uses theorems and corollaries to solve a geometric proof. A physician uses diagnostic principles to diagnose a patient's disease.

Legal deductive reasoning is the process of using rules from legal authorities to predict the outcome of a client's situation. To start, state the rule, whether from case law or codified law or both, in if/then form and then separate it into elements and legal consequences. Then you match your client's facts to the rule's elements and assess whether the elements required by the rule are present. The structure of the rule dictates what is required; that is, all elements of a conjunctive rule, only one of several disjunctive sub-elements, or some critical mass of the factors in aggregate and balancing rules. If the elements are met, then the rule's legal consequences will follow.

If the outcome is not clear, and often it is not, you may need to supplement your deductive reasoning with reasoning by example and policy analysis. Even so, deductive reasoning remains the core of legal analysis; everything else is supplementary.

C. LINKING ELEMENTS AND CLIENT FACTS

Deductive reasoning is structured; the rule's elements frame the analysis. Drawing out the relevant facts from the client's situation to align with each element is sometimes easy, sometimes rather difficult.

Each element of the rule directs your attention to some aspect of the client's situation; relevant facts pertain to that aspect. Most elements of a rule focus your attention on one or perhaps two of the six classic questions journalists ask: who, what, when, where, why, and how. An element describing an actor focuses on the "who" aspect of the situation. An element focusing on the action taken is a "what" element. An element focusing on the circumstances may be a "when," "where," "why," or "how" element.

If you are unsure of the factual focus of a case law element, reread the case, and study the facts that the court saw as relevant to that element. Similarly, if you are unsure of the factual focus of a statutory element, examine a case interpreting the statute, or consider the statute's paradigm case. Commentary may help you identify the focus of murky elements.

Sometimes, even when you understand an element well, discerning the relevant facts in your client's situation can be difficult.

- The facts may be complicated. If so, consider separating them according to the six classic journalist's questions; create a timeline; diagram the relationships between the main actors; divide the facts into logical clusters (e.g., people involved, events).
- The difficulty may arise because you are missing key facts. Note the omission and the uncertainty it creates; make one or more sensible assumptions and proceed on your assumption(s).
- The difficulty may arise because you have conflicting information, because different individuals perceived an event differently. You can handle a conflict in the same way as a missing fact.

As a simple example, consider the statutory prohibition on the unauthorized practice of law, which applies to any person except members of the Minnesota bar admitted and licensed to practice—a "who" element with a narrow focus. In analyzing the HomeElderCare facts, you would link this element to the non-lawyer social workers and conclude that this element is met.

For a more difficult example, consider the case law requirement that, to invalidate a contract on the grounds of unlicensed practice, the circumstances surrounding the contract must violate the reason for the licensing statute—a "how" element with a very broad sweep. In *Weatherston's,* the court considered the client's awareness of the non-licensure and the supervision of the unlicensed work by a licensed professional, among other facts. You can assume that the HomeElderCare clients will be informed that the social workers are not attorneys, but the social workers' competence is hard to assess. Therefore, you would pursue two analyses of HomeElderCare's situation.

D. Depicting Deductive Reasoning

As you work through your analysis, you can depict deductive reasoning various ways. Any depiction must use a rule of law as its point of departure and reflect the structure of the if-clause of the rule: conjunctive, disjunctive, aggregate, or balancing.

1. Syllogism

One option is, in essence, a syllogism. The major premise is the rule of law; the minor premise is the specific set of facts presented by the client. Deductive reasoning is the process of matching the minor premise to the major premise

EXHIBIT 8.1

SYLLOGISM

Major Premise: [rule of law]	IF (1)	a statute requires a person practicing a particular profession or engaging in a particular business to obtain a license, and
	(2)	a person in that profession or business lacks that license, and
	(3)	that person enters into a business or professional contract, and
	(4)	the circumstances surrounding the contract violate the reason for the statute's existence,
Minor Premise:	THEN	that contract is void.
	(1)	A statute requires persons practicing law to obtain a license; and
[relevant client facts]	(2)	the HEC social workers lack that licence; and
	(3)	they probably will be practicing law or entering into contracts to practice law in drafting living wills; and
	(4)	these contracts nonetheless would *not* violate the policy underlying the licensing statute, given the social workers' training and knowledge of their status by HEC clients.
Conclusion: [legal consequence]		Therefore, the contracts would *not* be void under this rule.

to generate a conclusion about the outcome of the client's case.[1] In other words:

Major Premise:	[rule of law]
Minor Premise:	[relevant client facts]
Conclusion:	Therefore [probable legal consequence]

As an example, in Exhibit 8.1, the major premise is the *Weatherston's* rule on enforcement of contracts for unlicensed professional services. Assume that the living will service would indeed amount to the practice of law. This conclusion and other relevant facts appear in the minor premise. Because the fourth element is not met, the prediction is that the contracts would not be void under this rule.

---

1. In the study of logic, this syllogism, known as modus ponens, can be expressed as "if P, then Q. P is true. Therefore Q is true."

EXHIBIT 8.2

COLUMN CHARTS

CONJUNCTIVE RULE

	Elements	Client Facts	Element Met/Not Met
IF	1 and	*xxxxxxxxx*	✓
	2 and	*xxxxxxxxx*	✓
	3	*xxxxxxxxx*	✓
THEN	Consequence x.	Consequence x results.	

MIXED CONJUNCTIVE AND DISJUNCTIVE RULE

	Elements	Client Facts	Element Met/Not Met
IF	1 and	*xxxxxxxxx*	✓
	2 and	*xxxxxxxxx*	✓
	3 or	*xxxxxxxxx*	✓
	3'	*xxxxxxxxx*	✓
THEN	Consequence x.	Consequence x does not result under this rule.	

AGGREGATE RULE

	Factors	Client Facts	Factor Present/Absent
IF	some but not necessarily all of the following are present:		
	a	*xxxxxxxxx*	++
	b	*xxxxxxxxx*	+
	c	*xxxxxxxxx*	−
	d	*xxxxxxxxx*	+++
	e	*xxxxxxxxx*	−
THEN	Consequence x.	Consequence x results.	

BALANCING RULE

	Factors	Client Facts	Factor Present/Absent
IF	a outweighs	*xxxxxxxxx*	++
	b	*xxxxxxxxx*	+
THEN	Consequence x.	Consequence x results.	

2. Column Chart

In a column chart, elements of the rule line up with relevant facts of your client's situation. If the required elements are met by the client's facts, then the legal consequences follow.

A column chart makes clear how the rule is structured. Exhibit 8.2 shows four formats for the four different forms of legal rules. With conjunctive and disjunctive elements, you can use a check mark to signify that an element is met. With aggregate and balancing rules, you can use plus and minus marks to represent the extent of the presence or absence of the factors.

Exhibit 8.3 is a sample HomeElderCare column chart addressing the unauthorized practice of law under section 481.02 and *Gardner*; it addresses only the legality of the living will service as giving legal advice or preparing a legal document. According to the analysis presented in Exhibit 8.3, some aspect of the living will service would constitute unauthorized practice; the possible legal consequences would be misdemeanor penalties or an injunction.

E. CAUTIONS ABOUT THE NEGATIVE OF THE RULE

When at least one element of a rule is not met, you might be tempted to recast the rule in a negative form, so that you can figure out the legal consequence of that element not being met. To do so, carefully follow these steps:

(1) Recast the if-clause in a negative form.
(2) Apply the recast if-clause to the client's facts.
(3) Recast the then-clause in a negative form.
(4) Evaluate the overall meaning of the analysis. Consider the application of other rules if the rule under analysis is not the only rule leading to the consequence.

First, recast the if-clause in a negative form. In recasting the elements of a conjunctive rule, "and" becomes "or,"[2] as shown below:

IF	1 and	becomes	IF	not 1 or
	2 and			not 2 or
	3			not 3

This change in connectors makes sense because a conjunctive rule can be defeated by *just one* element not being met.

The opposite change in connectors occurs when you recast the elements of a disjunctive rule into a negative form, as follows:

IF	1 or	becomes	IF	not 1 and
	2 or			not 2 and
	3			not 3

---

2. In logic, the change in connectors is based on De Morgan's Rules, which can be restated as follows: "Not (P and Q)" is equivalent to "not P or not Q." "Not (P or Q)" is equivalent to "not P and not Q."

EXHIBIT 8.3

HomeElderCare COLUMN CHART

	Elements	Client Facts	Element Met/Not Met
IF	any person/ass'n except members of MN bar admitted & licensed to practice does 1 OR 2 OR 3 (all in subd. 1)	social workers not members of MN bar	✓ (yes)
	1. gives legal advice or counsel or performs for or furnishes legal services to another for fee or consid'n	not clear if HEC is giving legal advice/counsel or performing/furnishing legal services; HEC will charge fee	? (maybe)
	• *Gardner*: unauthorized practice if legal acts are more than incidental; or if acts are incidental, they involve difficult/doubtful legal issues	acts will be incidental, but it's not clear whether there will be "difficult or doubtful legal issues"	
	2. prepares for another person/firm/corp any other legal document for fee or consid'n	living will is legal document; HEC is preparing it for a fee	✓ (yes)
	• common meaning of "legal" "document": official paper relied on as basis or proof, established by law or conforming to law		
	• in pari materia: § 145B.04 equates living will with "legal document"		
THEN	X. misdemeanor prosecuted by county atty in dist ct OR Y. injunction brought by county atty or atty gcn'l	HEC would be guilty of misdemeanor or subject to injunction	

This change in connectors makes sense because a disjunctive rule can be defeated only by *all* of the elements not being met.

Sometimes, negating an element that already contains a negative concept results in a pair of negatives, which—true to common sense—cancel each other out. For example, the negative of "a person in that profession or business *does not lack* a license" is "a person . . . *has* a license."

Because of the flexible nature of aggregate and balancing rules, you are less likely to recast them in negative form. If you were to do so, the elements would be expressed as follows:

IF enough of factors a, b, c	becomes	IF not enough of factors a, b, c
IF factors a, b, c outweigh d, e, f	becomes	IF factors a, b, c do not outweigh d, e, f

After negating the if-clause, the second step is to apply the re-drafted if-clause to the client's facts. If the client's facts meet the required elements of the re-drafted if-clause, then move on to the next step.

The third step is to recast the then-clause in a negative form. If the then-clause contains more than one consequence (plural or alternative), negate each consequence and change the connector(s): "and" becomes "or"; "or" becomes "and." For example, "then misdemeanor or injunction" becomes "then *not* misdemeanor *and not* injunction."

The fourth step is to evaluate the overall meaning of negating the then-clause. In most rules, the most you can conclude is that the consequence does not result under this rule. However, it might result under some other rule. For example, if the client's facts do not meet the elements of the rule invaliding contracts for professional services by an unlicensed person, the consequence of the rule (a void contract) would not result under that rule. However, you would need to perform additional research to determine whether the contract is void under other rules.

Occasionally, though, a rule will be the only rule with that particular legal consequence. Then you can safely negate the consequence without any caveats. You might think of these rules as exclusive rules.[3] For example, the following exclusive rule appears in section 145B.05 of Minnesota's Living Will Act:

IF   a living will is delivered to the declarant's physician or other health care provider,

THEN   the living will becomes operative upon delivery.

The negative of that rule would be the following:

IF   a living will is *not* delivered to the declarant's physician or other health care provider,

THEN   the living will does *not* become operative.

---

3. The exclusive rule is a variation of the "if and only if" rule. A non-exclusive rule can be rephrased as "if P, then Q," or "P is sufficient for Q." An exclusive rule can be rephrased as "if and only if P, then Q," or "P is sufficient and necessary for Q." Nonexclusive rules are not conclusive when restated in the negative. Accordingly, a non-exclusive rule represented by "if P, then Q" cannot be restated in the negative as "if not P, then not Q." To do so is the classic fallacy of denying the antecedent. On the other hand, exclusive rules are conclusive when restated in the negative, as in "if not P, then not Q."

In other words, no other rule makes the living will operative if it is not delivered to the physician or health care provider, so the negative of the consequence is true without any caveats.

F. REVIEW OF CHAPTER 8

Deductive reasoning—applying a rule to the facts of the client's situation to predict the legal consequence for the client—is the fundamental form of legal reasoning. Based on a careful reading of the law, deductive reasoning involves the following steps:

(1) Analyze each element in an if/then rule statement; focus on who, what, when, where, why, or how.
(2) Identify the facts in the client's situation that are relevant to each element.
(3) Analyze whether each element is met by the facts of the client's situation.
(4) If the necessary elements are not met, then the legal consequence does not result under this rule. If they are met, then the legal consequences of the rule follows.

The deductive reasoning process sometimes leaves unanswered questions. You may be able to answer those questions with the tools covered in Chapter 9: reasoning by example and policy analysis.

9

APPLYING A RULE

TO FACTS: REASONING

BY EXAMPLE AND

POLICY ANALYSIS

A. Introduction
B. Reasoning by Example
C. Policy Analysis
D. Meshing Deductive Reasoning, Reasoning by Example,
    and Policy Analysis
E. Review of Chapter 9

> We are all able to reason. Someone totally unable to assess
> claims and arrive at conclusions would believe anything and act
> in wild and arbitrary ways. That we do not generally behave in
> this fashion shows how we rely on reasoning to guide our
> actions and ground our beliefs.
> —David A. Conway and Ronald Munson
> *The Elements of Reasoning* (1990)

A. INTRODUCTION

Quite often, possibly more often than not, uncertainty remains at the end of
the deductive reasoning process. How do lawyers reduce, if not eliminate, that
uncertainty?

This chapter covers two tools: reasoning by example and policy analysis.
Both derive from legal authorities. Both are less structured than deductive
reasoning and require good judgment. They are in one key sense quite
different: reasoning by example is more concrete than deductive reasoning,
and policy analysis is more abstract.

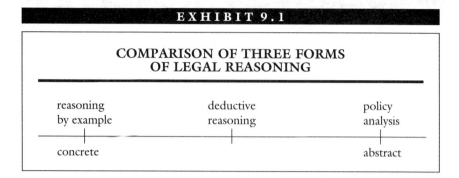

As always, this chapter draws examples from various parts of the HomeElderCare case file.

B. REASONING BY EXAMPLE

1. What Is Reasoning by Example?

Reasoning by example, or analogical reasoning, involves using the known outcome(s) of one or more resolved situations to draw a conclusion about a current situation with an unknown outcome. In law in particular, it is based on a formal principle of justice: that similar facts should be treated similarly.[1] Not insignificantly, the use of the decided case as an example adds a human side to the law and demonstrates how the rule has affected the lives of others.

Reasoning by example is common outside the law. For instance, a student who turns in a paper late expects that he or she will be treated similarly to other students who have turned in late papers. An employee who performs an employment obligation poorly or well expects to be treated like other similarly performing employees.

When you compare your client's situation to a decided case, one possibility is that your client's situation and the decided case are sufficiently similar that your client should experience the same outcome as the decided case. This analysis is called "drawing an analogy."

The other possibility is that your client's situation and the decided case are sufficiently different that your client should not experience the outcome of the decided case. This is called "distinguishing a case." Distinguishing a particular case does not necessarily allow you to conclude that a result opposite to that of the distinguished case would occur. For example, if the closest tort liability case to your client's situation is distinguishable, your client may not be required to pay tort damages; however, your client may have to pay contract damages.

Note our use of "should": there always is some uncertainty in reasoning by example. Inexactitude is inherent in the process of judging how much and

---

1. David A. Conway & Ronald Munson, *The Elements of Reasoning* 123-24 (1990).

what kind of similarity is needed for an analogy or how much and what kind of difference is needed to distinguish a case.

2. Judging Similarity and Difference
a. With a Single Case

To reason by example, you must first decide which case to work with, then evaluate its similarities to and differences from your client's situation, and then determine whether that case and your client's situation are analogous or distinguishable. All three steps require you to exercise considerable judgment.

As for the first step, a decided case is a possible candidate for reasoning by example if it meets two criteria:

- It must address the same or very nearly the same legal rule or element that you are analyzing in your client's situation.
- The facts pertaining to that rule or element should be similar to your client's facts, although they almost certainly will not be identical or even nearly so.

You should focus on the client's facts that are relevant to the rule or element you are analyzing and select a decided case with relevant facts similar to those client facts.

The second step is to thoroughly compare and contrast the decided case and your client's situation, focusing on the facts relevant to the rule or element under consideration. There inevitably will be both similarities and differences, and you should list both. Deciding whether a client's fact is similar or different to its parallel in the decided case requires careful thought. If your focus is too narrow, the decided case will appear utterly different from your client's situation. If your focus is broad, every decided case will begin to look similar to your client's situation. To judge how much elasticity is justifiable:

- Look to the court's language. If the decided case discusses the law or the facts in broad terms, then a broadly drawn comparison is justifiable; a narrowly drawn comparison is appropriate when the decided case is narrowly worded as to its law or its facts.
- Other authorities discussing the decided case may also help you decide how elastic it is.
- Avoid the temptation to stretch or constrict a comparison to bring your client's situation within a favorable decided case or to avoid the impact of an unfavorable decided case. Make the intellectually better judgment, especially in an advisory setting where caution can forestall future legal problems.

The third and final step is to conclude whether the case is overall analogous or distinguishable. After carefully reading the court's reasoning in the decided case, rank its facts from least to most weighty. Some facts will be basic facts that define the category of situations to which the rule applies; other facts will drive the outcome. With this weighting in mind, study your list of common and contrasting facts in your client's situation. Sometimes you will decide that your client's situation is analogous because there are more common than contrasting facts. Or a single key contrast may prompt you to distinguish your client's situation from the decided case.

For an illustration of reasoning by example, consider the *Gardner* case and the HomeElderCare situation. Both involve the unauthorized practice of law and the question whether the practitioner addressed "difficult or doubtful legal questions." A social worker case would be preferable, but *Gardner*, which involves tax preparation and a tax preparer, is fairly close. The relevant facts under the difficult-or-doubtful-legal-question element are the activities of the non-lawyer and the extent to which those activities are legal in nature. In a broad sense, the HomeElderCare tasks and the *Gardner* tasks are very similar, because both involve advice on matters with legal implications and the eventual filling out of forms. Yet in a narrow sense, the two activities are not the same; one involves taxes and the other involves medical treatment. The analysis should then focus on whether the legal dimensions of the two activities are comparably complicated. This is a close call.

b. With More than One Case

You may be uncertain at various points in reasoning by a single example. One way to resolve the uncertainty is to use more than one case for comparison by fusing several decided cases into a pattern and reasoning from that pattern to the client's situation. This process is known as "inductive generalization"— reasoning from specific (the decided cases) to a generalization (their pattern) to specific (the client's situation).

Inductive generalization rests on a case fusion that reveals a pattern on which the decisions rest (as discussed in Chapter 4). The strongest basis for an inductive generalization is a fact that differentiates two or more cases, i.e., case(s) with that fact or a version of that fact came out differently than case(s) without that fact or a different version of that fact. Splits in the facts and outcomes are not enough; the outcome split must be attributable at least in part to the fact split, as revealed in the court's reasoning. Once you have identified the cases with the fact and outcome splits, you can compare your client's fact to the two examples in the decided cases.

As an example, assume that the court decided that an unlicensed liquor seller could enforce his contract, while an unlicensed real estate broker and an unlicensed engineer could not. This splits suggest that if licensure assures technical competence, the unlicensed professional cannot enforce the contract; but if licensure merely generates revenue for the state, the unlicensed person can enforce the contract. The HomeElderCare social workers would have difficulty enforcing their contracts because licensure as an attorney assures technical competence.

3. Depicting Reasoning by Example

Just as with deductive reasoning, you can depict reasoning by example in various ways. In addition to text, you may want to consider diagrams.

Exhibit 9.2 is a Venn diagram. The purpose of a Venn diagram is to illustrate the areas of similarity and difference between two sets—in this

━━
EXHIBIT 9.2
━━

VENN DIAGRAM

Gardner   HomeElderCare

accounting   filling out form   social work

business/tax decisions   form has important legal   medical decisions
                            consequences

long and complicated   form could be done by   new, short statute with
statute with lots of case   client alone   little case law
law and regulations
                            separate field with training
                            and standards

instance, two sets of facts. It is less helpful for legal aspects of reasoning by example. The areas of similarity appear in the center, the areas of difference at the sides.

Exhibit 9.3 is a checkerboard chart that lines up the decided case's issue, facts, and holding with the client situation's issue facts, and predicted result. This chart forces you to think through not only the fact parallels but also the parallel in the legal issue.

C. POLICY ANALYSIS

1. What Is Policy Analysis?

Sometimes your deductive reasoning and reasoning by example may not prove conclusive. The rule may employ vague terms. There may be no decided cases to use, or your conclusion as to analogy or distinction may be tentative. The third phase of legal reasoning, policy analysis, is useful in these situations.

Policy analysis involves discerning and relying on an ultimate goal, often a goal chosen by an organization. You no doubt use policy analysis in non-legal contexts. For example, the policy supporting a penalty for turning in a paper late is fairness to all students, especially those who turned in theirs on time. One policy supporting merit pay is promoting excellent work by all employees.

In the context of legal reasoning, policy is the broad principle or societal goal to be achieved by application of a legal rule to various situations; a policy is more abstractly expressed than a rule of law. Policy considerations drive the creation of legal rules. Judges, especially in the highest court, derive rules and select outcomes in particular cases based in part on their judgment of how to further society's interests. Legislators enact statutes based on their conceptions of the social good.

EXHIBIT 9.3

CHECKERBOARD CHART

Decided Case—*Gardner*		Client's Situation
Issue(s)		Issue(s)
Will these laypersons be engaged in unauthorized practice of law? Will they be answering difficult or doubtful legal questions?	same? ⟶	same as *Gardner*
Facts		Facts
A tax preparer provided a client with advice on partnership, tax exemption, filing status, and deductions; the form has some instructions.	similar enough? ⟶	Yes, social workers will fill out a form and answer questions about living wills, e.g., guardian selection, choice of medical treatment; the form contains instructions.
Holding		Predicted Result
The advice on the four legal topics was unauthorized law practice because these were difficult or doubtful legal questions that require a legally trained mind.	analogy or distinction justified? ⟶	Analogy (probably). HEC social workers will be practicing law if they answer client questions about difficult or doubtful legal topics; living will issues may well be difficult or doubtful, given the newness of statute and related regulations.

In many areas of law, society has more than one competing interest. Lawmakers may select one interest to serve, and the resulting law arises out of a single and perhaps one-sided policy. Frequently, lawmakers seek to serve more than one interest, and the resulting law is more nuanced and complex. Competition among policies also causes jurisdictions to diverge in their choice of rules on the same subject. These jurisdictional splits occur in both the judicial and legislative branches.

Legal policy often is informed by other disciplines that also address how to achieve the public good. For example, legal rules about who should bear the risk of loss in accidents are informed by philosophical conceptions of fault and responsibility. As another example, economic principles about efficient markets underlie many rules of contract law.

2. Deriving Policy

To apply policy to a client's situation, you first must discern the policy underlying the law. In some situations, the court or legislature states its policy in so many words, in the reasoning portion of a judicial opinion or in the purpose section of a statute. Commentary writers often discuss the underlying policy of a rule in the process of describing and critiquing it.

When your research has not yielded a strong statement of policy, you may find stakeholder analysis useful. Stakeholder analysis is a method of discerning the ethical implications of a situation. It entails thinking broadly about the stakeholders in a situation, their respective interests, and possible resolutions. In the legal context, it also involves actual resolutions, because you are seeking to discern lawmakers' policy or policies, not your own. Policy analysis involves several steps:

(1) Select a major decided case or statute's paradigm case to analyze.
(2) Identify the immediate participants in the situation (the parties) as well as persons who are less immediately involved but nonetheless affected by the case's resolution.
(3) Identify the stakes, or interests, of each stakeholder, such as economic security.
(4) Identify the legal consequences that follow from application of the rule, such as payment or receipt of damages, and the impact of the rule's application on the various stakeholders' interests.
(5) The final step is to identify the actual winners and losers in the case. The winner's interest, stated in broad terms, constitutes the major policy behind the legal rule.

There are various ways to depict policy analysis. Exhibit 9.4 is the standard hub-and-spokes diagram.

Consider, as an example, the *Buckley* case. The two major stakeholders were the parties: the real estate agent, who sought his contract fee and the freedom to pursue his occupation, and the client, who sought to avoid paying the agent's fee and to be protected against possibly incompetent work. Less immediately involved were the buyer of the property, any company for which the agent worked, and other buyers and sellers in the real estate market. The client's interests won out, along with those of the real estate market.

3. Employing Policy Analysis

Once you have discerned the policy underlying a legal rule, you can incorporate this information into your reasoning about the client's situation. In doing so, ask how well each potential outcome in your client's situation would serve the policy you have identified. Policy analysis can be incorporated in various ways:

- If you are not certain of the elements in a rule, even after carefully reading the law, you can examine the possible versions in light of what you know about the rule's policy, then select the version that best serves the policy.
- If you have identified an element of the rule, matched it to your client's facts, and are uncertain whether your client's facts meet the requirements of the rule, you can test options by how well they serve the rule's policy.

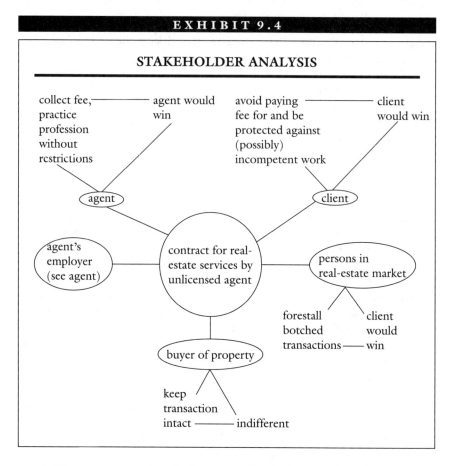

EXHIBIT 9.4

STAKEHOLDER ANALYSIS

- If you are uncertain whether your client's situation is analogous to or distinguishable from a decided case, policy analysis permits you to resolve the tie by helping you focus on the factual comparisons relevant to the law's policy.

You may find that more than one policy is inherent in a complex rule. The two chief questions to ask yourself are: First, is either policy preferred over the other by lawmakers? For example, has the court cited or relied on one policy more than the other recently? Second, which policy is more clearly served by the possible outcomes in the client's situation? If one outcome would clearly serve one policy while the other outcome would only somewhat serve the competing policy, the former outcome might be favored by the courts.

As always, there are various ways to depict your analysis. Exhibit 9.5 presents a simple flowchart.

By way of example, the policy regarding the unauthorized practice of law is to protect the public from the adverse consequences of incompetently performed legal work. If questions addressed in a living will are primarily legal, permitting the social workers to draft the living wills raises the potential of deficient legal work. On the other hand, the potential for deficient work is not large if the living will addresses primarily medical and moral topics and the social workers receive training.

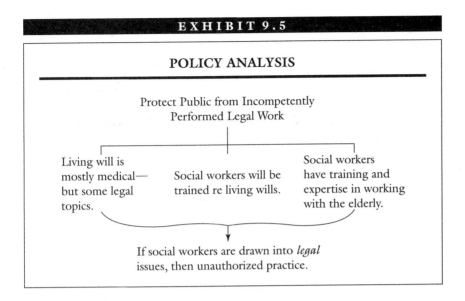

EXHIBIT 9.5

POLICY ANALYSIS

Protect Public from Incompetently
Performed Legal Work

Living will is
mostly medical—
but some legal
topics.

Social workers will be
trained re living wills.

Social workers
have training and
expertise in working
with the elderly.

If social workers are drawn into *legal*
issues, then unauthorized practice.

D. MESHING DEDUCTIVE REASONING, REASONING BY EXAMPLE, AND POLICY ANALYSIS

Reasoning by example and policy analysis enrich and reinforce your deductive reasoning. But they do not make difficult calls easy. You will need to exercise judgment in the end. As your experience increases, your judgment will improve. You will learn how to inform a client of the uncertainty in your analysis and how to develop options or arguments to minimize the risks and maximize the strengths of the client's position.

If you have proceeded through a fairly complex reasoning process, you may want to mesh major points in your analysis. Exhibit 9.6 is an example of how you might do so.

However you depict your meshed analysis, be sure to review it for compliance with the four criteria of sound legal writing:

- *Completeness:* Have you included all pertinent rules (their elements and factors) and all relevant facts?
- *Correctness:* Have you expressed the legal rules accurately? Have you depicted the facts accurately? Is your depiction of decided cases accurate?
- *Coherence:* Does the analysis hold together? Do the facts match the elements? Does your policy analysis fit with the other aspects of your reasoning? Is the probable outcome a sensible resolution of the case?
- *Comprehensibility:* Can you understand fully all steps of the analysis?

EXHIBIT 9.6

DEPICTION OF DEDUCTIVE REASONING, REASONING BY EXAMPLE, AND POLICY ANALYSIS

Rule	HomeElderCare Analysis
IF any person/association except members of MN bar admitted & licensed to practice gives legal advice, that is, • acts are more than incidental to other calling or • acts are incidental and involve difficult/doubtful legal issues . . .	HEC social workers are not licensed to practice law; they will be giving legal advice on living wills incident to their social work, and the issues probably involve difficult/doubtful legal issues because . . .
Gardner Case	Analogy/Distinction
Tax preparer not licensed in MN answered questions about tax treatment of transactions, e.g., marital status, business expenses; he was addressing difficult or doubtful legal issues; this conduct was unauthorized practice of law.	Analogy: there is a parallel between tax issues (complex statute) and living will issues (simpler statute, but complex and uncertain area of law).
Policy	Policy Analysis
1. Preclude provision of legal services by incompetent laypersons. 2. Promote living wills.	1. It is important to forestall mistakes by social workers, though they will be trained. 2. Living wills may be harder to draft if an attorney is required; living wills drafted by social workers will be valid, even if there is unauthorized practice of law.
Legal Consequence	Conclusion
Then the conduct is prohibited as the unauthorized practice of law; misdemeanor penalties or an injunction are possible.	*Probably* unauthorized practice of law.

E. REVIEW OF CHAPTER 9

Both reasoning by example and policy analysis can supplement deductive reasoning, to reduce uncertainty in the rule or its application to the client's situation. The process of reasoning by example, from specific to specific, involves the following steps:

    (1) Select a decided case involving the same legal rule and element that you are analyzing in your client's situation.

(2) Evaluate the similarities and differences between the relevant facts in the client's situation and those of the decided case.

(3) Determine whether the client's situation and the decided case are analogous or distinguishable.

Uncertainty in reasoning by example can be reduced by inductive generalization, that is, by reasoning from more than one decided case.

While reasoning by example is based on specifics, policy analysis entails application of broad principles to your client's case. The broad principle is the purpose of the legal rule—the goal sought by lawmakers. Policy analysis entails the following steps:

(1) Discern the policies from a statement in the law itself or from commentary on the law.

(2) If there is no satisfactory statement of policy, conduct a stakeholder analysis to draw out the policies; identify the stakeholders, their interests and preferred outcomes, and the interests favored by the law.

(3) Apply the policies to your client's situation by testing tentative outcomes against them.

Once you have read the law and commentary carefully and reasoned carefully about your client's situation, you are ready to communicate your analysis. The next chapter describes IRAC, the standard template used to present a legal analysis of a client's situation.

RULE-DRIVEN WRITING:

THE IRAC TEMPLATE

A. Introduction
B. Understanding IRAC
C. Deconstructing IRAC
D. Constructing IRACs
E. Review of Chapter 10

> Words after all are symbols, and the significance of the symbols
> varies with the knowledge and experience of the mind
> receiving them.
> —Benjamin N. Cardozo
> *Cooper v. Dasher*, 290 U.S. 106 (1933)

A. INTRODUCTION

The processes of briefing and fusing cases; briefing and interpreting statutes; reading commentary on your topic; and engaging in deductive reasoning, reasoning by example, and policy analysis can take a long time and a lot of energy. Even so, the task of capturing your work in writing remains.

How do lawyers write up their analysis in a way that captures what they have learned and considered and also serves the reader's interest in grasping the analysis quickly and accurately? Lawyers rely on a template that reflects the rule-driven nature of legal writing: IRAC (easily the most widely used mnemonic in legal education). As we present it here, IRAC stands for introduction + rule + application + conclusion.

Here are the facts for this chapter:

> A HomeElderCare social worker, who had worked with a client
> for several years, amended his testamentary will, at his direction, by
> changing the names of the nonprofit organizations that would

receive small bequests. She arranged for the will's execution as well. Six weeks before this occurred, the client was diagnosed with terminal lung cancer. Three days before the social worker amended his will, his condition deteriorated quickly, and he moved into a hospice for palliative care. The day after the will was amended, the client died.

A complete IRAC on this topic appears at the end of this chapter. You should read it before proceeding.

B. UNDERSTANDING IRAC

IRAC is a legal version of the standard template for expository writing:

Introduction	Topic
Rule	Elaboration
Application	Elaboration
Conclusion	Conclusion

In legal writing as in other types of writing, you should orient the reader by introducing the topic, then present the extended discussion, and bring the discussion to a close by presenting a conclusion.

Introductions are important in legal writing for several reasons. Legal writing can involve complicated material; when this is so, orienting the reader is critical. Reading the introduction should help the reader focus on the topic at hand (and help you do the same as you write your analysis). The introduction also helps the reader see the connections among the several or even many IRACs in your paper.

The rule + application portion resembles the legal reasoning process. You should think of those elements as R → A, which signifies that the rule comes before the application and is then applied to the client's facts (not the other way around). Note the organization of this text: reading the law, then reasoning about the client's situation in light of the pertinent rules. So, too, lawyers analyze clients' situations by applying rules to their clients' facts. When you use IRAC, you are conforming to the template of legally trained readers, who can thus process your analysis relatively quickly and efficiently. R → A is the essence of IRAC.

The conclusion is important in legal writing because the point of legal analysis is to discern the probable legal meaning of the client's situation. The conclusion presents this legal meaning, as explained by the IRA it follows.

IRAC is used in many types of analytical papers written by lawyers. In this text, you will see it in office memos, advice letters, demand letters, memoranda submitted to a trial court, and appellate briefs. IRAC looks a bit different in different genres, but the structures are either IRACs or variations on the IRAC theme.

C. DECONSTRUCTING IRAC

Within each of the four IRAC components, you can choose among several options. Your choice should reflect the material you are discussing.

Introduction: For some, "I" stands for issue. We have chosen a broader term: introduction. The introduction component orients the reader to the precise point you are about to discuss and is typically one sentence long. You may state any of the following:

- the topic—that is, a reference to the subject of the upcoming IRAC;
- the issue you are about to address—that is, a question linking law to facts;
- the conclusion you have come to—again, linking law to facts, but in statement form; and
- a transition—that is, a sentence linking the previous topic to the upcoming topic.

The topic option is shorter than the others. The issue and conclusion options tend to be longer than the others and thus work best at the start of a lengthy IRAC. The transition option is a good choice if consecutive topics have important links that the reader may miss unless they are pointed out. Consider using the same option for a series of IRACs, for stylistic coherence. See Exhibit 10.1 for several examples.

EXHIBIT 10.1

SAMPLE INTRODUCTIONS

Topic

The social worker's assistance with the will raises the issue of the unauthorized practice of law.

Issue

Did the social worker engage in the unauthorized practice of law when she amended the client's will the day before he died, three days after he was placed in a hospice for palliative care?

Conclusion

More likely than not, the social worker's conduct did not amount to the unauthorized practice of law.

Transition

The first and pivotal issue is the unauthorized practice of law.

Rule: The rule component informs the reader of the law pertinent to the client's situation. The derivation of the legal rule determines how you should present it:

- If your rule is derived from a *single case*, you will present the court's statement of the rule from the case, along with a summary of the facts and holding if the facts are similar enough to merit a comparison to your client's situation.
- If your rule is derived from a *set of cases*, you will state the fused rule and refer to the set of cases. You also might summarize the case that most resembles your client's situation, or you might briefly present two cases with different facts and outcomes.
- If your rule is derived *solely from a statute*, you will quote the pertinent statutory language.
- If your rule is derived from a *statute supplemented by case law or* other materials, you will first quote the statute and then present the supplementary material.

Whether your rule is from a statute or case law, if the reader would benefit from knowledge of the rule's underlying policy at this point, you could state that policy as well, typically at the end of the R component.

Each legal proposition you present must be supported by a citation to one or more authorities, ideally a statute or binding precedents. (Appendix III covers citation.). See Exhibit 10.2 for several examples of rules, followed by application to the client's facts.

EXHIBIT 10.2

SAMPLE RULES AND APPLICATIONS

Statute

It is unlawful for a person who is not admitted and licensed to practice law in Minnesota "for or without a fee or any considerations, to prepare, directly or through another, for another person, firm or corporation, any will or testamentary disposition or instrument of trust serving purposes similar to those of a will." Minn. Stat. § 481.02 subdiv. 1 (1992). However, a non-lawyer may "draw[ ] a will for another in an emergency if the imminence of death leaves insufficient time to have in drawn and its execution supervised by a licensed attorney-at-law." *Id.* subdiv. 3(2). Violation of the statute is a misdemeanor. *Id.* subdiv. 8.

[Application] HomeElderCare's social worker was not licensed to practice law. She amended the client's existing will by changing the names of several nonprofit organizations to receive small bequests. Although the statute does not cover amending a will, as distinct from writing a new will, this activity most likely qualifies as "preparing" a will, particularly since she also arranged for its execution.

However, the social worker's conduct most likely is protected under the exception for drawing wills in an emergency. The patient's condition deteriorated over the last few days, he was placed in hospice, and he died the day after he amended the will. This timeframe amounts to the imminence of death. With only hours to live, the client chose his social worker for assistance, a choice that was both practical and possibly the only feasible option with so little time left.

Case

In *Peterson v. Hovland (In re Peterson's Estate)*, 42 N.W.2d 59 (Minn. 1950), a bank cashier prepared and executed Mr. Peterson's will, upon his request. This occurred several weeks before Peterson died, and the trial court found that death was not so imminent that Peterson could not have had an attorney perform this service. *Id.* at 61. Thus, the cashier engaged in the unauthorized practice of law. *Id.*

[*Application*] The HomeElderCare social worker's situation is distinguishable from *Peterson*. As was true in *Peterson*, the social worker was not a lawyer, the client requested the assistance, and the assistance involved a will. However, the HomeElderCare social worker amended, rather than drafted, a will, and the amendments were straightforward. The social worker knew the client well. Finally and most importantly, the client was in hospice care and died the next day; thus death was imminent.

Policy

The policy behind the prohibition on the drafting of wills by non-lawyers, other than in an emergency, is to assure that wills are written by competent attorneys, rather than non-lawyers who mean well but know little about the law. *Peterson v. Hovland (In re Peterson's Estate)*, 42 N.W.2d 59, 63 (Minn. 1950). Through a non-lawyer's "bungling use of legal terms," the will might be invalid, bequests might fail, the estate might be over-taxed, and the testator's intent might not be realized. *Id.* On the other hand, the *Peterson* court permitted the will to stand, so that the testator's interests would not suffer because of the unauthorized practice. *Id.* at 64-66.

[*Application*] The HomeElderCare social worker was not as trained in the law as a lawyer, of course, However, the risk in this situation was minimal. The social worker changed only the names of nonprofit organizations on the list of small bequests. She did not alter the language creating the bequests. Nor did she make changes in any of the other provisions of the will. This minimal risk was offset by the policy favoring implementation of the client's dying wishes.

Application: The application component presents your reasoning about the client's facts in light of the law. Your goal is not simply to restate the facts, but rather to show how they do or do not meet the factual conditions in the rule under discussion. The application closely reflects the type of reasoning you are presenting:

- Sometimes the reasoning process involves only *deductive reasoning*. Set out the relevant facts of your client's situation and tell the reader whether they meet the elements.
- As you *reason by example*, identify the similarity or difference between the facts of the decided case and the client's situation, then tell the reader the significance of the comparison. To strengthen your analysis on a topic without a clear conclusion, you may want to present reasoning by *multiple examples*, showing how your client's situation is analogous to one case and distinguishable from another.
- As you deal with *policy*, spell out for the reader how the various possible outcomes would or would not serve the policy you have identified.

Although the application relies to a great extent on the development of the law in the rule component, the application may refer to and cite legal authorities to expand upon the opening statement of the rule.

Deductive reasoning usually comes first, followed by reasoning by example or policy analysis. If all three are presented, policy analysis generally comes last. On occasion, policy analysis may be used as a lead-in to deductive reasoning.

If there are good arguments on both sides of an issue, you generally will present both sides in parallel discussions, with differing implications. In objective writing, such as an office memo used to counsel a client, the conventional approach is to lead with the better argument (whether it favors the client or not), follow it with the weaker one, and then explain why you favor the first. When writing to a court, you will lead with and emphasize the argument favoring your client. Often, policy forms the basis for the choice among competing applications and thus is discussed near the end.

To test whether your analysis is explicit enough, ask yourself "why?" after each sentence, and add to your discussion until nothing remains to be stated. Review Exhibit 10.2 for several examples of various types of rule material applied to the same facts.

Conclusion: The IRAC discussion closes with a statement of your conclusion, that is, whether the requirements of the rule are met or not. The conclusion in an IRAC discussion does not, however, address the actions the client should take; that topic appears in a different component of the paper. For an example of a conclusion, see the complete IRAC at the end of this chapter.

D. CONSTRUCTING IRACs

The length of an IRAC varies depending on the complexity of the analysis.

1. One Main Rule

IRAC can be rather brief if a simple rule applies to the client's situation in a quite obvious way. A very standard pattern for this situation is:

Para. 1: Introduction (topic) and **R**ule
Para. 2: **A**pplication and **C**onclusion

Indeed, IRAC can be completed within a single paragraph, e.g., one sentence introducing the topic and presenting the rule, the second sentence applying the rule and stating the conclusion, when very little needs to be said.

On the other hand, IRAC likely will run several or more paragraphs where more needs to be stated, e.g., a statute and case law are involved, there are good arguments on both sides, an extended comparison to a decided case or lengthy policy analysis would be instructive. Then, IRAC requires a sequence of paragraphs, that is, a paragraph block. For example, a lengthy paragraph block might be divided as follows:

Para. 1: Introduction (issue) and statutory Rule
Para. 2: Rule/major case interpreting statute
Para. 3: Application/deductive reasoning
Para. 4: Application/parallel between case and client situation
Para. 5: Application/contrast between case and client situation
Para. 6: Application/policy analysis
Para. 7: Conclusion as to this element

As you construct an IRAC paragraph block, consider how much legal material the reader should be expected to process at one time. The sequence above works when the statute and case are both straightforward and succinct. When one or both are complicated, a better option could be:

Para. 1: Introduction (issue) and statutory Rule
Para. 2: Application of statute
Para. 3: Rule from case
Para. 4: Application/parallel between case and client situation
Para. 5: Application/contrast between case and client situation
Para. 6: Rule policy and Application/policy analysis
Para. 7: Conclusion

For an example of a multi-paragraph IRAC, see the complete IRAC at the end of this chapter.

One key to using IRAC effectively in all of these situations is to follow the IRAC sequence. In addition, use paragraph breaks to signal the end of one phase in the sequence, e.g., between the rule and the application, between the statute and an illustrative case, between one side and the other.

2. A Rule with Distinct, Significant Elements

Many rules have elements that are distinct from each other and significant in their own right. It often makes sense to discuss these elements in their own IRACs. You should package these IRACs so the reader properly sees them as connected to the same rule. The mechanisms for doing so are bookend paragraphs or sentences: a roadmap at the beginning with the main rule and an overall conclusion at the end. In other words:

Roadmap
IRAC for element #1
IRAC for element #2
IRAC for element #3
Overall conclusion

The overall conclusion, which follows the conclusion as to the last element, may begin with a brief summary of all intermediate conclusions and should then state what the legal consequences are. For an outline following this approach, see Exhibit 10.3.

Another way to see this situation is one big IRAC consisting of several small IRACs. The initial introduction and rule are followed by the irac sequences for each element of the rule. The IRAC package finishes with an overall conclusion. In other words:

> Introduction
> Rule
> irac for element 1
> irac for element 2
> irac for element 3
> Conclusion

To decide which IRAC comes first, second, etc., attend to the rule itself; following the rule's sequence is an obvious option. If, however, one or two elements are very easy to apply, you may want to lead with those even if they do not come first in the rule.

As you present your IRACs, be sure to flag their connections. The reader should know at the outset whether they are from a conjunctive, disjunctive, aggregate, or balancing rule. As the IRAC unfolds, the reader should have a sense of moving methodically through the rule.

EXHIBIT 10.3

IRAC OUTLINE

Introduction: unauthorized practice prohibited by § 481.02

R#1. general rule: non-lawyer drafting will for another

- § 481.02 subdiv. 1
- *Peterson* case
- Policy—avoid bungling that leads to failed will etc.
- Key facts for application: non-lawyer, amended will

R#2. exception: drafting will in emergency when death is imminent

- § 481.02 subdiv.8
- *Peterson* did not involve this
- Policy above is outweighed by testator having will
- Key facts for application: death was imminent, minimal amendment so little concern re bungling

Conclusion: conduct falls within exception to general rule.

E. REVIEW OF CHAPTER 10

IRAC is the building block of analytical legal writing. By following the IRAC template, you will present your legal analysis in a way that reflects legal reasoning and fits your reader's expectations. IRAC is structured but not rigid:

- Introduction: may be a topic, issue (question), conclusion, or transition.
- Rule: may involve statutes, cases, policy, depending on the law governing your topic.
- Application: always involves deductive reasoning and may involve reasoning by example and policy analysis.
- Conclusion: presents the legal meaning of the client's situation that you have derived through reading the law and reasoning about your client's situation.

As you complete an IRAC, check whether it meets the criteria for all legal writing:

- *Complete:* Have you included the pertinent law, the key relevant facts, the major policies? Have you discussed both sides of a debatable issue?
- *Correct:* Have you stated both the law and the facts accurately?
- *Coherent:* Does the application clearly connect the rule and the facts? Does the conclusion follow from the application? If your topic involves more than one legal authority, do they fit together?
- *Comprehensible:* Will your reader be able to understand your IRAC in one careful reading?

EXHIBIT 10.4

COMPLETE IRAC

Did the social worker engage in the unauthorized practice of law when she amended the client's will the day before he died, three days after he was placed in a hospice for palliative care?

It is unlawful for a person who is not admitted and licensed to practice law in Minnesota "for or without a fee or any consideration, to prepare, directly or through another, for another person, firm or corporation, any will or testamentary disposition or instrument of trust serving purposes similar to those of a will." Minn. Stat. § 481.02 subdiv. 1 (1992). However, a non-lawyer may "draw[ ] a will for another in an emergency if the imminence of death leaves insufficient time to have it drawn and its execution supervised by a licensed attorney-at-law." *Id.* subdiv. 3(2). Violation of the statute is a misdemeanor. *Id.* subdiv. 8.

In *Peterson* v. *Hovland (In re Peterson's Estate)*, 42 N.W.2d 59 (Minn. 1950), a bank cashier prepared and executed Mr. Peterson's will, upon his request. This occurred several weeks before Peterson died, and the trial court found that death was not so imminent that Peterson could not have had an attorney perform this service. *Id.* at 61. The supreme court ruled that the cashier engaged in the unauthorized practice of law. *Id.*

The policy behind the prohibition on the drafting of wills by non-lawyers, other than in an emergency, is to assure that wills are written by competent attorneys, rather than non-lawyers who mean well but know little about the law. *Id.* at 63. Through a non-lawyer's "bungling use of legal terms," the will might be invalid, bequests might fail, the estate might be over-taxed, and the testator's intent might not be realized. *Id.* On the other hand, the *Peterson* court permitted the will to stand, so that the testator's wishes would not be thwarted because of the unauthorized practice. *Id.* at 64-66.

At first glance, under both section 481.02 and *Peterson*, the Home-ElderCare social worker's actions seem to be prohibited. The social worker was not licensed to practice law. She amended the client's existing will by changing the names of several nonprofit organizations to receive small bequests. Although the statute does not cover amending a will, as distinct from writing a new will, this activity most likely qualified as "preparing" a will, particularly since she also arranged for its execution.

However, unlike *Peterson*, the social worker's conduct most likely was protected under the statutory exception for drawing wills in an emergency. The patient's condition had deteriorated over the last few days, he was placed in hospice, and he died the day after he amended the will. This time frame amounted to the imminence of death. With only hours to live, the client chose his social worker for assistance, a choice that was both practical and possibly the only feasible means to amend the will with so little time left.

In addition, although the HomeElderCare social worker was not trained in the law, the risk of bungled drafting in this situation was minimal. The social worker changed only the names of nonprofit organizations on the list of small bequests. She did not alter the language creating the bequests. Nor did she make changes in any of the other provisions of the will. This minimal risk was offset by the policy favoring implementation of the client's dying wishes.

In conclusion, although the law generally prohibits non-lawyers from drawing wills for others, the conduct of HomeElderCare's social worker likely was not the unauthorized practice of law because she made only minor changes in a pre-existing will when the death of the client was imminent.

ADVISORY WRITING:
THE FUNCTION
AND FORMAT
OF THE OFFICE MEMO

> You may write for the joy of it, but the act of writing is not
> complete in itself. It has its end in its audience.
> —Flannery O'Connor
> *The Habit of Being* (Sally Fitzgerald, ed., 1979)

A. INTRODUCTION

Once you have read the law and reasoned through your client's situation, you are ready to present your analysis to someone else. As discussed in Chapter 10, IRAC is a building block for analytical legal writing. Is IRAC all there is? What types of papers are built on IRACs?

The short answer is: it depends on the context. Some of the more common legal writing genres are the client letter, demand letter, motion practice memorandum, and appellate brief. Lawyers present their analyses orally as well; examples include meeting with clients, deal or dispute negotiation, and court proceedings.

Quite often, the office memo precedes these forms of communication. An office memo captures the lawyer's analysis of the client's matter as of the date the memo was written. It may be read by a fellow lawyer also working on the case, or it may be a file memo that the author turns to as the case proceeds.

Although the following chapters depict writing as a separate step, the reading, reasoning, and writing processes are not truly separable. For example, you may write a rough outline of a memo midway through the reasoning process, to record your thoughts or test your analysis.

This chapter discusses several topics: reader-centered prose, audience and purpose, and the framework of the office memo. Chapters 12 through 14 cover in more detail the components of the office memo.

You will find two sample office memos on the HomeElderCare case at pages 334 and 342. Please read them before reading the rest of this chapter. You will see that they come to both similar and different conclusions. This is not surprising. As is generally true of legal analysis, some issues are easy to call; others are close calls because the law is ambiguous, some facts are unknown, or application of the law to the facts is debatable.

The two memos read differently in part because their contents differ. The first memo analyzes a past event: the drafting of a living will for Roger Nelson, now contested by his son. The second analyzes HomeElderCare's plan to provide a living will service to its clients, before the plan is carried out. We have annotated the memos, the first more than the second.

B. READER-CENTERED WRITING AND THE WRITER'S VOICE

1. Reader-Centered Writing

The aim of legal writing is to communicate the writer's legal analysis of a situation—his or her research, reading of the law, and reasoning about the client's situation—to an interested reader. If the writer succeeds, the reader will fully understand the writer's analysis, understand the legal meaning of the client's situation, and take appropriate action.

Legal writers (indeed, all writers who wish to be understood) should keep in mind basic principles of communication. Communication, a form of social interaction, succeeds when the writer honors these principles:

(1) Give neither too much nor too little information.
(2) Keep to relevant points.
(3) Convey the truth as you see it.
(4) Try to be understood; write coherently and comprehensibly.
(5) Take the reader's characteristics into account.
(6) Produce a writing that is appropriate to the context and circumstances.
(7) Produce a message that is appropriate to your purpose.[1]

---

1. *See generally* C. Douglas McCann & E. Tory Higgins, *Personal and Contextual Factors in Communication: A Review of the "Communication Game," in Language, Interaction and Social Cognition* 144 (Gun R. Semin & Klaus Fiedler eds., 1992).

Some of these principles restate the four attributes of sound legal writing: complete (items 1 and 2), correct (item 3), and coherent and comprehensible (item 4). Others highlight the importance of the reader's characteristics (item 5) and the paper's context, circumstances, and purpose (items 6 and 7). In other words, you must attend to the paper's audience and purpose, which together determine its function.

From the overall format of the paper to the sequence of points in individual paragraphs to the design of each sentence, you should consider how the reader will peruse and use your paper:

- What will the reader already know? What does the reader still need to know?
- How can the information be presented so as to maximize understanding?
- How will the reader best grasp the big picture and still see the nuances?
- What should come first? Next? At the end?

To a significant extent, the answers to these questions are provided by the conventions of legal writing. Every discipline has its own writing conventions; law is no exception. Not surprisingly, legal writing conventions closely reflect the ways lawyers approach and solve problems. Thus, once you learn how lawyers approach legal issues and problems, following the conventions should be fairly natural. If you follow the profession's conventions, other lawyers will be able to follow your analysis, and they will view your work as credible.

2. The Writer's Voice

It may seem that focusing on the reader means that your voice, as a writer, is muffled. Admittedly, your aim in legal writing is not primarily self-expression, and your personal preferences may differ from the language and conventions of the law. Nonetheless, it is your analysis that is presented within the conventional form. Your analysis reflects your values, your creative way of thinking about problems, and your choice of phrasing. No two lawyers, writing about the same client's situation, would generate the same paper.

Many lawyers have been trained never to use the first person ("I think . . .") in legal writing. A typical explanation is that the reader does not care what you think but is concerned only with what the law is; without the first person, your analysis will seem more objective and, hence, more credible. A better explanation is that the reader does in fact care what you think, but the reader also realizes full well, without a reminder, that your paper reflects your thinking. In choosing whether to use the first person, consider the preferences of your particular audience; a fellow lawyer in your firm may consider the first person appropriate, while an appellate court will not consider it acceptable in a brief. In any event, your paper will bear your name, because most formats include the writer's name in a prominent location.

C. The Function and Format of the Office Memo

1. The Function of the Office Memo: Audience and Purpose

The office memo (also known as a file memo, intraoffice memo, or internal memo) is standard in most settings where more than one lawyer practices, whether in a law firm, corporate counsel office, or legal department of a government agency or other organization. Office memos are written for various purposes. Some simply record conversations with the client or opposing counsel, information recently obtained from other sources, or ideas generated in discussions among lawyers working on the case.

The analytical office memo presents the lawyer's legal analysis of the client's situation at a particular time. The analytical office memo records the facts of the client's situation as currently known; documents the research conducted on the case, along with citations to the sources; presents the lawyer's reading of the pertinent legal authorities; and sets out the lawyer's reasoning about the case. The memo sets out predictions about how a court would handle the client's case, should this come to pass, and recommendations for appropriate action.

The analytical office memo states the best judgment of the writer and permits informed judgment by other lawyers working on the case. The memo also forms the basis of advice to the client, which in turn leads to steps taken on the client's behalf, such as the structuring of a transaction, discussions to settle the dispute, or arguments made to courts or other tribunals.

The most obvious audience for the analytical office memo is the named recipient, typically the senior lawyer who has requested the memo from a junior lawyer. Other lawyers working on the case also may read it. Lawyers working on a different case raising the same issue may read the memo. The writer also is a member of the audience, because he or she is likely to return to the memo as the work on the case continues.

In writing the analytical office memo, a lawyer, even though acting on behalf of the client, must act objectively: a lawyer must assess both the strengths and weaknesses of the client's legal position in accord with the lawyer's role as an officer of the legal system. The requirement of objectivity also stems from considerations of practicality and trust. A lawyer best serves a client contemplating a legally risky transaction by telling the client the risks and how to avoid them, rather than permitting the transaction to go forward and hoping that liability will not follow. For a client in a difficult position in litigation, a lawyer's most valuable service is to alert the client to the difficulties and to help the client obtain a realistic outcome, rather than to pursue a losing position until the case is lost at great expense. A lawyer's job is to tell the client "yes" only if "yes" is warranted, and to say "no" or present options if "yes" is not warranted.

2. The Format of the Office Memo

There is no single office memo format on which lawyers everywhere agree. On the other hand, several components are common to almost every format.

This section discusses those components from the perspective of the reader; Chapters 12 through 14 describe how to write them.

Caption: A typical caption consists of the recipient's name, the writer's name, the date, and the subject. The date is important because every office memo is time-bound, reflecting only what the writer knew and thought about the client's situation and the law as of the date the memo was written. The subject of the memo usually consists of the client's name and file number, along with a brief description of the topic of the memo.

Issue(s): The issues orient the reader to the legal questions arising in the client's situation and to the organization of the memo. The issues link legal concepts to the relevant facts of the client's situation. They appear in the same order as the main topics appear in the discussion.

Short answer(s): The short answers further orient the reader and provide the reader with the writer's position on the issues, permitting the reader to read the rest of the memo in light of the writer's position. The short answers present bottom-line answers, an indication of the degree of certainty the lawyer can provide, and a phrase or two of explanation. They parallel the issues in number and sequence.

Taken together, the issues and short answers constitute the executive summary of the memo.

Facts: The fact statement tells the reader the client's story. If the lawyer has talked only to the client, the story is told through the client's eyes. If the lawyer has investigated the facts, the fact statement includes information from other sources. If the client has sought advice before taking action, the fact statement refers to present facts and future possibilities.

Discussion: The bulk of the office memo is the discussion, in which the writer systematically analyzes each issue and justifies each short answer for the reader. The discussion consists of IRACs on the various topics: an introduction, a presentation of the rule of law, application of the rule to the client's facts, and the writer's conclusion. Headings and sub-headings signal the major and minor topics.

Conclusion: The conclusion both summarizes the preceding material for the reader and recommends actions to be taken for or by the client. The recommendations should flow from the legal analysis in the discussion and may also be based on non-legal factors, which should be clearly stated.

It may seem that the office memo presents the same information over and over again. As Exhibit 11.1 shows, this is in some sense true: the facts appear in every major component, the law in five out of six components. Because an office memo assigns legal meaning to a client's situation, the facts and law should, of course, be prevalent. It is the way the facts and law are handled—the depth of treatment, as show in Exhibit 11.1, and manner of presentation—that varies from component to component.

Some office memos also contain attachments: key authorities, such as a key statute or new case, especially if the authority is not well known to the recipient of the memo; an important contract, map, or other document; a timeline if there are many specific events and their timing is crucial.

In some ways, office memos parallel judicial opinions. See Exhibit 11.2. A lawyer writing an office memo is, in essence, seeking to anticipate what a

---

EXHIBIT 11.1

FACTS AND LAW IN OFFICE MEMO

Components	Facts	Law
issues	brief	brief
short answers	brief	brief
facts	thorough	—
discussion	selected	thorough
conclusion	selected	selected

---

court would do when faced with the client's case. Indeed, one way to maintain objectivity is to imagine that you are a judge deciding the client's case.

3. An Analogy: The Architecture of a House

The upcoming chapters develop an analogy: An office memo resembles a building, specifically, a house. The issues and short answers together constitute the facade, the facts the foundation, the discussion the interior, the conclusion the roof. Just as one must attend to function and structure in building a house, so one must attend to function and structure in constructing an office memo.

EXHIBIT 11.2

PARALLELS BETWEEN JUDICIAL OPINIONS AND OFFICE MEMOS

Judicial Opinion	Office Memo
case name, court, date, docket number	caption (client's name, writer's name, date, file number, etc.)
issues	issues
holdings	short answers
fact statement	facts
reasoning	discussion
concluding paragraph with procedural outcome	conclusion with recommendations

D. WRITING THE OFFICE MEMO COMPONENTS

The next three chapters discuss the writing of office memo components in the following order: discussion; issues, short answers, and conclusion; facts. You may well write these components in this order, because the discussion flows most directly from your reasoning; the issues, short answers, and conclusion derive from the discussion; and the facts must support the rest of the memo. However, if you are a big-picture thinker, you might begin with the issues and short answers. If you are more fact-oriented, you might write the facts first.

No matter what order you choose, you should assemble the memo components in the order set out in this chapter. Then check each component for consistency with the other components. In a successful memo, the components work together well and meet the criteria discussed in the next three chapters.

E. REVIEW OF CHAPTER 11

As the foundational form of legal writing, the office memo communicates the writer's legal analysis of a client's situation to the reader. The audience consists of lawyers working on the case (the author included), and the purpose is to present an objective analysis that will support sound advice for the client. You will meet your audience's need and serve your purpose well if you structure the memo according to the following conventional format: caption, issues, short answers, facts, discussion, and conclusion.

THE OFFICE MEMO:

THE DISCUSSION

> Never be afraid to sit awhile and think.
> —Lorraine Hansberry
> *A Raisin in the Sun* (1958)

A. INTRODUCTION

The core, as well as the bulk, of the office memo is the discussion component. In the discussion, the writer systematically analyzes each issue and justifies each short answer by connecting the facts and the law. The reader has not come to know the case in detail as the author has, yet wants to know what needs to be known. How do lawyers present their analysis as efficiently and effectively as possible?

The key to an effective discussion is its organization, which directly reflects the rule of law, or rules of law, pertinent to the client's situation. Hence analysis and organization are intertwined. This chapter discusses how to organize the material within the discussion; how to deal with branchpoints at which the analysis could proceed in two (or more) directions; and how to use transitions and headings. While most of the chapter discusses a memo analyzing a dispute, it also covers a deal-oriented memo as well.

There are many ways to create a well organized discussion. Some prefer to write an outline first. Others prefer a more organic approach, writing small pieces that they eventually assemble into an organized discussion. Either way can work, especially if you follow the IRAC template (discussed in Chapter 10) as you fill in your outline or write your small pieces.

This chapter refers primarily to the discussion from the first sample HomeElderCare office memo, found at page 334, and secondarily to the second memo, at page 342. You may want to look them over before proceeding.

B. AN ANALOGY: THE INTERIOR OF A HOUSE

In the analogy between office memos and houses, the discussion constitutes the interior. Just as the interior of a house is organized at several levels, so is an office memo. In designing a house, the architect must decide how many stories there will be and how the rooms on a story will fit together to best serve the needs of the occupant. Each room has a distinct use and relates to the others in distinct ways. In home design, there are conventions that the architect may consider but is not compelled to follow.

Similarly, a lawyer must decide how to present the various topics in a discussion to best serve the reader. Each topic is important in itself and related to the others to form a complete legal analysis of the client's situation. Many lawyers generally follow the conventions discussed in this chapter.

C. ORGANIZATION OF DISPUTE-ORIENTED MEMOS

Many office memos cover several issues; thus, the discussion covers several topics and several IRACs or IRAC packages. Which topic should you discuss first? Which comes second? And so on.

You should order the parts of the discussion according to either the logic of the law or the factual logic of the client's situation. It is more common to follow legal logic; factual logic may be used if there is no clear legal logic to follow. Sometimes you can discern legal logic by examining the legal authorities you have read, for example, a commentary source or leading case. Of course, you should be sure that the borrowed organization is indeed logical and fits your client's situation. You also may find the standard legal conventions listed below helpful:

- *Intermediate to ultimate consequences:* Because the discussion of the ultimate-consequence rule presupposes the intermediate consequence, you should discuss the intermediate-consequence rule first.
- *Threshold topic first:* A threshold topic nearly always appears first because its application dictates whether analysis of the other rules is necessary. For example, if the court clearly lacks jurisdiction, issues of liability and remedies are beside the point. However, unless a threshold

topic unequivocally forecloses further analysis, you should discuss the remaining issues.

- *Pivotal topic first:* A pivotal topic comes first because the conclusion from that discussion sets up the analysis of related topics.
- *Claim/defense/remedy:* Many memos start with the topics applicable to the plaintiff's claim, proceed to the topics governing the defendant's defense, and then discuss any topics pertaining to remedies.
- *General to specific:* Generally, discussion of a broad topic precedes discussion of a narrower topic, such as an exception.
- *More to less important alternatives:* Some conduct is covered by more than one topic, e.g., overlapping common law and statutory rules. The discussion should begin with the rule that is more clearly applicable, better established, or more significant in consequence to your client.
- *Procedural/substantive or substantive/procedural:* Procedural topics often appear together, and substantive topics often appear together. Which set comes first depends on the logic of the law as applied to the client's situation.
- *Chronology:* Some topics arise chronologically. For instance, contract law parallels the unfolding of the transaction: formation, terms, performance, breach, and remedies.
- *Actors:* The discussion focuses first on all topics pertaining to a particular actor, then proceeds to the topics pertaining to another actor, and so on. This convention is most useful when you are analyzing a transaction involving multiple actors or a single complicated event.
- *Easy to difficult:* This approach is not based on logic but rather on the reader's approach to the memo. The discussion of an easy topic first helps the reader understand the client's situation better when the reader turns to the more difficult material.

Even in a simple memo, you may employ two or more of these conventions. For instance, you may proceed through procedural topics chronologically, then move to substantive topics by claim/defense/remedy.

Some complex discussions entail overlap between legal topics. For example, the same topic may apply to two different sets of parties involved in closely related transactions:

- One option is to discuss all claims involving one set of parties, then all claims involving the other set: A and B—claim 1, claim 2; then A and C—claim 1, claim 2.
- Another option is to discuss all instances of one claim, then all instances of the other claim: Claim 1—as between A and B, as between A and C; then Claim 2—as between A and B, A and C.
- A third option is a hybrid, e.g., to discuss the topics on which there is no difference across the parties, then discuss the topics that are unique to each party.

All options involve some repetition, but that is inherent in the situation. Whatever organization you choose, use shortened discussions and cross-references in the later portions of the discussion to reduce repetition.

If you are discussing a complex topic, you will need to order not only topics but sub-topics as well. The conventions listed above work not only for large-scale organization—the ordering of topics—but also middle-scale organization—the ordering of sub-topics within a topic. For example, if you are discussing a statutory claim along with a common law claim, you may decide at the large-scale level to lead with the statute, because it is more important. At the middle-scale level, in the discussion of the statute, you may decide to lead with the issue of scope, then discuss the statute's general rule, and conclude with the exceptions, because scope is a threshold matter and general precedes specific.

The analysis of each simple topic or sub-topic within your large- and middle-scale organization needs its own organization. This is where IRAC enters in; it serves, in essence, as the small-scale organization throughout the discussion. Thus, in discussing the scope of a statutory claim your client may have, you would identify the statute under discussion (introduction), set out its scope provision (rule), analyze whether the opponent fits within that scope (application), draw a conclusion on that issue (conclusion), and proceed to IRACs covering the statute's general rule and exceptions.

The discussion in the first HomeElderCare sample memo, sketched in Exhibit 12.1, follows several of these principles. The order is: (1) unauthorized practice of law, (2) enforcement of the contracts between HomeElder-Care and the clients, and (3) validity of the living wills. This organization presents the pivotal topic first and the intermediate consequence before the ultimate consequence. Within the discussion of unauthorized practice, the easy topic (legal document) precedes the harder topic (legal advice).

D. ORGANIZATION OF DEAL-ORIENTED MEMOS

Just as many lawyers help clients resolve disputes over past events, many lawyers assist clients in planning for the future. A catch-all term for the latter is "transactional practice." The two types of practice have much in common, e.g., reading the law, thinking through the client's situation in light of the rules, and discerning the legal meaning of the client's situation.

On the other hand, there are some differences. Even when there are missing or ambiguous facts, because events have occurred, the litigator has a more fixed set of facts to work with than does the transactional lawyer who must anticipate future events. A litigator's thinking resembles point-counterpoint: the court could rule for or against the client (although most cases settle for a sum between the two). A transactional lawyer thinks in terms of options the client has, with a focus on the legal benefits and drawbacks of each option. In considering a specific option, the transactional lawyer does think somewhat like a litigator: if the client takes this option and it is challenged in court, what would be the outcome? Even so, the fundamental difference remains: the litigator tries to fit the law to the client's dispute so as to yield a favorable outcome; the transactional lawyer fits the client's deal to the law to develop a legally beneficial transaction.

EXHIBIT 12.1

SAMPLE OUTLINE OF DISCUSSION OF DISPUTE-ORIENTED MEMO

I. **UNAUTHORIZED PRACTICE OF LAW** (eleven paragraphs)
   A. **Statutory quote with overall rule re non-attorney; application—non-attorney**
   B. **Drafting legal documents** (all one paragraph)
      1. Introduction: conclusion
      2. Rule: construing UPL and LW statutes together; dictionary definitions
      3. Application: living will as legal document, fee
      4. Conclusion: there is UPL
   C. **Giving legal advice or counsel** (eight paragraphs)
      1. Introduction: transition
      2. Rule: statute, *Gardner* rule and example
      3. Application in several stages
         • Review of activities and LW statute
         • Comparison to *Gardner*
         • Policy argument: protect public
         • Another policy: inconvenience, impracticality
         • Counter-argument
         • Charging fee
      4. Conclusion: there likely is UPL; consequences
   D. **Link between UPL and two remaining questions**

II. **CONTRACT ENFORCEABLITY** (seven paragraphs)
   [No A, B level because simpler rule]
      1. Introduction: topic
      2. Rule: *Buckley* and *Weatherston's;* summary of latter
      3. Application in several stages
         • Practice probably contrary to statute
         • Purpose of UPL statute
         • Protections against incompetence
         • No fraud or misrepresentation
         • Legal work incidental to other service
         • Supporting public policy
      4. Conclusion: enforceable contract

III. **VALIDITY OF LIVING WILL** (three paragraphs)
   [Again, no A, B]
      1. Introduction: conclusion
      2. Rule: UPL statute and *Peterson*
      3. Application in two stages
         • Comparison to *Peterson*
         • Policy analysis based on LW statute
      4. Conclusion: valid living wills

For this reason, a transactional lawyer's office memo may look different than a litigator's memo. The discussion may be organized around legal concerns, paralleling the litigator's issue-oriented approach, or it may be organized around options. The organization may blend the two: overall design by issue with options within an issue, or overall design by options with issues within options.

The second HomeElderCare memo is a transactional lawyer's memo. Its overall design is by issue, with the options explored within each issue. See Exhibit 12.2, and compare it to Exhibit 12.1, covering the first memo.

E. BRANCHPOINTS

The discussion thus far has skirted a major organizational challenge present in some memos: branchpoints. Branchpoints occur when an analysis can proceed down one of two roads, each with its own analysis and implications. Unlike the narrator in the Robert Frost poem about two roads diverging in a yellow

EXHIBIT 12.2

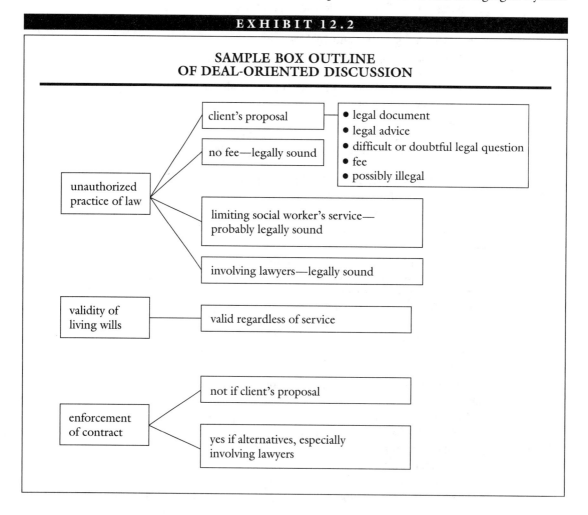

SAMPLE BOX OUTLINE
OF DEAL-ORIENTED DISCUSSION

wood,[1] a legal writer should proceed down the first road and loop back to proceed down the second. Otherwise, the analysis will not be complete.

Branchpoints commonly occur in the following situations:

- an *ambiguous rule*, so that you have to apply two or more possible versions of the law;
- an *unknown rule*, so that you have to consider two or more rules from persuasive authority;
- *unknown or disputed facts* or facts that have yet to occur because the client has sought advice before acting, so that you have to apply the law to two or more alternative versions of the facts;
- *facts that fit awkwardly* within the rule, so that your reasoning could lead to two or more results; and
- *interlocking rules*, such that the debatable outcome of the analysis of the pivotal rule dictates the analysis of the other rule(s).

Exhibit 12.3 presents these situations in flowchart form.

The organizational challenge is to make the branchpoint design clear to the reader. Generally, the most straightforward approach is to provide an initial roadmap, complete one path of the analysis, indicate that the discussion is about to loop back to an earlier point where the analyses diverged, pursue the second path, and conclude with a summary.

For example, in the first HomeElderCare sample memo, at the end of the first part of the discussion, a branchpoint arises. The memo begins the discussion with the unauthorized practice of law and ends the unauthorized practice discussion with a paragraph describing the branchpoint: If there is no unauthorized practice, the validity of the will and enforcement of the contract are not a concern. If there is unauthorized practice, both of these topics merit serious analysis.

F. HEADINGS, OVERVIEWS, AND TRANSITIONS

No matter how simple or complex your analysis, you should alert your reader to the discussion's structure. There are three tools for this purpose: headings, overviews, and transitions.

Headings: Office memos typically have headings, surrounded by white space, that demarcate portions of the memo. The most prominent headings announce the components of the office memo. Within the discussion, less

---

1. Two roads diverged in a yellow wood,
   And sorry I could not travel both
   And be one traveler, long I stood
   And looked down one as far as I could
   To where it bent in the undergrowth
   Then took the other, just as fair, . . .
   Oh, I kept the first for another day!
   Yet knowing how way leads on to way,
   I doubted if I should ever come back.
       —Robert Frost, "The Road Not Taken,"
       in *The Complete Poems of Robert Frost* (1949).

EXHIBIT 12.3

TYPES OF BRANCHPOINTS

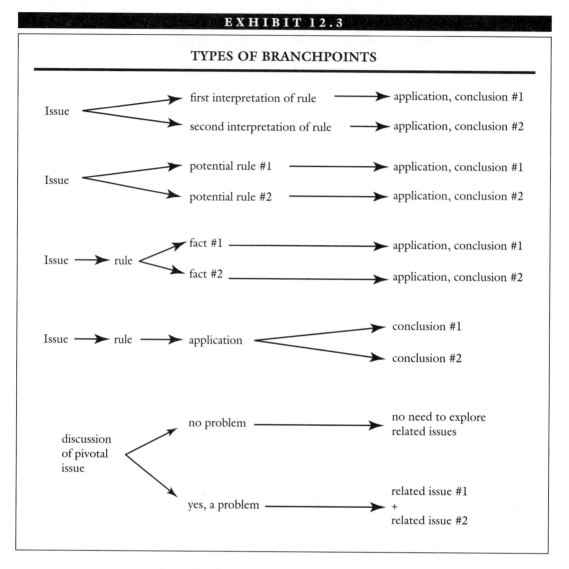

prominent headings announce the topics and sub-topics. Topic headings typically are words or phrases, not full sentences.

Overviews: An overview briefly states the points in the order they appear in the text. It usually does not contain any citations or reasoning. Overviews generally summarize the discussion, e.g., a few sentences identifying the main topics, a sentence or two identifying the elements of a complex rule. There are two types of overview: a roadmap, which appears at the outset of the material it previews, and a summary, which reviews the material just presented.

Transitions: A transition links segments, alerting the reader that one segment has finished and the next is starting. A transition can be a mere word, a phrase, a sentence, or even a paragraph, depending on the complexity of the material and the size of the units being linked. For example:

- *Between topics:* Although the enforcement of the living will contracts is debatable, the validity of the living will is clear.

- *Between elements:* Second, the non-lawyer must have engaged in certain behavior.
- *From point to counterpoint:* However . . .

If you have laid out a clear roadmap, brief transitions should suffice. In particular, text transitions following a heading can be brief. In all events, take care to use words that truly convey the nexus between the segments you are linking. Exhibit 12.4 lists transitional words and phrases, grouped by meaning.

The discussion in the first sample HomeElderCare memo uses headings for the three main topics; overviews, such as the introduction paragraph (roadmap); and transitions, including phrases ("first," "second," "finally," "in conclusion") and sentences ("The remaining questions are the enforceability of the contract and the validity of the living will.").

EXHIBIT 12.4

LIST OF TRANSITIONS*

Introducing	*Exemplifying*	*Adding or Amplifying*
first	for example	again
initially	for instance	furthermore
to begin	to illustrate	moreover
the first reason	in particular	additionally
primarily	namely	similarly
in general		also
	Emphasizing	alternatively
Sequencing	indeed	a further reason
first, second, third	certainly	
finally	above all	*Connecting Logically*
initially	especially	thereby
next	not only . . . but also	therefore
then		thus
last	*Contrasting*	as a result
before	however	hence
	but	accordingly
Restating	on the other hand	consequently
that is	yet	because
in other words	unlike *x*	
more simply	in contrast	*Concluding*
in brief	nevertheless	to conclude
as noted	nonetheless	in summary
	rather	to review
	although	finally
	despite	as a result
		as we have seen

*Adapted from Lynn B. Squires et al., *Legal Writing in a Nutshell* 95–98 (2d ed. 1996).

G. Sketching and Checking the Organization

Once you have tentatively committed yourself to an organizational scheme, you should sketch it somehow, at some point well before you write the bulk of your paper. The classic means is an outline; an alternative is to use a typeface outline. See Exhibit 12.1, which combines classic and typeface outlines. A quite different alternative is a flowchart in which the rules occupy large boxes, the elements middle-sized boxes, and so on. See Exhibit 12.2.

As you review your rough draft, ask yourself whether you can follow your organization without difficulty: Is anything omitted? Does any material appear more than once without a compelling reason? Do you need to know about a later point to understand an earlier point? Have you adhered to your organizational scheme? Indeed, you may wish to sketch out the organization of your actual draft discussion and check it against your pre-writing sketch.

Furthermore, review how you have allocated your space to various topics. Your sketch should demonstrate how complex each rule and element is as applied to your facts, and your draft should allocate space accordingly. Avoid overly long discussions of straightforward material and overly compact discussions of complex material. For your memo to be effective, each sentence must convey its fair share of the information to be communicated.

H. Overarching Consideratons

As you write your discussion, keep in mind the principles of communication presented in Chapter 11, as well as the four criteria for sound legal writing:

- *Completeness:* Have you covered the material completely?
- *Correctness:* Have you stated both the law and the facts accurately?
- *Coherence:* Does the analysis make sense? Does each part connect clearly to the others? Does each conclusion on each topic fit with the others?
- *Comprehensibility:* Will your reader be able to understand your discussion in one careful reading?

Furthermore, think carefully about issues of breadth, depth, and slant. You should present the information the reader needs to understand and evaluate your analysis of the client's case. On the other hand, you should not write the legal equivalent of an encyclopedia, providing more background on the law than a reader really needs. Nor should you write an epitaph, a cursory statement of your bottom line without an explanation. Nor should you write an editorial, with the primary aim of persuading the reader of the wisdom of your personal point of view. Rather, you should write an essay—a balanced, analytical paper.

For example, the reader of the HomeElderCare memo would not need a statement of the law of contract formation in the HomeElderCare analysis.

The reader would look for an assessment of why there is no concern about fraud, not simply a statement that there is none. Because the unauthorized practice issue is a close call, the reader will want to know about both views in some detail.

I.   REVIEW OF CHAPTER 12

The discussion in an office memo is as successful as its structure is sound. As you develop your discussion, use the tools listed below to assure that your discussion is well organized:

- an overall organization that reflects the logic of the subject or a legal organizational convention;
- clear expression of branchpoints; and
- well chosen headings, overviews, and transitions.

Also take care to present an objective analysis with sufficient breadth and depth to fully inform, but not overwhelm, your reader.

Once the discussion is drafted, you are ready to capture its key points by writing the opening and closing sections of the memo—the issues, short answers, and conclusion. Chapter 13 covers these three components.

THE OFFICE MEMO:

ISSUES, SHORT

ANSWERS, AND

CONCLUSION

> What is the answer? [no response] Then, what is the question?
> —Gertrude Stein's last words
>   quoted in Elizabeth Sprigge, *Gertrude Stein* (1957)

A. INTRODUCTION

Although the discussion constitutes the core of the office memo, it neither opens nor closes the memo. Rather, the memo opens with two closely linked sections—the issues and short answers—and closes with the conclusion. Why do lawyers include these components? How are they written?

This chapter uses as examples the issues, short answers, and conclusions of the sample office memos on the HomeElderCare case at pages 334 and 342. You may want to review those components and memos before continuing.

B. AN ANALOGY: PARTS OF A HOUSE

In the analogy between a house and an office memo, the exterior walls of the house parallel the issues and short answers. The issues and short answers link the main legal and factual concepts covered in each part of the discussion. They let you see the memo at a glance, just as the exterior walls allow you to deduce the basics of a house's design.

Similarly, the conclusion is like the roof. The roof rests on the rest of the house, can be constructed only after the house is framed, and protects the house's occupants and property. So, too, the conclusion in an office memo rests on the rest of the memo, can be written only after the rest of the memo is drafted, and presents recommendations that protect the client's interests.

C. ISSUES

In most memo formats, the caption is followed immediately by the issues. In some formats, this component is called the "questions presented." In general, questions attract and focus a reader's attention; the issues in an office memo focus the reader's attention on the key legal topics and facts addressed in the discussion. The issues also show the reader how the memo is organized, alerting the reader to the number and order of major topics and to the relationships among them.

The basic formula for an issue is *law + facts* in question form. In most situations, the issue links a major legal concept to the most important relevant fact(s) of the client's case. To maximize your reader's understanding, you generally should present the legal concept at one end of the issue and the factual material at the other, rather than interweaving the two. You can lead with the law and proceed to the facts, or vice versa: *Is [law] when [facts]? Do [facts] result in [law]?*

On occasion, your issue will be almost purely legal or factual. For example, when the rules of law are unsettled and your primary task is to determine what the rule is, with the application to your client's situation following as a matter of course, your issue will be primarily legal in content. On the other hand, when your task is to assess the facts under a straightforward rule, the issue will read as primarily factual.

Whichever situation applies, your goal is to state the topic(s) of the discussion clearly and in a question that is informative and fully readable the first time through:

- Chart a middle course between generality and specificity.
- Present only the most important legal concepts and facts, not every detail.
- Refer to the concepts in a pertinent rule, rather than using general terms like "liability" or "illegality" or presenting citations to specific authorities.

- Refer to actors by using labels that identify their roles under the rule, rather than using abstract references to "person" or proper names (except perhaps for the client, whose identity is known).

Furthermore, because the office memo should be objective, the issue should be phrased objectively. Avoid slanted language that plays on the reader's emotions; rather, use language that a neutral observer, such as a court, would use. Present the most important facts and legal concepts, whether they are favorable or unfavorable to your client.

Many memos cover more than one topic. Generally, you should write an issue for each topic, or rule, you cover in the discussion. The issues should signal the relationships among the topics through transitional phrases or cross-references; for example, where one topic follows from another, the second issue could begin with "if so" or "as a result." In some situations, you may want to reflect sub-topics as well. The classic approach is to present an introductory segment or question referring to the main topic, followed by specific questions referring to the sub-topics.

Most lawyers number issues and present each issue in its own paragraph. Finally, although some writers introduce an issue with "whether," this construction is undesirable because the result is a sentence fragment, which generally is difficult for the reader to understand.

The first sample HomeElderCare memo contains three issues, which appear in the order in which the topics appear in the discussion. The first issue begins with the legal concept (practicing law illegally) and closes with the key facts (elderly clients, living will, set fee). It is phrased objectively and uses labels rather than proper names. The second issue refers back to the first ("such a service"), the third refers to the second ("that contract"), so both are quite concise.

D. SHORT ANSWERS

In most memo formats, the issues are followed by short answers, labeled "brief answers" in some formats. Short answers not only continue to orient the reader to the memo, they also they tell the reader the legal meaning you would ascribe to the client's situation. Knowing your answers to the issues at the outset permits the reader to examine along the way how well the analysis supports the answers.

The basic formulas for a short answer are *law + facts + a reason* or *facts + law + a reason* in statement form. Not surprisingly, many of the principles of writing issues apply as well to the writing of short answers. There should be an answer for every issue. Short answers should combine facts and law, read well the first time through, and be phrased objectively. You should use transitional phrases, cross-references, and formatting to convey the relationships among the answers.

Short answers are more extensive than issues because they include brief statements of your reasoning. Take care not to synopsize all steps of your reasoning, or the answer will no longer be short. Rather, you should state, in simple and concise terms, the main reason for each answer. Ordinarily, you will not include citations in your short answers.

A challenge in writing short answers is to convey the certainty or uncertainty of your answer. In some situations, you will be certain how the law applies to your client's situation; in other situations, you will be quite unsure. In any event, you should clearly state your best prediction about how a court would handle your client's situation, should litigation actually arise. At the same time, you may phrase your short answer to reflect your uncertainty, possibly by using a hedging phrase, such as "probably" or "most likely." Some lawyers include probabilities in their predictions; for example, in stating that "there is a seventy-five percent chance" that a court will rule a particular way, a lawyer is opining that three out of four courts faced with the case would rule one way, while the fourth would rule differently. (Your instincts for predicting legal outcomes will develop as you develop expertise in a particular area of law.)

The first sample HomeElderCare memo contains three short answers, paralleling the three issues and the order the issues are covered in the discussion. All three short answers provide clear responses to the issues. Each short answer includes a brief explanation: the first refers to difficult or doubtful legal questions, the second to the absence of fraud and the promotion of living wills, and the third to statutory policy. The short answers are linked in subtle ways; for example, "this service" and "nonetheless" in the second answer refer back to the first. Each short answer reflects the writer's relative uncertainty or certainty ("likely," "probably," "is").

E. CONCLUSION

1. Writing the Conclusion

At the end of the memo comes the conclusion. In some formats, this component is labeled "summary" or "recommendations." The conclusion provides closure and should prompt the reader to make a final judgment about whether he or she accepts the writer's answers to the issues. In addition, the conclusion presents the writer's recommendations as to how the situation should be handled. Here the memo shifts from predicting how the legal system would respond to the client's situation to recommending actions that will lead to the best possible results for the client.

Unlike the issues and short answers, the conclusion is written in conventional paragraph form. You should begin with a restatement of the answers to the issues. Unless the memo is quite long, you need not restate the reasoning, and it is rare to include citations.

The bulk of the conclusion should be devoted to a discussion of the client's options, including the plan(s) identified by the client. For example, in a litigation context, the advice may cover such options as negotiating a settlement, employing alternative dispute resolution (such as mediation or arbitration), or filing a lawsuit. The probable outcome of each option should be noted.

In the conclusion in the first HomeElderCare sample memo, the first paragraph answers the three legal issues. The second paragraph suggests actions to take in light of HomeElderCare's legal position.

2. Giving Legal Advice

As you turn to the conclusion, keep in mind the following statement about legal advice, from the Model Rules of Professional Conduct: "In representing a client, a lawyer shall exercise independent professional judgment and render candid advice. In rendering advice, a lawyer may refer not only to law but to other considerations as well, such as moral, economic, social and political factors, that may be relevant to the client's situation."[1]

Legal advice is to be "candid" and based on "independent professional judgment." The lawyer's job is to inform the client about how the law governs the client's case, not only when the law favors the client's plans, but especially when the law constrains the client. Lawyers must know how to say "no" effectively. Of course, to the extent possible, the lawyer should also provide the client with alternatives that avoid or minimize the legal problems.

Although legal advice is grounded in the law, it also may incorporate non-legal factors. Many cases call for consideration of other disciplines: engineering for patent law, finance for corporate law, psychology for criminal law, and so on. It often is both practical and valuable for a lawyer to give advice mixing law and non-legal factors, especially when the lawyer has training in another relevant discipline and when the client has come to value the lawyer's counsel over time. The comments to the Model Rule also state that a lawyer should recommend that a client consult a professional in a different discipline if the situation calls for that expertise.

F. VARIATIONS ON THE THEME: THE DEAL-ORIENTED MEMO

As is true of the discussion, the issues, short answers, and conclusion of a deal-oriented memo differ in some ways from those in a memo discussing past events. The issues and short answers may be framed in terms of options or in terms of options combined with legal concerns.

The difference in context is especially pronounced in the conclusion component. In the litigation context, the conclusion discusses which of a fairly fixed set of steps should be pursued. In a transactional context, the client's situation is less fixed, so the conclusion should be more wide-ranging.

Thus, in the transactional context in particular, good legal advice typically entails creative and expansive thinking similar to that used in other forms of problem-solving. Although you should start with the client's proposal, you should then generate alternatives that have the potential of serving the client's interests. Once you have generated a list of possibilities, you should assess each and select those that best serve the interests of the client and conform to the law.

A useful way of sketching the options available to a client is a decision tree. A decision tree charts the client's options, linking each to the most likely legal outcome and non-legal outcomes. The decision tree in Exhibit 13.1 depicts the reasoning behind the conclusions in the second HomeElderCare sample memo.

---

1. Model Rules of Prof'l Conduct R. 2.1 (1983).

EXHIBIT 13.1

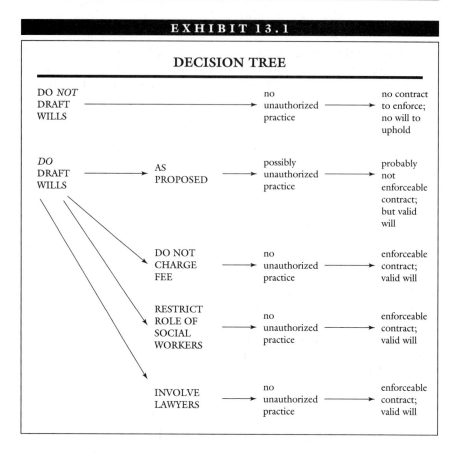

DECISION TREE

DO *NOT* DRAFT WILLS		no unauthorized practice	no contract to enforce; no will to uphold
DO DRAFT WILLS	AS PROPOSED	possibly unauthorized practice	probably not enforceable contract; but valid will
	DO NOT CHARGE FEE	no unauthorized practice	enforceable contract; valid will
	RESTRICT ROLE OF SOCIAL WORKERS	no unauthorized practice	enforceable contract; valid will
	INVOLVE LAWYERS	no unauthorized practice	enforceable contract; valid will

G. OVERARCHING CONSIDERATIONS

You should, of course, review all three components discussed in this chapter to verify that they fit the four criteria:

- *Completeness:* Does your work incorporate the important legal and factual concepts? Are the main topics in the discussion alluded to?
- *Correctness:* Have you referred to both facts and law accurately?
- *Coherence:* Do the components track each other, so that the same topics appear in all three? Do the short answers and the issues align with each other, does the conclusion match the short answers, and do the recommendations flow from the answers?
- *Comprehensibility:* Will your reader be able to follow your prose in one careful reading?

Finally, in assessing your advice to your client, consider whether you have approached your client's situation candidly, expansively, and creatively.

H. REVIEW OF CHAPTER 13

The issues, short answers, and conclusion share important attributes: All three orient the reader, by focusing his or her attention and by paralleling the organization of the discussion. All three advance the reader's understanding—the issue by posing a question, the short answer by answering the question, and the conclusion by tracing out the implications of that answer. More specifically:

The issues should:

- combine law and facts in question form,
- be neither too abstract nor too detailed,
- be phrased objectively, and
- reflect the organization of the discussion.

The short answers should:

- combine law, facts, and a brief reason in statement form;
- be neither too abstract nor too detailed;
- be phrased objectively;
- reflect the organization of the discussion; and
- convey your degree of certainty or uncertainty about the answer.

The conclusion should:

- briefly restate your answers to the issues,
- provide candid and creative advice,
- incorporate non-legal principles as needed, and
- present and assess your client's options.

Issues, short answers, and a conclusion fulfilling these criteria should serve the needs of your reader well.

THE OFFICE MEMO:

THE FACTS

> Fact and fancy look alike across the years that link the past with
> the present.
> —Helen Keller
> *The Story of My Life* (1903)

A. INTRODUCTION

Between the short answers and discussion in the office memo comes the fact statement, generally labeled "facts." The fact statement is precisely what the name suggests: a recounting of the important facts of the client's situation. How do lawyers figure out the facts and decide which to include and exclude? How do lawyers describe the client's situation?

The fact statements from both sample memos on the HomeElderCare case, at pages 334 and 342, serve as the examples in this chapter. You may want to review them before continuing.

B. FUNCTIONS OF THE FACT STATEMENT

The fact statement tells the client's story. The fact statement does not duplicate the coverage of the facts in the discussion. There, facts are interspersed among legal rules and elements. To serve a client with understanding, a lawyer must see the client's situation as a story, not merely as bits of factual material tied to legal rules.

If the reader of the memo is unfamiliar with the client's situation, the reader learns of it through the facts. If the reader is familiar with the client's situation but has learned it in bits and pieces through interviews and a review of documents, the fact statement helps the reader see the important facts, assembled and presented in a coherent narrative.

For the writer of the memo, writing the fact statement presents an opportunity to revisit the facts and think through them carefully. It is easy to lose track of the facts as you research the law, read it, and reason about the client's situation. Committing the facts to paper in a carefully organized narrative forces you to concentrate on them. Indeed, the importance of a particular fact may become clear for the first time during the drafting of the fact statement.

In addition, the fact statement serves as a record of the facts as of the date the memo is written. Often you will learn facts gradually, over days, weeks, months, or even years. A lawyer must take stock periodically to determine which facts are fully known, which facts are not known, and which are disputed. The legal analysis in the memo is tied to the facts known when the memo was written. When new facts come to light, not only the fact statement but also portions of the analysis may need revision.

C. An Analogy: Foundation of a House

In the analogy of an office memo to a house, the facts form the foundation on which the office memo is built. A house's foundation sets the shape for and supports the house. Similarly the fact statement sets the topics for the office memo, and the analysis is only as strong as the lawyer's understanding of the client's situation.

D. Assembling the Facts

Assembling the facts from the bits of factual information you have gathered entails two steps: (1) studying and organizing information from various sources and (2) sorting through the facts.

1. Studying and Organizing the Facts

Facts rarely come in a single tidy statement. Rather, you gather facts by talking to your client and other participants, reading documents, visiting the location of the events, handling the items, and so on. Then you must weave together these bits of information.

Of course, the first step is to read (or otherwise process) each source carefully, so that you have a very good idea of the information it provides.

As you work through the sources one by one, start a list of topics and, as needed, sub-topics. These topics may be relationships, communications, events, locations, etc. Once you know the territory covered in your sources, you should have an idea of the big picture. To systematically capture and organize what you are learning, you may want to develop codes for each topic and annotate the sources with the codes. As a next step, or possibly an initial step if the material you are dealing with is short and straightforward, you may develop a matrix chart like Exhibit 14.1; the boxes contain the information from each source or references to pages within a source.

Another classic way to organize factual information is the timeline, as shown in Exhibit 14.2. The line itself contains relevant dates; the material

EXHIBIT 14.1

FACTUAL MATRIX

	PARTICIPANT X	PARTICIPANT Y	DOCUMENT A	VISIT TO SITE
description of location				
background of X-Y relationship				
1st event				
2nd event				
etc.				

EXHIBIT 14.2

TIMELINES

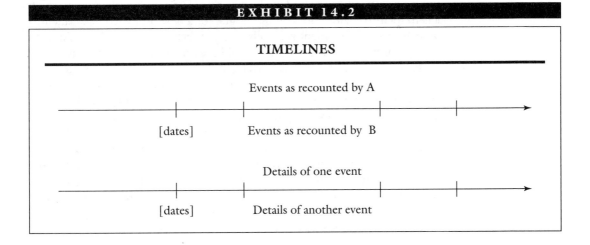

Events as recounted by A

[dates]   Events as recounted by B

Details of one event

[dates]   Details of another event

above and below the line consists of date-specific information. You can use the timeline as a dividing line, by writing information from one source above the line and information from another below the line, or by writing information about one of two simultaneous events above the line and information about the other below the line.

You may well discover not only overlap but also discrepancies in the information from various sources. Experienced lawyers expect this discrepancy. Participants or observers of an event often differ in their recollections of what they have experienced or perceived. They vary in their abilities to perceive, understand, and recall situations, as well as their perspectives and interests. Your task is to reconcile these discrepancies:

- If the discrepancy is minor, you may be able to cover both versions with a somewhat broadly phrased statement, such as a numerical range rather than a precise number.
- You may discern any core area of agreement and leave the details in dispute, as long as the details are not critical.
- If one source has greater credibility, a clearer perspective, or less self-interest than the other, you could choose the version provided by that source and state the reason for your selection.
- If these methods fail, you may need to state both versions and their sources—in which case, as discussed in Chapter 12, the discussion may come to a branchpoint and proceed along two paths.

2. Sorting Facts

Once you have organized the information from the various sources, you need to choose which facts to include in the fact statement. Facts fall into three categories: legally relevant facts, background facts, and residual facts. You should include the first and second, but not the third.

Legally relevant facts: These facts pertain directly to the elements in the legal rules; they are used in your deductive reasoning, reasoning by example, or policy analysis. As a court or legislature makes law, it sets the factual focus of the rule of law. The rule may not focus on every fact you would consider important, but you are bound by the court's or legislature's selection of which facts to focus on (although you may argue for a new or revised legal rule in a compelling case). To identify legally relevant facts, read your discussion. All facts appearing in your discussion should appear in the fact statement.

Background facts: These are facts that the reader needs to know to make sense of the client's situation, even though they do not pertain directly to the elements of the rule. To identify the background facts, ask yourself: What does the reader need to know to fit the relevant facts into a coherent narrative? Focus on what the reader needs to know, not on what might be interesting to know.

Residual facts: These are neither legally relevant nor background. You should exclude these facts, because they clutter the narrative and distract the reader's attention. Some residual facts are emotionally charged, causing one to feel sympathy or distaste for your client or another participant. You should take particular care to exclude these residual facts, which may cloud the reader's ability to assess the client's situation objectively.

Of course, you will be quite aware that some facts are favorable to your client and others are unfavorable. This distinction is not an appropriate basis on which to include or exclude facts. Both favorable and unfavorable facts belong in the fact statement, just as they do in the discussion, if they are legally relevant or needed for background.

As an example, in the first sample memo, most of the facts are legally relevant, especially the protocols of the living will service. There are some background facts, such as the elderly client's requests for the service. No residual facts are stated. Both favorable and unfavorable facts are stated.

3. Timing

You probably will find that you must work with the facts of your client's situation several times. In particular, you may study and organize the facts early on, before you write your analysis or conduct your research; you may even write an outline or tentative statement at that early stage. However, you should not sort your facts until you have analyzed the case in light of the law, because only at that point will you appreciate the legal significance of the various facts.

E. PRESENTING THE FACTS

1. Format

The relevant and background facts should appear in your fact statement in a sequence that makes for a coherent story. The classic organization entails an introductory paragraph, several paragraphs or pages of development, and a wrap-up or transition paragraph as needed.

The introductory paragraph sets the stage and orients the reader. It should identify the client and other important people or organizations and briefly synopsize the client's situation.

The body of the fact statement should be a well organized telling of the client's story:

- The most common organizational scheme is chronology: the fact statement begins with the first important event and moves forward in time to the most recent.
- Also very common is topical organization: each paragraph or paragraph block covers a facet of the situation, such as relationships among people or features of transactions.
- Least common is perceptual organization: the events are presented first from one person's perspective, then from another's.

A mixed organization may work well; for example, several topical paragraphs may be used to set the scene for a series of chronologically ordered paragraphs.

The last paragraph typically draws a link between the facts and the upcoming discussion of their legal implications. This paragraph should describe the client's current legal situation, e.g., the stage of litigation, the reason the client is seeking legal advice. The last paragraph may also note the client's non-legal concerns. This wrap-up paragraph may not be necessary if the fact statement is brief.

At various points, you should indicate where you derived your facts. Although you need not provide formal citations, you should inform the reader whose statement or which document yielded your information, for instance, "according to Ms. Smith," or "as indicated in the contract."

In the first sample memo, the first paragraph introduces the facts by describing HomeElderCare and the genesis of the legal concern. The overall organization is topical: HomeElderCare's business, living wills, staff competence and training, and the living will protocols. The paragraph detailing the protocol follows a chronological organization. A statement of the client's legal concerns concludes the fact statement.

2. Perspective and Flow

Your fact statement is unlikely to have the flair or drama of a prize-winning short story. A short-story writer can use tools that are inappropriate to memo writing, such as first-person point of view, shifts in time, symbolism, and ambiguity. Nonetheless, your fact statement need not be clinical or wooden; you are, after all, telling a story.

As the narrator, you have the advantage of an omniscient third-person point of view; you know whatever there is to be known for purposes of writing the memo and can recount the story fully. To help your reader fully understand the situation, show how one event led to another, why a participant selected the course of conduct he or she engaged in, and how an event affected a participant. In other words, link the events to each other and the participants to each other.

Strike a balance between detail and abstraction. Decide how much detail the reader needs on each topic, and condense the facts to provide only needed detail. Consider attaching material that would otherwise require a lengthy explanation, such as a contract or map.

In the first HomeElderCare sample memo, the focus throughout the fact statement is on the relationship between the clients and the social workers. The discussion begins with a broad description of that relationship and eventually brings the reader into the specific interaction between social worker and client as they engage in the preparation of a living will.

F. VARIATIONS ON THE THEME: THE DEAL-ORIENTED MEMO

When you write the fact statement for a deal-oriented memo, you will write both about fixed past or present facts and about future possibilities. The fixed facts are the client and its situation, e.g. its structure, its products; the other participants to the possible deal; and the context in which they all operate. Writing about these facts is very similar to writing about the facts in a dispute-oriented memo. This information generally appears in the beginning of the fact statement.

When you write about future possibilities, one challenge is selecting which possibilities to cover. You should cover at least the specific proposal(s) the client has framed. Whether to cover more depends on the circumstances, e.g., how many options the client has proposed, how clearly worth considering the other options are. Take your lead from the other components of the memo, e.g., cover an option not suggested by the client if the client's options are not permissible. Cover each option in as much detail as the reader needs to understand the proposal and follow the analysis presented in the discussion. Make clear whether the option is one the client has developed or one you have developed.

A fact statement in a deal-oriented memo generally follows a topical organization; the client's preferred option(s) should come first, followed by other possible options. In addition, to distinguish what is fixed and what may or may not come to be, use the subjunctive mood ("client would do . . . .") or future tense ("client will do . . . .") in your discussion of options.

The closing paragraph should focus on what has prompted the client to seek counsel. All clients seek counsel to avoid legal problems and secure a favorable legal position through the transaction. If you have more specific information about the client's legal concerns, stating them in the last paragraph can be an excellent transition to the discussion.

The fact statement in the second sample HomeElderCare memo exemplifies this approach. The first two paragraphs set the scene, the third describes HomeElderCare's plan, and the fourth sets up the discussion by stating the executive director's concerns.

G. OVERARCHING CONSIDERATIONS

First and foremost, you must state the facts accurately. While you may work off of your notes from various sources in writing the fact statement, checking what you have written against the sources themselves is very advisable.

Similarly, you must state the facts objectively, for the same reasons discussed in earlier chapters. Indeed, the harder you work on writing an objective fact statement, the more likely it is that the analysis presented in other components will be objective. If you follow these standard practices, your fact statement should meet this key criterion:

- Refer to all of the individuals in the story in a respectful way; use their names or neutral labels, such as the roles the individuals play in the situation.
- Use verbs with straightforward meanings, and use the proper tense. For example, use a past tense for events that occurred in the past, the present tense for the client's current situation or concerns.
- Avoid adverbs and adjectives.
- Avoid words that have legal connotations, such as "negligently."

- Use a detail from the story in lieu of words that carry some judgment on your part, e.g., numbers rather than "large" or "small," "fast" or "slow."

Finally, check your work against the four criteria for effective legal writing:

- *Completeness:* Have you included the favorable and unfavorable relevant and background facts your reader needs?
- *Correctness:* Are the facts stated true, according to their sources?
- *Coherence:* Does your fact statement present a story that could occur as you have stated it? Are the events, people, places, and times properly aligned?
- *Comprehensibility:* Will your reader follow the story in one careful reading?

In the first HomeElderCare sample memo, the facts are stated objectively, with neutral labels ("clients," "social workers") and few adjectives and adverbs. The reader can tell where the facts came from (the document, the social work director). The writer might have attached the form, if the reader would be unfamiliar with it. The statement is readable.

H. REVIEW OF CHAPTER 14

The facts statement informs the reader of the client's story and stands as a record, for the reader and writer, of the facts known at the time the memo was written. To assure that you fully understand the facts, you must first study and organize the information from various sources, reconcile any discrepancies, and then sort out the relevant and background facts from residual facts. A well presented fact statement:

- includes relevant and background facts, whether favorable or unfavorable to the client;
- begins with an introductory paragraph or paragraph block;
- follows a chronological, topical, or perceptual organization (or combination);
- closes with a wrap-up paragraph, as needed; and
- states the facts accurately, objectively, with attribution, and with appropriate detail.

This chapter is the last of four chapters on the office memo, the basic form of advisory writing. You may want to review the appendices on the writing process (Appendix I); paragraph design, sentence structure, and word usage (Appendix II); and citation (Appendix III. A or III. B). All three skill sets are critical to writing a polished office memo.

15

ADVISORY WRITING:

THE FUNCTION AND

FORMAT OF THE

ADVICE LETTER

> Letters are expectation packed in an envelope.
> —Shana Alexander
>   "The Surprises of the Mail," *Life* (1967)

A. INTRODUCTION

As important as the office memo is, it rarely serves as the final expression of the lawyer's analysis. The lawyer still must take the next critical step: sharing the lawyer's analysis and conclusions with the client. How do lawyers explain the legal meaning of a client's situation and obtain direction as to what steps to take on the client's behalf? Client counseling almost always involves a conversation and often also involves a written document—the advice letter.

The advice letter is only one of many types of letters lawyers write.[1] They also write letters to clients to ask for information, inform the client of new

---

1. For a discussion of other letters, such as a transmittal letter, see Helene S. Shapo, Marilyn R. Walters, & Elizabeth Fajans, *Writing and Analysis in the Law* 297-328 (4th ed. 2003).

developments, enclose documents related to the case, seek payment, and so forth. Lawyers write letters on behalf of clients to other people, demanding payment or other relief from opposing parties, seeking records or information from third parties, making arrangements with opposing counsel, enclosing briefs sent to courts, and similar matters. Some lawyers specialize in writing formal opinion letters; an opinion letter discusses the client's compliance with a particular rule and is used to induce others to transact business with the client.

This chapter focuses on advice letters because of their importance to the lawyer-client relationship. Moreover, the advice letter is a challenging letter to write well. If you can master the advice letter, most other types of client letters should come relatively easily.

A sample letter to HomeElderCare, drawing on the analysis in the second sample office memo, appears at page 349. This letter is written to HomeElder-Care when it is considering creating the living will service. You should read the letter before proceeding.

B. THE ADVISOR'S ETHICS

Model Rule of Professional Conduct 1.2 states: "[A] lawyer shall abide by a client's decisions concerning the objectives of representation and . . . shall consult with the client as to the means by which they are to be pursued." The client's case is just that—the *client's* dispute or transaction. The client sets the objectives of the representation, subject to legal constraints and the lawyer's professional obligations. According to the comment to Rule 1.2, the lawyer is to consult with the client about the means for obtaining the client's objectives, with the lawyer leading the way as to technical, legal, and tactical matters, and the client leading the way as to expenses to be incurred and the impact on third parties. In practice, lawyers and clients jointly delineate their respective roles, reflecting the client's desire for control or involvement, the degree of trust between client and lawyer, the lawyer's experience with the type of situation at hand, and similar factors.

As discussed in Chapter 13, Rule 2.1 makes two important points. First, "[i]n representing a client, a lawyer shall exercise independent professional judgment and render candid advice." Second, "[i]n rendering advice, a lawyer may refer not only to law but to other considerations such as moral, economic, social and political factors, that may be relevant to the client's situation." Although these dimensions may be primarily within the client's realm, the lawyer's objective observations may help the client assess these factors.

Lawyers and clients relate to each other in various ways. Thomas Shaffer and Robert Cochran have posited four models:[2]

- The hired gun acts as directed by the client without regard for the impact of the client's actions on others; the autonomy of the client is the key value.

2. Thomas L. Shaffer & Robert F. Cochran, Jr., *Lawyer, Clients, and Moral Responsibilities* (1994).

WHAT HAPPENS WHEN YOU FAIL TO FULLY INFORM YOUR CLIENT?

In re Thonert,
733 N.E.2d 932 (Ind. 2000).

. . .

The parties agree that the respondent represented a client charged with operating a motor vehicle while intoxicated. Prior to the client's initial hearing and before the client met with or hired the respondent, the client was advised by videotape of his rights. He pleaded guilty to the charge, and the matter was set for sentencing hearing. Prior to that hearing, the client met with the respondent to discuss the possibility of withdrawing his guilty plea. During their meeting, the respondent told the client of another criminal case, *Snowe v. State,* 533 N.E.2d 613 (Ind. Ct. App. 1989), in which the respondent had prevailed on appeal for the defendant. He provided a copy of the Indiana Court of Appeals decision to his new client. The respondent agreed to represent the client for $5,000, which the client paid.

Snowe also involved a prerecorded videotaped televised advisement of rights, but the record in that case failed to indicate whether the defendant had ever viewed the tape advising him of his rights. Further, the opinion held that a trial court judge cannot rely solely on displaying a videotape advisement of rights, but instead must also determine whether the defendant knows of and understands his rights, the nature of the charge or charges against him, the full import of the rights waiver in his guilty plea, and the sentencing possibilities for the charges against him. *Snowe,* 533 N.E.2d at 617.

At the client's initial hearing, it was established that he had viewed the videotape, that the videotape advised him of his rights and the sentencing possibilities under the charges filed against him, that he understood the charge against him and his rights as explained in the videotape, and that he voluntarily waived those rights and pleaded guilty.

On May 30, 1996, the respondent entered an appearance on behalf of the client and filed a motion to withdraw the guilty plea. The trial court denied the motion without hearing. The respondent appealed that ruling, alleging that his client had a right to withdraw the plea because, due to the absence of counsel at the time he entered it and the fact that the record did not reflect that the trial court property examined the client as to waiver of his rights, the client had not made it knowingly, intelligently, or voluntarily. The respondent further argued that the client had a right to a hearing on his motion to withdraw the plea.

The respondent represented the defendant in *Fletcher v. State,* 649 N.E.2d 1022 (Ind. 1995). In that case, this Court addressed the questions that the respondent raised in his client's case. The ruling in *Fletcher* was adverse to the arguments that the respondent offered on appeal of his client's case. [footnote omitted] The respondent had served as counsel of record for defendant Fletcher in the appeal before this Court. This Court's ruling in *Fletcher* was issued on May 1, 1995, over one year before the respondent filed his appeal on behalf of the client. In his appellate brief filed on behalf of the client, the respondent failed to cite to *Fletcher* or argue that its holding was not controlling authority in the client's case. The respondent also failed to argue that the holding in *Fletcher* should be changed or extended. Although he advised his client of the *Snowe* case, he failed to advise him of *Fletcher* or explain any impact *Fletcher* might have on his case. Opposing counsel had not previously disclosed *Fletcher* to the Court of Appeals. . . .

Professional Conduct Rule 1.4(b) provides that a lawyer shall explain a matter to the extent reasonably necessary to permit a client to make informed decisions regarding a representation. A client should have sufficient information to participate intelligently in decisions concerning the objectives of the representation. *Comment* to Prof. Cond. R 1.4. By failing to advise his client of a ruling in the controlling jurisdiction that was adverse to the legal arguments contemplated for his client's case on appeal, and instead choosing only to advise the client of an earlier appellate decision favorable to his position, the respondent effectively divested his client of the opportunity to assess intelligently the legal environment in which his case would be argued and to make informed decisions regarding whether to go forward with it. Accordingly, we find that the respondent violated Prof. Cond. R 1.4(b). . . .

The parties agree that the respondent should be publicly reprimanded for his misconduct. We agree that a public admonishment is appropriate in this case, given the negative impact on the efficient resolution of the client's appeal occasioned by the respondent's lack of disclosure and its attendant deception of the client as to the viability of any efforts to withdraw the guilty plea. Accordingly, we accept the parties' agreement and the discipline called for therein.

- The godfather, focusing on client victory, makes choices, with fairly little client involvement, so as to produce victory for the client.
- The guru, focusing on client rectitude, makes choices, with fairly little client involvement, so as to prompt the client to do what the lawyer sees as the right thing.
- The friend, focusing on client goodness, engages the client in a discussion of what is good for the client and others affected by the case.

In reality, lawyers often use a blend of these models, switching from one to another, depending on the client and the situation. As you learn more about being a lawyer, you may want to consider which models are true to practice, professional principles, and your own values.

Finally, Model Rule 1.4 requires a lawyer to "promptly inform the client" of key decisions, "reasonably consult with the client about the means" of the representation, "keep the client reasonably informed about the status" of the case, and "promptly comply with reasonable requests for information." In other words, communication with clients is critical to the ethical practice of law. The rule sets this standard for lawyer-client communication: "A lawyer shall explain a matter to the extent reasonably necessary to permit the client to make informed decisions regarding the representation."

C. THE FUNCTION OF THE ADVICE LETTER: AUDIENCE AND PURPOSE

If the client is an individual, the primary reader of the advice letter is, of course, the client. If the client is an organization, such as a corporation or government agency, the primary reader is the person empowered to act for the client in the case.

Every reader has his or her own preferences, which the lawyer must take into account. Some readers prefer considerable detail about legal authorities; for others, summary information suffices. Some readers prefer extensive discussion of the non-legal dimensions of the case; others view such analysis as overstepping by the lawyer. Some readers prefer a no-nonsense approach; others prefer a more empathetic style. And so on. These preferences reflect the reader's personal attributes and the client's situation. For example, a reader with legal training may prefer a detailed legal analysis. A reader who has suffered personal injury or lost a loved one typically looks for empathy as well as legal analysis.

Thus, an important first step in writing an advice letter is analyzing the situation and thinking about the client. Take care not to act on stereotypes. For instance, the elderly widow with little formal education and no paid work experience may be a savvy reader due to her volunteer work or civic activities. Learn what you can about your reader's preferences by getting to know the reader before writing the letter.

Some advice letters will be read by more than one reader. For example, a letter advising a corporation may be read by its president, in-house counsel, board members, and key managers. Sometimes it is possible for a single letter to address both primary and secondary readers. In other instances, you may need to write to the primary reader and cover the different needs of the secondary reader another way, for example, by providing a more detailed memo for a more sophisticated secondary reader.

Regardless of exactly who reads the advice letter, it has two main purposes:

- to inform the reader of the lawyer's legal analysis of the client's situation, that is, to convey to the reader the legal meaning of the client's situation; and
- to persuade the client to take action that has sound legal support, whether resolving an existing dispute or framing an upcoming transaction.

Subsidiary purposes include establishing rapport with the client, verifying the facts and tasks the client has presented to the lawyer, and seeking direction from the client. On occasion, these purposes may conflict. For example, it may be difficult to establish rapport with a client who strongly desires to engage in behavior that is illegal or legally risky. When a conflict among purposes arises, be sure to serve the main purposes of informing the client and persuading the client to take legally sound actions.

D. THE FORMAT OF THE ADVICE LETTER

The format of the advice letter is similar in several ways to that of the office memo. First, its format is governed not by rule, but by convention. Second, it differs from law office to law office and across client situations. Third, as Exhibit 15.1 shows, the conventional components parallel those of the office memo. In a long or formal letter, headings may be used to set off some of these components; in short or less formal letters, transitional phrases or sentences are used instead.

Heading: As with any business letter, the heading includes the sender's letterhead; the date of the letter; the name, position, and address of the reader (or readers); and the salutation. The heading also may include a one-line reference to the topic of the letter; this feature makes the letter more formal

EXHIBIT 15.1

COMPARISON OF ADVICE LETTER AND OFFICE MEMO

Advice Letter	Office Memo
heading • letterhead • date • addressee • topic reference • salutation	caption • to • from • date • topic
introduction	issues short answers
summary of facts	facts
explanation	discussion
advice and closing	conclusion

and is most common when the letter is sent to an organization or individual that has frequent contact with lawyers.

Introduction: The introduction has two purposes: to establish rapport with the reader and to provide an overview of the main points made in the letter.

The first sentence or two typically refers to the previous contact between the lawyer and the client and to the occasion for the request for legal advice. You should personalize this opening; do not use a canned sentence such as "This letter is in response to yours of October 14th."

The next part of the introduction is the overview of the legal points covered in the letter. Often, the reader will have asked an open-ended bottom-line question; the overview helps the reader to see how the law frames the client's concern. You may state the conclusion you have come to, the topics you have analyzed, the issues you have addressed, or some combination. Generally, stating your conclusions at the outset will benefit the reader. However, if the conclusions are complex or significantly adverse, it may be wiser to present an overview of the topics or issues instead.

The overview is not stated as completely or technically as the issues and short answers in an office memo. See Exhibit 15.2. Nonetheless, be sure to state the overview with great care. The scope of the advice should be apparent to the reader. If you state your conclusions, take care to convey how (un)certain they are.

EXHIBIT 15.2

SHORT ANSWERS VERSUS INTRODUCTION

Short Answers

1. The living will service as proposed by HomeElderCare probably would not constitute the unauthorized practice of law, but this is a very close call. Variations on the current plan would be more clearly legal.
2. Even if the service is the unauthorized practice of law, especially if the will closely follows the form in the Minnesota Living Will Act, the living will would be valid so as not to penalize the declarant.
3. If the service is the unauthorized practice of law, the contract between HomeElderCare and its clients may well be unenforceable out of concerns about the social workers' competence.

Introduction

. . . as this letter explains, there could be some legal risks. One concern is avoiding the unauthorized practice of law, which could lead to prosecution for a misdemeanor or a court order prohibiting the service. If the living will service is not designed carefully enough to ensure competence as to legal matters, the contracts with the clients may be unenforceable. In any event, the living wills would be valid.

Some lawyers include a third part in the introduction: a brief paragraph stating the ground rules of a legal advice letter:

- Most likely, you will alert the client to the need to keep the letter confidential.
- You may want to note that the letter states the facts of the client's case, identify the source of the facts, and ask the client to verify those facts.
- You also might note that the conclusions are based on the facts currently known or assumed as well as on current law, and that the conclusions could change with changes in the facts or law.
- If you have any reason for concern that you have not addressed all of your client's issues, you could urge the client to contact you if there seem to be omissions.

You could state these points in the summary of the facts or in the explanation, or you could omit these points if it is likely the reader is well aware of them.

The introduction in the sample advice letter takes this tripartite approach. The first paragraph seeks to establish rapport with the client's executive director, the second provides an overview of the three topics, and the third alerts her to the limitations of the letter. Because theirs is not a longstanding relationship, the writer chose to state the ground rules of an advice letter.

Summary of facts: As with the fact statement in the office memo, the summary of facts tells the reader the facts of the client's situation. You may wonder why this is necessary, if the reader is the client or represents the client. The summary of facts serves the following critical purposes:

- to show the reader you have heard the story;
- to permit the reader to verify your account;
- to help the reader see the facts from an objective point of view;
- to identify for the reader which facts are important from the law's perspective; and
- where applicable, to show the reader how information from various sources comes together.

You should include legally relevant facts and important background facts, whether favorable or unfavorable. You also may want to include residual facts that are very significant to the client; do so sparingly, so as not to blur your focus on what is legally relevant. The sources of the facts should be noted informally. The organization should be clear and logical; chronological and topical approaches typically work well. When you know the differing perspectives of two or more people regarding the situation, you may employ perceptual organization.

Some lawyers also include caveats about the facts. In addition to the points mentioned above, you may want to note that you have not yourself investigated the facts, especially if you have doubts about them or believe your client may assume that you have investigated them yourself.

In the sample HomeElderCare summary of facts, virtually all facts are either legally relevant facts or important background facts. The summary notes that the source of the facts is the conversation with the client. The overall organization is topical, with a chronological scheme in the second facts paragraph.

Explanation: The explanation presents your objective legal analysis of the client's situation. It should proceed in a logical way through the issues, presenting the legal rules and linking them to the relevant facts. It should explore both sides of issues as to which there is a reasonable debate. The organization should be made clear through transitions, especially if there are branchpoints in the analysis.

The explanation differs from the discussion in an office memo primarily in how it presents the law. See Exhibit 15.3, which shows portions of each. The explanation focuses not on the legal authorities, but on the key legal concepts. Those concepts typically are stated in concrete terms paralleling the client's case. Indeed, where the legal concept is fairly straightforward and its link to the facts is obvious, you may merge the law and relevant facts into a single statement. On the other hand, if similar situations may arise in the future for the same client or if the law is complex, you should state the law in abstract terms first, then link it to the facts. Unless the reader is a lawyer or otherwise sophisticated in the law, the explanation does not include citations.

The explanation in the sample HomeElderCare letter proceeds logically through the three issues. It raises the unauthorized practice issue first, because it plays a part in the analysis of the other two issues and has the most serious

---

EXHIBIT 15.3

DISCUSSION VERSUS EXPLANATION

Discussion

According to Minnesota's unauthorized practice statute, "[i]t shall be unlawful for any person . . . except members of the bar of Minnesota admitted and licensed to practice as attorneys at law . . . for a fee . . . to prepare for another person . . . any . . . legal document . . . ." Minn. Stat. § 481.02 subdiv. 1 (1992). Here, the living will probably is a "legal document" under the unauthorized practice statute, because the living will statute says that it is a "legal document." Minn. Stat. § 145B.04 (1992). Thus, HomeElderCare's social workers would be preparing legal documents for their clients, in return for fees.

Explanation

The Minnesota statute on the unauthorized practice of law states that preparing legal documents for someone else for a fee constitutes practicing law. The living will form itself indicates that the living will is a "legal document."

consequences for HomeElderCare. The law is stated precisely, simply, and concisely, without citations. The legal rules on unauthorized practice are stated in abstract terms because this client should know the rules outside the living will context. Other rules are stated in the context of this particular situation. The uncertainty in the unauthorized practice analysis is revealed in a paragraph of counterarguments, while the analysis of the validity of the living wills is presented as much more certain. Because the explanation is fairly involved, the letter features various transitional devices.

Advice: The purpose of the advice component is to link the legal analysis presented in the letter to concrete actions to be taken by or on behalf of the client. The advice component typically has two, sometimes intertwined, parts: a summary of the legal analysis and a discussion of the client's options.

The summary helps the reader recall the conclusions you have drawn. You may not need to include one if the explanation is fairly brief and clearly states your conclusions. Another approach is to reiterate your conclusions as they arise in your discussion of the client's options. In either event, the summary generally parallels the order of topics in the introduction, and you should convey whatever uncertainty you may have.

Most clients have more than one option. The client may have suggested one or more options; you may have thought of others. Your conclusion should present the relative legal advantages and disadvantages of each option. If you know the client has nonlegal concerns, you may bring these into the discussion as well.

Whether to advance a particular option as the best option is a matter of considerable judgment. The law may decide for you—that is, there may be only one good option from a legal perspective. Where various options are legally sound, in deciding whether to indicate your preference, you should think about your relationship with the client. For instance, do you know all of the facts regarding the client's financial situation? Do you know for sure how the client weighs various non-legal factors? Do you have an established relationship of trust with the client? If you do indicate your preference, you should take care to convey that the choice is ultimately the client's.

The advice conveyed in the HomeElderCare sample letter has two prongs. First, the letter clearly, but gracefully, tells the client not to pursue the proposal it brought to the lawyer. Second, the letter suggests some options with fewer legal risks and leaves non-legal factors for the client to consider.

Closing: The closing is not simply the end of the letter but also the basis of the continuation of the representation. It has three parts: an indication of what you plan to do next, instructions as to what the client should do next, and the signature block. Your next step should be to contact the client so you are sure that the client fully understands the letter. After that, the client may contact you to implement the client's choice of action, such as sending a demand letter to the opponent in a dispute, proceeding with a transaction, or doing nothing further.

The closing in the sample HomeElderCare letter simply refers to a follow-up phone conversation, initiated by the lawyer or the client.

E. OVERARCHING CONSIDERATIONS

The artistry of an advice letter derives from its tone. Its tone conveys much about the lawyer as a person and directly influences the relationship between the lawyer and the client. The letter should convey that the lawyer is professional, focused, thorough, analytical, objective, careful, involved, creative, cooperative, and reasonable. Other impressions may be more or less appropriate in particular settings: assertive and efficient, for example, or sympathetic and supportive, as another example.

These impressions are created through subtle stylistic variations. Consider, for example, how to use personal pronouns. A certain intimacy results when the letter uses the first person ("I recommend . . ."), perhaps even drawing the client into the first-person plural ("We could contact their lawyer . . ."). Distance results when an organizational client is referred to by name ("HomeElderCare could take the following actions . . ."), rather than second-person pronoun ("You could take the following actions . . .").

As a second example, consider the use of active versus passive voice. The active voice has a harder edge to it than the passive voice, especially when used to refer to the actions of the client. Active voice ("The county attorney will prosecute") may be appropriate if the lawyer wants to appear emphatic or business-like, whereas passive voice may be appropriate if the lawyer wants to appear compassionate and empathetic ("HomeElderCare may be prosecuted").

As always, be sure that the letter fulfills the following four criteria:

- *Completeness:* Does the letter address all topics brought to you by the client? Have you covered the pertinent legal rules and relevant facts?
- *Correctness:* Have you stated the client's facts with scrupulous accuracy? Do your statements of the law fairly reflect the concepts pertinent to the client's case?
- *Coherence:* Do the various components mesh well? Do the conclusions make sense in light of the rules and facts? Do they fit with each other?
- *Comprehensibility:* Will your reader probably be able to understand the letter in one careful reading? Is the letter written to fit the reader's attributes and situation?

F. REVIEW OF CHAPTER 15

The advice letter is a critical document because it communicates your legal advice to your client and forms a basis for the client's future actions. To write it successfully, you should follow these steps:

(1) Respect the relative roles of yourself and your client.
(2) Carefully consider how best to communicate with the probable reader(s) of the letter.
(3) Present the information in the following components: heading, introduction, summary of facts, explanation, advice, and closing.

    (4) Bring creativity to your advice; develop various options for the client and assess their wisdom in light of the law and non-legal factors.

    (5) Write it so your work meets the criteria of completeness, correctness, coherence, comprehensibility, and creativity.

Following these steps should enable you to meet your professional obligation to communicate with your client and your client to make well informed decisions about its case.

16

PERSUASIVE WRITING: THE FUNCTION AND FORMAT OF THE DEMAND LETTER

> And do as adversaries do in law—Strive mightily, but eat and
> drink as friend.
> —William Shakespeare
> *The Taming of the Shrew* I, 2

A. INTRODUCTION

Lawyers communicate not only with their clients, of course, but also with others on the client's behalf.[1] Generally, the goal is to persuade someone else to take some action that benefits the client. For example, litigators seek to resolve disputes by convincing the other party to settle or by obtaining a favorable ruling from a judge, a jury, or a decision-maker in an informal

---

1. For a wide-ranging discussion of various types of correspondence, see Mary Barnard Ray & Barbara J. Cox, *Beyond the Basics: A Text for Advanced Legal Writing* 312-70 (2d ed. 2003).

proceeding such as arbitration. Lawyers lobby legislatures and agencies to create laws that benefit their clients. A transactional lawyer seeks to persuade the other party to a potential transaction to agree on terms that favor the client.

Each of these situations typically entails some type of written communication. The content and presentation vary by context, of course. This chapter focuses on the early stages of bringing about resolution of a past dispute. How does a litigator approach the other side to begin the process of dispute resolution?

The typical answer is: by sending a demand letter. A demand letter apprises the opponent of the client's factual and legal positions relative to the dispute and the client's proposed resolution. Typically it is sent just as the dispute has become serious enough to have lawyers involved. The recipient may send a letter in response. Ideally, and frequently, these letters lead to amicable negotiation and a quick and fair settlement.

A sample demand letter written directly to HomeElderCare by the local county attorney appears at page 353. A portion, the client's situation and legal position, of a letter written to HomeElderCare's attorney follows at page 355. You should read both before proceeding.

B. The Advocate's Ethics

When most people think about lawyers, they see them as zealous advocates for their clients. As explained in the Preamble to the Model Rules, this is indeed one role of a lawyer, but there are limits. Lawyers are to follow the rules of the adversary system and, in negotiation, deal honestly with others. Several legal ethics rules address demand letters, all reflecting the risk that a demand letter could prove unduly coercive.

First, Model Rule of Professional Conduct 4.2 provides that if the lawyer knows that the opponent is represented by a lawyer, the demand letter, indeed all communication, must be sent to that lawyer, not the opponent. Model Rule 4.3 provides that when a lawyer does communicate with an unrepresented opponent, the letter must identify the lawyer's role in the dispute and avoid giving legal advice, other than suggesting that the opponent seek representation.

Second, under some ethics codes, a demand letter may not threaten to instigate a criminal case or similar proceedings, such as a disciplinary action before a licensing board or an investigation of a business for consumer fraud, except in fairly narrow situations.[2]

---

2. *See* Margaret Z. Johns, *Professional Writing for Lawyers: Skills and Responsibilities* 70–76 (1998).

WHAT ARE THE BOUNDS OF ZEALOUS ADVOCACY IN A DEMAND LETTER?

In re Glavin,
107 A.D.2d 1006, 484 N.Y.S.2d 933 (1985).

MEMORANDUM DECISION.

In this disciplinary proceeding respondent, an Albany attorney admitted to practice in this Department in 1929, is charged with one count of misconduct arising out of an April 6, 1984 letter which he sent to an individual who had apparently done some unsatisfactory repair work at the home of one of his clients. The petition charges respondent with violating several provisions of the Code of Professional Responsibility in that his letter, *inter alia*, threatens the recipient with arrest and/or jail in an effort to obtain a refund of moneys paid by the client and implies that respondent possessed the authority to impose or withhold these criminal sanctions.

Following the filing of respondent's answer, we vacated his demand for a bill of particulars and denied petitioner's motion for a reference noting that respondent did not deny sending the letter and no other factual issues of any substance were presented. In accordance with 22 NYCRR 806.5 of our rules, respondent was permitted to appear and be heard in mitigation.

Respondent's one-page letter, written on behalf of his client, charges the recipient with having "conned her out of $1,000 before you did a lick of work." The letter further informs the recipient, *inter alia*, that "you will return the money or go to jail," "you will be arrested," and "I will have a warrant issued for your arrest." In addition, the letter advises the recipient that "If you return her money and just don't do any work *then I will tell the City not to punish you*" (emphasis added). We conclude that these statements, read together, could be construed as suggesting that respondent possessed authority to impose or withhold criminal sanctions and thus constituted misrepresentation in violation of the Code of Professional Responsibility, DR 1-102(A)(4). We also find respondent's letter to be improper in that it threatens to use the criminal process to coerce the adjustment of a private civil claim (see Code of Professional Responsibility, DR 7-105, EC 7-21; *Matter of Beachboard*, 263 N.Y.S. 492; *Matter of Gelman*, 230 App. Div. 524, 245 N.Y.S. 416; *Matter of Hyman*, 226 App. Div. 468, 235 N.Y.S. 622).

Although respondent believed he was justified in sending the correspondence in question, his behavior constituted unprofessional conduct for which, considering all of the circumstances, censure is the appropriate sanction.

Respondent censured.

Third, a demand letter must be truthful, under Model Rule 4.1. In communicating with a third party, a lawyer "shall not knowingly . . . make a false statement of material fact or law." The duty to disclose information is more limited, arising when necessary to avert a crime or fraud on the part of the client. Some points that may be covered in a letter—including a party's intentions as to settlement—are not deemed "material facts" and thus are not held to as high a standard of truthfulness, as noted in comment 1. Of course, shading the truth in a demand letter may cause the lawyer for your client's opponent to distrust you, which may prove troublesome in the negotiations that follow the demand letter.

Finally, some bar associations have created guidelines that are not legally binding but seek to set standards of ethical conduct. For example, the 1996 Guidelines for Conduct of the American Bar Association Section of Litigation state: "We will treat all other counsel, parties, and witnesses in a civil and courteous manner, not only in court, but also in all other written and oral communications." A lawyer who seeks to resolve a client's dispute enters into a conflict that may already be bitter and protracted. The lawyer should not only avoid exacerbating the conflict but also, through his or her integrity and moderation, decrease the level of animosity.

C. THE FUNCTION OF THE DEMAND LETTER: AUDIENCE AND PURPOSE

A demand letter has two audiences: (1) the opponent, including the opponent's lawyer and people who can approve settlement of claims against the company, and (2) the client and individuals connected to the client.

The primary audience of the demand letter is the opponent or the opponent's lawyer. If you do not know the opponent and do not know whether the opponent has a lawyer, the issue of audience is complicated. For example, figuring out how much detail to provide in the statement of the client's legal position can be challenging. Learning what the client knows about the opponent is one way to minimize this uncertainty. Writing a standard letter for the particular area of practice, such as personal injury or construction litigation, is another. As with the advice letter, another option is preparing more than one letter, an initial letter pitched at the opponent and a second letter pitched at the opponent's lawyer once you know that the opponent is represented.

However the letter is pitched, it has three main purposes:

- to introduce yourself, your client, and the dispute;
- to inform the opponent of your client's situation and legal position; and
- to persuade the opponent to accede to your client's demand for a remedy.

In addition, a demand letter begins a conversation, whether orally or in writing, with the opponent or the opponent's lawyer. Thus the letter, in effect, elicits factual information, the opponent's view of the law as applied to the situation, and the opponent's initial thoughts about acceptable resolutions to the dispute.

D. THE FORMAT OF THE DEMAND LETTER

There is no fixed format for demand letters. On the other hand, the sequence set out below is fairly standard. Note that it tracks, to a certain extent, the sequence of components in the office memo and the advice letter. See Exhibit 16.1. It is the content within the various components that differentiates the demand letter from objective analytical writing. If the letter is lengthy, you may want to provide headings that track the components of the letter.

Introduction: Unless the opponent has reason to expect the demand letter and knows that you represent your client, the letter may be something of a surprise. So the introduction should clearly identify who you are; who your client is; what is in dispute; and, very generally, what you are seeking on behalf of your client. Although other parts of the letter make assertions adverse to the opponent and thus will read as adversarial, the introduction should be measured in tone so as to begin to develop the working relationship, if not rapport, necessary to resolve the dispute with a minimum of rancor and energy. If the letter is long and the reader is not a lawyer, the introduction may also provide a roadmap of the rest of the letter.

If you are writing directly to your client's opponent, you should include a statement that you are representing your client, not the opponent, and that the opponent should hire a lawyer if he or she wants legal representation to assist with resolving this dispute.

Your client's situation and legal position: For the opponent to be willing to provide a remedy to your client, you must convey that there is a wrong to be remedied. The opponent must see the facts from your client's perspective and understand the legal meaning of those facts.

EXHIBIT 16.1

COMPARISON OF THE OFFICE MEMO, ADVICE LETTER, AND DEMAND LETTER

Office Memo	Advice Letter	Demand Letter
caption	heading	heading
issues & short answers	introduction	introduction
facts	summary of facts	client's situation
discussion	explanation	client's legal position
conclusion	advice & closing	demand & closing

When you state the facts, tell the story in a logical manner, e.g., chronologically. Note how the problem that led to the dispute has affected and continues to affect your client. Include facts from sources other than your client that support your client's position. Avoid melodramatic language; let the story itself make your client's case. The length and level of detail of the story should be determined by how many facts you know with confidence and how much of the story is favorable to your client. You need not include unfavorable facts. However, you may do so; noting and defusing unfavorable facts in the demand letter may prompt an early and favorable settlement.

When you write your legal analysis, think through how to organize it. It must, of course, be logical; it is hard to persuade someone who is very puzzled. If you can see more than one logical organization, consider the following strategies:

- Start with the major basis for your client's claim.
- Start with points that are indisputable or very tilted in your client's favor.
- Start with points that are not as critical of the opponent as others.
- Start with points that are easily understood, especially if you are writing to an opponent, not a lawyer.

If your client has a number of potential claims against the opponent so that the letter would be unduly lengthy if all were discussed in depth, consider presenting one or two in full and listing the rest with a line or two of explanation.

In addition, consider carefully how to pitch your analysis. Obviously, if you are writing to a lawyer, the analysis may be technical and lengthy, and you should include citations for major propositions. If you are writing to the opponent, not a lawyer, the analysis should be less technical and extensive. As with the facts, you need not include unfavorable legal points, but doing so and defusing them may be a good strategy, especially if you are writing to a lawyer.

As to both facts and law, take care not to inadvertently undermine your case. Check for statements that are inaccurate, ambiguous, overly revealing, or too conciliatory as well as statements that could be viewed as admissions of fault by your client.

The demand: Ideally, by the time your reader gets to the actual demand, he or she should feel that some remedy is in order, although probably not the full remedy your client is seeking. Setting out the demand in an effective, rather than off-putting, way is not easy. Consider the following strategies, which rest on understanding human nature:

- Frame your demand in terms of common goals; the opponent will benefit along with the client.
- Frame your demand as a fair solution to a problem both sides are facing and will continue to face unless they settle.
- Frame the opponent's situation as an opportunity to benefit, not only because your client's situation will be resolved but also, for example, because the opponent will be better off with others similar to your client, such as future customers.

- Offer various ways that the opponent can meet the demand.
- Pair the demand with an incentive.
- Pair the demand with warnings—within reason and ethical constraints, of course—of what will occur if the demand is not met.

The demand itself should be well defined and expressed in a straight-forward way.

Often, the client seeks damages. You may want to set a high but tenable figure (the maximum the client could recover) or invite the opponent to make a serious offer. Breaking down a monetary demand into components provided for by the applicable law may induce a higher settlement because the demand is, in a certain sense, objective. Keep in mind that courts may follow formulas for setting damages, but the parties may settle for a sum that reflects their compromise rather than a formula.

The demand may be for non-monetary relief as well. Parties can fashion remedies that a court cannot order; indeed this is a major advantage of settling disputes. Examples of non-monetary relief are re-writing the parties' contract, erasing an adverse performance evaluation, alterations in the opponent's business practices, a training program for the opponent's employees, and creation of a fund for aiding others who may be in the same situation as your client.

Conclusion: You should include a date by which the opponent needs to contact you and indicate what action you will take if there is no contact. An option is to indicate that you will call the opponent, if the opponent does not have a lawyer, or the opponent's lawyer on a specific date in the not-too-distant future. Conclude the letter in a courteous manner and with optimism that the dispute can be resolved satisfactorily and soon.

Responding to a demand letter: When your client receives a demand letter, you may choose to respond. At the least, the responsive letter informs the opponent's lawyer that you are representing your client, so all future communications should come to you. You may also choose to state your client's perspective on the factual and legal positions stated in the opponent's demand letter along with your client's reaction to the demand itself. Rarely does a client assent to the full relief specified in the demand letter. More likely, your client may want to make a counter-proposal to begin the process of negotiation.

E. OVERARCHING CONSIDERATIONS

Achieving the proper tone in a demand letter can be challenging. You want the opponent to understand the claim, so you should avoid legal jargon and unnecessary complexity. You want the opponent to realize that your client's demand is serious and you are confident about the claim, so your tone should be direct and firm. You want the opponent to see that working with you to resolve the claim will be productive, so you want to seem professional and reasonable. You want the opponent to feel respected, so you should avoid condescension and irritation.

To achieve these goals, generally use short affirmative sentences with strong verbs; use adverbs and adjectives sparingly. You should use a diplomatic approach, such as passive voice and the subjunctive mood, in stating the demand itself. A demand letter is a formal letter, so you should use titles and last names, and avoid colloquialisms and shorthand references.

Finally, keep in mind that you are voicing your client's claim. You should definitely confer with your client about the content of the letter and may also find it helpful to confer about the letter's tone as well.

A well written demand letter fulfills the criteria for all good legal writing:

- *Completeness:* Although it does not purport to cover all of the facts or present your full legal analysis, does it cover enough to inform the opponent of the client's situation and support the demand?
- *Correctness:* Are the facts and the law stated accurately, albeit favorably?
- *Coherence:* Do the various components—the client's situation, legal position, and demand—fit together? Does the demand flow naturally from the preceding material?
- *Comprehensibility:* Can the probable reader—the opponent or the opponent's lawyer—understand it in one careful reading?

As you write so as to fulfill these criteria, aim to fulfill another criterion: *convincing.* The suggestions stated in this chapter should serve you well on this score.

F. REVIEW OF CHAPTER 16

The demand letter is a critical document because you are stating your client's claim against your client's opponent, ideally in such a way that prompt resolution of the dispute will follow. To write a successful demand letter:

- Conform to the ethical principles governing communication on behalf of a client.
- Discern whatever you can about the likely reader(s) of the letter, and pitch the letter accordingly.
- Organize the letter by these components: the introduction, your client's situation and legal position, the demand itself, and the conclusion.
- Write the opening segments so the reader sees why a demand is being made.
- Set out a well defined demand, framed to prompt the reader to accede to it or respond with a reasonable counter-offer.
- Write the letter so that the opponent will want to work with you to settle the dispute, e.g., by conveying that you are professional and reasonable, and by treating the opponent respectfully.

17

ADVOCACY WRITING IN THE PRE-TRIAL AND TRIAL SETTING: THE FUNCTION AND FORMAT OF THE MOTION PRACTICE MEMORANDUM

> Of every hundred cases, ninety win themselves, three are won
> by advocacy, and seven are lost by advocacy.
> —A. Fountain
> *Wit of Wig*, 1980

A. INTRODUCTION

Litigation—the process of resolving disputes, whether civil or criminal, within the courts—involves formal advocacy. Litigation follows certain steps, and the protocols for each step are specified. Many of the protocols address written and oral arguments. How do lawyers, operating within these constraints, advocate effectively for their clients?

They operate strategically: They abide by ethical rules governing the lawyer as advocate. They know what is at stake and what the possible outcomes are at every step, so they choose their moves carefully. They frame their arguments not only to appeal to the judge but also to convince the opposing party and to express the client's thoughts and concerns.

The remaining chapters explain these points in more detail as follows:

- This chapter—the pre-trial and trial settings, that is, motion practice;
- Chapter 18—the fundamentals of legal advocacy;
- Chapter 19—the appellate setting;
- Chapter 20—advanced advocacy; and
- Chapter 21—oral argument.

This chapter draws on motion practice materials in the HomeElderCare case, which begin at page 357. The State is seeking a temporary injunction to prohibit the living will service during the lawsuit. You should read through those materials before reading further in this chapter.

B. THE ADVOCATE'S ETHICS

According to the preamble to the Model Rules of Professional Conduct, the lawyer who serves as a client's zealous advocate simultaneously takes on two roles: "an officer of the legal system and a public citizen having special responsibility for the quality of justice." At times, you may perceive conflict, or at least tension, between these roles. But they are intended to be complementary; clients should be interested in a fair process and just outcome, as well as a favorable result.

A lawyer, as an officer of the legal system, may pursue only non-frivolous claims and defenses. Model Rule 3.1 states: "A lawyer shall not bring or defend a proceeding, or assert or controvert an issue therein, unless there is a basis in law and fact for doing so that is not frivolous, which includes a good faith argument for an extension, modification or reversal of existing law." A lawyer who violates this rule faces professional sanctions such as reprimand and disbarment. Similarly, Federal Rule of Civil Procedure 11 provides for sanctions when a lawyer signs a document that is not, according to the lawyer's informed belief, "warranted by existing law or by a non-frivolous argument" for a change in the law. Many states have similar rules.

A lawyer must be candid with the court. According to Model Rule 3.3, it is a violation of professional ethics to knowingly make a false statement of fact, fail to correct a previous false statement of material fact, or offer evidence the lawyer knows to be false. Similarly, it is a violation to knowingly fail to disclose known and adverse legal authority not disclosed by opposing counsel.

Finally, a lawyer must expedite litigation and refrain from engaging in unfair, harassing, or delaying tactics. Examples of the latter under Model

WHAT HAPPENS WHEN YOU FAIL TO FULFILL THE OBLIGATION OF CANDOR TOWARD THE COURT?

In re Thonert,
733 N.E.2d 932 (Ind. 2000).

[Review the facts of this case in Chapter 15, page 149.]

Indiana Professional Conduct Rule 3.3(a)(3) provides that a lawyer shall not knowingly fail to disclose to a tribunal legal authority in the controlling jurisdiction known to the lawyer to be directly adverse to the position of the client and not disclosed by opposing counsel. The concept underlying this requirement of disclosure is that legal argument is a discussion seeking to determine the legal premises property applicable to the case. *Comment* to Ind. Professional Conduct Rule 3.3. The respondent's intimate familiarity with *Fletcher* is established by his having served as counsel to the defendant. Accordingly, we find that the respondent violated the rule by failing to disclose *Fletcher* to the Court of Appeals in his legal arguments on behalf of the client.

. . .

[The court accepted the parties' agreement that the respondent be publicly reprimanded.]

Sobol v. Capital Management Consultants, Inc.,
726 P.2d 335 (Nev. 1986).

[Saul Sobol developed a medical practice under the name Physicians Medical Center. Capital Management Consultants, a competitor, sought to use the name Physician's Medical Center. Sobol sued and sought a preliminary injunction. The Nevada Supreme Court reversed the trial court's denial of the injunction and further stated:]

Additionally, some discussion of the brief submitted by respondents is in order. This court recently warned the bar that "[w]e expect and require that *all* appeals brought in this court . . . will be pursued in a manner meeting high standards of diligence, professionalism, and competence." *State, Emp. Sec. Dep't v. Weber,* 100 Nev. 121, 123, 676 P.2d 1318, 1319 (1984) (emphasis in original). In the answering brief, CMC strenuously argues that Sobol affirmatively admitted and acknowledged in a statement of stipulated facts issued prior to the preliminary hearing that the term "Physicians Medical Center" was "not capable of tradename [sic] or copyright registration and is in the public domain." This is a blatant misrepresentation of the stipulated facts. The supposed "admission" provides in pertinent part:

18. The sole and only basis upon which Defendants claim a legal right to the name "Physician's Medical Center" is by virtue of the filing of the fictitious name certificate in March of 1985, the issuance of a county business license in May of 1985 and that said name is not capable of trade name or copyright registration and is in the public domain.

CMC also quotes language from *Frederick Gash, Inc. v. Mayo Clinic*, 461 F.2d 1395 (C.C.P.A. 1972), as though it were the holding of the case, when in fact the language comes from the dissent. While vigorous advocacy of a client's cause is expected and encouraged, these representations transcend the outer limits of zeal and become statements of guile and delusion. In light of CMC's disregard of the rules and professional standards established by this court, we have determined that the imposition of sanctions on respondents is warranted. *See* NRAP 38(b). Accordingly, CMC shall pay the sum of $5,000.00 to the Clark County Law Library Contribution Fund within thirty (30) days from the date of the issuance of this opinion, and shall promptly provide the clerk of this court with proof of such payment.

Rule 3.4 are obstructing access to potentially relevant material and resisting proper requests for information from opposing counsel.

For many lawyers, these rules serve as minimum standards. Their own personal values prompt them to act according to even more stringent standards of respect for the law, candor, and fairness.

C. CIVIL LITIGATION

The central purpose of litigation is to resolve disputes through the application of legal rules to proven facts carried out by decision-makers empowered by the government. The following discussion presents a generic model of civil litigation; the details vary by jurisdiction.

In general terms, as illustrated in Exhibit 17.1, civil litigation entails framing the case, ascertaining the facts through discovery, and obtaining a decision. At various points in the litigation, one side or the other may bring a motion requesting the court to act as desired by the moving party, or movant, against the opposing party. The movant may seek to move the litigation along (a non-dispositive motion), or the movant may seek a resolution of the case in its favor (a dispositive motion). Courts either grant or deny motions. Exhibit 17.1 lists common motions.

Framing the case. In the first phase of litigation, the parties frame the case through the plaintiff's complaint and the defendant's answer. The two sides name the persons or entities involved, assert various facts to be true or deny the opponent's assertions, identify legal claims or defenses arising out of those facts, and state their desired outcomes. In complicated cases, there may be three or more parties, or the defendant may sue the plaintiff as well as be sued, or a group of similarly situated individuals may sue as a class.

Motions are quite common at this initial stage of litigation. For example, the defendant may seek to dismiss the case on various grounds, such as the court's lack of jurisdiction (power to decide the case), the plaintiff's excessive delay in bringing the lawsuit, or inadequate legal support for the plaintiff's claim. The plaintiff may seek certification of a class. Or the plaintiff may seek a

EXHIBIT 17.1

OUTLINE OF CIVIL LITIGATION

Phases of Litigation	Illustrative Motions
Framing the Case	
• complaint • answer • joinder of parties • counterclaims • class certification	• dismissal for lack of jurisdiction • dismissal for failure to state a claim • class certification • temporary injunction
Ascertaining Facts Through Discovery	
• depositions • production of documents • interrogatories • admissions	• compel discovery
Obtaining a Decision	
• summary judgment (pre-trial) trial Trial • selection of jury • opening statements • presentation of evidence • closing arguments • instruction of jury • deliberations by jury • entry of judgment	• summary judgment Trial • in limine • judgment as matter of law • new trial
Appeal (See Exhibit 19.2)	

temporary injunction to preserve the status quo or prevent certain activity during the litigation.

Ascertaining facts. In discovery, the second phase of litigation, which may overlap somewhat with the first, the parties exchange information about the relevant facts through several methods: depositions (interviews) of parties and witnesses, production of documents or other items, answers to interrogatories (written questions), and admissions (statements of agreement as to certain facts).

Motions arise during discovery if the parties are unable to manage the process themselves. A party may resist discovery if it believes the opposing party is seeking irrelevant or protected information or is asking for discovery that is exceedingly burdensome. Then the party seeking discovery brings a motion to compel discovery.

Obtaining a decision. Discovery concludes as the case nears the trial date. The parties may avoid trial in various ways. They may settle the case based on what they have learned through discovery, or they may resolve it with the assistance of a third-party neutral, through processes such as mediation and arbitration. If one party believes the key facts to be undisputed and its position to be supported by the law, it may move for summary judgment. Summary judgment is a decision by the court based on the pleadings, factual documents supporting the motion (such as a deposition or an affidavit, a sworn statement of facts), and arguments of counsel. Summary judgment may cover all claims or defenses in the case or only some portions of the case. A grant of summary judgment obviates the need for trial on that portion of the case.

If the case has not been resolved during the pre-trial phases, it will proceed to trial. The trial process consists of selection of the jury; opening statements by the lawyers; each side's presentation of evidence through witnesses, documents, and items; closing arguments; the judge's instruction of the jury on the law; jury deliberations; and the verdict. The judge then reviews the jury's work and decides whether to enter judgment on the verdict. Some cases are tried to a judge without a jury (a bench trial), in which case the judge determines what the facts are and applies the law to the facts.

Motions are common at various phases of trial. For example, one party may bring a motion in limine, to obtain a ruling on the admissibility of certain evidence. The defendant may bring a motion for judgment as a matter of law at the end of the plaintiff's case, seeking a ruling that the plaintiff failed to carry its burden of proof and that the defendant therefore wins. Or either party may move for judgment as a matter of law before the case goes to the jury. The party that lost before the jury may seek a new trial based on erroneous rulings by the judge on such matters as admissibility of evidence.

If a party that loses at the trial court is sufficiently disturbed by the loss and wants to pursue the case further, it may appeal. The appeals process is described in Chapter 19.

The sample memoranda in the HomeElderCare file are based on a fictional lawsuit brought by the county attorney of LaSalle County, Minnesota, on behalf of the State of Minnesota. Assume that the complaint asserted that HomeElderCare was engaging in the unauthorized practice of law and that this conduct should be enjoined. HomeElderCare's answer admitted some of the county's factual assertions, denied others, presented facts HomeElderCare deemed important, and asserted that HomeElderCare was not violating the statute. The county attorney moved for a temporary injunction restraining HomeElderCare from continuing to draft living wills pending the resolution of the litigation.

D. MOTION PRACTICE

1. Procedures

Motion arguments can be made orally, in writing, or both. Some motions are first made and argued orally, frequently on the spot. For example, an evidentiary motion generally is made and argued orally while the trial is in progress.

More typically, the movant brings a motion by filing a notice of motion and motion. See the sample at page 357. The notice alerts the opponent to the motion and provides information about the time and location of the hearing. The motion requests the court to take the action desired by the movant. Generally the movant also provides a proposed order for the court's consideration, should the court grant the motion. See the sample at page 358.

The movant and opponent typically write memoranda of law for and against the motion. The movant writes first, filing the memorandum in support of the motion with the court and serving it on opposing counsel. The party opposing the motion writes its memorandum in opposition to the motion, in response to the movant's memorandum, and then serves and files it. The movant then may prepare, serve, and file a reply memorandum if the memorandum in opposition raises matters unaddressed by the movant's initial memorandum. Motion practice memoranda set out and analyze the law governing the case, apply that law to the facts of the case, and cite to the factual record to support statements about the facts of the case.

In addition to submitting written materials, the lawyers usually argue orally before the judge. Motion practice arguments may be very formal (in the courtroom with each lawyer standing at a lectern and arguing in turns) or quite informal (with the lawyers seated around the judge's desk in his or her chambers, or office). Formal oral arguments typically follow the same sequence as the memoranda: movant, opponent, movant. Informal oral argument resembles a discussion. Oral arguments are based on the material in the memoranda and include questions by the judge.

Judges are assigned to hear motions under one of several systems. In a block system, each case is assigned to a judge to handle from the very earliest stages through trial; that judge hears motions in the case. In a calendar system, each judge rotates through a schedule in which he or she hears all motions scheduled for a specific day. Furthermore, in federal court, judges typically hear and decide dispositive motions while magistrates (assistant judges) typically hear and decide non-dispositive motions.

2. Court Rules

Federal and state rules of procedure define the types of motions that can be made and state the standards for granting them. In addition, court or local rules, which supplement the rules of procedure and are drafted by a single court or by a set of trial courts, cover matters of detail. For example, in the state courts in Minnesota, memoranda can be no longer than thirty-five pages, exclusive of facts. The parties must file their memoranda at fixed intervals before the date of the hearing, e.g., the movant's initial memorandum is due twenty-eight days before the hearing on a dispositive motion. If the deadlines are not met, adverse consequences may follow, e.g., loss of the opportunity to argue orally, imposition of attorney fees.[1]

The message should be clear: Know and comply with both the rules of procedure and the court rules in your jurisdiction.

---

1. Minn. Gen. R. Prac. Dist. Ct. 115.03-.06.

HOW IMPORTANT ARE COURT RULES?

Kano v. National Consumer Cooperative Bank,
22 F.3d 899 (9th Cir. 1994).

The opening brief filed on behalf of appellant violated Fed.R.App.P. 32(a) in that the lines were not double-spaced, but were spaced only one-and-one half spaces apart. Furthermore, the footnotes were of a typeface much smaller than that permitted by the rule, and contained approximately eight lines per inch as opposed to six lines per inch in a normal single-spaced format. We estimate that the opening brief was the equivalent of at least sixty-five pages in length, far exceeding the fifty-page limit.

Counsel for appellant took full responsibility for the form of the brief. However, it is apparent from the reply brief filed by counsel that he knows what the spacing requirements are, even though the footnotes in the reply brief also do not comply with Rule 32. Consequently, we impose sanctions against counsel for the appellant in the amount of $1,500. *See Adriana Intern. Corp. v. Thoeren,* 913 F.2d 1406, 1417 (9th Cir. 1990), *cert. denied,* 498 U.S. 1109, 111 S.Ct. 1019, 112 L.Ed.2d 1100 (1991) (imposing sanctions for failure to comply with Fed.R.App.P. 32(a)); *see also* 28 U.S.C. 1927 (authorizing sanctions for failure to comply with rules governing form of briefs). The court acknowledges payment of the sanction.

3. Strategy

Bringing a motion should reflect a well considered choice. The most obvious reason for bringing a motion is to obtain the relief sought, whether it be dismissal of the case, a temporary injunction, or a discovery order. In addition, if the case has been assigned to a specific judge, motions provide an opportunity to educate the judge about the case and, in turn, to see how the judge assesses the case. Furthermore, because the opponent typically defends against the motion, motions provide an opportunity to learn the opponent's strategy.

Nonetheless, there are distinct disadvantages to motions, especially ill-considered ones. Bringing a motion takes time, energy, and therefore money. A premature or weakly supported motion presents a poor impression of the case (and the lawyer) to the judge. Finally, excessive use of motions can undermine the relationships among the lawyers and between them and the judge, who must work together throughout the litigation.

The opponent party typically chooses to defend against the motion. Alternatively, the opponent may offer to negotiate about the matter in dispute. For example, a party facing a summary judgment motion may offer to settle the case.

In the hypothetical HomeElderCare case, the county attorney moved for a temporary injunction for several reasons: to preclude preparation of living wills by HomeElderCare social workers during the litigation, to begin to sway the court in the State's favor, to ascertain the court's first reaction to the case, and to learn of HomeElderCare's approach to the case. HomeElderCare probably would oppose against the motion, which goes to the heart of the dispute—HomeElderCare's ability to provide its living will service.

E. THE FUNCTION OF THE MOTION PRACTICE MEMORANDUM: AUDIENCE AND PURPOSE

As you prepare your motion practice memorandum, keep in mind who will read it and why: the judge and his or her law clerk, opposing counsel, and your client.

WHAT DO TRIAL JUDGES SEEK IN MOTION PRACTICE MEMORANDA?

A brief should be an essay with a clear train of thought, advancing only as many cohesive, well-supported arguments as necessary that, taken together, make up a unified whole—while rebutting the opposition's counterarguments. The brief should marshal the relevant precedent but need not address irrelevant arguments. Also, it must include contrary authority that is on point and controlling.

. . .

Credibility is an extremely important component of a good brief. Misleading or incorrect citations, however unintentional, detract from the persuasiveness of the brief. The brief-writer should carefully draft and edit for correct citations, as well as for punctuation, grammar, and syntax. . . . Mark Twain once said: "Easy writing makes damned hard reading." How true this is in legal writing.

—*Hon. Duross Fitzpatrick*
United States District Court
for the Middle District of Georgia

Memoranda of law are called *briefs* rather than *encyclopedias* for a reason. A brief presents the elements of an argument concisely with references to the sources of law and with descriptions of the particular facts that define the transaction. . . .

Briefs are a medium for articulation and presentation—goals assisted by clarity, precision, and *brevity.*

—*Hon. Lynn N. Hughes*
United States District Court
for the Southern District of Texas

Judges on Briefing: A National Survey 5, 7 (Bryan A. Garner comp., 2001).

Judges, of course, are familiar with the law in general and the legal system. Every judge has a few areas of expertise and some areas that he or she has not studied since law school (if then). Typically, law clerks are recent law school graduates who assist judges by researching cases and writing memos analyzing the cases; most law clerks have only general knowledge of issues that are presented to the court.

To render a correct decision by assigning the proper legal meaning to the case, the judge and clerk need to know the facts of the dispute, the applicable substantive and procedural law, and the application of the law to the facts of the case. They need to know the complete picture, not just the material favoring your client. To find in your favor, they need to believe your position; they need to find you and your client credible. And they need to understand the case with a minimum of time and effort; most judges are very pressed for time because of heavy caseloads.

As for opposing counsel, your primary purpose is to convince him or her of the merits of your position. If your opponent becomes at least somewhat convinced of your position, settlement in your client's favor becomes more likely. Even if the case does not settle, your opponent may contest fewer points in pre-trial or at trial. Your secondary purpose is to develop a good working relationship; modern litigation requires considerable cooperation between the lawyers, even as they pursue their clients' divergent interests.

As for your client, your purpose is to earn the client's confidence. Your client should see his or her story told in an effective way, and your client should understand the main legal arguments, if not the intricacies of the law. Furthermore, your client should see that you believe in his or her position and want the court to do so as well.

F. The Format of the Motion Practice Memorandum

As diverse as these readers' perspectives are, you can serve all of your audiences and your purposes well by writing your memorandum to meet the criteria developed earlier in this book, as well as one new criterion. Legal advocacy should be complete, correct, coherent, comprehensible— and convincing.

1. Format Choices

No single format for the motion practice memorandum is used in courts across the country. Although most courts do not dictate a format, you should check for any applicable local rules. You also should consult other attorneys about any informal local practices. As shown in Exhibit 17.2, the motion practice memorandum bears a certain resemblance to the office memo.

EXHIBIT 17.2

COMPARISON OF OFFICE MEMO AND
MOTION PRACTICE MEMORANDUM

Office Memo	Motion Practice Memorandum
caption	caption
issues	introduction or summary
short answers	issues
facts	facts
	procedure
discussion	argument
conclusions and recommendations	conclusion with signature

The movant's initial memorandum typically follows this sequence: caption, opening components, argument, conclusion with signature. The variation comes in the opening components: Some begin with issues, others with an introduction, yet others with a summary. Virtually all formats include a fact statement. Some cover the procedural history of the case within the fact statement; others include a separate procedure statement.

The formats for the opponent's memorandum are similar. The opponent need not follow the format selected by the movant. The opponent generally does not include a procedure statement. Also, the opponent occasionally elects not to include a fact statement if the movant's statement is acceptable, as occurs when the parties are not disputing the facts and may even have an agreed-upon (stipulated) fact statement. More often, the opponent tells its own story in a fact statement.

The movant's reply memorandum is the most flexibly structured. Its purpose is to respond to points raised by the opponent that are not addressed in the movant's initial memorandum. It is fairly common to include an introduction; address factual matters in a short fact statement, legal matters in a short argument, or both; and close with a conclusion and a signature.

As for the sample memoranda, the State's memorandum opens with a summary and then the facts. On the other hand, HomeElderCare's memorandum introduces the court to the facts first and then turns to the legal issues.

2. Seven Components

This section discusses the seven components in the order the reader generally encounters them. You need not write the motion practice memorandum in this order. For example, you may write the argument before the facts, or you may write the introduction last.

Caption: The chief purpose of the caption is to permit easy recognition and accurate processing of the document. The caption lists the parties, the court in which the case is venued, the docket number for the case, and the title of the document. Local rules may require additional information, such as the type of case and the judge's name, and specify the layout of the caption.

Note that the captions of the two HomeElderCare sample memoranda are nearly identical. Only the documents' titles differ.

Most memoranda have either an introduction or a summary or a statement of the issues. All serve to frame the central point of the motion and orient the reader.

Introduction or Summary: When done well, the introduction serves two very important purposes: it orients the reader to the motion, and it begins to persuade the reader to adopt the client's position. The introduction should briefly identify the parties, the nature of their dispute, and the relief sought by the movant or the result sought by the opponent. It also should present a key point or two, whether a key fact or legal point. If you also present an overview of the legal arguments in the memorandum, "summary" is the preferred title.

In the HomeElderCare file, the sample State's memorandum includes a summary, which acquaints the reader with the factual dispute, identifies the legal dispute, and provides an overview of the argument.

Issues: The issue statement, which poses questions answered in the memorandum, begins to persuade the reader and reveals the scope and sequence of the points covered in the memorandum. The issues should reflect the facts and law accurately, but they need not necessarily be objective in tone. Rather, each issue should be subtly phrased so as to suggest the answer desired by the client. Furthermore, the issues should be relatively concise, so that the reader's attention does not flag.

In most situations, the issues link the law to key facts. Many issues refer both to the law of the motion under consideration (procedural law) and to the law governing the parties' claims or defenses (substantive law). Some issues involve only procedural law, as in a discovery motion, or a pure legal issue, as in an argument that a jurisdiction does not recognize a cause of action.

The classic approach is to frame an issue in a single sentence. However, if a single sentence would be very long or unwieldy, and deleting content is not a good option, you may want to write a two- or three-sentence issue: the law (major premise), the facts (minor premise), then a question about the conclusion.[2] Exhibit 17.3 presents a conventional one-sentence issue and a three-sentence issue on the same topic.

---

2. *See* Bryan A. Garner, *Legal Writing in Plain English: A Text with Exercises* 58–61 (2001).

EXHIBIT 17.3

SHORT-FORM AND LONG-FORM ISSUES

Short Form: Single Sentence

Is it likely that the State will ultimately succeed in convincing the court that HomeElderCare's living will service constitutes the unauthorized practice of law?

Long Form: Three Sentences

Minnesota law permits a non-lawyer professional to touch on legal matters so long as this is incidental to her professional services and does not involve difficult or doubtful legal questions. HomeElderCare's geriatric social workers assist their clients in filling out a living will form, which addresses medical and ethical decisions. Will the State likely succeed in convincing the court that this service is the unauthorized practice of law?

The issues as a set should reflect the organization of the argument. There should generally be an issue for each major point in the argument, and you may want to flag minor points in the argument with sub-issues. Use outlining levels (I, II; A, B, C) and transitional words to convey the relationships among the issues and sub-issues.

HomeElderCare's sample memorandum uses the classic short form. This statement signals the scope and sequence of the upcoming argument: an initial threshold requirement (I) and then a series of three factors (II A, B, and C). The issues incorporate procedural law, substantive law, and facts; they focus on the service of preparing living wills for elderly clients.

Facts: The fact statement informs the reader of the events that gave rise to the litigation. Equally important, the fact statement prompts the reader to see the situation from the client's point of view, empathize with the client, and perhaps begin to lean toward the client's legal position.

The key to a successful fact statement is the careful selection of facts. Your two goals are that the reader understands the situation and also sees your client as acting responsibly and reasonably under the circumstances. As synopsized in Exhibit 17.4, you should include legally relevant (related to the elements of the rule) and background (necessary for the reader to understanding the story) facts—regardless of whether they are favorable or unfavorable to your client. As tempting as it may be to omit unfavorable facts, you must include them to fulfill your ethical responsibility to the court. To assist your client, place unfavorable facts in the best light possible, e.g., show why your client acted in a way that harmed the other party. You need not include any residual facts; however, you may want to include favorable residual facts, within limits so that your fact statement does not become

EXHIBIT 17.4

COVERAGE OF FACTS STATEMENT

	Must Include	May Include	Need Not Include
favorable relevant facts	✓		
unfavorable relevant facts	✓		
favorable background facts	as needed to make story understandable		
unfavorable background facts	as needed to make story understandable		
favorable residual (emotional facts)		✓	
unfavorable residual (emotional facts)			✓

an appeal to emotion. Residual facts with no persuasive content should be excluded.

As the case proceeds through the court system, the pleadings, transcripts of oral proceedings, and other material filed with the court become the record of the case. In the fact statement, you must cite to the pertinent portion of the record for each fact. You need not quote the record verbatim, although you may want to quote some material if the precise wording is important or persuasive. Your presentation must be faithful to the record. For example, inferences drawn from the facts should be clearly identified as inferences, lest they be taken to be stated facts.

The fact statement should have a clear beginning, body, and end. The opening paragraph should identify the important participants in the situation and establish the labels used for them in the memorandum. If the memorandum does not have an introduction or summary, the opening paragraph also should present a very brief synopsis of the parties' dispute.

The body of the fact statement chronicles what happened between these participants. The common modes of organization are chronological, topical, and perceptual. The first two approaches are more strictly objective, while the third introduces an element of subjectivity. In a chronological presentation, events are told in the order they occurred. A topical presentation proceeds from one aspect of the facts, such as location or relationships, to another.

In the perceptual mode, the events are presented as a key participant experienced or learned of them; then a competing perspective is presented. The perceptual organization should be used when the participants' perspectives are critical and differ fundamentally. You should choose the organization that best permits you to tell your client's story, from your client's perspective, in a coherent and interesting narrative. Lengthy fact statements may have subject headings.

The end of the fact statement generally states the pertinent procedural history of the litigation up to the point at which the motion was made. There need not be much detail about unimportant procedural matters. If the memorandum includes a procedure component, the procedural history appears there instead.

The two sample fact statements contain very much the same facts. Both writers have presented their clients' favorable and unfavorable facts. Nearly all are legally relevant or background facts. Some details, such as Mr. Nelson's condition, are residual and stated primarily for persuasive effect. Both memoranda use a primarily topical organization, with some chronological passages. Both fact statements contain cites to the record.

Procedure: This component is most commonly used for cases with complex procedural histories and for motions that are predominantly procedural (such as a motion to compel discovery), rather than substantive (such as a motion to dismiss for failure to state a claim).

This component sets out the history of the litigation, up to the current motion. It identifies the main events, typically in chronological order, and provides citations to pertinent documents, such as the complaint or request for admissions.

Neither sample memorandum in the HomeElderCare case file has a procedure component.

Argument—in general: As the longest component of most memoranda, the argument's purpose is to prove that the client's position is the better one on the facts and the law. The argument presents a legal meaning for the client's situation and provides the judge with the legal reasoning needed to support that legal meaning. Indeed, the judge may use portions of the successful argument in writing his or her opinion.

To prove its points, the argument first must state the law accurately, as synopsized in Exhibit 17.5. Ethics rules require counsel to discuss and cite the legal authorities that the court will deem important in deciding the motion—not only favorable authorities but also unfavorable authorities not covered by opposing counsel. The argument must present mandatory authority where it exists, of course; it also may present persuasive precedent and commentary that may be useful to the court and is favorable to the client. If no mandatory authority exists, the argument should demonstrate how to use persuasive authority and commentary to decide the case and how to handle unfavorable persuasive precedent. The argument should present all analytical steps necessary to develop the applicable rule of law. As appropriate, it should show how to fuse several cases or interpret an ambiguous statute.

EXHIBIT 17.5

LEGAL CONTENT OF ARGUMENT

mandatory authority—favorable	required
mandatory authority—unfavorable	required if opponent does not raise it; should be included
persuasive precedent	may be used; no need to cite unfavorable
commentary	may be used; no need to cite unfavorable

The argument should show how the substantive law and the procedural law interact. This varies:

- Some procedural rules operate relatively independently of the substantive law governing the case; an example is a motion to compel discovery where the issue is burdensomeness.
- Other procedural rules are nearly entirely dependent on the substantive law; an example is a motion to dismiss for failure to state a claim recognized by the law.
- Still other procedural rules include elements that rely heavily on substantive law along with elements that operate relatively independently of substantive law. An example is a motion for a temporary injunction, which involves consideration of the likelihood of success on the merits (fixed by substantive law) as well as the burden of harms to the parties from various results (not so fixed).

A well written argument clearly demonstrates how to view the facts in light of the substantive law (as needed) and the procedural law.

In all of these situations, you need to do more than present a statement of the law; the argument must connect the law and the facts. The argument should discuss the relevant facts—both favorable and unfavorable—in depth and demonstrate why the court should draw the desired conclusion. This task requires clear deductive reasoning; in many cases, it also requires reasoning by example and policy analysis.

On debatable issues, your argument also should address the opposing argument. This discussion commonly arises in one of two postures. If the conflict relates to which rule should apply, you would state the favorable rule and address the unfavorable rule. If the conflict relates to how the rule should be applied, you would state the favorable application and address the unfavorable application. Your discussion of the opposing argument may be woven into your main argument, or it may follow your main argument.

Of course, you must fully and properly cite the law in your argument. In general, the citations to the record in the fact statement support references to the facts within the argument. However, you should provide record citations in the argument when you use a direct quote from the record or want the court to look at a key page.

In the sample memoranda from the HomeElderCare case, both arguments present and fully develop the procedural law (through five or seven mandatory precedents) and the substantive legal topics (through two main statutes, the two leading cases, and commentary; the State relying as well on additional cases, including persuasive precedents, and a related statute). Both use the elements of the procedural rule (the elements of an injunction) as the procedural framework, with the substantive law presented in the context of the procedural framework and the facts in the context of the law, although the schematics differ. See Exhibit 17.6. Both arguments include deductive reasoning, reasoning by example, and policy arguments; both subtly refute the other's argument, e.g., the State's discussion of the policy against technical restrictions and HomeElderCare's handling of the fee and "legal document."

Argument—point headings: An argument cannot be persuasive if it cannot be followed. Point headings throughout the discussion reveal the structure of the arguments and make a full-sentence assertion. Taken together, the point headings state the handful of assertions the court must accept (in total or in part) to rule in the client's favor.

In most situations, each major point heading ties together the substantive and procedural law and the key facts relevant to the assertion. Each point heading should be a single sentence and persuasively worded. The sentence can be compound but should not be so complex that its readability suffers. For complicated or lengthy topics, the major point heading is a broad assertion, and minor point headings state the subsidiary assertions, which may combine law and facts, or refer only to the law, or refer only to the facts. If an argument is primarily legal or procedural, the point headings will be, too.

Multiple headings and sub-headings should be numbered and lettered in outline form. Point headings should stand out from the text; use white space (open lines) above and below the heading, underlining, italics, boldface, initial capital letters, or a different font (if not too flamboyant). All capital letters is also an option, but studies have shown that readers have to work harder and retain less information when reading sentences in all capital letters.

To guide your reader through what can be a complex analysis, use roadmaps, topic sentences, and appropriate transitions. Roadmaps may appear in various places, such as between the argument heading and point heading I, or between point heading I and sub-point heading A. Topic sentences and transition sentences function as they do in office memos.

The structures of the two sample arguments are apparent from their point headings, reprinted as Exhibit 17.7. Each major heading makes a main assertion, and most combine law and facts. The minor headings elaborate on the points in the major headings.

EXHIBIT 17.6

SCHEMATIC OF ARGUMENTS

STATE'S (PLAINTIFF'S) MEMORANDUM
Temporary injunction is warranted because

| State likely will succeed on merits, and public policy in statutes favors injunction. | Absent an injunction, clients will suffer irreparable harm outweighing harm to HEC from injunction: | Injunction will be straightforward to enforce |

Unauthorized practice statute prohibits non-lawyers
- social workers
■ from drafting legal documents
   - living wills
■ or providing legal advice on difficult or doubtful questions
   - advice re physician duties, proxies, etc.
■ for a fee.
   - HEC charges fee.

■ improper receipt or denial of medical treatment

vs.

■ impairment of only one of HEC's many services.

Unauthorized practice statute calls for injunction
■ short-term version of statutory remedy
■ notice to employees
■ review of HEC bills

Injunction will promote purposes of unauthorized practice statute
■ prohibit incompetent practice by non-lawyers
and living will statute
■ promote accurate expression of declarant wishes.

HOMEELDERCARE'S (DEFENDANT'S) MEMORANDUM
Temporary injunction is improper because

State has not proved threshold requirement of great and irreparable injury

- ■ laudable service
- ■ one allegedly erroneous will is not significant
- ■ clients seek assistance.

State has not met its burden as to three requirements

■ balance of harms
   - clients want and need service
   - HEC will suffer business disruption
■ unlikelihood of State succeeding on merits
   - law prohibits legal advice only as to difficult or doubtful legal questions; HEC fills in form; does not deviate from form; refers questions to lawyers
   - law prohibits drafting legal documents; no legal document here—only filling in form
■ public interest will not be served by injunction
   - elderly will not obtain living wills
   - burden on health care system.

EXHIBIT 17.7

POINT HEADINGS

PLAINTIFF'S MEMORANDUM

I. The State likely will succeed in demonstrating that **Defendant's preparation of and counseling about living wills for its elderly clients** *constitutes the illegal practice of law* and affronts the public policies stated in the statutes on *living wills and the unauthorized practice of law.*

    A. **Defendant's living will service** *constitutes the unauthorized practice of law, for a fee,* **by social workers.**

    B. **Defendant's living will service** affronts the public policies stated in the *unauthorized practice and living will statutes.*

II. **If Defendant incompetently prepares living wills that inaccurately reflect its elderly clients' choices concerning medical treatment or death, its clients** will suffer irreparable harm, with no adequate remedy at law, and this harm will outweigh **Defendant's loss of income** if the injunction is granted.

III. The temporary injunction **sought by the State** will be straightforward to enforce.

DEFENDANT'S MEMORANDUM

I. The State has failed to prove that it will suffer great and irreparable injury if **HomeElderCare continues to offer living will assistance to its clients.**

II. The State has not met its burden as to the factors needed for a temporary injunction to issue.

    A. The State's alleged harm in the absence of a temporary injunction does not outweigh the harm to **HomeElderCare's elderly clients and to the relationships between HomeElderCare and its clients** if an injunction is granted.

    B. The State is not likely to succeed in convincing this Court that **HomeElderCare's provision of living will services to its clients** *constitutes the unauthorized practice of law.*

    C. The public interest will not be served by **prohibiting HomeElderCare's living will service** during the pendency of the case.

Key: procedural law
      substantive law
      facts

Conclusion and signature: The purpose of the conclusion is to remind the reader of the outcome desired by the client. It typically follows a simple formula, in which the writer respectfully requests that the court act in the client's favor. Some writers also synopsize the argument. The closing is usually "Respectfully submitted," followed by the lawyer's signature, as an endorsement of the preceding material. The signature block also includes the lawyer's name, client, firm affiliation, contact information, attorney registration number, and the date.

Both sample memoranda contain conclusions. The State's conclusion is a short statement of its main points and the relief desired, and HomeElder-Care's conclusion includes a slightly longer review of its three main points.

G. REVIEW OF CHAPTER 17

Lawyers advocate for clients in a range of settings, all governed by the ethical principles of respect for the law, candor, and fairness. These principles reflect the lawyer's dual role as advocate and public servant. In the setting of civil litigation, motion practice memoranda serve multiple audiences by persuading the judge, opposing counsel, and indeed the client that the client's position is the better one. The format of the motion practice memorandum is as follows:

(1) The caption provides identifying information.
(2) The introduction or summary orients the reader by providing basic information about the case and begins to persuade the reader by featuring a key point or two. The issues frame the legal/factual questions to be decided, signal the organization of the argument, and subtly suggest the desired answer.
(3) The fact statement tells the client's story and generates understanding if not empathy.
(4) The procedure component recounts the important events in the litigation to date. It may appear at the end of the fact statement.
(5) The argument proves that the client's position is the better one on the facts and the law (both substantive and procedural) and employs point headings as succinct statements of the major propositions.
(6) The conclusion states the relief desired by the client and carries the lawyer's signature and the date.

The resulting memorandum should be complete, correct, coherent, comprehensible, and convincing. Chapter 18 develops several foundational principles of legal advocacy to help you accomplish the goal of convincing your readers.

18

FUNDAMENTALS OF

ADVOCACY

> Among attorneys in Tennessee the saying is: When you have
> facts on your side, argue the facts. When you have the law on
> your side, argue the law. When you have neither, holler.
> —Albert Gore, Jr.
> *Washington Post* (July 23, 1982)

A. INTRODUCTION

How does a lawyer convince a court to rule in the client's favor, when the probable outcome is far from clear? Lawyers conceive of this process as "making the case" on the client's behalf.

According to principles of Aristotelian rhetoric, persuasion is a function of three elements: logos, pathos, and ethos. In simple translation, these three elements are an appeal to logic or proof, an appeal to emotion, and reliance on the writer's good character. An argument must be logically sound, it must appeal to the reader's sense of what is right on the facts, and the advocate must appear credible and trustworthy.[1]

---

1. *See generally* Louis J. Sirico, Jr. & Nancy L. Schultz, *Persuasive Writing for Lawyers and the Legal Profession* 1–20 (2d ed. 2001).

Similarly, Karl Llewellyn, a prominent legal scholar in the first half of the twentieth century, said that a successful lawyer must "bring in a technically perfect case on the law" and "make the facts talk" to be persuasive.[2] In both of these tasks, the lawyer must fulfill the ethical obligation of candor toward the court, discussed in Chapter 17. If the court is to adopt an advocate's view of the legal meaning to be assigned to the case, the advocate must present the facts and the law in a compelling and credible combination.

Making a case involves careful selection and development of points to be made on the client's behalf and then artful presentation of those points. This chapter focuses on the former; Chapter 20 focuses on the latter. The topics discussed in this chapter are applicable to all advocacy settings, including appellate arguments.

The examples in this chapter are from the sample motion practice memoranda in the HomeElderCare case at pages 359 and 369, which you should read over before continuing.

B. An Analogy: Photography

Photographers and lawyers share this task: to present what exists or has happened in a way that informs the observer about the subject and generates a particular response. For the photographer, the subject is the scene, and the goal is to produce the desired response—curiosity, sorrow, amusement—in the viewer. For the lawyer, the subject is the case, and the goal is to convince the reader to assign to the case the legal meaning the client desires.

Both the photographer and the lawyer must accept their subjects as they are. For both, the subject has features that will incline the observer toward the desired response and features that may produce the opposite response. Both the photographer and the lawyer have the opportunity, within limits, to set boundaries, to decide what is included in the photograph or memorandum and what is not. And both can choose which aspects of the subject to bring into focus and which to leave in the background.

C. Creating a Theory of Your Case

The steps discussed in this chapter serve one main goal: to develop a convincing "theory of the case." The theory of a case is what the case is about, in simple (but not simplistic) terms. If you were to write a newspaper article about your case, the headline or first paragraph would state the theory of the case. If you were to make a movie about your case, the poster or preview would present the theory of the case.

The theory of a case provides a theme for your argument, indeed for your entire memorandum. A theme is important for you as a writer and for your

---

2. K. N. Llewellyn, *The Modern Approach to Counseling and Advocacy—Especially in Commercial Transactions*, 46 Colum. L. Rev. 167, 182–83 (1946).

readers. For you, the theory of the case suggests language to use throughout the memorandum, provides a basis for ultimately deciding which assertions to make or emphasize and which to exclude or downplay, and permits you to unify what might otherwise seem to be disparate assertions. For the reader, who is unlikely to be able to truly absorb and recall all the distinct assertions of the memorandum, a well communicated theory of the case provides an idea about the case that can be easily grasped and adopted.

Because a case meshes facts, substantive law, procedural law, and policy, the ideal theory of the case partakes of all of these. However, one or the other may dominate. For example, your central concept may be a key factual detail or a phrase representing the pertinent legal rule. Less commonly, a public policy may be your central concept. Whatever your central concept, the court's appreciation of your theory should lead directly to the outcome desired by your client and away from the outcome desired by your opponent.

There are various ways to develop a theory of a case. You might build a theory on whatever struck you as very compelling when you first learned of the case. You might build a theory on your client's statement of why the case is so important. Or you might derive the theory from the insights you gain through the processes described in the rest of this chapter. However you develop the theory, consider it as you make your final decisions about interpreting the facts, presenting legal arguments, and writing the memorandum so as to emphasize the strengths of your client's case while downplaying its weaknesses.

One way to depict a theory of the case is a pie chart, divided into quarters, with key phrases allocated to segments labeled "facts," "policy," "law," and "procedure." See Exhibit 18.1. As you assign each phrase to its appropriate sector, you should see concepts that parallel each other fall into alignment around the circle.

In the sample HomeElderCare memoranda, the theories of the case are as sketched in Exhibit 18.1 and the following statements in the memoranda:

- For the State: "Defendant has illegally drafted legal documents and provided legal counsel for a fee to elderly citizens—and erroneously so in at least Mr. Nelson's case."
- For HomeElderCare: "In fact, a laudable service has been done—for the client, for his or her family, and for society. . . . Yet, the State wants to put a halt to this service. . . ."

D. INTERPRETING THE FACTS

Rarely are the facts of a case fixed. Rather, most records consist of bits of information that suggest a set of relationships and series of events. Thus the information requires interpretation. Judges expect you to help them understand the facts from your client's perspective.

You must, of course, fully and fairly inform the court. The court needs to be apprised of all relevant facts and necessary background facts. You may include persuasive residual facts, as long as you do so judiciously. Keep in

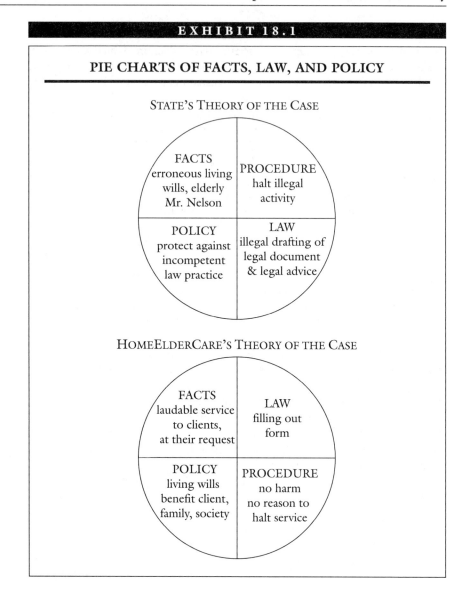

EXHIBIT 18.1

PIE CHARTS OF FACTS, LAW, AND POLICY

STATE'S THEORY OF THE CASE

FACTS
erroneous living
wills, elderly
Mr. Nelson

PROCEDURE
halt illegal
activity

POLICY
protect against
incompetent
law practice

LAW
illegal drafting of
legal document
& legal advice

HOMEELDERCARE'S THEORY OF THE CASE

FACTS
laudable service
to clients,
at their request

LAW
filling out
form

POLICY
living wills
benefit client,
family, society

PROCEDURE
no harm
no reason to
halt service

mind that ethical obligations require you to present unfavorable as well as favorable facts.

One situation requiring interpretation is inconsistency, which may arise, for example, between the statements of two observers, between the early and later statements of the same observer, or between a document and a witness. Some inconsistencies are not significant, because, for example, the fact is not relevant or the inconsistency relates to a detail while the general fact is all that matters. Other inconsistencies are significant and can be handled in various ways:

- You may be able to show that the two sources are only apparently, not truly, in conflict.

- You may be able to show that one source is the more credible, based on capacity to perceive the events or lack of bias.
- A legal rule may dictate how you handle an inconsistency. For example, the court must take the plaintiff's view of the facts on a motion to dismiss the complaint for failure to state a claim.
- Or you may have to discuss both ways of seeing the fact in your analysis.

Often, seemingly fixed facts can give rise to various inferences, depending on whose perspective is taken, and the inferences may be as important as the known fact itself. In such situations, you must take care to delineate what the record itself says. You may then go on to present the inference favored by your client if it is an obviously reasonable one or you can explain it well.

Finally, it may be significant that evidence of a specific fact does not appear in the record. If this is to your advantage, you may want to note its absence and who could have testified to it, were that fact true. Of course, absent "facts" are not as weighty as facts that are stated in the record.

In the two sample memoranda, the facts presented in the fact statements and analyzed in the arguments are nearly identical. The key fact requiring interpretation is the cause of the error in Mr. Nelson's living will. HomeElderCare's fact statement (at page 370) states what is known and delicately but fairly intimates that Mr. Nelson may have erred ("Perhaps he did not fully process . . ."). The State's fact statement (at page 360) identifies the error, notes that a lawyer corrected it, and underscores that the original erroneous will was drafted by a non-lawyer.

E. DEVELOPING YOUR AFFIRMATIVE LEGAL ARGUMENTS

As you research and reason through your client's case, you may develop a long list of legal topics that could be discussed and points that could be made, and you may want to include them all, lest you omit the winning argument. But if you try to develop too many points, you are unlikely to develop any fully, and you may seem to be relying on quantity, rather than quality, of argument. As judges know, one convincing argument suffices; no number of unconvincing arguments can suffice.

To identify the topics you need to address, consider the structure of the various rules involved in the case, for they both impose requirements on the memorandum and offer you options. For example, if the substantive rule governing the plaintiff's claim is conjunctive, as plaintiff's counsel, you must present an argument for each element; as defendant's counsel, you need only prevail on one element and could omit discussion of one or possibly more elements. As another example, if the situation is governed by an aggregate or balancing rule, both plaintiff and defendant may select the factors to be discussed.

SHORT AND SWEET, OR THE KITCHEN SINK?

In the summer of 2000, Bryan Garner surveyed state and federal trial and appellate judges about their preferences as to motion practice memoranda and appellate briefs.[3] He posited two options, and the nearly sixty judges voted as follows:

1. "A brief should be an essay that advances two or three cohesive, well-supported arguments . . . while rebutting the opposition's counter-arguments" and run short if possible.
     50 judges (86%)
2. "A brief should be a repository of all the information that a curious judge might want to know about a case" and use all the allotted space.
     0 judges
3. Neither view is quite right.
     8 judges (14%)

---

3. *Judges on Briefing: A National Survey* iii–iv (Bryan A. Garner comp., 2001).

Because motions involve substantive law in combination with a procedural rule, you must also consider the requirements and options of the procedural law. For example, the party seeking a temporary injunction must show a likelihood of success on the merits. The opponent may be able to deflect the injunction by demonstrating that the movant is unlikely to succeed or that the balance of harms favors denial of the injunction.

Once you have selected the topics to cover, you should consider the various assertions to make on each topic. If you have more than one argument to make on a topic, think first about the relative power of each. A legal argument derives its power from the law, the facts, and the strength of the link between them. Ask yourself:

- Does the law unambiguously say what I am asserting, or is some interpretation necessary?
- Are my important facts uncontroverted and sympathetic?
- Is the link between the law and the facts obvious, or is there some murkiness?
- How well does this assertion defeat my opponent's argument?
- Would I be convinced if I were the judge or opposing counsel?

As you prepare your motion practice memorandum, as at other times, you should consult with your client about the arguments to be made. While the client may not fully grasp the fine points of an argument, the client should be aware of and endorse the gist of the argument. The client may feel strongly about making some arguments or forgoing others, based on important considerations other than the law.

Ideally, your best assertions will form a coherent whole argument. Each legal and factual assertion will flow smoothly from the previous assertion and lead naturally into the upcoming assertion. Not infrequently, however, your best assertions will not be consistent with each other. There may be a break between two assertions: "X is true. Whether X is true or not, Y is true." Or there may be a conflict: "X is true. Even if X is false, Y is true."

Although it may seem intellectually dishonest to make two such arguments, lawyers commonly argue in the alternative. Arguing in the alternative is common in the law because both facts and law are malleable enough that more than one legal meaning may reasonably be ascribed to a situation. For example, a statute may be amenable to two interpretations; a fact may be unknown or ambiguous. Judges are accustomed to arguments in the alternative; indeed, they use reasoning in the alternative to justify some of their own decisions.

Nonetheless, arguing in the alternative does have its drawbacks. It entails complexity and risks confusing the reader. The alternative argument may suggest that the initial assertion or argument is not strong enough to stand on its own. In general, alternative arguments involving breaks are more convincing than alternative arguments involving conflicts.

The key to a successful argument in the alternative is clarity of presentation. You should begin with a clear roadmap, and you should introduce each assertion or argument with a signpost calling attention to the alternative relationship, such as, "Even if the Plaintiff's conduct were covered by the statute, it nonetheless would be permissible because . . . ."

In the HomeElderCare sample memoranda, both parties discussed the same procedural rule and opted not to cover one factor from the aggregate injunction rule—the parties' previous relationship—on the grounds it is not apt and would only clutter already intricate arguments. The State addressed one factor—ease in enforcing the injunction—that HomeElderCare chose to skim by in one line; that factor favors the State. Both parties focused on the obviously central concerns: harm to the parties, likelihood of success on the merits, and statutory expressions of public policy.

An argument in the alternative in the sample memoranda appears in HomeElderCare's argument about Mr. Nelson's living will on page 373. It is phrased in fairly subtle terms; the transition phrase is "in any event." A more obvious phrasing would be: "But even if HomeElderCare erred, one inaccurate living will out of forty does not amount to great harm."

F. ACCOUNTING FOR YOUR OPPONENT'S ARGUMENTS

Legal advocacy has both offensive and defensive aspects. Not only must you convince the court of the merits of your argument; you also must deflect your opponent's arguments. Thus, an important step in developing your argument is to take stock of your opponent's arguments.

Often this entails anticipating your opponent's argument, for instance, when your memorandum is the first to be written. Ask yourself: What would I argue if I were counsel for my client's opponent? If I were the judge analyzing this case, what are the assertions that I would discuss that would lead me to hold in favor of my client's opponent?

Next, compare your opponent's probable or actual arguments to your own. You very probably will discern both points of concurrence and points of clash. Points of concurrence are propositions on which you and your opponent agree; points of clash are propositions on which you and your opponent disagree. Both may involve various matters:

- You may agree or disagree as to what the governing legal rule is on a topic, how (or whether) to fuse a given set of cases, how to interpret a statute.
- You may agree or disagree about what the relevant facts are, especially inferences to be drawn from the facts.
- You may agree or disagree about how the rule applies to the facts, how policy analysis plays out, or whether a leading case is analogous or distinguishable.

You should take care to discern the points of concurrence and clash with precision because your memorandum should be focused accordingly. Your memorandum should focus on the points of clash, providing the court with compelling reasons to resolve them in your client's favor. Although your memorandum should cover the points of concurrence enough to provide context for your discussion of the points of clash, you should not allocate much space to those points.

A useful tool for depicting this analysis is the T-chart, in which you state the main arguments and significant assertions of the two sides in juxtaposition. See Exhibit 18.2. You can use symbols, such as X for points of clash.

In Exhibit 18.2, a T-chart of the HomeElderCare case, note that the parties concur on what the governing legal authorities are, what the rules and elements are, and how some of them apply to the facts. The parties clash as to the application of key elements to their facts, the role of public policy, and the wisdom of granting an injunction.

G. STRESSING STRENGTHS AND WORKING AROUND WEAKNESSES

1. Discerning Strengths and Weaknesses

Once you have sorted through the assertions, both legal and factual, that you want to make and thought through your opponent's arguments, you should assess the overall strengths and weaknesses of your case. Every case in litigation has its strengths and weaknesses; truly one-sided cases generally are

EXHIBIT 18.2

T-CHART OF ASSERTIONS

State's Assertions		HomeElderCare's Assertions
various factors re injunction		various factors re injunction
• death etc. is irreparable	X	• no irreparable harm
• bungled living wills outweigh impairment of HomeElderCare business	X	• halting of useful service outweighs single incident
• no administrative burden		• no administrative burden
• no prior relationship		• no prior relationship
• will succeed on merits	X	• will not succeed on merits
unauthorized practice prohibitions apply to non-lawyers		unauthorized practice prohibitions apply to non-lawyers
social workers are not lawyers		social workers are not lawyers
social workers draft documents	X	social workers fill in form
living will is legal document	X	living will is not legal document
• 145B says so	X	• two statutes are separate
• will has legal effect	X	• issues are medical and ethical
social workers give legal advice	X	social workers avoid giving legal advice
• service is incidental to non-legal matters		• service is incidental to non-legal matters
• test is whether Q is difficult or doubtful		• test is whether Q is difficult or doubtful
• legal issues abound	X	• social workers avoid law
• *Gardner* is analogous	X	• *Gardner* is distinguishable
public policy is important		public policy is important
• protect elderly from incompetence in provision of legal service	X	• assist elderly with living wills that address medical and ethical issues
• ensure accurate living wills	[X]	• encourage living wills
• protect public now from incompetent legal work	X	• continue valuable non-legal service

resolved before litigation by the parties or their lawyers. Of course, one side's strength is usually the other side's weakness.

Some cases are said to be "strong on the law," while others are "strong on the facts" or "strong on policy." A case is strong on the law when the rule is well established, clearly addresses the client's situation, and calls for the client's desired outcome. A case is strong on the facts, or equities, when a reasonable observer easily empathizes with the client and sees the client's desired outcome as sensible and fair. A case is strong on policy when the client's goals reflect an important societal interest.

If the case raises multiple issues, the strengths and weaknesses may vary across issues. For example, the plaintiff may have the stronger legal position as to one claim, while the defendant has the stronger position as to another.

Or the plaintiff's case may be strong on facts as to liability but weak on facts as to damages. Moreover, one party may have the advantage on the substantive law, while the other may have the advantage on the procedural law.

In the HomeElderCare case, the two sides have interesting mixes of strengths and weaknesses. Generally, the rule on temporary injunctions favors the party opposing the motion, although the State can counter with the authorization of injunctions in the unauthorized practice statute. The State has a strong legal-document argument, while HomeElderCare has a strong argument under the difficult-or-doubtful-legal-question test. Mr. Nelson's situation is a strength for the State, especially because it illustrates the public policy behind the unauthorized practice statute. However, HomeElderCare has a strong record of client service (apart from Mr. Nelson) in an area of articulated client need and legislative concern.

2. Stressing Your Strengths

As you draft your memorandum, you should, of course, stress the strengths highlighted in your theory of the case. The tools for doing so depend on the nature of your strong-suit material. If your case is strong on the law, overall or in part, emphasize the legal rule by presenting the strongest authority possible and developing it fully:

- If the rule emanates from a statute, quote and paraphrase the statute, discuss its underlying policy, and provide an illustrative case.
- If the rule emanates from case law, present the rule itself, and also describe one or two cases in some depth. You could cite an early case to underscore the rule's long standing, and you could cite a recent case to underscore its continued authority.

If your case is strong on the facts, overall or in part, emphasize the facts:

- Quote from the record.
- Stack evidence on a key fact by showing that it appears in multiple sources.
- Note not only what the evidence shows, but also what it does not show.
- If possible, develop an extended comparison to a decided case, or present several case comparisons, but not so many that the reader loses sight of your client's case.

If your case is strong on policy, overall or in part:

- Quote from cases, a statutory purpose section, or commentary that states the policy clearly.
- Show how the policy plays out in the facts of your case.
- Refute any opposing policy statements by your opponent by citing authority that downplays that policy, showing its inconsistency with your policy, or demonstrating its irrelevance to the case.

These methods may be used in various parts of your memorandum. You likely will seek to emphasize favorable law or policy in the introduction or summary, issues, and argument. In all of these areas, and also in the fact statement, you will seek to emphasize favorable facts.

In the sample HomeElderCare memorandum, you will note an essential contrast in the State's reliance on the law versus HomeElderCare's emphasis on the facts and equities. This contrast is apparent in the parties' discussion of the equities element of the injunction rule: HomeElderCare leading with two versions of the harm factor (starting at pages 372 and 373), the State presenting a short discussion of this factor well into the argument (starting at page 366).

3. Working Around Your Weaknesses

You cannot simply wish that the weaknesses in your client's case will go away and ignore them; they certainly will appear in your opponent's memorandum. On the other hand, you should not dwell on the weaknesses, lest the court also do so. Rather, dispel the weaknesses, even as you make the points you want to make. How to do so depends on the nature of the weakness.

Some weaknesses may be matters of law. If the authority is not mandatory, you should downplay it as merely persuasive and non-binding; you also should criticize any weaknesses in its reasoning or policy. If the authority is mandatory case law, you have a range of options:

- Distinguish the case by showing that the facts or issues differ from your case.
- Narrow the scope of the case by confining its holding to facts not present in your case.
- Show that the adverse statement is dictum, not a holding.
- Demonstrate that the case is inconsistent with other binding precedent and should be discounted.
- If needed, argue that the case should be overruled because it relies on weak reasoning, the trend of the law is against it, or the holding is contrary to public policy.

If the adverse mandatory authority is a statute or procedural rule or regulation, you have several options:

- Argue that your case falls outside its scope, based on definitions or other scope sections.
- Focus on cases interpreting the statute if they afford more favorable material.
- Demonstrate that the law is ambiguous given the facts of your case; then provide a favorable interpretation based on legislative history or intent, canons of construction, or policy.
- The most difficult option is to establish that the law is unconstitutional or outside the power of the lawmaking body; a less radical form of this option is to argue for a limiting interpretation that would avoid unconstitutionality and favor the client.

WHAT HAPPENS WHEN YOU TRY TO IGNORE THE WEAKNESSES OF YOUR CASE?

Northwestern National Insurance Co. v. Guthrie,
No. 90 C 4050, 1990 WL 205945 (N.D. Ill. Dec. 3, 1990).

[Northwestern National sought a declaratory judgment that it had no duty to defend or indemnify Guthrie. The parties contested whether the court could look to matters outside the complaint against Guthrie.]

[T]he Court is deeply troubled by the manner in which [Guthrie's] counsel argued this motion. . . . Counsel's memorandum in support of the motion faithfully recites the *Maryland Casualty Co. v. Peppers* line of cases explicating the general rule. Counsel neglects, however, to discuss the exception to that general rule that is directly on point here—a failure that strikes us as something more than mere oversight. For example, counsel quotes a lengthy passage from *State Farm Fire & Casualty Co.,* Defendants' Memorandum at 5, that sets forth the general rule that the court may not look beyond the allegations of the complaint. *State Farm Fire & Casualty Co.,* 176 Ill. App.3d at 866–67, 531 N.E.2d at 919. The *very next sentence,* explaining the exception to the rule in the declaratory judgment context, is not disclosed by counsel. Nor does counsel mention anywhere in the memorandum that such an exception exists. This failure to disclose relevant legal authority borders perilously close to a violation of the legal profession's ethical canons. *See* Illinois Rules of Professional Conduct 3.3(a)(3) ("In appearing in a professional capacity before a tribunal, a lawyer shall not: . . . (3) fail to disclose to the tribunal legal authority in the controlling jurisdiction known to the lawyer to be directly adverse to the position of the client and not disclosed by opposing counsel"). We will assume that counsel's glaring omission is the result of sloppy research and writing, and not an intentional effort to mislead or misdirect this Court. We request that the head of the Litigation Department of [Guthrie's] law firm write to the Court in response to this concern.

Some weaknesses may be matters of fact, as to which you may have several options:

- If there is conflicting evidence on the fact, emphasize the helpful evidence.
- Discuss other facts that put the unfavorable fact into context, without altering the unfavorable fact. For example, if the client acted unwisely, show why the client did so.
- Show that the record does not present an even worse scenario.

Some weaknesses may be matters of policy; again, you have several options:

- Show that your case does not truly implicate the policy.
- Show that the policy is outdated or needs re-evaluation.
- Shift the focus to a competing policy that is well served by the outcome your client seeks.
- If the law is clear and favors your client, point out that the law must be followed even if the court would favor a different policy.

These methods for handling weaknesses may be used as follows: the law and policy methods in the introduction or summary, issues, and argument; the fact methods in all those components of the memorandum and additionally in the fact statement.

Of the two sample memoranda, HomeElderCare's memorandum better illustrates how to deal with adverse law. The memorandum downplays the unauthorized practice statute by focusing on case law; pointing out ambiguities in its connection to the living will statute; and distinguishing *Gardner,* the leading case, which has a favorable rule but adverse outcome (at page 374). HomeElderCare's memorandum deals with the adverse facts regarding Mr. Nelson's situation by subtly suggesting he may have been at fault and pointing out that no real harm occurred (at page 372-73). The State's memorandum deals with the adverse policy of encouraging living wills by showing how this policy is undercut by incompetent assistance by social workers (at page 365-66).

H. REVIEW OF CHAPTER 18

To write a convincing legal argument, a lawyer must make the case for the client by developing and delivering a strong theory of the case. The steps toward that end include:

(1) Interpret the facts fairly yet persuasively.
(2) Select legal assertions that are well grounded in the law and facts.
(3) Discern the points of concurrence and points of clash between the client's and the opponent's views of the case, and focus on the latter.
(4) As you draft your memorandum, stress your strengths and work around your weaknesses.

By following these steps, you will carefully select and develop the arguments to be made on your client's behalf. Chapter 20 covers techniques for artful presentation of the points you have thus developed.

19

ADVOCACY WRITING IN THE APPELLATE SETTING: THE FUNCTION AND FORMAT OF THE APPELLATE BRIEF

> Be brief, be pointed, let your matter stand
> Lucid in order, solid and at hand;
> Spend not your words on trifles but condense;
> Strike with the mass of thought, not drops of sense;
> Press to the close with vigor, once begun,
> And leave—how hard the task!—leave off when done.
> —Joseph Story
> *Advice to a Young Lawyer*

A. INTRODUCTION

Although the vast majority of legal disputes end in settlement or a trial court judgment, some do not, for various reasons. One party may simply be unwilling to abide by the trial court judgment, for financial, emotional, or reputational reasons. One party may believe that the trial court committed a serious error that affected the outcome. In other cases, the law governing the dispute may be uncertain, two public policies may conflict, and the issue may have very wide repercussions. Appellate litigation is the means of handling these cases.

How does a lawyer, in handling an appeal, reverse a loss or defend a win in the trial court? And how does a lawyer participate in making law? The adept appellate lawyer knows how to operate in a procedurally and intellectually complex system, refines the theory of the case to incorporate its appellate posture, and delivers the client's argument with nuance and sophistication. This chapter describes the appellate process and practice; Chapter 20 presents advanced advocacy tools.

For examples, this chapter draws on two opposing briefs in the fictional case of *Nelson v. HomeElderCare*, a lawsuit over the enforceability of a contract for drafting living wills between HomeElderCare and a disgruntled client, Roger Nelson. The briefs appear at pages 378 and 390. You should read them in conjunction with this chapter.

B. The Appellate Setting

1. The Purpose of Appeals in the Legal System

Appeals provide a check on the trial courts. The trial judge is engaged in a venture with some potential for error, which may be due to inadvertence, mistakes in judgment, or, less commonly, bias. Hence, the case may benefit from a second analysis by a somewhat removed observer, the appellate court.

Appeals also benefit the legal system by providing a mechanism for making and standardizing the law. Appellate courts are collegial bodies of experienced and respected judges who have gained broad perspective on legal issues from seeing a range of lower court results. Thus, appellate courts have the authority to make precedent. The appellate court seeks to promote uniformity and predictability in the law so that the law in each new case accords with the law in similar or related decided cases.

Yet the appellate system has several disadvantages. Appeals add delay to judicial resolution of disputes and prolong the strain of litigation. They impose costs on the parties and society: salaries for the judges and court personnel, building and equipment costs, and additional attorney and filing fees for the parties.

2. Differences Between Appeals and Trials

All courts seek to assure that the process is fair, the parties receive a just result, and the law is well served. As shown in Exhibit 19.1, the various types of courts contribute in different ways to these goals.

A trial court is the court of first impression. Trial judges see the case unfold in person before them, as the parties, experts, other witnesses, documents, and other exhibits come before them. Trial courts focus primarily on ascertaining the facts of the case and applying the law to the facts; they focus only secondarily on making law. The parties are known as "plaintiff" and "defendant," based on who sued whom. Possible outcomes include dismissal

EXHIBIT 19.1

COMPARISON OF TRIALS AND APPEALS

	Trial Court	Appeals Courts Intermediate	High
Primary Role of Court	initial determination through application of law to fact	review of trial court outcome and procedure	policy and lawmaking
Decisionmakers	trial judge; sometimes jury	usually panel of judges	usually entire court
Parties	plantiff defendant	appellant (petitioner) respondent (appellee)	
Presentation of Case	pleadings, motions, memoranda, witnesses, exhibits, oral arguments	transcript of trial, pleadings, motions, memoranda, exhibits; briefs and oral argument; lower court opinion(s)	
Possible Outcomes	dismissal, judgment for plaintiff, judgment for defendant	affirm, reverse, modify, remand to trial court	

with or without prejudice, judgment for plaintiff or defendant, or a mixed outcome on various counts.

Appellate courts determine whether the trial court drew supportable factual findings and focus on whether the trial court properly applied the substantive and procedural law. Cases arrive at the appellate court in file folders and boxes (or, increasingly, electronically submitted files) containing the transcript of the trial and hearings, the pleadings and other discovery, and the briefs of the parties. The only in-person contact is the oral argument and perhaps a pre-argument conference between the attorneys and a judge. The parties are known as "appellant" (or "petitioner") and "respondent" (or "appellee"). The appellant is the party bringing the appeal against the respondent, regardless of their roles in the lower court. The appellate court may affirm, reverse, or modify the trial court judgment or may remand the case back to the trial court with instructions.

Most jurisdictions have two levels of appellate courts. While the high court supervises the lower and intermediate courts, it focuses on the task of making the law and its underlying policies. (For brevity's sake, this chapter generally uses "judges" to include both judges of the intermediate court and justices of the supreme court.)

In the fictional HomeElderCare case, Roger Nelson is the plaintiff and respondent, while HomeElderCare is the defendant and appellant. The trial court entered a declaratory judgment in favor of Mr. Nelson, stating that his contract with HomeElderCare was invalid because the living will service constituted the unauthorized practice of law. HomeElderCare has appealed that ruling, seeking to have the declaratory judgment reversed.

3. Mandatory and Discretionary Review

Some appeals arise as a matter of right. In almost every jurisdiction, the intermediate appellate court must take nearly every appeal because a constitution or statute guarantees the right to one appeal. In many jurisdictions, some very serious cases, such as capital punishment or life imprisonment cases, are granted appeal to the high court as a matter of right.

In a two-tier appellate system, as to most cases, the high court exercises its discretion as to which appeals to hear. The would-be appellant petitions to the high court for a writ of certiorari compelling a lower court to transfer the record to the high court for review of alleged errors; the writ is either granted or denied. In other jurisdictions, the labels are "grant of review" or "denial of review." The justices vote on which cases to hear; for example, four or more of the nine members of the United States Supreme Court must vote in favor of review for the petitioner to obtain a writ of certiorari.

Various factors influence a high court's decision to grant discretionary review:

- Rulings among the intermediate courts of appeals conflict, undermining the predictability of the law.
- The case involves important or pressing questions.
- The lower court has ruled on the constitutionality of a statute.
- The lower court departed from an established line of precedent or practice.
- The high court seeks to harmonize policies or rules across a line of related cases.

The factors prompting discretionary review may be published in the court's rules, provided for by a statute on the court's jurisdiction, developed on a case-by-case basis, or presented in articles written by the justices. Because the decision to deny review is not a decision on the merits of the case, there is no precedential value to the denial of review.

In recognition of the federalist system, federal courts sometimes decline, or abstain from, deciding cases in a range of situations, thereby deferring to state courts. For example, the United States Supreme Court generally will not review a state supreme court decision that a government action violates both the state and federal constitutions, because the violation of the state constitution as interpreted by the high court of that state is sufficient to uphold the judgment.

The HomeElderCare appeal is an appeal as of right to the intermediate appellate court, the Minnesota Court of Appeals. In Minnesota, the state constitution guarantees the right to one appeal, generally to that court.

4. The Range of an Appeal

Usually one party is the winner, the other the loser, and the appeal is brought by the party that lost at the trial court level. The appellant may appeal all adverse rulings of the trial court. However, sometimes the appellant appeals only a portion of the final judgment, because there is no reversible error (explained below) in the unappealed portions of the case, a successful appeal as to certain matters would not have enough impact to be worth the cost, or a portion of the case is better left as is (because, for example, the factual record is weak).

In complex cases, both parties may be winners and losers as to different facets of the case. For example, the plaintiff may win on liability but lose on damages. If both parties are unhappy with the trial court ruling, both parties may appeal. In a cross-appeal, both parties are simultaneously appellants and respondents.

In the sample case, only HomeElderCare lost and appealed the trial court's adverse ruling.

5. The Scope of Appellate Review

Rules on the scope of appellate review define which trial court rulings, facts, and issues are properly before the appellate court. These rules preserve the proper roles of the trial and appellate courts and reduce the likelihood of appeals.

a. The Final Judgment Rule

Most appeals are taken from a "final judgment," which means that the trial court judgment was final as to the entire case (or perhaps as to a claim or party). A final judgment may be, for example, a grant of a motion to dismiss the whole case or a jury verdict followed by a judgment. Decisions that are not final include such actions as denial of a motion to dismiss and rulings on evidence to be admitted at trial. The final judgment rule gives the trial court an opportunity to conclude the case (or a significant portion of it) before the appeal stage.

Occasionally, a party will want to appeal a non-final ruling of the trial court; this type of appeal is called an "interlocutory appeal." Appellate courts routinely grant some interlocutory appeals, such as an appeal from an order granting, denying, or dissolving an injunction. Generally, however, appellate rules discourage interlocutory appeals because the would-be appellant could nonetheless go on to win the case and because a more completely adjudicated case will have a stronger factual record for the court to review on appeal.

When a trial court considers a major issue in the case to be unsettled by mandatory precedent, it may seek an appellate ruling early in the case. "Certifying" or "reserving" a question can occur within the federal court system, within the state court system, or from a federal district court to the high court of the state whose law governs the question. Court rules vary as to when certified questions are allowed.

In the HomeElderCare case, the trial judge granted summary judgment based on the record developed during discovery, because the important facts were virtually uncontroverted and the law could be applied without trial. The declaratory judgment disposed of the entire case and constituted a final judgment.

b. No New Facts on Appeal

An appeal is not a second trial; the appeals court does not receive new evidence. The appellate court reviews only whether the evidence at trial supports the factfinder's determination. If not, the appellate court may reverse the trial court judgment or remand the case to the trial court for re-determination.

In the HomeElderCare case, the parties submitted the case to the trial court and then to the appellate court on stipulated (agreed-upon) facts.

c. No New Issues or Theories on Appeal

The appellate court generally does not hear legal issues or theories that the trial court did not have a chance to address. The trial court need not have been apprised of every case, argument, and alternative line of reasoning presented on appeal, but the trial court must have had a chance to address the basic issues. This rule gives parties the incentive to present the case fully to the trial court and maximizes the likelihood of a correct ruling in the first instance.

For any issue one may want to raise on appeal, there is a means of preserving the issue for appeal during the trial court proceedings. These means include motions, such as a motion for a new trial, and objections to evidence during trial.

In the HomeElderCare case, as shown in the issue and statement of the case in HomeElderCare's brief, at page 382, the issues and legal theories presented on appeal are very similar to the issues presented to the trial court.

d. The Reversible Error Rule

The appellate court is interested only in errors that are substantial enough to justify reversal (in whole or in part) of the trial court ruling. An error meeting this test is called "reversible error," "prejudicial error," or "material error." An error not meeting this test is known as "harmless error," "non-prejudicial error," or "immaterial error." An error is not a reversible error if the trial court reached the right result, albeit based on incorrect reasoning. Thus, the appellate court focuses on matters of real consequence.

In the sample case, HomeElderCare argued that the trial court misapplied the law regarding the unauthorized practice of law and the validity of contracts for services not authorized by statute. Either, if established, would lead to reversal of the trial court judgment.

6. Standards of Appellate Review

An appellate court's discretion varies depending on the posture of the case. The "standard of review" expresses the appellate court's degree of discretion in reviewing the trial court's work and is a key element in the lawyers' arguments as well as the appellate court's analysis. In other words, appellate courts defer to the trial court to a greater or lesser degree based on the type of ruling or judgment under appeal:

- Rulings within the discretion of the trial court, such as whether to allow the plaintiff to amend the complaint a second time, can be overturned only if the ruling was an abuse of discretion—that is, arbitrary, capricious, based on the wrong law, or based on a clearly erroneous factual determination.
- A jury verdict is upheld unless as a matter of law reasonable minds could not have reached the jury's conclusions.
- Findings of fact by a trial judge can be overturned if they are clearly erroneous or contrary to the manifest weight of evidence.
- A judge's rulings on questions of law can be overturned if the lower court ruled incorrectly on the law and the error was material.

In the HomeElderCare case, because of the stipulated facts, appellant did not allege any errors in factfinding. The alleged errors were either questions of law or mixed questions of law and fact. Thus, the standard of review was whether the trial court correctly applied the law to the facts when it ruled that Mr. Nelson was entitled to summary judgment as a matter of law.

7. Appellate Procedure

As you prepare an appeal, you should research the appellate rules of your jurisdiction. For instance, your failure to file a brief within the prescribed briefing period may deprive your client of the right to oral argument. Although the details of appellate procedure differ among jurisdictions, the major steps do not. See Exhibit 19.2.

The initial preparation for an appeal actually occurs during the trial court stage. An appeal is grounded in the pleadings, discovery, motions, and trial, where the important facts and legal theories are first brought to the attention of the court and any errors are preserved for the appeal.

Within a specified time after the trial court has ruled, the appellant must file a notice of appeal with the appellate court and serve it on the opponent, as well as notify the trial court administrator. Shortly thereafter, if the respondent also wants to appeal some issues, it can initiate a cross-appeal.

Meanwhile, the appellant must arrange for compilation of the record. The typical record of a fully litigated case contains pleadings, motions, orders of the court, exhibits, a transcript of the trial proceedings, the charge to the jury, the verdict, the judgment, and the notice of appeal. The respondent may identify additional portions to be included in the record. The trial court administrator then forwards the record to the appellate court.

Also during this time, the appellate court may require a pre-hearing conference between one of the appellate judges or the court's designee and the parties' counsel, to focus or narrow the issues and to discuss what material the court would like covered. During this period, as well as later, settlement talks may occur between counsel.

EXHIBIT 19.2

STAGES OF CIVIL APPELLATE LITIGATION*
(CONTINUATION OF EXHIBIT 17.1)

Preparing for Appeal

- drafting and amending pleadings
- making all appropriate pre-trial motions
- getting all needed facts into evidence or, if the judge rules a fact inadmissible, noted in the record
- making needed objections and motions to preserve issues for appeal
- briefing all issues thoroughly

Framing the Appeal

- appellant files and serves notice of appeal (sixty days after trial court order or judgment)
- appellant requests trial court to prepare record and forward it to appellate court (ten days after filing notice of appeal)
- respondent may cross-appeal (fifteen days after service of notice of appeal)
- respondent may add to record (within ten days of appellant's notification of transcript)
- appellate court judge may hold a pre-hearing conference

Presenting the Argument

- appellant files its brief (thirty days after delivery of transcript)
- respondent files its brief (thirty days after service of appellant's brief or delivery of transcript ordered by respondent)
- appellant may file its reply brief (ten days after service of respondent's brief)
- amici may file briefs, if allowed by the court
- counsel present oral arguments

*The timeline is that of the Minnesota state appellate courts. *See* Minn. R. App. P. 104.01, 106, 110.02, 131.01.

On a specified date, the appellant must file and serve its brief. The brief asks the court to reverse or modify the judgment of the trial court and sets out the legal bases for the request.

The respondent's brief responds to appellant's arguments. It also sets forth affirmative arguments as to why the trial court ruled correctly in respondent's favor. Many respondents' attorneys write a rough draft of the respondent's brief during the appellant's briefing period and then add arguments on any unexpected topics after appellant's brief has arrived. This practice prompts respondent's counsel to argue the case affirmatively, as well as react to the appellant's brief.

The appellant may file a reply brief, which addresses any unexpected points in the respondent's brief that merit rebuttal.

Some appeals involve a brief by an amicus curiae—"friend of the court." An amicus brief is written by a non-party with a strong stake in the outcome of the case; the amicus typically is an organization with a broad perspective on the public policy aspects of the case. The appellate court decides whether to let amici participate in the case, based on whether they will contribute a viewpoint or arguments that the parties are not likely to present.

Following the exchange of briefs, the parties may engage in oral arguments before the court. Oral arguments are mandatory before some courts, rare before others; the practices of most courts fall somewhere in between. The oral argument is counsel's last chance to convince the court, but it certainly does not take the place of well written briefs.

8. Appellate Strategy and Ethics

The appeal of a case may be handled by the trial lawyer(s), or the case may pass to a new lawyer, or lawyers, for the appeal. Although the trial lawyer knows the case very well, a new lawyer may be more objective or have new insights, and the new lawyer will see the case as the appellate court will see it—through the record, not the trial itself. Furthermore, litigation at the trial-court level involves rather different skills than appellate practice; some lawyers specialize in appellate practice.

WHAT HAPPENS WHEN THE COMPUTER FAILS?

Martinelli v. Farm-Rite, Inc.
785 A.2d 33 (N.J. Super. Ct. App. Div. 2001).

Plaintiff, who operates a farm in Hammonton, New Jersey, claims defendant supplied him with a defective water pump resulting in the loss of his blueberry crop in 1993. Suit was filed on October 30, 1998 and the case was referred to arbitration on May 19, 2000. . . .

Upon completion of the arbitration proceeding, the arbitrators assessed liability at eighty percent upon defendant and twenty percent upon plaintiff; they awarded plaintiff damages of $150,000. Neither party filed a notice of rejection of the award and demand for a trial *de novo* within thirty days after the arbitration award was filed. See *R.* 4:21A-6(b)(1). On June 20, 2000 plaintiff filed a motion to confirm the arbitration award, *R.* 4:21A-6(b)(3), which defense counsel received on June 22, 2000. Upon receipt of the motion defense counsel reviewed his file. He discovered that due to an apparent system failure, his computerized diary had not alerted him to file a demand for a trial *de novo* within the thirty-day time period as required by *R.* 4:21A-6(b)(1).

Defense counsel's office was in the end stage of converting from an Alpha-Micro Mainframe Computer System to a local area network (LAN) PC Service System. Counsel relied on the computer "markup" system to diary statutes of limitations and other deadlines, including a diary notation to alert him when to file a demand for a trial *de novo*. Counsel had no backup diary system. Without dispute, counsel had no reason to suspect, in advance of the incident, that the system would not operate correctly. Not until counsel received the motion to confirm the arbitrators' award did the system failure become known and was the loss of the diary notation discovered.

At oral argument defense counsel acknowledged that he was unaware of any other circumstance in which the system failed. Although the reason for the system failure has not been conclusively determined, counsel suspects it was a malfunction of the system's software. . . .

A fact-sensitive analysis is necessary in each case to determine what constitutes an extraordinary circumstance [justifying a late filing]. *Hartsfield*, 149 *N.J.* at 618, 695 *A.2d* 259. In *Hartsfield*, the attorney's failure to supervise his secretary and review his diary was not considered an extraordinary circumstance. *Id.* at 619, 695 *A.2d* 259. . . .

We agree that a computer malfunction is not sufficient justification for late submission of documents to the court, whether required by statute, court rule or court order. One does not need to be an expert to recognize that computers do not always work. It is not uncommon for previously accessible data to suddenly disappear. There can be any number of reasons why a computer system fails. There can be human errors inputting and accessing the data, electrical failures, power surges, and computer viruses. Not all programs are as dependable as others. Quite simply, systems fail regularly and do not always perform to their specifications. Such an occurrence is neither exceptional, unusual, nor without precedent. . . .

Computer failures, not unlike human failures, must be anticipated. Just as with a manual diary system, where it is commonplace to have at least one backup system available in anticipation of mistakes which are bound to be made by attorneys and other office staff, the same should hold true when a diary system is computerized. In today's environment a computer failure, which results in the late filing of a demand for trial *de novo*, must be treated the same as a wrong date marked on a calendar or the failure of an attorney to properly supervise staff. It is an occurrence that can be anticipated and guarded against. . . .

An attorney is compelled to determine the appropriate method to assure compliance with the thirty-day rule. To permit a computer failure to constitute an excuse to file late is contrary to the underlying goals of the arbitration process—to bring about an inexpensive, expeditious adjudication of disputes and to help ease the caseload of the courts. *Behm*, 286 *N.J. Super.* at 573–74, 670 *A.2d* 40. . . .

When you are considering whether to appeal a case, you should look at the case carefully and objectively, to assess the areas of continuing controversy. The process of choosing whether to appeal and on which grounds entails several steps.

First, you must review the record to ascertain what did in fact occur in the trial court, compared to what you remember or others have told you. You should verify that witnesses stated what you think they did, the necessary motions were made, and so on.

Second, you must apply the substantive and procedural law to the court's rulings to discern whether any errors occurred and then evaluate whether any errors are within the appellate court's scope of review. As noted above, appellate courts typically do not review errors based on facts not presented to the trial court; errors based on issues or theories not raised at the trial level; and errors which, if corrected by the appellate court, would not result in at least a partial reversal, remand, or modification.

Next, you must evaluate each error according to the applicable standard of appellate review. Some rulings are extremely unlikely candidates for reversal, because the applicable standard of review gives considerable deference to the trial court ruling. In light of the standard of review, you should evaluate the quality of the law, policy, and facts on both sides:

- Do both sides have plausible arguments?
- Are your client's arguments supported by statute, mandatory precedent, persuasive precedent, commentary?
- Which side does public policy favor?
- How strong are the facts?

You should set aside errors that could not overcome the applicable standard of review or could not do so without a stretch that the court is unlikely to make.

Once you have thus discerned the potential bases for appeal, you should explore the scope of the appeal with your client, of course. Your client may not want to pursue one or more points, or your client may have a strong desire to pursue a particular point.

Finally, you should consider how many and which arguments to make. Few briefs contain more than three or four major arguments, because including more reduces the space for, and dilutes the effectiveness of, the stronger arguments. (Recall the survey summarized in Chapter 18 at page 192.) On occasion, you may make a large number of small arguments, in hopes of casting doubt on the overall fairness of the trial court proceedings; this tactic is common in the appellant's brief for a convicted criminal defendant.

Your choice of arguments should reflect your theory of the case. Appellate courts as well as trial courts seek a coherent and compelling understanding of your case to rule in your favor. As best you can, weave the appellate court's role and standard of review into your theory of the case. See Exhibit 19.3, an expanded theory-of-the-case diagram. For example, if the jury favored your client, stress the deference appellate courts afford juries. Or highlight the legal and policy facets of the case—these are significant concerns to an appellate court, especially the high court.

Much of the respondent's task is to respond to the grounds for appeal selected by the appellant. If the appellant does not raise an anticipated issue,

EXHIBIT 19.3

COMPONENTS OF AN APPELLATE THEORY OF THE CASE

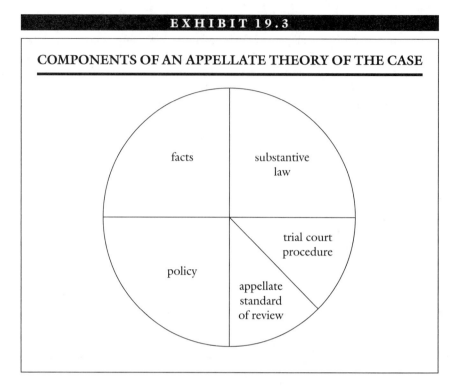

you need not address it. If, as respondent's counsel, you are considering a cross-appeal, you would follow the process just described. Whether shaping a cross-appeal or deciding which arguments to make on an issue under appeal, you should refine your theory of the case to incorporate the appellate posture.

In selecting grounds for appeal as well as points to cover in the brief, both appellant's and respondent's counsel must comply with the ethical principles regarding legal advocacy. The rules (detailed in Chapter 17) preclude pursuing frivolous claims or defenses, knowingly presenting false statements of fact, and knowingly failing to disclose known and adverse precedent not disclosed by opposing counsel. These rules are specific expressions of the lawyer's general duty to the legal system and justice, as well as to the client, to act with candor and with respect for the law.

The HomeElderCare appeal raises one major ground for appeal: the invalidity of the living will contract due to the unauthorized practice of law. The issue is within the scope of appellate review, and the standard of review is fairly favorable. HomeElderCare's case has some favorable law, public policy, and facts. HomeElderCare cares about this issue, especially because its resolution affects more than just Mr. Nelson's contract. And a single ground for appeal makes for a well focused brief.

C. THE FUNCTION OF THE APPELLATE BRIEF: AUDIENCE AND PURPOSE

The primary audience of an appellate brief is, of course, the court: the judges and their clerks. At the intermediate appellate court, cases typically are heard

HOW DO APPELLATE COURTS REACT
TO MERITLESS APPEALS?

Federated Mutual Insurance Co. v. Anderson,
920 P.2d 97 (Mont. 1996).

[Jones Equipment leased a feller buncher machine to Brent Anderson, doing business as Conifer Logging. The machine was delivered to Conifer on June 17, 1991, and it was destroyed by fire on July 17, 1991. Conifer notified its insurer, John Deere, of the loss on July 18, 1991. The insurance contract between John Deere and Conifer provided automatic coverage for new equipment provided that Conifer reported the acquisition and paid a new premium within thirty days of the acquisition.

Federated Mutual insured Jones Equipment and paid Jones for its loss. Federated then sought to recover from Conifer, which filed a third-party complaint against John Deere. The trial court denied John Deere's motion for summary judgment and granted Conifer summary judgment. John Deere appealed.]

As a final matter, Conifer requests that this Court sanction John Deere pursuant to Rule 32, M.R.App.P. Sanctions on appeal are appropriate when this Court "is satisfied from the record and the presentation of the appeal in a civil case that the same was taken without substantial or reasonable grounds." Rule 32, M.R.App.P.

This Court does not readily impose sanctions upon parties for filing frivolous appeals. However, given the inconsistent and conflicting positions John Deere has taken throughout this matter, its inaccurate citations to authority, and the lack of support for its claims on appeal, we conclude that sanctions are necessary and appropriate in this case.

. . .

John Deere's . . . argument . . . is that no automatic coverage existed because the feller buncher was destroyed thirty-one days after Conifer acquired it. According to John Deere, the day that the feller buncher was delivered must be counted in calculating the thirty-day period of automatic coverage. John Deere's argument, however, is contrary to the universal rule that, unless a contrary intent is clearly manifested, the first day or the day upon which the act was done or the event occurred is generally excluded in computing periods of time. Even more troubling is the fact that, as part of its effort to urge this Court to adopt a different method of calculation, John Deere cites four cases in support of its position; however, three of those cases actually cite the general rule that the first day should be excluded in calculating the thirty-day grace period in insurance contracts and the fourth case was effectively overruled more than 120 years ago. For example, John Deere cites *American National Bank v. Service Life Insurance Co.* (7th Cir. 1941), 120 F.2d 579, 582, *cert. denied* (1941), 314 U.S. 654,

62 S.Ct. 104, 86 L.Ed. 524, to further its argument; however, on the same page to which John Deere cites, the court states: "[W]e think the weight of authority supports the rule of excluding the first day and including the last where no other or different method has been indicated by the parties."

. . .

Finally, John Deere's sincerity on appeal must be questioned in light of its inconsistent theories for denial of coverage which have culminated in this meritless appeal. For example, on July 18, 1991, John Deere's insurance agent wrote on the property loss notice that the policy's "30 day coverage extension should apply." On August 21, 1991, however, one of John Deere's insurance adjusters notified Conifer that John Deere was denying coverage because the thirty-day "waiting period" would not have been satisfied until July 24, 1991.

. . .

Because of John Deere's meritless appeal, Conifer has incurred unnecessary and substantial legal fees to obtain the coverage to which the District Court determined it was entitled under each of its theories. In addition, Conifer has been caused unnecessary delay during the pendency of this appeal. As we stated in *Reilly v. Farm Credit Bank of Spokane* (1993), 261 Mont. 532, 535, 863 P.2d 420, 422: "When an appeal is entirely unfounded and causes delay, the respondent is entitled to reasonable costs and attorney's fees."

Therefore, on the basis of the inconsistent and conflicting positions John Deere has taken throughout this matter, its baseless claims on appeal, and its inaccurate citations in its appellate brief, we assess sanctions against John Deere pursuant to Rule 32, M.R.App.P., and order it to pay Conifer's reasonable costs and attorney fees incurred in defending this appeal.

by a panel of judges; three is the most common number. Intermediate courts hear only particularly important cases en banc, i.e., as a full court; sometimes after a panel hears a case initially, a full court may rehear the case if the losing party convinces the full court of its significance. Interlocutory appeals may be decided by a single judge or a panel. As a general rule, the high court hears all cases en banc, which typically involves seven or nine justices. Whatever the number of judges hearing your case, they are likely to have a range of backgrounds, areas of expertise, world views, and preliminary leanings in cases like yours.

The primary purpose of the appellate brief is, of course, to persuade the court to rule in your client's favor and to do so based on sound legal and factual bases. To persuade the court, you must educate those who know little about the area of law involved, inform all of the judges about your client's situation, and demonstrate the justness of your client's position to those who are skeptical.

Your brief will also be read by opposing counsel and your client. The brief should convince opposing counsel of the strengths of your case, thereby enhancing the chances of settlement, if that possibility exists at such a late stage. For your client, your brief should demonstrate your continuing commitment to the case and provide insight into its legal strengths and weaknesses.

D. The Format of the Appellate Brief

Every court has its own rules as to appellate brief format, so you should always read and follow the applicable rules. The format featured in this part is based on Minnesota's appellate rules, because the sample HomeElderCare case is on appeal to the Minnesota Court of Appeals.[1] Other courts may require different components or sequences of components; the text below discusses some of the more common variations. Regardless of the required format, you should aim for a brief that is complete, correct, coherent, comprehensible, and convincing.

An important court rule to know is the rule on how long a brief may be. In Minnesota, for example, a principal brief may be forty-five pages long, exclusive of tables and appendices, or 1,300 lines or 14,000 words. The lawyer must certify that the line or word count is met.[2]

While the appellate brief is the most formal and elaborate of the various documents used to present legal analysis, it has strong parallels to the office memo and the motion practice memorandum, as shown in Exhibit 19.4.

1. Classic Components of the Main Brief

The following text discusses the components in the appellate brief as they appear to the reader. Of course, you need not write them in this order; indeed, you should save the table of contents and table of authorities until last. As you read this text, you should refer to one or both of the sample briefs at pages 378 and 390.

a. Opening Components

The title page contains the docket number of the case; the name of the appeals court; the case name; the title of the document, such as "Appellant's Brief"; and the names, addresses, phone numbers, and attorney registration numbers of the lawyers. The plaintiff typically is listed first, and both parties' roles in the trial court as well as on appeal are noted. The terms used to identify the parties should be consistent throughout the brief and may be governed by convention or court rule. The title page may be color-coded by the identity of the party.

---

1. *See* Minn. R. App. P. 128.02.
2. Minn. R. Civ. App. Pro. 132.02 subdiv. 3.

EXHIBIT 19.4

COMPARISON OF OFFICE MEMO, MOTION PRACTICE MEMORANDUM, AND APPELLATE BRIEF

Office Memo	Motion Practice Memorandum	Appellate Brief
caption	caption	title page
		table of contents
		table of authorities
issues	introduction or summary	statement of issues
	issues	
short answers	facts	statement of the case (covering facts and procedure)
facts	procedure	summary of argument
discussion	argument	argument
conclusion	conclusion with signature	conclusion with signature

The table of contents lists the brief components, including all of the point headings within the argument (described below) and starting pages for each item listed. The table of contents may be the first page the reader consults, so if the point headings are written with care, the reader will have a clear, concise, and logically ordered overview of the argument.

The table of authorities lists cases, statutes, rules, and other authorities cited in the brief. The table also lists the pages on which each source is cited; "passim" follows the initial page number for a very frequently cited source. Generally, authorities are grouped by type and presented in alphabetical or numerical order within groups. As the rules permit, you may be able to order or group authorities so as to emphasize certain types of authorities, thereby driving home a particular view of the case. For example, you may choose not to break out mandatory and persuasive precedent if you are seeking a change in the law and thus relying heavily on persuasive precedent.

For example, note that HomeElderCare's brief (at page 380) lists cases first, then statutes, reflecting HomeElderCare's emphasis on the common

---

WHAT DO APPELLATE JUDGES SEEK
IN APPELLATE BRIEFS?

A brief will be most helpful to the judge, and net the brief-writer the greatest gain, if the judge can use the brief to compose an opinion in the brief-writer's favor. A kitchen-sink presentation may confound and annoy the reader more than it enlightens her. In busy courts, judges work under the pressure of a relentless clock. If a brief runs too long, the judge may not read beyond the summary of the argument. The same fate may attend a brief that makes arguments a judge cannot reasonably be expected to buy. Of prime importance, a brief should be trustworthy. If authorities are not accurately described, the judge will lose confidence in the reliability of the brief and its author; if the judge reads on at all, she will do so with a skeptical eye.

  —*Hon. Ruth Bader Ginsburg*
   Supreme Court of the United States

A judge, when writing an opinion, strives to craft precise and well-formulated legal holdings that derive from careful analysis of the facts, the procedural posture of the case, interpretation of relevant documents and application of relevant authority. A brief must adhere to those same standards of precision and care.

  —*Hon. E. Norman Veasey*
   Chief Justice, Supreme Court of Delaware

The purpose of the brief is to persuade me that the outcome the writer wants the court to reach is the correct outcome, and the path to that outcome is the correct one. Careful, cogent thought, clearly and cogently expressed, is what convinces me. The brief-writer is most helpful to me when she tells me not only what decision to reach but how to get there.

  Never loosely speculate about what the judge might think is important. Brief-writers should make it so clear that the judge will instantly know what is important and why. Discuss that and little else.

  —*Hon. John M. Duhé Jr.*
   United States Court of Appeals for the Fifth Circuit

Judges on Briefing: A National Survey 6, 17, 4 (Bryan A. Garner comp., 2001).

---

law test of unauthorized practice. Mr. Nelson's brief (at page 392) uses the reverse order, emphasizing the statutes on unauthorized practice and guardianship.

  Other appellate formats merge the information in the tables of contents and authorities into a single table, the table of points and authorities. This table lists the major components of the brief as well as the point headings from the argument, along with page numbers. Each point heading is followed by a list of several or all of the authorities cited.

b. Issue

This component poses the questions the court must answer to resolve the case. Most issues combine law and facts; the law may be either substantive or procedural or both. The trial court's answer is stated after each issue as is a short list of the most pertinent primary authorities.

The issues are closely related to the point headings in the argument (discussed below). Both reflect the organization of the argument, and the major point headings usually answer the issues. Some briefs include sub-issues, which mirror the minor point headings.

The issues usually should be a full question (not a phrase introduced by "whether") and as concise as possible given the ideas to be conveyed. By tradition, they should be answerable with "yes" or "no." Some courts, Minnesota included, require that the issues be phrased neutrally; you can slant the issues only as far as the court would if it were writing an opinion in your favor.

The issues from the two HomeElderCare sample briefs are reprinted in Exhibit 19.5, along with the point headings from the two briefs. Both sets of issues are neutral enough to be stated by a court, yet both clearly suggest what the favored answer is. HomeElderCare's fact-centered issue focuses on how HomeElderCare serves its clients and promotes their self-determination. Mr. Nelson's issues focus on the unauthorized practice of law.

In other jurisdictions, the statement of issues may be called "questions presented." Some court rules do not require the trial court's position and the listing of authorities.

c. Statement of the Case

This component contains two portions: (1) the procedural history of the case and (2) the real-world facts of the case. Under the Minnesota rules, this component begins with one or two paragraphs specifying the nature of the case, the court and judge at the trial level, and the procedural history of the case.

The procedural history should reflect the direct line of procedural events leading from the outset of the case to the appeal. The appellant may want to show that he or she preserved the right to appeal the pertinent issues, by making the required motions or objections, for instance. The respondent emphasizes the favorable ruling and reasoning of the trial court, the respondent's hidden ally. The statement of the case must contain citations to the record to support each procedural fact.

The second portion of the statement of the case, the statement of the real-world facts, can be one of the most persuasive parts of the brief. Facts must be stated fully and fairly:

- Relevant and background facts must be presented; you may include persuasive residual facts, as long as you do so judiciously.

EXHIBIT 19.5

APPELLATE ISSUES AND POINT HEADINGS

Appellant HomeElderCare's Brief

Issues	Point Headings
Is a service contract between Appellant, a nonprofit geriatric services agency, and Respondent, an elderly client, invalid on the grounds that a trained social worker practiced law when she helped the elderly client fill in the blanks on a living will form?	This Court should reverse the summary declaratory judgment in favor of Respondent and should instead grant Appellant's cross-motion for summary judgment, thereby upholding the contract under which a trained social worker for a nonprofit geriatric services agency helped an elderly client fill in the blanks on a living will form.

    A.   The trained social worker did not practice law when she helped the client fill in the blanks on a living will form.

    B.   Even if the social worker practiced law, the contract is valid because the social worker provided the living will service without fraud or incompetence and incidentally to non-legal professional services.

    C.   Public policy favors living wills and therefore also favors a service provider who assists a client in filling in the blanks on the statutory living will form.

Respondent Mr. Nelson's Brief

Issues	Point Headings
I. Did a social worker—who is neither trained nor licensed to practice law—engage in the unauthorized practice of law when she prepared a defective living will for an elderly client for a fee?	I. The trial court properly ruled that Appellant HomeElderCare's social worker engaged in the unauthorized practice of law when she prepared Respondent Mr. Nelson's living will for a fee.
II. In light of this unauthorized practice of law, is the contract between the social work agency and the client unenforceable, so as to excuse the client from paying for the defective document?	II. Because of this unauthorized practice of law, the contract between Appellant HomeElderCare and Respondent Mr. Nelson for preparation of the living will is unenforceable, as the trial court property held.

- Ethical and tactical considerations clearly dictate that unfavorable facts be presented.
- The brief is on firmest ground when stating facts that are plainly and indisputably stated in the record.
- However, the fact statement may note what seems to have been true based on what is known (inferences).
- The fact statement may note what is not in the record but presumably would have been if the opposing party could have brought the evidence forward.
- Argumentative statements and legal conclusions should be avoided in the statement of the case. For instance, it would be improper to characterize an act as "negligent."
- Of course, favorable "facts" may not be created to suit an advocate's purpose.
- The fact statement should contain all facts discussed in the argument, at least in general terms; in complicated cases, factual details may be reserved for the pertinent portions of the argument.

Your presentation of the facts should help the court see the events from your client's perspective. For example, although the classic organizational theme for facts is chronology, you may decide to open with a paragraph that highlights the critical event from your client's perspective, even if it did not occur first. Alternatively, you may use topical organization to emphasize the important facts from your client's perspective. You may use perceptual organization to tell the story the way your client experienced it and then present the perspectives of others.

In the appellate setting, you must refer the court to the evidence of a fact, for example, a witness' testimony at trial or deposition, or a document admitted at trial. You also may refer to the trial judge's fact findings or the jury's verdict. Indeed, if the case is on its second round of appeal, you also can refer to the intermediate appellate court's statement of the facts.

In both HomeElderCare sample briefs, the statement of the case begins with the case's procedural history. Both sample briefs convey essentially the same information, yet they convey different subtexts. The HomeElderCare statement (at page 382) underscores the effect of the declaratory judgment in shutting down its living will service for all clients, while Mr. Nelson's statement (at pages 393-94) focuses on the favorable trial court ruling.

Both presentations of the real-world facts convey the necessary information from the stipulated record, including unfavorable facts. Through seemingly minor differences, they create contrasting impressions. For example, HomeElderCare's brief suggests that Mr. Nelson was responsible for the error, while Mr. Nelson's brief intimates the opposite. HomeElderCare's statement begins with a description of the valuable services HomeElderCare provides for its clients, while Mr. Nelson's statement begins with Mr. Nelson's ill health and mis-drafted living will. The HomeElderCare fact statement proceeds topically, while Mr. Nelson's follows in a loosely chronological organization.

In other jurisdictions, the two portions of the statement of case may be separate labeled components. Another variation is to present the procedural information at the conclusion of the real-world facts.

d. Summary of Argument

More than any other component of the brief, the summary of the argument is written to capture the attention of the reader. One to three paragraphs long, it signals what is really at stake, presents your theory of the case, and provides an overview of the argument to come, which should appear sensible and straightforward. The tone of the summary should be affirmative; it should not be framed as a rebuttal.

The HomeElderCare briefs each contain a summary of the argument, HomeElderCare's as a separate component (at page 384) and Mr. Nelson's as the first part of the argument (at page 396). Both preview the legal arguments. Both also weave in their theories of the case: HomeElderCare's summary posits the living will service as carefully designed, responsive to clients' wishes, primarily moral and ethical in content, and in accord with the public policy favoring living wills. Mr. Nelson's brief states: "A social worker should not be paid for defective legal work."

Jurisdictions differ on whether a summary is required. Even if it is not required, you often will want to include this material, whether in a separate component so labeled or at the outset of the argument.

e. Point Headings

Point headings in appellate briefs present the main assertions the court must accept to rule in that party's favor. Read as a set, the point headings should provide a clear and logical outline of the brief, showing the order of and relationships among the arguments. Indeed they appear in the table of contents as an outline; this is what many readers look to first. They also appear at the appropriate places within the argument.

Each point heading should be a single sentence. It should be forcefully phrased: concise, to the point, affirmative in tone. Generally, a major heading combines legal rules and facts to form a distinct conclusion that the court should reach to rule for the client. Most major headings reflect procedural as well as substantive law, because cases arise in particular procedural postures. Minor point headings provide steps of the analysis, policy, or reasons. They need not always be complete fact + law combinations.

You should strive to make your point headings informative. Very general point headings are of little help to the court, because they do not focus on a specific legal problem and do not arise from the facts of the case. Too many facts or legal principles make for point headings that are unduly lengthy, clumsy, and hard to grasp. If the reader must read the heading more than once to understand it, it needs rewriting: rephrase it into multiple major point headings, convert it to a major heading with minor headings, or keep the main point in the heading and leave subordinate points to the text of the argument.

Point headings are organized in outline form, preceded by Roman numerals (I, II), capital letters (A, B), and Arabic numerals (1, 2). Take care not to use headings more detailed than these three levels, or you may lose your reader. As in outlining, if there is no "B," you should not use an "A."

To set point headings apart from the text and show their hierarchical relationships, use the format, if any, that is required by your court. If the court does not require a particular format, use any of the following or a combination: open lines above and below the heading, indentation, underlining, boldface, italics, initial caps, and all capital letters. Use the latter option sparingly, if at all, because it reduces readability.

The point headings from the two HomeElderCare sample briefs, which appear in Exhibit 19.5, are assertive, but not overwrought. Taken together, they link facts, law (both procedural and substantive), and policy (HomeElderCare's more so than Mr. Nelson's). The relationships among the headings are clear: by the overall issue and A, B, and C in HomeElderCare's brief; by a transitional phrase and I, II in Mr. Nelson's brief. The point headings convey the key dimensions of the case, the parties, living will drafting, fee, contract validity, unauthorized practice of law.

The point headings differ, as they should. Only Mr. Nelson's point headings refer to the rulings of the trial court. HomeElderCare's point headings posit the case as a contract case which includes a sub-topic of unauthorized practice of law, while Mr. Nelson's headings posit the case as involving two equal issues.

f. Argument

This component explains why the court should rule for your client. The appellant concentrates on undermining the trial court's reasoning and rulings, while the respondent uses the trial court as its ally on appeal. That is, the appellant's brief tries to demonstrate reversible error, while the respondent's brief tries to maintain the status quo. Appellate advocacy is four-dimensional involving the facts, substantive law, policy, and two-pronged procedural law (trial-court procedure and appellate review). See Exhibit 19.6.

Legal advocacy entails convincing the court to apply substantive legal rules to the facts of the case so as to favor your client. To do this, you must cite to and explain pertinent mandatory authority; you may cite helpful persuasive authority and may discuss unfavorable persuasive authority. You must reason deductively from the law to the facts, and you should bolster your deductive reasoning with reasoning by example where appropriate. You should directly or indirectly refute the competing authorities and assertions of your opponent, whether they pertain to what the law is or how to apply the law to the facts.

In many cases, the argument also discusses public policy, especially when the case is in the jurisdiction's high court and challenges the current state of the law. Even in a routine case briefed for an intermediate appellate court, policy can be important; intermediate appellate courts sometimes create precedent and seek to do so based on solid policy grounds.

In addition, at the appellate level the interaction between procedural law and substantive law is complex. The standard of appellate review envelops

EXHIBIT 19.6

PROCEDURAL AND SUBSTANTIVE LAW + FACT + POLICY DIAGRAM OF APPELLATE BRIEF

declaratory judgement → granted on summary judgment by trial court; so, standard of review =
- any genuine issues of material facts? no; see stipulation
- did trial court err in applying law?

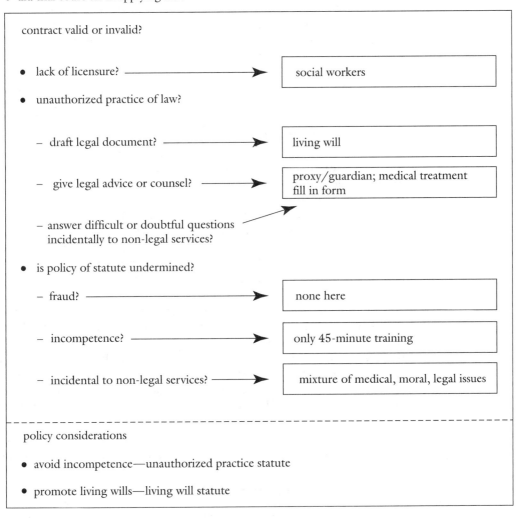

trial-level procedural law, which in turn envelops the substantive law, which in turn is applied to the facts.

The brief should present and reflect the applicable standard of appellate review. If the same standard of review governs all of the issues, it can be stated at the outset of the argument. If different standards govern different issues, then the discussion of each topic should begin with a paragraph or so on the applicable standard of review. If both sides agree on the applicable standard of review and it is a common one, the statement of the standard of review can be very brief.

Of course, legal propositions must be fully and accurately cited. The traditional location for these citations is in the text, immediately after the legal propositions. With the advent of word processing and widespread use of computers, some lawyers now choose to provide citations in footnotes. In a brief with citations in footnotes, the argument itself is easier to read, but the reader sees the authority for a proposition more immediately in a brief with citations in the text. Neither approach is obviously better.

Generally, you need not provide citations to the record as you refer to facts within the argument, because the citations in the fact statement suffice. However, you should provide appropriate citations to the record if you quote from the record, provide more detail than in the fact statement, or want to highlight a particular passage.

Footnotes are routinely used to present content that is tangential to the main text. A footnote may convey information that is needed to make the brief more complete, yet would interrupt the argument's flow. The reader should not lose any essential meaning by not reading a footnote.

To promote the flow of your argument, you should be especially careful to use not only point headings, but also transitional words or phrases, overviews, and summaries to signal the relationships among the parts of the argument.

The arguments in the HomeElderCare briefs both address the package of procedural and substantive law, policy, and facts depicted in Exhibit 19.6. (Exhibit 19.6 is phrased neutrally; the same diagram can be used to sketch arguments to be made for one party or the other.) Both briefs grapple with statutory language, rely on case law, and reason by example from the leading case to the facts of this case—arriving at different conclusions, of course. Both briefs use policy arguments; although the court is not the high court, policy is especially important where the issue is new and the rule of law itself calls for policy analysis. Given the nearly de novo standard of review (which appears near the opening in both briefs), neither brief emphasizes the trial court's opinion, although Mr. Nelson's brief refers to the trial court's ruling more often than does HomeElderCare's brief. Both briefs use footnotes— HomeElderCare's only for tangential points, Mr. Nelson's also for citations.

g. Closing Components

The conclusion is a concise statement of the relief requested. It need not, but may, restate the argument, although conclusions rarely cite authority and should not raise any new arguments. Keep it short. A signature block follows the conclusion. The closing typically reads "Respectfully submitted," followed by the attorney's signature and information (name, client representation, firm affiliation, contact information, and attorney registration number).

The conclusions of the two sample briefs contain straightforward statements of the respective clients' desired outcomes. Mr. Nelson's conclusion briefly restates his two main arguments, framed as favorable trial court rulings.

h. Other Components

One or more of the following may be required in your jurisdiction:

- a request for (or waiver of) oral argument, if oral argument is not automatically granted;
- a statement of the appellate court's jurisdiction;
- a statement certifying that the brief has been served;
- a citation to any published opinions of lower courts;
- a preliminary statement, which typically covers the identities of the parties, the nature of the case, and its disposition below; and
- citations to or quotations from statutes or constitutional provisions.

Nearly every jurisdiction requires an appendix at the end of the appellant's brief that contains pertinent parts of the record. The respondent's brief may include additional appendix material if the needed parts of the record are not in the appellant's appendix. In some jurisdictions, the appendix includes constitutional or statutory provisions. Be sure to read the appellate rules on brief format for details of these components.

2. Respondent's Brief and the Reply Brief

As intimated above, in general, the respondent's brief follows the same form as the appellant's brief. The statement of the issues, real-world facts, and procedural posture may be optional, but a savvy advocate usually does not let opposing counsel have the only say on these matters.

The reply brief has no particular format. Its purpose is to respond to points in the respondent's brief that are not covered in appellant's main brief. Thus most common format includes a summary, the argument, and the conclusion. It is less common to include a fact or issue statement.

E. REVIEW OF CHAPTER 19

Appeals provide an important safeguard against trial court error as well as a mechanism for making law. The following rules preserve the proper roles of the trial and appellate courts: the final judgment rule, the prohibition against new facts and theories on appeal, the reversible error rule, standards of review, and mandatory and discretionary review.

An important step in the appellate process is the preparation of the appellate brief, written to convince the court (as well as opposing counsel and the client) of the justness of the client's position. A typical appellate brief format includes the following components:

(1) The title page identifies the case, the court, the lawyers, and the document.

(2) The tables orient the reader to the points made and legal authorities relied on in the brief.

(3) The statement of issues frames the questions to be decided by the appellate court.

(4) The statement of the case informs the court of the real-world and procedural facts of the case.

(5) The summary of argument presents the theory of the case and a brief distillation of the legal arguments.

(6) The argument draws together substantive and procedural law, policy, and facts to make the case for the client's desired outcomes, with point headings flagging the main assertions.

(7) The conclusion states the relief desired by the client and includes the lawyer's signature.

The resulting brief should be complete, correct, cohesive, comprehensible, and convincing. Further strategies for achieving these criteria appear in Chapter 18 (fundamentals of advocacy) and Chapter 20 (advanced advocacy).

ADVANCED ADVOCACY

> Tell all the Truth but tell it slant—
> Success in Circuit lies—
>   —Emily Dickinson

A. INTRODUCTION

Truly successful legal advocacy entails not only careful selection and development of points to be made on the client's behalf, but also artful presentation of those points. Chapter 18 focuses on the former. This chapter focuses on the latter, answering this question: What makes legal prose persuasive? The topics discussed in this chapter generally are applicable to other advocacy settings as well.

For examples, this chapter draws on the sample briefs in the fictional HomeElderCare appeal at pages 378 and 390.

B. AN ANALOGY: PHOTOGRAPHY

Photographers and lawyers share the same opportunity: to use the tools of their trade to present what exists or has happened in a certain light, to make a point about their subjects. Of course, the tools of the two trades are rather different. Photographers use lighting, lenses, film, and development processes in various ways. Lawyers use only words, but words are remarkably powerful and flexible tools.

Ultimately, photographers and lawyers can alter how the observer sees a subject. In a compelling photograph, a photographer can alter the viewer's understanding of the subject. In a compelling argument, the lawyer can alter the court's understanding of the law and, indeed, bring about a change in the law.

C. SLANTING YOUR PROSE

The way something is said often determines its impact. This part discusses five aspects of writing style that you can use to maximize the persuasive impact of your prose: space allocation, sequence, syntax, semantics, and special sentences.

1. Space Allocation

The more we read about a topic, the more we attend to it, the more we recall about it, and the greater the importance we attach to it. Hence you should allocate more space to the material you want the reader to remember and less space to the material you need to include yet want to de-emphasize.

This strategy applies to various components of the brief. For example:

- In the statement of case or facts, you could write several paragraphs on your client's circumstances and motivations, while covering the adverse effect of the client's actions on the opponent in only a few lines.
- The summary of argument should be devoted almost entirely to the strong points of your client's case, and only a phrase or two should refer to the weak points, if even that.
- In the argument, you could present several paragraphs on a favorable element of the rule and only one paragraph on a more troublesome element.
- You could state a favorable rule in some detail, quoting and paraphrasing and illustrating it (without undue repetition), and provide a terser statement of an adverse rule.

If you must state your opponent's argument for candor or rebuttal purposes, do so very briefly.

One way to implement this strategy is to allocate percentages to various topics before you write and then monitor how well your draft complies with your allocation. Or, after you have completed a draft, run a word count of the brief's components, and compare the results to your desired allocation.

The HomeElderCare sample briefs reveal contrasting space allocations. For example, HomeElderCare's statement of the case allocates only two lines to the trial court ruling, while Mr. Nelson's brief explains that ruling in four lines. As shown in Exhibit 20.1, Mr. Nelson's argument

EXHIBIT 20.1

SEQUENCE AND SPACE ALLOCATION IN ARGUMENTS

# lines	Appellant HomeElderCare	# lines	Respondent Nelson
7	Standard of review	5	Standard of review
94	No unauthorized practice	120	Unauthorized practice
68	* • no legal advice; not difficult or doubtful	11	* • policy is to protect public
		3	* • social worker, not attorney
11	• not "legal document"	14	* • "legal document"
13	* • not will	63	• legal advice; difficult or doubtful questions
33	Valid contract		
7	* • no fraud	3	* • charging fee
10	• no incompetence	10	* • persuasive precedent
3	* • incidental to professional services	46	Contract unenforceable
45	Public policy	5	• general rule invalidating contract by unlicensed practitioner
16	* • right to privacy and control of body	9	• exception based on legislative intent
19	* • role of living wills in allocating health care resources	24	• incompetence
8	• HEC's role in completing living will forms	9	* • public policy of unauthorized practice statute
		8	* • financial gain
	* strong topics		

regarding unauthorized practice runs 94 lines; HomeElderCare's, 120 lines. Mr. Nelson's argument includes 10 lines on persuasive precedent; Home-ElderCare's brief has none.

2. Sequence

According to the primacy effect, we process most thoroughly and remember best the information that appears at the start of a text. According to the recency effect, we process and remember nearly as well the information that appears last. Information in the middle of a text recedes in memory.

As you organize your brief, you must, of course, follow format requirements, and you must present the material within each component in a logical order. For instance, chronological, topical, or perceptual sequences generally work best for fact statements. In devising your sequence of legal topics, threshold issues generally precede other issues, claims precede defenses, etc.

If several sequences are permissible and logical, you should take advantage of the primacy and recency effects. You may choose to follow one of these sequences:

- The sandwich sequence: Present your strongest material first, sandwich your weakest material in the middle, and finish with your second strongest material. This sequence reflects both the primary and recency effects.
- The running-start sequence: Present your strongest material first, so that it makes a strong impression and dispels most of the doubts the reader might have. Then present your next strongest material, so as to dispel most remaining doubts. And so on, until the last doubt is dispelled.
- The momentum sequence: Start with weaker material and finish with the strongest, thereby starting slowly but finishing with your strongest material.

These sequences can be used in various components: opening and closing the statement of the case, ordering the issues and hence the main legal topics (or rules) within the argument; ordering the elements within a legal rule.

The sample HomeElderCare briefs demonstrate these strategies. Mr. Nelson's statement of the case's facts begins with his situation, while HomeElderCare's begins with the services HomeElderCare provides; both authors led with the client's strong facts. As synopsized in Exhibit 20.1, HomeElderCare's argument on the unauthorized practice of law sandwiches the most difficult topic (legal document) between favorable topics (legal advice and testamentary wills). Mr. Nelson's argument on contract invalidity displays the momentum sequence: a few lines of general principles, the leading adverse precedent, a discussion of policy, and the clearly favorable argument about HomeElderCare's charging of fees.

At the small-scale level, although you usually will follow the introduction-rule-application-conclusion (IRAC) sequence, you may deviate from this pattern for persuasive purposes. For example, you may lead with a fact discussion or policy if these are your client's strengths.

For example, in footnote 3 of the HomeElderCare brief (at page 385), the facts on charging a fee precede the statement of the rule because the facts are far more favorable than the rule. Mr. Nelson's argument on unauthorized practice (at page 396) begins with a discussion of the policy underlying that rule and Mr. Nelson's situation; the rule and its application follow.

3. Syntax

Readers respond more to ideas presented in a strongly framed sentence than to ideas couched in an obscure manner. Careful use of syntax allows you to highlight material you want the reader to remember and downplay material you want to de-emphasize. For instance, you should de-emphasize concessions and your opponent's arguments that need to be stated for rebuttal purposes. Here are some specific methods:

- State favorable material in short, simple sentences, and state unfavorable material in long, complex (but still understandable) sentences.

Complex sentences draw attention to the structure of the sentence and away from the sentence's content.

- Place unfavorable material in dependent clauses and favorable material in main clauses. Main clauses demand more attention than dependent clauses.
- Use the active voice for verbs relating favorable material, and use the passive voice for verbs relating unfavorable material. Active voice demands more attention than passive voice. Also, with passive voice, you can obscure the actor; this strategy is appropriate where the actor is unknown or unimportant or where you do not want to highlight who the actor is.
- Similarly, use nominalization, instead of a simple verb, for unfavorable information. Nominalization and passive voice have similar purposes and effects.

Exhibit 20.2 shows how these strategies are used for persuasive effect in the HomeElderCare sample briefs' fact statements.

EXHIBIT 20.2

SYNTAX

Sentence length

- These social workers are not lawyers. (Nelson brief)
- When Mr. Nelson was hospitalized, his son realized that the living will nominated Roger Nelson's proxy for medical decisions to be his guardian for financial decisions, although Roger Nelson now desires otherwise. (HomeEldercare brief)

Dependent/main clauses

- While neither Ms. Hall nor Mr. Nelson can remember the details of their interaction leading up to the defective document [dependent clause], HomeElderCare social workers, including Ms. Hall, have followed certain procedures [main clause]. (Nelson brief)

Active/passive voice

- The social workers do not deviate from the form. . . . [active] (HomeElderCare brief)
- In this living will, Mr. Nelson's minister was designated as the proxy authorized to make medical decisions. . . . [passive] (Nelson's brief)

Nominalization

- Ms Hall's practice is to provide a standard explanation of the roles of proxies, guardians, and conservators. . . . (HomeElderCare brief)

4. Semantics

Readers respond more to concepts stated in vivid terms than to concepts stated in bland terms. Use vivid words for material you want your reader to notice and recall, and use nondescript language for material you want your reader to notice less.

Perhaps the most important semantic choice is how to label the parties, where court rules do not mandate or forbid certain labels.

- One option is to use procedural labels, such as Plaintiff and Defendant or Appellant and Respondent. This first option is the most abstract, and the reader may feel rather distanced from the situation or even confused about who plays which roles in the litigation.
- A middle ground is to use labels reflecting the parties' roles in the dispute, such as buyer and seller, landlord and tenant. In most situations, this option comes closest to the way the court needs to think about the parties.
- A third option is to use their proper names. This option personalizes the parties the most, especially if they are individuals.

If you are writing about individuals and using their names, you have several further options. Some legal writers prefer to use only last names, which sounds matter-of-fact, while others prefer Mr. Nelson or Dr. Richards, for example, which sounds more respectful. You should use first names only if the individual is a child. If two or more individuals have the same last name, you should use differentiating words such as "Mr." and "Ms." or both the first and last names.

Less obvious but equally important are the labels you use for the key legal concepts in the case. Most legal concepts can be referred to by more than one name, and some labels carry more serious connotations than others. Generally you will want to use the serious label for a cause of action if your client is the wronged party and the milder label if your client is the defendant.

Finally, pay close attention to the verbs you use to describe the actions of various parties. Some verbs are more vivid than others. Adding an adverb to a dull verb to make it stronger is less effective than using a more vivid verb.

In the sample HomeElderCare briefs, both authors chose to employ proper names for the parties. They did, however, choose different phrases for various other concepts, as shown in Exhibit 20.3.

5. Special Sentences

Some statements are more memorable than others, because of the way they present their messages.[1] Within limits, it is appropriate to use rhetorical flourish in legal advocacy. Be sure to use it to make your most important

---

1. *See* Louis J. Sirico, Jr. & Nancy L. Schultz, *Persuasive Writing for Lawyers and the Legal Profession* App. A (2d ed. 2001) for many nonlegal examples.

EXHIBIT 20.3

SEMANTIC CHOICES

HomeElderCare's Phrasing	Mr. Nelson's Phrasing
filling in the blanks on the living will form	preparation of Mr. Nelson's living will
medical and ethical issues	legal obligation of doctors legal issues re client autonomy
validity of contract	enforcement of contract

assertions; do not draw undue attention to a minor assertion in this way. Indeed, you may want to express your theory of the case early on by use of one of the following eight devices; you would then return to that phrasing in key locations throughout the brief.

First, *juxtaposition* involves a sharp contrast between two ideas presented one after another. The second idea is somewhat startling, given the first.

Second, *allusion* involves an implied or indirect reference to a commonly known situation, typically drawn from history or literature. The allusion prompts the reader to draw the lesson from that situation into the case.

Third, an *aphorism* is a terse statement of a point, designed to draw the reader's attention and linger in the reader's mind. A maxim is an aphorism conveying an important truth or precept.

Fourth, *anaphora* involves the repeated use of a few words or a phrase at the outset of several consecutive clauses or sentences, so as to underscore that phrase and strengthen the connection among the ideas.

Fifth, *epistrophe* is the same as anaphora except that the repetition occurs at the end of the clauses or sentences.

Sixth, *alliteration* involves repeated use of a starting letter, typically a consonant, in neighboring words to make a phrase stand out.

Seventh, a *rhetorical question* involves asking a question without answering it. The reader notices the question because we generally attend more closely to questions than to statements and because the paper is mostly statements. The question may imply an answer, or it may have no good answer. Either way, the reader ponders the answer or lack thereof. Rhetorical questions should be used for smaller points. Some lawyers avoid rhetorical questions on the ground that they are too showy, so you should use this technique sparingly.

Eighth and last, consider selective use of *quotes*. To some extent, you must quote the law, especially as to statutory material and key phrases from the common law. You also may quote portions of the record and nonessential passages from legal authorities, such as key portions of the reasoning in a case or helpful commentary. However, if you quote too much, the reader will not take special note of any of your quotes, and your brief will not flow well. If you quote sparingly, the quotes will stand out.

The brief of Mr. Nelson in the HomeElderCare case has several examples of rhetorical flourish, albeit fairly restrained. These appear in Exhibit 20.4. Note that both briefs quote the statutory language at issue in the case. Both quote the court's reasoning in the leading unauthorized practice case—but different language for different purposes. See pages 385-86 and 398-99. HomeElderCare's brief also quotes material about the right to privacy (at page 388), and Mr. Nelson's brief quotes a case law passage about the dangers of unauthorized practice (at page 398).

D. Setting the Proper Tone and Pitch

Words make or break legal arguments by setting proper or improper tones. Tone is in part a matter of your personal style or voice as a writer and in part a reflection of the needs of the specific case. Some writers routinely choose a measured tone, others a more impassioned tone. Some cases call for a matter-of-fact tone, others for more emotion. Within a range of reason, you may choose the tone for your brief.

One tone is unacceptable, however: sarcasm. You may be tempted to use sarcasm toward the opposing party or opposing counsel (especially if the case has been in acrimonious litigation for some time). Or you may be tempted to use sarcasm toward the lower court that ruled against your client. You should not succumb to these temptations. Sarcasm would deflect the court from its task, which is to decide between conflicting arguments, not to decide who is the better person. Furthermore, the court may wonder whether you are resorting to sarcasm because your arguments are not strong enough to stand on their own. To treat the court, your opponent, or others in the case with disrespect is unprofessional.

To avoid sarcasm, focus your brief on the law and facts of the case; do not write about opposing counsel. Read your brief with this question in mind: If I were opposing counsel, would I find the tone of this brief to be appropriate?

EXHIBIT 20.4

SPECIAL SENTENCES

As a consequence of the actions of Ms. Hall, Mr. Nelson designated his minister as both his proxy and guardian—even though this arrangement was not what he desired. (juxtaposition)

A social worker should not be paid for defective legal work. (aphorism)

These social workers are not lawyers. These social workers do not have law degrees. These social workers have not been admitted to practice law in Minnesota or anywhere else. (anaphora)

HOW DO COURTS RESPOND
TO INTEMPERATE LANGUAGE?

Henry v. Eberhard,
832 S.W.2d 467 (Ark. 1992).

[Willene Henry and Richard Roth, employees of the Arkansas Department of Human Services, took a minor child into protective custody rather than permit supervised visitation with the child's father ordered by the judge handling the parents' divorce. The trial court held Henry and Roth in contempt of court. The Arkansas Attorney General was permitted to intervene in the appeal of the contempt orders.]

[A]ppellants make numerous accusations of the lower courts which are disrespectful. Appellants state that a concise picture of what happened in Benton County cannot be presented to this court because they "sincerely believe a spark was ignited that turned into a blaze for reasons other than the administration of justice." Appellants accuse the trial court of "pursuing an independent agenda" and characterize its conduct as "calculated to lead to the public humiliation of the officials of the Department of Human Services."

The above-quoted language from appellants' brief is so offensive that it prompted the intervenor, the Attorney General, to request that the language be stricken from the briefs. Pursuant to Ark.Sup.Ct.R. 6, and *McLemore v. Elliot,* 272 Ark. 306, 614 S.W.2d 226 (1981), we conclude the intervenor's motion is well-taken. In *McLemore,* as a sanction for violating Ark.Sup.Ct.R. 6, we struck the briefs containing the language that was disrespectful to the trial court from the records of this court. The language used in the present case is far more inflammatory and disrespectful than the language used in *McLemore.* Accordingly, we grant the intervenor's request to strike pages 462–67 of appellants' brief from our records.

Related to tone is the issue of pitch. Generally, by the time you write a brief, you are well immersed in the facts and law of the case, as are two of your audiences, your opposing counsel and your client. However, the case will be unknown to your primary reader, the court. You should see yourself as writing for an intelligent but not yet informed reader. A useful strategy is to ask yourself: What did I need to know about the facts and law when I first took on this case? And what has been difficult for me to sort out as I have worked on this case? Your brief should include the former, in compact form, at the outset of a topic, then proceed to focus on the latter.

Both HomeElderCare sample briefs employ a moderate tone. Mr. Nelson's is, not surprisingly, more impassioned about his situation than HomeElderCare's. HomeElderCare maintains an even-handed tone in the passages about Mr. Nelson's situation, to avoid the impression that HomeElderCare is attacking Mr. Nelson, its own client, and reserves a passionate tone for the concluding policy argument.

The brief written for HomeElderCare maintains a fairly consistent pitch throughout; the most abstract material relating to privacy rights and allocation of medical resources appears last. The brief written for Mr. Nelson reflects a rising pitch in both main arguments: the unauthorized practice argument starting with the basic concept applied to the facts before proceeding to application of the statute, the contract argument presenting hornbook material before exploring the jurisdiction's cases.

E. Handling Concessions and Rebuttals

Many legal arguments entail two potential troublespots: concessions and rebuttals of the opponent's argument. While both enable the court to fully understand the case, they also distract from the affirmative argument you want to make on the client's behalf. Hence, both should be handled with care.

1. Concessions

The need to present a concession arises when the two sides concur on a point and that point favors your client's opponent. Concessions may be handled several ways. The first two are true concessions, while the third is a limited-purpose concession.

First, you may by omission implicitly concede the point, neither stating the point nor presenting an argument to the contrary. For example, you could note that the issue concerns a statute and begin your argument with a discussion of the exceptions, implicitly conceding that your client's case falls within the scope and general rule of the statute.

Other techniques for handling concessions involve explicit statements of the conceded point. In the technique known as "confession and avoidance," you state the conceded point but move on to an argument that nullifies the harmful impact of the concession. For example, you could state that the client's conduct falls within a statutory definition, yet argue that the client's conduct is permitted by a statutory exception.

In a third technique known as "assuming arguendo," you state the conceded point for purposes of the present argument only, and you emphasize that the point is not conceded beyond the present argument. For example, you would argue first that your client is outside the scope of the statute, then assume arguendo that the client falls within the statute's scope to show how its conduct is governed by a statutory exception.

Whenever you are stating a concession, you would use the methods described in this chapter to deflect the reader's attention from the concession. For example, you could allocate little space to the concession, place it in a dependent clause, or state it in passive voice or nominalization. Indeed, if you deem the concession unnecessary to the logical flow of your argument, you could place it in a footnote. Meanwhile, you would allocate more space to your argument responding to the concession, place that argument in the main clause, or use active voice to express it.

In the sample briefs in the HomeElderCare case, several concessions appear. HomeElderCare implicitly conceded that its social workers are not licensed as lawyers; its argument proceeds directly from a quotation of the unauthorized practice statute to the prohibition against giving legal advice (at page 385). Exhibit 20.5 presents two explicit concessions; note how affirmative arguments tightly frame both concessions.

EXHIBIT 20.5

CONCESSIONS AND REBUTTALS

Confession and Avoidance (in Mr. Nelson's brief)

The *Gardner* rule must be applied in "a common sense way which will protect the public and not hamper or burden that public interest with impractical and technical restrictions which have no reasonable justification." [citation omitted] The restriction on social workers preparing living wills may burden the social worker who wishes to practice law. [confession] But the restriction is not impractical or merely technical; it is more than reasonably justified when viewed from the proper perspective—the client's. [avoidance]
(Sentences developing the client's perspective follow.)

Assuming arguendo (in the HomeElderCare brief)

To avoid the rendering of legal advice, HomeElderCare policy calls for the social worker to suggest that the client consult an attorney if the client wishes to deviate from the form or has legal questions. Thus, the social worker did not provide legal advice. [affirmative argument]

However, even if the social worker touched on legal matters, [concession for purposes of proceeding], the service would not constitute the unauthorized practice of law under Minnesota case law. [next affirmative argument]

Rebuttal (in a footnote in the HomeElderCare brief)

As it does for all its services, HomeElderCare charged a fee for its living will services. [factual introduction] The charging of a fee should not render this service the practice of law [Mr. Nelson's argument], any more than the charging of a fee for home maintenance services would render that service the practice of law. *Cf. Cardinal v. Merrill Lynch Realty/Burnet, Inc.* . . . . [rebuttal]

2. Rebuttals

Most of your argument should address points of clash in the case, the topics on which the two sides disagree. As to many points of clash, you will find that stating your affirmative argument suffices to rebut your opponent's argument, that the relationship between the two arguments will be apparent to any reader of the brief, and that little if anything needs to be said in so many words about the opponent's argument.

In other situations, you will determine that your brief should refer to, or perhaps even state, your opponent's argument because the relationship between the two arguments is subtle and will not otherwise be clear to the reader. Or your rebuttal to your opponent's argument may be understandable only as a negation of the opponent's argument, rather than an affirmative assertion. In either situation, an effective rebuttal will boost your credibility.

When you determine that your brief should indeed state or refer to your opponent's argument, do so with care. You will accentuate your opponent's argument if you state it in a position of primacy, at length, in vivid language, or with noteworthy quotes. You should instead minimize the opponent's argument by, for example, referring to it rather than fully stating it, placing the reference in a dependent clause, or sandwiching the reference in the middle of the passage on the topic. Another option is to rebut your opponent's argument in a footnote. Even if you think the opponent's argument is very weak, take care to criticize it in a professional tone, taking aim at the ideas rather than the author.

For example, Exhibit 20.5 presents HomeElderCare's rebuttal of Mr. Nelson's well taken argument that charging a fee suggests unauthorized practice. The brief downplays this topic; it appears in a footnote. Mr. Nelson's legal assertion is stated briefly, sandwiched between two sensible factual assertions.

F. CONCEPTUALIZING A CHANGE IN THE LAW

Some disputes become litigation because of the parties' inclinations to carry on the dispute. However, most lengthy litigation occurs because the parties (and their lawyers) assign different legal meanings to their dispute. That is, the parties (and their lawyers) disagree about what happened, how the law applies to what happened, what the law is, or what it should be. In the latter two situations, when the law is uncertain, the lawyers have the privilege and responsibility of contributing to the development of the law by proposing a rule of law. The lawyers' task entails not only arguing the client's case but also conceptualizing a change in the law.

1. Traditional Steps in Advocating for a Rule of Law

Because courts adhere to stare decisis, and because courts are bound to follow statutory language in most situations, it is preferable to argue a case by showing how it fits within established law. You should engage in a discussion of what the rule should be only when your case does not fit an established rule or when an alternative to the established rule would provide a strong basis for your desired outcome.

Generally, the less radical your position, the more likely it is to be adopted by the court. Hence an important step is to identify how your rule connects to existing law. For example, show how your rule simply adds an element or defense to an existing common law claim, or show how your rule adapts a common law claim from one setting to your client's setting. Alternatively, you might show how your interpretation of a statute is necessitated by, intimated in, or resolves ambiguity in an existing interpretation of the statute, or show that your approach has been taken by the court in interpreting other statutes.

Another option is to rely on persuasive precedent and legal commentary. This route may be your only option, or you may use these materials to bolster your argument based on binding authority. Select the strongest persuasive material you can, based on its source, reasoning, factual parallel to your case, and currency. If there is an opposing strand of persuasive authority, you should acknowledge it, to fulfill your obligation of candor toward the court, and then show its weaknesses, to bolster your argument.

If the court properly perceives that your request is to make new law, it is likely to be concerned about the wisdom of doing so in your particular case. You therefore must show how the proposed rule would apply to your case, yielding a clearly equitable result. You should dispel the court's concern over ambushing the opposing party with an unforeseen rule, by showing that the opposing party should have foreseen the change you are proposing; by showing that the existing rule improperly favors your client's opponent; or by showing that the opponent does not deserve sympathy, given its actions.

The court also is likely to be concerned about the rule's impact beyond your case. The court may worry that the rule will be taken too far and will be thought to cover related yet different situations, the proverbial "slippery slope." You must show, as best you can, where the limits of your rule are, so the court will be able to provide guidance for future situations and need not fear a rash of cases exploring the new rule. You should show how the proposed rule yields sound results in the situations it would govern. You also should show how the rule accords with public policy, by identifying those policies and using your case as an illustration of them.

While the fictional HomeElderCare case involves a new application of existing law, it does not involve making new law. The *Weatherston's* case cited by both parties did entail the making of new law. The lawyer for Weatherston's needed to convince the court that it should uphold a contract in violation of a statute that regulates a profession to safeguard the public, although the court's previous case law suggested otherwise. Weatherston's lawyer might have cited the current rule, noted its essential purpose as protecting clients, posited that there could be a case involving a technical statutory violation but no harm to or misleading of the client, highlighted the interests of the unlicensed professional in such a situation and the windfall to the client if the contract is not upheld, and then crafted a rule to reflect the new approach and applied it to the *Weatherston's* facts. If persuasive precedent in favor of the new rule were available, it would be presented for the court's consideration.

2. Stepping Outside the Law

Disciplines other than law also consider issues of justice and fairness, and scholars in those disciplines may have information that could assist a court seeking to make law. Near the turn of the twentieth century, Louis Brandeis (who later became a justice of the United States Supreme Court) submitted a brief that presented social science research on the detrimental effects of long work hours on the health of women.[2] Henceforth, a brief presenting non-legal information has been known as a "Brandeis brief."[3] Should you be interested in presenting non-legal perspectives on your client's legal problem, you might turn to economics or psychology.

a. Economics

Economic analysis is premised on the assumption that people usually make rational choices in allocating and using their resources to achieve the best possible result for themselves, whether in terms of wealth as it is traditionally defined or in terms of utility—that is, intangible benefits such as satisfaction or security. Society benefits as individual members engage in transactions, each maximizing their utilities. Transactions are desirable if both parties gain ground, or one gains and the other does not lose ground, or one gains more ground than the other loses. Accordingly, legal rules that disturb the rational and voluntary distribution of resources are inefficient and therefore undesirable. Legal rules should constrain behavior only when defects in the relationship between the parties impair their ability to make rational and voluntary choices.[4]

If this perspective were brought to bear on the *Weatherston's* case, it would provide a strong rationale for the outcome sought by Weatherston's. Presumably the contract between Weatherston's and Minnesota Mutual was formed because both parties found it beneficial. The evidence did not show that defects in their relationship impaired their contract formation; indeed, Minnesota Mutual was fully informed at the time of contract formation of the facts it later cited in refusing to perform the contract. If Minnesota Mutual could shirk its responsibilities without more grounds than it actually had, the efficacy of contracts would be undercut.

b. Psychology

An important branch of psychology is the study of moral reasoning. According to one school of thought, often associated with Carol Gilligan,[5] difficult issues are not easily decided by yes/no answers based on ranking of interests according to abstract principles. Rather, moral reasoning involves

---

2. The case was *Muller v. Oregon*, 208 U.S. 412 (1908), and the brief can be found at 16 *Landmark Briefs and Arguments of the Supreme Court of the United States: Constitutional Law* 63 (Philip B. Kurland & Gerhard Casper eds., 1975).
3. For further discussion, *see* Ellie Margolis, *Beyond Brandeis: Exploring the Uses of Non-Legal Materials in Appellate Briefs*, 34 U.S.F. L. Rev. 197 (2000).
4. A classic in the field of law and economics is Richard A. Posner, *Economic Analysis of Law* (4th ed. 1992).
5. *See* Carol A. Gilligan, *In a Different Voice: Psychological Theory and Women's Development* (1982).

consideration of a wide range of concerns held by various participants in the situation and then seeking a solution that accommodates as many of these interests as possible.

This approach has strong parallels to the stakeholder analysis discussed in Chapter 9's discussion of policy analysis. In *Weatherston's*, this approach would call for consideration of the interests of at least Weatherston's, Minnesota Mutual, the individuals who would work in or visit the building, and the general public. A ranking of the respective interests of Weatherston's and Minnesota Mutual might suggest that Weatherston's should be paid and Minnesota Mutual should pay according to the contract. But this result does not take into account the safety or welfare of people occupying the building or the public need for effective enforcement of the engineering licensure statute. A solution that would accommodate these less visible interests would be to pay Weatherston's a figure representing the value of the materials provided or hours expended, for example, but not recovery of his anticipated profit. This outcome would deter unlicensed professionals from crossing the line to the detriment of the public.

G. REVIEW OF CHAPTER 20

This chapter has explored the artistry of legal advocacy, showing how you can use the tools of the lawyer's trade—words—to convey the client's case in a convincing way. The methods available to the legal advocate include space allocation, sequence, syntax, semantics, and special sentences (such as aphorisms and juxtaposition). Your wording choices fix the tone of your brief to reflect your personal voice, the nature of the case, and your respect for all participants in the litigation. You should pitch the arguments to reflect the needs of your primary reader, the court. The methods discussed in this chapter can be used to present concessions and rebuttals persuasively.

In addition, this chapter has briefly explored the steps of legal analysis and the use of other disciplines involved in carrying out one of the special responsibilities of the lawyer: bringing about change in the law.

21

ORAL ADVOCACY

> Proceed. You have my biased attention.
> —Learned Hand
>   speaking to a counsel who sought to re-argue a motion
>   quoted in M. Frances McNamara, *2000 Famous*
>   *Legal Quotations*

A. INTRODUCTION

After the memoranda or briefs have been filed and served, the advocates may have a chance to present oral arguments to the court. Oral arguments occur in both trial courts and appellate courts. Why does the legal system provide for oral argument? How do lawyers make the case for their clients in this quite different setting?

The examples in the text of this chapter are drawn from a sample oral argument on appeal to the Minnesota Court of Appeals in the fictional case of *Nelson v. HomeElderCare*. You should read the transcript, starting at page 403, before reading further in this chapter.

B. THE FUNCTION OF ORAL ARGUMENT: AUDIENCE AND PURPOSE

An oral argument is a conversation with the court, not a speech to the court. You should welcome it as a chance to talk with the judge or judges about the arguments in your brief or memorandum, to find out the court's concerns and misgivings, and to dispel them. Rather than give a book report on your brief, you should take advantage of the dialogue, fully and truthfully answering the judges' questions and focusing on the interests of the court.

Your attitude should be one of "respectful intellectual equality" toward the court.[1] Try to think of the court not as an adversary, but rather as individuals who remain to be convinced of the correctness of your arguments. Your goal is to convince them to adopt your reasoning as their own.

Similarly, you have an ethical duty to show respect for opposing counsel. Opposing counsel has a duty to raise arguments that conflict with yours. Your dialogue will be with the court, not opposing counsel, and should focus on the events and the law of the case, not on opposing counsel.

Oral arguments help judges to clarify the facts, law, and policies, especially in close cases. United States Supreme Court justices have found oral arguments to be most effective when characterized by clarity, adaptability, and strategy.

- The first factor, clarity, derives from effective organization, language usage, and delivery.
- The second factor, adaptability, is counsel's ability to respond to points raised in questions by the court.
- The third factor, strategy, is how well the argument can withstand tough questioning from the court and attacks by opposing counsel.[2]

The potential scope of an oral argument is the material covered in the parties' briefs. Either party can raise any point or authority covered in any of the briefs, but no new material can be added in oral argument. Courts strongly discourage surprises in oral argument. On rare occasions, newly discovered material may be presented in a supplementary brief, if the court allows it.

Rarely will you present the full content of a brief in oral argument. Instead, the oral argument usually focuses on the highly contested issues. Chief Justice Rehnquist commented:

> Many litigators . . . mistakenly approach the two instruments of appellate advocacy, the brief and the oral argument, "as the functional equivalent of one another." Many counsel, the justice contends, view an oral argument as no more than a "brief with gestures." . . . Rather, like the preview of a movie that consists of "dramatic or interesting scenes that are apt to catch the interest of the viewer and make him

---

1. Fredrick Wiener, *Briefing and Arguing Federal Appeals* § 101 (1967).
2. Nicholas M. Cripe, *Fundamentals of Persuasive Oral Argument,* 20 Forum 342 (1985).

HOW INFLUENTIAL IS ORAL ARGUMENT?

In two studies, oral arguments were helpful to the judges in 80 to 82% of argued cases. Moreover, oral arguments influenced the judges' eventual outcomes in 22 to 31% of the cases heard.[1]

---

1. Myron H. Bright & Richard S. Arnold, *Oral Argument? It may Be Crucial!*, A.B.A. J., Sept. 1984, at 68, 70.

---

want to see that entire movie," oral argument should have "flesh and blood . . . insert[ed] into it."[3]

Oral argument gives you a chance to bring the case to life for the court, to humanize the case by using the spoken medium to impart your personality and credibility. The court naturally assesses the lawyer's commitment to the arguments being raised. Furthermore, you can use voice inflection, gestures, body stance, and other means to impart meaning that the written word cannot convey.

At the same time, the spoken medium carries with it some challenges, because it occurs in the moment. Thus, the listener must learn the structure of the presentation from oral roadmaps and signposts, changes in inflection, gestures, and pauses. And the ideas must be presented in terms that the listener can process as quickly as the oral advocate presents them.

Another challenge of an oral argument is that the oral advocate does not control the argument—in sharp contrast to the virtually complete control of the writer over the written brief. With its questions, the court can set the direction and coverage of the argument.

C. ORAL ARGUMENT PROCEDURES

1. The Context of Oral Argument

Motion Arguments: In the trial court, an oral argument is presented to a single judge. It may occur any time a motion is pending or the judge is about to make a ruling (for instance, on an evidentiary matter or a point of procedure). It may be part of a trial, or it may come up on the motion calendar along with other pending motions. In many jurisdictions, dispositive pre-trial motions, such as summary judgment or dismissal, are argued both in writing and orally, while less critical motions are submitted in writing. In other settings, the trial judge has the discretion whether to ask for briefs and whether to hear oral arguments. In yet others, the practice is to permit oral arguments on all motions.

The amount of time allowed for an oral argument on a motion can vary considerably, from a few moments to an hour. Some oral arguments occur in

---

3. *Justice Rehnquist Emphasizes Importance of Oral Argument*, The Third Branch, Dec. 1983, at 1, 2, 4 (quoting excerpts from two speeches by Chief Justice Rehnquist in October 1983).

the courtroom; others occur in the less formal setting of the trial judge's chambers, with counsel seated before the judge's desk.

Appellate Arguments: In some appellate courts, all cases are granted oral argument. However, because of increasing caseloads, the trend is toward restricting oral arguments. In some appellate courts, counsel must request and justify oral argument, and the court has full discretion to grant or deny that request.

Appellate oral arguments take place in an appellate courtroom; a bench with seats for all of the judges faces a lectern for counsel. The argument may be heard by the full court or a smaller panel, typically three judges. The proceeding generally is amplified and audiotaped. Most appellate courts set a fixed time limit for all but the most unusual cases; these limits usually range from fifteen to thirty-five minutes per side. The time limit may or may not include questions by the court and counsel's answers.

The preparation level of the judge(s) hearing an oral argument can vary considerably. At the trial level, the oral argument may be heard by the motion calendar judge, who may not be familiar with the case, or it may be heard by a judge who has worked on the case for some time. In some appellate courts, before the oral argument, the chief or presiding judge tentatively assigns a judge to write the opinion; one judge may be extremely well prepared, while others may have done very little preparation. In other courts, the assignment is not made until after the oral argument; so all, none, or some of the judges may be well prepared. Lawyers describe these situations as "hot bench" and "cold bench."[4]

The fictional sample HomeElderCare oral argument took place at the appellate level and was heard by three judges. Appellant's counsel was limited to fifteen minutes, and respondent's counsel was limited to twelve minutes. It is difficult to gauge the judges' preparation levels from their questions, but the judges all appear fairly familiar with the case and so may be termed a "warm bench."

2. The Format of Oral Argument

You always should study the rules on oral argument before the court hearing your case. You also may want to consult the clerk of the court and local attorneys to learn of any unwritten traditions.

Motion Arguments: In formal oral arguments at the trial level, the movant speaks first, followed by the non-movant; sometimes the movant is allowed a rebuttal argument as well. The format of these oral arguments is highly variable, although tradition and logic dictate that the issues and the relevant facts be stated near the beginning of the oral argument. Less formal arguments at the trial level resemble a discussion, with the judge asking questions and the lawyers responding to those questions and to each other.

Appellant's Arguments: At the appellate level, as appellant's counsel, you would open with an introduction. You may begin with the formal opening, "May it please the court," or you may bypass the formal phrase and directly

---

4. Myron H. Bright, *How to Win on Appeal: The New Ten Commandments of Oral Argument,* Trial, July 1996, at 68, 69.

introduce yourself and your client. You should state right away how much time you want to reserve for rebuttal. Then introduce the case, by stating your theory of the case and providing a roadmap of the issues or arguments that you plan to cover and in what order.

It is customary for the appellant to state the facts and procedural posture. This statement should be whittled down to minimal length and stress facts pertinent to the issues being addressed in the oral argument. A longer fact statement is appropriate when the case pivots on a factual dispute or the client's case is strong on the facts and weak on the law. The statement should be fairly balanced, for both ethical and strategic reasons.

Most of your time will be spent discussing the legal arguments, discussed in detail in Parts D and E below.

The conclusion should be very brief, with any recapping limited to only a few sentences, if that. You should conclude with the disposition you want the court to grant (reversal, remand, affirmance, modification).

Respondent's Argument: As respondent's counsel, you usually will use this same format. You can choose whether to give your view of the facts and the procedural posture; most respondents' advocates do state additional or reframed facts near the beginning of the argument. Otherwise, you will open with a roadmap of the issues or arguments and then proceed directly to the body of the argument.

With rebuttal, appellant is allowed to end the oral argument. Rebuttal is appellant's chance at the end of the oral argument to refute respondent's arguments and to present the final conclusion. You should not raise new arguments in a rebuttal. You need not answer all of the respondent's points and, indeed, should not address more than two or three topics. For example, you could point out the respondent's omissions or select one or two major topics on which appellant has strong counterarguments. You should conclude by reiterating the relief your client seeks from the court.

The time devoted to rebuttal should be proportional to the length of the argument. Two or three minutes is the norm, but five minutes is appropriate if the argument is long and contains many issues. If appellant's counsel fails to reserve rebuttal time, some courts treat rebuttal as waived.

Exhibits 21.1 and 21.2 present comparisons of oral argument components to the components of motion practice memoranda and appellate briefs.

In the sample HomeElderCare oral argument, appellant's counsel used the formal opening, "May it please the court," before introducing herself and her client. Appellant's counsel then reserved three minutes for rebuttal and gave a quick roadmap of the two main issues. Her fact statement focused on the crucial points and reflected a balanced view of the facts. She then recounted the procedural events that led to this appeal and stated the standard of review. See pages 403-04.

Respondent's counsel began with the traditional opening and then stated the theory of his case. After clarifying the facts in three sentences, he gave a roadmap of his two main arguments. See pages 406-07.

The main portions of both arguments are discussed below. Both counsel concluded their arguments by summarizing their points and requesting the appropriate relief from the court (see pages 406 and 410).

EXHIBIT 21.1

COMPARISON OF MOTION PRACTICE
MEMORANDUM AND ORAL ARGUMENT

Motion Practice Memorandum	Oral Argument
Caption	introduction (who I am & whom I represent)
Introduction, Summary, Issues	theory of cases; roadmap of issues or arguments
Facts Procedure (optional)	facts (with or without procedure)
Argument	argument (more selective)
Conclusion	conclusion

EXHIBIT 21.2

COMPARISON OF APPELLATE BRIEF
AND ORAL ARGUMENT

Appellate Brief	Oral Argument
cover page Table of Contents Table of Authorities	introduction (who I am & whom I represent)
Issues	theory of case; roadmap of issues or arguments
Statement of Case and Facts	statement of facts and procedure (albeit briefer)
Summary of Argument	
Argument	argument (more selective)
Conclusion	conclusion
Appendix	

Appellant's counsel began her rebuttal by stating her theory of the case; she then responded to respondent's assertions as to the two main issues. She concluded her argument by emphasizing the public policy in her client's favor (see pages 410-11).

D. Preparing for the Oral Argument

Although oral argument is a conversation and not a speech, you nonetheless should prepare carefully for it. You should have a plan for what you hope to accomplish, even though you will not be able to control the course of the argument and must defer to the court's direction.

1. Selecting Arguments to Present

Experts suggest presenting one or two, not more than three, major arguments. The court does not expect the oral argument to cover all topics covered in the briefs.

In choosing arguments for oral presentation, you should consider various factors.

- Try to present a coherent picture of your client's case; your arguments should draw in the key facts and outline your theory of the case.
- Choose your strongest arguments; if you cannot win on the strongest argument, you are not likely to win on the weakest.
- Consider which arguments are better suited for oral presentation—generally policy, factual, or equitable arguments, not technical or complex legal questions.
- Focus on points of clash, the issues on which the parties' positions conflict and which pose the greatest challenge to the court. You will greatly assist the court, and thereby enhance your credibility, by dealing with adverse precedent and troublesome arguments raised by opposing counsel.
- Some of your arguments may affirmatively advance your client's case, while others merely refute opposing arguments. Make sure that the affirmative arguments outweigh the refutations.
- If you still need to pare down your list of arguments, carefully examine arguments in the alternative to see whether you can omit one or more of the alternatives.

In the sample oral argument, both counsel selected the same two major issues—unauthorized practice and contract validity—because the scope of the appeal dictated those two issues and because those issues constituted the points of clash. Both addressed these issues in that order because logic compels it. However, their arguments differed quite a bit. For example, at the outset, HomeElderCare's lawyer stressed the difficult-or-doubtful test and holdings in favor of the non-lawyer (beginning at page 404). In contrast, Mr. Nelson's lawyer stressed the statute, the living will as a legal document, Ms. Hall's status, and the fee (beginning at page 407).

2. Setting the Pitch of the Argument

You generally will not know how prepared your judges will be. Thus, you should frame your arguments so you can educate the trial judge or a majority (at least) of the appellate court. Consider covering the basics initially, then elevating the level of discussion as soon as you are reasonably certain that the judges will be able to follow the more complicated aspects of the case.

In the appellate setting, resist the temptation to pitch the entire argument to the least prepared judge. You may thereby limit the depth of your argument and its effectiveness for the more informed judges. On the other hand, you do not want to converse exclusively with the judge who seems to understand the case best. This tactic may result in only a muddled understanding among the members of the court who did not follow your argument and, perhaps, a spirited dissent from the judge with whom you conversed at length.

In the HomeElderCare oral argument, appellant's counsel started with the basics and then steadily elevated the level of discussion through the progression of arguments stated above. Respondent's counsel did not need to vary the pitch of his arguments because he could build on the material already presented by appellant's counsel.

3. Allocating Time

Just as you should analyze your briefs and memoranda for allocation of space to various components and topics, so too should you plan how to allocate your oral argument time to particular components and topics.

In preparing for your argument, time the fact statement you plan to deliver. In a five-minute motion argument at the trial level, the fact statement may need to be less than a minute long. In a fifteen-minute appellate oral argument, fact statements rarely run longer than three minutes. In a thirty-minute argument, the facts ordinarily would not exceed five minutes. To fit within these limits, consider the following:

- Condense facts that do not need to be presented in detail.
- Omit facts that pertain to topics you do not intend to argue orally.
- Present general facts in your fact statement, and save the more detailed facts for the body of the argument, when they will mean more to the listener and make the legal argument more understandable.
- Limit the procedural history to the rulings that are relevant to the legal issues covered in your oral argument.

In planning the body of your argument, reserve approximately a third of your time for responses to the court's questions, or allocate that time to a less important argument that can be omitted if need be. Of the remaining time, determine how much time to devote to each argument, based on its relative importance and controversy. You may be able to cover some arguments in one or two sentences; other arguments may require factual analogies, extensive development of public policies, or fusion of related cases. For each argument, you must judge how much time you need to make the argument clearly and persuasively, so you can decide whether to attempt the argument if time is running out.

In the sample oral argument, appellant's counsel spent less than three of her fifteen minutes on her introduction and fact statement. Respondent's counsel spent less than a minute on his introduction and facts. Both counsel focused on the essential facts and omitted the unneeded ones; appellant's counsel saved some of the specific facts for the body of her argument. Both oral advocates spent most of their time on the unauthorized practice of law, the crucial issue in this lawsuit. Both were able to present far more than the bare minimum on this topic, while they reduced their coverage of the contract issue to the bare minimum.

4. Planning for Flexibility

Of course, you never should count on being able to proceed through your argument without adapting it to respond to the judges' questions and concerns. Furthermore, you will want to account for the arguments made by your opponent. As the argument unfolds, you may need to switch the order of topics, drastically expand or condense the coverage of a particular topic, or even change which briefed topics you cover.

In planning for adaptability, you first should determine what material to present if you receive no questions. Then you should decide which topics and which arguments on each topic you want to cover, at a bare minimum, if you receive many questions. You also should plan how to make transitions between arguments if you are forced to cover the arguments in less-than-optimal order.

Adaptability also entails responsiveness to the arguments of your opponent. You must master the authorities and arguments in his or her brief and be prepared to answer questions on topics raised there. In the course of your argument, you may want to address some of the questions asked of opposing counsel in the preceding argument.

In the HomeElderCare oral argument, the court's questions indicated that the court was interested in two topics: the actions of HomeElderCare's social workers in filling out the living wills and legislative intent. Both counsel tailored their arguments accordingly.

5. Preparing Written Materials

You should not deliver your argument from a written script, because your presentation will be stilted, and you may fail to respond well to questions. Nor are note cards advisable, because you will find it difficult to adjust your organization or see the entire argument at a glance, and because you may distract the court if you nervously shuffle your cards.

Rather, you should prepare a bare-bones outline of the major issues and arguments, as well as abstracts of the leading cases or statutes, quotations from the important legal rules, and notes of the key facts or policies.

You might place the outline on one side of an open manila file folder. On the other side, tape a flip-card index of key authorities, both favorable and adverse. Each card has the citation on the bottom of the card and the important facts, quotations, and reasoning on the rest. See Exhibit 21.3.

EXHIBIT 21.3

FLIP-CARD AND OUTLINE

Sources

	May it please the court. My name is ----------------; I represent ---------------- ------------------------. My argument will cover -- --
"-------------------------------------" --	
treatise	The facts are uncontested:
1. rev.	• ------------------------------------
treatise	• ------------------------------------
Rule 12	• ------------------------------------
Rule 56	• ------------------------------------
§333	• ------------------------------------
§222	I. -----------------------------------
§111	A. ---------------------------------
K v. L	B. ---------------------------------
I v. J	II. ----------------------------------
G v. H	A. ---------------------------------
E v. F	1. ------------------------------
C v. D	2. ------------------------------
A v. B	B. ---------------------------------
	In conclusion, ---------------------------- --.

Some lawyers assemble a notebook containing an outline of the argument, followed by tabbed sections containing the record and important authority. This technique should be used only for very complex cases, because the turning of pages can be distracting.

Whatever method you use, you should bring the record or a detailed summary of the record with you, in case the court asks you a question about a particular page in the record.

6. Practicing

Write out, memorize, and practice your introduction and your conclusion, so that you can open and close the argument cleanly and with confidence. For example:

- Appellant's introduction might read as follows: "May it please the court. My name is _____, and I represent the Appellant, _____ I wish to reserve _____ minutes for rebuttal. I will be addressing the following issues in my argument: . . ."

- Respondent's conclusion might read as follows: "In conclusion, both of Appellant's arguments are unsupported by law. I urge the court to affirm the trial court holding and rule in favor of _____."

You also may want to memorize the opening segment of the fact statement, if it is short.

Then practice talking about the case. First, present your entire oral argument without interruptions, perhaps recording it once or twice. Practice presenting your arguments in differing orders. You also should rehearse for the possibility that the court will ask you to skip the facts and proceed to the body of the argument. (This practice is especially common in arguments delivered in law school.) Time your fact statement and each argument, and examine those times for conformance to your desired time allocations, as discussed above. Try to discern how easy or difficult it is to follow your presentation.

Next, find someone to quiz you on the case. Ask your colleagues to ask tough questions and help you figure out how best to handle the tougher questions. Work on connecting your answers to the arguments you want to make.

Consider presenting in front of a video recorder; then review your performance from the perspective of the listening judges. Watch for distracting nervous mannerisms, like jingling coins in your pocket. Also evaluate your posture, general demeanor, and body language. Do you appear forthright and confident in your client's case at all times?

If possible, visit the courtroom in which you will be presenting. Evaluate the distance between yourself and the judges; the adequacy of the lighting; the sightlines of each of the judges; and the range of the microphone, if there is one.

E. DELIVERING THE ARGUMENT

1. Making Spoken Communication Clear

A judge listening to an oral argument cannot re-listen to a portion that occurred some minutes ago or stop the argument to consider a statement just made. To help the judges assimilate what is being said, speak at a medium tempo with occasional pauses. These pauses provide you and the judges with time to think; pauses also serve as aural cues equivalent to punctuation and paragraph breaks in written communication. You should pause briefly between sentences, rather than running the sentences into each other, and pause a bit longer between paragraphs.

In addition to tempo and pauses, use roadmaps and signposts to assist the listener. These semantic roadmaps and signposts can be emphasized by inflections, pauses, and gestures.

In the sample HomeElderCare oral argument, counsel gave the following roadmaps:

- There are two issues that we will discuss today. The first deals with whether . . . . The second issue is whether . . . .

- Respondent must prove two issues to establish the invalidity of the contract. First, . . . Even if . . . .
- [T]he . . . statute was violated . . . in two ways. First, . . . Second, . . .

They used the following signposts to mark the beginning of a new topic or subtopic:

- The facts have been stipulated . . . .
- While opposing counsel has generally stated the facts accurately, I would like to make a few clarifications . . . .
- The main point that I would like you to remember is . . . .
- The first issue addresses . . . .
- The second issue deals with . . . .

They also used the following signposts to mark the end of a topic:

- Therefore, . . .
- So . . . .
- In short, . . .
- In conclusion, . . .

Sometimes visual aids, such as a timeline, map, or diagram, may be helpful to the court. You should ask the clerk whether the court permits visual aids and, if so, in what form. You may choose to present the material in an appendix to the brief, on an easel, or through a document projection system. Of course, the information must have appeared in the briefs or record in some form and must be within the scope of the court's review.

2. Presenting Quotations

Generally, quotations are difficult for a listener to process. You are unlikely to read a quotation as naturally as you speak in your own words, and the listener must adjust to the style of the quotation and then back to your speaking style. If the quotation was meant to be read, not heard, it may be complex in syntax or semantics. So if the point you want to make can be made equally well by paraphrasing, do so.

Some material may be so important that it merits a direct quotation, for example, the key phrase of a statute in a statutory interpretation case or the telling statement of a critical witness. Above all else, be sure you state it accurately. Formally introduce the quotation by indicating its source, and be sure to close the quotation.

In the sample HomeElderCare argument, both counsel used brief and accurate quotations, which they marked by a pause, a change in inflection, and the use of "quote" and "un-quote."

3. Answering Questions

In most oral arguments, the court will ask you questions. In no circumstance should you treat the court's questions as interruptions. Rather, as a famous appellate advocate exhorted, "Rejoice when the court asks questions."[5] Questions can be of great assistance to a well prepared advocate; like weather vanes, they tell you which way the wind is blowing. Without questions from the court, you are left delivering a speech that may not address the court's real concerns.

Court etiquette dictates that you stop your presentation whenever a member of the court begins a question, even if you are in mid-sentence. Do not interrupt the judge; listen to the entire question; give yourself time to think. Then answer the question, even if the topic is out of the order in which you planned to present your arguments. It is not acceptable to delay the answer to a question, unless the judge asking the question signals that you may do so.

Some questions require only a few words by way of response. Others call for a potentially lengthy response. Once you have answered, you should not wait for the court for a sign of permission to proceed. Rather, you should maintain eye contact with the court so that you can gauge the reaction of the judges to your answer. If the judges seem to have followed your initial response, you should conclude the answer and move on. However, if much of the bench looks puzzled by your answer, you might want to elaborate on it. If the reaction is one of skepticism, you might decide that discretion is the better part of valor and move to an alternative argument or even another topic that the court may view more favorably. If the reaction is mixed, you might quickly count heads and decide whether a majority of the court is with you. When you move back to your prepared comments, try to link your answer to the argument you are about to make.

Above all, do not take tough questioning personally. A seemingly hostile judge may in fact favor your client and may take a devil's advocate stance. At worst, tough questioning represents criticism of your legal arguments, not you personally. The members of the court are usually trying out the reasoning you propose to see whether they are comfortable enough with it to adopt it for the holding.

As the court asks questions, try to discern which of the following types of questions the court is asking and respond accordingly.

a. Questions About the Facts

Judges ask questions about the facts primarily to lock in their understanding of the dispute they are asked to resolve. The judge may not remember a key fact and may simply seek a reminder from you. Or the judge may ask you to clarify or synthesize evidence that is muddled or conflicting; your answer must be supported by the record and should be as favorable to your client as it can be. Or the judge may ask you about facts that are not in the record; you must respond that the fact is not in the record, and you may draw an inference if the inference is a strong one based on facts in the record. As much as possible, follow up your answer with a comment about the significance of the fact to the legal analysis or equities of the case.

---

5. John Davis, *The Argument of an Appeal*, 26 A.B.A. J. 895, 897 (1940).

In the sample oral argument, for example, the judges asked respondent's counsel the following purely factual question:

Judge 1: Well, don't the facts of this case indicate that the friends and relatives or other people that you mentioned are apparently not filling this need, because HomeElderCare apparently did do some forty wills and charged, at least in this case, $80, and that shows that there is a need for this service, doesn't it?

Respondent's Counsel: It shows that they did that. I don't know that it shows that that is the only alternative that was available. They do provide other services that require legal expertise in those areas—for example, testamentary wills, with real-estate transactions. There they have also provided service to the HomeElderCare clients, and there they have acted primarily as a liaison with attorneys, recognizing that they really don't have the skill and ability to engage in this sort of activity.

b. Questions About the Law

Judges ask questions about the law as they seek to resolve an ambiguity about the legal rule or its application to the facts of the case. In response, you first should state what the law says, as viewed from your client's perspective and within the confines of ethical principles regarding candor with the court. You may need to disagree respectfully with a judge who does not see the law your way; if so, provide a clear rationale for your viewpoint, whether a succinct quotation or policy argument or later legal development. Next, be sure to draw a connection between the law as you have stated it and the facts of your case. In many instances, the law is not clear in the abstract, but becomes so when applied to a specific situation.

In the sample oral argument, the following exchange typifies this kind of question and response:

Judge 2:   Counsel, don't you also have to show fraud or incompetence in order to prevail on the contract claim?

Respondent's Counsel: That is true, your honor, and we believe that we have clear evidence of incompetence here. The proof of this is that the living will had to be redone; it had to be revised so that the interests of Mr. Nelson were met, so that his desires were satisfied. So we believe that indeed we do have evidence of incompetence in this case.

c. Questions About Public Policy

Especially at the highest court, judges ask questions about the societal implications of possible rulings. Your response should show how a ruling in your favor will lead to positive outcomes for similar disputes, by showing why the ruling would promote justice in your client's case. Your response also should show that any concerns about adverse by-products are either founded on speculation or outweighed by the positive outcomes. For example, if a new cause of action provides recovery for a class of injured individuals, would-be defendants can avoid liability by reforming their harmful practices, and the courts can avoid excessive litigation by crafting the rule carefully.

In the sample oral argument, the following discussion of public policy occurred:

> *Judge 3:*   Counsel, my understanding is that the legislature enacting the living will statute intended for the document to be very easily executed. It did adopt two different ways to execute the document. Wouldn't it be appropriate for this court to authorize persons other than lawyers, such as social workers, to help with the execution of these documents? The legislature has indicated that it is the policy of the state to encourage this document for persons.

> *Respondent's Counsel:*   It is true that the legislature has made clear that it believes it is good public policy to encourage the use of living wills. We don't see that there is really any conflict between that policy and the policy underlying the unauthorized practice of law statute. We think the two can coexist very comfortably. What we have here, though, is a situation where the policies that guide the unauthorized practice of law statute—namely, to protect the public from the very serious harm that can result from activities or actions by individuals who are not lawyers—that should be given the primary consideration.

d. Questions About Hypothetical Situations

Under stare decisis, judges must write decisions that will work well in the future, lead to just and predictable outcomes, and avoid undue administrative burdens. Thus, judges are concerned with, and ask about, hypothetical future situations. Answers to hypotheticals help the judges to foresee the future operation of the holding in your case.

Hypothetical questions are challenging because they often involve facts, law, and policy in a situation you may not have fully contemplated while preparing for oral argument. The key to a good answer is to take time to think, so that you can provide not only a conclusion, but also an analysis of why the hypothetical would and should be resolved a particular way, in light of the elements of the rule and its policy. If you deem the hypothetical a close call, you should phrase your answer tentatively or provide more than one response and rationale.

If the court asks multiple hypotheticals or engages you in an extended discussion of a single hypothetical, you may feel that your case has become lost in the fray and that you are on unsure ground. If so, you may want to observe that your client's case does not raise the problem in the hypothetical and then show how the court could rule so as to avoid the problem in the hypothetical.

In the sample oral argument, a judge and respondent's counsel had the following exchange on a hypothetical situation:

Judge 3:   Counsel, I'm a bit concerned as to where you would have us draw the line. Are you saying that if a person were brought to a hospital losing consciousness—about to lose the capacity to execute a document of this sort—that the people at the medical facility could not assist in the execution of the document? We'd have to wait until an attorney was called to come?

Respondent's Counsel: No, I don't think that we would say that that was the case. I think if a person in that situation—a hospital worker, for example—just wrote down exactly what the patient wanted, there was no discussion of what the terms mean but basically did it in a sort of clerical way, I don't think that we would have the unauthorized practice of law in such a situation.

Judge 3:   But isn't that what happened here?

Respondent's Counsel: Well, we don't believe that it is. In fact, we have the record which indicates that they explain the document to the doctors, they explain it to the proxies, they explain it to the witnesses, and they actually oversee the execution of the document. So we have something very much more involved here than simply completing a form.

e. Questions Seeking Concessions

A judge may signal that one of your assertions or arguments is not credible and thereby exert pressure on you to concede that point. Your response to a question seeking a concession can take various forms. Least common is outright retreat, when you say, "That's correct, your honor. We no longer are basing our case on that argument." This response may improve your credibility with the court and thereby strengthen the court's support for your other arguments. For instance, as a plaintiff, you may be able to concede one cause of action, so long as another cause of action secures the recovery sought by your client. As a defendant, you may be able to concede that the plaintiff has a good case on one element of a conjunctive rule, so long as you maintain that another element can be defeated. Of course, to the extent possible, you should know your client's views as to these matters before you enter the courtroom.

More often, oral advocates seek to minimize the impact of any concessions they make by pairing the concession or apparent concession with a strong assertion. You engage in confession and avoidance by saying, "That may be true, your honor, but it doesn't matter because this other [fact or argument] is controlling, rather than the one you raise." You assume arguendo by saying, "Let's assume, for the sake of argument, that these [facts were true or elements were met]. Even if they were, my client would still prevail because. . . ."

In the sample oral argument, the following examples are of the confession-and-avoidance form:

Judge 3:   So that any deviation from the form would constitute the practice of law, you think?

Appellant's Counsel: It could be. It's reaching that fuzzy line of what may be the difficult and doubtful question, but it's really not an issue here because our social workers do not deviate from the form whatsoever.

Judge 3:   But don't the issues that arise under the content of the living will—they are medical issues, are they not, not legal issues— decisions as to what kind of medical care someone might take? Isn't it true that geriatric social workers might indeed have more knowledge of medical issues than would a lawyer?

Respondent's Counsel: It is true that there are certainly a lot of medical issues involved in the living will form, but there are also a good number of legal issues as well that we believe require expertise in order to provide a proper service to these clients. We see a social worker discussing the role of proxies, guardians, and conservators; explaining the legal obligations of doctors; explaining the document to the client's witness and proxy.

In every case, there are points you cannot concede without sacrificing your client's claim or defense. If the court presses you to concede such a point, you should gracefully convey that you must disagree with the court and perhaps state (or restate) your most persuasive reasons.

In the sample oral argument, respondent's counsel followed this course:

Judge 1:   Are those really such difficult and doubtful issues? Isn't it fairly simple to explain in everyday language what a proxy or a conservator is?

Respondent's Counsel: Well, we think that it is difficult and doubtful, and we think the proof of that is actually the fact of this case. And we had a situation here where the person that Mr. Nelson wanted to be his guardian was in fact not made his guardian as a result of the actions of HomeElderCare. So we believe that indeed there are difficult and doubtful legal questions being addressed here, and therefore, the actions of the HomeElderCare social workers did indeed constitute the unauthorized practice of law.

f. Questions About Your Opponent's Argument

Judges naturally ask counsel to respond to the opponent's argument. Your three basic options are to present your client's approach to the topic; to show the fallacies or weaknesses in the opposing argument; or, less commonly, to make a concession. In any case, you must convey respect for opposing counsel and his or her client, even as you convey disagreement with their assertion, by framing your response in terms of the assertion, not the people involved.

In the sample oral argument, the following exchange occurred:

Judge 1:   Well, opposing counsel indicates that the record is unclear as to whether it was maybe Mr. Nelson's own misunderstanding that caused this. We don't really have it clear on the record that it was the HomeElderCare worker's incompetence that produced this. Isn't that true?

Respondent's Counsel: I think that we can make the assumption that indeed it was the incompetence of the HomeElderCare social worker. I think that this further demonstrates why you need somebody with a trained legal background to make these kinds of decisions so that these kinds of questions are not at issue after we have the living will being formed.

g. Nudging Questions

A question may amount to a direction to move on. Oftentimes, this type of question is a so-called "soft toss"—that is, a question in which the judge makes a point favorable to your client and thereby encourages you to discuss that point. Resist the cynic's temptation to look for a trap in the question. Rather, to continue the baseball analogy, you should hit the ball out of the ballpark by first concurring with the judge and then developing the point further by citing authority, or referring to relevant facts, or both.

In the sample oral argument, for instance, the following question, if asked, would have given either counsel the chance to move to the second topic:

Judge 1:   Counsel, even if there were unauthorized practice of law, wouldn't there also have to be some incompetence or fraud shown for this contract to be invalid?

h. Unclear, Irrelevant, or Unanswerable Questions

If the court asks an unclear question, politely tell the court that you are not sure what point the court means to raise and that you need a clarification. For instance, "Your honor, could you rephrase that question? I'm not sure that I understand it."

If the court asks an irrelevant question, consider asking the judge to repeat the question so you can be sure you have not misunderstood it. Then answer briefly, or tactfully explain what the more relevant question is, and answer it.

If the court asks a question you cannot answer, say so candidly, and offer to submit a supplemental brief on the point. For instance, "I'm sorry, your honor; I'm not familiar with that statute. I would be glad to research it and submit a supplemental brief on it, if that would be helpful." Of course, this approach is appropriate only if you are completely unprepared to answer the question. This response likely will decrease your credibility with the court, but it is better to candidly admit lack of knowledge than to risk an erroneous or ill-considered response.

4. Being Your Best Self

Courtroom demeanor varies considerably. Some oral advocates are fairly passionate and demonstrative. Others are more reserved and moderate. To a great extent, your courtroom demeanor will be a matter of your personal style. You also may consider matching your demeanor to the situation, as determined by the nature of the case, the type of argument you are making (equitable arguments calling for more passion than technical legal arguments), and the temperament of the court.

In all cases, of course, you must convey respect for the court, opposing counsel, and the law. Address judges with deference, never familiarity. You may disagree with the merits of opposing counsel's arguments, but you should never convey personal disdain for opposing counsel. Furthermore, oral argument is not an occasion for emotional appeals, pejoratives, abstract speeches about justice, or irrelevant humor. Nor is it an occasion for stating your personal views of the client's case or the state of the law. Indeed, most experts caution against first-person references ("I believe . . ."). Rather, your argument should be grounded in the facts as found in the record, the law as it exists or should be, and well founded public policy.

Finally, in all cases, you should convey both credibility and a commitment to the client's cause. Ideally, you actually will believe your client's arguments, and this belief will come through naturally. To maximize the appearance of credibility and commitment during the argument, take care in framing your points so you neither overreach nor understate matters. As much as possible, focus on the material you personally find most compelling. Answer questions honestly; do not try to bluster through awkward situations. Rather than acting according to your image of a lawyer, be yourself.

F. THE DAY OF THE ARGUMENT

1. Before the Argument

You should dress neatly and appropriately, so that your appearance does not distract from your argument. Consult with a lawyer who argues often before that court as to local dress conventions.

Bring to the courtroom the transcript, record, all briefs, your notes, and any other materials to which you may need to refer. You need not bring all of these materials to the lectern, but you should have them on the counsel's table, where you can retrieve them if you need them.

Arrive early to scout out the courtroom, if it is unfamiliar to you. You will want to note the acoustics, the height of the lectern, and the timing system. Check with the bailiff or clerk for hints as to the procedures of that particular court and the preferences of the judge(s).

The timing system in an appellate courtroom may consist of a conventional countdown timer or a set of lights—green for go, yellow for x number of minutes remaining, and red for stop. Or you and the court may keep track of the time yourselves. You always should bring an easy-to-read watch and place it on the lectern.

2. During the Argument

Rise when the court enters and leaves, as well as when you address the court. Wait for the presiding judge to give you permission to begin your argument. Refer to the judge as "your honor," "Judge," or "Justice" (if you are before the high court of the jurisdiction).

To achieve your goal of a conversation, maintain eye contact as much as possible. Give the name of the case or the section number of the statute only if needed to avoid confusion. Do not read citations unless asked for them. Avoid distracting conduct, like jingling coins in your pocket, covering your mouth, or flipping pages over the front edge of the lectern.

According to the recency principle, the last words said carry particular weight, so it is important to conclude well. You need not use all of the allotted time. Courts really do appreciate brevity and may be impressed with the simplicity of a short argument. If you finish early, ask the court if it has any more questions, and, if not, conclude and sit down. If you represent the appellant, you may be able to add your leftover time to your reserved rebuttal time. On the other hand, if you run out of time, you should conclude the sentence or the answer in very brief form, then ask the court if you may have an additional thirty to sixty seconds in which to deliver a very brief conclusion. If the court grants the extension, take care not to exceed the time given. If the court refuses the request, thank the court for its attention, and sit down.

G. REVIEW OF CHAPTER 21

Oral argument is not a speech or book report, but rather a conversation with the court in which your primary goal is to address the court's concerns. Oral argument procedures vary considerably from trial to appellate courts, and you should research the rules and practices of a court before arguing before it.

The movant or appellant argues first. Although oral argument is less fixed than written advocacy, most arguments follow a sequence that bears a loose resemblance to memoranda or briefs: introductory material, facts and procedure, development of the legal argument, and conclusion. Counsel for the party opposing the motion or appeal speaks next, responding to the points made by opposing counsel and stating his or her own view of the case. The movant or appellant may conclude the argument with a brief rebuttal.

To prepare for an oral presentation, you must select the arguments you want to present, typically your strongest arguments, the areas of sharpest conflict between the parties, and arguments that can be stated easily in oral form. In addition, you should think through the pitch of your argument, the allocation of time among your various topics, and ways to maintain flexibility during the argument. For significant arguments, it is important to prepare written materials to have at the lectern and then to practice.

As you deliver your presentation, speak clearly, use inflection, and employ verbal signals so that your listeners can easily understand your arguments and follow your organization. Analyze the questions you receive by type, for example, as hypotheticals or policy questions; respond accordingly and fully; then move back into your argument as smoothly as possible. Finally, be sure to follow court etiquette and procedures during the argument so that the court focuses not on your personal mannerisms but rather on the content of your argument.

Your argument will be complete if it addresses what the court wants to know. It will be comprehensible if the court can follow your issues, fact statement, and argument. It will be correct and cohesive if the facts, law, and policy are accurately stated and mesh together into a coherent whole. Lastly, your argument will be convincing if you advocate your client's position with confidence and sincerity.

HomeElderCare Case File
TABLE OF CONTENTS

PREFACE TO

HomeElderCare

CASE FILE

This case file contains materials pertinent to a fictitious case, the HomeElderCare case. The central issue in the case is whether a HomeElderCare social worker commits the unauthorized practice of law by preparing a living will, or health care directive, for an elderly client for a fee. The case file covers both advice to HomeElderCare before it created the service and litigation of complaints arising out of the service.

---

1. Consultation before the Living Will Service Is Created

Meeting with Mary Mahoney, Executive Director of HomeElderCare, Sept. 9, 1992
HomeElderCare (HEC)
not-for-profit corporation
    clients = elderly
    250 clients
    staff = 10 social workers, variable # of volunteers
    social worker duties:
        initial interview to find needs (finances, family concerns, home cleaning, etc.)
        set up schedule
        monthly check-in
        liaison to atty or physician is possible
    fee per service, differs for each client
legal concern
    some clients want living wills & help with health care decisions

has form living will that looks straightforward (gave me copy)
>   is it?
>   does atty need to do it?
>   if not done by atty, will it be valid?
> will HEC's fees be collectible?
> social workers' role (not volunteers)
>>   need training
>>   would ask Qs on form & fill in client's answers
>>   would help get form notarized
>>   would charge fee for those services
> client would save $ by not hiring atty
> client already knows social workers, so easier than hiring atty
> social workers' background/training
>>   minimum = bachelor's degree in social work, licensed (5 staff)
>>   some have master's degree + second-level licensing (5 staff)
>>   4 possible levels of licensing
>>   some master's degree classes focus on care of elderly
>>   do they need additional 1-2 seminars?
> I'll send her opinion letter soon, before her trip, then call re additional Qs.

2. Representation in a Dispute between HomeElderCare and Client Roger Nelson

- HomeElderCare did create and implement a living will service not involving a lawyer.
- Nelson's living will nominates his medical proxy to be his guardian. This is contrary to his current desires.

The first component of the case file is the legal research file: four cases and corresponding case briefs, two additional case briefs, the leading statute and a statute brief, a related statute, and excerpts from five commentary sources.

The second component consists of two analytical office memos and an advice letter. The first office memo analyzes the living will service in light of the dispute with Mr. Nelson; it is a dispute-oriented memo. The second office memo advises HomeElderCare about a potential living will service; it is a deal-oriented memo. The advice letter is based on the second memo.

The third component consists of five documents pertaining to an action brought by the State of Minnesota to enjoin, or stop, HomeElderCare's preparation of living wills. The documents are:

- the demand letter, written to HomeElderCare by the county attorney on behalf of the State, seeking a quick resolution of the case;
- the State's notice of motion and motion for a temporary injunction;
- its proposed order;
- the State's memorandum in support of its motion; and
- HomeElderCare's memorandum in opposition to the State's motion.

Note that in a real litigation file, there would be other documents as well, such as the pleadings and certificates of service.

The fourth component, drawing on the dispute between HomeElderCare and Mr. Nelson's son and the first office memo, consists of three documents pertaining to an appeal from a trial court ruling in favor of Mr. Nelson who sought to invalidate his contract with HomeElderCare. The three documents are:

- HomeElderCare's brief
- Mr. Nelson's brief, and
- the transcript of the oral argument.

Again, in a real litigation file, there would be other documents as well, such as the stipulation of facts and the trial court's order and memorandum.

In brief, the documents pertain to the two stages as follows:

Stage One—Deal-Oriented Consultation:

- the first component
- the second office memo
- the advice letter

Stage Two—Dispute-Oriented Representation:

- the first component
- the first office memo
- the demand letters
- the third component re an action by the state
- the fourth component re an action by a HomeElderCare client

Although the case is fictitious and the files are incomplete, we hope that the materials help you appreciate the end-products of the legal reading, reasoning, and writing processes described in the text. To promote your understanding, we have annotated some of the documents in the margin and have provided space in the margins of the other documents for your own annotations.

We have written the office memos, motion practice memoranda, and appellate briefs so as to illustrate various approaches to certain matters. For example, some documents follow *The Bluebook: A Uniform System of Citation,* while others follow *ALWD Citation Manual: A Professional System of Citation.* The box on the first page of each of these documents alerts you to the approaches taken therein.

One final and important note: The case file was written in the early 1990s and takes place in Minnesota. Although the law has changed since then, we decided to freeze the case file as of that time because it works better, from an educational standpoint, under 1993 law than under current law. In addition, we used procedural rules that fit our teaching purposes, not necessarily the most applicable rules. The law of your state may be fairly similar to or very different from what is presented here.

Dick Weatherston's Associated Mechanical Services, Inc. v. Minnesota Mutual Life Insurance Company, 100 N.W.2d 819 (Minn. 1960).

DICK WEATHERSTON'S A. M. SERV. v. MINNESOTA M. L. I. CO. Minn. **819**
Cite as 100 N.W.2d 819

DICK WEATHERSTON'S ASSOCIATED MECHANICAL SERVICES, INC., Respondent,

v.

MINNESOTA MUTUAL LIFE INSURANCE COMPANY, Appellant.

No. 37730.

Supreme Court of Minnesota.

Jan. 22, 1960.

Action was brought for breach of contract between plaintiff's assignor and defendant for installation of air-conditioning equipment by assignor in defendant's building. The District Court, Ramsey County, Ronald E. Hachey, J., entered an order denying defendant's motion in the alternative for judgment notwithstanding the verdict or a new trial, and the defendant appealed. The Supreme Court, Murphy, J., held that contract between plaintiff's assignor and defendant for installation of air-conditioning equipment by assignor in defendant's building, was not illegal under statute providing that it is unlawful for a person to practice, among other occupations, architecture and professional engineering unless such person is qualified by registration under law, though contract involved elements of engineering work by preparation of plans and estimates, and though assignor was not licensed as an engineer under the statute, where plans, specifications, and estimates were furnished with understanding that they would be subject to approval by defendant's architect and engineer and were to be installed under supervision of that architect and engineer, and such professional work was incidental to and part of the contract for the entire job and was approved and accepted by defendant's architect and engineer.

Affirmed with directions.

1. Appeal and Error ☞930(1)

Conflicts in evidence are to be resolved upon appeal by stating controlling facts as jury, in light of whole evidence, reasonably could and must have found them in arriving at its verdict, and reviewing court is controlled by such elementary rule, even though reviewing court might have, on basis of record, reached a different conclusion.

2. Contracts ☞28(3)

In action to recover for breach of alleged contract between plaintiff's assignor and defendant for installation of air-conditioning equipment in defendant's building, evidence sustained jury's findings that a valid contract had been made by plaintiff's assignor and defendant.

3. Appeal and Error ☞994(2, 3)

Question whether certain witnesses are worthy of belief is primarily for jury and trial court.

4. Licenses ☞39.1

Generally, where a license or certificate is required by statute as a requisite for one practicing a particular profession, an agreement of professional character without such license or certificate is ordinarily held illegal and void.

5. Licenses ☞39.40

Statute providing that it is unlawful for a person to practice, among other occupations, architecture and professional engineering unless such person is qualified by registration under law, is founded on sound public policy and has as its purpose the public health and welfare as well as the protection of the public against incompetence and fraud. M.S.A. § 326.02.

6. Licenses ☞39.1

Justice and sound public policy do not always require literal and arbitrary enforcement of a licensing statute, and though general rule is that a contract executed in violation of a statute imposing a prohibition against carrying on of a business or occupation without first having secured a license is void, that rule is not to be

---

❶	case name	❸	court	❻	West's headnotes
❷	docket number	❹	date of decision	❼	citation
		❺	West's editorial matter		

820   Minn.   **100 NORTH WESTERN REPORTER, 2d SERIES**

applied in a particular case without first examining the statute as a whole to determine whether or not the Legislature intended such contract to be illegal.

7. Licenses ⬰39.40

Contract between plaintiff's assignor and defendant for installation of air-conditioning equipment by assignor in defendant's building, was not illegal under statute providing that it is unlawful for a person to practice, among other occupations, architecture and professional engineering unless such person is qualified by registration under law, though contract involved elements of engineering work by preparation of plans and estimates, and though assignor was not licensed as an engineer under the statute, where plans, specifications, and estimates were furnished with understanding that they would be subject to approval by defendant's architect and engineer and were to be installed under supervision of that architect and engineer, and such professional work was incidental to and part of the contract for the entire job and was approved and accepted by defendant's architect and engineer. M.S.A. § 326.02.

8. Damages ⬰40(2)

Generally, where breach of contract consists in the repudiation of the contract or prevention of performance of contract, party who is ready to perform may recover profits he would have realized had contract been performed.

9. Damages ⬰45

In action for breach of contract between plaintiff's assignor and defendant for installation of air-conditioning equipment by assignor in defendant's building, it was proper for jury in determining amount of plaintiff's damages to consider $1,500 item representing time consumed by plaintiff's assignor, not only in preparation of plans and designs for approval by defendant's architect, but expense involved as well in time expended in conferences and in investigating prices and costs of components required for installation of the equipment.

10. Appeal and Error ⬰221, 1178(6)
   Costs ⬰238(2)

Where appellant fails to call trial court's attention to error in jury's computation resulting in an excessive verdict, such error ordinarily will not be considered on appeal for the first time, but where apparent error in computation is substantial, question may be remanded for review by trial court in interests of justice without prejudice to respondent's rights to recover costs on appeal.

Syllabus by the Court.

1. Conflicts in the evidence are to be resolved upon appeal by stating the controlling facts as the jury in the light of the whole evidence reasonably could and must have found them in arriving at its verdict. An appellate court is controlled by this elementary rule even though it might have, on the basis of the record, reached a different conclusion.

2. It is the general rule that where a license or certificate is required by a statute as a requisite for one practicing a particular profession, an agreement of professional character without such license or certificate is ordinarily held illegal and void.

3. M.S.A. § 326.02, which requires persons engaged in the occupation of architecture and professional engineering to qualify by registration, is founded upon sound public policy, having as its purpose the public health and welfare as well as the protection of the public against incompetence and fraud.

4. Where an air-conditioning contractor enters into a contract for the installation of air-conditioning equipment, which contract involves elements of engineering work by preparation of plans and estimates, such contract is not rendered illegal within the meaning of § 326.02, even though the contractor is not licensed as an engineer under § 326.02, where the plans, specifications, and estimates are furnished with the understanding that they will be subject to approval by the architect and engineer re-

court's editorial matter

DICK WEATHERSTON'S A. M. SERV. v. MINNESOTA M. L. I. CO.   Minn.   821
Cite as 100 N.W.2d 819

tained by the other party and are to be installed under the supervision of the other party's architect and engineer. Such professional work was incidental to and part of the contract for the entire job and was approved and accepted by the architects and engineers responsible for the supervision of such construction.

5. The court correctly instructed the jury in accordance with the general rule that where a breach consists in repudiating the contract or preventing its performance the party who is ready to perform may recover the profits he would have realized had the contract been performed and that expenditures made in preparation to execute the contract may be recovered.

6. Where the appellant fails to call the trial court's attention to an error in computation by the jury resulting in an excessive verdict, such error ordinarily will not be considered on appeal for the first time. However, where the apparent error is substantial, the question may be remanded for review by the trial court in the interests of justice without prejudice to the respondent's rights to recover costs on appeal.

———————

 Richard J. Leonard and Eugene M. Warlich, St. Paul, Doherty, Rumble & Butler, St. Paul, of counsel, for appellant.

B. Jerome Loftsgaarden, Loftsgaarden & Loftsgaarden, St. Paul, for respondent.

MURPHY, Justice.

This case comes to us on appeal from an order denying the defendant's motion in the alternative for judgment notwithstanding the verdict or for a new trial. The plaintiff recovered a verdict in the sum of $5,691 in an action brought for breach of contract. The principal issue involved in this case requires a construction of M.S.A. § 326.02 as it applies to the particular facts before us. We are asked to determine if a contract which includes professional engineering services is in violation of that

statute and illegal so as to preclude recovery thereon under circumstances where the contractor is an unlicensed engineer whose services are rendered subject to the approval and supervision of an architect and engineer retained by the other party.

 Viewing the record in the light most favorable to the verdict, the jury could have found these facts: The plaintiff's assignor, Dick Weatherston, at the time of the events involved in this action, was a contractor in the air-conditioning business. He had received a bachelor of science degree in mechanical engineering from the University of Michigan, after which he was employed by various companies, including General Mills and the Seeger Refrigerator Company, as a plant engineer. For some years before engaging in the contracting business in Minnesota he was employed as a project engineer, and in the course of that work he was registered in that profession under the laws of the States of Ohio and Texas. As a contractor he expected to receive work on projects designed and supervised by registered architects and engineers, and he stated in his testimony that in order to avoid a conflict of interest and to obviate the possibility of being considered a competitor with such architects and engineers he did not register as an engineer in Minnesota.

In the fall of 1956 the Minnesota Mutual Life Insurance Company was in the process of completing the construction of a large home office building in St. Paul. They had retained as their architects the firm of Ellerbe & Company. It appears that during the process of construction of this building the company determined to install certain electronic computing equipment on one of the upper floors of the building. Because of the great amount of heat this machine would give off in operation, there arose a serious problem in providing ventilation and air conditioning in the particular area where the equipment was to be installed.

In the fall of 1956 certain officers of the defendant company discussed the problem

822   Minn.   100 **NORTH WESTERN REPORTER, 2d SERIES**

with plaintiff. He was advised that the plans submitted by Ellerbe & Company as to this particular phase of the construction and installation would involve costs in excess of the budget set up by the company. They asked him if he would be in a position to give them a proposal, including a design and cost price, to solve the air-conditioning problem in the particular area involved. After being told that Ellerbe & Company were the architects and engineers retained by the builder, Weatherston informed the defendant through its officers that a large part of his business was derived from architectural firms and that if these firms knew that he engaged in designing and engineering work they would discontinue dealing with him. He told them accordingly that he could not compete with Ellerbe in designing the system, but he could submit plans if he obtained the contract for the entire installation. He was told that an arrangement had been made whereby Ellerbe had withdrawn from the "air conditioning phase" of the installation but that they would remain as "consultant" to supervise and approve the system used. Weatherston agreed to this arrangement.

Preliminary plans and specifications were drawn up by Weatherston and submitted to the company with an offer about January 1, 1957. When these plans were submitted to the officers of the defendant company, Weatherston again explained that he was a contractor and did not want to conflict with Ellerbe in doing designing or engineering work. He was told that the company understood his position and that the plans submitted by him would have to be approved by Ellerbe. After some discussion and examination of his proposals, another plan was drawn up and submitted with a new offer for approval by Ellerbe & Company. Later, modifications were made which were suggested by Ellerbe and a final proposal appears to have been submitted some time in February 1957. During the course of these negotiations there were at least three conferences with Ellerbe & Company, the defendant's architects. The final plan, ex-

cept for some minor changes, proved satisfactory to Ellerbe & Company, and after a meeting at their office, it was agreed that the plaintiff would install the necessary equipment and furnish the materials for a price of $16,203. Weatherston testified that, after the final meeting with Ellerbe, the corporate officer who acted for the defendant company told him "to proceed with the work and get the equipment ordered, and then to, just to go ahead and get the job rolling." In the proposals Weatherston submitted, the sales price of all component parts of the air-conditioning system was included. So far as appears from the record no charge for design or plan was made. Weatherston considered the contract as one for the sale of an entire system and none of his actions in submitting the proposals are inconsistent with that conclusion.

On March 2, 1957, about 2 weeks after Weatherston claims his plans were submitted and his offer was accepted, he was informed that the defendant company had determined to give the work to another air-conditioning contractor. No loss was sustained by the plaintiff in the purchase of materials specified for the job. He was able to cancel the orders before delivery. The work was finally performed by Holmsten Refrigeration, Inc. It appears from the evidence that the latter company was not a registered architect or engineer.

[1–3] 1. There is a sharp conflict in the evidence in this case. The evidence of the defendant tended to show that no contract was ever entered into between the parties; that the plaintiff was one of a number of contractors invited to submit a bid or proposal setting forth the materials and labor he would furnish and the price he would charge for the proposed work; and that there was no acceptance of any proposal made by the plaintiff. On the other hand, there was evidence supporting the finding of the jury that an offer and acceptance constituting a valid contract had been made by the parties. Under the circumstances we are controlled by the well- ⑮

⑮ discussion of first issue: evidence supporting contract formation

DICK WEATHERSTON'S A. M. SERV. v. MINNESOTA M. L. I. CO.   Minn.   **823**
Cite as 100 N.W.2d 819

established rule that conflicts are to be resolved upon appeal by stating the controlling facts as the jury, in the light of the whole evidence, reasonably could and must have found them in arriving at its verdict. An appellate court is controlled by this elementary rule even though it might have, on the basis of the record, reached a different conclusion. Hardy v. Anderson, 241 Minn. 478, 63 N.W.2d 814; 1 Dunnell, Dig. (3 ed.) § 415b; 14 Id. §§ 7144, 7159. Whether certain witnesses are worthy of belief is primarily for the jury and the trial court. Becker v. Thomson, 208 Minn. 332, 294 N. W. 214.

[4] 2. It is the contention of the defendant that the contract involved is one for professional engineering services and, since the plaintiff was unlicensed as an engineer, the contract is illegal so as to preclude recovery. It may be generally stated that where a license or certificate is required by statute as a requisite for one practicing a particular profession, an agreement of professional character without such license or certificate is ordinarily held illegal and void.[1]

1. 53 C.J.S. Licenses, § 59; 33 Am.Jur., Licenses, §§ 68 to 74, 4 Dunnell, Dig. (3 ed.) § 1873.

2. Section 326.02, subd. 1, provides:
   "In order to safeguard life, health, and property, and to promote the public welfare, any person in either public or private capacity practicing, or offering to practice, architecture, professional engineering, or land surveying in this state, either as an individual, a co-partner, or as agent of another, shall be registered as hereinafter provided. It shall be unlawful for any person to practice, or to offer to practice, in this state, architecture, professional engineering, or land surveying, or to solicit or to contract to furnish work within the terms of sections 326.02 to 326.16, or to use in connection with his name, or to otherwise assume, use or advertise any title or description tending to convey the impression that he is an architect, professional engineer (hereinafter called engineer) or land surveyor, unless such person is qualified by registration under sections 326.02 to 326.16."

[5] 3. It is specifically provided by M.S.A. § 326.02 that it is unlawful for a person to practice, among other occupations, architecture and professional engineering unless such person is qualified by registration under law.[2] This statute is founded upon sound public policy, having as its purpose the public health and welfare as well as the protection of the public against incompetence and fraud.[3] It has been held in accordance with this principle that contracts made in violation of statutes requiring registration or licensing of engineers or architects are illegal and unenforceable because inimical to both the public policy and the actual, though implied, intent of the legislature.[4]

[6] 4. While it is true that certain elements of the preliminary work performed by the plaintiff, such as calculations and design submitted by the plaintiff to the defendant and its architects, required an expertise in the area of engineering as defined by § 326.02, subd. 3,[5] the transaction as a whole must be considered in connection with its particular facts to determine if it comes within the prohibition of § 326.02.

3. In re Estate of Peterson, 230 Minn. 478. 42 N.W.2d 59, 18 A.L.R.2d 910; Leuthold v. Stickney, 116 Minn. 299, 133 N.W. 856, 39 L.R.A.,N.S., 231; cf. Vercellini v. U. S. I. Realty Co., 158 Minn. 72, 196 N.W. 672; Restatement, Contracts, § 580; 6 Corbin, Contracts, § 1512; 4 Dunnell, Dig. (3 ed.) § 1873; Annotations, 42 A.L.R. 1226 to 1228 and 118 A.L.R. 646.

4. Baer v. Tippett, 34 Cal.App.2d 33, 92 P.2d 1028; American Store Equipment & Const. Corp. v. Jack Dempsey's Punch Bowl, Inc., 174 Misc. 436, 21 N.Y.S.2d 117, affirmed 258 App.Div. 794, 16 N.Y.S. 2d 702, affirmed 283 N.Y. 601, 28 N.E.2d 23; 6 Williston, Contracts (Rev. ed.) § 1766.

5. Designing the plans and specifications called for knowledge of heating units (called British Thermal Units) which the equipment would give off when operating; calculating the amount of air conditioning needed to carry off the heat and control the room temperature; locating and installing the various component parts of the system; designing

---

⑯   discussion of second issue: legality of contract   ⑰   general rule

824 Minn. **100 NORTH WESTERN REPORTER, 2d SERIES**

Justice and sound public policy do not always require the literal and arbitrary enforcement of a licensing statute.[6] While recognizing the general rule that a contract executed in violation of a statute imposing a prohibition against the carrying on of a business or occupation without first having secured a license is void, that rule is not to be applied in a particular case without first examining the statute as a whole to determine whether or not the legislature intended such contract to be illegal.[7]

[7] If we apply the terms of the statute to the particular facts in this case we must readily come to the conclusion that the agreement between the parties was in no way inimical to life, health, property, or public welfare; nor should there by any difficulty in conceding that the transaction before us is free from any element of fraud, incompetence, or misrepresentation. Viewing the relationship of the parties, it must be recognized at the outset that the plaintiff was sought out by the defendant for his services as an air-conditioning contractor. It was clearly understood by the defendant that the plaintiff was engaged in the air-conditioning business and that in addition to his qualifications as a contractor he had a background and education giving him a certain competence in the area of engineering. The plaintiff, however, made it clear to the defendant that he was not a registered engineer and architect. It is equally clear that the defendant had its own architects and engineers and did not wholly rely upon the qualifications of the plaintiff in that area. Because of the nature of the work to be performed, it was necessary for the plaintiff in order to give the defendant an estimate of the cost of the proposed work to specify the materials needed with plans and details of how the work was to be carried out. The defendant company was interested in having the work done at a price which would come within its budget. Since the plan for this work prepared by its own architects and engineers exceeded the budget, it was not surprising that it consulted a contractor who, because of his business, had specialized knowledge of methods of installing air-conditioning equipment. The design and plan he submitted to accomplish this purpose were approved by the defendant's architects and in effect were adopted by it and became its own plans.[8]

---

methods to comply with city ordinances on water regulation, all for the protection of the machinery and health and comfort of defendant's employees. Section 326.02, subd. 3, provides:

"Any person shall be deemed to be practicing professional engineering within the meaning of sections 326.02 to 326.16 who shall furnish any technical professional service, such as planning, design or supervision of construction for the purpose of assuring compliance with specifications and design, in connection with any public or private structures, buildings, ultilities, machines, equipment, processes, works, or projects wherein the public welfare or the safeguarding of life, health, or property is concerned or involved, when such professional service requires the application of the principles of mathematics and the physical sciences, acquired by education or training."

6. 6 Corbin, Contracts, § 1512, p. 968.

7. 4 Dunnell, Dig. (3 ed.) § 1873; see, In re Estate of Peterson, 230 Minn. 478, 42 N.W.2d 59, 18 A.L.R.2d 910; Minter

Brothers Co. v. Hochman, 231 Minn. 156, 42 N.W.2d 562; Brimhall v. Van Campen, 8 Minn. 13, Gil. 1.

8. The necessity of examining the particular facts in each case so as to determine whether or not there is a violation of the statute becomes apparent from the testimony of Richard Holmsten, who was eventually awarded the contract for the work. He was not registered as an engineer or architect, yet he testified there were two methods by which air-conditioning contractors received work. He said, "One is to receive from a registered engineer a set of plans and specifications whereby he will outline the problem involved and we submit our quotation to accomplish this problem." The other, he said, is to call upon the customer and "ask him for the opportunity to design and work up a proposal to accomplish for the problem which we quote a sum of money to accomplish this." He further testified that his company prepared plans where the job was of sufficient size "that it is to our benefit." It is

---

18 broadly stated exception

19 application of rule to facts

DICK WEATHERSTON'S A. M. SERV. v. MINNESOTA M. L. I. CO.   Minn.   **825**
Cite as 100 N.W.2d 819

[20] Since the professional work performed by the plaintiff in this case was incidental to and part of a contract for an entire job which was approved and accepted by architects and engineers responsible for the supervision of such construction, it is our view that it comes within those numerous exceptions which hold generally that the prohibitions of the statute involved are no broader than its purpose in protecting the public from misrepresentation and deceit.[9] The scope of the statute coincides with the reasons for its existence. Since those reasons have no bearing upon the transaction involved herein, the statute is without application. 6 Corbin, Contracts, § 1512; In re Estate of Peterson, 230 Minn. 478, 42 N.W.2d 59, 18 A.L.R.2d 910.

[21] 5. In support of its contention that the plaintiff violated the statute, the defendant points to the allegation of the plaintiff's amended complaint claiming damages in the sum of $1,500 for "work performed in designing and preparing drawings for said mechanical work" and to the testimony of the plaintiff to the effect that his contract price included the sum of $1,500 for that particular work. It argues that this evidence alone is determinative of the character of the work as being an architectural and engineering service requiring registration under the law.

[22] [8,9] In discussing this point it is necessary to keep in mind that this is not a suit to collect for an architectural or engineering fee. It is a suit to recover damages suffered by the plaintiff as a result of the defendant's alleged breach of contract. The only out-of-pocket expense involved in this transaction grew out of loss of the plaintiff's time in conferences with the defendant and its architects and in preparation of plans for the execution of the contract. We think the trial court correctly

perceived the issues as appears from his instructions. He told the jury that under the laws of Minnesota "an unregistered person is not permitted to practice professional engineering" and that "plaintiff would not be permitted to recover for the engineering services, that is, the consultation service, the drawing of plans, and the proposals standing alone because plaintiff is not a registered engineer in this state." He told the jury that the plaintiff could not recover for the services performed unless he could show that under the agreement "he was to prepare the plans and drawings or any other proposal and make the complete installation for a price certain and that the same was accepted by the defendant * * *." On the issue of damages he correctly instructed the jury in accordance with the general rule that where the breach consists in repudiating the contract or preventing its performance the party who is ready to perform may recover the profits he would have realized had the contract been performed. 15 Am.Jur., Damages, § 151; 5 Dunnell, Dig. (3 ed.) § 2568a. Further, with reference to expenditures made in preparation to execute the contract, the jury was instructed that recovery may be had for expense incurred in part performance or in preparation for performance, providing, of course, such items of damage are proven. Swanson v. Andrus, 83 Minn. 505, 86 N.W. 465; Periodical Press Co. v. Sherman-Elliott Co., 143 Minn. 489, 174 N.W. 516; Johnson v. Wright, 175 Minn. 236, 220 N.W. 946; 5 Dunnell, Dig. (3 ed.) § 2568a. In determining plaintiff's damage we think it was proper for the jury to take into consideration actual costs incurred by the plaintiff in connection with this work. We think it satisfactorily appears from the evidence that the $1,500 item represents time consumed by the plaintiff, not only in the preparation of the plans and designs

conceivable that under the latter method, depending upon the particular circumstances, the contractor might find that he is in fact engaging in professional engineering work without having registered as required by law.
100 N.W.2d—52½

9. Kennoy v. Graves, Ky., 300 S.W.2d 568; Edmonds v. Fehler & Feinauer Const. Co., 6 Cir., 252 F.2d 639; Dow v. United States, 10 Cir., 154 F.2d 707; Fischer v. Landisch, 203 Wis. 254, 234 N.W. 498.

---

[20] holding; specific rule   **[21]** defendant's secondary argument   **[22]** court's analysis of secondary argument

for approval by the defendant's architect but expense involved as well in time expended in conferences and in investigating prices and costs of the components required for the installation of the work. We agree with the trial court that it was proper for the jury to consider the $1,500 item as an out-of-pocket expenditure in establishing the amount of plaintiff's damages.

6. In addition to the $1,500 representing the work performed in designing and preparing the drawings, the plaintiff claimed the further sum of $4,191.21 for loss of profit in the performance of the work. His total claim was $5,691.21. The jury awarded him $5,691, of which $4,191 appears to have been attributable to profit.

The record strongly supports the company's claim that the verdict is excessive. The plaintiff testified as to the cost of the various components, including two air conditioners, pneumatic controls, humidifiers, electrical wiring, and other items including labor and freight. He testified that his profit was $4,191.21, which was the difference between his cost price of $12,011.79 and his selling cost of $16,203. It appears from the record, however, that the plaintiff's estimated cost was $13,011.80, not $12,011.79. His profit, accordingly, would not be $4,191.21, but $3,191.20, or exactly $1,000.01 less than the error in addition showed it to be.

The defendant accordingly argues that a new trial should be granted on the ground that the verdict on the issue of damages is contrary to law and is not sustained by the evidence.

It must be noted, however, that the defendant made no motion in the trial court for a correction of this error. The trial court should have first been given the opportunity to examine the verdict and the record to determine how the error was made, if there was one, for the error could have been made in other ways than excessive computation by the jury. La Nasa v. Pierre, 225 Minn. 189, 30 N.W.2d 32; Fletcher v. German-American Ins. Co., 79 Minn. 337, 343, 82 N.W. 647, 649; Barnard-Curtiss Co. v. Minneapolis Dredging Co., 200 Minn. 327, 274 N.W. 229.

[10] In view of the substantial amount involved, we are of the view that in the interests of justice this particular issue should be remanded to the district court to give it an opportunity to pass upon the matter of the apparent error. The order of the trial court is affirmed and the case is remanded to the district court for the purpose only of reviewing the issue relating to the asserted error in computation. The case is remanded, however, only on condition that the appellant pay the full costs and disbursements on this appeal and such further costs as may be incurred on remand to the district court.

Affirmed with directions.

㉓ discussion of third issue: excessive damages   procedural outcome

Weatherston's Brief

Dick Weatherston's Associated Mechanical Services v. Minnesota Mutual Life Insurance Co., Minnesota Supreme Court, 1960, 100 N.W.2d 819.

FACTS: P is air conditioning contractor in MN. Although P's assignor Dick Weatherston (DW) had B.S. in mechanical engineering, he was not registered as engr in MN. D needed air conditioning for new building & asked P to submit design plans & pricing. DW told D he wasn't licensed & raised concern about conflict w/Ellerbe, D's architects & engrs. Ellerbe agreed to act as consultant. P submitted plans; they were modified after review by Ellerbe & approved. No charge for design or plan was included. P was told to start, but 2 weeks later, P was informed that D had given project to different contractor (also not regd engr).

PROCEDURE: P sued D for damages for breach of K. Jury found offer & acceptance & awarded damages. D moved for new trial or JNOV; denied. D appealed.

*ISSUE: Is K illegal, or can unregd engr recover damages for breach of K, where statute requires regn as engr to practice engrg, work covered by K includes prof'l engr services, engr has training as engr, services are subject to approval of architect/engr retained by D, & D knows engr isn't regd?

HOLDING: Affirmed & remanded to trial ct w/directions re damages. Unregd engr can recover damages for breach of K including engr services where engr has training, D's engr approves plans, & engr tells D of non-regd.

REASONING: Rule: Ks made in violation of licensing statutes typically are illegal & void. But statute & transaction must be viewed as whole to determine whether legislature intended K to be illegal.
   Statute: Minn. Stat. § 326.02 requires that person who practices as prof'l engr be registered in MN. Statutory purpose is protect public against fraud & incompetence & promote public health & welfare.
   Application: Here K should be enforced: Engr work was incidental to & part of entire job. DW had training. Work was approved by regd engrs. D sought out P, & DW told D of unregd status. Case does not raise concerns about incompetence, harm to public welfare, fraud. Nor does P's claim for "designing & preparing drawings" establish P's work was illegal engrg practice.
   Policy: Assure that parties who K for engr services are not harmed by fraud or work done by incompetent persons. Safeguard public welfare (through properly engrd buildings presumably).

PERTINENCE: Look into statute re practice of law, training & oversight of social workers.

---

*Challenges to jury verdict & damages award are not covered.

Buckley v. Humason, 52 N.W. 385 (Minn. 1892).

BUCKLEY v. HUMASON *et al.*

(Supreme Court of Minnesota. June 15, 1892.)

VALIDITY OF CONTRACT—DOING BUSINESS WITHOUT LICENSE—REAL-ESTATE AGENTS.

1. Transactions in violation of law cannot be made the foundation of a valid contract.

2. Where a statute or an ordinance, duly authorized and enacted, makes a particular business unlawful for unlicensed persons, any contract made in such business by one not authorized is void.

3. Where, by a valid city ordinance, it was made unlawful for any person to exercise within the city the business of a real-estate broker without a license, *held*, that a person so engaged in negotiating the sale or exchange of real property, in violation of such ordinance, could recover no commissions for his services.

(Syllabus by the Court.)

Appeal from district court, Ramsey county; EGAN, Judge.

Action by Thomas A. Buckley against Emma A. Humason and others to recover commissions for services as real-estate agent. From an order dismissing the case on plaintiff's showing he appeals. Affirmed.

Stevens, O'Brien & Glenn and *Armand Albrecht,* for appellant. *Otis & Godfrey,* for respondents.

VANDERBURGH, J. This action is brought by plaintiff to recover commissions for services as a real-estate agent or broker in procuring a purchaser for certain real estate in Chicago. The cause of action is stated as follows in the complaint: "During the year 1890 the plaintiff, at the special instance and request of the defendants, performed services for said defendants in the city of Chicago, in the state of Illinois, in and about procuring a purchaser for certain property in the state of Illinois, which said services were then and there of the reasonable value of $4,375, and which said sum the defendants agreed and promised to pay plaintiff therefor." The plaintiff testified that at the time of the alleged services he resided in the city of Chicago. The transactions referred to occurred there, and the negotiations were there concluded, and the contract and purchase were consummated in that city, and the plaintiff claims to be entitled to the usual commissions charged and received in Chicago for such services. He also testified that he had been previously engaged in the real-estate business in Chicago, as an agent, and sold and exchanged property for others on commission; and the transaction in question appears clearly enough to have been in the line of his regular business as a real-estate agent or broker. In this connection we must observe that it is admitted in the pleadings that during the year 1890, and prior thereto, an ordinance of the city of Chicago, enacted in pursuance of a statute of that state, was in force, which provided that it should not be lawful for any person to exercise within that city the business of real-estate broker, without a license therefor, and defined a "real-estate broker" as a person who, for commissions or other compensation, is engaged in the selling of or in negotiating sales of real estate belonging to others. A license fee of $25 per annum is required to be paid by such broker, and any person violating the provisions of the ordinance is subject to a penalty of not less than $25, and to the same penalty for every subsequent violation thereof. The testimony shows that the plaintiff was using and exercising the business of a real-estate broker in the city of Chicago during the time in question, and in performing the services for which a recovery is sought in this action. It was made unlawful for him to do so by the terms of the ordinance referred to. It was not at all material that the parties for whom he negotiated a sale agreed to take property in St. Paul in payment or exchange for the Chicago property of which plaintiff negotiated a sale, and for which he found a purchaser. The ordinance, which is set out in full in the answer, was valid, and the case as presented by the evidence clearly falls within it. Braun v Chicago, 110 Ill. 187. It has the force of law within the city of Chicago. Bott v. Pratt, 33 Minn. 323, 23 N. W. Rep. 237. The particular transaction in question was therefore in violation of law, unless he was duly licensed, which was not shown. On the contrary, the answer alleges, and it stands admitted, for want of a reply, that the plaintiff was not duly licensed as a broker. The plaintiff cannot, therefore, recover his commissions. Hustis v. Pickands, 27 Ill. App. 270; Johnson v. Hulings, 103 Pa. St. 501; Holt v. Green, 73 Pa. St. 198. Business transactions, in violation of law, cannot be made the foundation of a valid contract; and the general rule is that where a statute makes a particular business unlawful generally, or for unlicensed persons, any contract made in such business by one not authorized is void, (Bish. Cont. §§ 471, 547; 1 Pom. Eq. Jur. § 402;) and the contract, being void where it was made and to be performed, will be so held here, (Bish. Cont. § 1383.) The case was properly dismissed upon the evidence.

Order affirmed.

Buckley Brief

Buckley v. Humason, Minnesota Supreme Court, 1892, 52 N.W. 385.

FACTS: D hired P, real-estate broker & resident of Chicago, to find purchaser for D's property in Chicago in 1890. P was not licensed as RE broker during contract with D. P found purchaser; D promised to pay P his commission. D did not pay P's commission.

PROCEDURE: P sued D to recover commission. Trial ct dismissed P's suit. P appeals.

ISSUE: Can person acting as RE agent w/o license in violation of city ordinance recover unpaid commission?

HOLDING: Affirmed. P cannot recover commission.

REASONING: Rule: Where statute makes business unlawful for unlicensed persons, contract by person not authorized is void.
　　Statute: 1890 Chicago ordinance: RE broker must obtain license to lawfully conduct RE business in Chicago.
　　Application: Business transaction between P & D was unlawful because P was not licensed. P cannot enforce void K.

PERTINENCE: Bright-line rule; contract is void if license is required & practitioner is not so licensed.

Solomon Brief

Solomon v. Dreschler, Minnesota Supreme Court, 1860, 4 Minn. 278.

FACTS: Merchant P sold goods to D. Goods included "spirituous liquors" & other items. P was not licensed to sell spirituous liquors.

PROCEDURE: P sued D to recover for price of goods sold to D. Lower ct held for D. P appealed.

ISSUES: (1) Can seller recover under K for sale of liquor & other goods if K violates statute that imposes fine for selling liquor w/o license?

(2) If sale of goods would be invalid w/o license, does burden of proof lie with P to show no violation of licensing statute, or with D to show violation of statute?

HOLDINGS: (1) K for sale of liquor & other goods in violation of statute may not be enforced.

(2) If sale of goods would be invalid w/o license, burden of proof lies with P to show P's authority & legal capacity to sell goods.

REASONING: Rule: K in violation of licensing statute is valid if statute's purpose is to raise revenue; K in violation of licensing statute is invalid if statute's purpose is to protect public health or morals or prevent fraud.

Statute: Territorial statute of 1855 required seller of liquors to obtain license, post bond of $5000, sell only in designated building, not sell on Sabbath or to certain people, not permit gambling for money on premises, keep quiet & orderly house.

Application: Statute of 1855 is more than purely revenue statute; policy is to protect public against problems that may result from unrestrained sale of "spirituous liquors." Violation of licensing statute may result in imprisonment & fine.

Policy: Ct should not enforce K that violates licensing statute.

Therefore, K for sale of goods that violates licensing statute may not be enforced. Violator may be exposed to fine & imprisonment. P must show legal claim against D.

PERTINENCE: K may be invalid if license is designed to protect public.

Minn. Stat. § 481.02 (1992).

481.01 ATTORNEYS-AT-LAW   24

CHAPTER 481

ATTORNEYS-AT-LAW

title

scope & definition

general rule
(elements 1–5)

481.02 UNAUTHORIZED PRACTICE OF LAW.

Subdivision 1. **Prohibitions.** It shall be unlawful for any person or association of persons, except members of the bar of Minnesota admitted and licensed to practice as attorneys at law ● to appear as attorney or counselor at law in any action or proceeding in any court in this state to maintain, conduct, or defend the same, except personally as a party thereto in other than a representative capacity, or, ● by word, sign, letter, or advertisement, to hold out as competent or qualified to give legal advice or counsel, or to prepare legal documents, or as being engaged in advising or counseling in law or acting as attorney or counselor at law, or in furnishing to others the services of a lawyer or lawyers, or, ● for a fee or any consideration, to give legal advice or counsel, perform for or furnish to another legal services, or, ● for or without a fee or any consideration, to prepare, directly or through another, for another person, firm or corporation, any will or testamentary disposition or instrument of trust serving purposes similar to those of a will, or, ● for a fee or any consideration, to prepare for another person, firm, or corporation, any other legal document, except as provided in subdivision 3.

Subd. 2. **Corporations.** No corporation, organized for pecuniary profit, except an attorney's professional corporation organized under chapter 319A, by or through its officers or employees or any one else, shall maintain, conduct, or defend, except in its own behalf when a party litigant, any action or proceeding in any court in this state, or shall, by or through its officers or employees or any one else, give or assume to give legal advice or counsel or perform for or furnish to another person or corporation legal services; or shall, by word, sign, letter, or advertisement, solicit the public or any person to permit it to prepare, or cause to be prepared, any will or testamentary disposition or instrument of trust serving purposes similar to those of a will, or hold itself out as desiring or willing to prepare any such document, or to give legal advice or legal services relating thereto or to give general legal advice or counsel, or to act as attorney at law or as supplying, or being in a position to supply, the services of a lawyer or lawyers; or shall to any extent engage in, or hold itself out as being engaged in, the business of supplying services of a lawyer or lawyers; or shall cause to be prepared any person's will or testamentary disposition or instrument of trust serving purposes similar to those of a will, or any other legal document, for another person, firm, or corporation, and receive, directly or indirectly, all or a part of the charges for such preparation or any benefits therefrom; or shall itself prepare, directly or through another, any such document for another person, firm, or corporation, except as provided in subdivision 3.

Subd. 3. **Permitted actions.** The provisions of this section shall not prohibit:

(1) any person from drawing, without charge, any document to which the person, an employer of the person, a firm of which the person is a member, or a corporation whose officer or employee the person is, is a party, except another's will or testamentary disposition or instrument of trust serving purposes similar to those of a will;

(2) a person from drawing a will for another in an emergency if the imminence of death leaves insufficient time to have it drawn and its execution supervised by a licensed attorney-at-law;

(3) any insurance company from causing to be defended, or from offering to cause to be defended through lawyers of its selection, the insureds in policies issued or to be issued by it, in accordance with the terms of the policies;

(4) a licensed attorney-at-law from acting for several common-carrier corporations or any of its subsidiaries pursuant to arrangement between the corporations;

(5) any bona fide labor organization from giving legal advice to its members in matters arising out of their employment;

(6) any person from conferring or cooperating with a licensed attorney-at-law of another in preparing any legal document, if the attorney is not, directly or indirectly, in the employ of the person or of any person, firm, or corporation represented by the person;

(7) any licensed attorney-at-law of Minnesota, who is an officer or employee of a corporation, from drawing, for or without compensation, any document to which the corporation is a party or in which it is interested personally or in a representative capacity, except wills or testamentary dispositions or instruments of trust serving purposes similar to those of a will, but any charge made for the legal work connected with preparing and drawing the document shall not exceed the amount paid to and received and retained by the attorney, and the attorney shall not, directly or indirectly, rebate the fee to or divide the fee with the corporation;

(8) any person or corporation from drawing, for or without a fee, farm or house leases, notes, mortgages, chattel mortgages, bills of sale, deeds, assignments, satisfactions, or any other conveyances except testamentary dispositions and instruments of trust;

not pertinent

exception

not pertinent

exception

not pertinent

not pertinent

(9) a licensed attorney-at-law of Minnesota from rendering to a corporation legal services to itself at the expense of one or more of its bona fide principal stockholders by whom the attorney is employed and by whom no compensation is, directly or indirectly, received for the services;

(10) any person or corporation engaged in the business of making collections from engaging or turning over to an attorney-at-law for the purpose of instituting and conducting suit or making proof of claim of a creditor in any case in which the attorney-at-law receives the entire compensation for the work;

(11) any regularly established farm journal or newspaper, devoted to general news, from publishing a department of legal questions and answers to them, made by a licensed attorney-at-law, if no answer is accompanied or at any time preceded or followed by any charge for it, any disclosure of any name of the maker of any answer, any recommendation of or reference to any one to furnish legal advice or services, or by any legal advice or service for the periodical or any one connected with it or suggested by it, directly or indirectly;

(12) any authorized management agent of an owner of rental property used for residential purposes, whether the management agent is a natural person, corporation, partnership, limited partnership, or any other business entity, from commencing, maintaining, conducting, or defending in its own behalf any action in any court in this state to recover or retain possession of the property, except that the provision of this clause does not authorize a person who is not a licensed attorney-at-law to conduct a jury trial or to appear before a district court or the court of appeals or supreme court pursuant to an appeal;

(13) any person from commencing, maintaining, conducting, or defending on behalf of the plaintiff or defendant any action in any court of this state pursuant to the provisions of section 566.175 or sections 566.18 to 566.35 or from commencing, maintaining, conducting, or defending on behalf of the plaintiff or defendant any action in any court of this state for the recovery of rental property used for residential purposes pursuant to the provisions of section 566.02 or 566.03, subdivision 1, except that the provision of this clause does not authorize a person who is not a licensed attorney-at-law to conduct a jury trial or to appear before a district court or the court of appeals or supreme court pursuant to an appeal, and provided that, except for a nonprofit corporation, a person who is not a licensed attorney-at-law shall not charge or collect a separate fee for services rendered pursuant to this clause;

(14) the delivery of legal services by a specialized legal assistant in accordance with a specialty license issued by the supreme court before July 1, 1995;

(15) the sole shareholder of a corporation from appearing on behalf of the corporation in court; or

(16) an officer, shareholder, director, partner, or employee from appearing on behalf of a corporation, partnership, sole proprietorship, or association in conciliation court in accordance with section 487.30, subdivision 4a, or in district court in an action that was removed from conciliation court.

Subd. 3a. **Real estate closing services.** Nothing in this section shall be construed to prevent a real estate broker, a real estate salesperson, or a real estate closing agent, as defined in section 82.17, from drawing or assisting in drawing papers incident to the sale, trade, lease, or loan of property, or from charging for drawing or assisting in drawing them, except as hereafter provided by the supreme court.

Subd. 4. **Mortgage foreclosure fees.** It shall be unlawful to exact, charge or receive any attorney's fee for the foreclosure of any mortgage, unless the foreclosure is conducted by a licensed attorney at law of Minnesota and unless the full amount charged as attorney's fee is actually paid to and received and retained by such attorney, without being, directly or indirectly, shared with or rebated to any one else; and it shall be unlawful for any such attorney to make any showing of receiving such a fee unless the attorney has received the same or to share with or rebate to any other person, firm, or corporation such fee, or any part thereof, received by the attorney; but such attorney may divide such fee with another licensed attorney at law maintaining the other's place of business and not an officer or employee of the foreclosing party, if such attorney has assisted in performing the services for which the fee is paid, or resides in a place other than that where the foreclosure proceedings are conducted and has forwarded the case to the attorney conducting such foreclosure.

not pertinent

Subd. 5. **Corporate fiduciary agents.** It shall be unlawful for any corporation, appearing as executor, administrator, guardian, trustee, or other representative, to do the legal work in any action, probate proceeding or other proceeding in any court in this state, except through a licensed attorney at law of Minnesota maintaining the attorney's own place of business and not an officer or employee of such executor, administrator, guardian, trustee, or representative. No attorney's fee shall be charged or paid or received in any such case, unless actually paid to and received and retained by such an attorney at law maintaining the attorney's own place of business and not an officer or employee of such executor, administrator, guardian, trustee, or representative; and it shall be unlawful for such attorney to represent in any manner receiving any sum as a fee or compensation unless the same has been actually received or, directly or indirectly, to divide with or rebate to any person, firm, or corporation any part of any such fee or consideration received by the attorney in any such case; but such attorney may divide such fee with another licensed attorney at law maintaining the other's own place of business and not an officer or employee of such executor, administrator, guardian, trustee, or other representative, if such attorney has assisted in performing the services for which the fees are paid, or resides in a place other than that where the action or proceedings are conducted and has forwarded the case to the attorney conducting the action or proceedings.

Subd. 6. **Attorneys of other states.** Any attorney or counselor at law residing in any other state or territory in which the attorney has been admitted to practice law, who attends any term of the supreme court, court of appeals, or district court of this state for the purpose of trying or participating in the trial or proceedings of any action or proceedings there pending, may, in the discretion of the court before which the attorney appears in the action or proceeding, be permitted to try, or participate in the trial or proceedings in, the action or proceeding, without being subject to the provisions of this section, other than those set forth in subdivision 2, providing the state in which the attorney is licensed to practice law likewise grants permission to members of the state bar of Minnesota to act as an attorney for a client in that state under the same terms.

Subd. 7. **Lay assistance to attorneys.** Nothing herein contained shall be construed to prevent a corporation from furnishing to any person lawfully engaged in the practice of law, such information or such clerical service in and about the attorney's professional work as, except for the provisions of this section, may be lawful, provided, that at all times the lawyer receiving such information or such services shall maintain full, professional and direct responsibility to the attorney's clients for the information and services so received.

exception

Subd. 8. **Penalty; injunction.** Any person or corporation, or officer or employee thereof, violating any of the foregoing provisions shall be guilty of a misdemeanor; and, upon conviction thereof, shall be punished as by statute provided for the punishment of misdemeanors. It shall be the duty of the respective county attorneys in this state to prosecute violations of this section, and the district courts of this state shall have sole original jurisdiction of any such offense under this section.

consequences & enforcement

In lieu of criminal prosecution above provided for, such county attorney or the attorney general may, in the name of the state of Minnesota, or in the name of the state board of law examiners, proceed by injunction suit against any violator of any of the provisions above set forth to enjoin the doing of any act or acts violating any of said provisions.

Subd. 9. Nothing in subdivision 3a shall be construed to allow a person other than a licensed attorney to perform or provide the services of an attorney or be construed to otherwise conflict with this section.

not pertinent

History: *(5687-1) 1931 c 114 s 1; 1959 c 476 s 1; 1969 c 9 s 87; 1974 c 406 s 49; 1981 c 168 s 1; 1983 c 247 s 173,174; 1986 c 444; 1987 c 377 s 6; 1988 c 695 s 3-5; 1991 c 299 s 1; 1992 c 376 art 1 s 1; 1992 c 497 s 1; 1992 c 591 s 1*

§ 481.02 Brief

IF any person/ass'n except members of MN bar admitted & licensed to practice

A. does 1 OR 2 OR 3 (all in subd. 1)

1. gives legal advice or counsel or
   performs for or furnishes legal services
   to another
   for fee or consid'n

2. prepares directly or thru another
   for another person/firm/corp
   any will or testamentary disp'n or instrument of trust serving pur-
     poses similar to will
   (for or w/o fee or consid'n)

3. prepares for another person/firm/corp
   any other legal document
   for fee or consid'n

   - common meaning of "legal document": official paper relied on as
     basis or proof, established by law or conforming to law
   - in pari materia: § 145B.04 equates living will with "legal
     document"

B. AND NOT person drafting will
    for another
    in emergency leaving insuff time for atty superv'n
    subd. 3(2)

C. AND NOT person conferring or cooperating
    with licensed atty of another
    in preparing any legal document
    where atty is not emp'd by that person or by person/firm/corp rep'd
      by that person
    subd. 3(6)

D. AND NOT corp furnishing
    lawful info or clerical services
    to atty who maintains responsibility to clients for info & services
    subd. 7

THEN   misdemeanor prosecuted by county atty in dist ct OR injunction
       brought by county atty or atty gen'l—subd. 8.

   - *Peterson:* illegally drafted document is *not* voided
     —policy of statute is to penalize drafter, not testator
     —expressio unius

Minn. Stat. §§ 145B.01-.06 (1992).

CHAPTER 145B

ADULT HEALTH CARE DECISIONS

145B.01 CITATION.

This chapter may be cited as the "Minnesota living will act."

History: *1989 c 3 s 1; 1991 c 148 s 1*

145B.02 DEFINITIONS.

Subdivision 1. **Applicability.** The definitions in this section apply to this chapter.

Subd. 2. **Living will.** "Living will" means a writing made according to section 145B.03.

Subd. 3. **Health care.** "Health care" means care, treatment, services, or procedures to maintain, diagnose, or treat an individual's physical condition when the individual is in a terminal condition.

Subd. 4. **Health care decision.** "Health care decision" means a decision to begin, continue, increase, limit, discontinue, or not begin any health care.

Subd. 5. **Health care facility.** "Health care facility" means a hospital or other entity licensed under sections 144.50 to 144.58; a nursing home licensed to serve adults under section 144A.02; or a home care provider licensed under sections 144A.43 to 144A.49.

Subd. 6. **Health care provider.** "Health care provider" means a person, health care facility, organization, or corporation licensed, certified, or otherwise authorized or permitted by the laws of this state to administer health care directly or through an arrangement with other health care providers.

Subd. 7. **HMO.** "HMO" means an organization licensed under sections 62D.01 to 62D.30.

Subd. 8. **Terminal condition.** "Terminal condition" means an incurable or irreversible condition for which the administration of medical treatment will serve only to prolong the dying process.

History: *1989 c 3 s 2; 1991 c 148 s 6*

145B.03 LIVING WILL.

Subdivision 1. **Scope.** A competent adult may make a living will of preferences or instructions regarding health care. These preferences or instructions may include, but are not limited to, consent to or refusal of any health care, treatment, service, procedure, or placement. A living will may include preferences or instructions regarding health care, the designation of a proxy to make health care decisions on behalf of the declarant, or both.

Subd. 2. **Requirements for executing a living will.** (a) A living will is effective only if it is signed by the declarant and two witnesses or a notary public.

(b) A living will must state:

(1) the declarant's preferences regarding whether the declarant wishes to receive or not receive artificial administration of nutrition and hydration; or

(2) that the declarant wishes the proxy, if any, to make decisions regarding the administering of artificially administered nutrition and hydration for the declarant if the declarant is unable to make health care decisions and the living will becomes operative. If the living will does not state the declarant's preferences regarding artificial administration of nutrition and hydration, the living will shall be enforceable as to all other preferences or instructions regarding health care, and a decision to administer, withhold, or withdraw nutrition and hydration artificially shall be made pursuant to section 145B.13. However, the mere existence of a living will or appointment of a proxy does not, by itself, create a presumption that the declarant wanted the withholding or withdrawing of artificially administered nutrition or hydration.

(c) The living will may be communicated to and then transcribed by one of the witnesses. If the declarant is physically unable to sign the document, one of the witnesses shall sign the document at the declarant's direction.

(d) Neither of the witnesses can be someone who is entitled to any part of the estate of the declarant under a will then existing or by operation of law. Neither of the witnesses nor the notary may be named as a proxy in the living will. Each witness shall substantially make the following declaration on the document:

"I certify that the declarant voluntarily signed this living will in my presence and that the declarant is personally known to me. I am not named as a proxy by the living will."

Subd. 3. **Guardian or conservator.** Except as otherwise provided in the living will, designation of a proxy is considered a nomination of a guardian or conservator of the person for purposes of section 525.544.

History: *1989 c 3 s 3; 1991 c 148 s 6*

145B.04 SUGGESTED FORM.

A living will executed after August 1, 1989, under this chapter must be substantially in the form in this section. Forms printed for public distribution must be substantially in the form in this section.

"Health Care Living Will

Notice:

This is an important legal document. Before signing this document, you should know these important facts:

(a) This document gives your health care providers or your designated proxy the power and guidance to make health care decisions according to your wishes when you are in a terminal condition and cannot do so. This document may include what kind of treatment you want or do not want and under what circumstances you want these decisions to be made. You may state where you want or do not want to receive any treatment.

(b) If you name a proxy in this document and that person agrees to serve as your proxy, that person has a duty to act consistently with your wishes. If the proxy does not know your wishes, the proxy has the duty to act in your best interests. If you do not name a proxy, your health care providers have a duty to act consistently with your instructions or tell you that they are unwilling to do so.

(c) This document will remain valid and in effect until and unless you amend or revoke it. Review this document periodically to make sure it continues to reflect your preferences. You may amend or revoke the living will at any time by notifying your health care providers.

(d) Your named proxy has the same right as you have to examine your medical records and to consent to their disclosure for purposes related to your health care or insurance unless you limit this right in this document.

(e) If there is anything in this document that you do not understand, you should ask for professional help to have it explained to you.

TO MY FAMILY, DOCTORS, AND ALL THOSE CONCERNED WITH MY CARE:

I, ..., born on .... (birthdate), being an adult of sound mind, willfully and voluntarily make this statement as a directive to be followed if I am in a terminal condition and become unable to participate in decisions regarding my health care. I understand that my health care providers are legally bound to act consistently with my wishes, within the limits of reasonable medical practice and other applicable law. I also understand that I have the right to make medical and health care decisions for myself as long as I am able to do so and to revoke this living will at any time.

(1) The following are my feelings and wishes regarding my health care (you may state the circumstances under which this living will applies):

....
....
....
....

(2) I particularly want to have all appropriate health care that will help in the following ways (you may give instructions for care you do want):

....
....
....

(3) I particularly do not want the following (you may list specific treatment you do not want in certain circumstances):

....
....

(4) I particularly want to have the following kinds of life-sustaining treatment if I am diagnosed to have a terminal condition (you may list the specific types of life-sustaining treatment that you do want if you have a terminal condition):

....
....
....

(5) I particularly do not want the following kinds of life-sustaining treatment if I am diagnosed to have a terminal condition (you may list the specific types of life-sustaining treatment that you do not want if you have a terminal condition):

....
....
....

(6) I recognize that if I reject artificially administered sustenance, then I may die of dehydration or malnutrition rather than from my illness or injury. The following are my feelings and wishes regarding artificially administered sustenance should I have a terminal condition (you may indicate whether you wish to receive food and fluids given to you in some other way than by mouth if you have a terminal condition):

....
....
....
....

(7) Thoughts I feel are relevant to my instructions. (You may, but need not, give your religious beliefs, philosophy, or other personal values that you feel are important. You may also state preferences concerning the location of your care.)

....
....
....
....

(8) Proxy Designation. (If you wish, you may name someone to see that your wishes are carried out, but you do not have to do this. You may also name a proxy without including specific instructions regarding your care. If you name a proxy, you should discuss your wishes with that person.)

If I become unable to communicate my instructions, I designate the following person(s) to act on my behalf consistently with my instructions, if any, as stated in this document. Unless I write instructions that limit my proxy's authority, my proxy has full power and authority to make health care decisions for me. If a guardian or conservator of the person is to be appointed for me, I nominate my proxy named in this document to act as guardian or conservator of my person.

Name: ....

Address: ....

Phone Number: ....

Relationship: (If any) ....

If the person I have named above refuses or is unable or unavailable to act on my behalf, or if I revoke that person's authority to act as my proxy, I authorize the following person to do so:

Name: ....

Address: ....

Phone Number: ....

Relationship: (If any) ....

I understand that I have the right to revoke the appointment of the persons named above to act on my behalf at any time by communicating that decision to the proxy or my health care provider.

I (have) (have not) agreed in another document or on another form to donate some or all of my organs when I die.

DATE: ....

SIGNED: ....

STATE OF ....

....

COUNTY OF ....

Subscribed, sworn to, and acknowledged before me by .... on this ..... day of ...., 19...

....

NOTARY PUBLIC

OR

(Sign and date here in the presence of two adult witnesses, neither of whom is entitled to any part of your estate under a will or by operation of law, and neither of whom is your proxy.)

I certify that the declarant voluntarily signed this living will in my presence and that the declarant is personally known to me. I am not named as a proxy by the living will, and to the best of my knowledge, I am not entitled to any part of the estate of the declarant under a will or by operation of law.

Witness .... Address ....

Witness .... Address ....

Reminder: Keep the signed original with your personal papers.

Give signed copies to your doctors, family, and proxy."

History: *1989 c 3 s 4; 1991 c 148 s 6; 1992 c 535 s 1*

145B.05 WHEN OPERATIVE.

A living will becomes operative when it is delivered to the declarant's physician or other health care provider. The physician or provider must comply with it to the fullest extent possible, consistent with reasonable medical practice and other applicable law, or comply with the notice and transfer provisions of sections 145B.06 and 145B.07. The physician or health care provider shall continue to obtain the declarant's informed consent to all health care decisions if the declarant is capable of informed consent.

History: *1989 c 3 s 5; 1991 c 148 s 6*

145B.06 COMPLIANCE WITH LIVING WILL.

Subdivision 1. **By health care provider.** (a) A physician or other health care provider shall make the living will a part of the declarant's medical record. If the physician or other health care provider is unwilling at any time to comply with the living will, the physician or health care provider must promptly notify the declarant and document the notification in the declarant's medical record. After notification, if a competent declarant fails to transfer to a different physician or provider, the physician or provider has no duty to transfer the patient.

(b) If a physician or other health care provider receives a living will from a competent declarant and does not advise the declarant of unwillingness to comply, and if the declarant then becomes incompetent or otherwise unable to seek transfer to a different physician or provider, the physician or other health care provider who is unwilling to comply with the living will shall promptly take all reasonable steps to transfer care of the declarant to a physician or other health care provider who is willing to comply with the living will.

Subd. 2. **By proxy.** A proxy designated to make health care decisions and who agrees to serve as proxy may make health care decisions on behalf of a declarant to the same extent that the declarant could make the decision, subject to limitations or conditions stated in the living will. In exercising this authority, the proxy shall act consistently with any desires the declarant expresses in the living will or otherwise makes known to the proxy. If the declarant's desires are unknown, the proxy shall act in the best interests of the declarant.

History: *1989 c 3 s 6; 1991 c 148 s 6*

Peterson v. Hovland (*In re Peterson's Estate*)
42 N.W.2d (Minn. 1950).

IN RE PETERSON'S ESTATE   Minn.   59
Cite as 42 N.W.2d 59

In re **PETERSON'S ESTATE.**

PETERSON et al. v. HOVLAND.
No. 35108.

Supreme Court of Minnesota.
March 31, 1950.

Proceeding in the matter of the estate of Peter H. Peterson, decedent, by Hans H. Peterson and others, heirs at law, against George M. Hovland, wherein validity of will was challenged. From a judgment of the District Court, Freeborn County, Martin A. Nelson, J., affirming an order of the probate court allowing the last will and testament of decedent, the heirs at law appealed. The Supreme Court, Matson, J., held that a will drawn for testator by bank cashier in

60   Minn.   42 NORTH WESTERN REPORTER, 2d SERIES

violation of statute against the unlicensed practice of law is not invalid.

Judgment affirmed.

1. Contracts ⬬107

Generally, a contract in violation of statute which imposes prohibition and penalty is void, but before so ruling in a particular case, statute should be examined as a whole to determine whether legislature so intended.

2. Contracts ⬬105

Validity of instrument executed in violation of statute does not depend on whether the acts involved are malum in se or merely malum prohibitum.

3. Contracts ⬬108(1)

Generally, a contract is not void as against public policy unless it is injurious to interests of the public or contravenes some established interests of society, but contracts are contrary to public policy if they clearly tend to injure public health or morals, the fundamental rights of the individual, or if they undermine confidence in impartiality of the administration of justice.

4. Contracts ⬬107

If an act is expressly forbidden and a penalty is imposed for violation, intent of legislature is controlling factor in determining to what extent, in order to preserve requirements of public policy, contracts and other instruments made in connection with such violation are to be held illegal.

5. Contracts ⬬107

An inference of invalidity of contract executed in violation of statute does not necessarily follow from fact that statute prescribes a penalty.

6. Statutes ⬬181(2)

Where language of statute is not explicit and admits of construction, the courts in determining legislative intent will consider occasion and necessity for the law, mischief to be remedied, object to be obtained, and consequences of a particular interpretation. M.S.A. § 645.16.

7. Statutes ⬬241(1)

Where statute specifically prohibits and penalizes a certain act by members of one class, for protection of members of another class, a statutory construction which attributes to legislature an intent to bring about a consequence that is inconsistent with the protective purpose should not be adopted.

8. Statutes ⬬241(1)

Where legislature has carefully designated offense, offender, and the penalty and has made specific provisions to insure enforcement, inference is that legislature has dealt with subject completely and did not intend, in addition thereto, that by mere implication drastic consequences of invalidity should be visited upon victim of offender.

9. Courts ⬬107

No decision has authoritative value beyond the proportions established by its controlling facts.

10. Wills ⬬84

Will drawn by bank cashier for testator, at a time when no emergency existed which would leave insufficient time to have it drawn and its execution supervised by an attorney at law, was not invalid because it was prepared in direct violation of the statute which prohibits and penalizes as a misdemeanor the act of an unlicensed practitioner in preparing a will for another. M.S.A. § 481.02.

Syllabus by the Court.

1. Although the general rule is that a contract executed in violation of a statute which imposes a prohibition and a penalty for the doing of an act—such as the pursuit of an occupation, business, or profession without being possessed of a license as required by law for the protection of the public—is void, such rule is not to be applied in any particular case without first examining the statute as a whole to find out whether or not the legislature so intended.

2. The distinction between acts which are *malum in se* and those which are merely *malum prohibitum* is no longer controlling in this jurisdiction in determining the validity of an instrument executed in violation of statute.

IN RE PETERSON'S ESTATE   Minn. **61**
Cite as 42 N.W.2d 59

3. If an act is expressly forbidden and a penalty is imposed for a violation, the intent of the legislature is the controlling factor in determining to what extent, in order to preserve the requirements of public policy, contracts and other instruments made in connection with such act of violation are to be held illegal, if at all.

4. An inference of invalidity does not necessarily follow from the fact that a statute prescribes a penalty.

5. Where a statute specifically prohibits and penalizes a certain act by the members of one class, for the protection of the members of another class, a statutory construction should not be adopted which attributes to the legislature an intent to bring about a consequence that is inconsistent with the protective purpose for which the law was enacted.

6. Where the legislature has carefully designated the *offense*, the *offender*, and the *penalty* and *has made specific provisions to insure enforcement*, the inference is that the legislature has dealt with the subject completely and did not intend, in addition thereto, that drastic consequences of invalidity should be visited upon the victim of the offender by mere implication.

7. No decision has authoritative value beyond the proportions established by its controlling facts.

8. A will does not become invalid and void by reason of the sole fact that it was drawn for the testator—when no emergency existed which left insufficient time to have it drawn and its execution supervised by a licensed attorney at law—by a layman in direct violation of M.S.A. § 481.02, which prohibits and penalizes as a misdemeanor the act of an unlicensed practitioner in preparing a will for another.

————◆·————

Moonan, Moonan & Friedel, Waseca, for appellants.

Peterson & Peterson, Albert Lea, for respondent.

MATSON, Justice.

Appeal from a district court judgment affirming an order of the probate court allowing decedent's last will and testament.

Peter H. Peterson, decedent, on September 7, 1948, which was several weeks prior to his death, executed his last will and testament, which, upon his request, had been drawn by the cashier of the Twin Lakes State Bank, a layman, who had never been admitted to the practice of law. The trial court specifically found that at the time the will was drawn "no emergency existed nor had the imminence of death left insufficient time to have this Will drawn and its execution supervised by a licensed attorney at law."

Appellants are heirs at law for whom no provision was made in the will. The only issue raised is whether a will which is otherwise valid is invalid and should be given no legal effect by reason of the *sole* fact that it was drawn by a layman—who at the time the will was drawn was not admitted and licensed to practice as an attorney at law—in direct violation of M.S.A. § 481.02, which provides:

Subd. 1. "It shall be unlawful for any person or association of persons, except members of the bar of Minnesota admitted and licensed to practice as attorneys at law, * * * *for or without a fee or any consideration*, to prepare, directly or through another, for another person, * * * any will or testamentary disposition or instrument of trust serving purposes similar to those of a will, * * *."[1] (Italics supplied.)

Subd. 8. "Any person or corporation, or officer or employee thereof, violating any of the foregoing provisions *shall be guilty of a misdemeanor;* and, upon conviction thereof, shall be punished as by statute provided for the punishment of misdemeanors. *It shall be the duty of the respective county attorneys in this state to prosecute violations of this section,* * * *

---

1. Subd. 3 of said statute permits a layman to draw a will for another in an emergency wherein the imminence of

death leaves insufficient time to have the same drawn and its execution supervised by a licensed attorney at law.

62 **Minn.** **42 NORTH WESTERN REPORTER, 2d SERIES**

"In lieu of criminal prosecution above provided for, such county attorney or the attorney general may, * * * proceed by injunction suit against any violator of any of the provisions above set forth to enjoin the doing of any act or acts violating any of said provisions." (Italics supplied.)

Does it follow that the will itself is tainted with such illegality as to be void by reason of having been drafted in a prohibited manner? Did the testator, in employing an unlicensed layman, so participate in the performance of a crime that his attempt to make a will resulted in a nullity? In considering the issue, it should be borne in mind that the direct **violator** of the statute, the unlicensed scrivener, is not a beneficiary under the will and is not a party to this litigation. He is in no manner seeking a fee for his services or any other benefit from his unlawful act. In other words, we are not asked to aid the wrongdoer himself. See, 5 Williston, Contracts (Rev.Ed.) § 1630; Bosshard v. County of Steele, 173 Minn. 283, 217 N.W. 354; Goodrich v. N. W. Tel. Exch. Co., 161 Minn. 106, 201 N.W. 290. A different situation arises where an unlicensed practitioner seeks to recover fees for his performance of legal services. See, Annotations, 4 A.L.R. 1087 and 42 A.L.R. 1228; Gionti v. Crown Motor Freight Co., 128 N.J.L. 407, 26 A.2d 282.

In most instances, decisions concerned with the validity of instruments executed in violation of a statute involve the issue of the enforceability or nonenforceability of contracts. Where an attempt is made to enforce a contract which was made in violation of a statute, many considerations enter which are not present where the validity of a will is assailed on the sole ground that it was drawn by an unlicensed scrivener. Nevertheless, the contract cases are illustrative of certain fundamental principles which are controlling.

See, 5 Williston, Contracts (Rev.Ed.) § 1630.

[1-6] 1-2-3-4. Although the general rule is that a contract executed in violation of a statute which imposes a prohibition and a penalty for the doing of an act—such as the pursuit of an occupation, business, or profession without being possessed of a license as required by law for the protection of the public—is void, such rule is not to be applied in any particular case without first examining the statute as a whole to find out whether or not the legislature so intended.[2] It is not an arbitrary rule which is applicable to all instruments executed in violation of statutory prohibitions. Its applicable scope coincides with the reason for its existence, and when that reason ceases the rule itself ceases to have a basis and becomes inoperative. See, Webster v. U. S. I. Realty Co., 170 Minn. 360, 363, 212 N.W. 806, 807; cf. Restatement, Contracts, §§ 598-604. In construing such a statute, the inference is that the legislature did not intend that an instrument executed in violation of its terms should be void unless that be necessary to accomplish its purpose. Barriere v. Depatie, 219 Mass. 33, 106 N.E. 572. Usually the rule that a contract so made is void finds application where the acts or things prohibited by statute are *malum in se,* in that they are by their nature iniquitous and void. Laun v. Pacific Mut. Life Ins. Co. of California, 131 Wis. 555, 111 N.W. 660, 9 L.R.A.,N.S., 1204; Walter A. Wood Mowing & Reaping Machine Co. v. Caldwell, 54 Ind. 270, 23 Am.Rep. 641. No longer, however, is the distinction between acts which are *malum in se* and those which are merely *malum prohibitum* controlling in this jurisdiction in determining the validity of an instrument executed in violation of a statute. Holland v. Sheehan, 108 Minn. 362, 122 N.W. 1, 23 L.R.A.,N.S., 510, 17 Ann. Cas. 687; 2 Dunnell, Dig. & Supp. § 1868.

2. Solomon v. Dreschler, 4 Minn. 278 (Gil. 197); Miller v. Ammon, 145 U.S. 421, 12 S.Ct. 884, 36 L.Ed. 759; Harris v. Runnels, 53 U.S. 79, 12 How. 79, 13 L.Ed. 901; Pangborn v. Westlake, 36 Iowa 546;

Barriere v. Depatie, 219 Mass. 33, 106 N.E. 572; see, 2 Dunnell, Dig. & Supp. § 1873; Annotations, 30 A.L.R. 834 and 42 A.L.R. 1226.

IN RE PETERSON'S ESTATE   Minn.   63
Cite as 42 N.W.2d 59

Where contracts or other instruments which are merely *malum prohibitum* have been made in violation of statutory provisions—as in the instant case—they may or may not be void.[3] Generally speaking, a contract is not void as against public policy unless it is injurious to the interests of the public or contravenes some established interest of society. On the other hand, contracts are contrary to public policy if they clearly tend to injure public health or morals, the fundamental rights of the individual, or if they undermine confidence in the impartiality of the administration of justice. See, Solomon v. Dreschler, 4 Minn. 278 (Gil. 197); 2 Dunnell, Dig. & Supp. § 1870. These general principles are of little direct aid in a specific case and are but reflections of what the legislature has usually declared public policy to be. Primarily, it is the prerogative of the legislature to declare what acts constitute a violation of public policy and the consequences of such violation. Mathison v. Minneapolis St. Ry. Co., 126 Minn. 286, 148 N.W. 71, L.R.A.1916D, 412. If an act is expressly forbidden and a penalty is imposed for a violation, the intent of the legislature is the controlling factor in determining to what extent, in order to preserve the requirements of public policy, contracts and other instruments made in connection with such act of violation are to be held illegal, if at all. 3 Sutherland, Statutory Construction (3 ed.) § 5608. An inference of invalidity does not necessarily follow from the fact that a statute prescribes a penalty. De Mers v. Daniels, 39 Minn. 158, 39 N.W. 98. Each statute must be judged by itself as a whole. Solomon v. Dreschler, 4 Minn. 278 (Gil. 197); Bowditch v. New England Mut. Life Ins. Co. 141 Mass. 292, 4 N.E. 798, 55 Am.Rep. 474.

In construing a statute where the language is not explicit and admits of construction, in determining legislative intent the courts will consider the occasion and the necessity for the law, the mischief to be remedied, the object to be attained, and the consequences of a particular interpretation. M.S.A. § 645.16.

Section 481.02 had its origin with G.S. 1866, c. 88, § 8, which simply prohibited any person not a lawyer to appear, to maintain, or defend in any proceeding in court.[4] Although the wording was changed from time to time in certain inconsequential particulars, no major change was made until the enactment of L. 1901, c. 282, when it was made unlawful for an unlicensed practitioner not only to appear in court but also to hold himself out as competent to furnish legal services or to perform any legal services for a consideration. Undoubtedly this amendment by its application generally to the practice of law made it unlawful for a layman to prepare another's will for a fee. It was not, however, until the enactment of L. 1931, c. 114, § 1, that this statute was amended to apply in *express* terms to wills. Undoubtedly, the necessity for expressly prohibiting any person not licensed to practice as an attorney at law from preparing a will for another, *whether for or without a fee,* arose out of the deplorable situation frequently created for widows and children of testators whose wills had been drawn by laymen who meant well but had only a superficial knowledge of law. Through the bungling use of legal terms and an improper knowledge of estate planning, poorly drawn wills frequently were held invalid, specific bequests failed, estates were needlessly depleted by burdensome taxation, or the testator's intent was otherwise defeated.

3. De Mers v. Daniels, 39 Minn. 158, 39 N. W. 98; Pangborn v. Westlake, 36 Iowa 546; John E. Rosasco Creameries, Inc. v. Cohen, 276 N.Y. 274, 278, 11 N.E.2d 908, 909, 118 A.L.R. 641 (wherein a milk dealer was permitted to recover sale price of milk sold without having statutory license); Hartford Fire Ins. Co. v. Knight, 146 Miss. 862, 867, 111 So. 748; Irwin v. Curie, 171 N.Y. 409, 64 N.E. 161, 58 L.R.A. 830; Niemeyer v. Wright, 75 Va. 239, 40 Am.Rep. 720;

Warren People's Market Co. v. Corbett & Sons, 114 Ohio St. 126, 151 N.E. 51; 2 Dunnell, Dig. & Supp. § 1873.

4. Derivation of M.S.A. § 481.02: Mason St.1940 Supp. § 5687-1; L. 1931, c. 114, § 1; Mason St. 1927, § 5687; G.S. 1923, § 5687; G.S. 1913, § 4947; R.L. 1905, § 2280; L. 1901, c. 282; G.S. 1894, § 6179; L. 1891, c. 36, § 8; G.S. 1878, c. 88, § 8; G.S. 1866, c. 88, § 8.

Incompetency was accompanied by irresponsibility, in that these laymen, unlike members of the bar, by reason of their unlicensed status were not subject to the direct supervision and discipline of the courts. See, Matter of Co-operative Law Co., 198 N.Y. 479, 92 N.E. 15, 32 L.R.A.,N.S., 55, 139 Am.St.Rep. 839, 19 Ann.Cas. 879; cf. State v. Nowicki, 256 Wis. 279, 40 N.W.2d 377. The need for remedial legislation was acute. It was met by the enactment of an express statutory prohibition and penalty, *not against any act of the testator or against the drafting or making of wills generally,* but solely against the act of the *unlicensed* will draftsman, whose unskilled services and irresponsible status could no longer be tolerated. As a result, we have a typical example of legislation designed to protect one class of the public, those persons in need of a will, from imposition by another class, those individuals who, without adequate legal training, offer their services to the unwary. Similar protective legislation is not new to this jurisdiction.[5] In De Mers v. Daniels, 39. Minn. 158, 39 N.W. 98, we held a contract for the sale of certain lots to be valid and enforceable though the vendor was subject to a statutory penalty for having failed to execute and file the townsite plat as required by G.S. 1878, c. 29. In the De Mers case we said, 39 Minn. 159, 39 N.W. 99: "It must be conceded to be an established principle of law that when a statute prescribes a penalty for the doing of a specific act, that is *prima facie* equivalent to an express prohibition; and that, *when the object of such an enactment is deemed to have been the protection of persons dealing with those in respect to whose acts the penalty is declared,* or the accomplishment of purposes entertained upon grounds of public policy, not pertaining to mere administrative measures, such as the raising of a revenue, the act thus impliedly prohibited will, in general, be treated as *unlawful and void as to the party who is subjected to the penalty.* This rule is not, however, without qualification. The question is one of interpretation of the legislative intention. *The imposing of a penalty does not necessarily give rise to an implication of an intention that, where an act is done which subjects a party to the penalty, the act itself shall be void, and of no legal effect;* and if it seems more probable, from the subject and the terms of the enactment, and from the consequences which were to be anticipated as likely to result from giving such an effect to the penal law, that it was not the intention of the legislature to make the transaction void, but only to punish the offending party in the manner specified, the law should be so construed. * * * *The fact that no penalty, forfeiture, or disability is declared with respect to purchasers, under any circumstances, is worthy of being considered* in this connection." (Italics supplied.)

In the De Mers case, as in the instant case, a specific penalty was imposed for the wrongful act of one party, but the statute was silent as to the consequences to the other party and as to the validity of a written instrument executed in connection with or in reliance upon such wrongful act. In ascertaining legislative intent under such circumstances, we may well apply the maxim that "the expression of one thing is the exclusion of another." Sacketts Harbor Bank v. Codd, 18 N.Y. 240; Laun v. Pacific Mut. Life Ins. Co., 131 Wis. 555, 111 N.W. 660, 9 L.R.A.,N.S., 1204; 6 Dunnell, Dig. & Supp. § 8980. As indicative of legislative intent to rely upon the penalty alone for accomplishing the statutory purpose, without holding the will itself void, is the statutory emphasis placed upon the enforcement of the penalty. By express terms, the statute declares it to be the positive duty of county attorneys to institute criminal proceedings against any unlicensed practitioners who draw wills—in the absence of an actual emergency when no lawyer is available. The only alternative in lieu of criminal prosecution is the initiation of proceedings to enjoin future acts of violation.

[7, 8]   5-6. Where a statute specifically prohibits and penalizes a certain act by the members of one class, for the protection of the members of another class, a statutory

---

5. De Mers v. Daniels, 39 Minn. 158, 39 N.W. 98; Webster v. U. S. I. Realty Co., 170 Minn. 360, 212 N.W. 806.

construction should not be adopted which attributes to the legislature an intent to bring about a consequence that is inconsistent with the protective purpose for which the law was enacted. Where a penalty is imposed upon one party and not upon the other, they are not to be regarded as *in pari delicto*. Irwin v. Curie, 171 N.Y. 409, 414, 64 N.E. 161, 162, 58 L.R.A. 830. A testator is not *in pari delicto* with an unlicensed practitioner. He is a member of the class the statute was designed to protect. See, Webster v. U. S. I. Realty Co., 170 Minn. 360, 212 N.W. 806. Protective legislation is to be construed so that it does not become just another hazard for the unwary. If, by implication, we were to attribute to the legislature an intent that a will drawn by an unlicensed practitioner should in all cases be void, we would visit upon the unfortunate victims of unskilled draftsmen a penalty far greater than, and out of all proportion to, the penalty imposed upon the wrongdoer himself. Where the legislature has carefully designated the *offense,* the *offender,* and the *penalty* and *has made specific provisions to insure enforcement,* the inference is that the legislature has dealt with the subject completely and did not intend, in addition thereto, that drastic consequences of invalidity should be visited upon the victim of the offender by mere implication. See, Laun v. Pacific Mut. Life Ins. Co., 131 Wis. 555, 570–571, 111 N.W. 660, 665, 9 L.R.A.,N.S., 1204; Bowditch v. New England Mut. Life Ins. Co., 141 Mass. 292, 4 N.E. 798, 55 Am.Rep. 474.

Appellants cite Buckley v. Humason, 50 Minn. 195, 52 N.W. 385, 16 L.R.A. 423, 36 Am.St.Rep. 637, in support of their contentions. In that case the plaintiff, who conducted a Chicago real estate brokerage business without having the license required by an ordinance of that city, was denied the right to recover his brokerage commissions, on the ground that where a business is made unlawful for unlicensed persons any contract made in such business is void. In the Buckley case, the wrongdoer himself was

seeking, *to his own advantage,* to enforce a contract made in violation of law. In the instant matter we do not have that situation. It is also significant that the earlier De Mers decision, 39 Minn. 158, 39 N.W. 98, was not called to the attention of or considered by the court. In a much later decision, Vercellini v. U. S. I. Realty Co., 158 Minn. 72, 196 N.W. 672, the court, after citing Buckley v. Humason, supra, expressly took notice of the error in the assumption that all contracts made in violation of law are necessarily void. In that case, the purchaser of certain lands under an investment contract made in violation of the blue sky law, L. 1917, c. 429, as amended by L. 1919, c. 105, was permitted to recover what he had paid. The court said therein that the purchaser was a member of the protected class and that he was not *in pari delicto* with the seller, who was the only party guilty of violating the statute. See, also, Marin v. Olson, 181 Minn. 327, 232 N.W. 523.

[9] 7. Our attention is directed to In re Estate of Calich, 214 Minn. 292, 8 N.W.2d 337, wherein this court discussed the serious losses resulting to innocent people from the unlicensed practice of law by laymen, and then, after vigorously condemning such unlawful practice, urged the prompt and aggressive prosecution of all violators. This court therein expressed a reluctance to give effect to a will drawn by a layman in violation of the statute, but it is significant to note that the alleged will was drawn by a layman who stood to profit by his own wrongful act, in that he was the sole beneficiary. What is of more significance is that the actual decision therein was not based upon any illegality resulting from an unauthorized practice of law, but on a determination that the finding of the trial court that no will had ever been executed was sustained by the evidence. It is elementary that no decision has any authoritative value beyond the proportions established by its controlling facts.[6]

---

6. Certain cases cited by appellants should be distinguished. In Waddell v. Traylor, 99 Colo. 576, 64 P.2d 1273, involving a

suit upon a promissory note which, in violation of a penal statute, prescribed an unlawful rate of interest, the court

42 N.W.2d—5

Appellants cite certain cases wherein unlicensed practitioners have appeared in court, and in consequence thereof the proceedings have been set aside and spoken of as void. These cases illustrate the confusion which results when the distinction between the words "void" and "voidable" is not observed. They also illustrate that the authoritative value of a decision is limited to the scope of its controlling or decisive facts. In practically all these decisions, the courts have either granted a new trial or taken other steps to protect the rights of the wrongdoer's clients and the interest of opposing parties. No purpose will be served by attempting to distinguish or discuss such decisions, in that the task has already been ably performed in Schifrin v. Chenille Mfg. Co. Inc., 2 Cir., 117 F.2d 92. In certain instances, court proceedings have failed for want of jurisdiction where the only effort made to invoke the court's jurisdiction has been by the issuance of a summons which was fatally defective in not having been subscribed by the plaintiff or by an officer of the court in his behalf, as required by statute. See, Jacobs v. Queen Ins. Co., 51 S.D. 249, 213 N.W. 14.

[10] 8. It follows that a will does not become invalid and void by reason of the sole fact that it was drawn for the testator —when no emergency existed which left insufficient time to have it drawn and its execution supervised by a licensed attorney at law—by a layman in direct violation of § 481.02, which prohibits and penalizes as a misdemeanor the act of an unlicensed practitioner in preparing a will for another.[7]

The judgment of the trial court is affirmed.

Affirmed.

FRANK T. GALLAGHER, J., took no part in the consideration or decision of this case.

---

held the note invalid *only* to the extent of the unlawful interest and allowed a recovery of the money actually loaned, together with lawful interest thereon. The court refused to increase the penalty beyond that expressly prescribed by the statute. In Hancock Co. Inc. v. Stephens, 177 Va. 349, 14 S.E.2d 332, the wrongdoer himself, an unlicensed real estate broker, was denied a right of recovery. Cf. Restatement, Contracts, §§ 598–604.

7. There is a question whether appellants are in a position to raise the issue of illegality. Usually the issue or defense of illegality may be raised only by the parties or those claiming under them and not by third parties. See, Marx v. Lining, 231 Ala. 445, 165 So. 207; Ferris v. Snively, 172 Wash. 167, 19 P.2d 942, 90 A.L.R. 278; White v. Little, 131 Okl. 132, 268 P. 221; Matta v. Katsoulas, 192 Wis. 212, 212 N.W. 261, 50 A.L.R. 291.

Peterson Brief

Peterson v. Hovland (In re Peterson's Estate), Minnesota Supreme Court, 1950, 42 N.W.2d 59.

FACTS: Decedent Peterson executed will several weeks before death. At his request, will was drawn by cashier of bank, layperson never admitted to practice of law. No emergency involving imminent death existed. (Cashier is not beneficiary under will or seeking fee.)

PROCEDURE: Heirs at law not provided for in will challenged it. Probate ct allowed will; dist ct affirmed. Heirs appealed.

ISSUE: Is otherwise valid will rendered invalid solely because it was drawn by layperson, where no emergency involving imminent death of testator existed?

HOLDING: Affirmed. Will is not invalid solely because it was drawn by layperson, even where no emergency existed.

REASONING: Statutory rule: Unauthorized practice statute prohibits non-lawyer from drawing will for another w/ or w/o fee; stated penalties are misdemeanor & injunction. § 481.02.
    This case is different from suit by layperson to secure fee; there wrong-doing layperson is seeking to benefit. Compare contract enforceability cases: general rule is that contract in violation of licensing statute is void—but one must examine legis intent behind statute to be sure voiding contract accords w/legis purpose. Contract is void where enforcement would injure public health or morals, harm fundamental rights of individual, undermine confidence in justice system. Cites to MN cases.
    It is legis task to declare acts in violation of public policy & to set consequences. Where statute is not explicit as to consequences, consider legis intent, derived from need for law, mischief to be remedied, object to be attained, & consequences of particular interpretation, etc. (Cite to § 645.16.)
    § 481.02 is aimed at harm to widows & kids—where well meaning but bungling layperson drafted defective will. Such laypeople are outside supervision of cts. So statute's purpose is to protect testators from drafters, & penalty operates against drafters.
    Where statute imposes penalty on wrongdoer & is silent as to effect of transaction, silence is significant. See expressio unius. Where penalty is imposed on one party & not on other, do not deem them in pari delicto. Here penalty goes against drafter. Do not penalize testator by invalidating will.
    Buckley is distinguished as involving attempt by wrongdoer to benefit from transaction. Similarly, case in which unlicensed drafter was sole beneficiary of will & will was declared invalid is distinguishable. Cases involving litigation are distinguishable.

PERTINENCE: Addresses living will itself—valid. Touches on enforcement of contract; lists many factors. Stresses public policy.

Gardner v. Conway, 48 N.W.2d 788 (Minn. 1951).

GARDNER et al. v. CONWAY.
No. 35317.

Supreme Court of Minnesota.

July 6, 1951.

Action by Clifford W. Gardner and others, as constituting all the members of a committee on the unauthorized and illegal practice of the law, being a subcommittee of the Committee on Practice of the Law of the Ramsey County Bar Association, etc., against James L. Conway to perpetually enjoin defendant from further engaging in the unauthorized practice of law and to adjudge him in contempt of court therefor. The District Court, Ramsey County, Albin S. Pearson, J., entered an order denying defendant's motion for a new trial and defendant appealed. The Supreme Court, Matson, J., held that the resolution by tax expert of difficult legal questions incidental to the preparation of income tax return for another for a consideration constituted the practice of law and that a layman may not hold himself out to the public as a tax consultant or tax expert or describe himself by any similar phrase which implies that he has a knowledge of the law.

Order affirmed.

1. Attorney and client ⊙=11

A proceeding to adjudge a person in contempt of court for unauthorized practice of law, regardless of whether such unauthorized practice occurred within or outside the presence of the court, is punitive and criminal in its nature and is primarily brought in the public interest to vindicate the authority of the court and to deter other like derelictions.

2. Contempt ⊙=66(1)

A conviction for a criminal contempt, as distinguished from a civil contempt, must be reviewed by certiorari and is not appealable.

3. Injunction ⊙=89

The district court has jurisdiction to enjoin the unauthorized practice of law, regardless of whether such practice takes place within or outside the presence of the court, and such jurisdiction is not destroyed by the criminality of defendant's misconduct which neither gives nor ousts jurisdiction in chancery. M.S.A. § 481.02.

4. Injunction ⊙=89

Where purported acts of unauthorized practice of law were intentionally performed by defendant upon the mistaken assumption that he was advising a bona fide taxpayer and was preparing for him a tax return for use in reporting an actual taxpayer's income, action to enjoin unauthorized practice of law presented a justiciable issue, though the evidentiary basis of action consisted primarily of professional acts and service furnished for a consideration for a private investigator acting under a fictitious name upon a hypothetical state of facts in connection with preparation of an income tax return which was never intended to be filed. M.S.A. § 481.02.

5. Injunction ⊙=22

In action to enjoin unauthorized practice of law, the controversy was not moot, since judgment would have a swift and definite impact upon defendant by forever enjoining him from giving regular advice and service in connection with the preparation of income tax returns. M.S.A. § 481.02.

6. Attorney and client ⊙=11

The development of any practical criterion for determining what constitutes the practice of law, as well as the application of such criterion, must be closely related to the purpose for which attorneys are licensed as the exclusive occupants of their field. M.S.A. § 481.02.

7. Attorney and client ⊙=11

The purpose for which attorneys are licensed as the exclusive occupants of their field is to protect the public from the intolerable evils which are brought upon people by those who assume to practice law without having the proper qualifications.

8. Attorney and client ⊙=4

The law practice franchise or privilege is based upon the threefold requirements of ability, character, and responsible supervision. M.S.A. § 481.02.

9. Attorney and client ⊙=36(1)

Attorneys as officers of the court are subject to its inherent supervisory jurisdiction, which embraces the power to remove from the profession those practitioners who are unfaithful or incompetent in the discharge of their trust.

10. Attorney and client ⚖4

While professional standards for safeguarding the public interest must be sufficiently flexible to allow for adaptation to changes in conditions, they must in any event be of such stability and permanence as to protect the individual practitioner in the enjoyment of his professional franchise, in order to induce men of ability and character to undergo the years of training necessary to qualify them as attorneys.

11. Attorney and client ⚖11

A layman's legal service activities constitute the "practice of law" unless they are incidental to his regular calling, but the mere fact that they are incidental is not decisive. M.S.A. § 481.02.

> See publication Words and Phrases, for other judicial constructions and definitions of "Practice of Law".

12. Attorney and client ⚖11

What constitutes the practice of law may be determined only from a consideration of the acts of service performed in each case.

13. Attorney and client ⚖11

Generally, whenever, as incidental to another transaction or calling, a layman, as part of his regular course of conduct resolves legal question for another at his request and for a consideration by giving him advice or by taking action for and in his behalf, the layman is "practicing law" if difficult or doubtful legal questions are involved which, to safeguard the public, reasonably demand the application of a trained legal mind. M.S.A. § 481.02.

> See publication Words and Phrases, for other judicial constructions and definitions of "Practicing Law".

14. Attorney and client ⚖11

What is a difficult or doubtful question of law demanding the application of a trained legal mind is not to be measured by the comprehension of a trained legal mind but by the understanding thereof which is possessed by a reasonably intelligent layman who is reasonably familiar with similar transactions. M.S.A. § 481.02.

15. Attorney and client ⚖11

In restricting laymen from unauthorized practice of law, the difficult question of law criterion is to be applied in a common sense way which will protect primarily the interests of the public and not hamper or burden such interest with impractical and technical restrictions which have no reasonable justification. M.S.A. § 481.02.

16. Broker ⚖4

As ancillary to the closing of a real estate transaction, a real estate broker may draw the ordinary instruments of conveyance.

17. Attorney and client ⚖11

A layman may not draw another's will, except where dire emergency prevents the calling of an attorney. M.S.A. § 481.02.

18. Attorney and client ⚖11

When an accountant or other layman who is employed to prepare an income tax return is faced with difficult or doubtful questions of the interpretation or application of statutes, administrative regulations and rulings, court decisions or general law, it is his duty to leave the determination of such questions to an attorney. M.S.A. § 481.02.

19. Attorney and client ⚖11

The work of an accountant disassociated from the resolving of difficult or doubtful questions of law is not the practice of law. M.S.A. § 481.02.

20. Attorney and client ⚖11

Where income tax expert incidental to the preparation of income tax return for a consideration resolved difficult legal questions as to whether taxpayer was in partnership with common-law wife in operation of a truck farm, whether he was entitled to claim as an exemption the woman with whom he had been living without ceremonial marriage, whether taxpayer and such woman should file a joint or separate returns, and whether cost of improvement of buildings on farm and produce losses sustained by frost and flood were deductible while preparation of return was not of itself the practice of law, the services rendered, taken as a whole, constituted the "practice of law". M.S.A. § 481.02.

21. Attorney and client ⊜11

A layman, regardless of whether he is an accountant, may not hold himself out to the public as a tax consultant or tax expert or describe himself by any similar phrase which implies that he has a knowledge of the law. M.S.A. § 481.02.

Syllabus by the Court.

1. A proceeding to adjudge a person in contempt of court for the unauthorized practice of law—whether such unauthorized practice occurred within or outside the presence of the court—is punitive and criminal in its nature and is primarily brought in the public interest to vindicate the authority of the court and to deter other like derelictions.

2. A conviction for a criminal contempt, as distinguished from a civil contempt, is not appealable, but must be reviewed by certiorari.

3. The district court has jurisdiction to enjoin the unauthorized practice of law, whether such practice takes place within or outside the presence of the court, and such jurisdiction is not destroyed by the criminality of the defendant's misconduct.

4. A justiciable issue may arise although the purported acts of unauthorized practice of law were intentionally performed by defendant upon the mistaken assumption that he was then advising a bona fide taxpayer and was preparing for him a tax return for use in reporting an actual taxpayer's income.

5. The purpose for which lawyers are licensed as the exclusive occupants of their field is to protect the public from the intolerable evils which are brought upon people by those who assume to practice law without having the proper qualifications.

6. The law practice franchise or privilege is based upon the threefold requirements of *ability, character,* and *responsible supervision.*

7. A layman's legal service activities are the practice of law unless they are incidental to his regular calling; but the mere fact that they are incidental is by no means decisive.

8. Generally speaking, whenever, as incidental to another transaction or calling, a layman, as part of his regular course of conduct, resolves legal questions for another—at the latter's request and for a consideration—by giving him advice or by taking action for and in his behalf, he is practicing law if difficult or doubtful legal questions are involved which, to safeguard the public, reasonably demand the application of a trained legal mind.

9. What is a difficult or doubtful question of law is not to be measured by the comprehension of a trained legal mind, but by the understanding thereof which is possessed by a reasonably intelligent layman who is reasonably familiar with similar transactions.

10. In restraining laymen from improper activity, *the difficult question of law criterion* is to be applied in a common-sense way which will protect primarily the interest of the public and not hamper or burden that interest with impractical and technical restrictions which have no reasonable justification.

11. When an accountant or other layman who is employed to prepare an income tax return is faced with difficult or doubtful questions of the interpretation or application of statutes, administrative regulations and rulings, court decisions, or general law, it is his duty to leave the determination of such questions to a lawyer.

12. The work of an accountant disassociated from the resolving of difficult or doubtful questions of law is not law practice.

13. Although the preparation of the income tax return was not of itself the practice of law, defendant herein, incidental to such preparation, resolved certain difficult legal questions which, taken as a whole, constituted the practice of law.

14. A layman, whether he is or is not an accountant, may not hold himself out to the public as a tax consultant or a tax expert, or describe himself by any sim-

ilar phrase which implies that he has a knowledge of tax law.

———

Bundlie, Kelley, Finley & Maun, St. Paul, for appellant.

Clifford W. Gardner, C. Paul Smith, Calvin Hunt, Alric Anderson, Irving Gotlieb, Fred Kueppers, and Worth K. Rice, all of St. Paul, for respondents.

Fontaine C. Bradley, Washington, D. C. (American Institute of Accountants), Best, Flanagan, Rogers, Lewis & Simonet, Minneapolis (Minn. Assn. of Public Accountants and National Soc. of Public Accountants), Fowler, Youngquist, Furber, Taney & Johnson, G. Aaron Youngquist and John R. Goetz, all of Minneapolis (Minnesota Soc. of Certified Public Accountants), Robert J. Nowack, Minneapolis (Minnesota State Bar Assn., by its Standing Committee on Unauthorized Practice of Law), John D. Randall, Chairman, Cedar Rapids, Iowa, Cuthbert S. Baldwin, New Orleans, La., Thomas J. Boodell, Chicago, Ill., A. J. Casner, Cambridge, Mass., Edgar N. Eisenhower, Tacoma, Wash., Edwin M. Otterbourg, New York City and Warren H. Resh, Madison, Wis. (American Bar Assn., by its Standing Committee on Unauthorized Practice of Law), amici curiæ.

MATSON, Justice.

Defendant appeals from an order denying his motion for a new trial.

This action, to have the defendant perpetually *enjoined* from further engaging in the unauthorized practice of law and to have him *adjudged in contempt* of court therefor, was brought by the plaintiffs[1] in their own behalf as licensed lawyers and in a representative capacity in behalf of every other licensed lawyer in Minnesota, as well as in behalf of the courts and the public.[2]

1. Plaintiffs are the members of a committee on the unauthorized and illegal practice of law, which is a subcommittee of the Committee on Practice of Law of the Ramsey County Bar Association.

2. As *amici curiae* the following organizations have filed briefs with the court:

Defendant, who is possessed of only a grade-school education, has never been admitted to the practice of law in Minnesota or elsewhere. During a two-year period immediately prior to the time of trial, he followed the occupation of a public accountant. Prior thereto, he served for three years as a United States deputy collector of internal revenue. Before that, he had worked for six years as the credit manager of a hardware company, about five years as the operator of a collection agency, and for four years as an insurance solicitor and risk inspector.

At and prior to the time with which we are concerned, defendant held himself out to the public by newspaper advertisements and by other advertising media as an "Income Tax Expert," duly qualified to give advice, aid, and assistance to the public generally in the discharge of a taxpayer's duty to make accurate returns of income to the federal government. Defendant alleges that he is thoroughly familiar with income tax rules and regulations. He has used a business card on which he describes himself as a "Tax Consultant" and prominently calls attention thereon to the fact that he was a former deputy collector of internal revenue.

On or about March 4, 1948, Cecil G. Germain, a private investigator employed by plaintiffs to obtain information as to whether defendant was engaged in the practice of law, went to the office of defendant under the assumed name and identity of an alleged taxpayer, George Heinl. Germain, as George Heinl, informed defendant that he operated a truck farm, that he had come to have his income tax return prepared, and that he needed help with certain questions. For a cash consideration, defendant prepared the income tax return and gave Germain professional advice for the determination of the following questions:

Minnesota Association of Public Accountants, National Society of Public Accountants, Minnesota Society of Certified Public Accountants, American Institute of Accountants, Minnesota State Bar Association, and the American Bar Association.

(a) Whether the taxpayer, who himself had exclusive control of the operation of the truck farm, was in partnership with his wife, who had contributed one-half of the purchase price, who helped with the work, and who received one-half the profits.

(b) Whether the taxpayer was entitled to claim his wife as an exemption, since he had never been ceremonially married, though maintaining a common-law marriage status.

(c) Whether the taxpayer should file his separate return and advise his so-called common-law wife to file a separate return.

(d) Whether certain money expended on improvements of buildings on the truck farm was deductible from his earnings.

(e) Whether a certain produce loss sustained by frost and subsequent flood was a deductible item.

Aside from the fundamental issue of whether defendant's activities constituted the unauthorized practice of law, we are concerned with these procedural issues:

(1) Does the *district court* have the power to adjudge defendant in contempt of court and to punish him for the unauthorized practice of law?

(2) Does the district court have jurisdiction to enjoin the unauthorized practice of law where defendant's acts of purported law practice did not involve any act or appearance before said court?

(3) Is a justiciable issue presented when the evidentiary base of an action to enjoin the unauthorized practice of law consists primarily of professional acts of advice and service which were furnished for a consideration to a person who was not a bona fide taxpayer, upon a fabricated

and hypothetical state of facts, and in connection with the preparation of an income tax return which was never intended to be filed?

[1, 2] 1–2. We shall dispose of the procedural matters first. A proceeding to adjudge a person in contempt of court for the unauthorized practice of law—whether such unauthorized practice occurred within or outside the presence of the court—is punitive and criminal in its nature and is primarily brought in the public interest to vindicate the authority of the court and to deter other like derelictions. In re Frederick Bugasch, Inc., 175 A. 110, 12 N.J. Misc. 788, State ex rel. Indianapolis Bar Ass'n v. Fletcher Trust Co., 211 Ind. 27, 5 N.E.2d 538; Dangel, Contempt, National Lawyers' Manual (1939), §§ 353, 436; 7 C.J.S., Attorney and Client, § 16c. Although a prosecution for the unauthorized practice of law, as an offense against society, inures incidentally to the individual benefit of properly licensed lawyers, the criminal nature of the proceeding is unaffected. In re Frederick Bugasch, Inc., supra; see, Root v. MacDonald, 260 Mass. 344, 367, 157 N.E. 684, 692, 54 A.L.R. 1422.[3] Defendant, contending that the supreme court of Minnesota has the sole and exclusive jurisdiction to adjudge a person in contempt for the unauthorized practice of law, asks us upon this appeal to determine whether the district court had the power to adjudge him in contempt. This we cannot do. We have repeatedly held that a conviction for a criminal contempt, as distinguished from a civil contempt, is not appealable, but must be reviewed by certiorari. Swift & Co. v. United Packing House Workers, 228 Minn. 571, 37 N.W.2d 831, and cases cited therein.[4]

---

3. As to the distinction between a contempt proceeding, even though its object and result are wholly punitive, and an ordinary criminal proceeding, see Root v. MacDonald, 260 Mass. 344, 365, 157 N.E. 684, 691, 54 A.L.R. 1422; Dangel, Contempt, National Lawyers' Manual (1939) § 161.

4. As to contempt proceedings generally for the unauthorized practice of law, see Bump v. District Court, 232 Iowa 623, 5 N.W.2d 914; State ex rel. Wright v.

Barlow, 131 Neb. 294, 268 N.W. 95; State ex rel. Johnson v. Childe, 147 Neb. 527, 23 N.W.2d 720; People ex rel. Illinois State Bar Ass'n v. Peoples Stock Yards State Bank, 344 Ill. 462, 176 N.E. 901; People v. Securities Discount Corp. 361 Ill. 551, 198 N.E. 681; In re Frederick Bugasch, Inc., 175 A. 110, 12 N.J. Misc. 788; Matter of New York County Lawyers Ass'n (Bercu) 273 App.Div. 524, 78 N.Y.S.2d 209, 9 A.L.R.2d 787, affirmed, 299 N.Y. 728, 87 N.E.2d 451;

GARDNER v. CONWAY   Minn.   793
Cite as 48 N.W.2d 788

[3] 3. The district court has jurisdiction to enjoin the unauthorized practice of law, whether such practice takes place within or outside the presence of the court, and such jurisdiction is not destroyed by the criminality of the defendant's misconduct. The criminal nature of unauthorized practice neither gives nor ousts jurisdiction in chancery. Fitchette v. Taylor, 191 Minn. 582, 254 N.W. 910, 94 A.L.R. 356; Cowern v. Nelson, 207 Minn. 642, 290 N.W. 795; see, Miller v. Minneapolis Underwriters Ass'n, Inc. 226 Minn. 367, 371, 33 N.W.2d 48, 51; M.S.A. § 481.02.

[4] 4. Does a justiciable issue arise when the purported acts of unauthorized practice of law were intentionally performed by defendant upon the mistaken assumption that he was then advising a bona fide taxpayer and was preparing for him a tax return for use in reporting an actual taxpayer's income? Defendant's intentional acts were performed when plaintiffs' private investigator provided the occasion and the opportunity for such performance by calling at defendant's office under an assumed name with a purely fictitious and hypothetical state of facts. Although such investigator employed defendant's services for the sole purpose of obtaining evidentiary information as to the nature of defendant's regular activities, defendant did intentionally give his advice in the same manner as if a bona fide taxpayer had actually appeared. The fact that the income tax return was based upon fictitious facts and figures is not of itself a defense. Frequently decoy letters and other fictional devices have been employed in law enforcement cases, not to induce the commission of an unlawful act, but to secure information as to whether unlawful acts had been and were being committed. United States v. Lindenfeld, 2 Cir., 142 F.2d 829. Defendant here assumes that because the tax return which he prepared

was not authentic he could not have committed any offense. He is mistaken. The leading case upon this point is Grimm v. United States, 156 U.S. 604, 609, 15 S.Ct. 470, 472, 39 L.Ed. 550, 552, where the court said:

"* * * it is insisted that the conviction cannot be sustained, because the letters of defendant were deposited in the mails at the instance of the government, and through the solicitation of one of its officers; that they were directed and mailed to fictitious persons; that no intent can be imputed to defendant to convey information to other than the persons named in the letters sent by him; and that, as they were fictitious persons, there could in law be no intent to give information to any one. * * *

"* * * The mere facts that the letters were written under an assumed name, and that he was a government official,—a detective, he may be called,—do not of themselves constitute a defense to the crime actually committed. The official, suspecting that the defendant was engaged in a business offensive to good morals, sought information directly from him, and the defendant, responding thereto, violated a law of the United States by using the mails to convey such information, and he cannot plead in defense that he would not have violated the law if inquiry had not been made of him by such government official."

This court followed the Grimm case in State v. Gibbs, 109 Minn. 247, 123 N.W. 810, 25 L.R.A., N.S., 449. When the investigator called at defendant's office he did not thereby induce or originate defendant's intent to perform the alleged acts of unauthorized practice, but merely provided the opportunity for defendant to exercise the intent which he already possessed.[5]

State ex rel. Indianapolis Bar Ass'n v. Fletcher Trust Co., 211 Ind. 27, 5 N.E.2d 538; In re Morse, 98 Vt. 85, 126 A. 550, 36 A.L.R. 527, with Annotation at page 533; Rhode Island Bar Ass'n v. Automobile Service Ass'n, 55 R.I. 122, 179 A. 139, 100 A.L.R. 226, with Anno-

48 N.W.2d—50½

tation at page 236; In re McCallum, 186 Wash. 312, 57 P.2d 1259; Appeal of Cichon, 227 Wis. 62, 278 N.W. 1.

5. United States v. Lindenfeld, 2 Cir., 142 F.2d 829; United States v. Becker, 2 Cir., 62 F.2d 1007; Flunkin v. United States, 9 Cir., 265 F. 1; Rothman v.

[5] An actual intent by defendant to hold himself out to the public as willing to do and as customarily and regularly doing the acts which are here alleged to constitute the unauthorized practice of law is the very basis of these proceedings. In view of the evidentiary establishment of his intent and his regular doing of such acts, does it follow that no justiciable issue is presented simply because the evidence was obtained by the device of a fictitious tax return and a purely hypothetical set of facts? There is nothing fictitious or hypothetical about the basic issue between the parties. Instead of a fictitious, academic, or hypothetical issue, we have an actual, genuine, and live controversy as to whether defendant is guilty of the unauthorized practice of law. We are not concerned with some contingent or threatened event which may never occur. We are dealing with acts of alleged unlawful practice which have occurred. Furthermore, a controversy is not moot where, as here, the judgment of the court will have a swift and definite impact upon defendant by forever enjoining him from giving regular advice and service in connection with the preparation of income tax returns.

5. Was defendant, however, practicing law when, as a preliminary to and as part of his preparation of an income tax return, he advised the purported taxpayer as to whether he had acquired a partnership status, a valid marriage for exemption purposes, whether he should file a joint return with a woman to whom he had never been ceremonially married, and whether certain building and truck farm improvements, as well as certain losses sustained by frost and subsequent flood, were deductible items?

Much of what is law practice is conducted outside the courtroom, and as to that field of activity we have said: " * * * The line between what is and what is not the practice of law cannot be drawn with precision. Lawyers should be the first to recognize that between the two there is a region wherein much of what lawyers do every day in their practice may also be done by others without wrongful invasion of the lawyers' field." Cowern v. Nelson, 207 Minn. 642, 646, 290 N.W. 795, 797.

[6, 7] Although it is difficult to draw any precise dividing line, the task is ours to find some criterion for distinguishing that which is from that which is not law practice. The development of any practical criterion, as well as its subsequent application, must be closely related to the purpose for which lawyers are licensed as the exclusive occupants of their field. That purpose is to protect the public from the intolerable evils which are brought upon people by those who assume to practice law without having the proper qualifications. See, 29 Mich.L.Rev. 989. The need for public protection is not of new origin. As early as 1292,[6] the problem was recognized when Edward I, by royal ordinance, limited the number of attorneys and directed his justices "to provide for every county a sufficient number of attornies and apprentices from among the best, the most lawful and the most teachable, so *that king and people might be well served.*" (Italics supplied.) 1 Pollock and Maitland, History of English Law, p. 194. See, Herbert, Antiquities of the Inns of Court and Chancery, pp. 166, 167. The limitation and selection of lawyers, without strict regulation, proved inadequate.

" * * * The evil finally became so great that in the year 1402 Parliament this time took cognizance of it and enacted the now famous statute, 4 Henry IV, Ch. 18, which provided that all attorneys should be examined by the justices, and in their discretion, only those found to be good and virtuous, and of good fame, learned and sworn to do their duty, be allowed to be

---

United States, 2 Cir., 270 F. 31; Sorrells v. United States, 287 U.S. 435, 53 S.Ct. 210, 77 L.Ed. 413; see, People v. Alfani, 227 N.Y. 334, 125 N.E. 671.

6. What is probably the first Anglo-Saxon statute regulating the practice of the law was passed in 1275 as the Statute of

Westminster, the First, 3 Edward I, c. 29 (1 Stat. at Large, p. 94). The professional lawyer, however, began to appear in Anglo-Saxon England shortly after the Conquest. See, Cohen, The Law:—Business or Profession? (1924) pp. 84–86.

GARDNER v. CONWAY
Cite as 48 N.W.2d 788

put upon the roll and all others put out." Rhode Island Bar Ass'n v. Automobile Service Ass'n, 55 R.I. 122, 133, 179 A. 139, 144, 100 A.L.R. 226. These early English statutes illustrate that a licensed bar subject to the supervision of the courts originated with a public demand for the exclusion of those who assumed to practice without being qualified therefor.

[8–10] 6. The protection of the public, as the purpose of confining law practice to a licensed bar, ancient as it is in its origin, is of vital importance today. See, In re Estate of Peterson, 230 Minn. 478, 42 N. W.2d 59; Cowern v. Nelson, 207 Minn. 642, 290 N.W. 795; M.S.A. 481.02. Any criterion for distinguishing law practice from that which belongs to other fields can be properly geared to the public welfare only if we keep in mind the manner in which the licensing of lawyers serves its purpose. The law practice franchise or privilege is based upon the threefold requirements of *ability, character,* and *responsible supervision.* The public welfare is safeguarded not merely by limiting law practice to individuals who are possessed of the requisite ability and character, but also by the further requirement that such practitioners shall thenceforth be officers of the court and subject to its supervision. See, 40 Dickinson L.Rev. 225, 229. In consequence, lawyers are not merely bound by a high code of professional ethics, but as officers of the court they are subject to its inherent supervisory jurisdiction, which embraces the power to remove from the profession those practitioners who are unfaithful or incompetent in the discharge of their trust. In re Tracy, 197 Minn. 35, 266 N.W. 88, 267 N.W. 142; see, In re Opinion of the Justices, 289 Mass. 607, 194 N.E. 313. This is in itself an important reason why law practice should be confined to members of the bar. Protection of the public is set at naught if laymen who are not subject to court supervision are permitted to practice law. Although professional standards for safeguarding the public interest must be sufficiently flexible to allow for adaptation to changes in conditions, they must in any event be of such stability and permanence as to protect the

individual practitioner in the enjoyment of his professional franchise; otherwise men of ability and character will find no inducement to undergo the years of training necessary to qualify them as lawyers. This principle, as a part of the public weal, is applicable to any profession which demands of its members high skill and proficiency based upon years of intensive preparatory training. State v. Bailey Dental Co., 211 Iowa 781, 234 N.W. 260; 5 Fordham L. Rev. 207.

[11] 7. If we bear in mind that any choice of criterion must find its ultimate justification in the interest of the public and not in that of advantage for either lawyer or nonlawyer, we soon cease to look for an answer in any rule of thumb such as that based upon a distinction between the incidental and the primary. See, People v. Title Guarantee & Trust Co., 227 N. Y. 366, 379, 125 N.E. 666, 670; Merrick v. American Security & Trust Co. 71 App.D. C. 72, 107 F.2d 271. Any rule which holds that a layman who prepares legal papers or furnishes other services of a legal nature is not practicing law when such services are incidental to another business or profession completely ignores the public welfare. A service performed by one individual for another, even though it be incidental to some other occupation, may entail a difficult question of law which requires a determination by a trained legal mind. See, 33 Minn.L.Rev. 445. Are we to say that a real estate broker who examines an abstract of title and furnishes an opinion thereon may not be held to practice law merely because the examination of a title is ancillary to a sale and purchase of real estate? Can we say that a lawyer employed to bring a suit for damages for personal injuries is competent to diagnose the nature of his client's injuries and that he is not practicing medicine merely because such diagnosis is incidental to a proper presentation of his client's case? The drawing of a simple instrument or the application of an elementary legal principle is one thing in the incidental classification, but it is wholly another when such incidental act or service requires professional skill. The incidental test has no value ex-

cept in the negative sense that if the furnishing of the legal service is the primary business of the actor such activity is the practice of law, even though such service is of an elementary nature. In other words, a layman's legal service activities are the practice of law unless they are incidental to his regular calling; but the mere fact that they are incidental is by no means decisive. In a positive sense, the incidental test ignores the interest of the public as the controlling determinant.

[12–14] 8–9. In rejecting the incidental test, it follows that the distinction between law practice and that which is not may be determined only from a consideration of the nature of the acts of service performed in each case. No difficulty arises where such service is the primary business of the actor. We then have law practice. Difficulty comes, however, when the service furnished is incidental to the performance of other service of a nonlegal character in the pursuit of another calling such as that of accounting. In the field of income taxation, as in the instant case, we have an overlapping of both law and accounting. An accountant must adapt his accounting skill to the requirements of tax law, and therefore he must have a workable knowledge of law as applied to his field. By the same token, a lawyer must have some understanding of accounting. In the income tax area, they occupy much common ground where the skills of both professions may be required and where it is difficult to draw a precise line to separate their respective functions. The public interest does not permit an obliteration of all lines of demarcation. We cannot escape reality by hiding behind a facade of nomenclature and assume that "taxation," though composed of both law and accounting, is something *sui*

generis and apart from the law. See, Matter of New York County Lawyers Ass'n (Bercu) 273 App.Div. 524, 78 N.Y.S.2d 209, affirmed, 299 N.Y. 728, 87 N.E.2d 451. If taxation is a hybrid of law and accounting, it does not follow that it is so wholly without the law that its legal activities may be pursued without proper qualifications and without court supervision. The interest of the public is not protected by the narrow specialization of an individual who lacks the perspective and the orientation which comes only from a thorough knowledge and understanding of basic legal concepts, of legal processes, and of the interrelation of the law in all its branches.[7] Generally speaking, whenever, as incidental to another transaction or calling, a layman, as part of his regular course of conduct, resolves legal questions for another—at the latter's request and for a consideration—by giving him advice or by taking action for and in his behalf, he is practicing law if difficult or doubtful legal questions are involved which, to safeguard the public, reasonably demand the application of a trained legal mind. What is a difficult or doubtful question of law is not to be measured by the comprehension of a trained legal mind, but by the understanding thereof which is possessed by a reasonably intelligent layman who is reasonably familiar with similar transactions. A criterion which designates the determination of a difficult or complex question of law as law practice, and the application of an elementary or simple legal principle as not, may indeed be criticized for uncertainty if a rule of thumb is sought which can be applied with mechanical precision to all cases. Any rule of law which purports to reflect the needs of the public welfare in a changing society, by reason of its essen-

7. The shortcomings of a narrow specialization is well illustrated by the service given by the respondent to his client in Matter of New York County Lawyers Assn. (Bercu) 273 App.Div. 524, 78 N.Y. S.2d 209, affirmed, 299 N.Y. 728, 87 N.E. 2d 451. On the other hand, the value of a well-rounded legal training in the income tax field was demonstrated by two Minnesota lawyers in Albright v. United States,

8 Cir., 173 F.2d 339, wherein the court held that sales of all dairy and breeding animals used in a farmer's business and owned more than six months were entitled, under § 117(j) of the Internal Revenue Code, 26 U.S.C.A. § 117(j), to be treated as sales of capital assets. It has been said that this decision has saved farmers millions of dollars in income taxes. See, 35 Iowa L.Rev. 49.

GARDNER v. CONWAY
Cite as 48 N.W.2d 788

tial and inherent flexibility, will, however, be as variable in operation as the particular facts to which it is applied.

[15–17] 10–11–12. In restraining laymen from improper activity, *the difficult question of law criterion* is to be applied in a common-sense way which will protect primarily the interest of the public and not hamper or burden that interest with impractical and technical restrictions which have no reasonable justification. Cowern v. Nelson, 207 Minn. 642, 290 N.W. 795. We are therefore not concerned with a technical application which would ban the giving of any and all legal advice or the taking of any and all action for another.[8] Whether a difficult or doubtful question of law is resolved by the giving of advice to, or the doing of an act for, another must in each case depend upon the nature of the problem involved. As ancillary to the closing of a real estate transaction, a real estate broker may draw the ordinary instruments of conveyance. Cowern v. Nelson, supra. No layman, however, except when dire emergency prevents the calling of a lawyer, may draw another's will. In re Estate of Peterson, 230 Minn. 478, 42 N.W.2d 59; M.S.A. § 481.02. As applied to the preparation of income tax returns, it has been well said: " * * * Federal income taxation is founded on statute, elaborated and interpreted by administrative regulations and rulings, and construed by court decisions. Matters in this field, as in other statutory subjects, will at times involve difficult questions of interpretation of statute or court decision, and the validity of regulations or statute; they will also involve doubtful questions of nontax law on which the tax issues may depend, and questions of liability for criminal or civil penalties or of statutes of limitation or of liability as transferee for the taxes of another. Such questions, in general, are the

kind for which lawyers are equipped by training and practice." [9]

[18, 19] When an accountant or other layman who is employed to prepare an income tax return is faced with difficult or doubtful questions of the interpretation or application of statutes, administrative regulations and rulings, court decisions, or general law, it is his duty to leave the determination of such questions to a lawyer. In so holding that the determination of difficult or doubtful questions is the practice of law, it does not follow that the entire income tax field has been preempted by lawyers to the exclusion of accountants. The work of an accountant disassociated from the resolving of difficult or doubtful questions of law is not law practice. See, Opinion of the Justices, 289 Mass. 607, 615, 194 N.E. 313, 318. In the determination of income—the subject of taxation—difficult accounting problems may arise by presenting "such aspects as inventory pricing methods (last-in-first-out, first-in-first-out, retail method, cost determination, actual costs, standard costs, cost of in-process merchandise, market price valuation, etc.), accrual and installment accounting, carryover and carryback of net operating losses, depreciation, depletion and corporate distributions. The taxation of such income may involve such concepts as consolidated returns, taxable years of less than twelve months, invested capital, etc. All of these are concepts of accounting, * * *." 36 Iowa L.Rev. 227, 229.

Where difficult accounting questions arise, the careful lawyer will naturally advise his client to enlist the aid of an accountant. In the income tax field, the lawyer and the accountant each has a function to perform in the interest of the public.[10]

[20] 13. In the instant case, the evidence sustains the trial court's findings and

---

8. " 'Giving any legal advice' would include telling a man whether it is lawful to write 'Please do not open until Christmas' on a parcels post package. 'Any action taken for others in any matter connected with the law' would include parking a man's automobile for him parallel to the curb not over six inches from it." 19 American Bar Assn. Journal 652.

9. Maurice Austin, Relations Between Lawyers and Certified Public Accountants in Income Tax Practice (1951), 36 Iowa L.Rev. 227, 228.

10. See, 1 Catholic University of America L.Rev. 21.

conclusions that defendant was engaged in the practice of law. For a consideration, and as part of his regular income tax work, defendant advised and determined for the taxpayer whether the latter had attained the status of a lawful marriage with a woman with whom he had been living but to whom he had never been ceremonially married. He further gave advice as to whether such taxpayer and his consort should file separate or joint returns. The purported taxpayer was likewise uncertain as to whether he occupied the status of a partner with his so-called common-law wife in the operation of a truck farm, over which he himself exercised exclusive control but in which the latter shared equally in the labor, investment, and profit. This question, the answer to which obviously required legal training, he also resolved. We do not here have the case of a taxpayer whose legal status was established or known beforehand. In addition, defendant gave advice as to the deductions which the taxpayer might claim for certain farm improvements and for certain produce loss by frost and subsequent flood. Although the preparation of the income tax return was not of itself the practice of law, defendant, incidental to such preparation, resolved certain difficult legal questions which, taken as a whole, constituted the practice of law.

[21] 14. In further confirmation of the conclusion that defendant was practicing law, the evidence establishes that he advertised and held himself out as a "Tax Consultant," which by reasonable implication advised the public that he was competent to give legal advice on the law of taxation. A layman, whether he is or is not an accountant, may not hold himself out to the public as a tax consultant or a tax expert, or describe himself by any similar phrase which implies that he has a knowledge of tax law. It should be noted that lawyers, by the canons of ethics of the American Bar Association and the opinions thereto pertaining, are likewise prohibited from advertising any special branch of law practice. Canons of Professional and Judicial Ethics, American Bar Association, Canons 27 and 45, and see Opinion 260.

The order of the trial court is affirmed.

Affirmed.

Gardner Brief

Gardner v. Conway, Minnesota Supreme Court, 1951, 48 N.W.2d 788.

FACTS: D held himself out to public through newspaper & other advertisements as "income tax expert" qualified to assist public in filing of federal income tax returns. D attained formal education through grade school & was never admitted to practice law in any state. Ps are members of Ramsey County Bar Ass'n.

Detective hired by Ps went to D under assumed name as alleged taxpayer. Detective told D he operated truck farm, needed to have income tax return prepared, requested D to resolve questions: (1) whether he had formed partnership with his wife, (2) whether he could claim his common law wife as exemption, (3) whether he & common law wife should file joint or separate returns, (4) whether certain business expenditures & certain business losses could be deducted from his income. D answered these questions for detective & prepared his tax return.

PROCEDURE: Ps sued D to have him perpetually enjoined from further engaging in unauthorized practice of law & to have him adjudged in contempt of ct. Dist ct found D illegally engaged in practice of law & denied D's motion for new trial. D appealed.

ISSUE: Did D engage in practice of law when he answered questions of detective about tax implications of marital & business relations?

HOLDING: Affirmed. Evidence sustains dist ct's finding that D was engaged in practice of law when answering questions about tax implications of marital & business relations.

REASONING: Rule: If legal services are primary business of actor, then law practice. When layperson as part of regular course of conduct incidentally resolves legal questions for another upon request & for consideration, layperson practices law if difficult or doubtful legal questions are involved which reasonably demand application of trained legal mind.

Policy: Lawyers must be licensed to practice law to protect public from intolerable evils brought upon people by those who assume to practice law w/o having proper qualifications. Public welfare is safeguarded by limiting law practice to individuals who possess requisite ability & character & are officers of ct & subject to its supervision. Focus of rule must be interest of public & not advantage for either lawyer or non-lawyer.

More discussion of rule: Rule permitting layperson to prepare legal papers or perform other legal services whenever such services are incidental to another business completely ignores public welfare. Incidental act of performing legal services may require professional skill which actor does not possess. Thus, focus on nature of acts of service performed in each case.

What is difficult or doubtful question of law is to be determined by reasonably intelligent layperson familiar with similar transactions. Criterion is not to be applied in impractical or technical manner. Application of rule demands common sense dependent on facts of each case.

Application: Here preparation of income tax return was not in itself practice of law. However, incidental to completion of return, D resolved difficult legal questions regarding partnership law, marital status, & business deductions which, taken as whole, constituted practice of law. Further, D held himself out to public that he was competent to give legal advice on tax law.

PERTINENCE: Living will service is incidental to social work; tougher question is doubt & difficulty of issues.

Cardinal Brief

Cardinal v. Merrill Lynch Realty/Burnet, Inc., Minnesota Supreme Court, 1988, 433 N.W.2d 864.

FACTS: MLRB is licensed real-estate broker. Closing department provided services for sellers, incl. review of conditions, ordering searches & abstracts, notifying mortgagees & contract-for-deed vendors, reviewing title insurance & opinion. MLRB charged flat fee of $250 for drafting, recording, & closing services. MLRB closer—licensed neither for real estate nor law—handled closing for Cardinal on sale of her home; she paid $250 fee. (Also another test case involving Ormans.)

PROCEDURE: Ps sued as uncertified class. Based on stipulated facts, dist ct ruled for Ps & ordered D to refund $250 minus fee MLRB paid to record or file documents. Sup ct granted accelerated review.

ISSUE: Does charging fee for real-estate closing services where no difficult or doubtful legal issues arise constitute unauthorized practice of law? Note: case does not raise underlying issue whether services were complex enough to require lawyer.

HOLDING: No, charging of fee alone does not render real-estate closing services unauthorized practice of law where no difficult or doubtful issues arise.

REASONING: Rules: Minn. Stat. § 481.02 subd. 1 precludes non-lawyer from preparing legal document for another; subd. 2 so provides as to for-profit corp. But subd. 3(3) & 3(9) exempt certain real-estate services.* Ct held in *Cowern v. Nelson*, 290 N.W. 795 (Minn. 1940), that real-estate broker could handle ordinary conveyancing w/o committing unauthorized practice of law—but could not charge for it. Ct developed difficult-or-doubtful-legal-question test in *Gardner v. Conway*, 48 N.W.2d 788 (Minn. 1951).
    Policy: Protect public against non-lawyer performing service for which perspective & orientation of lawyer is needed.
    Application: Here no allegation of difficult or doubtful legal question or incompetence. Only assertion is that charging fee made for unauthorized practice. Not so. Fee covered some clearly non-legal activities. Charging for service is not alone determinative; but charging for service is relevant to & factor in unauthorized practice analysis, cuz fee reflects parties' judgment of value of services.

DISSENT (THREE JUSTICES): Services were complex & implicated legal judgment, so services + fee constituted unauthorized practice of law.

PERTINENCE: Fee is not helpful for HEC—but not determinative either, especially if covers non-legal task too.

---

*NOTE: *Cardinal* arose under older version of § 481.02. In 1988 former subd. 3(3) was deleted, former subd. 3(9) became subd. 3(8), & subds. 3a & 9 were added.

Annotation, *Activities of Law Clerks as Illegal Practice of Law*, 13 A.L.R.3d 1137 (1967).

ANNOTATION

ACTIVITIES OF LAW CLERKS AS ILLEGAL PRACTICE OF LAW

TABLE OF JURISDICTIONS REPRESENTED
Consult POCKET PART in this volume for later case service

§ 1. Introduction

[a] Scope

This annotation[1] collects the cases discussing the nature of activities by a law clerk which constitute the illegal practice of law. For purposes of this annotation, "law clerk" includes clerical personnel employed by an attorney but not admitted to the bar.

Attention is called to the fact that this annotation discusses statutes only insofar as they are reflected in reported cases within the scope of the annotation. The reader is advised to consult the most recent statutes of his jurisdiction.

---

1. Insofar as the earlier annotations in 111 ALR 19, 125 ALR 1173, and 151 ALR 781, contain cases within the scope of this annotation, such cases have been included herein.

Consult POCKET PART in this volume for later case service

[13 ALR3d]—72

[b] Related matters

Power of court to enjoin attorney from prosecuting actions secured through chasers or runners. 14 ALR2d 740.

Services in connection with tax matters as practice of law. 9 ALR2d 797.

Handling, preparing, presenting, or trying workmen's compensation claims or cases as practice of law. 2 ALR3d 724.

What amounts to practice of law. 111 ALR 19, 125 ALR 1173, 151 ALR 781.

Liability of attorney for services rendered to him by one not admitted to bar as affected by the fact that they amounted to practice of law by the latter. 90 ALR 288.

§ 2. Preparatory or ministerial work

In the following cases, it was held that the activities of an unlicensed law clerk did not constitute the practice of law where such acts were limited to work of a preparatory or ministerial nature.

Thus, it was held that an unlicensed law clerk was not engaged in the unlawful practice of law where the clerk was hired by an attorney to take charge of the management of the work to be done in his office to the extent of drawing pleadings and papers necessary to be drawn by such attorney in his practice, in Johnson v Davidson (1921) 54 Cal App 251, 202 P 159, ovrld on other grounds Crawford v State Bar of California, 54 Cal 2d 659, 7 Cal Rptr 746, 355 P2d 490, the court, in affirming a judgment which held that the law clerk owned an undivided interest in certain property purchased by the attorney-employer with firm funds, simply stating that it was lawful for the attorney to employ the clerk to perform such functions.

An unlicensed law clerk who prepared and presented an order to the court that a jury had disagreed on a case, appeared before a court at a later date, and in-

formed the court that the case had not been settled and that his employer, an attorney representing one of the parties to the suit, was engaged in a trial in another court, was held not to have engaged in the unauthorized practice of law in People v Alexander (1964) 53 Ill App 2d 299, 202 NE2d 841, 13 ALR3d 1132, the court reversing an order adjudging the law clerk guilty of contempt of court for the unauthorized practice of law. In holding that the clerk's preparation of the order showing the mistrial was not an unauthorized practice of law, the court noted that the order had been prepared with the collaboration of opposing counsel and at the request of the court, and then stated that the preparation of the order was a ministerial act for the benefit of the court and a mere recordation of what had transpired. As to the law clerk's appearance before the court regarding the availability of counsel and the status of the case as not constituting the unauthorized practice of law, the court said that they agreed with the trial court that clerks should not be permitted to make motions or participate in other proceedings which could be considered as "managing" the litigation, but if apprising the court of an employer's engagement or inability to be present constituted the making of a motion, then they must hold that clerks could make such motions for continuances without being guilty of the unauthorized practice of law.

And while Toth v Samuel Phillipson & Co. (1928) 250 Ill App 247, is not within the scope of this annotation in that the question whether activities of an unlicensed law clerk constituted an unauthorized practice of law was not considered, the court stated that it was well known that where numerous trial courts were sitting at the same time the exigencies of such a situation required that trial attorneys be represented by their clerical force to respond to some of the calls, that the court acted upon their response the same as if the attorneys of record themselves appeared in person, and that the litigant, or his attorney, in such instances was treated as having appeared, it being recognized that it was impracticable and impossible under such circumstances for the trial attorney to respond to each call in person or to employ a force sufficient to try every case as it was called.

And see Ferris v Snively (1933) 172 **Wash** 167, 19 P2d 942, 90 ALR 278, infra § 3, wherein the court in holding that a law clerk had been engaged in the unlawful practice of law stated that a law clerk would not be engaged in the practice of law if he limited his functions to work of a preparatory nature, such as research, investigation of details, assemblage of data, and like work that would enable the attorney-employer to carry a given matter to a conclusion through his own examination, approval, or additional effort.

§ 3. Performance of functions requiring legal knowledge

In the following cases, it was held that an unlicensed law clerk was involved in the unauthorized practice of law where he engaged in activities requiring legal knowledge or training, such as handling probate matters, examination of abstract titles, and preparation of wills, leases, mortgages, bills of sale, or contracts, without supervision from his employer.

A disbarred attorney working as an alleged law clerk in the office of his attorney son was found to be engaged in the unlawful practice of law in Crawford v State Bar of California (1960) 54 **Cal** 2d 659, 7 Cal Rptr 746, 355 P2d 490, where the court, in reproving the son for permitting his father to engage in such activities, noted that the father

had given advice concededly legal in nature directly to a client regarding certain mining claims, had handled an entire probate matter, including conferences with the client, handled an escrow that involved considerable controversy as to compliance with the underlying contract, and performed various routine services for tax clients. As to the son's contention that the acts complained of were not improper for they were within the functions of a law clerk, the court stressed the fact that the father had acted independently of the son, both in regard to matters involving legal advice and to matters that could be characterized as such because performed in a law office, and that the son merely had knowledge of the existence of them but not of their progress or disposition.

In Clements v State (1940) 141 **Tex** Crim 108, 147 SW2d 483, the court sustained a conviction for "practicing law" illegally where, without being admitted to the bar, an individual was associated with an attorney's office, and received and consulted with one who came there as a client, giving her advice which resulted in her filing a suit for divorce asking for alimony and a division of community property, and accompanied her to the courthouse or to the office of her husband's attorney, where she introduced him as her attorney, and upon the letterhead of the attorney with whom he was associated appeared his name, with that of the attorney, over the designation "law offices," followed by the address of the office, and a letter upon such a letterhead was addressed to the husband's attorney submitting terms of settlement, which was signed by a firm designation which included the defendant, and was followed by his name as agent, notwithstanding the defendant did not collect a fee but was paid a salary by the attorney in whose office he was working.

The activities of an unlicensed law clerk which included his handling uncontested probate matters, giving oral opinions on abstracts of title, and preparing wills, leases, mortgages, bills of sale, and contracts, upon his own initiative, with no supervision from his employer, a licensed attorney, were held to amount to the practice of law within the meaning of a statute providing that no person should be permitted to practice as an attorney or counselor at law or to do work of a legal nature for compensation unless he had been admitted to practice law in the state in Ferris v Snively (1933) 172 Wash 167, 19 P2d 942, 90 ALR 278, the court holding, however, that the clerk's violation of the statute as to the practice of law by an unlicensed person did not preclude him from enforcing a contract against the estate of his employer for services rendered. In thus holding, the court stated that it recognized that the nature of work performed by law clerks approached in a degree that of their employers, and that the line of demarcation as to where their work began and where it ended could not always be drawn with absolute distinction or accuracy. The court went on to say that the activities of a law clerk would not constitute the practice of law so long as they were limited to work of a preparatory nature, such as research, investigation of details, assemblage of data, and like work that would enable the attorney-employer to carry a given matter to a conclusion through his own examination, approval, or additional effort.

The preparation, drafting, or drawing of wills and the giving of advice with respect thereto by an unlicensed law clerk was held to constitute the unauthorized practice of law in violation of a statute which required that any person practicing law must be admitted to the state bar in State ex rel. Wyoming State Bar v Hardy (1945) 61 Wyo 172, 156 P2d 309, the court, however, dismissing the proceeding against the defendant for contempt for unlawful practice of law in view of the circumstances involved in the case. In dismissing the proceeding, the court noted that the defendant had been engaged in the preparation of wills, etc., for a number of years, that this fact was known to members of the bar residing in the vicinity and yet no suggestion of impropriety or warning was given the defendant and no steps were taken to stop such practices until the present proceeding was instituted, and that the defendant did not intend to engage in the unauthorized practice of law. The court went on to say that inasmuch as this was the first case of this character before them they preferred to refrain from being unduly severe with defendant notwithstanding he had mistakenly transgressed the boundaries that subsisted between lay and professional action in the matter of drawing wills.

✦

8 Dunnell's Minn. Digest *Contracts* § 3.20, at 163-64 (4th ed. 1990).

3.20 Contracts contrary to statutes

As a general rule, contracts in violation of a statute that imposes a penalty for the doing of an act are unlawful,[48] but they are not always so.[49] An inference of invalidity of an act or document does not necessarily follow from the fact that a statute prescribes a penalty.[50] Although the general rule is that a contract entered into in violation of a statute that imposes a prohibition and a penalty for the doing of an act, such as the pursuit of a business, profession, or occupation without procuring a license or permit required by law for the protection of the public, is void, the rule is not to be applied without first examining the nature and circumstances of the contract in light of the applicable statute or ordinance.[51] It is a question of legislative intention.[52]

48. *See* Lew Bonn Co v. Herman, 271 Minn. 105, 135 N.W.2d 222 (1965); *In re* Peterson's Estate, 230 Minn. 478, 42 N.W.2d 59 (1950); Suess v. Arrowhead Steel Prod Co, 180 Minn. 21, 230 N.W. 125 (1930) (statutes for protection of employees); Vercellini v. U S I Realty Co, 158 Minn. 72, 196 N.W. 672 (1924); Johnstown Land Co v. Brainerd Brewing Co, 142 Minn. 291, 172 N.W. 211 (1919) (contract for introduction of liquor into territory made dry by treaty with Indians); Thomas v. Knapp, 101 Minn. 432, 112 N.W. 989 (1907) (statute prescribing conditions of foreign corporations doing business in Minnesota); Berni v. Boyer, 90 Minn. 469, 97 N.W. 121 (1903) (lease of property to be used as brothel); Swedish-American Nat'l Bank v. First Nat'l Bank, 89 Minn. 98, 94 N.W. 218 (1903) (statute regulating pledges); G Heileman Brewing Co v. Peimeisl, 85 Minn. 121, 88 N.W. 441 (1901) (statute imposing restrictions on foreign corporations); National Inv Co v. National Sav Loan & Bldg Ass'n, 49 Minn. 517, 52 N.W. 138 (1892) (statute forbidding building associations from leasing money to certain persons); Bisbee v. McAllen, 39 Minn. 143, 39 N.W. 299 (1888) (statute regulating weights and measures); Ingersoll v. Randall, 14 Minn. 400 (Gil. 304) (1869) (statute for boxing knuckles and tumbling rods of threshing machine); Brimhall v. Van Campen, 8 Minn. 13 (Gil. 1) (1862)

(statute regulating observance of Sun.); Solomon v. Dreschler, 4 Minn. 278 (Gil. 197) (1860) (statute regulating sale of liquors).

49. *In re* Peterson's Estate, 230 Minn. 478, 42 N.W.2d 59 (1950); Tolerton v. Barck, 84 Minn. 497, 88 N.W. 19 (1901) (statute requiring foreign corporations to appoint local agent); De Mers v. Daniels, 39 Minn. 158, 39 N.W. 98 (1888) (statute relating to town plats).

50. *In re* Peterson's Estate, 230 Minn. 478, 42 N.W.2d 59 (1950).

51. Lew Bonn Co v. Herman, 271 Minn. 105, 135 N.W.2d 222 (1965) (failure of electrical contractor to file with city building inspector copy of plans and specifications as required by ordinance did not render contract illegal where failure was no more than slight breach relating to collateral duty and did not involve bad motives or design to deny protection of law to one of class for whose benefit ordinance was enacted). *See* Dick Weatherston's A M Serv v. Minnesota Mut Life Ins Co, 257 Minn. 184, 100 N.W.2d 819 (1960); Minter Bros Co v. Hochman, 231 Minn. 156, 42 N.W.2d 562 (1950); *In re* Peterson's Estate, 230 Minn. 478, 42 N.W.2d 59 (1950).

52. *In re* Peterson's Estate, 230 Minn. 478, 42 N.W.2d 59 (1950); Tolerton v. Barck, 84 Minn. 497, 88 N.W. 19 (1901) (statute requiring foreign corporations to appoint local

§ 3.20 CONTRACTS

The intent of the legislature is the controlling factor in determining to what extent, in order to preserve the requirements of public policy, contracts and other instruments made in connection with the act of violation are to be held illegal, if at all.[53] In construing a statute or ordinance, courts will infer that the legislature did not intend that an instrument executed in violation of its terms should be void unless that is necessary to accomplish its purpose.[54] A statute is not to be construed as abridging freedom of contract unless such an intention is clearly expressed.[55] For example, in the absence of fraud or mistake, the doctrine that invalidates contracts contemplating illegal performance does not prohibit a sale from a vendor to a vendee merely because the property has only limited value.[56]

Where a statute or an ordinance makes a particular business unlawful for unlicensed persons, a contract made in that business by an unlicensed person is unlawful.[57] Justice and sound public policy do not always require the literal and arbitrary enforcement of a licensing statute.[58] A party who enters into a contract, such as leasing out an airplane, by which he is required to perform an act or service for which a license or permit is required by statute does not forfeit his right of recovery on the contract because of his failure to have the permit or license, unless it appears clearly that this result was intended by the legislative authority specifying such a requirement.[59]

If a party agrees to do a thing that it is lawful for him to do and it becomes unlawful by an act of the legislature, the act avoids the promise.[60] A contract entered into in contravention of express law is wholly void.[61] A provision in a lease, authorizing the lessee to operate a theater under a license issued to and held by the lessor, has been held illegal as contrary to

---

agent); De Mers v. Daniels, 39 Minn. 158, 39 N.W. 98 (1888) (statute relating to town plats).

53. *In re* Peterson's Estate, 230 Minn. 478, 42 N.W.2d 59 (1950).

54. Lew Bonn Co v. Herman, 271 Minn. 105, 135 N.W.2d 222 (1965). *See In re* Peterson's Estate, 230 Minn. 478, 42 N.W.2d 59 (1950).

55. Johnson v. Central Life Assur Soc'y, 187 Minn. 611, 246 N.W. 354 (1933).

56. Bernard v. Schneider, 264 Minn. 104, 117 N.W.2d 755 (1962) (purchasers were bound by terms of covenant in deed permitting no building except dwelling in spite of zoning ordinance excluding dwellings from areas zoned commercial).

57. Buckley v. Humason, 50 Minn. 195, 52 N.W. 385 (1892) (ordinance

licensing real estate brokers); Solomon v. Dreschler, 4 Minn. 278 (Gil. 197) (1860) (sale of liquor without license). *See* Gunnaldson v. Nyhus, 27 Minn. 440, 8 N.W. 147 (1881).

58. Dick Weatherston's A M Serv v. Minnesota Mut Life Ins Co, 257 Minn. 184, 100 N.W.2d 819 (1960).

59. North Cent Co v. Phelps Aero, 272 Minn. 413, 139 N.W.2d 258 (1965).

60. Seaman v. Minneapolis & R R Ry, 127 Minn. 180, 149 N.W. 134 (1914).

61. Swedish-American Nat'l Bank v. First Nat'l Bank, 89 Minn. 98, 94 N.W. 218 (1903). *See* Schmidt v. Prudential Ins Co, 190 Minn. 239, 251 N.W. 683 (1933).

Howard Orenstein, David Bishop & Leigh D. Mathison,
Minnesota's Living Will . . .,
Bench & B. Minn., Aug. 1989, at 21.

Howard Orenstein, David Bishop and Leigh D. Mathison

Minnesota's Living Will...

One of the most controversial questions faced by medical providers and by families of the critically ill is whether and when to withdraw care from patients who are too sick to make that choice for themselves. Society continues to wrestle with questions of how to allocate scarce medical resources and whether care should be provided to a patient who has not requested it and does not want it. While there appears to be a consensus that competent adults have the right to refuse medical treatment, there is not a similar consensus regarding how that right should be extended to incompetent adults — especially on the question of withholding or withdrawing artificially provided nutrition and hydration.

After several unsuccessful attempts in previous years, in 1989 the Minnesota Legislature joined 39 other states and the District of Columbia in passing "living will" legislation. The so-called Adult Health Care Decisions Act, Laws 1989, chapter 3 (to be codified at Minn. Stat. §145B.01 et seq.), provides a statutory framework for competent adults to give advance direction as to the health care they wish to receive or not receive should they later become unable to make such decisions. This legislation, while certainly not dispositive of the controversial social issues surrounding the withdrawal of medical care, does give new direction to families, medical providers, and judges as they struggle with questions of medical ethics.

ILLUSTRATION BY REG SANDLAND

The Adult Health Care Decisions Act of 1989 provides a statutory framework for addressing several of the key issues regarding living wills in Minnesota but the law in this area will likely be unsettled for the forseeable future.

The Legal Bases

While the Adult Health Care Decisions Act was 12 pages long in its final legislative form, the legal principle underlying the act is simple and basic: each individual has the right to control his or her own body. As discussed below, that principle finds consistent support in the common law, the Constitution of the United States and the constitution of the state of Minnesota.

At common law, the right of each individual to control his or her body was recognized through the tort of battery. The simple law school definition of battery — an unconsented touching — goes directly to the question involved with living wills. The common law of battery requires a physician to obtain a patient's informed consent prior to rendering invasive medical treatment to the patient. However, if the patient has made a living will, the physician presumably knows the kind of treatment the patient is willing to accept and may render that treatment without committing a battery.

The United States Supreme Court has recognized the right to control one's body as a fundamental constitutional right. As early as 1891, the U.S. Supreme Court held that a plaintiff in a civil suit could not be required to submit to a surgical examination. The Court stated:

No right is held more sacred, or is more carefully guarded by the common law, than the right of every individual to the possession and control of his own person, free from all restraint or interference of others. . . . The right to one's person may be said to be a right of complete immunity: to be let alone. *Union Pacific Railroad Company v. Botsford,* 141 U.S. 250, 251 (1891), citations omitted.

The "right to be let alone" was described by Justice Brandeis as "the most comprehensive of rights and the right most valued by civilized men. . . ." *Olmstead v. United States,* 277 U.S. 438, 478 (1928) (dissenting opinion). *Also see, e.g., Rochin v. California,* 342 U.S. 165, 174 (1952) (forced stomach pumping is "brutal and offensive to human dignity"); *Schmerber v. California,* 384 U.S. 757, 772 (1966) ("the integrity of an individual's person is a cherished value

of our society"); and *Winston v. Lee,* 470 U.S. 753, 762 (1985) (compelling a criminal defendant to submit to surgery was unconstitutional since such an intrusion "damages the individual's sense of personal privacy and security").

This federally protected right to control one's health care has previously been given effect in Minnesota through statute and case law. The Patients' Bill of Rights, Minn. Stat. §144.651, guarantees the right of patients to participate in the planning of their health care (subd. 10) and to refuse treatment (subd. 12). The Minnesota Supreme Court relied on the Patients Bill of Rights and the federally recognized right of privacy in upholding a conservator's decision to order removal of life-sustaining treatment from a comatose man who had previously told friends and relatives he would not want such treatment. *In re Torres,* 357 N.W.2d 332 (Minn. 1984). *See also Price v. Sheppard,* 307 Minn. 250, 239 N.W.2d 905 (1976) (the right to privacy recognized in the federal Constitution requires that physicians obtain court approval in an adversary proceeding prior to administering intrusive medical treatment to a committed patient who either refuses to give consent or is incompetent to give consent).

Minnesota courts have recently recognized the right to privacy as a state constitutional right distinct from the federal Constitution. In *State v. Gray,* 413 N.W.2d 107 (Minn. 1987), the Minnesota Supreme Court, without elaborating on the breadth of such a right, held that Minnesotans do derive a right of privacy from the state constitution.

Just two months later, the Court held that the right to privacy under the Minnesota constitution includes the right not to receive invasive medical care without consent. *Jarvis v. Levine,* 418 N.W.2d 139 (Minn. 1988). In *Jarvis,* a man involuntarily committed to a security hospital challenged the right of his physicians to administer neuroleptic drugs to him without his consent. The Court held that absent extraordinary situations, a competent person has a constitutional right to refuse to accept invasive medical treatment. 418 N.W.2d at 149. More important for the living will debate, the Court held that where a person is incompetent to give consent to

invasive medical treatment, a court hearing must be held before such treatment can be given.

The effect of *Jarvis* was to recognize that a person's incompetence does not negate the person's right to bodily control; rather, the Court held, physicians must still obtain consent — albeit from some source other than the contemporaneous words of the patient — before administering invasive medical treatment. The Court stated: ". . . the final decision to accept or reject a proposed medical procedure and its attendant risks is ultimately *not* a medical decision, but a personal choice." 418 N.W.2d at 148, emphasis in original. The right to privacy, the Court held, "begins with protecting the integrity of one's own body and includes the right not to have it altered or invaded without consent." *Id.*

It seems clear from the reasoning and dicta in *Jarvis* that absent extraordinary circumstances, a physician would be prohibited from administering invasive medical treatment to an adult who, while competent, had made an advance directive refusing such treatment. Living will legislation provides a statutory framework for individuals to assert this constitutionally recognized right to control their own health care.

The Minnesota Adult Health Care Decisions Act was passed in the spirit of *Jarvis* and was intended by its authors to be construed liberally so as to give full effect to the constitutional right to privacy enunciated in *Jarvis.* While the act was, of course, the product of compromise within the legislative process, we believe nothing in the act should be read as the intent of the Legislature to restrict an individual's right to bodily integrity. Section 17 of the act (Minn. Stat. §145B.17) states explicitly:

Nothing in this chapter impairs or supersedes the existing rights of any patient or any other legal right or legal responsibility a person may have to begin, continue, withhold, or withdraw health care.

The Legislative Battle

Living will legislation has been introduced in the Minnesota Legislature since 1984. Only this year did a number of forces converge to enable passage of the Adult Health Care Decisions Act.

Various legal issues were battled out in the four previous legislative sessions. These disputes involved, on the one hand, a coalition of senior citizen groups, the bar association, and almost all medical provider associations in the state as proponents of the final 1989 bill, and, on the other hand, a vigorous opposition led by the Minnesota Citizens Concerned for Life (MCCL), widely regarded as the most politically potent special interest lobbying force in the Legislature.

The MCCL was successful in 1984 in defeating a prior bill in committee and in 1985 prevented the bill from even getting a hearing in the House. Another version in 1986 was stopped by the MCCL in a House committee. In 1987, extensive efforts were made to revise the bill and work out problems through mediation arranged and paid for by the House Judiciary Committee chairman, Rep. Randy Kelly. The MCCL decided in 1987 to offer its own bill, one that would mandate food and nutrition, unless shown to be medically counterproductive, for all incompetent patients. This aggressive proposal by the MCCL resulted in a virtual deadlock for living will legislation.

During the 1987-88 legislative interim, approximately 35 hours of hearings were held around the state by the House Judiciary Committee on the two opposing proposals. Again in the 1988 session, a deadlock between the two powerful forces resulted in no bill being approved, although the coalition proposal reached the floors of both the Senate and House. The House Judiciary Committee rejected the MCCL version as an amendment to the coalition bill by a margin of one vote. The MCCL then claimed it had the votes lined up on the floor to reverse that result. This became moot when the MCCL amendment effectively gutted the coalition bill on the floor of the Senate and its chief author, Sen. Clarence Purfeerst, pulled the bill.

During 1988, the battle over living will legislation raged on in many aspects of the political scene in Minnesota, from the June Independent Republican convention platform to the questionnaires

sent out by the MCCL and the Berean League to all the candidates for the Minnesota House of Representatives. The senior citizens were urged to respond with similar political pressure and did so with their own questionnaires and meetings. They put together a much broader and more active coalition of supporting organizations than previously existed. In the fall elections, the defeat of Rep. Allen Quist, the chief House leader for the MCCL, sent a signal to other legislators that the coalition in favor of the bill had mustered respectable political clout.

> "The new Minnesota law is unusual in that it does not specifically provide immunity to health care providers who comply with the declaration."

After the elections, the living will coalition enlisted a new chief author in the Senate, Sen. Ember Reichgott, an attorney who studied the various issues involved and prepared for another vigorous battle in the 1989 session.

As the 1989 legislative session opened, the chief House author, Rep. David Bishop, devised a new strategy: to line obtain a substantial commitment of support from sufficient members long in advance of the final voting. Rep. Bishop and supporters of the legislation were successful in obtaining 66 separate members as coauthors.

The House Judiciary Committee chair announced that the bill would not get a hearing in the House until it had cleared

the Senate, since so much time had previously been devoted to the issue in House hearings in 1988. Sen. Reichgott then proceeded in the Senate, needing only a bit of collaboration on clarifying amendments which were acceptable to the House author and to the coalition.

At this point, several amendments or changes in the bill occurred, which were followed and expanded upon as it then proceeded through the House committee and on the House floor. These changes reflect legislative intent and may be of particular interest to lawyers.

First, the clause granting medical providers legal immunity from malpractice claims if they relied in good faith on a declaration was eliminated in a Senate committee and was never reinstated in the House. This bill thus became the only living will law, in the 40 states that now have adopted similar legislation, not to grant provider immunity. The representatives of the medical profession indicated to the Senate committee that they did not consider such a clause legally necessary as long as the threshold for choice and applicability of a living will remained as stated — "reasonable medical practice."

Another amendment responded to extensive opposition by the MCCL and other groups who claimed that the law would apply to every incompetent patient, regardless whether the patient had made a written declaration. Those groups also claimed that the bill would apply to every medical condition regardless whether the condition was terminal. Amendments were therefore offered in both the Senate and the House, making it clear that only those patients who had signed declarations would be affected, and only terminal conditions as defined in the bill and as diagnosed by an attending physician would qualify.

In addition, negotiations with representatives of the Minnesota Catholic Conference of Health Care Facilities resulted in some changes in the bill. The opposition of the Catholic Conference that had surfaced at the end of the 1988 session was thus removed.

These developments led, after ten hours of hearings in the House Judiciary Committee, to a 13-to-12 vote that defeated the same MCCL amendment that had stalled the bill in the Senate in 1988. The way was thus cleared and the bill was sent to the House floor.

Finally, an amendment on the House floor attempted to specify the form that should be used to make an advance health care declaration (the term "living will" is never used in the act). The document form, originally intended only to be "suggested," was made practically mandatory on the floor of the House by inclusion of a clause in Section 4 (Minn. Stat. §145B.04) that "a declaration executed after August 1, 1989 under this Chapter must be substantially in the form in this Section."

The authors believe that notwithstanding these statutory provisions relating to the form of the declaration, advance declarations using a different form from that in the statute will be given effect by courts reviewing them. As discussed above, abundant precedent exists to support construction of the new statute consistent with the underlying constitutional right to privacy which prevents administration of medical treatment contrary to the patient's expressed wishes.

A Practitioner's Guide

While a person need not obtain legal assistance before making an effective advance health care declaration under the new Adult Health Care Decisions Act, it seems likely that attorneys will be involved in advising both patients and health care providers in how best to comply with the act. The following practice pointers are offered to assist attorneys and the general public in understanding and effectively using the Adult Health Care Decisions Act.

When Is An Advance Declaration Effective? Section 2, subd. 3 of the act (Minn. Stat. §145B.02, subd. 3) restricts the definition of "health care" to mean "care, treatment, services or procedures to maintain, diagnose, or treat an individual's physical condition *when the individual is in a terminal condition*" (emphasis supplied), while subdivision 8 sets forth a definition of terminal condition in the law which was not included in the original bill. The definition of terminal condition is important because

The 20 organizations that compose the Living Will Coalition, of which the Minnesota State Bar Association is a member, have produced a booklet entitled "Questions & Answers about the Adult Health Care Decisions Act." This booklet includes the form and instructions to assist people in completing a health care declaration. Copies are being prepared for distribution at a nominal charge. For further information, contact the MSBA at (612) 333-1183 or (800) 292-4152.

the opening paragraph of the statutory form states that the declaration applies "when you are in a terminal condition." This narrows the scope of situations in which a person's advance directive is effective under the statute.

A terminal condition is defined as "an incurable or irreversible condition for which the administration of medical treatment will serve only to prolong the dying process." Section 2, subd. 8 (Minn. Stat. §145B.02, subd. 8). This definition is broader than that which is included in some other states' statutes in that it includes an irreversible coma and a permanently unconscious or persistent vegetative state. Therefore, if a person does not want to include these conditions within the scope of a declaration, the definition should be narrowed in paragraph (1) of the form wherein the declarant is to state the circumstances under which the declaration applies. Likewise, if a person specifically wants the declaration to cover an irreversible coma, although it is included under the present definition of terminal condition, it might be wise to so state, both for clarity and to be prepared in the event that the definition of "terminal condition" is narrowed in the future.

Executing an Effective Declaration. Section 3 of the act (Minn. Stat. §145B.03) sets forth the scope and requirements for a declaration. It is also important because pursuant to Section 15 (Minn. Stat. §145B.15), a declaration executed prior to August 1, 1989, is effective only if it "substantially

complies" with the requirements set forth in that section. The declaration may include preferences or instructions regarding health care, the designation of a proxy decision maker, or both. Because many health care providers feel that appointment of a proxy is a superior way to provide for decision making, completion of that part of the form should be encouraged. Subdivision 2 of that section provides that the declaration must be signed by the declarant and two witnesses or a notary public, none of whom may be named as a proxy. In addition, neither of the witnesses may be entitled to any part of the declarant's estate by will or by intestacy, and must make a certification to that effect. Subdivision 2(b) also requires the declarant to state either his or her preferences regarding the administration of artificial nutrition and hydration ("tube feeding") or that the declarant wishes a proxy to make that decision. However, it goes on to state that if the declaration does not include the declarant's preferences regarding artificial nutrition and hydration, the declaration is still enforceable and the decision as to the administration of artificial nutrition and hydration will be made consistent with reasonable medical practice as outlined in Section 13 (Minn. Stat. §145B.13). The proxy may not be able to participate in the decision in that event.

What Form To Use. Section 4 of the Act (Minn. Stat. §145B.04) is the statutory form. Although the section is entitled "suggested form," the prefatory language states that "a declaration executed after August 1, 1989 under this Chapter must be substantially in the form in this Section," possibly precluding the use of a different form (but see the discussion of constitutional issues, *supra*).

The form contains a notice and instructions to the person executing the form. It utilizes a fill-in-the-blank format, wherein the declarant may state not only the circumstances under which the declaration applies, but also instructions for care and treatment the person wants or does not want. A person may complete any or all of the blanks.

For example, paragraphs (2) and (4) of the form ask what care the person wants. The person may wish to state in paragraph (2) that he or she wants "medical procedures or medication to provide comfort care and to alleviate pain." If the person wishes to have a more aggressive course of treatment, this should be so stated. Paragraphs (3) and (5) of the form enable the person to specify what treatment he or she does not want. If a traditional "living will" format is desired, the person may wish to state that he or she does not want any treatment that would serve only to prolong the dying process.

Paragraph (6) of the form is particularly important in that it requires the person to state his or her feelings regarding the provision of artificial nutrition and hydration. It should be completed whenever possible, since failure to complete this paragraph may mean that the proxy cannot make this decision for the declarant. Paragraph (8) is the provision for appointment of a proxy, and may be completed whether or not the person has specified instructions earlier in the form. It should be kept in mind that the person named as proxy will have priority for appointment as a guardian or conservator of the person if such a proceeding is required. Section 3 of the act (Minn. Stat. §145B.03) gives the proxy priority for appointment as guardian or conservator of the person of the declarant as permitted by Minn. Stat. §525.544.

Health Care Provider's Obligations. A declaration becomes operative when it is delivered to the declarant's physician or other health care provider and the declarant can no longer give informed consent. Unless the declaration is revoked, a physician or other health care provider is required to follow the declaration, consistent with reasonable medical practice, or comply with the notice and transfer provisions of Section 6 (Minn. Stat. §145B.06).

The new Minnesota law is unusual in that it does not specifically provide immunity to health care providers who comply with the declaration. However, as discussed above, no liability should result so long as the health care provider complies with reasonable medical practice as set forth in Section 13 (Minn. Stat. §145B.13). That section provides, in part, that care to provide comfort and alleviate pain must always be given, and requires oral administration of food or water to a patient who accepts it, "except for clearly documented medical reasons."

Exclusions and Open Issues. The law states in several places that it has no effect upon a person who has not executed a declaration, and creates no presumption regarding the appropriate medical treatment to be provided to such a person. The law also states that it is not to be construed to condone, authorize, or approve mercy killing, euthanasia, suicide, or assisted suicide.

Practitioners should in all instances remember the underlying constitutional principle that each individual has the right to control his or her own health care. Where the new Minnesota statute results in some substantive or procedural roadblock to the effectuation of that constitutional right, practitioners may wish to assert their clients' rights to the full extent allowed by the Constitution and, where appropriate, litigate those issues for the clients' benefit.

Conclusion

The issues involved in the new Minnesota Adult Health Care Decisions Act are so deep and so pervasive that they will likely be with us in legislation and litigation in years to come. Already in 1989, the MCCL has indicated it intends to continue the fight in the legislative arena and attack the definition of "terminal." In addition, the whole subject of forced or natural supply of food and fluids is being litigated all over the country by organizations such as the MCCL.

The prospect of continued controversy surrounding these issues suggests taht the law in this area will not be settled soon. What is clear is that clients will require careful and informed counsel from attorneys from time to time, interpreting both the existing legislation and the underlying constitutional rights of medical patients. 🏃

Restatement (Second) of Contracts § 181 (1979)
with comments and illustrations

Ch. 8   GROUNDS OF PUBLIC POLICY   § 181

§ 181.   Effect of Failure to Comply with Licensing or Simi-
            lar Requirement

If a party is prohibited from doing an act because of
his failure to comply with a licensing, registration or
similar requirement, a promise in consideration of his
doing that act or of his promise to do it is unenforceable on grounds of public policy if

(a) the requirement has a regulatory purpose,
and

(b) the interest in the enforcement of the promise
is clearly outweighed by the public policy behind the
requirement.

Comment:

a. *Scope.* One of the most frequent applications of the general
rule stated in § 178 occurs where a party seeks to enforce an agreement although he has failed to obtain a license, to register or to comply
with a similar requirement. This Section states a specific version of

§ 181   CONTRACTS, SECOND   Ch. 8

that general rule as it applies to such cases. Whether there has been a violation of legislation that imposes the requirement is a matter of interpretation of the legislation itself and is beyond the scope of this Restatement.

b. Regulatory purpose. In deciding whether a party can enforce an agreement in spite of his failure to comply with such a requirement, courts distinguish between requirements that have a regulatory purpose and those that do not. The policy behind a requirement that has a regulatory purpose may be regarded as sufficiently substantial to preclude enforcement, while the policy behind one that is merely designed to raise revenue will not be. In determining whether a measure has a regulatory purpose, a court will consider the entire legislative scheme, including any relevant declaration of purpose. Common indications of regulation include provisions for examination or apprenticeship to ensure minimum standards on entrance and provisions for the posting of a bond or procedures for license revocation to ensure that standards are maintained.

Illustration:

    1. A, an unlicensed broker, agrees to arrange a transaction for B, for which B promises to pay A $1,000. A city ordinance requires persons arranging such transactions to be licensed as a result of paying a fee, with no inquiry into competence or responsibility. A arranges the transaction. Since the licensing requirement is designed merely to raise revenue and does not have a regulatory purpose, enforcement of B's promise is not precluded on grounds of public policy.

c. Balancing where purpose is regulatory. If the court decides that the requirement has a regulatory purpose, it must then weigh the interests favoring enforcement of the promise against the public policy behind the requirement. The factors listed in § 178 are taken into account in this process. If the party who has failed to comply with the requirement has done nothing by way of preparation or performance, the interest in enforcement of the promise is easily outweighed. But if, as is usually the case, he has completely performed and is seeking the promised compensation for that performance, forfeiture to himself and enrichment to the other party may result from a refusal to enforce the other party's promise. In determining the extent to which forfeiture and enrichment will result, a court will consider the possibilities that part of the agreement may be enforceable (see § 183 and Illustration 1 to that section) and that restitution may be available (see § 197 and Illustration 4 to that section). In evaluating the gravity of the public policy involved, the court will look to the interest that the regulation is designed to protect and will give greater weight, for example, to a measure intended to protect the public health or safety than one intended to have only an economic effect. Compare Illustrations 2 and 3. It will consider the magnitude of the penalty provided by the legislature as some indication of the weight that it attached to that interest. It will also take account of the extent to which the misconduct was deliberate or inadvertent. See Illustration 4.

Illustrations:

2. A, an unlicensed plumber, agrees to repair plumbing in B's home, for which B promises to pay A $1,000. A state statute, enacted to prevent the public from being victimized by incompetent plumbers and to protect the public health, requires persons doing plumbing to be licensed on the basis of an examination, the posting of a bond, and the payment of a fee, and makes violation a crime. A does the agreed work. A court may decide that the public policy against enforcement of B's promise outweighs the interest in its enforcement, and that B's promise is unenforceable on grounds of public policy. Compare Illustration 1 to § 183.

3. A, an unlicensed milk dealer, promises to deliver to B, a licensed milk dealer, milk for which B promises to pay $20,000. A state statute designed for the purpose of economic regulation of the milk industry provides that "no dealer shall buy or sell milk without a license," and makes violation a misdemeanor punishable by a fine of up to $500 and imprisonment for up to 6 months. A delivers the milk to B, but B refuses to pay the price. In view of all the circumstances, including the discrepancy between the forfeiture by A if B's promise were not enforced and the penalty provided by the statute, a court may decide that the public policy against enforcement of B's promise does not outweigh the interest in its enforcement and that enforcement of B's promise is not precluded on grounds of public policy.

4. The facts being otherwise as stated in Illustration 2, A had once been licensed but his license had expired the week before because, unknown to him, his clerk had inadvertently forgotten to send in the renewal fee, although the bond had been extended. The court may decide that in all the circumstances including A's ignorance of the fact that he was unlicensed, enforcement of B's promise is not precluded on grounds of public policy.

E. Allan Farnsworth, *Contracts* § 5.6, at 377-79 (2d ed. 1990).

. . . .

In cases of this second type, a party **Unlicensed**
who seeks to recover the price of goods delivered or services performed **claimant cases**
under an agreement is met with the defense that the party failed to comply with a licensing requirement. Analogous problems arise under registration and similar requirements,[15] but most of the leading cases involve licensing.

In deciding the licensing cases, courts have traditionally distin- **Regulatory or**
guished between requirements that have a regulatory purpose and those **other purpose**
that do not. A court may regard the policy underlying a licensing requirement that has a regulatory purpose as sufficiently strong to justify a refusal to enforce the agreement, even though forfeiture will result.[16] A court will not, however, regard the policy underlying a requirement designed merely to raise revenue as sufficiently strong to justify a refusal.[17]

[15]For cases involving other types of requirements, *compare* Amoco Oil Co. v. Toppert, 56 Ill. App. 3d 595, 371 N.E.2d 1294 (1978) (since failure of seller of fertilizer to provide statement of chemical analysis as required by Fertilizer Act was "not seriously injurious," seller could recover price of fertilizer delivered) *with* Brooks v. R.A. Clark's Garage, 117 N.H. 770, 378 A.2d 1144 (1977) (failure of garage to give customer written estimate as required by consumer protection statute barred garage from recovering for repairs). *See also* Fields v. Hunter, 368 A.2d 1156 (D.C. App. 1977) (taking of postdated check by seller of liquor violated statute prohibiting sale of liquor on credit and barred him from recovering amount of check); Mascari v. Raines, 220 Tenn. 234, 415 S.W.2d 874 (1967) (taking of note by seller of liquor violated statute prohibiting sale of liquor on credit and barred him from recovering on note).

[16]Derico v. Duncan, 410 So. 2d 27 (Ala. 1982) (where "regulation and protection are the goal" of licensing statute, consumer loan in violation was "null, void, and unenforceable"); Truitt v. Miller, 407 A.2d 1073 (D.C. App. 1979) (unlicensed home improvement contractor could not recover for renovation of house); William Coltin & Co. v. Manchester Sav. Bank, 105 N.H. 254, 197 A.2d 208 (1964) (where statute requiring brokers to be licensed is "an exercise of the police powers and is designed to protect the public against fraud and incompetence, the lack of license will not only subject a violator to the express statutory penalties but he will be unable to enforce his bargain and collect his commission").

[17]M. Arthur Gensler, Jr., & Assocs. v. Larry Barrett, Inc., 7 Cal. 3d 695, 499 P.2d 503 (1972) (at most, failure to apply for amended building permit "affected only the revenue-raising provisions of the code and not those directed at public protection").

377

§5.6   Unenforceability on Grounds of Public Policy

In deciding whether the purpose is regulatory, a court will consider the
entire legislative scheme, including any legislative declaration of purpose and provisions for examination, apprenticeship, posting a bond,
and license revocation.[18]

**Balancing of
interests**

Even if the court concludes that the purpose is regulatory, it will not
refuse to enforce the agreement unless the policy underlying the licensing requirement clearly outweighs the interest in enforcing the agreement. Courts have been increasingly reluctant to refuse enforcement on
the ground of mere noncompliance with some regulatory law. A court
may disregard the noncompliance if the regulation is intended to serve
only an economic interest, and not an interest in health or safety,[19] if the
penalty provided by the legislature for violation is relatively modest,[20]
or if there has been substantial compliance with the licensing requirement.[21] And it may infer, from the legislation's silence on the question of
unenforceability when compared with explicit provisions in similar legislation, that this additional sanction is inappropriate.[22]

---

[18]Wilson v. Kealakekua Ranch, 551 P.2d 525 (Haw. 1976) ("while the provisions of
the statute requiring initial registration [of architects] are clearly designed to protect
the public from unfit and incompetent practitioners of architecture, we think that the
provision requiring renewal . . . is purely for the purpose of raising revenue" where no
reexamination or reinvestigation was required).

[19]John E. Rosasco Creameries v. Cohen, 276 N.Y. 274, 11 N.E.2d 908 (1937) (although
milk dealer was unlicensed, violation of statute did "not endanger health or morals").

[20]Town Planning & Engr. Assocs. v. Amesbury Specialty Co., 369 Mass. 737, 342
N.E.2d 706 (1976) (firm that performed engineering services without being registered
as professional engineers not barred from recovery under contract since any violation
"was punishable as a misdemeanor [and] we have to ask whether a consequence, beyond the one prescribed by statute, should attach"); John E. Rosasco Creameries v.
Cohen, *supra* note 19 (violations were punishable as misdemeanors, by fine of up to
$200 and imprisonment of up to six months, whereas denial of enforcement will "punish
the plaintiff to the extent of a loss of approximately $11,000 and permit the defendants
to evade the payment of a legitimate debt"). *But cf.* Gene Taylor & Sons Plumbing Co.
v. Corondolet Realty Trust, 611 S.W.2d 572 (Tenn. 1981) (distinguishing *Rosasco
Creameries* where statute providing penalty took effect subsequently).

[21]Asdourian v. Araj, 38 Cal. 3d 276, 696 P.2d 95 (1985) (contractor operated as sole
proprietorship using own name instead of name of business under which he obtained
license); Northwest Cascade Constr. v. Custom Component Structures, 83 Wash. 2d 453,
519 P.2d 1 (1974) (although employees of registered subcontractor completed job, subcontractor remained obligated and sufficiently involved).

[22]Mountain States Bolt, Nut & Screw Co. v. Best-Way Transp. Co., 116 Ariz. 123, 568
P.2d 430 (Ct. App. 1977) (where legislature expressly barred recovery by improperly
licensed contractors, but did not do so in the case of deficiently licensed carriers, such
a carrier was not barred from recovering for services); Murphy v. Mallos, 59 A.2d 514
(D.C. App. 1948) (where a related statutory provision barred suit by unlicensed broker,
but provision in question did not, court had "no right to read such additional punitive
provision into the section"). For a more extreme view, *see* Hiram Ricker & Sons v. Students Intl. Meditation Socy., 342 A.2d 262 (Me. 1975) ("In the absence of any *express*

C. Policies Derived from Legislation §5.6

That an agreement is unenforceable by an unlicensed party does not necessarily mean that it is unenforceable by the other party. If the regulatory legislation is designed to protect persons in a particular class, a court may conclude that the policy underlying the legislation will best be served by allowing a claimant who is a member of that class to hold the unlicensed party in damages for any defective performance.[23] It may also conclude that the claimant is entitled, in the alternative, to restitution of any payments made.[24]

May be enforceable by other party

---

legislative intention to declare contracts made and performed by unlicensed innkeepers void, we will not infer such intention."), appeal dismissed, 423 U.S. 1042 (1976). For a case holding a contract enforceable in spite of legislative history suggesting the contrary, *see* Davenport & Co. v. Spieker, 197 Cal. App. 3d 566, 242 Cal. Rptr. 911 (1988). *See* Restatement Second §181.

[23]Hedla v. McCool, 476 F.2d 1223 (9th Cir. 1973) (owners could recover damages for delay caused by inadequacy of plans furnished by architects who were unlicensed, though owners did not know this); Cohen v. Mayflower Corp., 196 Va. 1153, 86 S.E.2d 860 (1955) (owner could recover damages for defective waterproofing by contractor who had failed to get license since "to deny relief . . . would defeat the purpose of the statute and penalize the person intended to be protected"). *But cf.* In re Mahmoud & Ispahani, [1921] 2 K.B. 716 (C.A.) (unlicensed buyer who misrepresented that he was licensed not liable to seller for refusal to take delivery of goods).

[24]Truitt v. Miller, *supra* note 16 (owners of house entitled to restitution of payments made to unlicensed home improvement contractor before they knew he was not licensed).

SECOND COMPONENT

OFFICE MEMO #1

- This sample discusses an existing dispute in its early stages.
- This sample follows *The Bluebook: A Uniform System of Citation.*
- It uses underlining (rather than italics).
- This sample takes the more conventional approach to the following matters: avoidance of the first person, single-sentence issue formulation, and placement of citations within the text.

TO: Partner
FROM: Associate
RE: HomeElderCare: drafting of living wills
DATE: October 20, 1992

ISSUES

law + facts

1. Did a social worker illegally practice law when, at the request of an elderly client, she drafted a living will for him, advised him about it, and charged a fee?

facts + law

2. Is a contract to provide such a service for a fee enforceable?

facts + law

3. Is the product of that contract, the living will, valid?

SHORT ANSWERS

law + facts + reasons

1. The social worker likely did practice law when she prepared the living will and advised the client because she addressed difficult or doubtful legal questions.

facts + law + reason

2. Nonetheless the contract to provide this service probably is enforceable because no fraud was involved and the legislative purpose of promoting living wills was furthered.

facts + law + reason

3. The living will is valid, based on the intent of the legislature in enacting the Minnesota Living Will Act and the unauthorized practice of law statute.

FACTS

introduction

As related by Mary Mahoney, executive director of our client Home-ElderCare (HEC), HEC is a private, nonprofit corporation in Minnesota that provides various services for elderly persons who still live in their own homes. Recently HEC began a new service: preparing living wills for its clients. Albert Nelson, a lawyer and the son of HEC client Roger Nelson, has challenged the legality of this service, in a letter to HEC's executive director.

Each HEC client contracts for the services he or she desires. Standard services include shopping, transportation, home maintenance, and assistance with personal finances. A staff of geriatric social workers coordinates these services for clients. The social workers provide some services; volunteers provide others. The social workers also serve as liaisons between clients and lawyers working on legal transactions for the clients and between clients and their health-care providers.

1st topic: HEC's services generally

Two to three months ago, several clients, concerned about their health, asked whether the social workers would help the clients complete living wills. A living will is a document that specifies the signer's desires regarding medical treatment in the event the signer is incapacitated. One social worker located a form living will, which presents blanks to be filled in and indicates fairly clearly how the document is to be signed, witnessed, and notarized. According to the form's introduction, the form complies with the requirements of Minnesota law.

2nd topic: living will

The social work staff and executive director discussed the idea and concluded that preparation of living wills would be a logical extension of the liaison work done with doctors and other health care providers. HEC's executive director assessed the demand for living wills among HEC clientele and investigated ways to train the social workers for this new task. All interested social workers attended a two-hour seminar on the topic.

3rd topic: staff competence and attitudes

The protocol is as follows: The client is interviewed by a social worker, who also talks through the significance of the living will, and the social worker then prepares a draft based on the form. The client is encouraged to review the document with his or her physician before signing it. The social worker arranges for the signing, including notarization. Finally, the social worker delivers the living will to the client's primary-care physician. Each client pays a fee based on the time the social worker spends on the living will. The clients know and are reminded that the social workers are not lawyers or doctors. Kimberly Hall, the social worker who worked on Mr. Nelson's will, followed this protocol.

4th topic: HEC's protocol in chronological form

In light of the client's son's letter, HEC's director now wonders whether the preparation of living wills by the social workers violates the law. She also wonders whether HEC's contracts with its clients for the drafting of living wills are enforceable and whether the living wills themselves are valid.

client's concerns

DISCUSSION

Introduction

roadmap

The Minnesota unauthorized practice of law statute prohibits individuals who are not members of the bar and licensed to practice law from providing legal services. The drafting of living wills by HEC social workers most likely is the unauthorized practice of law, and the counseling service also is unauthorized if answers to difficult or doubtful legal questions are given to clients. Despite the illegal practice of law, the contracts between HEC and its clients most likely are enforceable, on public policy grounds. Finally, the living wills are valid, in light of public policy and the limited penalty provisions of the unauthorized practice of law statute.

Unauthorized Practice of Law

first part
statute as overview

Under the Minnesota unauthorized practice of law statute, it is unlawful for any person

> except members of the bar of Minnesota admitted and licensed to practice as attorneys at law, . . . for a fee or any consideration, to give legal advice or counsel, perform for or furnish to another legal services, or, for or without a fee or any consideration, to prepare, directly or through another, for another person, any will or testamentary disposition or instrument of trust serving purposes similar to those of a will, or, for a fee or any consideration, to prepare for another person, firm, or corporation any other legal document.

beginning of application; easy element

Minn. Stat. § 481.02 subdiv. 1 (1992). The HEC social workers, including Ms. Hall, are not licensed or admitted attorneys in Minnesota. HEC's protocol violates this statute in two respects.

major subpart A: IRAC in one paragraph

First, HEC social workers, Ms. Hall included, have prepared "legal documents" for a fee by preparing living wills for their clients. Although the unauthorized practice of law statute does not define "legal document," the Minnesota Living Will Act provides a suggested form for living wills that plainly states that the form is a legal document, Minn. Stat. § 145B.04 (1992) (notice provision). This interpretation accords with the dictionary definitions of "legal" and "document": "an original or official paper relied on as the basis, proof, or support" of matters that are "established by law; statutory; conforming to or permitted by law or established rules." Webster's New Collegiate Dictionary 333, 651 (1981). A living will is the basis of a doctor's duty to respect the patient's health care preferences. HEC's social workers have drafted these legal documents for clients, and HEC has charged a fee for this service, thereby violating the statute.

Second, Ms. Hall and other HEC social workers may have given "legal advice or counsel" for a fee in the course of preparing living wills. See § 481.02 subdiv. 1. Although "the line between what is and what is not the practice of law cannot be drawn with precision," an individual who engages in legal practice activities incidental to his or her non-legal career practices law if "difficult or doubtful legal questions are involved which, to safeguard the public, reasonably demand the application of a trained legal mind." *Gardner v. Conway*, 48 N.W.2d 788, 794, 796 (Minn. 1951). For example, an accountant engaged in the unauthorized practice of law when he provided information on various tax issues in the course of preparing a tax return for a client. Id. at 797-98. He provided advice and analysis on business partnerships, the status of a common law wife on joint tax returns, and the deductibility of various expenditures. Id. at 798.

major subpart B: introduction; rule: general statement & case brief

The preparation of living wills is an activity incidental to HEC's social work. HEC social workers most likely have faced difficult or doubtful legal questions when discussing the significance of a living will with a client, preparing a draft of the document, and presenting it to the client. The sample form provided in the Living Will Act, which Ms. Hall used in preparing Mr. Nelson's living will, contains numerous examples of terms that could easily give rise to questions of a legal nature, such as "limits of reasonable medical practice," "terminal condition," "legally bound," and "willfully and voluntarily." See § 145B.04. Furthermore, the suggested form in the Living Will Act specifically states that a professional should be consulted if there are any questions pertaining to the document, an indication that the form may not be as simple as it appears at first glance. Id.; see also Howard Orenstein, David Bishop & Leigh D. Mathison, Minnesota's Living Will . . . , Bench & B. Minn., Aug. 1989, at 21, 24-25 (legislators deemed lawyers' involvement in drafting of living wills likely).

application

The questions involved in living wills are at least as complex as those in Gardner relating to tax issues. Both involve legal interpretations of statutory terms. The living will statute is shorter and simpler than the tax code, but the questions it raises may be more difficult given the relatively brief history of living wills. The Living Will Act is three years old, see Act of Mar. 3, 1989, ch. 3, 1989 Minn. Laws 8, and no appellate courts have addressed or settled the legal issues it raises. Furthermore, it is only part of a broader body of law on patient autonomy. See generally Orenstein, Bishop & Mathison, supra, at 22.

more application: comparison to case

Interpreting the unauthorized practice statute to bar this service accords with the primary purpose of the prohibition on unauthorized practice. That purpose is to "protect the public from the intolerable evils which are brought

more application: policy

upon people by those who assume to practice law without having the proper qualifications." Gardner, 48 N.W.2d at 794. If HEC's social workers err, the consequences for the clients would be significant, because the living will addresses issues of health care and guardianship. See § 145B.04.

more application: another policy

On the other hand, the Gardner rule must be applied in "a common-sense way which will protect the public and not hamper or burden that public interest with impractical and technical restrictions which have no reasonable justification." Id. at 797; see also Cardinal v. Merrill Lynch Realty/Burnet, Inc., 433 N.W.2d 864 (Minn. 1988) (involving charging of a fee for simple real estate transactions). Completing a living will form does not necessarily require legal knowledge; declarants may complete the form themselves. Many of the issues addressed in a living will are medical or ethical, not primarily legal. Furthermore, the authors of the living will statute sought to facilitate the use of living wills as a means of effectuating the patient's right to choose his or her health care options, Orenstein, Bishop & Mathison, supra, at 21, and prohibiting social workers from assisting clients could deter some clients from using living wills.

more application: counter-argument

However, a prohibition against social workers preparing living wills is neither impractical nor merely technical. The burden on the clients is reasonably justified because very significant legal issues are involved, as in the context of regular wills. Cf. § 481.02 subdiv. 1 (explicit prohibition against testamentary will drafting). These issues literally involve "matters of life and death" and, therefore, warrant particularly careful attention from a legal perspective.

more application: final element

Finally, the charging of a fee suggests that an activity involves the resolution of difficult legal questions. Cardinal, 433 N.W.2d at 869. HEC charges a fee.

conclusion; consequences

Thus, Ms. Hall likely did violate the unauthorized practice of law statute when she prepared Mr. Nelson's living will and counseled him about it. The statute provides for misdemeanor penalties or an injunction. § 481.02 subdiv. 8.

branchpoint & transition

The remaining questions are the enforceability of the contract and the validity of the living will. If preparing the living will is *not* an unauthorized practice of law, then the contract is enforceable, and the living will is valid. If the drafting and advising *did* constitute unauthorized practice, further analysis is necessary.

second part introduction; rule: general statement

Contract Enforceability

For some years, Minnesota courts deemed a contract void if a statute requires licensing to perform professional services and an unlicensed practitioner enters into a contract to perform those services. See, e.g., Buckley v. Humason, 52 N.W. 385 (Minn. 1892) (a real estate broker was held unable to recover a fee for real estate services because he was not licensed as required by statute). The rule, however, has been modified, and courts in Minnesota now examine the legislative intent behind the licensing statute rather than automatically hold the contract to be void. See Dick Weatherston's Assoc'd Mech. Servs. v. Minn. Mut. Life Ins. Co., 100 N.W.2d 819, 824 (Minn. 1960).

In Weatherston's, the court enforced a contract on behalf of an engineer who was not licensed as required by statute, although he was trained as an engineer. The court determined that the legislative intent behind the engineering licensing statute was to protect the public against incompetence and fraud. Id. at 823. The air-conditioning installation contract at issue did not violate those statutory goals for several reasons. The building owner sought out the engineer's services and clearly knew of his unlicensed status. Id. at 824. The building owner had its own architects and engineers who approved, supervised, and eventually accepted the engineer's work. Id. Although unlicensed, the engineer had a bachelor's degree in engineering as well as pertinent experience. Id. at 821, 824. The engineering and design work at issue was incidental to a much larger contract for air-conditioning installation. Id. at 824. Thus, the transaction involved neither danger to the public health and welfare nor fraud, the purpose of the licensing statute was not violated by the contract at issue, and the contract was valid. Id. at 825.

more rule: case brief

Here, too, the statute on unauthorized practice of law prohibits certain unlicensed professional services, and the contemplated living will service may well constitute unauthorized practice.

application: first two elements

The purpose of the unauthorized practice statute is to protect the public from the potentially serious harm that can result from the practice of law by incompetent individuals not subject to the direct supervision and discipline of the courts. Peterson v. Hovland (In re Peterson's Estate), 42 N.W.2d 59, 63-64 (Minn. 1950). The competence of Ms. Hall and the other social workers is debatable. They have general experience in health care and legal matters, they received training in drafting living wills, and their work is guided by a legally sanctioned form. However, unlike in Weatherston's, the social workers have not been educated as attorneys and are not supervised by licensed attorneys.

more application: third element

In HEC's favor, the HEC clients, including Mr. Nelson, are not the target of fraud or misrepresentation; the social workers inform clients that they are not lawyers. The social workers are responding to client requests and are doing so in a responsible manner. In addition, the legal services are incidental to

more application: counter-argument

legitimate non-legal services, namely the provision of emotional support and guidance as to medical and moral issues.

more application: policy

Furthermore, as noted above, the legislature, in enacting the Living Will Act subsequent to the unauthorized practice of law statute intended to encourage the use of living wills. Permitting the social workers to assist their clients will promote this legislative purpose.

conclusion

As noted in Weatherston's, "[j]ustice and sound public policy do not always require the literal and arbitrary enforcement of a licensing statute." 110 N.W.2d at 824. The legislature would not intend the HEC contract to be unenforceable as a consequence of the violation of the unauthorized practice of law statute.

Validity of Living Will

third part introduction; rule; statute and case law

The living wills of Mr. Nelson and other HEC clients are very likely valid notwithstanding any unauthorized practice by the social workers. The unauthorized practice of law statute provides for the prosecution and enjoining of individuals who engage in the unauthorized practice of law. Minn. Stat. § 481.02 subdiv. 8 (1992). The statute makes no reference to voiding the product of such acts. Interpreting the statute accordingly, the Minnesota Supreme Court held that a testamentary will drawn by a layperson in violation of the statute was nevertheless valid. Peterson v. Hovland (In re Peterson's Estate), 42 N.W.2d 59, 64 (Minn. 1950).

application

Similarly, Mr. Nelson's living will and those of other HEC clients are valid. HEC might be penalized for its breach of the law through unauthorized practice proceedings, but the clients, who are not at fault, should not be punished. Furthermore, the purpose of the Living Will Act is to encourage and support individuals who want to complete such documents. Presumably the living wills prepared by HEC social workers express the desires of the clients. Holding the living wills invalid would be contrary to the underlying philosophy of the Living Will Act.

conclusion

Analysis of both statutes leads to the conclusion that the living wills are valid, even if their drafting would constitute the unauthorized practice of law.

CONCLUSION AND RECOMMENDATIONS

conclusion

Ms. Hall's preparation of Mr. Nelson's living will likely did constitute the unauthorized practice of law, as his son asserts. However, for reasons of public policy, the contract between HEC and Mr. Nelson is enforceable, and the living will is valid.

HEC should acknowledge Mr. Nelson's son's concern, thank him for bringing the issue to light, and refund the fee received from Mr. Nelson. HEC also should reconsider the current living will service. For example, HEC social workers could operate as liaisons between the clients and their attorneys, with the drafting and advising performed by the attorneys.

recommendations

OFFICE MEMO #2

- This sample discusses a plan to provide a new service.
- This sample follows *ALWD Citation Manual: A Professional System of Citation.*
- It uses italics rather than underlining.
- This sample takes the more conventional approach to most matters, although it does use the first person.

TO: Senior Attorney
FROM: Associate
DATE: October 20, 1992
RE: HomeElderCare's proposal to draft clients' living wills,
             File No. H-53

ISSUES

1. Will the preparation of living wills constitute the unauthorized practice of law if a geriatric social worker employed by HomeElderCare (a nonprofit corporation) interviews the declarant, a HomeElderCare client; explains the will; prepares a draft; and arranges for the signing and notarization?

2. Will these living wills prepared by social workers be valid?

3. Will HomeElderCare be able to enforce its contracts with its clients for the preparation of living wills?

SHORT ANSWERS

1. The living will service as proposed by HomeElderCare probably would not constitute the unauthorized practice of law, but this is a very close call. Variations on the current plan would be more clearly legal.

2. Even if the service is the unauthorized practice of law, especially if the will closely follows the form in the Minnesota Living Will Act, the living will would be valid so as not to penalize the declarant.

3. If the service is the unauthorized practice of law, the contract between HomeElderCare and its clients may well be unenforceable out of concerns about the social workers' competence.

FACTS

Our client, HomeElderCare, serves an elderly population by providing the services that each client picks from a menu of services, including transportation, shopping, home maintenance, bill-paying and other financial services, and liaison work with the client's physician and attorney. HomeElderCare is a private, nonprofit corporation that employs a staff of social workers trained and experienced in working with geriatric clients; volunteers provide some services.

Now several of HomeElderCare's clients have asked for an additional service: assistance in completing living wills. A living will gives its declarants control over some choices of medical treatment, especially extraordinary measures, in the event the declarant becomes incapacitated.

HomeElderCare would like to honor its clients' wishes by adding this service. The service would begin with an interview by the social worker assigned to work with the client, which would include a discussion of the purpose and importance of a living will. Then the social worker would present the client with a living will form, ask the client the questions on the form, and prepare a draft. The social worker would encourage the client to discuss the draft with the client's physician before signing it. Then the social worker would arrange to have the living will signed and notarized. Later, HomeElderCare would bill the client an hourly fee for its services.

The HomeElderCare social workers are enthusiastic about this proposed new service. They see the value of living wills to their clients and are confident that they can be trained to competently provide this service by attending one or two seminars. However, HomeElderCare's executive director wonders whether there are legal barriers to this proposal, which is the only proposal she has developed to date. In particular, she wants to know whether social workers can legally prepare living wills, whether the living wills would be effective, and whether HomeElderCare could enforce its contracts for this service with its clients.

DISCUSSION

Unauthorized Practice of Law: The Proposed Approach

According to Minnesota's unauthorized practice statute, "[i]t shall be unlawful for any person . . . except members of the bar of Minnesota admitted and licensed to practice as attorneys at law . . . for a fee . . . to prepare for another person . . . any . . . legal document." Minn. Stat. § 481.02 subdiv. 1 (1992). Here, the living will probably is a "legal document" under the unauthorized practice statute, because the form in the Minnesota Living Will Act says that it is a "legal document." *See* Minn. Stat. § 145B.04 (1992). Thus,

HomeElderCare's social workers would be preparing legal documents for their clients, in return for fees.

In addition, the unauthorized practice statute prohibits anyone but a licensed Minnesota attorney from "giv[ing] legal advice or counsel" for a fee. Minn. Stat. § 481.02 subdiv. 1. HomeElderCare's social workers might be in a position to give legal advice or counsel to some clients on some aspects of living wills, in return for the hourly fee to be charged for the living will service.

However, both of these activities—document drafting or advice giving— could be permissible under *Gardner v. Conway*, 48 N.W.2d 788 (Minn. 1951), which adds a judicial gloss to the statutory rule. Under *Gardner*, if a service is an incidental part of a person's business, it is unauthorized only if the person answers "difficult or doubtful legal questions." *Id.* at 796. What is a difficult or doubtful legal question is measured by a reasonably intelligent person who has knowledge in similar transactions. *Id.* This test is to be "applied in a common-sense way which will protect primarily the interest of the public and not hamper or burden that interest with impractical and technical restrictions which have no reasonable justification." *Id.* at 797. The difficult-or-doubtful-legal-question test is flexible and demands a case-by-case analysis. *Id.* In *Gardner,* an accountant familiar with income tax rules and regulations gave advice on business partnerships, the status of a common law wife on a joint tax return, and the deductibility of various expenses. These were deemed answers to difficult or doubtful legal questions, and therefore the accountant was engaged in the unauthorized practice of law. *Id.* at 798.

HomeElderCare's living will service would be only one of many services it provides; its primary business is social work. If the social workers focus on the statutory form, they will avoid difficult or doubtful legal questions. The living will form is provided in the Living Will Act, poses a series of questions, and gives instructions as to its completion. *See* Minn. Stat. § 145B.04. By following the instructions, the social workers could lead their clients through the preparation of the living will without interpreting the statute. The information to be written into the form involves, for example, preferences regarding life-sustaining treatment and designation of a proxy for health-care decisions. *Id.* Thus, the social workers would discuss primarily medical and ethical, not legal, judgments with the clients. Because the social workers would not need to answer difficult or doubtful legal questions, they therefore would not engage in the unauthorized practice of law.

However, there are some legal subtleties to the form. For example, the designation of a proxy operates as a nomination of a guardian or conservator. *Id.* at § 145B.03 subdiv. 3. I am also concerned that some elderly persons may find that the living will form is not suited to their needs. *See* Dallas M. High, *Who Will Make Health Care Decisions for Me When I Can't?* 2 J. Aging & Health 291, 307 (Aug. 1990). If a HomeElderCare client wishes to deviate from the form, the social workers may cross the line into difficult or doubtful legal questions; this situation requires the skills of an attorney.

In other contexts, the court has found the charging of a fee to be an indication of the practice of law. *Cardinal v. Merrill Lynch Realty/Burnet, Inc.,* 433 N.W.2d 864, 869 (Minn. 1988). Yet HomeElderCare charges a fee for all of its services, and the fee would be for non-legal services. Hence it should not pose problems here.

In summary, the unauthorized practice statute seems to prohibit the proposed living will service. Under the leading supreme court decision, however, the service may be permissible if the social workers confine their work to medical and ethical issues and avoid discussion of difficult or doubtful legal questions. The statutory form provides a way for the social workers to do this and may help to tip the scales towards HomeElderCare should litigation occur. Even so, this is a close call.

Unauthorized Practice of Law: Other Approaches

still first topic: other options

Because the unauthorized practice of law is a misdemeanor and may lead to an injunction, Minn. Stat. § 481.02 subdiv. 8 (1992), HomeElderCare may want to revise the living will service to fully and clearly avoid these consequences. Section 481.02 suggests several possibilities.

Providing the service without charge. The prohibitions against drafting legal documents and providing legal advice include "for a fee or any consideration." *Id.* at subdiv. 1. And the supreme court has indicated that a fee suggests that the service is the practice of law. *Cardinal,* 433 N.W.2d at 869. Thus, if HomeElderCare were not to charge a fee, the living will service is less likely to be prohibited.

Limiting the scope of the service. Another approach is to develop the service so as to minimize the risks that the social worker would take on difficult or doubtful legal questions under *Gardner*—and thus avoid the incompetence that is the chief concern behind the unauthorized practice of law statute. *See In re Est. of Peterson,* 42 N.W.2d 59, 63 (Minn. 1950). Requiring the social workers to inform the clients of their non-lawyer status, training the social workers to spot legal problems, limiting their work to the statutory form, having a lawyer available to take questions, and providing for a referral to a lawyer when a client seeks services beyond this narrow realm would be key elements of this approach.

Involving lawyers. Two exceptions to the prohibition on unauthorized practice permit non-lawyers to assist lawyers. Section 481.02 subdivision 3(6) permits a person to "confer[] or cooperate[] with a licensed attorney-at-law of another in preparing any legal document" so long as the attorney is not employed by that person. In addition, section 481.02 subdivision 7 permits corporations to:

> furnish[] to any person lawfully engaged in the practice of law, such information or such clerical service in and about the attorney's professional work . . . provided, that at all times the lawyer receiving such information or such services shall maintain full, professional and direct responsibility to the attorney's client for the information and services so received.

Much of what HomeElderCare proposes to do comes within the activities listed in these provisions: conferring, cooperating, providing information or clerical service. These provisions operate when a lawyer is working with a client. Thus this approach resembles the liaison work HomeElderCare now provides in other areas involving a lawyer.

Involving lawyers may not be all that costly and complicated. Lawyers may be willing to assist on a pro bono basis. Or a law school clinic or pro bono program could participate.

second topic

Validity of Living Wills

I assume that the HomeElderCare social workers would use a living will form that complies with the requirements of the Living Will Act, Minn. Stat. § 145B.04 (1992). By following the instructions given in the form, the Home-ElderCare social workers would produce valid wills for HomeElderCare's clients—even if the living will service violated the unauthorized practice of law statute.

In deciding whether such a living will is valid, the court would seek to protect the best interests of the client. *See In re Est. of Peterson,* 42 N.W.2d 59, 65 (Minn. 1950). The unauthorized practice statute prohibits a non-lawyer from drafting a will without an emergency. Minn. Stat. § 481.02 subdiv. 1 (1992). In *Peterson*, a bank cashier drafted a testamentary will for Peterson several weeks before Peterson's death without any known emergency. *Id.* at 61. The will protected the interests of Peterson and was held valid; otherwise the innocent testator would be punished. *Id.* at 65-66.

Likewise, the purpose of a living will is to communicate the declarant's health care decisions if the declarant becomes incapacitated. If the living will were deemed invalid, the declarant's health care decisions could be violated.

Accordingly, I am confident that the living wills prepared by the social workers according to the form's instructions will be deemed valid, regardless of whether HomeElderCare's preparation of the wills constitutes the unauthorized practice of law.

Enforceability of Contracts

third topic

As discussed above, HomeElderCare's living will service can be designed to avoid the unauthorized practice of law. However, if the social workers do cross the boundary into the practice of law, the contracts with the clients probably would be unenforceable.

A century ago, the Minnesota Supreme Court ruled that a contract for professional services provided by an unlicensed professional is not enforceable. *Buckley v. Humason,* 52 N.W. 385, 386 (Minn. 1892). In *Buckley,* an unlicensed real estate broker entered into a contract with a client who refused to pay the broker's commission; the broker sued for recovery of the commission. *Id.* The court held that a contract is invalid if it is founded on an unlawful business transaction. *Id.*

In a more recent case, however, a contract for professional services by an unlicensed professional was deemed valid because the activities to be undertaken were not the sort of activities the licensing statute was adopted to preclude. *Dick Weatherston's Assocd. Mech. Servs. v. Minn. Mut. Life Ins. Co.,* 100 N.W.2d 819 (Minn. 1960). There, a contractor with a degree but no license in engineering was asked to provide an air-conditioning system; the job required some professional engineering tasks. The defendant knew that the contractor was not a licensed engineer. The defendant gave the contractor the job, including the engineering work, subject to review and approval by defendant's licensed engineer. *Id.* at 821-22. The court held that this contract was not the type of contract that the licensing statute was meant to prevent. *Id.* at 824-25.

Here, the unauthorized practice of law statute is designed to protect people from incompetent service by unlicensed professionals. *In re Est. of Peterson,* 42 N.W.2d 59, 63 (Minn. 1950). The social workers are not only unlicensed; they do not have law degrees. Even if the social workers do not mislead the clients about their expertise, their competence remains a real concern. If an attorney does not supervise or review the resulting living wills, the safety net present in *Weatherston's* will not be present here. One or more living wills may be misdrafted, leading to the argument that these are the kind of contracts that the unauthorized practice statute was designed to prohibit. Then the contracts between HomeElderCare and its clients for such services would be unenforceable.

On the other hand, the alternatives suggested above, which involve attorneys to a greater or lesser extent, would provide protections against incompetence similar to the *Weatherston*'s situation. Most likely the contract would then be enforced.

CONCLUSION

HomeElderCare's current plan to provide living wills through its social workers may not be the unauthorized practice of law—but not by much. To avoid the risks of legal proceedings, HomeElderCare should consider revisions that will strengthen the plan by involving lawyers. For example, the social worker could serve as a liaison between the client and the client's lawyer. As another example, the social worker could assist the client until legal issues arise and then refer the client to a lawyer.

HomeElderCare need not be concerned about the validity of the living wills. If the wills are prepared according to the statutory instructions, they will be valid, without regard to any unauthorized practice by HomeElderCare social workers.

On the other hand, if HomeElderCare wants to enforce its contracts with its clients, it should adopt the revisions suggested above. Doing so will address the courts' concern about incompetent performance of professional services by people without licenses to practice law.

Irwin & Associates, P.A.
123 Main Street, Suite 400
Great Lake MN 50000
(210) 555-6543

Heading

November 6, 1992

Ms. Mary Mahoney, Executive Director
HomeElderCare, Inc.
678 Great Lake Boulevard
Great Lake MN 50000

**CONFIDENTIAL
ATTORNEY-CLIENT
COMMUNICATION**

Re: Drafting of living wills

Dear Ms. Mahoney:

    I enjoyed talking with you about HomeElderCare last week, and I appreciate the opportunity to advise you on the preparation of living wills by HomeElderCare social workers for your elderly clients. From what you have told me, I certainly can see why your staff favors providing this service.

Introduction: rapport, previous contact

    However, as this letter explains, there could be some legal risks. One concern is avoiding the unauthorized practice of law, which could lead to prosecution for a misdemeanor or a court order prohibiting the service. If the living will service is not designed carefully enough to ensure competence as to legal matters, the contracts with the clients may be unenforceable. In any event, the living wills would be valid.

overview

    To help you understand these conclusions, I have first restated HomeElderCare's situation and the proposal, as I understand them from our conversation. Please be sure to contact me if my understanding is mistaken, because my advice rests on the stated facts. Then I have explained my conclusions under the law as it now stands. As you no doubt can appreciate, the law in this area is evolving fairly rapidly, and my conclusions could change if the law changes. I have concluded with a discussion of HomeElderCare's options. Please keep this letter confidential.

ground rules

    Summary of facts. As I understand it from our conversation, HomeElderCare is a private, nonprofit corporation that provides various services for hourly fees to elderly persons who still live in their own homes. The services are provided by geriatric social workers and volunteers, none of them lawyers.

Summary of facts: HEC

proposal

In response to client requests, the social work staff would like to prepare living wills for clients who desire them. The social worker would attend a seminar or two first. The social worker would interview the client and talk through the significance of a living will. The social worker would then prepare a draft based on the form you have found, which indicates that it complies with Minnesota law. The social worker would encourage the client to confer with a doctor before signing the will. The social worker would arrange for the signing and notarizing of the will and then deliver it to the client's doctor. As with other HomeElderCare services, the client would pay a fee based on the time that the social worker spent on the service.

Explanation:
overview

Explanation. As I recall, you expressed several legal concerns: that the service might be prohibited by law, that HomeElderCare's contracts with the clients might not be enforceable by HomeElderCare, and that the living wills drafted by HomeElderCare social workers might not be valid. The first two concerns are well founded; the third is less troublesome.

1st topic

Unauthorized practice. As for your first concern, Minnesota law prohibits persons who are not licensed lawyers from practicing law. The statute is commonly known as the "unauthorized practice of law statute." The non-lawyer can be prosecuted for a misdemeanor, or the court may issue an order prohibiting the activity. Because your social workers lack licenses as lawyers, a very important question is whether the proposed service would amount to practicing law. The answer depends on exactly how your living will service would operate.

The Minnesota statute on the unauthorized practice of law states that preparing legal documents for someone else for a fee constitutes practicing law. The living will form itself indicates that the living will is a "legal document." In addition, providing legal advice or counsel for a fee constitutes practicing law.

However, the Minnesota courts have recognized that the border between the law and some professions is quite blurry; social work probably would be viewed as such a profession. In these professions, non-lawyers are permitted to handle easy and clear legal questions but not difficult or doubtful ones. Most questions that might arise during the preparation of a living will would be primarily medical or moral, not legal, and the legal ones may be straightforward, especially if the social workers adhere closely to the questions in the form. If so, the service would not entail practicing law.

HomeElderCare also can point to public policy should it need to justify the service. The Minnesota statute setting out the living will form shows that living wills are desirable; permitting your staff to prepare living wills would encourage their use. In addition, the statute permits an individual to draft his or her own living will, unassisted.

Because this is a close call, other options suggested in the unauthorized practice statute merit consideration. For example, HomeElderCare could drop the fee. HomeElderCare could cooperate or provide information to lawyers who would actually provide the service. Another option is to offer the living will service through the social workers with many safeguards aimed at minimizing their discussion of difficult or doubtful legal questions.

Because it is not clear whether the preparation of the living wills would entail practicing law, we need to look at your second and third questions in both lights. *transition/branchpoint*

Enforcement of contracts. If the preparation of the living wills would *not* entail practicing law, the courts would not deny enforcement of HomeElderCare's contracts with the clients. *2nd topic*

But if the service *would* entail practicing law and thus violate the prohibition against non-lawyers practicing law, HomeElderCare may not be able to enforce its contracts with its clients. The courts look not only at whether the professional lacks a license to do the work but also at several other factors. The service your staff provides would be incidental to legitimate non-legal services of providing emotional support and guidance on medical and moral issues. And the clients would not be the target of fraud, because (I assume) the social workers would identify their professional status and indicate the limits of their expertise. However, a service that would constitute the unauthorized practice of law would also raise concerns about the social workers' competence, so that the courts would not permit HomeElderCare to profit financially.

Validity of Living Wills. Finally, whether the living will services does or does not entail practicing law, an otherwise properly prepared living will would almost certainly be valid. The courts would not wish to invalidate the living will, thus depriving the client of the opportunity to make his or her wishes known, merely because the social worker acted illegally. *3rd topic*

<u>Advice.</u> Your current proposal might draw the social workers into practicing law, and the contracts between HomeElderCare and the clients probably would be unenforceable. The living wills would be valid, however. I suggest that you consider other options. *Advice: client proposal*

One option is not to charge a fee for the living will service. This option may not be economically feasible and does not really address the underlying issue of the social workers' competence to address legal issues. *other options*

A better option is to construct the service to minimize the possibility that the social workers would address difficult legal questions: The social workers should be trained in drafting living wills and identifying topics with significant legal dimensions. They should adhere to the form, including the signing process, and refer clients to attorneys when a client wants a will that goes beyond or is different from the form. They should make clear that they are neither lawyers nor doctors and urge clients to consult these professionals.

A third option is that HomeElderCare would provide a more modest service, with the social workers serving as liaisons between the clients and their lawyers. The law does permit a non-lawyer to cooperate with a licensed lawyer who is providing legal services.

Involving lawyers may be less complicated and costly than one would think. Many lawyers perform pro bono work, providing free legal services to people of limited means; law schools offer opportunities to supervised law students to do pro bono work. To begin to explore this opportunity, I would contact the elder law section of the bar association and the clinical and pro bono program directors at local law schools.

Closing:

These alternatives no doubt have practical and economic advantages and disadvantages for HomeElderCare as well as your clients. I hope that this letter is helpful to you and your staff. I will call you in a week or so to answer any questions and explore any options you may want to pursue. If you wish to talk with me before then, please feel free to call my direct dial number, 555-6543.

Sincerely,

Ann Irwin

Ann Irwin

THIRD COMPONENT

This demand letter is directed to HomeElderCare because the sender understands that HomeElderCare is not represented.

Office of LaSalle County Attorney
1234 Sherburne Avenue
LaSalle, Minnesota 55555
(507) 555-4567

Heading

August 3, 1993

Ms. Mary Mahoney, Executive Director
HomeElderCare, Inc.
678 Great Lakes Boulevard
Great Lake MN 50000

Dear Ms. Mahoney:

As one of the attorneys in the office of the LaSalle County Attorney, I am *introduction* looking into a concern raised by the son of Roger Nelson, one of your clients. The concern is the possibility that HomeElderCare's preparation of living wills may be the unauthorized practice of law. County attorneys, acting on behalf of the State of Minnesota, enforce the unauthorized practice statute.

Please be aware that I represent the State, not Mr. Nelson or HomeElder-Care. This is a matter for which you may want to hire an attorney to represent HomeElderCare.

My understanding is that HomeElderCare social workers, who are not *facts of the situation* lawyers, prepare living wills for elderly clients. A social worker discusses the matters recorded in the will, drafts it as specified by the client, explains the will to the client's proxy, and supervises its execution. It appears that, at least in Mr. Nelson's case and perhaps more often, the result is a living will that does not, in fact, state the client's preferences as to important legal matters, such as Mr. Nelson's legal guardian.

Minnesota has a statute that prohibits non-lawyers from practicing law. *legal analysis* The prohibition includes giving legal advice and drafting legal documents for another for a fee. The living will is a legal document; indeed the form in the Minnesota Living Will Act so states. Discussion of the living will involves legal matters, such as the naming of the proxy and a doctor's legal duty to follow the living will's instructions. Although social workers may touch on simple legal matters as they practice social work, the HomeElderCare living will service goes well beyond what is permitted.

The statute prohibiting the unauthorized practice of law calls for one or the other of two legal proceedings, as chosen by the county attorney acting on behalf of the State. One option is prosecution for a misdemeanor; the other is an injunction against the activity.

demand

These options will be unnecessary if we resolve the situation ourselves. I believe that we have the same goal: providing high-quality care to the elderly living in LaSalle County. Various professions need to be involved for this goal to be met, and each should operate within its expertise. Just as lawyers should not practice social work, so should HomeElderCare social workers not practice law. There may be ways in which social workers can legally facilitate the preparation of the living wills by lawyers; I look forward to exploring this possibility with you or your attorney. In the meantime, I ask that HomeElder-Care discontinue its involvement in the living will area.

conclusion

This is a matter of some urgency, given the vulnerability of the elderly served by HomeElderCare. Accordingly, if I have not heard from you or your attorney by September 1st, I will take the first steps provided in the unautho-rized practice statute for enforcing the statute. However, my hope, as stated above, is that through negotiation we come to an acceptable solution very soon.

Sincerely,

Andrew McCampbell

Andrew McCampbell
Office of LaSalle County Attorney

> This partial letter presents the legal analysis as it may be presented to the lawyer representing HomeElderCare.

As you no doubt know, Minnesota Statutes section 481.02 (1992) prohibits non-lawyers from engaging in various activities. I understand that HomeElderCare social workers are not lawyers. Thus HomeElderCare's conduct falls squarely within the reach of the statute. HomeElderCare's living will service violates the statute in two respects.

First, HomeElderCare is preparing "legal documents." The Minnesota Living Will Act plainly states, in its suggested form, that the living will is an "important legal document." Minn. Stat. § 145B.04 (1992). A living will is an official statement proving the declarant's wishes in the event of incapacitation, conforming to the requirements of the Minnesota Living Will Act, so it is a legal document in the plain meaning of the term. Furthermore, a living will is similar to a testamentary will, which is the reference point for the phrase "any other legal document." Like a testamentary will, a living will states the declarant's intentions about important personal matters to be carried out near the time of death and is enforceable through legal mechanisms.

Thus when HomeElderCare's social workers prepare the living wills—by eliciting information from the clients, typing that information into a form or typing the entire document, and arranging for the living will's execution—and charge a fee, they are engaging in the unauthorized practice of law.

Second, the unauthorized practice statute also prohibits giving legal advice or counsel for a fee. This activity occurs when a non-lawyer engages in counseling activities incidental to another calling "if difficult or doubtful legal questions are involved which, to safeguard the public, reasonably demand the application of a trained legal mind." *Gardner v. Conway*, 48 N.W.2d 788, 796 (1951).

The social workers' counseling of clients about the living wills may be an incident of the general social services provided to clients—but it also is unauthorized law practice because it involves difficult and doubtful legal questions that require a trained legal mind. These questions may pertain to phrases used in the living will, or they may pertain to the living will's effect. For example, the social workers counsel clients about the client's status as an adult of sound mind, acting willingly and voluntarily; the obligations of a physician to follow the directives of the living will; the concurrent obligation of the physician to comply with reasonable medical practice; the role of the proxy; and the declarant's power to revoke the living will. These matters are regulated in the Minnesota Living Will Act, Minn. Stat. §§ 145B.01-.17 (1992), and other statutes, such as Minnesota's guardianship statute, Minn. Stat. §§ 525, 532-.6198 (1992). A non-lawyer is unlikely to perceive or fully understand these legal dimensions of living wills.

HomeElderCare has charged a fee for its living will services. The statute identifies charging a fee as an element of unauthorized practice. § 481.02 subdiv. 1. Furthermore, the Minnesota Supreme Court has noted that charging a fee suggests that the counseling involves a difficult or doubtful legal issue. *See Cardinal v. Merrill Lynch Realty/Burnet, Inc.*, 433 N.W.2d 864, 869 (Minn. 1988).

STATE OF MINNESOTA   DISTRICT COURT

COUNTY OF LASALLE   SEVENTEENTH JUDICIAL COURT

State of Minnesota, Plaintiff, vs. HomeElderCare, Inc., Defendant	)))))))))

Other Civil: Practice of Law

NOTICE OF MOTION
AND MOTION
FOR TEMPORARY INJUNCTION

File No. CIV93-893

Notice of Motion

TO: Ms. Katherine Crawford, Attorney for Defendant HomeElderCare, Inc.:

Please take notice that the undersigned will move the Court for a temporary injunction at the Courthouse in the city of LaSalle on the 1st day of November, 1993, at 9:00 a.m. or as soon thereafter as counsel can be heard.

Motion

Pursuant to Minnesota Rule of Civil Procedure 65, Plaintiff State of Minnesota moves this Court to temporarily enjoin Defendant from engaging in the drafting of living wills and all counseling services related to living wills. This motion is based on the pleadings, discovery record, and memorandum and argument in support of this motion.

Date: Oct. 1, 1993   *Andrew McCampbell*
                                        Andrew McCampbell
                                        Counsel for Plaintiff State of Minnesota
                                        LaSalle County Attorney
                                        1234 Sherburne Avenue
                                        LaSalle MN 55555
                                        (507) 555-4567
                                        Attorney Reg. No. 11111

STATE OF MINNESOTA   DISTRICT COURT

COUNTY OF LASALLE   SEVENTEENTH JUDICIAL COURT

State of Minnesota, Plaintiff, vs. HomeElderCare, Inc., Defendant	Other Civil: Practice of Law PROPOSED ORDER File No. CIV934-893

This matter came before this Court on November 1, 1993, on Plaintiff's Motion for Temporary Injunction. This Court, having read the record and counsels' memoranda, having heard arguments of counsel, and being fully apprised in the matter, hereby ORDERS:

Pursuant to Minnesota Rule of Civil Procedure 65, Defendant HomeElderCare, Inc., is hereby temporarily enjoined from engaging in the drafting of living wills and all counseling services related to living wills. This Order takes effect immediately and continues in effect until lifted by this Court or until judgment is entered in this case.

Date: _____   _____

Judge _____
Special Term Judge
District Court for Seventeenth
Judicial District

- This sample follows *The Bluebook: A Uniform System of Citation*.
- It uses underlining rather than italics.
- It includes parallel citations to state cases, where available.
- It begins with a summary, followed by the facts.
- Please note: The motion is for a temporary injunction. A memorandum relating to a different motion would not use temporary injunction elements, such as likelihood of success and irreparable harm, but rather the elements of the applicable rule.

STATE OF MINNESOTA   DISTRICT COURT

COUNTY OF LASALLE   SEVENTEENTH JUDICIAL COURT

State of Minnesota, Plaintiff, vs. HomeElderCare, Inc., Defendant	Other Civil: Practice of Law PLAINTIFF'S MEMORANDUM SUPPORTING TEMPORARY INJUNCTION File No. CIV93-893

SUMMARY

Kimberly Hall is not a lawyer. Rather, Ms. Hall is a geriatric social worker employed by HomeElderCare, Inc., a nonprofit provider of social services for elderly individuals. Despite her lack of admission to the bar of any state and despite her lack of legal training, Ms. Hall has drafted living wills for Home-ElderCare clients, for a fee, without the assistance of a lawyer. Furthermore, she has counseled these clients about the legal effect of their living wills. So have other HomeElderCare social workers. *[opening with factual emphasis]*

These activities violate Minnesota's unauthorized practice of law statute, which prohibits non-lawyers from drafting legal documents for others for a fee and from providing legal counsel to others for a fee. The statute explicitly provides for actions brought by a county attorney to enforce the statute and for injunctions against further unauthorized practice. *[legal significance of facts]*

A temporary injunction is warranted here. First, the State likely will succeed in demonstrating that Defendant's preparation of and counseling *[summary of arguments (roadmap)]* about living wills for its elderly clients constitute the illegal practice of law and affront the public policies underlying the statutes governing the unauthorized practice of law and living wills. If Defendant prepares living wills that inaccurately reflect its elderly clients' choices concerning medical treatment or death, its clients will suffer irreparable harm, with no adequate remedy at law, and this harm will outweigh Defendant's loss of income if the injunction is granted. Finally, enforcement of the injunction will be straightforward.

FACTS

opening: introduction of parties & claim

The State, through the LaSalle County Attorney, has brought this action against HomeElderCare, Inc., a nonprofit social services agency serving elderly individuals. The State has acted because the Defendant has overstepped its bounds as a social service agency and has illegally practiced law by drafting living wills for clients and providing related counseling. (Compl.)

1st topic: living wills

As the living will itself indicates, it is "an important legal document." (Hall Dep. Ex. A.) This label is apt. A living will states the declarant's wishes as to medical care in the event he or she is incapacitated and unable to make those wishes known. The living will states the declarant's views as to treatment in general, life-sustaining treatment, and sustenance. The living will identifies a proxy, who may act on behalf of the declarant and is thereby nominated to be the declarant's guardian. (Hall Dep. Ex. A.)

2nd topic: example of HEC incompetence

By way of example, Roger Nelson is seventy-eight years old, in declining health because of diabetes, and a widower. (R. Nelson Dep. 2.) Several months before a recent hospitalization, Mr. Nelson had executed a living will. (R. Nelson Dep. 6.) The living will made the family's minister his proxy and thereby nominated the minister as his guardian. (R. Nelson Dep. Ex. A.) Yet Mr. Nelson wanted his minister to serve only as his proxy for medical decision-making; he wanted his son, Albert Nelson, to serve as his guardian. (R. Nelson Dep. 10.) When Albert Nelson discovered the error, he arranged for a correct substitute living will drafted by the family's attorney. (A. Nelson Dep. 6.)

3rd topic: HEC social worker's experience & training

The elder Mr. Nelson's original, erroneous living will was drafted by Kimberly Hall. (R. Nelson Dep. 8.) Ms. Hall is a geriatric social worker employed by HomeElderCare. (Hall Dep. 2.) HomeElderCare offers its clients assistance in maintaining their homes, managing personal finances, obtaining home maintenance and transportation, shopping, working with lawyers, and other aspects of their lives. These services are provided by social workers and volunteers. (Mahoney Dep. 3-4.) Ms. Hall is an experienced social worker.

However, Ms. Hall is not a lawyer, she has not attended law school, and she has never been admitted to practice in Minnesota or elsewhere. (Hall Dep. 2-4.) Neither have any of the other HomeElderCare social workers. (Mahoney Dep. 5-6.)

Nonetheless, Ms. Hall has prepared about ten living wills for Home-ElderCare clients, including Mr. Nelson. (Hall Dep. 8-9.) In all of these situations, Ms. Hall has actually prepared the living will by typing the entire document herself or typing multi-line insertions into a blank form. She has discussed the wishes of the client and sought to represent them in the living will. She has inquired whether the client is an adult of sound mind, acting willingly and voluntarily. She has explained how the living will should be used by doctors and other medical personnel, in conjunction with the requirements of reasonable medical practice, in the event of incapacitation. She has explained the form to the client's witnesses and proxy and answered their questions. She has supervised the execution of the living will. She also has charged a fee for these services, which varies according to the time spent on the project. (Hall Dep. 14-15.)

4th topic: HEC living will service

Ms. Hall has undertaken all of these tasks without the involvement of a lawyer. (Hall Dep. 16.) She is aware of the legal issues surrounding living wills because she heard a presentation—lasting forty-five minutes—by a lawyer on living wills at a workshop on social work for the terminally ill. (Hall Dep. 19.) Furthermore, Ms. Hall is aware that the forms and the living wills she herself has written indicate that the will is "an important legal document." (Hall Dep. 18; Hall Dep. Ex. A.)

5th topic: HEC awareness of legal aspect

The ten living wills Ms. Hall has drafted constitute only a quarter of the forty or so living wills prepared by HomeElderCare social workers. (Mahoney Dep. 12.) Ms. Hall's services are typical of those provided in the thirty other situations. (Mahoney Dep. 22.) Eight HomeElderCare clients have been hospitalized, and the living wills have been shown to their doctors. Fortunately, no client has yet been incapacitated so as to bring any of the living wills into effect. (Mahoney Dep. 25-26.)

6th topic: HEC track record

The State sued HomeElderCare on July 12, 1993, seeking an end to the practices just described, before HomeElderCare prepares more wills or the wills become effective. (Compl.) HomeElderCare answered, denying that its practices violate the law. (Answer.) Based on the pleadings, the documents produced during discovery, and the depositions of HomeElderCare staff and clients, the State now moves for a temporary injunction. (Pl.'s Temp. Inj. Mot.)

7th topic: procedure

ARGUMENT

The party seeking an injunction must prove that it has no adequate remedy at law and that it would suffer irreparable injury if the injunction were not issued. Sanborn Mfg. Co. v. Currie, 500 N.W.2d 161, 163 (Minn. Ct. App. 1993) (citing Cherne Indus., Inc. v. Grounds & Assoc., 278 N.W.2d 81, 92 (Minn. 1979)). The court must take into account the following five factors when deciding whether to grant a temporary injunction:

> (1) [t]he likelihood that one party or the other will prevail on the merits when the fact situation is viewed in light of established precedents fixing the limits of equitable relief[;]
>
> (2) [t]he aspects of the fact situation, if any, which permit or require consideration of public policy expressed in the statutes, State and Federal[;]
>
> (3) [t]he harm to be suffered by plaintiff if the temporary restraint is denied as compared to that inflicted on defendant if the injunction issues pending trial[;]
>
> (4) [t]he administrative burdens involved in judicial supervision and enforcement of the temporary decree[; and]
>
> (5) [t]he nature and background of the relationship between the parties preexisting the dispute giving rise to the request for relief[.]

Dahlberg Bros. v. Ford Motor Co., 272 Minn. 264, 274-75, 137 N.W.2d 314, 321-22 (1965) (five factors reordered above). The third factor, the balance of harms, incorporates the Sanborn and Cherne requirements of inadequate remedy and irreparable injury. Yager v. Thompson, 352 N.W.2d 71, 75 (Minn. Ct. App. 1984).

roadmap

In this case, the law and public policy as expressed in state statutes (factors 1 and 2) favor the injunction. The harm suffered by the state's elderly citizens without the injunction is irreparable and easily outweighs any harm to Defendant from grant of an injunction (factor 3). And the temporary injunction would be straightforward to enforce (factor 4). The fifth Dahlberg factor is irrelevant because the parties do not have a pre-existing relationship. Thus, this Court should grant the requested temporary injunction.

1st major heading (procedural & substantive law + facts)

I. The State likely will succeed in demonstrating that Defendant's preparation of and counseling about living wills for its elderly clients constitutes the illegal practice of law and affronts the public policies stated in the statutes on living wills and the unauthorized practice of law.

1st minor heading A

A. Defendant's living will service constitutes the unauthorized practice of law, for a fee, by social workers.

Minnesota's statute on the unauthorized practice of law states in pertinent part:

> It shall be unlawful for any person or association of persons, except members of the bar of Minnesota admitted and licensed to practice as attorneys at law, . . . [1] for a fee or any consideration, to give legal advice or counsel, perform for or furnish to another legal services, or, [2] for or without a fee or any consideration, to prepare, directly or through another, for another person, firm, or corporation, any will or testamentary disposition or instrument of trust serving purposes similar to those of a will, or, [3] for a fee or any consideration, to prepare for another person, firm, or corporation, any other legal document.

Minn. Stat. § 481.02 subdiv. 1 (1992) (enumeration added). This prohibition is enforced through misdemeanor penalties or, as here, by an injunction action brought by the State, acting through county attorneys. Id. subdiv. 8.

Defendant falls squarely within the reach of the statute. Ms. Hall is not a member of the bar of Minnesota, nor are the other HomeElderCare social workers. No exception is applicable. See id. § 481.02 subdivs. 3-7. Furthermore, Defendant's actions violate two statutory prohibitions: against drafting legal documents (number 3 above) and against giving legal advice and counsel (number 1 above).

First, living wills are "legal documents" within the scope of the unauthorized practice statute. See id. subdiv. 1. While the unauthorized practice statute does not define the phrase "legal document," the Minnesota Living Will Act plainly states, in its suggested form, that the will is "an important legal document." Minn. Stat. § 145B.04 (1992). In addition, the plain meaning of "legal" is "conforms to rules or the law," Webster's New Collegiate Dictionary 656 (1976), and the plain meaning of "document" is "an original or official paper relied on as the basis, proof, or support of something," id. at 336. A living will is an official statement proving the declarant's wishes in the event of incapacitation, conforming to the requirements of the Minnesota Living Will Act, so it is a legal document in the plain meaning of the term.

Furthermore, a living will is similar to a testamentary will, which is expressly covered by the preceding prohibition (number 2 above) and is the reference point for the phrase "any other legal document." See § 481.02 subdiv. 1. Like a testamentary will, a living will states the declarant's intentions about important personal matters to be carried out near the time of death and is enforceable through legal mechanisms. See §§ 145B.03-.05.

In light of this definition, Defendant has illegally prepared legal documents for other people for a fee. Defendant's employees prepare the wills when they elicit information from the clients, type that information into a form

overall rule from statute

beginning application & roadmap

1st sub-topic: drafting legal document

or draft or type the entire document, and arrange for the will's execution. Furthermore, clients pay Defendant a fee for these services—even when, as in Mr. Nelson's case, the living will is erroneous.

2nd sub-topic: giving legal advice

Second, a non-lawyer engages in unauthorized law practice when she "give[s] legal advice or counsel" for a fee. § 481.02 subdiv. 1. This activity occurs when the non-lawyer engages in counseling activities incidental to another calling "if difficult or doubtful legal questions are involved which, to safeguard the public, reasonably demand the application of a trained legal mind." Gardner v. Conway, 234 Minn. 468, 481, 48 N.W.2d 788, 796 (1951). In Gardner, an accountant engaged in unauthorized law practice when he provided information on various tax issues in the course of preparing a tax return for a client. The accountant covered business partnerships, the status of a common law wife in joint tax returns, and the deductibility of various expenditures. Id. at 472, 48 N.W.2d at 797-98.

Defendant's employees' counseling of clients about the living wills may be an incident of the general social services provided to clients—but it also is illegal law practice because it involves difficult and doubtful legal questions that require a trained legal mind. These questions may arise during the initial consultation, during the drafting process, or at the time of the will's execution. These questions may pertain to phrases used in the will form or the will drafted by the social worker, or they may pertain to the will's effect. For example, the social workers counsel clients about the client's status as an adult of sound mind, acting willingly and voluntarily; the obligations of a physician to follow the directives of the living will; the concurrent obligation of the physician to comply with reasonable medical practice; the role of the proxy; and the declarant's power to revoke the will. Ms. Hall has admitted to counseling her clients on many of these topics.

All of these matters are regulated in the Minnesota Living Will Act, Minnesota Statutes sections 145B.01-.17 (1992). Furthermore, living wills implicate legal concerns extending well beyond the Living Will Act. In Mr. Nelson's case, for example, the error arose because his identification of a proxy affected his choice of a legal guardian. Guardianship is, of course, extensively regulated by Minnesota law; this regulation covers both the powers and appointment of guardians. Minn. Stat. §§ 525.532-.6198 (1992). More broadly, a living will is a manifestation of the declarant's constitutional right to privacy in the sense of bodily autonomy. See Howard Orenstein, David Bishop & Leigh D. Mathison, Minnesota's Living Will . . . , Bench & B. Minn., Aug. 1989, at 22; Note, Pamela B. Goldsmith, Live and Let Die: The Constitutional Validity of a Living Will, 5 N.Y.L. Sch. J. Hum. Rts. 477, 486-90 (1988).

A non-lawyer is unlikely to perceive or fully understand these legal dimensions of living wills. Indeed, the brief training that Defendant provided Ms. Hall on living wills was conducted by a lawyer.

These issues and areas of law are certainly as difficult and doubtful as the tax issues addressed by the accountant in Gardner. They involve the drawing of fine lines with significant consequences. Indeed, the questions addressed by Defendant's social workers may be even more difficult than the tax questions addressed by the accountant in Gardner. The Living Will Act is four years old, see Act of Mar. 3, 1989, ch. 3, 1989 Minn. Laws 8, and its subtleties have yet to be interpreted by the appellate courts. Legal regulation of medical decision-making is in a phase of rapid change. See generally Orenstein, Bishop & Mathison, supra, at 22, 25.

In addition, HomeElderCare has charged a fee for its drafting and counseling services. The statute identifies charging a fee as an element of the unauthorized practice of law. § 481.02 subdiv. 1. Furthermore, the Minnesota Supreme Court has noted that charging a fee suggests that the counseling involves a difficult or doubtful legal issue. Cardinal v. Merrill Lynch Realty/Burnet, Inc., 433 N.W.2d 864, 869 (Minn. 1988).

3rd sub-topic: fee

Thus, Defendant has illegally drafted legal documents and provided legal counsel for a fee to elderly citizens—and erroneously so in at least Mr. Nelson's case. To secure a temporary injunction, the State need not demonstrate that it will win this case, but only that it is likely to. Dahlberg Bros, Inc. v. Ford Motor Co., 272 Minn. 264, 275, 137 N.W.2d 314, 321 (1965). The State has successfully demonstrated that the Defendant has violated the unauthorized practice statute.

theory of the case

conclusion to sub-topic A & reference to procedural rule

B. Defendant's living will service affronts the public policies stated in the unauthorized practice and living will statutes.

2nd minor heading B

The purposes of the unauthorized practice statute would be furthered by a temporary injunction precluding Defendant's preparation of living wills and related counseling services. The statute is designed to forestall poorly drawn legal documents caused by a non-lawyer's "bungling use of legal terms and . . . improper knowledge" of the law that result in documents that either are invalid or operate contrary to the client's intent. Peterson v. Hovland (In re Peterson's Estate), 230 Minn. 478, 484, 42 N.W.2d 59, 63 (1950) (involving drafting of a testamentary will). When Ms. Hall prepared Mr. Nelson's living will and counseled him, precisely these problems occurred—and they were corrected when an attorney drafted a revised living will.

1st policy

Other jurisdictions faced with the issue of non-lawyers completing and advising clients about legal forms have ruled in favor of protecting the public.

The Florida Supreme Court has held that a non-lawyer may distribute legal forms and type in material as directed by the client, but the non-lawyer may not provide specific assistance in the preparation of the form, answer questions, or correct errors or omissions. Fla. Bar v. Brumbaugh, 355 So. 2d 1186, 1194 (Fla. 1978). Other courts have similarly ruled that distributing legal forms is permissible, but personal contact between a non-lawyer and a client involving explanation, advice, or assistance is the unauthorized practice of law. E.g., State Bar of Mich. v. Cramer, 249 N.W.2d 1, 8-9 (Mich. 1976); N.Y. County Lawyers Ass'n v. Dacey, 234 N.E.2d 459 (N.Y. 1967); Or. State Bar v. Gilchrist, 538 P.2d 913, 919 (Or. 1975).

Certainly, the unauthorized practice statute should not be used so as to impose "impractical and technical restrictions which have no reasonable justification." Gardner, 234 Minn. at 481-82, 48 N.W.2d at 797; see also Cardinal, 433 N.W.2d at 868-69. The restrictions imposed by the statute on Defendant's social workers are not technical and impractical; they have a more than reasonable justification—implementation of the policy expressed in the living will statute.

2nd policy

The Living Will Act evinces a strong public policy in favor of giving a competent adult the means by which to

> make a living will of preferences or instructions regarding health care. These preferences or instructions may include, but are not limited to, consent to or refusal of any health care, treatment, service, procedure, or placement. A living will may include preferences or instructions regarding health care, the designation of a proxy to make health care decisions on behalf of the declarant, or both.

§ 145B.03 subdiv. 1. This statute allows individuals to assert their constitutional right to control their own health care. See Orenstein, Bishop & Mathison, supra, at 22. If a person filling out a living will receives incompetent assistance, the intent of the statute and the underlying constitutional right will not be implemented.

conclusion

Thus, the public policies of both statutes support a temporary injunction.

2nd major heading (procedural law + facts)

II. If Defendant incompetently prepares living wills that inaccurately reflect its elderly clients' choices concerning medical treatment or death, its clients will suffer irreparable harm, with no adequate remedy at law, and this harm will outweigh Defendant's loss of income if the injunction is granted.

rule

The party seeking an injunction must show irreparable harm, while the opposing party need show only substantial harm to bar the injunction. Yager v. Thompson, 352 N.W.2d 71, 75 (Minn. Ct. App. 1984). Irreparable harm is defined as an injury that cannot be compensated by money alone. <u>Morse v. City of Waterville</u>, 458 N.W.2d 728, 729-30 (Minn. Ct. App. 1990).

The State is acting in this case on behalf of Defendant's clients. They are *client's factors* elderly individuals, faced with their own mortality, contemplating difficult issues of how to bring a close to their lives in a way that is legally, medically, morally, and socially responsible. They must depend not only on the good faith and efforts of Defendant's social workers but also on the professional competence of those social workers. Yet Defendant's social workers are not fully professionally competent for the task they have undertaken and for which they are charging fees. The clients' vulnerability justifies judicial intervention.

As already noted, a living will sets out a person's instructions as to how medical treatment should be administered at his or her life's end in certain situations, as well as who has the authority to speak for the declarant. Minn. Stat. §§ 145B.01-.17 (1992). If these instructions are recorded inaccurately, the declarant may receive unwanted medical treatment or may not receive the treatment he or she wanted. Worse yet, if the living will is drafted so poorly that it is unenforceable, <u>id</u>. § 145B.03 subdiv. 2 (requirements for valid living will), the person's wishes will be totally disregarded, except insofar as the person's family members convey those wishes and the doctor honors those wishes. There is a grim and very real possibility that a client will die prematurely or be kept alive against his or her wishes as a consequence of a bungled living will.

In each of these scenarios, the declarant who is near life's end would suffer irreparable harm. Anxiety, confusion, worsened quality of life, pain and suffering, and possibly death are very difficult—if not impossible—to value and compensate. Death, by definition, is irreparable. For these losses, there is no adequate remedy at law.

By contrast, Defendant will suffer little harm from grant of the injunction. *opponent's factors* Although it will not be able to provide this single service pending the resolution of the litigation, it can, of course, maintain its client relationships by continuing to offer its other services, such as assistance with home maintenance, personal finances, and transportation. Therefore, the balance of harms *conclusion* favors the State.

III. The temporary injunction sought by the State will be straightforward to enforce.

3rd major heading (procedural law)

The relief requested in this motion is nothing more than a short-term version of the remedy provided by the legislature—a permanent injunction against the unauthorized practice of law, requested by the State. <u>See</u> Minn.

Stat. § 481.02 subdiv. 8 (1992). The State requests that this Court temporarily prohibit the living will services offered by Defendant. The injunction can be effected by Defendant notifying its own employees of the prohibition. Monitoring, if needed, could be accomplished by examining Defendant's billings to its clients. Thus, granting a temporary injunction in this case will not impose an excessive administrative burden on this Court.

CONCLUSION

summary relief requested

The State has established that the relevant factors weigh strongly in favor of a temporary injunction against Defendant, to preclude its further violation of the unauthorized practice of law statute and to protect the elderly citizens of this state, who otherwise might be irreparably harmed during the pendency of this case. Therefore, the State respectfully requests that this Court grant a temporary injunction against the living will services provided by Defendant.

Respectfully submitted,

Dated: Oct. 1, 1993   *Andrew McCampbell*

Andrew McCampbell
Counsel for Plaintiff State of Minnesota
LaSalle County Attorney
1234 Sherburne Avenue
LaSalle MN 55555
(507) 555-4567
Attorney Reg. No. 11111

- This sample follows *ALWD Citation Manual: A Professional System of Citation.*
- It uses italics rather than underlining.
- It does not include parallel citations to state cases.
- It begins with the facts, followed by issues.
- Please note: The motion is for a temporary injunction. A memorandum relating to a different motion would not use temporary injunction elements, such as likelihood of success and irreparable harm, but rather the elements of the applicable rule.

space for your notes

STATE OF MINNESOTA

DISTRICT COURT

COUNTY OF LASALLE

SEVENTEENTH JUDICIAL COURT

State of Minnesota, Plaintiff,	)))	Other Civil: Practice of Law
vs.	))	DEFENDANT'S MEMORANDUM OPPOSING
HomeElderCare, Inc., Defendant	)))	TEMPORARY INJUNCTION
	)	File No. CIV93-893

FACTS

HomeElderCare, Inc., is a private, nonprofit corporation with a staff of geriatric social workers who provide services to help their elderly clients in their day-to-day activities. (Margaret Mahoney Depo. 2 (Sept. 11, 1993).) HomeElderCare has been sued by the State of Minnesota to terminate HomeElderCare's valuable service of assisting its clients with filling in the statutory living will form. (Compl. (July 12, 1993).) The State's pending motion for a temporary injunction would prevent HomeElderCare's clients from obtaining that service during this litigation. (Pl.'s Temp. Inj. Mot. (Oct. 1, 1993).)

HomeElderCare has many clients who are on fixed incomes. (Mahoney Depo. 6.) When requested, HomeElderCare social workers assist clients in obtaining transportation, shopping, maintaining their homes and apartments, and managing personal finances. Volunteers provide some services. The social workers also serve as liaisons between clients and their lawyers working on such matters as wills and real estate transactions. (*Id.* at 3-4.) Each client contracts with HomeElderCare for the services he or she desires and pays a modest fee based on the amount of time that the social worker spends on the services. (*Id.* at 5.)

Several clients recently asked HomeElderCare to fill a gap in the services provided to them by providing assistance in preparing living wills; the clients sought the emotional support of a social worker while completing the form. (*Id.* at 10.) A living will is a document that specifies the signer's desires regarding medical treatment in the event the signer is incapacitated. (*Id.* at 12.) In Minnesota, a state statute includes a living will form that is easily prepared by filling in blanks; the form also indicates how the document is to be signed, witnessed, and notarized. (Ex. A to Mahoney Depo.)

To date, HomeElderCare social workers have prepared about forty living wills, relying on a living will form that complies with Minnesota law. (Mahoney Depo. 12.) The social workers decline to prepare wills deviating from the form, and they refrain from influencing clients' personal choices or pressuring clients to complete living wills. Furthermore, if a client demands a living will that does not adhere to the form, the social workers advise the client that this action is beyond the scope of their service, and they recommend that the client seek expert legal advice from a licensed lawyer. (*Id.* at 15-17.) Eight of the forty HomeElderCare clients have been hospitalized since their living wills were drafted. The living wills were shown to their doctors, but the clients were not incapacitated enough to bring any of the living wills into effect. (*Id.* at 25-26.)

Kimberly Hall is a social worker at HomeElderCare. She has a master's degree in social work and has worked in the field for twelve years. Kimberly (Hall Depo. 2-4 (Sept. 11, 1993).) She attended a one-day HomeElderCare workshop on care issues involving the terminally ill; this workshop included a training session on preparing living wills. (*Id.* at 19.) Thus far, she has prepared ten living wills for HomeElderCare clients. (*Id.* at 9.)

When one of those clients, Roger Nelson, was hospitalized, Mr. Nelson's son realized that his father's living will nominated Mr. Nelson's proxy as his guardian, (Albert Nelson Depo. 5 (Aug. 4, 1993),) but Mr. Nelson instead wanted his son to be his guardian, (Roger Nelson Depo. 10 (Aug. 5, 1993).) Roger Nelson, a seventy-eight-year-old widower, is in declining health because of diabetes. (*Id.* at 2.) Perhaps he did not fully process Ms. Hall's standard explanation of the roles of proxies, guardians, and conservators; he apparently did not consult a lawyer with his questions, as she believes she suggested to him. (*See* Hall Depo. 13-15.)

In any event, Mr. Nelson's son contacted the LaSalle County Attorney about HomeElderCare's living will service. (A. Nelson Depo. 8.) The county attorney, representing the State of Minnesota, has sued HomeElderCare, seeking to end its living will services. Compl. HomeElderCare believes that its living will services are legal, (Ans. (July 27, 1993)), and now asks this Court not to prohibit HomeElderCare from offering this service to its clients.

ISSUES

I. Has the State proved, as it must to obtain a temporary injunction, that it will suffer great and irreparable injury if HomeElderCare continues to offer assistance with living wills to its elderly clients?

II. Has the State met its burden as to the following requirements for a temporary injunction:

A. Would the State's alleged harm in the absence of a temporary injunction outweigh the harm both to HomeElderCare's elderly clients and to the relationships between HomeElderCare and its clients if an injunction is granted?

B. Is it likely that the State will ultimately succeed in convincing this Court that HomeElderCare's living will service constitutes the unauthorized practice of law?

C. Will the public interest be served by prohibiting HomeElderCare's living will services during the pendency of the case?

ARGUMENT

A temporary injunction is an extraordinary equitable remedy that preserves the status quo pending a trial on the merits. *Sunny Fresh Foods, Inc. v. Microfresh Foods Corp.*, 424 N.W.2d 309, 310 (Minn. App. 1988). "A party seeking the injunction must establish that [the] legal remedy is not adequate . . . and that the injunction is necessary to prevent great and irreparable injury." *Id.* (quoting *Cherne Indus., Inc. v. Grounds & Assoc., Inc.*, 278 N.W.2d 81, 92 (Minn. 1979)). Here, the State has failed to prove that a great and irreparable injury will result if a temporary injunction is not granted; this failure alone is sufficient ground to deny the injunction.

Furthermore, this Court must consider and weigh the following factors:

(1) the relationship between the parties before the dispute;
(2) the harm the plaintiff will suffer if [the injunction] is denied compared with the harm inflicted on the defendant if the injunction is issued;
(3) the likelihood that one party or the other will prevail on the merits;
(4) the public policy involved, if any;
(5) the administrative burdens involved in enforcing the [injunction].

Overholt Crop Ins. Serv. v. Bredeson, 437 N.W.2d 698, 701 (Minn. App. 1989) (citing *Dahlberg Bros., Inc. v. Ford Motor Co.*, 137 N.W.2d 314, 321-22 (Minn. 1965)).

The State has failed to carry its burden as to these factors, especially in light of the stringent standard of proof required of the movant. "Injunctive relief should be awarded only in clear cases, reasonably free from doubt. . . . The burden of proof rests upon the complainant to establish the material allegations entitling him to relief." *Sunny Fresh Foods*, 424 N.W.2d at 310 (citing *AMF Pinspotters, Inc. v. Harkins Bowling, Inc.*, 110 N.W.2d 348, 351 (Minn. 1961)).

Most important to this case are the second, third, and fourth factors. The State has failed to establish that its alleged harm outweighs HomeElderCare's harm if an injunction is granted, that it likely will prevail on the merits at trial, and that the various public interests in this dispute favor a temporary injunction. (The first factor is irrelevant because the State and HomeElderCare had no relationship before this dispute. The fifth factor is not at issue, because neither party foresees any administrative burden from a temporary injunction in this case.)

I. The State has failed to prove that it will suffer great and irreparable injury if HomeElderCare continues to offer living will assistance to its clients.

The *Cherne* test requires the movant to show that an injunction would prevent a "great and irreparable injury" from occurring. *Cherne Indus. Inc. v. Grounds & Assoc., Inc.*, 278 N.W.2d 81, 92 (Minn. 1979). "[F]ailure to show irreparable harm [or injury] is, by itself, a sufficient ground upon which to deny an injunction." *Carl Bolander & Sons Co. v. City of Minneapolis*, 488 N.W.2d 804, 811 (Minn. App. 1992).

theory of the case

When a HomeElderCare social worker assists a client with a living will by helping the client to record his or her wishes in the blanks on the living will form, no injury occurs. In fact, a laudable service has been done—for the client, for his or her family, and for society. And in thirty-nine instances, that is exactly what happened.

Yet the State wants to put a halt to this service for the duration of the litigation. The State's only factual ground for doing so is a disputed single incident. HomeElderCare's social worker believes that she helped an elderly gentleman in failing health accurately record his wishes, as he stated them, in response to the questions on the living will form. She also believes that she suggested that he discuss any questions with his lawyer. The client apparently did not consult a lawyer. His living will was amended when the client reviewed his living will with his family, a step many people signing living wills probably take. No action adverse to the client occurred pursuant to the living will. In any event, this one incident is not sufficient to establish that great and irreparable harm will occur to HomeElderCare's clients (and therefore to the state's citizens) if this Court denies the State's motion for a temporary injunction.

Furthermore, the State argues that HomeElderCare's clients will suffer harm, but the clients have expressed a need for assistance with the form. The State, in seeking an injunction, is acting contrary to the voiced wishes of HomeElderCare's clients. Thus, the State has failed to clearly prove the crucial element of great and irreparable injury.

II. The State has not met its burden as to the factors needed for a temporary injunction to issue.

A. The State's alleged harm in the absence of a temporary injunction does not outweigh the harm both to HomeElderCare's elderly clients and to the relationships between HomeElderCare and its clients if an injunction is granted.

One of the five temporary injunction factors is that, absent the injunction, the State would suffer greater injury than would HomeElderCare and its clients upon the grant of the injunction. *See Dahlberg Bros., Inc. v. Ford Motor Co.*, 137 N.W.2d 314, 321-22 (Minn. 1965). The party seeking to trigger the injunction must show irreparable harm, but the opposing party must show only substantial harm to bar it. *Yager v. Thompson*, 352 N.W.2d 71, 75 (Minn. App. 1984).

Here, the State has failed to show that HomeElderCare's living will service is causing irreparable harm; to the contrary, the service provides clients invaluable assistance with the crucial issues covered by a living will. HomeElderCare seeks to help its elderly clients fill in the blanks of the living will form. The form calls for difficult emotional, moral, social, and even religious decisions that may determine a person's quality of life in his or her final days. The resolution of these issues may also have a significant impact on the person's family members and friends. Many elderly people find it helpful to discuss these issues with an informed person who does not have an emotional stake in their resolution yet understands the range of factors at issue. HomeElderCare is not influencing its clients in any way, nor is it pressuring its clients to complete living wills. In fact, the elderly clients originally requested HomeElderCare to provide this service to them.

If an injunction forced HomeElderCare to temporarily eliminate this service, its clients likely would not seek out lawyers to assist them in filling out the living will form because their needs as to the form are not legal needs; their needs are instead emotional and moral. Moreover, clients on fixed incomes might not have the resources to hire a lawyer for this service. Nor would the HomeElderCare clients who request this service be likely to complete the living wills on their own without the emotional support of the HomeElderCare social workers.

In addition, HomeElderCare would suffer substantial harm because of an undeserved hindrance of its relationships with its clients. In *Dahlberg*, the court ruled that the potential harm resulting from a dealer's temporary interruption of business outweighed the manufacturer's potential harm from not being able to terminate the dealer's franchise right away, because the dealer's "[l]iaison with the buying public will be interrupted." 137 N.W.2d at 322. Similarly, HomeElderCare would have to terminate this requested service and somehow explain that it cannot offer living will assistance until this trial is concluded.

The interests of HomeElderCare and its clients are far stronger than any interests that the State purports to represent. Accordingly, the State has not met its burden in proving that the State would suffer irreparable harm outweighing the substantial harm to HomeElderCare.

B. The State is not likely to succeed in convincing this Court that HomeElderCare's provision of living will services to its clients constitutes the unauthorized practice of law.

Non-lawyers may not, of course, practice law in Minnesota. *See* Minn. Stat. § 481.02 (1992). But a non-lawyer may touch on legal matters incidental to her profession so long as she does not answer difficult or doubtful legal questions. *See Gardner v. Conway*, 48 N.W.2d 788, 796 (Minn. 1951). What is a difficult or doubtful legal question is measured by a reasonably intelligent person who has knowledge of similar transactions. *Id.* This test is "applied in a common-sense way which protects primarily the interests of the public and does not hamper or burden that interest with technical restrictions." *Id.* at 797. The test is flexible, and its application entails a case-by-case analysis. *Id.* In *Gardner*, an accountant familiar with income-tax rules and regulations answered difficult and doubtful legal questions in preparing a tax return and, therefore, violated the unauthorized practice of law statute. *Id.* at 792.

HomeElderCare social workers use a straightforward living will form that meets the requirements of the Minnesota Living Will Act and gives instructions as to its completion. *See* Minn. Stat. § 145B.04 (1992). Indeed, the statute anticipates that many declarants will complete their own living wills. *See id.* § 145B.03. The form addresses various medical topics and designation of decision-makers for the declarant should he become incompetent. *Id.* By leading their clients through the statutory living will form, the social workers meet their elderly clients' desire to complete that form. More important for this case, by this process, the social workers avoid interpreting the living will statute and thereby avoid answering any difficult or doubtful legal questions. They thereby avoid engaging in the unauthorized practice of law.

The possibility of the social workers engaging in the unauthorized practice of law might exist if the social workers deviated from the living will form or interpreted the statute. However, the HomeElderCare social workers have done neither. The social workers do not alter the form. If a client demands a living will that does not adhere to the living will form, the HomeElderCare social workers advise the client that this action is beyond the scope of their service, and they recommend that the client seek expert legal advice from a licensed lawyer—unlike the accountant in *Gardner.* A single HomeElderCare client's disregard of the suggestion to seek a lawyer to answer his legal questions does not convert the social worker's actions into the unauthorized practice of law.

Although charging a fee for services has in the past been seen as an indication that an issue may be difficult or doubtful, *Cardinal v. Merrill Lynch Realty/Burnet, Inc.*, 433 N.W.2d 864, 869 (Minn. 1989), HomeElderCare's fee is not for legal services. HomeElderCare charges a reasonable fee for all of its services. The preparation fee for living wills is an hourly rate charged all clients who select this service.

The State has argued that living wills are "legal documents" within the statutory prohibition against drafting "legal documents." *See* Minn. Stat. § 481.02. This argument fails for several reasons. There is no evidence that the reference in the living will form to "legal document" was meant to relate to the unauthorized practice statute. To the contrary, had the legislature intended this connection, it would have alerted declarants to the need for legal advice, whereas the form refers more broadly to seeking "professional advice." *See* Minn. Stat. § 145B.04.

Furthermore, the difficult-or-doubtful-legal-question test was developed in response to a non-lawyer practicing in another form-driven setting—tax. *See Gardner*, 48 N.W.2d at 792. Hence this test would apply to HomeElderCare's filling out a living will form. As already argued, the living will service passes the Gardner test.

Because the living will service does not involve difficult or doubtful legal questions, it is not prohibited by the unauthorized practice of law statute. Therefore, the State is not likely to succeed on the merits of the case.

C. The public interest will not be served by prohibiting HomeElderCare's living will service during the pendency of the case.

The persons most affected by any temporary injunction granted in this case would be elderly persons and persons in failing health. These persons often are vulnerable, in need of emotional support, and on fixed incomes. Many lawyers are not as well prepared as social workers who work with the elderly to provide emotional support to clients considering the difficult issues in a living will; furthermore, the cost of obtaining these services from lawyers would not be an efficient use of these clients' meager or fixed incomes. Elderly and ill clients ought to be able to use this service now; they should not have to await the outcome of trial.

Ultimately, the public is served well by HomeElderCare's assistance in preparing living wills. The service enhances the possibility that elderly persons will have living wills in place when and if they are needed. It is Minnesota's public policy to encourage living wills. *See* Minn. Stat. §§ 145B.03, 145B.06 (1992).

Furthermore, living wills enable the health care system to better serve the needs of its patients and to better allocate scarce health care resources. "Patients without [living wills] have significantly higher terminal hospitalization charges than those with [living wills]." William Weeks, *Advance Directives and the Cost of Terminal Hospitalization*, 154 Archives Internal Med. 1 (1994) (available at DIALOG ARCHINTMED 2077). "[T]he preferences of patients with [living wills] are to limit care and these preferences influence the cost of terminal hospitalization." *Id.* The possible total savings in the cost of health care if living wills were completed by all in the nation is somewhere between thirty-five and sixty percent. *Id.* at 6. Therefore, both the patient and the health care system benefit from the use of living wills.

The living will service provided by HomeElderCare serves the public interest. Thus the public interest will not be served by prohibiting this service.

CONCLUSION

The State has not met its burden of proving its entitlement to the extraordinary equitable remedy of a temporary injunction. It has not demonstrated great and irreparable harm. It will not suffer a greater harm upon the denial of the injunction than HomeElderCare would suffer upon the grant of the injunction. Nor is the State likely to succeed on the merits of this case, because the living will service does not constitute the unauthorized practice of law. Finally, the public interest would not be served by a temporary injunction. Thus, the State's motion should be denied.

Respectfully submitted,

Dated: Oct. 10, 1993   _Katherine Crawford_

Katherine Crawford
Counsel for HomeElderCare, Inc.
5678 Sherburne Avenue
LaSalle MN 55555
(507) 555-4321
Attorney Reg. No. 12541

FOURTH COMPONENT

- This sample follows *The Bluebook: A Uniform System of Citation* (18th ed. 2005).
- It uses underlining rather than italics.
- It includes parallel citations to state cases, where available.
- In this sample, citations are interspersed in the text. Footnotes are used only for tangential points.

APPELLATE COURT CASE NO. 94-1234

STATE OF MINNESOTA

IN COURT OF APPEALS

Roger Nelson,
      Plaintiff-Respondent,

vs.

HomeElderCare, Inc.,
      Defendant-Appellant

APPELLANT'S BRIEF

Katherine Crawford (No. 12541)   Albert Frank (No. 14711)
Attorney for Appellant   Attorney for Respondent
Crawford & Larson   Law Offices of Albert Frank
12 Main Avenue   672 Oak Street
Versailles, MN 50000   Versailles, MN 50001
Telephone: (222) 555-1234   (222) 777-7771

TABLE OF CONTENTS

TABLE OF AUTHORITIES

PERIODICALS:

STATEMENT OF THE ISSUE

facts + law + more
facts

Is a service contract between Appellant, a nonprofit geriatric services agency, and Respondent, an elderly client, invalid on the grounds that a trained social worker practiced law when she helped the elderly client fill in the blanks on a living will form?

trial court holding &
procedural posture

The trial court ruled in the affirmative, granting Respondent summary declaratory judgment and denying Appellant's cross-motion for summary judgment.

key authorities

Minn. Stat. § 481.02 (1992).
Minn. Stat. §§ 145.B.01-07 (1992).
Dick Weatherston's Assoc'd Mech. Servs. v. Minn. Mut. Life Ins. Co.,
        257 Minn. 184, 100 N.W.2d 819 (1960).
Gardner v. Conway, 234 Minn. 468, 48 N.W.2d 788 (1951).

STATEMENT OF CASE AND FACTS

The Case

commencement of suit

cause of action

On July 20, 1993, the Respondent, Roger Nelson, sued the Appellant, HomeElderCare, Inc., seeking to void his own contract with HomeElderCare for preparation of a living will—and, in effect, to prohibit HomeElderCare from offering its living will service to other HomeElderCare clients. (Compl.)

remedy sought

Mr. Nelson's suit sought a declaratory judgment (Compl.), HomeElderCare and Mr. Nelson stipulated to the facts (Stip'n.), and both parties moved for summary judgment (Pl.'s Mot. for Summ. J.; Def.'s Cross-Mot. for Summ. J.).

trial court order

Judge Annelise Burton of the LaSalle County District Court granted Mr. Nelson's motion and issued a declaratory judgment in his favor. (Order

appeal

for Decl. J.) HomeElderCare appeals.

The Facts

1st topic: HEC and its
services

Appellant HomeElderCare is a private, nonprofit corporation with a staff of geriatric social workers who provide services to help their elderly clients with day-to-day activities. Volunteers assist with some services. Available services include shopping, transportation, home maintenance, and assistance with personal finances. The social workers also serve as liaisons between clients and attorneys working on such matters as testamentary wills and real estate transactions. (Stip'n. ¶ 2.[1]) Each client contracts with HomeElderCare

---

1. The Stipulation of Facts appears in the Appendix beginning at page 10. Citations to the record are presented as stipulation paragraphs because these references are more specific than page references.

1

for the services he or she desires and pays a modest fee based on the services rendered. (Stip'n ¶ 3.)

Several clients recently asked HomeElderCare to fill a gap in the services provided to them by offering the service of preparing living wills. Home-ElderCare decided to respond to its clients' requests and began preparing living wills for its clients. (Stip'n ¶ 7.) As with its other services, HomeElderCare charges a modest fee that varies with the time the social worker puts in on the project. (Stip'n. ¶ 7.)

2nd topic: living will service

A living will is a document that specifies the signer's desires regarding medical treatment in the event the signer is incapacitated. In Minnesota, a state statute includes a living will form that is easily prepared by filling in the blanks; the statute also indicates how the document is to be signed, witnessed, and notarized. See Minn. Stat. § 145B.04 (1992). HomeElderCare's social workers use the living will form that complies with Minnesota law. The social workers do not deviate from the form but rather advise clients to consult with attorneys in such situations. (Stip'n. ¶ 7.)

definition of living will & use of statutory form

Appellant Kimberly Hall is a social worker at HomeElderCare. She has a master's degree in social work and has worked in the field for twelve years. (Stip'n. ¶ 6.) As is true of her colleagues, she attended a one-day HomeElder-Care workshop on care issues involving the terminally ill; this workshop included a forty-five-minute presentation by an attorney about preparing living wills. (Stip'n. ¶ 6.) With this training, thus far, she has prepared ten living wills for HomeElderCare clients. (Stip'n. ¶ 11.)

3rd topic: social worker's training

Ms. Hall prepared a living will for Roger Nelson. (Stip'n. ¶ 8.) When Mr. Nelson was hospitalized, his son, an attorney, realized that the living will nominated Roger Nelson's proxy for medical decisions to be his guardian for financial decisions, although Roger Nelson now desires otherwise. (Stip'n. ¶ 8.) Mr. Nelson, who is a seventy-eight-year-old widower, is in declining health due to diabetes. (Stip'n. ¶ 1.) It is unknown how the terms of Mr. Nelson's living will came to diverge from his present desires. Ms. Hall's practice is to provide a standard explanation of the roles of proxies, guardians, and conservators, and Mr. Nelson did not consult an attorney with his questions, as Ms. Hall believes she suggested to him. (See Stip'n. ¶ 8.)

4th topic: Roger Nelson's situation

To date, the HomeElderCare social workers have prepared forty living wills. Eight clients have since been hospitalized. The living wills were shown to their doctors, but no client was incapacitated enough to bring his or her living will into effect. Other than Mr. Nelson, HomeElderCare's clients have registered no objections to their living wills. (Stip'n. ¶ 11.)

5th topic: other clients served

2

SUMMARY OF ARGUMENT

summary of substantive arguments

—main argument

HomeElderCare responsibly designed a service to provide assistance to its elderly clients who requested help in filling in the blanks on a living will form. Because the social worker confined her service to filling out the statutory form and would refer clients to attorneys as needed, there was no provision of legal advice. The living will form has many medical and ethical implications, but relatively few legal implications and no testamentary effect. Hence a living will is not a legal document that an attorney must draft. The service in question did not constitute the unauthorized practice of law.

—argument in the alternative

However, even if the social worker's assistance was the practice of law, the social worker provided the living will service as an incident of her social work, competently and without fraud. The service did not contravene the purpose of the statute on the unauthorized practice of law. Moreover, public policy favors living wills and therefore supports the agency's living will service. Thus, the service contract between the client and the agency was valid.

procedural argument

In the trial court, both parties, having stipulated to the facts, moved for summary judgment. The trial court erroneously granted summary judgment to Mr. Nelson. That judgment should be reversed, and HomeElderCare's cross-motion for summary judgment should be granted.

ARGUMENT

overall point heading (procedural law + facts)

This Court should reverse the summary declaratory judgment in favor of Respondent and should instead grant Appellant's cross-motion for summary judgment, thereby upholding the contract under which a trained social worker for a nonprofit geriatric services agency helped an elderly client to fill in the blanks on a living will form.

standard of review

A declaratory judgment "may be reviewed as other orders, judgments and decrees." Minn. Stat. § 555.07 (1992). When reviewing an appeal from summary judgment, this Court determines whether there are any genuine issues of material fact and whether the trial court erred in its application of the law. See Offerdahl v. Univ. of Minn. Hosp. & Clinics, 426 N.W.2d 425, 427 (Minn. 1988); Minn. R. Civ. P. 56.03. Because the parties stipulated to the facts, this Court need decide only whether the trial court correctly applied the law.

1st main topic point heading (law + facts)

A. The trained social worker did not practice law when she helped the client fill in the blanks on a living will form.

When HomeElderCare's social worker assisted its client, Mr. Nelson, in filling in the blanks on a state-approved living will form, she did not engage in

3

the unauthorized practice of law because she neither gave legal advice nor drafted a legal document. In Minnesota:

> It shall be unlawful for any person . . . except members of the bar of Minnesota admitted and licensed to practice as attorneys at law . . . [1] for a fee . . . to give legal advice or counsel, perform for or furnish to another legal services, or, [2] for or without a fee . . . , to prepare . . . for another person . . . any will or testamentary disposition or instrument of trust serving purposes similar to those of a will, or, [3] for a fee . . . to prepare for another person . . . any other legal document.[2]

overall rule: statute

Minn. Stat. § 481.02 subdiv. 1 (1992) (enumeration added).

Clause 1 forbids a layperson from giving legal advice or counsel, or performing for or furnishing to another legal services, for a fee. The Home-ElderCare social worker assisted her elderly client with the medical and ethical issues in the living will form set out in the statute. The form asks the declarant questions about health care preferences, life-sustaining treatment, artificially administered sustenance, designation of a health care proxy, and organ donation; the answers take effect when the declaratant has an incurable or irreversible condition and is no longer able to participate in decisions regarding his or her health care. Minn. Stat. § 145B.04 (1992). To avoid the rendering of legal advice, HomeElderCare policy calls for the social worker to suggest that the client consult an attorney if the client wishes to deviate from the form or has legal questions. Thus, the social worker did not provide legal advice.[3]

1st topic
first argument

However, even if the social worker touched on legal matters, the service would not constitute the unauthorized practice of law under Minnesota case law. The Minnesota Supreme Court held that a layperson can dispense legal advice in the course of her or his business so long as it is incidental (not primary) to the business and the layperson does not answer "difficult or doubtful legal questions." Gardner v. Conway, 234 Minn. 468, 480-81, 48 N.W.2d 788, 796 (1951). A legal question is difficult or doubtful if it must be answered by someone with a trained legal mind, in order to safeguard the public. Id. In Gardner, an accountant gave a client opinions on tax questions concerning lawful marital status, joint versus separate returns, and partnership status,

2nd argument, in the alternative

• rule

---

2. The exceptions do not apply to these facts. See § 481.02 subdiv. 3.
3. As it does for all of its services, HomeElderCare charged a fee for its living will service. The charging of a fee should not render this service the practice of law, any more than the charging of a fee for home maintenance services would render that service the practice of law. Cf. Cardinal v. Merrill Lynch Realty/ Burnet, Inc., 433 N.W.2d 864, 869 (Minn. 1988) (charging a fee suggests, but does not establish, practice of law).

tangential points
• statutory exceptions
• fee charged

all of which required analysis by someone with legal training. Thus, the accountant was engaging in the unauthorized practice of law. Id. at 483-84, 48 N.W.2d at 797-98. The court emphasized that the test of what is a difficult or doubtful legal question should be

> applied in a common-sense way which will protect primarily the interest of the public and not hamper or burden that interest with impractical and technical restrictions which have no reasonable justification. We are therefore not concerned with a technical application which would ban the giving of any and all legal advice or the taking of any and all action for another.

Id. at 481-82, 48 N.W.2d at 797 (citations omitted).

• application

It is not common sense to bar a HomeElderCare social worker from helping a client fill in the blanks on a statutory form dominated by medical and ethical questions, just because the form includes some incidental legal topics. So long as the social worker declines to answer any difficult or doubtful questions of law, there is no unauthorized practice of law. Here there is no evidence that Ms. Hall addressed such questions. She provided an explanation of proxies, guardians, and conservators—concepts that must not be that difficult, because these roles are routinely filled by laypeople. See generally Minn. Stat. §§ 145B.06 subdiv. 2; 145B.08; 525.539 subdivs. 2, 3; 525.56 (1992). There is no evidence that she counseled Mr. Nelson about how to apply these concepts to his individual situation. HomeElderCare's practice calls for referral to attorneys when clients raise questions or wish to deviate from the form.

• conclusion

Thus, unlike the tax accountant in Gardner, Ms. Hall did not exceed her bounds, and HomeElderCare did not violate the statutory prohibition against giving legal advice or counsel.

2nd topic

The living will form that HomeElderCare fills in for its clients is not a "legal document" under clause 3 of the unauthorized practice statute, as numbered above. See § 481.02 subdiv. 1. Although the form states that it "is an important legal document," the form is designed to provide medical and ethical instructions to medical caregivers. It focuses mostly on medical concepts such as "specific treatments," "life-sustaining treatments," "artificially administered sustenance," and death from "dehydration or malnutrition." § 145B.04. The form suggests that a declarant seek "professional help" to understand unclear provisions, id.; the legislature could have specified an attorney's assistance, but did not. Thus, the living will form in question is not a "legal document" within the meaning of the unauthorized practice statute.

3rd subtopic

Nor does the living will come within the scope of clause 2, as numbered above, which pertains to "any will or testamentary disposition or instrument of trust serving purposes similar to those of a will." See § 481.02 subdiv. 1. A living will does not convey any rights posthumously, nor is it designed to be filed in a court of law. It deals only with the patient's wishes in the event of a terminal illness that renders the patient unable to communicate his or her wishes as to medical treatment.[4]

In summary, Ms. Hall did not violate the Minnesota statute on the unauthorized practice of law.

conclusion to 1st topic

B. Even if the social worker practiced law, the contract is valid because the social worker provided the living will service without fraud or incompetence and incidentally to non-legal professional services.

2nd main topic point heading (law + facts)

A contract for professional services by an unlicensed professional is enforceable if the activities under the contract are not the kind of activities that the licensing statute was meant to preclude. See Dick Weatherston's Assoc'd Mech. Servs. v. Minn. Mut. Life Ins. Co., 257 Minn. 184, 191, 100 N.W.2d 819, 824 (1960). In Dick Weatherston's, the court upheld the validity of an engineering contract with an unlicensed engineer because the licensing statute was intended to protect the public from fraud and incompetence, neither of which were present in that case. The client knew the engineer's status, the client had its own engineers and architects who approved and accepted the services, and the engineering services were incidental to an air-conditioning contract. Id. at 190-92, 100 N.W.2d at 823-25.

• rule: case

Similarly, the law defining the unauthorized practice of law is intended to safeguard the public from fraud and incompetence. See Gardner, 234 Minn. at 478, 48 N.W.2d at 795. There is no evidence that Ms. Hall fraudulently held herself out as having legal expertise. Furthermore, HomeElderCare policy calls for a referral to an attorney should the client have questions or wish to deviate from the form, and Ms. Hall believes she so referred Mr. Nelson. He could not have been mistaken as to her professional status.

• application

Nor is there any clear evidence of incompetence. Although the client's living will contained a misstatement of his current preferences, the evidence does not show that he accurately stated his preference to Ms. Hall at the time the living will was drafted. Nor does the evidence show that Ms. Hall, rather

---

4. Peterson v. Hovland (In re Peterson's Estate), 230 Minn. 478, 42 N.W.2d 59 (1950), is inapplicable to this case because it deals with a bank cashier who drafted a customer's testamentary will, rather than a living will. The Peterson court allowed the will to stand, even though the act of drafting it violated the unauthorized practice statute. However, this appeal does not address a testamentary will or raise the question of the living will's validity. Thus, this case is distinguishable from Peterson on both its facts and its legal issues.

distinguish adverse case

6

than the client himself, was responsible. Moreover, there is no evidence of incompetence or even a single misunderstanding in the other thirty-nine living wills prepared with HomeElderCare's assistance. HomeElderCare trained its social workers for this specific service, and HomeElderCare instructed its social workers to urge clients with legal questions to consult an attorney, as Ms. Hall believes that she instructed Mr. Nelson.

Furthermore, as in Dick Weatherston's, HomeElderCare's allegedly legal services were incidental to its provision of primarily non-legal services, namely assistance with medical care and ethical decisionmaking. Thus, this case is analogous to Dick Weatherston's. Accordingly, the contract for living will services between HomeElderCare and its client is valid.

• conclusion

3rd main topic point heading (policy + facts)

C. Public policy favors living wills and therefore also favors a service provider who assists a client in filling in the blanks on the statutory living will form.

1st policy

Minnesota's state constitution recognizes the right to privacy and a derivative "right not to have [one's body] altered or invaded without consent." Jarvis v. Levine, 418 N.W.2d 139, 149 (Minn. 1988). If the patient is incompetent and cannot give consent, the physician cannot administer invasive medical treatment without first obtaining consent "from some source other than the contemporaneous words of the patient." Id. at 147. This rule is based on the "right of every individual to the possession and to control of his own person, free from all restraint or interference of others, unless by clear and unquestionable authority of law." Union Pac. R.R. Co. v. Botsford, 141 U.S. 250, 251 (1891), cited in Howard Orenstein, David Bishop & Leigh D. Mathison, Minnesota's Living Will . . . , Bench & B. Minn., Aug. 1989, at 21, 22. The Living Will Act furnishes a legal mechanism by which a patient can give advance instructions and preferences to the physician while the patient is still competent. It allows "a competent adult [to] make a living will of preferences or instructions regarding . . . health care, treatment, service, procedure, or placement." § 145B.03 subdiv. 1.

2nd policy

Furthermore, living wills enable the health care system to better serve the needs of its patients and to better allocate scarce health care resources. "Patients without [living wills] have significantly higher terminal hospitalization charges than those with [living wills]." William Weeks, Advance Directives and the Cost of Terminal Hospitalization, 154 Archives Internal Med. 1 (1994) (available at DIALOG ARCHINTMED 2077). "[T]he preferences of patients with [living wills] are to limit care and these preferences influence the cost of terminal hospitalization." Id. The possible total savings in the cost of health care if living wills were completed by all in the nation is somewhere between thirty-five and sixty percent. Id. at 6. Therefore, both the patient and the health care system benefit from the use of living wills.

To maximize the use of living wills in light of these public policies, the Living Will Act includes a suggested form for a living will and mandates that "[f]orms printed for public distribution . . . be substantially in the form in this section." § 145B.04. The Act does not restrict these forms to the offices of attorneys but instead promotes public distribution so that the forms can be made widely available—most probably by hospitals, physicians, and geriatric care organizations. Of course, many of the persons filling out these forms will be elderly. *connection of statute to policies*

HomeElderCare has sought to effectuate public policy and the Living Will Act through its living will service. Responding to the requests of elderly clients, it has sought to make living wills more available to the elderly, who have an undeniable interest in self-determination as to medical issues and an equally clear potential for unduly protracted medical care. Mr. Nelson himself sought out the help of a HomeElderCare social worker when he made out his living will. That social worker had been trained in how to fill in the blanks on the form and knew to refer legal questions to the client's attorney. *application*

Thus, the trial court's declaratory judgment invalidating the contract in this case is contrary to public policy and should be reversed. *conclusion*

CONCLUSION

HomeElderCare respectfully requests this Court to vacate the trial court's summary declaratory judgment in favor of Mr. Nelson and grant summary judgment to HomeElderCare. *conclusion with relief requested*

Dated: *Jan. 8, 1994*

Respectfully submitted, *signature block*

By: *Katherine Crawford*
Katherine Crawford (No. 12541)
Crawford & Larson
12 Main Avenue
Versailles, MN 50000
Telephone: (222) 555-1234
ATTORNEY FOR APPELLANT
HomeElderCare, Inc.

- This sample follows *ALWD Citation Manual: A Professional System of Citation* (3d ed. 2006).
- It uses italics rather than underlining.
- It does not include parallel citations to state cases.
- In this sample, citations appear in footnotes. One footnote also makes a tangential point.

APPELLATE COURT CASE NO. 94-1234

STATE OF MINNESOTA

IN COURT OF APPEALS

Roger Nelson,
    Plaintiff-Respondent,

vs.

HomeElderCare, Inc.,
    Defendant-Appellant

RESPONDENT'S BRIEF

Albert Frank (No. 14711)   Katherine Crawford (No. 12541)
Attorney for Respondent   Attorney for Appellant
Law Offices of Albert Frank   Crawford & Larson
672 Oak Street   12 Main Avenue
Versailles, MN 50001   Versailles, MN 50000
(222) 777-7771   Telephone: (222) 555-1234

TABLE OF CONTENTS

TABLE OF AUTHORITIES

ISSUES

space for your notes

I. Did a social worker—who is neither trained nor licensed to practice law—engage in the unauthorized practice of law when she prepared a defective living will for an elderly client for a fee?

The trial court held that the social worker violated the Minnesota statute on the unauthorized practice of law.

Minn. Stat. § 481.02 (1992).

Cardinal v. Merrill Lynch Realty/Burnet, Inc., 433 N.W.2d 864 (Minn. 1988).

Gardner v. Conway, 48 N.W.2d 788 (Minn. 1951).

In re Est. of Peterson, 42 N.W.2d 59 (Minn. 1950).

II. In light of this unauthorized practice of law, is the contract between the social work agency and the client unenforceable, so as to excuse the client from paying for the defective document?

The trial court held that, because of the violation of the statute on the unauthorized practice of law, the contract is not enforceable.

Dick Weatherston's Assocd. Mech. Servs. v. Minn. Mut. Life Ins. Co., 100 N.W.2d 819 (Minn. 1960).

In re Est. of Peterson, 42 N.W.2d 59 (Minn. 1950).

Buckley v. Humason, 52 N.W. 385 (Minn. 1892).

STATEMENT OF CASE AND FACTS

Statement of Case

Plaintiff Roger Nelson commenced this action against Defendant HomeElderCare, Inc. in LaSalle County District Court on July 20, 1993. Mr. Nelson sought a declaratory judgment that he is not legally obligated to pay HomeElderCare for preparing his living will on the grounds that HomeElderCare engaged in the unauthorized practice of law, rendering the contract unenforceable.[1] The parties stipulated to the facts[2] and filed cross-motions for summary judgment.[3]

---

1. Compl. (July 20, 1993).
2. Stip. of Facts (Sept. 15, 1993).
3. Pl.'s Mot. S.J. (Oct. 1, 1993); Def.'s Mot. S.J. (Oct. 8, 1993).

On November 3, 1993, Judge Annelise Burton granted summary judgment in favor of Mr. Nelson. The Order for Declaratory Judgment states:

(1) HomeElderCare's social workers engaged in the unauthorized practice of law.

(2) The contract between Mr. Nelson and HomeElderCare is not enforceable, so that Mr. Nelson is not legally obligated to pay HomeElderCare for preparing his living will.[4]

HomeElderCare appealed.[5]

Statement of Facts

Roger Nelson is seventy-eight years old and a widower. He is in declining health because of diabetes.[6] Contemplating the time when his condition might worsen and he would become incapacitated, Mr. Nelson set out to arrange his personal affairs as he wished. Among other steps, Mr. Nelson wrote a living will, a statement of his desires regarding health care when he is in a terminal state.[7] Unfortunately, Mr. Nelson initially turned to Defendant HomeElderCare, Inc., to prepare his living will.[8]

HomeElderCare is a private, non-profit corporation that provides various social services for elderly persons. Among the useful services provided by HomeElderCare are shopping, transportation, and home maintenance. The social workers also serve as liaisons between clients and other professionals, such as attorneys working on the clients' testamentary wills and real-estate transactions.[9] The elderly clients contract for the particular services desired, HomeElderCare's staff makes the necessary arrangements, and the clients pay a fee for the services.[10] Volunteers also provide some free services.[11]

As befits a social work agency, HomeElderCare is staffed by social workers. These social workers are not lawyers. These social workers do not have law degrees. These social workers have not been admitted to practice law in Minnesota or anywhere else.[12]

---

4. Or. Decl. Judm. 3 (Nov. 3, 1993).
5. Notice App. (Nov. 15, 1993).
6. Stip. ¶ 1.
7. *Id.* at ¶ 8.
8. *Id.* at ¶¶ 8, 9.
9. *Id.* at ¶ 2.
10. *Id.* at ¶ 3.
11. *Id.* at ¶ 4.
12. *Id.* at ¶ 5.

Nonetheless, HomeElderCare social workers have prepared at least forty living wills for their clients.[13] For some reason, HomeElderCare chose not to follow its established practice and serve as liaison between the clients and their lawyers, as it does with other legal transactions,[14] but rather elected to prepare the living wills itself.[15] The sole training received by the social workers was a forty-five minute seminar taught by a lawyer.[16]

In particular, social worker Kimberly Hall, a non-lawyer, prepared a living will for Mr. Nelson on October 10, 1992. In this living will, Mr. Nelson's minister was designated as the proxy authorized to make medical decisions on behalf of Mr. Nelson should he become mentally incapacitated.[17] The proxy is also, by operation of statute, nominated to be the declarant's guardian.[18] Mr. Nelson actually wanted his minister to serve only as his proxy for medical decisionmaking; he wanted his son, Albert Nelson, to serve as his guardian.[19] Thus the living will drafted by Ms. Hall fundamentally misstated Mr. Nelson's wishes about the handling of his affairs in the last days of his life.

While neither Ms. Hall nor Mr. Nelson can remember the details of their interaction leading up to the defective document,[20] HomeElderCare social workers, including Ms. Hall, have followed certain procedures. First, the social worker talks with the client, and then a draft of the living will is prepared by the social worker. The social worker explains various legal implications of the living will, such as the doctor's obligation to follow its provisions and the role of the proxy. The social worker also explains the living will to the proxy and then arranges for it to be signed and notarized. The social worker then delivers the living will to the client's primary care physician.[21]

The client is charged a fee that is based on the amount of time the social worker spends on the project.[22] Mr. Nelson paid $80 for his defective living will.[23]

---

13. *Id.* at ¶ 11.
14. *Id.* at ¶ 2.
15. *Id.* at ¶ 7.
16. *Id.* at ¶ 6.
17. *Id.* at ¶ 9.
18. Minn. Stat. § 145B.04 (1992).
19. Stip. ¶ 9.
20. *Id.* at ¶ 8.
21. *Id.* at ¶ 7.
22. *Id.* at ¶ 3.
23. *Id.* at ¶ 8.

Fortunately, Mr. Nelson's son, who is an attorney, became concerned when he realized that his father did not agree with the terms of the living will that had been prepared for him. The younger Mr. Nelson arranged for a substitute living will to be drafted by the family's attorney. The revised will accurately states Mr. Nelson's wishes.[24]

ARGUMENT

Summary

The trial court properly concluded that HomeElderCare's social worker engaged in the unauthorized practice of law and that the contract between Mr. Nelson and HomeElderCare thus is unenforceable.

To protect the public, the Minnesota statute on the unauthorized practice of law prohibits non-lawyers from practicing law. Yet HomeElderCare's social worker did precisely that when she drafted Mr. Nelson's defective living will, counseled him about it, and charged him for it. Because enforcement of the contract between HomeElderCare and Mr. Nelson for the preparation of his living will is contrary to the intent of the legislature, the contract is unenforceable. A social worker should not be paid for defective legal work.

Standard of Review

When reviewing an appeal from summary judgment, this Court determines whether there are any genuine issues of material fact and whether the trial court erred in its application of the law.[25] In the present case, there are no genuine issues of material fact because the parties stipulated to the facts. Therefore, the sole issue is whether the trial court correctly applied the law.

I. The trial court properly ruled that Appellant HomeElderCare's social worker engaged in the unauthorized practice of law when she prepared Respondent Mr. Nelson's living will for a fee.

Minnesota's unauthorized practice of law statute is designed to forestall poorly drawn legal documents due to "bungling use of legal terms and improper knowledge" of the law by non-lawyers.[26] Such poorly drawn documents may be invalid or operate contrary to the client's intent, yet

---

24. *Id.* at ¶ 10.
25. *Offerdahl v. U. of Minn. Hosp. & Clinics*, 426 N.W.2d 425, 427 (Minn. 1988).
26. *In re Est. of Peterson*, 42 N.W.2d 59, 63 (Minn. 1950) (involving drafting of a testamentary will).

their non-lawyer authors would not be subject to the supervision of the courts.[27] The situation involving Mr. Nelson is, unfortunately, a perfect example of the sort of situations that gave rise to the prohibition on the unauthorized practice of law. As a consequence of the actions of Ms. Hall, Mr. Nelson designated his minister as his proxy and guardian—even though this arrangement was not what he desired. It took a lawyer to correct the defective document to properly implement his desires.

More precisely, the Minnesota unauthorized practice of law statute renders it unlawful for non-lawyers to engage in the following activities:

> [1] for a fee or any consideration, to give legal advice or counsel, perform for or furnish to another legal services, . . .
>
> [2] for or without a fee or any consideration, to prepare, directly or through another, for another person . . . any will or testamentary disposition or instrument of trust serving purposes similar to those of a will, or
>
> [3] for a fee or any consideration, to prepare for another person, firm, or corporation, any other legal document.[28]

HomeElderCare social worker Kimberly Hall is not a lawyer. She has not been trained as a lawyer, has not passed the bar, and is not subject to the supervision of the Minnesota courts. Nonetheless, Ms. Hall practiced law in two respects.

First, contrary to the third prohibition (quoted above), social worker Hall prepared a legal document when she prepared Mr. Nelson's living will. While the unauthorized practice statute does not define "legal document," the Minnesota Living Will Act provides a suggest form for living wills which plainly states that the form is an "important legal document."[29] Furthermore, Mr. Nelson's living will is a "legal document" according to the plain meaning of the term. *Merriam-Webster's Collegiate Dictionary* defines "document" as "an original or official paper relied on as the basis, proof, or support of something" and "legal" as "conforming to or permitted by the law."[30] A living will is an official statement proving the declarant's wishes in the event of incapacitation, conforming to the requirements of the Minnesota Living Will Act, and imposing upon physicians the responsibilities set out

---

27. *Id.*
28. Minn. Stat. § 481.02 subdiv. 1 (1992) (numbers added).
29. Minn. Stat. § 145B.04 (1992).
30. *Merriam-Webster's Collegiate Dictionary* 342, 664 (10th ed., Merriam-Webster 1994).

in that statute.[31] In addition, HomeElderCare charged Mr. Nelson a fee for this service, thereby completing the violation of the third clause.

Second, contrary to the first prohibition (quoted above), social worker Hall gave legal advice and counsel to Mr. Nelson in the course of preparing his living will. The line between what is and what is not "legal advice and counsel" cannot be drawn with precision, because the practice of law overlaps with many other professions. For instance, in *Gardner v. Conway,*[32] the Minnesota Supreme Court observed that

> [i]n the field of income taxation, . . . we have an overlapping of both law and accounting. An accountant must adapt his [or her] accounting skills to the requirements of tax law, and therefore he [or she] must have a workable knowledge of law as applied to his [or her] field. By the same token, a lawyer must have some understanding of accounting . . . . The public interest does not permit an obliteration of all lines of demarcations. We cannot escape reality by hiding behind a facade of nomenclature and assume that "taxation," though composed of both law and accounting, is something *sui generis* and apart from the law . . . . If taxation is a hybrid of law and accounting, it does not follow that it is so wholly without the law that its legal activities may be pursued without proper qualifications and without court supervision.[33]

The *Gardner* court ruled that "whenever, as incidental to another . . . calling, a lay[person] . . . resolves legal questions for another . . . by giving . . . advice or by taking action . . . , he [or she] is practicing law if difficult or doubtful legal questions are involved which, to safeguard the public, reasonably demand the application of a trained legal mind."[34] The tax accountant in *Gardner* illegally practiced law when, in the course of preparing a tax return for a client, he provided information on various tax issues: tax treatment of business partnerships, the status of a common law wife on joint tax returns, and the deductibility of various expenditures.[35]

Ms. Hall, a social worker, similarly ventured into the realm of legal advice. Neither she nor Mr. Nelson can recall exactly what advice she gave Mr. Nelson when she prepared his living will. The parties have, however, stipulated that Ms. Hall would normally discuss the roles of proxies, guardians, and conservators. It also has been her practice to explain the legal obligations of doctors and other medical personnel in the event of a client's incapacitation. Furthermore, she has

---

31. Minn. Stat. § 145B.03 subdiv. 1.
32. 48 N.W.2d 788 (Minn. 1951).
33. *Id.* at 796 (citation omitted).
34. *Id.*
35. *Id.* at 792, 797-98.

explained the document to the client's witness and proxy, explained their roles to them, and supervised the execution of the living will.

These legal topics are as difficult and doubtful as the tax issues covered by the accountant in *Gardner*. They are legal matters covered in detail in the Minnesota Living Will Act.[36] Because the living will statute was enacted in 1989[37] and has yet to be interpreted by the appellate courts, its application to specific situations is uncertain. In addition, the specific issue on which Ms. Hall failed Mr. Nelson—the appointment of a guardian—is regulated not only by the living will statute but also by a separate extensive and complex statute on guardianship.[38] In general, legal regulation of medical decisionmaking is in a phase of rapid change, with both statutory and constitutional dimensions.[39]

The *Gardner* rule must be applied in a "common sense way which will protect the public and not hamper or burden that interest with impractical and technical restrictions which have no reasonable justification."[40] The restriction on social workers preparing living wills may burden the social worker who wishes to practice law. But the restriction is not impractical or merely technical; it is more than reasonably justified when viewed from the proper perspective—the client's. The client's need for legal assistance is recognized in the statutory living will form itself, which states that a professional should be consulted if there are any questions.[41] That professional should be a lawyer because very significant legal issues are covered in the document. These issues touch on important aspects of client autonomy, as in Mr. Nelson's case, and also—literally—matters of life and death.

The living will resembles a testamentary will. Only lawyers may prepare testamentary wills for other people.[42] So too should a lawyer be consulted for assistance in preparation of a living will. The proper role for a social worker is to serve as a liaison with the client's lawyer for a client needing assistance in obtaining legal services, a role permitted by the unauthorized practice statute.[43]

---

36. Minn. Stat. §§ 145B.01-.17.
37. 1989 Minn. Laws 8.
38. *See* Minn. Stat. §§ 525.532-.6198 (1992).
39. *See generally* Howard Orenstein, David Bishop & Leigh D. Mathison, *Minnesota's Living Will . . . ,* 46 Bench & B. Minn. 21, 21-25 (Aug. 1989) (citing *Jarvis v. Levine,* 418 N.W.2d 139 (Minn. 1988)).
40. *Gardner,* 48 N.W.2d at 797.
41. *See* Minn. Stat. § 145B.04.
42. Minn. Stat. § 481.02 subdiv. 1 (second prohibition stated above).
43. See *id.* at subdiv. 3(6), subdiv. 7. Of course, in both testamentory and living will situations, the client can also choose to draft the document himself, for reasons of cost or personal choice.

Furthermore, the charging of a fee suggests that the services offered involve a difficult or doubtful legal issue.[44] HomeElderCare charged Mr. Nelson a fee for the preparation of his living will.

The trial court's ruling in favor of Mr. Nelson is consistent with the law in other jurisdictions. For example, the Florida Supreme Court held that a non-lawyer could distribute and type standardized legal forms, but the court prohibited the non-lawyer from providing any specific assistance in the preparation of the forms, answering questions on how to complete the form, or correcting any errors and omissions made by her customers.[45] Other courts also have held that distributing standardized legal forms with general instructions may be permitted, but personal contact between a non-lawyer and a client is the unauthorized practice of law when there is explanation, advice, or assistance in filling out the form.[46]

In summary, social worker Hall violated the unauthorized practice statute when she prepared Mr. Nelson's defective living will and again when she counseled him about it, both for a fee. The declaratory judgment should be affirmed so as to protect Mr. Nelson and others like him from the potentially very serious consequences of incompetent legal practice.

II. Because of this unauthorized practice of law, the contract between Appellant HomeElderCare and Respondent Mr. Nelson for preparation of the living will is unenforceable, as the trial court properly held.

If a statute requires a license to perform a professional service and an unlicensed practitioner enters into a contract to perform that service, that contract is generally void.[47] However, the courts also examine the legislative intent behind the licensing statute to determine whether the contract should be illegal and void.[48]

---

44. *Cardinal v. Merrill Lynch Realty/Burnet, Inc.*, 433 N.W.2d 864, 869 (Minn. 1988).
45. *Fla. Bar v. Brumbaugh*, 355 So. 2d 1186, 1194 (Fla. 1978).
46. *E.g., State Bar of Mich. v. Cramer*, 249 N.W.2d 1, 8-9 (Mich. 1976); *Or. State Bar v. Gilchrist*, 538 P.2d 913, 919 (Or. 1975).
47. E. Allan Farnsworth, *Contracts* § 5.6, at 377-79 (2d ed., Little, Brown & Co. 1990).
48. *E.g., Buckley v. Humason*, 52 N.W. 385 (Minn. 1892) (real-estate broker held unable to recover fee for real-estate services because he was not licensed as required by statute).

In *Dick Weatherston's Associated Mechanical Services v. Minnesota Mutual Life Insurance Co.*,[49] on an unusual set of facts, the court enforced a contract involving an engineer who was not licensed as required by statute.[50] The contract involved installation of an air-conditioning system and associated incidental design work. The court there found that the agreement between the customer and the engineer was "free from any element of fraud, incompetence, or misrepresentation" and was "in no way inimical to life, health, property or public welfare."[51] The same, unfortunately, cannot be said about the contract between HomeElderCare and Mr. Nelson.

There are significant factual differences between the situation in *Weatherston's* and the present case as to the critical issue of competence. Mr. Weatherston, though unlicensed, was nonetheless competent and supervised. He had a bachelor of science degree in mechanical engineering, several years of experience in project engineering, and licensure in other states. He clearly was a competent professional. In addition, he was supervised by another engineer and an architect on behalf of the client; his proposals were actually subject to their approval.[52]

By contrast, social worker Hall is not well trained in the law. She is not licensed as a lawyer in Minnesota or any other state. She has not attended law school. She simply heard a brief presentation on the general subject of living wills. Having completed only ten living wills, Ms. Hall can boast of only minimal experience in this area. Thus, unlike the engineer in *Weatherston's*, Ms. Hall is not a fully competent professional. Furthermore, Hall works independently and is not under the supervision of a lawyer.

The issue of competence is critical, given *Weatherston's* focus on legislative purpose[53] and the intent of the legislature in enacting the unauthorized practice statute. The purpose of that statute is to protect the public from the very serious harm that can result from the practice of law by incompetent individuals not subject to direct supervision of the courts.[54] The error in Mr. Nelson's living will, drafted by social worker Hall, is a clear example of the type of harm the legislation is designed to prevent. Enforcement of the contract would effectively endorse activity that harmed Mr. Nelson and runs contrary to the public interest as determined by the legislature.

---

49. 100 N.W.2d 819 (Minn. 1960).
50. *Id.* at 824-25.
51. *Id.* at 824.
52. *Id.* at 821-22.
53. *See id.* at 823-24.
54. *Peterson,* 42 N.W.2d at 63-64.

Finally, HomeElderCare clearly stands to gain from enforcement of the contract as a result of the fee charged Mr. Nelson. Although the living will itself might be enforceable, the Minnesota Supreme Court indicated that "a different situation arises where an unlicensed practitioner seeks to recover fees for his performance of legal services."[55] And unlike Mr. Weatherston's business, HomeElderCare is seeking payment precisely for unauthorized legal services, not for a broader contract that incidentally includes legal services. A social worker should not be paid for defective legal work.

In summary, the contract between HomeElderCare and Mr. Nelson is tainted by incompetence, thus violates the statutory purpose of protecting the public from defective legal work performed by non-lawyers, and yet provides compensation to HomeElderCare for that work. The trial court properly deemed the contract unenforceable, and the declaratory judgment should be affirmed.

CONCLUSION

The trial court's grant of summary declaratory judgment for Mr. Nelson should be affirmed because the trial court properly ruled that:

(1)   HomeElderCare engaged in the unauthorized practice of law, and
(2)   the contract between HomeElderCare and Mr. Nelson is thus unenforceable.

Dated: _Feb. 1, 1994_   Respectfully submitted,

                                             By: _Albert Frank_
                                             Albert Frank (No. 14711)
                                             Attorney for Respondent Roger Nelson
                                             Law Offices of Albert Frank
                                             672 Oak Street
                                             Versailles, MN 50001
                                             (222) 777-7771

---

55. *Id.* at 62.

Nelson v. HomeElderCare Oral Argument
Before the Minnesota Court of Appeals

This is a transcript of a mock appellate oral argument for *Nelson v. HomeElderCare* at the Minnesota Court of Appeals, which is the intermediate appellate court in Minnesota. The judges were portrayed by Professors Ken Kirwin, Denise Roy, and Curt Stine, of William Mitchell College of Law. Arguing the case were law students Katie Crosby Lehmann and Tony Massaros. The time limits being observed in this case were twelve minutes for the appellant's main argument, twelve minutes for the respondent's argument, and three minutes for the rebuttal.

As you read each question from the judge, ask yourself how you would have answered the question; then read the advocate's answer and evaluate it against your own.

Judge 2: You may begin, counsel.

CHIEF JUDGE RECOGNIZES APPELLANT'S COUNSEL

Appellant's Counsel: May it please the court. My name is Katie Crosby Lehmann, and I represent appellant HomeElderCare. I wish to reserve three minutes for rebuttal.

introduction of self & client; reserve time for rebuttal

roadmap

There are two issues that we will discuss today. The first deals with whether HomeElderCare social workers engage in the unauthorized practice of law while preparing living wills for their clients. The second issue is whether Respondent Nelson's contract for the living will preparation is valid due to unauthorized practice of law concerns, fraud, and incompetency concerns.

The facts have been stipulated to by the parties. HomeElderCare is a private, nonprofit corporation that employs a staff of geriatric social workers. The social workers provide various services to their clients upon their clients' request.

fact statement HomeElderCare

HomeElderCare clients asked HomeElderCare to offer them an additional service: the service of preparing living wills for them. HomeElderCare agreed with their clients' request and now offers the service. The fee for this service is based on the time of completion. The fee is no different for this service than any other service.

living will service

Kimberly Hall is a social worker for HomeElderCare. She is highly educated and trained in living will preparation. She has been a social worker for over twelve years. She prepared Mr. Nelson's living will. A living will states the signer's medical treatment desires if and when the signer becomes incapacitated. Mr. Nelson is 78 years old and in declining health due to diabetes. Mr. Nelson's living will did not exactly reflect his wishes. However, there is no evidence that it was Ms. Hall versus Mr. Nelson himself who caused this misstatement. Ms. Hall believes she suggested Mr. Nelson to see an attorney if he had any further questions regarding his living will. Mr. Nelson's own son is an attorney, and he did not speak to his son or any other attorney.

Mr. Nelson's living will

procedure
procedural posture

standard of review

1st argument: unau-
thorized practice of law
difficult or doubtful
legal question
UPL statute

Respondent sued HomeElderCare seeking to void his contract for the living will preparation service and requested a declaratory judgment to determine the validity of the contract. Both parties moved for summary judgment. The district court granted Respondent declaratory judgment and summary judgment. The district court held that the living will preparation service constituted the unauthorized practice of law and that the contract for such services was invalid. HomeElderCare appeals. The standard of review of appeal is de novo.

The first issue addresses the unauthorized practice of law concern, joined with the difficult-and-doubtful-legal-question test. The Minnesota Supreme Court held that when a person's primary business is not to provide legal services, a person may dabble in the law so long as he or she is not answering difficult or doubtful legal questions. The unauthorized practice of law statute states that "it shall be unlawful for any person except members of the bar of Minnesota for a fee to give legal advice or counsel or to prepare for another person any other legal document." The unauthorized practice of law statute must be analyzed with the supreme court's difficult-and-doubtful-legal-question test. This test is measured by a reasonably intelligent person, not a lawyer, with knowledge of similar transactions. The test is to be applied in a common-sense way with the goal of protecting primarily the interests of the public without burdening the public with technical restrictions. It is a flexible test and demands a case-by-case analysis.

three examples

What is and what is not a difficult and doubtful question is not crystal clear. The following examples, all involving the charging of a fee, have been held to not be difficult and doubtful legal questions. The first is preparing a tax return, including calculating income in taxable years. The second is preparing documents for a real-estate closing, answering questions on the real-estate closing documents, and lastly, completing an affidavit and assignment for contract for deed.

question: real-estate
example vs. HEC
practice

Judge 3: Counsel, my understanding is that real-estate documents are pretty fixed in their content, whereas the living will statute talks about the form being substantially in the form as in the statute. Doesn't that suggest that deviation from the form is permitted so that's somewhat different from the real-estate documents?

answer

Appellant's Counsel: That's a question that really is beyond what the HomeElderCare service does. HomeElderCare social workers do not deviate from the forms. They think that if they deviate or interpret the form at all, then you could be reaching the line of what is a difficult and doubtful question.

question: risks in HEC
practice

Judge 3: But if they don't deviate from the form, is it possible that they are channeling people into a particular format, whether it fits that particular person's needs or not?

answer

Appellant's Counsel: The form they use is the statutorily approved living will form. This is the only service that they offer their clients. The clients come to them, and they ask them to help them guide them through the completion of this form. If their clients wish to alter or deviate, or if they have any concerns about following the form, then the social worker stops what they are doing and directs the person to see an attorney.

question: UPL rule on
hypothetical

Judge 3: So that any deviation from the form would constitute the practice of law, you think?

answer

Appellant's Counsel: It could be. It's reaching that fuzzy line of what may be the difficult and doubtful question, but it's really not an issue here because our social workers do not deviate from the form whatsoever.

An example of what is a difficult and doubtful legal question is when a person holding himself out as a tax expert gives advice on partnerships, valid marriages, common-law marriages, and improvements. Considering these examples, it is clear that a person can complete legal documents or guide another through a legal document as long as it is only an incidental part of the person's business and it does not involve answering difficult and doubtful legal questions.

another example of UPL

Judge 1: Well, counsel, doesn't the last page of the living will form refer to such concepts as proxy and guardian and conservator? Aren't those just as difficult or complicated concepts as the ones that you just referred to?

question: legal concepts in living will

Appellant's Counsel: Those are legal terms, but the social workers have been trained by an attorney on the definitions of those terms. The social workers in return offer those definitions to their clients. If that does not satisfy their clients' needs, the social worker recommends that the client seek an attorney's advice for further explanation. Because they are limiting themselves on what they do explain to the clients, they are not reaching the line of a difficult and doubtful legal question; the social workers simply lead their clients through the living will form. They answer simple questions on definitions, and, therefore, because they are not deviating from the form or altering the form in any way, they do not reach the line of answering difficult and doubtful legal questions and are not practicing law.

answer

Judge 2: Can you help us by telling us what kind of problems the clients have in filling out the forms? Why do they need assistance at all in going through the form?

question: client's need for assistance

Appellant's Counsel: The clients came to HomeElderCare and asked them to offer this service to them. They want HomeElderCare to provide the statutorily approved form to them, read through the form with them, and answer simple questions as they go along. What the social workers do is take the client's answers to the forms and fill in the form. After it is filled in, the client and the social worker go over the form to make sure it fits the client's needs. At the end, the social worker recommends that if the client has any further questions, they seek an attorney for more detailed explanation.

answer

HomeElderCare does charge a fee for this service. The fee in the past has triggered the difficult-and-doubtful-legal-question test. However, it is only a factor in the unauthorized practice of law analysis. Charging a fee cannot convert an otherwise lawful transaction into the unauthorized practice of law. Because the service is lawful and the fee is reasonable, the service is valid.

relevance of fee

Judge 1: Excuse me, counsel. Isn't this quite different from the previous cases where the work was really incident to some other transaction, like preparing a tax return or closing a real-estate transaction? Here the work is actually just doing the document.

question: incidental service

Appellant's Counsel: It is different from the previous examples; however, it is different in a better way. The HomeElderCare clients are only being charged for exactly the time it takes a social worker to lead them through the forms. In the real-estate example, the client was being charged whether or not the work was performed or not. So we think this is an even fairer way to establish the fee-calculation system.

answer

The beginning of the statutory living will form states that the living will is a legal document. A driver's license, employee handbook, and purchase agreements are also legal documents. The unauthorized practice of law statute refers to legal

legal document

documents, but surely it does not require all legal documents to be completed by attorneys.

The purpose of the unauthorized practice of law statute is to protect the public from fraudulent legal service. This purpose is not served by limiting the living will preparation to attorneys only. Requiring attorneys to complete the living will form runs counter to the purpose of the living will statute; the living will is to be distributed and used by members of the public. Therefore, completing the living will does not constitute the unauthorized practice of law.

2nd argument: contract validity

UPL factor

The second issue deals with the validity of Mr. Nelson's contract with HomeElderCare for the living will preparation service. Respondent must prove two issues to establish the invalidity of the contract. First, Respondent must prove that the contract constitutes unauthorized practice of law and second that the contract involved fraudulent or incompetent service. The unauthorized practice of law has already been discussed, and it's clear that social workers are not answering difficult and doubtful legal questions and are not engaging in the unauthorized practice of law. Even if it is found that the unauthorized practice of law exists, the contract is valid if there is no harm to the public due to fraudulent or incompetent service. The social workers have completed over forty forms for satisfied clients. There is no evidence that it was Ms. Hall versus Respondent himself who caused misstatement of Respondent's living will.

incompetence & fraud

question: other clients' situations

Judge 3: Counsel, have any of the living wills executed under the supervision of your client's employees actually been used? Have any of the persons who executed them become terminal and, therefore, someone had to take a careful look at the document?

answer

Appellant's Counsel: None of the clients have become terminal; however, we are confident in our social workers' ability to complete the living will forms competently.

question: role of attorneys

Judge 2: Counsel, does anyone such as an attorney periodically review the forms that have been completed to see how the social workers are performing?

answer

Appellant's Counsel: No. The social workers follow all the instructions on the living will form, and that is not one of the instructions included on the form.

There is no evidence of fraudulent or incompetent service by the social policy workers. If we deem the living contracts invalid, we are only harming the people who ask for the service—the elderly clients in need of the emotional support of HomeElderCare social workers. The social workers can ably perform this service and provide their clients with the emotional support.

conclusion and request for relief

In conclusion, HomeElderCare and Ms. Hall request the court to vacate the district court's declaratory judgment, reverse the summary judgment in favor of Respondent, and rule that HomeElderCare's preparation of Mr. Nelson's living will does not involve unauthorized practice of law or incompetent service, and rule that the contract is valid.

CHIEF JUDGE RECOGNIZES RESPONDENT'S COUNSEL

Judge 2: All right, counsel. Go ahead.

introduction of self & client

Respondent's Counsel: May it please the Court, my name is Tony Massaros, and I am counsel for Mr. Roger Nelson.

The issue in this case is whether a social worker should be paid for incompetent legal work.

theory of case

While opposing counsel has generally stated the facts accurately, I would like to make a few clarifications so as to make perfectly clear what it is we are dealing with in this case. In light of Mr. Nelson's age and condition, he desired to put his affairs in order now so that if he became incapacitated his wishes would be respected. A HomeElderCare social worker, a non-lawyer, prepared a living will in a way that did not reflect Mr. Nelson's wishes as to the person to be designated as his guardian. Fortunately, a lawyer corrected the document before any serious harm occurred to Mr. Nelson.

fact statement

My argument today has two points. First, HomeElderCare engaged in the unauthorized practice of law. Second, the contract between HomeElderCare and Mr. Nelson is, therefore, unenforceable. In short, the decision by the district court was correct and should be affirmed by this court. The main point that I would like you to remember is that a social worker should not receive payment for poorly performed legal work.

transition to argument

roadmap

Beginning first with the unauthorized practice of law: the Minnesota unauthorized practice of law statute was violated by HomeElderCare in two ways. First, non-lawyer Kimberly Hall prepared a legal document. Second, she provided legal advice and counsel. Either one of these actions is sufficient to find a violation of the statute.

1st argument: unauthorized practice of law

overview

The Minnesota unauthorized practice of law statute makes it unlawful for non-attorneys to prepare legal documents for a fee. A living will is a legal document. Indeed, the legislature specifically characterized the sample form as "an important legal document." The plain meaning of the term also supports such an interpretation.

legal document

Kimberly Hall is not an attorney. She is a social worker who prepared a living will for a fee and thereby engaged in the unauthorized practice of law.

social worker & fee

Secondly, while opposing counsel characterizes the social worker's actions as merely guiding the elderly patients through the process of creating a living will, a more accurate characterization is that the social worker in this case actually gave legal advice and counsel to Mr. Nelson. An individual practices law if difficult or doubtful legal questions are involved which, to safeguard the public, require legal expertise.

legal advice & counsel

Judge 3: Counsel, my understanding is that the legislature enacting the living will statute intended for the document to be very easily executed. It did adopt two different ways to execute the document. Wouldn't it be appropriate for this court to authorize persons other than lawyers, such as social workers, to help with the execution of these documents? The legislature has indicated that it is the policy of the state to encourage this document for persons.

question: legislative intent & policy

Respondent's Counsel: It is true that the legislature has made clear that it believes it is good public policy to encourage the use of living wills. We don't see that there is really any conflict between that policy and the policy underlying the unauthorized practice of law statute. We think the two can coexist very comfortably. What we have here, though, is a situation where the policies that guide the unauthorized practice of law statute—namely, to protect the public from the very serious harm that can result from activities or actions by individuals who are not lawyers—that should be given the primary consideration.

answer

Judge 3: But don't the issues that arise under the content of the living will—they are medical issues, are they not, not legal issues—decisions as to what kind of

question: medical issues in living will

medical care someone might take? Isn't it true that geriatric social workers might indeed have more knowledge of medical issues than would a lawyer?

answer

Respondent's Counsel: It is true that there are certainly a lot of medical issues involved in the living will form, but there are also a good number of legal issues as well that we believe require expertise in order to provide a proper service to these clients. We see a social worker discussing the role of proxies, guardians, and conservators; explaining the legal obligations of doctors; explaining the document to the client's witness and proxy.

question: difficult or doubtful legal questions
answer

Judge 1: Are those really such difficult and doubtful issues? Isn't it fairly simple to explain in everyday language what a proxy or a conservator is?

Respondent's Counsel: Well, we think that it is difficult and doubtful, and we think the proof of that is actually the fact of this case. And we had a situation here where the person that Mr. Nelson wanted to be his guardian was in fact not made his guardian as a result of the actions of HomeElderCare. So we believe that indeed there are difficult and doubtful legal questions being addressed here, and therefore the actions of the HomeElderCare social workers did indeed constitute the unauthorized practice of law.

question: purpose of living will statute

Judge 1: Isn't it likely that if we don't allow this to be done by the social workers that it won't be done at all? Wouldn't that run contrary to the legislature's purpose to encourage living wills?

answer

Respondent's Counsel: We believe that there are certainly a lot of other options, a lot of other ways, that the living will can be completed for these individuals. What we're saying here is that in this case the HomeElderCare social workers should not be providing legal advice and counsel in the process of creating those living wills. We believe that the individuals themselves could easily do it—could complete the form. They could have friends and family do it.

policy behind unauthorized practice statute

But the key that we have here is, we have legal advice and counsel being provided by somebody who is not authorized and licensed to practice law. And that's really the issue that we have here, not so much the question of whether or not living wills are appropriate or whether or not the legislature is encouraging the use of living wills. What we have here is a need to protect the public from people practicing law who are not competent to practice law. We believe that the difficult and doubtful questions are clearly evidenced by the facts of this case and that it took somebody trained in the law to fix the document that was drafted by the HomeElderCare social workers.

question: need for HEC service

Judge 1: Well, don't the facts of this case indicate that the friends and relatives or other people that you mentioned are apparently not filling this need, because HomeElderCare apparently did do some forty wills and charged, at least in this case, $80, and that shows that there is a need for the service, doesn't it?

answer

Respondent's Counsel: It shows that they did that. I don't know that it shows that that is the only alternative that was available. They do provide other services that require legal expertise in those areas—for example, testamentary wills, with real-estate transactions. There they have also provided service to the HomeElder-Care clients, and there they have acted primarily as a liaison with attorneys, recognizing that they really don't have the skill and ability to engage in this sort of activity.

Judge 3: Counsel, I'm a bit concerned as to where you would have us draw the line. Are you saying that if a person were brought to a hospital losing consciousness—about to lose the capacity to execute a document of this sort—that the people at the medical facility could not assist in the execution of the document? We'd have to wait until an attorney was called to come?

question: hypothetical emergency situation

Respondent's Counsel: No, I don't think that we would say that that was the case. I think if a person in that situation—a hospital worker, for example—just wrote down exactly what the patient wanted, there was no discussion of what the terms mean but basically did it in a sort of clerical way, I don't think that we would have the unauthorized practice of law in such a situation.

answer

Judge 3: But isn't that what happened here?

question: this case

Respondent's Counsel: Well, we don't believe that it is. In fact, we have the record which indicates that they explain the document to the doctors, they explain it to the proxies, they explain it to the witnesses, and they actually oversee the execution of the document. So we have something very much more involved here than simply completing a form.

answer

The second point that I would like to cover is the question of the enforceability of the contract between HomeElderCare and Mr. Nelson. It's clearly established that if a statute requires licensing a person to perform a professional service and a person who is unlicensed enters into a contract to do that, then that contract is generally considered void. And we believe that that's what we have here and that the contract between HomeElderCare and Mr. Nelson should therefore be unenforceable.

2nd argument: contract validity

Judge 2: Counsel, don't you also have to show fraud or incompetence in order to prevail on the contract claim?

question: requirements of legal rule

Respondent's Counsel: That is true, your honor, and we believe that we have clear evidence of incompetence here. The proof of this is that the living will had to be redone; it had to be revised so that the interests of Mr. Nelson were met, so that his desires were satisfied. So we believe that indeed we do have evidence of incompetence in this case.

answer

Judge 1: Well, opposing counsel indicates that the record is unclear as to whether it was maybe Mr. Nelson's own misunderstanding that caused this. We don't really have it clear on the record that it was the HomeElderCare worker's incompetence that produced this. Isn't that true?

question: record on key issue

Respondent's Counsel: I think that we can make the assumption that indeed it was the incompetence of the HomeElderCare social worker. I think that this further demonstrates why you need somebody with a trained legal background to make these kinds of decisions so that these kinds of questions are not at issue after we have the living will being formed.

answer

Judge 3: Counsel, real-estate agents often execute legal documents related to real estate; they have expertise in the area. Here we're dealing with social workers who have expertise in this particular area. Why shouldn't we treat them like real-estate agents, who are authorized to conduct these affairs?

question: analogy to real-estate agents

Respondent's Counsel: Well, I think the difference, your honor, is that with the real-estate transactions the legislature has chosen to carve out an exception for real-estate agents who engage in certain activities such as closing and other real-estate

answer

related matters. So I think that we have a very different situation there than we do in the situation involving HomeElderCare.

conclusion & request for relief

In conclusion, the district court's decision should be affirmed. There was an unauthorized practice of law, and the contract between HomeElderCare and Mr. Nelson is therefore unenforceable. A social worker should not be paid for incompetent, unlicensed, irresponsible legal work.

Thank you.

CHIEF JUDGE RECOGNIZES APPELLANT'S COUNSEL FOR REBUTTAL
theory of case

Judge 2: You may begin.

Appellant's Counsel: HomeElderCare social workers do not hold themselves out as attorneys. The social workers simply want to offer their clients a complete range of services to meet their clients' medical and emotional needs.

1. not legal advice

Opposing counsel stated that Ms. Hall gave legal advice and counsel to Mr. Nelson. In order to practice law, Ms. Hall and any HomeElderCare social worker would need to answer difficult and doubtful legal questions and violate the unauthorized practice of law statute. Ms. Hall and all HomeElderCare social workers do not make deviations or alterations to the living will form. They simply provide the form to their clients, read the form through with their clients, and fill in the blanks with the answers the clients provide them. They are not answering difficult or doubtful legal questions, and they are not engaging in the unauthorized practice of law.

suitability of social workers

The social workers are exactly the people who should provide this service to their elderly clients. They can build on their existing relationship with their clients. They are trained in medical and ethical issues affecting the elderly and the terminally ill. The social workers are better qualified than an attorney to answer these medical and ethical questions. There is no need for an attorney to complete this living will form because the social workers are competent, and they are not engaging in the unauthorized practice of law or answering difficult and doubtful legal questions.

clients' needs

The living will service by HomeElderCare is a service created at their HomeElderCare clients' request. The social workers do not answer difficult and doubtful legal questions; therefore, there is no concern about the unauthorized practice of law.

2. cause of error in Mr. Nelson's case

Mr. Nelson is 78 years old and in declining health. There is no evidence that the misstatement in his living will was due to Ms. Hall's incompetence versus an answer Mr. Nelson provided to Ms. Hall when Ms. Hall completed Mr. Nelson's living will.

question: vulnerability of clients & trust in HEC

Judge 2: Counsel, I'm concerned about the trust level that the HomeElderCare clients have in the social workers. It seems to me that the very trust that they place in those workers could lead them to give undue weight to any kind of—it wouldn't be legal advice, but—legal definitions provided by the social workers, and that they could be lulled into a sense of security in filling out these forms where they ought to be more questioning about what the meaning of the form is.

answer

Appellant's Counsel: At the end of the preparation of each living will, the social worker does recommend that the client seek an attorney's advice if they have any further questions or concerns. HomeElderCare does provide their social workers with training and education in the preparation of these forms. The training was done by an attorney, so there really is no concern that the definitions would be inaccurate.

The social workers are protecting their client's interest and serving the public interest by offering this living will preparation service. Without this service it is likely that the clients will not have a living will if and when they become incapacitated.

Judge 2: Counsel, your time's up. Thank you.

Appellant's Counsel: Thank you.

*CHIEF JUDGE ENDS
ORAL ARGUMENT*

APPENDIX I

THE WRITING PROCESS

A. The Inventor Stage
B. The Architect Stage
C. The Costume-Maker Stage
D. The Critic Stage

The writing process actually is several processes, which are more or less sequential. To write well, you must succeed in all of the following stages, each symbolized in this appendix by a non-legal profession:

- figuring out what to say—the inventor stage,
- designing the paper—the architect stage,
- crafting the first draft—the costume-maker, and
- refining the paper—the critic.[1]

A. THE INVENTOR STAGE

In this early stage, you figure out what to say. As an inventor, you understand and analyze the raw materials available to you (the facts, the primary authorities, helpful commentary), consider what you are trying to accomplish (your client's interests as well as the audience and purpose of your paper), and conceptualize a viable and creative solution (the legal meaning of the client's situation).

One key to being a successful inventor is fully understanding the raw materials available to you. In the practice of law, this entails reading, briefing, and fusing cases; reading, briefing, and interpreting statutes; reading commentary; and assembling and understanding your client's facts. Another key to being a

---

1. *See* Betty S. Flowers, *Madman, Architect, Carpenter, Judge: Roles and the Writing Process,* 44 Proceedings of the Conference of College Teachers of English 7–10 (1979) (cited and discussed in Bryan A. Garner, *Legal Writing in Plain English: A Text with Exercises* 5–10 (2001)).

successful inventor is combining your raw materials systematically. In law this entails reasoning deductively, reasoning by example, and policy analysis; in advisory contexts, also developing and assessing options for the client to consider; and in advocacy contexts, also developing a theory of the case. Yet another key to being a successful inventor is considering what you are trying to accomplish. In law this entails analysis of the audience and purpose of your paper.

Inventors are not only systematic and thorough thinkers; they also are creative thinkers. Here are some strategies that may be useful as you build your capacity for creativity in the legal context:

- When you first learn of a client's situation, that is, before you research and analyze it, mull it over a bit, decide what you would do if you were in charge of making the rules, and write out your impression of the case or matter.
- If you are handling a dispute, consider: What are the equities? Which facts are truly compelling? What seems right or wrong?
- If you are handling a deal, consider: Why is this a deal that the law should enforce? What are the risks that should be addressed? What would make the deal fair to both sides?
- Leave behind everything you have in writing or on your computer, take a walk (or jog, or ski, or ride a bike, etc.), and let yourself think about the situation and your legal analysis in an unstructured way.
- Engage in a continuous writing exercise. Take pen in hand or turn on your computer, set a timer for five minutes, and write for five solid minutes, uncritically but continuously.
- Within the bounds of professional responsibility rules, talk about the client's situation. Although most of us enjoy and benefit from talking to another person about a problem, legal rules about confidentiality of client information will ordinarily prohibit you from talking to persons outside your firm. In any event, you can talk to the mirror or to a tape recorder; you may find that you think more creatively when you speak than when you write.
- Keep a small notepad or PDA with you. You may find that an idea pops into your head when you least expect it, e.g., when you are shopping for groceries or reading a book. Be sure to capture those ideas for your file.

B. The Architect Stage

In this stage, you design the paper. You organize the many factual and legal points to be made into logical and effective frameworks: for the paper as a whole, for each component of the paper, for each part, etc. Recall the extended house analogy, developed in Chapters 11 through 14, all pertaining to the office memo.

To a certain extent, the overall structure of your paper will be set by standard conventions of legal writing or indeed by format requirements of the courts. Within each major component, you will have considerable latitude in structuring the material. Standard approaches include chronological, topical, and perceptual approaches to organizing the facts; the IRAC template; principles such as claims/defenses and substantive/procedural rules for organizing the discussion of the office memo; and strategic organizing principles in the advocacy setting, such as the sandwich sequence.

As you decide how to structure the paper, be sure that you fully develop each point you plan to make. To do so, ask yourself two questions: Does this point presuppose any other point? What is the implication of this point? Try various ways of depicting the organization of your material, such as an outline, flowchart, and timeline.

Depending on whether you are a big-picture or detail-oriented thinker, you may prefer to develop your framework and fit your points into it, or you may prefer to organize your points into clumps that give rise to the framework. Here are some mechanisms that may be useful:

- Label each source (whether factual or legal) with the main topics from your framework (again, whether factual or legal) covered therein. Many sources will address more than one topic.
- Create file folders (on paper or in your computer) for the main topics, and file your sources and ideas accordingly.
- Select several colors of highlighters for your main topics, and highlight key passages accordingly.
- Make actual piles of your ideas, and lay them out in a logical sequence or set of piles of related thoughts.
- Try out more than one organizing principle, especially if you are having difficulty coming up with a perfectly logical approach.
- You most likely will have some material that does not seem to fit into the framework or any of your piles. Do not discard that material; simply set it aside for consideration at a later stage of the writing process.

C. The Costume-Maker Stage

In this stage, you create the first draft. As a costume-maker executes with care the design drawn by the costume-designer, so you will follow the design developed in the second stage. And as a costume-maker makes adjustments as needed in the design, so you may find as you write the first draft that revisions in the initial design are warranted.

For people who love to write, this is the most exhilarating stage. But for many writers, this is the most difficult step. You may find it difficult to get started. Or you may be exasperated by the time it takes to create a first draft of even the smallest part of the paper. You probably will become aware of omissions or mistakes in your work to date and begin to lose confidence. You may tire out well before you reach the last component. Here are some suggestions that may ease the burden of this third stage:

- Most important, be sure that you take the time and put in the effort to accomplish the first two stages well.

- Almost as important, trust that you will be able to improve your draft later on; do not require perfection in your first draft.
- Think about how you prefer to generate text. The obvious choice is to start writing on your computer. Less obvious approaches are to write a few pages longhand, to talk into a tape recorder and then transcribe your tape, and to type with your monitor off (so you are not drawn into fussing too much over each sentence).
- There are three standard approaches to choosing where to start. First, start at the beginning—the logical choice. Second, start with whichever component seems the most achievable, even if that component does not come first—the easiest-first choice. Third, start with the most challenging or core material, even if that material does not come first—the get-it-over-with choice. All of these can work.
- Put a pad of paper beside you on which to note minor concerns or questions to address later. Or write those questions into your paper in a distinctive font or in footnotes. Do not try to resolve all of your minor questions along the way.
- On the other hand, if you encounter a major concern or question, put your draft aside, write out the question, take a brief break, and try to solve the question before you go on. You will not want to continue too far down a perilous road.
- Plan to spend several sessions writing the paper, even if it is short. Develop a plan for how much you hope to accomplish during each session. In other words, pace yourself.
- Stop working when fatigue sets in. You will lose confidence and probably generate inferior text if you push yourself too long.

D. THE CRITIC STAGE

In this last stage you refine the paper. Like a theatre, art, or book critic, you approach the paper as a work of art, seeking to discern its strengths and weaknesses, fundamental and minute. Unlike the critic of theatre, art, or books, you act on your observations to refine, if not perfect, the paper.

This stage is generally called "editing." To edit your own work effectively, you must both distance yourself from your draft and immerse yourself thoroughly in it. This is an apparent, but not actual, paradox. You must distance yourself emotionally from your draft, so that you are able to review it dispassionately. Then you must immerse yourself in it intellectually, reviewing every aspect of the draft and reforming what needs improvement.[2]

1. Distancing Yourself from Your Draft

Editing your own work generally is much more difficult than editing someone else's work. It is difficult to see your work as someone else sees it. It is difficult

___
2. For further editing suggestions, see Mary Barnard Ray & Jill J. Ramsfield, *Legal Writing: Getting It Right and Getting It Written* 122–27 (4th ed. 2005).

to delete or revise a passage on which you expended significant time and effort.

An excellent means of gaining the necessary perspective on your work is, of course, to ask an intelligent and careful reader to review your draft and give you suggestions. If your situation does not permit this assistance, or even if it does, you may want to try the following strategies:

- Leave your draft for a few days. It will seem less familiar, less a part of you when you return to it—and some good ideas may come to you during your respite.
- Try editing the draft somewhere other than where you wrote it. Similarly, try shifting from one mode of writing to another. For example, if you wrote the draft at the computer, start your editing on a printout of the paper.
- Re-read the assignment, and think again about your various audiences and their needs in reading the paper. As you turn to the draft, imagine you are a member of each audience.
- Imagine an intelligent and interested but uninformed reader looking over your shoulder. What questions would he or she ask? What problems would he or she see?
- When you begin your editing, read your draft aloud.

2. Immersing Yourself in Your Draft

It almost always helps to work through a draft several times, with a specific task for each run-through. Different people begin and end with different tasks. Some are big-picture tasks that fall within the category of "revising"; others are detail-oriented tasks that fall within the category of "polishing." See Exhibit App. I.1.[3] Presented in the order that generally is the most efficient, the tasks are:

Verify the accuracy of the factual and legal assertions you have made, and make any needed corrections. Look over the factual material on which the paper is based, and review your legal research. Then you should compare your draft to the content of these materials. If you have any doubt about the accuracy of a factual or legal point, you should look it up.

Discern and affirm or re-work the major and minor points of the paper. Read the draft fairly quickly, put it aside, and then jot down the major and minor points you can remember. Then think about whether the points make sense:

- Do they fit the facts, conform to the law, and lead to a just and sensible result?
- Do they relate to each other in a logical and consistent way? If your points are in the alternative, they should be discernible as alternatives.
- Can you proceed through the analysis without wondering "why" or "how" for more than a short time?

---

3. Adapted from Brooke E. Bowman, *Learning the Art of Rewriting and Editing—A Perspective*, 15(1) Perspectives: Teaching Legal Research and Writing 54 (fall 2006).

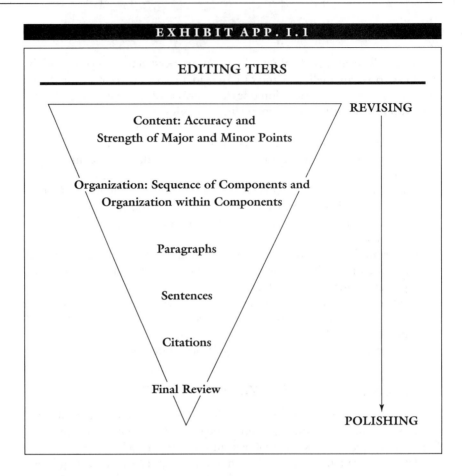

EXHIBIT APP. I.1

EDITING TIERS

Content: Accuracy and
Strength of Major and Minor Points

REVISING

Organization: Sequence of Components and
Organization within Components

Paragraphs

Sentences

Citations

Final Review

POLISHING

If any answer is "no," the next step is to re-think and re-work your analysis so that all answers are "yes."

Review the organization of the paper, and revise it as needed. To edit carefully, you should consider each organizational level in a separate step of the editing process. So first check the draft against the format requirements for the paper, making sure you have written all necessary components and that each component conforms to the requirements of the format.

Then make a retrospective outline (or flowchart or other depiction) of the longer sections, typically the discussion or argument as well as the facts. You might work through the paper highlighting major topics in yellow, minor ones in pink, and so on. Another preparatory step is to label portions of the draft in the margin. You then can write a traditional outline, or you can extract the topic or thesis sentences from each paragraph. Then review the retrospective outline:

- Is there a sensible overall organizing scheme? For example, does the fact statement flow chronologically or topically? In the discussion, are any threshold or pivotal topics handled first?
- Is each sub-topic assigned to its corresponding topic?
- Are there excessive cross-references or redundancies?

You may well find that your organization needs adjustment. In general, it is more efficient to reorganize the outline first and then proceed to make changes in the draft itself.

Next, examine the headings and transitions between topics and sub-topics; make sure that they clearly convey how this topic relates to what is coming and what has come before. Also, examine whether the facts and discussion have adequate introductory or roadmap paragraphs at the beginning and wrap-ups at the end. If the discussion is complex, check for a roadmap at the start of each major topic.

Refine your paragraphs. Review each paragraph against the guidelines of Appendix II, both as a distinct unit and in relation to adjacent paragraphs:

- Does the paragraph have a distinct point or topic? Does all material pertain to this point or topic?
- Where is the thesis or topic sentence? Is it clear?
- Do the sentences providing development or support proceed logically?
- Are there clear transitions linking this paragraph to the preceding and following paragraphs?

To sharpen your focus on individual paragraphs, you may find it helpful to work on them out of order.

Refine your sentences. Check each sentence against the guidelines of Appendix II. Look especially carefully at long sentences, where the risk of grammar errors and poor readability rises. As you gain practice in editing your own work, make note of the grammatical rules and guidelines you are prone to violate; focus on them. At this stage, you also should review your spelling and typing. If you edit initially on paper, the following standard editing symbols may be useful:

red	insert word, letter, punctuation mark
read	delete word, letter, punctuation mark
raed	invert order of letters or words
court	capitalize
Court	lower case
court	close space
it and	insert space

As with paragraphs, you may find that working on sentences out of order helps you to focus on the details of each sentence.

Refine your citations. You should include rough citations in your first draft, but you should wait to perfect your citations until your paper is nearly finished because some citation aspects (such as long versus short forms and signals) may change as the text evolves.

Once your text is in close-to-final form, you should verify that you have provided citations for your factual and legal points and have done so properly. Appendix III, which covers citation, suggests various steps in crafting citations: formulating the proper citation form for the source, placing the citation in your text, inserting a signal, appending information, and assembling string cites (where appropriate). Review each citation to be sure you have accomplished these steps correctly.

Computer-assisted editing. You most likely will have available to you various computer-assisted programs to check your spelling, composition, or citation. You should run your text through these programs (especially a spell-check program), but remember they are neither infallible nor as intelligent as you are. For example, a spell-check program will not correct the following sentence, because it does not understand context: "The trail court red the case narrowly."

3. Your Final Responsibility

Once you have refined your paper, you most likely will rely on some form of technology to produce your paper. Of course, technology can fail: word processors and printers can delete text or adjust margins; photocopiers can skip pages. Your paper is not done until you have checked over the final product, as it clears these machines, to be sure it is printed and copied correctly. Ultimately, you are responsible for the quality of your written work.

Finally, be sure to keep both a paper copy and an electronic record, as any responsible lawyer would do.

APPENDIX II

PARAGRAPH DESIGN,

SENTENCE STRUCTURE,

AND WORD USAGE

Easy Reference List

A. Paragraph Design
1. Cohesion Among Sentences
2. Paragraph Length
3. Links Between Paragraphs

B. Sentence Structure
1. Reader Expectations and Energy Expenditures
2. The Relationship Between Subject and Verb
3. Verbs
4. Nouns and Pronouns
5. Relationships Among Clauses and Phrases
6. Punctuation

C. Word Usage
1. Consistent and Distinct Wording Choices
2. Nominalization
3. Unneeded Adverbs
4. Multiple Negatives
5. Surplus Words
6. Precise Word Choices
7. Gender-Neutral Wording

EASY REFERENCE LIST FOR APPENDIX II

This appendix examines paragraph design, sentence structure, and word usage from the perspective of reader expectation theory—that is, how to construct paragraphs and sentences to meet the reader's underlying linguistic assumptions and preferences, to produce text that the reader can easily read and understand. This appendix first sets out principles of paragraph design and then highlights issues of sentence structure and word usage that frequently pose problems for legal writers. If you have questions about topics not covered here, consult a grammar or usage text.

HOW DO COURTS RESPOND TO WRITING ERRORS?

In re Hawkins,
502 N.W.2d 770 (Minn. 1993).

Hawkins' repeated disregard of the Local Bankruptcy Rules, coupled with the incomprehensibility of his correspondence and documentation, constitutes a violation of Rule 1.1, Minnesota Rules of Professional Conduct.[1] Although it is quite true that the deficiencies in the documents submitted to the bankruptcy court did not, as the referee concluded, cause harm to Hawkins' clients, the lack of harm is fortuitous. . . .

Moreover, harm has occurred: even though Hawkins' clients have not been harmed, administration of the law and the legal profession have been negatively affected by his conduct. Public confidence in the legal system is shaken when lawyers disregard the rules of court and when a lawyer's correspondence and legal documents are so filled with spelling, grammatical, and typographical errors that they are virtually incomprehensible. . . .

Respondent Patrick W. Hawkins is hereby publicly reprimanded for unprofessional conduct. He is ordered to pay costs and disbursements incurred in this proceeding in the amount of $250. Within two years after issuance of this opinion respondent shall successfully complete the following described CLE or other educational programs and shall report quarterly to the Director his progress in complying with these educational requirements:

(1) A program on bankruptcy rules, or if none is available, on the law of bankruptcy;
(2) A program of at least 10 hours in legal writing; and
(3) A program of at least 5 hours on law office management.

Public reprimand with conditions imposed.

---

1. Rule 1.1, Minnesota Rules of Professional Conduct, provides as follows: A lawyer shall provide competent representation to a client. Competent representation requires the legal knowledge, skill, thoroughness and preparation reasonably necessary for the representation.

A. PARAGRAPH DESIGN

Although each sentence should contain a complete thought, for many good writers the paragraph is the most important unit. Each paragraph should fully develop a topic through one or more related sentences. To craft strong paragraphs, you should attend to three features of paragraph design: cohesion among the sentences, paragraph length, and links between paragraphs. This discussion draws on the HomeElderCare advice letter (starting at page 349) for examples; several paragraphs from that letter are reprinted as Exhibit II.1.

EXHIBIT II.1

ILLUSTRATIVE HomeElderCare PARAGRAPHS

First

I enjoyed talking with you about HomeElderCare last week, and I appreciate the opportunity to advise you on the preparation of living wills by HomeElderCare social workers for your elderly clients. From what you have told me, I certainly can see why your staff favors providing this service.

However, as this letter explains, there could be some legal risks.

Second

In response to client requests, the social work staff would like to prepare living wills for clients who desire them. The social workers would attend a seminar or two first. The social worker would interview the client and talk through the significance of a living will. The social worker then would prepare a draft based on the form you have found, which indicates that it complies with Minnesota law. The social worker would encourage the client to confer with a doctor before signing the will. The social worker would arrange for the signing and notarizing of the will and then deliver it to the client's doctor. As with other HomeElderCare services, the client would pay a fee based on the time that the social worker spent on the service.

Third

As I recall, you expressed several legal concerns: that the service might be prohibited by law, that HomeElderCare's contracts with the clients might not be enforceable by HomeElderCare, and that the living wills drafted by HomeElderCare social workers might not be valid. The first two concerns are well founded; the third is less troublesome.

As for your first concern,

EXHIBIT II.1 (continued)

Fourth

But if the service *would* entail practicing law and thus violate the prohibition against nonlawyers practicing law, HomeElderCare may not be able to enforce its contracts with its clients. The courts look not only at whether the professional lacks a license to do the work but also at several other factors. The service your staff provides would be incidental to legitimate non-legal services of providing emotional support and guidance on medical and moral issues. And the clients would not be the target of fraud, because (I presume) the social workers would identify their professional status and indicate the limits of their expertise. However, a service that would constitute the unauthorized practice of law would also raise concerns about the social workers' competence, so that the courts would not permit HomeElderCare to profit financially.

1. Cohesion Among Sentences

Every paragraph should have a purpose, whether to cover a topic, support an assertion, or guide the reader through the document. Compare, for example, the paragraphs reprinted in Exhibit II.1: the first paragraph of the HomeElderCare advice letter, intended to establish rapport with the client; the second paragraph from the summary of facts describing the planned living will service; the third paragraph providing an overview of the explanation; and the fourth making and supporting the point that the contracts would be invalid.

Every sentence in a paragraph should further its purpose. Sentences that diverge from the paragraph's purpose are likely to distract and may confuse the reader. To ensure that all sentences in a paragraph further its purpose, plan carefully, and check your work. Before you write a paragraph, decide what you are trying to accomplish, and sketch out what is necessary to that task. After you have written a significant portion of a document, such as your argument on an issue in an appellate brief, go through each paragraph, identifying its purpose and checking all sentences against that purpose.

Paragraph cohesion also is a function of the order of the sentences within the paragraph. The classic paragraph design is TEC: topic, elaboration, conclusion. That is, the paragraph begins with a sentence announcing the topic, several sentences elaborating on that topic follow, and the paragraph concludes with a sentence wrapping up the topic. This classic design works well in many situations; consider, for example, the fourth sample paragraph in Exhibit II.1. Indeed, the classic legal mnemonic IRAC is a variation on TEC.

Some paragraphs can be cohesive without following TEC. When the paragraph is fairly short and its organizing scheme is very apparent, you may be able to dispense with the T or C elements or both. For example, the second sample paragraph, which recounts events in a chronological sequence, has no C concluding sentence. The first sample paragraph, which simply seeks to establish a connection between the lawyer and the reader, has neither a T nor a C sentence.

Finally, paragraph cohesion is furthered by links between sentences, including repeated words or concepts and transitional words or phrases. For example, in the second sample paragraph in Exhibit II.1, *social work* or *social workers* appears in every sentence; the third sample paragraph uses numerical concepts *(several, first, second, third)*.

2. Paragraph Length

In general, a paragraph should be as long as it needs to be to accomplish its purpose. Because some purposes are easy and others difficult to accomplish, you should expect to see paragraphs of varying length in the same document. Indeed, a one-sentence paragraph is acceptable so long as it accomplishes its purpose, which should be quite obvious. Note the wide variation in paragraph length in the four samples in Exhibit II.1—two to seven sentences.

If a paragraph is overly long, it will tax the reader, even if all of the sentences serve the paragraph's purpose. When you have written a very long paragraph, consider whether you can subdivide its purpose and the paragraph as well. If this is not possible, be sure that the paragraph's cohesion is very strong—it has strong topic and concluding sentences, and the flow from sentence to sentence is clear. The fourth sample paragraph in Exhibit II.1 is a long paragraph. It is not easily subdivided, and the reader already knows most of the information, so the writer opted for a long TEC paragraph.

As you work on writing fairly short paragraphs of varying lengths, keep in mind the results of a study of paragraph length in significant legal treatises and articles of the last fifty years: The averages ranged from 74 to 153 words. In one sample, the longest paragraph was 231 words; the shortest a single sentence of 14 words.[2]

3. Links Between Paragraphs

No matter how cohesive a paragraph is, if the reader cannot discern its connection to the discussion at hand, the reader will be puzzled. Every paragraph under a heading or subheading should, of course, obviously deliver what the heading or subheading promises.

Equally important is the connection between one paragraph and the next—the flow of the discussion. There are various ways to link a new paragraph to the preceding paragraph, including a transitional word or phrase and repetition of a key word or phrase from the last sentence of the preceding paragraph. Note, for example, what follows the first and third HomeElder-Care sample paragraphs, presented in Exhibit II.1. The first sample uses

---

2. Bryan A. Garner, *Legal Writing in Plain English: A Text with Exercises* 72–73 (2001).

a simple transition word—*however.* The second sample repeats a key word and uses enumeration—*as for your first concern.*

B. SENTENCE STRUCTURE

1. Reader Expectations and Energy Expenditures

Readers come to the activity of reading with expectations about grammar, punctuation, and word usage. The more formal the prose, the more likely its readers will expect their expectations to be honored. Legal writing is fairly formal prose, so reader expectations are high. To increase your awareness of reader expectations, imagine a crowd of prospective readers hovering over your shoulder, asking you questions like the following: "Must I really read this long sentence?" "What does this word mean?"

Legal readers are well educated, so they have acquired extensive and precise expectations about the prose they read. And legal readers value (and often bill) their professional time, so they want writing that they can read quickly. If the prose is grammatically correct and easy to read, the reader will think more highly of the written analysis. The opposite is also true: the higher the number of composition errors, the greater will be the reader's skepticism toward the analysis. This is due to the halo effect: If we judge a person positively or negatively on one aspect, we have a tendency to judge that person similarly on other aspects.

Reader expectations can be requirements or preferences. *Requirements* outrank all other writing considerations. Writing that does not meet these requirements jars the reader, prompts the reader to re-read some material, and causes a major break in the reader's progress. For example, read the following sentence:

A reader expect that a singular verb will follow a singular noun.

Was your attention jarred at some point? Did you re-read a portion of the sentence? What is its defect? (A plural verb following a singular noun.)

Other reader expectations are merely *preferences.* Writing that does not conform to these preferences may slow down and distract the reader, who then devotes mental energy to figuring out the sentence's structure and therefore pays less attention to the sentence's meaning. For example, read the following sentence:

Although the validity of the patient's living will is debatable because its form deviates from the form in the statute, it is doubtful that there will be any challenge to its validity because everyone knows that the wishes in the living will are clearly those of the patient.

Did your attempts to decipher the structure distract your attention from the meaning?

In other words, requirements are unavoidable, while preferences are norms that occasionally can be disregarded in favor of countervailing considerations. This appendix covers both.[3]

2. The Relationship Between Subject and Verb

The core of the sentence is the subject and its verb. A reader starts to read a sentence by looking for these: a subject, because it usually tells who the actor is, and a verb, because it usually tells what the actor is doing. Everything else in the sentence is secondary.

a. Subject-Verb Agreement

Rules of grammar *require* that a plural verb will be used with a plural subject and that a singular verb will be used with a singular subject. Subject-verb disagreement often occurs when many words intrude between subject and verb. For example:

> The living will form that appears in the statute and that was used by the clients are valid.

The easiest way to catch this error is to find the core of the sentence and then match subject to verb. In the example above, the word *clients* lured the writer into using a plural verb instead of the required singular verb. The true subject is *form,* and its verb should be *is.*

b. Subject-Verb Proximity

Readers *prefer* the subject and verb of a sentence to be close together, so their connection is clear. If too many words appear between the subject and verb, the reader probably will skim over the intervening words. For example:

> The *contract* for payment, **the illegality of which may not be raised by a non-party to the contract,** *may be enforced* by the unpaid party if the contract does not violate public policy.

The subject and its verb (in italics) are separated by a lengthy intervening clause (in boldface) that seems like a parenthetical remark.

Sentences with many words between subject and verb can be revised in various ways:

- Reduce the number of words between subject and verb.
- Move the intervening words elsewhere in the sentence.
- Break the sentence into two sentences, and add an appropriate connector.

---

3. For additional help with grammar, consult a college-level text or a grammar text written for lawyers, e.g, Linda Bahrych & Marjorie Dick Rombauer, *Legal Writing in a Nutshell* (3d ed. 2003); Richard Wydick, *Plain English for Lawyers* (4th ed. 1998).

In the sample sentence above, the intervening clause cannot be shortened without losing meaning. However, the intervening clause (in boldface) can be moved elsewhere in the sentence, so that the main subject and verb (in italics) are now close together:

> The *contract* for payment *may be enforced* by the unpaid party if the contract does not violate public policy, **and the illegality of the contract may not be raised by a non-party to the contract.**

Or you could break the sentence in two:

> The *contract* for payment *may be enforced* by the unpaid party if the contract does not violate public policy. **The illegality of the contract may not be raised by a non-party to the contract.**

Because subject-verb proximity is a preference, not a requirement, you might decide that some material between the subject and its verb is workable. For example, the following sentence reads well:

> The *living will*, **which the patient drew up more than fifteen years ago,** *may not reflect* the patient's current views.

The clause between the subject and its verb is brief enough that the reader can process it easily. In addition, the intervening clause provides information that links the subject and verb.

c. Active and Passive Voice

Each core sentence follows one of five patterns, as shown in Exhibit II.2.

EXHIBIT II.2

SENTENCE PATTERNS

1. subject The client	intransitive verb agreed.		
2. subject The client	linking verb is	subject complement satisfied.	
3. subject The client	transitive verb wrote	direct object a will.	
4. subject The lawyer	transitive verb wrote	indirect object the client	direct object a letter.
5. subject The client	transitive verb deems	direct object the will	object complement accurate.

All of these patterns are in active voice because the subject noun is the actor of the verb and the verb is in active voice. Active-voice sentences are easy to read because the verb describes the actions of the sentence's subject. Hence readers *prefer* active voice.

The latter three patterns (those with transitive verbs) can be transformed into passive voice when an object (direct object, indirect object, or object complement) rather than the actor occupies the position of the subject and the verb is in passive voice. Below are the passive-voice versions of the latter three patterns:

3. The will was written by the client.
4. The letter was written to the client by the lawyer.
5. The will is deemed accurate by the client.

Passive voice is more difficult for the reader than active voice for five reasons. First, contrary to the reader's expectation, the verb does not describe the actions of the subject of the sentence. Second, the passive-voice form of the verb (*was written, is deemed*) is more complex; it consists of a *to be* helping verb (*is, are, was, were, has been, had been*) and the past participle of the verb. Third, passive voice is wordier than active voice. Fourth, the true actor sometimes appears in a prepositional phrase (*by the lawyer*) and sometimes does not appear at all in a passive-voice sentence. For example:

The will is deemed accurate. (By whom? The court? The client's relatives?)

Unless the actor is apparent from the context, the reader wonders who did the action in the sentence. Fifth, passive voice increases the chance of a misplaced modifier, which is a word or phrase that seems to modify an adjacent word but really modifies a more distant word. For example:

Active: Satisfied with the will, the *client paid* the lawyer.
Passive: Satisfied with the will, the lawyer was paid by the *client.*

The reader expects the subject of the sentence also to be the actor of this introductory verb clause. The active-voice sentence above meets that expectation (*satisfied with the will* modifies *client*), but the passive-voice sentence does not (*satisfied with the will* should not modify *lawyer*).

You can test for passive voice in two ways: First, discern whether the verb is passive voice (*to-be* helping verb + past participle of verb). Note that in subtle passive-voice sentences, the *to-be* verb may be implied. Note also that a *to-be* verb without a past participle is not a passive-voice construction. For example:

Implied to-be verb: The social workers heard it suggested by some clients that . . . (It *was* suggested by some clients . . .)
No past participle: The unauthorized practice statute is applicable.
(Compare: The statute is applied by the courts [passive].)

Or locate the verb in question and ask who or what is taking that action. If that actor is in the subject position, the sentence is in active voice, but if that actor is missing or is elsewhere in the sentence (usually in a prepositional phrase), the sentence is in passive voice.

Active voice is a *preference*, not a requirement, but you should use passive voice only for a good reason. Here are eight settings in which passive voice is useful: First, use passive voice when the actor (in italics) of the actions is unknown. For example:

Active: *Someone* delivered the living will to the physician.
Passive: The living will was delivered to the physician.

Second, use passive voice when you want to de-emphasize the true actor (in italics) of the verb. Third, use passive voice when you want to dilute the power of the verb (in boldface). For example:

Active: *My client* **drafted** a defective living will.
Passive: A defective living will **was drafted.**

Fourth, use passive voice when you want to emphasize or lead with the direct object (in italics). For example:

Active: Only the parties to the contract can raise this *defense.*
Passive: This *defense* can be raised only by the parties to the contract.

Fifth, use passive voice to avoid some misplaced modifiers. For example, an introductory verb clause should modify the word in the subject position (in italics); if the introductory clause really modifies the direct object (in boldface), passive voice can avoid this problem. For example:

Active: Being of sound mind but weak body, the *lawyer* urged the **testator** to update her will. (misplaced modifier)
Passive: Being of sound mind but weak body, the *testator* was urged to update her will. (no misplaced modifier)

Sixth, use the passive voice to facilitate the use of pronouns or to avoid pronoun confusion (in italics). For example:

Active: The testator's brother urged the testator to cancel *his* bequest. (Does *his* mean the bequest going to the brother, or does it mean some other bequest by the testator?)
Passive: The testator was urged to cancel *his* bequest. (Now *his* can mean only the testator's.)

Seventh, use passive voice to avoid awkward gender-based pronouns (in italics). For example:

Active: The social worker drafts the living will. *He* or *she* then notifies the proxy when the signing will be.

Passive: The social worker drafts the living will. The proxy then is notified when the signing will be.

Eighth, use passive voice so that you can use a single subject for two verbs (in italics). For example:

Both active: The legal community *had anticipated* the ruling for years. Therefore, the ruling *raised* nary an eyebrow.
Passive, then active: This ruling *had been anticipated* for years and therefore *raised* nary an eyebrow.

Thus, passive voice can have a place in carefully crafted prose.

d. Postponed Subjects

Some sentences mimic the effect of passive voice because the true actor is not in the subject position. Instead, the main clause of the sentence begins with *there is, there exists,* or *it is [adjective] that* . . . . The remainder of the sentence contains the true actor and its action. For that reason, this type of construction is called a "postponed subject." For example:

There is a living will form in the statute.
There existed some concern that the living will was not accurate.
It is possible that the client will not understand the form.

Such a sentence sounds weak because the opening clause has little or no meaning. And the reader must expend mental energy looking for the real actor and the real action, buried later in the sentence. Thus, it is *preferable* to avoid postponed subjects.

The solution is to delete the weak opening and re-write the remainder. For example:

The statute contains a living will form.
The client's family was concerned that the living will was not accurate.
The client may not understand the language of the form.

3. Verbs

Verbs are the most powerful words in the English language and hence have considerable impact on readers. Legal readers expect legal writing to follow both general conventions for verb tense and the conventions of the legal profession.

a. Verb Tenses

All readers expect consistency in verb tense, so that a particular event is always discussed in the same tense, such as past or present, throughout the paper. Experienced legal readers also expect the conventions stated in Exhibit II.3 to be followed.

EXHIBIT II.3

LEGAL VERB CONVENTIONS

Rules of law, reasoning
      former (repealed, overturned)   past tense
      current (in force, used, valid)   present tense
      future (not yet in effect, proposed)   future tense

Actions of courts and legislatures
      past actions   past tense
      pending actions   present tense
      future actions   future tense

Real-world facts
      past events   past tense
      present events   present tense
      future events   future tense

The following passage demonstrates these tenses:

In 1960, the *Weatherston's* court *held that* the contract between an unlicensed professional and a client *was* enforceable. The court *based* its holding on the policy that the public should be protected against certain kinds of hazards but that other contracts should remain valid. Since this case, the rule in Minnesota *is* that an unlicensed professional *can* enter into a valid contract if the following conditions *are* met: . . .

Mr. Weatherston *was not licensed* but *was supervised* by a licensed engineer. HomeElderCare social workers *are not licensed* as lawyers. They *will not be supervised* by a lawyer.

Sometimes a writer needs more time frames than just the simple tenses of past, present, and future. The writer also can use the perfect tenses, which show completion of an action before a particular time (*had held, has held, will have held*) and the progressive tenses, which show that an action continues over a particular time period (*was holding, is holding, will be holding*). Exhibit II.4 shows these verb tenses, ordered from distant past to future. Note that the transition words such as *at that time* make your gradations of time even clearer to the reader.

Verb tense consistency is a *requirement*. Using the verb tense conventions of the legal profession is a *preference*.

EXHIBIT II.4

VERB TENSES

Tense	Examples	Timing
past perfect	had held	action completed in past before another action
past perfect progressive	had been holding	action continuing and completed in past before another past action
past progressive	was holding	continuing action in past
simple past	held	past action
present perfect	has held	action that began in past and is linked to present
present perfect progressive	has been holding	action that began in past and is continuing in present
present progressive	is holding	continuing action in present
simple present	holds	present
future perfect	will have held	action that will be completed before another future action
future perfect progressive	will have been holding	action that will be continuing and completed before another future action
future progressive	will be holding	continuing action in future
simple future	will hold	future

For example, a fact statement might include the following tenses:

past perfect	HomeElderCare *had instituted* a living-will service three years before Mr. Nelson's contract.
past perfect progressive	At that time its social workers *had been providing* other services for ten years.
past progressive	It *was delivering* its services through geriatric social workers.
simple past	When Mr. Nelson and the HEC social worker *met*, she *explained* to him his responsibilities.
present perfect	Throughout its history, HomeElderCare *has worked* hard to maintain trust with clients.

present perfect progressive	HomeElderCare social workers *have been* anxiously *awaiting* our opinion on the legality of the living will service.
present progressive	The district attorney *is contemplating* whether to seek an injunction.
simple present	The client *claims* that the living will *is* inaccurate.
future perfect	The social workers *will have received* specific training before completing any living wills for clients.
future perfect progressive	Each social worker also *will have been practicing* social work for five to ten years before providing living will services.
future progressive	HomeElderCare *will be supervising* all social workers closely during the two-year trial period.
simple future	HomeElderCare *will review* this plan two years after its implementation.

b. Verb Moods

Verb mood gives additional information about the verb beyond its tense. The three verb moods are indicative, imperative, and subjunctive, as illustrated in Exhibit II.5.

The rules about verb mood are *requirements*. There is an exception: A hypothetical condition contrary to fact may or may not be stated in subjunctive mood. A hypothetical sounds more likely when stated in indicative mood and less likely when stated in subjunctive mood, as shown below:

> Indicative: If a social worker *drafts* a living will erroneously, the client and the client's family *will suffer*.
> Subjunctive: If a social worker *were to draft* a living will erroneously, the client and the client's family *would suffer*.

Either statement is correct, so your choice of mood for hypotheticals depends on how likely or unlikely you want the hypothetical to sound. The subjunctive mood can be a powerful tool of persuasion, used to state a condition contrary to a client's interest, so as to make it sound as unlikely as possible.

c. Split Infinitives and Other Verb Phrases

Generally, a verb phrase (in italics) can be interrupted with a single-word adverb (in boldface) without disrupting the sentence. For example:

> The client *had* **recently** *asked* the social workers about a living will.

However, lengthier interruptions (in boldface) generally dilute the power of the verb and read awkwardly. For example:

> HomeElderCare *had,* **based on input from a dozen clients over two months,** *instituted* a living will service.

EXHIBIT 11.5

VERB MOODS

Mood	Attitude	Example
indicative	fact, opinion, or question	The contract *is* valid. *Is* the contract valid?
imperative	command or direction	*Ignore* irrelevancies. *Be* unbiased.
subjunctive	suggestion, desire, requirement, possibility, or hypothetical condition contrary to fact	She suggested that he *consult* . . . The statute requires that signatures *be notarized* . . . If she *were to draft* the living will, . . . *Had* she *advised* him otherwise, . . .

The solution is to move the interruption elsewhere in the sentence:

Based on client input from a dozen clients over two months, HomeElderCare *had instituted* a living will service.

The same problem occurs with infinitives, which are verbs preceded by the word *to* (for example, *to draft, to argue*). A split infinitive occurs when one or more words appear between *to* and the verb. Split infinitives regularly occur in spoken English and are acceptable under modern grammar rules when the interruption is small and the result is not awkward.[4] For example:

To **boldly** *go* where no man has gone before . . .

Larger interruptions should be avoided. For example:

Split: Are the social workers trained well enough *to,* **in every instance,** *draft* an accurate living will?
Unsplit: Are the social workers trained well enough *to draft* an accurate living will **in every instance?**

Because some readers may think poorly of a writer who splits any infinitive, in some sense, the safest course is never to split an infinitive. However, some sentences become more awkward when the infinitive is not split, and you should take this into account. For example:

Split: The issue is whether the social workers are trained well enough *to* **competently** *draft* living wills.

---

4. *See* H. W. Fowler, *A Dictionary of Modern English Usage* 429, 579–82 (2d ed. Ernest Gowers, ed. 1965) (out of the frying pan, split infinitives); Maxine Hairston & John J. Ruskiewicz, *The Scott, Foresman Handbook for Writers* 316–17 (4th ed. 1996).

Unsplit: The issue is whether the social workers are trained well enough *to draft* **competently** living wills.

4. Nouns and Pronouns

Nouns are words that name people, places, and things. A pronoun can take the place of a nearby noun.

a. Pronoun-Antecedent Agreement

A pronoun must agree with its antecedent in number, person, and gender. This is a *requirement* of good writing. Number is whether the pronoun is singular or plural (for instance, *it* or *they*). Person is whether the pronoun is in first-, second-, or third-person (for instance, *we, you,* or *they*). Gender is whether a third-person pronoun is feminine, masculine, or neuter (for instance *she, he,* or *it*).

Except in rare circumstances, two or more antecedents (in italics) joined by *and* take a plural pronoun (in boldface), regardless of the number of either antecedent. For instance:

When *HomeElderCare and its clients* initiated the living will service, **they** believed that it was a valuable addition.

However, when two or more antecedents are joined by *or* or *nor*, the pronoun must agree with the antecedent nearer to the pronoun. For instance:

Neither *HomeElderCare nor its clients* believed that **their** contract was void.

b. Collective Nouns

Legal writing contains many collective nouns that are singular because the group represented by the collective noun functions as a single entity. Proper treatment of collective nouns is a *requirement*. For example:

Collective noun (singular)	*Noun representing group members (plural)*
jury	jurors
court	judges or justices
legislature	legislators
board	board members
commission	commissioner
corporation	shareholders
partnership	partners

Once you know whether you are discussing the group or the persons in the group (in boldface), you can write the verbs (in italics), pronouns (also in italics), and the rest of the sentence correctly. For example:

HomeElderCare (a corporation) *offers its* clients the services of *its* social workers.

The **supreme court** *has ruled* against the appellants. But several **justices** *have written* concurring opinions to express *their* concern about the policy implications of the court's holding.

Note the agreement between noun and pronoun, as well as the agreement between subject and verb.

c. Indefinite Pronouns

Indefinite pronouns do not refer to a specific person or thing. Although grammar books differ as to which are singular and which are plural, the chart below reflects formal and college usage:[5]

Singular	*Either* *(singular or plural)*	*Plural*
any-body,-one, -thing	all	few
each	any	many
every-body,-one,-thing	either	several
no-body,-one,-thing	more	
some-body,-one,-thing	most	
	neither	
	none	
	some	

The following examples are correct:

Either of the employees *is* willing to serve this client.
None of the employees *is* willing to serve this client.
Each of the clients *was* satisfied with *his or her* living will.

To view these sentences properly, focus on the pronoun as the subject of the verb. For example, *either . . . is . . . .*

d. Implied Antecedents

When *this* and *that* are used as free-standing pronouns, they often result in unclear implied antecedents. Because the reader has to surmise the unnamed antecedent of the pronoun, readers *prefer* greater clarity. In the example below, *this* could be *this defective drafting, this defect,* or *this kind of living will.*

If defectively drafted, the living will may not represent the wishes of the patient as to his or her treatment for the final illness or injury preceding death. This can trigger difficult questions about mortality and medical practices.

The solution is to place the appropriate noun after the word *this.* You also may need to reword the preceding sentence to make the connection clearer.

---

5. Maxine Hairston & John J. Ruskiewicz, *supra* note 4, at 343.

5. Relationships Among Clauses and Phrases

This part discusses how clauses are joined with each other and how their structure affects the meaning of the sentence.

a. One Point Per Sentence

A short sentence is more readable than a long sentence because the reader does not have to work so hard to locate the subject and verb of the sentence. A reader who is confronted with a long, bulky sentence may slow down to process the sentence, or the reader may just move on to the next sentence. Consider the following sentence, which is grammatically correct but very bulky:

> Although the validity of the patient's living will is debatable because its form deviates from the form in the statute, no one likely will challenge its validity because everyone knows that the wishes in the living will are clearly those of the patient.

This sentence is trying to get the following two points across to the reader: (1) the form deviates from the statute so the living will may not be valid and (2) no one will challenge it because it states the patient's wishes. To make this sentence more readable, break the sentence into two sentences, as follows:

> The form of the patient's living will deviates from the form in the statute, so it may not be valid. However, no one likely will challenge the will's validity because it clearly states the patient's wishes.

Sometimes this reader *preference* must be disobeyed to meet a format requirement or reader expectations in a particular setting. For instance, a point heading in a brief to the court may be a long sentence, rather than two shorter sentences, if the format demands (and the reader expects) a single sentence.

b. Short Introductory Clauses

Short introductory clauses can be very effective. But long introductory clauses keep the reader from easily locating the core of the sentence. If the introductory clause is too long, the reader probably will skim over it. Sentences with overly long introductory clauses can be revised as follows:

- Delete unnecessary words from the introductory clause.
- Move the introductory clause to the end of the sentence.
- Make the introductory clause into the main clause, and make the former main clause into a dependent clause.
- Break the sentence into two sentences, and add an appropriate connector.

Consider the introductory clause (in italics) in the following sentence:

If the company carefully trains its social workers not to give legal or medical advice, the company can safely allow its social workers to assist clients in filling out living wills.

This introductory clause cannot be shortened without losing meaning, so the first solution is not possible. Under the second approach, the dependent clause moves to the end of the sentence, and the main subject and verb appear at the outset of the sentence, a position that enhances the sentence's readability:

The company can safely allow its social workers to assist clients in filling out living wills *if it carefully trains its social workers not to give legal or medical advice.*

Under the third approach, the introductory clause becomes the main clause, and the main clause becomes a dependent clause, as follows:

The company may be able to carefully train its social workers not to give legal or medical advice, so that the company can safely allow its social workers to assist clients in filling out living wills.

Under the fourth approach, the sentence breaks in two:

The company may be able to carefully train its social workers not to give legal or medical advice. With this training, the company can safely allow its social workers to assist clients in filling out living wills.

Readers prefer short introductory clauses. You should choose the solution that best fits with the surrounding text and the emphasis you want to convey.

c. *That, Which,* and *Who*

"That" and "which" are relative pronouns; they introduce dependent clauses modifying nouns. Using them properly is a *requirement* of sound writing. In the following correct examples, the relative pronouns are in underlined italics, the dependent clauses are in italics, and the modified nouns are in boldface:

The client's **intent** *that she not remain in an extended coma* was noted in the living will.
The client's **living will,** *which was drafted in her home,* accurately reflects her intent.

The choice between the two depends on whether the clause narrows or elaborates on the modified noun. Clauses that narrow the modified noun begin with *that,* are known as "restrictive clauses," and are not set off from the rest of the sentence with commas. Clauses that do not narrow the modified noun, but rather describe some aspect of that noun, begin with *which,* are known as "non-restrictive clauses," and are set off from the rest of the sentence with commas.

In the first example above, the that-clause narrows the client's intent to focus on her wishes as to an extended coma. In the second example above, the which-clause provides tangential information about the living will.

Who is used to introduce a dependent clause that modifies a noun describing a person. Who-clauses can be either restrictive or non-restrictive. For example:

> The **client** <u>*who wanted a living will*</u> was pleased with the social worker's assistance.

In this example, the who-clause is not set off from the rest of the sentence with commas because it is restrictive; it specifies which client was pleased.

d. Misplaced and Dangling Modifiers

The reader usually links a modifying word or phrase to the nearest word that could be modified. When the word seemingly modified is the wrong one, the modifier is misplaced. Avoiding misplaced modifiers is a *requirement* of good writing. In the following examples, the phrase in italics modifies the noun in boldface, for better or for worse:

> Misplaced: The social worker drafted the form for the **client** *using a computer*. (Is the client using the computer?)
> Correct: *Using a computer,* the **social worker** drafted the form for the client.

Limiting modifiers—*only, hardly, merely, nearly,* etc.—frequently are misplaced. They should appear immediately before the word or phrase being modified. In the three correct sentences below, the placement of *only* changes the meaning:

> The social workers *only* drafted the living wills in the first month.
> (They did not do anything besides draft.)
> The social workers drafted *only* the living wills in the first month.
> (They did not draft anything else.)
> The social workers drafted the living wills *only* in the first month.
> (After the first month, they did not draft living wills.)

A common instance of a misplaced modifier involves a verb phrase, a phrase with a verb but not a subject. The implied subject of an introductory verb phrase (in italics) is the subject of the sentence (in boldface). If it is not, the phrase is misplaced. For example:

> Misplaced: *Trying not to give legal advice,* the **client** was referred to an attorney by the social worker.
> Correct: *Trying not to give legal advice,* the **social worker** referred the client to the attorney.

The misplaced phrase above is caused by passive voice; the corrected sentence is in active voice. The misplaced phrase below is caused by a postponed subject, eliminated in the corrected sentence:

> Misplaced: *Assuming the living will form to be adequate,* **there** was no motivation for the client to raise any other topics.
> Correct: *Assuming the living will form to be adequate,* the **client** was not motivated to raise any other topics.

When a modifier does not seem to modify anything in the sentence, the modifier is dangling, rather than misplaced. In the example below, passive voice is involved:

> Dangling: *Wondering whether the contracts would be valid,* **counsel** was hired to research the question.
> Correct: *Wondering whether the contracts would be valid,* **Home-ElderCare** hired counsel to research the question.

e. Parallel Structure

Readers expect compound sentence elements to use a similar grammatical form. This *requirement* of parallel structure applies to lists and to series. A series is a collection of two or more items joined by a coordinating conjunction (*and, or, nor, but, yet.*) In the following correct examples, the series are in italics, and the coordinating conjunctions are in boldface:

> The form was *accurate, available,* **and** *helpful.* (series of three adjectives)
> The attorney *drafted* the will **and** *met* with the client to make sure the will was accurate. (series of two verbs, both in same tense)
> The social worker approached the counseling session *efficiently* **yet** *compassionately.* (series of two adverbs)

When parallel structure is missing, the result is awkward, jarring, or confusing. For example:

> The living will form in the statute asks the signer to state preferences about desired health care, life-sustaining treatment, giving artificially administered sustenance, and explains the proper use of the form.

A re-write that contains two properly parallel series (one in boldface, one in italics) is:

> The living will form in the statute **explains** the proper use of the form and **asks** the signer to state preferences about desired health *care,* life-sustaining *treatment,* and artificially administered *sustenance.*

Most lists are series and therefore should be in parallel structure. For example:

> The statute has four parts: (1) *purpose,* (2) *definitions,* (3) *duties of the officers,* and (4) *damages and penalties.* (all nouns)

However, the following enumerated sentence does not contain compound sentence elements joined by a conjunction, so it is not required to be in parallel structure:

> The maker of the living will must (1) sign it (2) in the presence of a witness (3) who is not the proxy.

The numbers above merely segment the sentence into non-coordinate parts.

Parallel structure also is *required* for items joined by correlative conjunctions (*either/or, neither/nor, both/and, not only/but also*). Note the following correct use of parallel structure (in italics) with correlative conjunctions (in boldface):

> The living will was **both** *valid* under the statute **and** *accurate* about the maker's wishes. (two adjectives)
> The contract **not only** *set* the flat rate for the living will service **but also** *specified* that a living will form would be used. (two verbs)

Parallel structure also is required between items being compared or contrasted. Note the following correct sentences:

> The living will was **better** *judged* invalid **than** *acted* upon in error. (comparison of two verbs in same tense)
> The clients wanted help from *social workers,* **rather than** *attorneys.* (comparison of two nouns)
> The clients wanted help *from* social workers, **rather than** *from* attorneys. (comparison of two prepositional phrases)

In the third sentence, the second, optional *from* emphasizes the parallel structure.

6. Punctuation

Punctuation marks are compact signals, each conveying a specific message to the reader about the connections among words. If you use a punctuation mark incorrectly, you will send the wrong signal, so proper punctuation is *a requirement* of good writing.

a. Choosing Among Stops: Commas, Semicolons, Periods, Dashes, Parentheses, and Colons

Stops are the punctuation marks that signal a pause; they are periods, semicolons, commas, dashes, parentheses, and colons. A key punctuation dilemma for most legal writers is which stop to choose in the three situations shown in Exhibit II.6.

i. Joining Main Clauses

One choice among stops occurs when you want to join two or more main clauses. You can use a period, a semicolon, or a comma for this task. Your choice should reflect how closely you want to link the two clauses. If you want to link the two clauses very closely, you should use a comma and a coordinating conjunction (*and, but, or, nor*). For example:

> The living wills likely will be valid, *but* the social workers cannot advise clients how to revise the form.

If you want to link the two clauses less closely but still show their connection to each other, you should use a semicolon but no coordinating conjunction. You might also choose to add some other connecting word or phrase (in italics):

> The living wills likely will be valid; *however,* the social workers cannot advise clients how to revise the form.

If you want a distinct break between the clauses, you should use a period, creating two separate sentences. Again, no conjunction should be used, but you might choose to add a connecting word or phrase (in italics):

EXHIBIT II.6

CHOICES AMONG STOPS

Purpose	Stop (listed in each box from smallest to largest pause or impact)
Joining two or more main clauses	• comma (and coordinating conjunction) • semicolon • period
Setting apart an interrupting word or phrase	• parentheses • commas • dashes
Introducing quote, list, or other material set off from sentence	• no stop • comma • colon

The living wills will be valid. *However,* the social workers cannot advise how to revise the form.

Generally, two short sentences are more readable than one longer sentence, so you should opt for one long sentence with two independent clauses only if both clauses are fairly short.

When two independent clauses are joined incorrectly, the result is known as a "run-on sentence" or "fused sentence." For example:

Incorrect: The living wills likely will be valid, the social workers cannot advise clients how to revise the form.

The first three examples in this discussion are all correct alternatives. Avoiding run-on sentences is a *requirement.*

ii. Interrupting the Text

Another choice among stops occurs when an interrupting word or phrase needs to be set apart from the rest of the sentence by a pause on either side. For this task, you can use parentheses, a pair of commas, or a pair of dashes. Your choice should reflect how much you want the reader to focus on the interrupting word or phrase. If you want the interruption de-emphasized, use parentheses. If you want more attention paid to the interruption, set off the interruption with a comma on either side (known as "parenthetical commas"). If you want maximum emphasis, use a dash on either side. For example (the interruptions are in italics):

The living will (*also known as an "advance directives declaration"*) was delivered to the maker's primary physician.
The living will, *once shown to be authentic,* was delivered to the maker's primary physician.
The living will—*although disputed by the patient's relatives*—was delivered to the patient's primary physician.

A dash can be made with two hyphens if your word processing program or printer will not generate a dash. Dashes are flush against adjacent text with no open spaces on either side.

iii. Introducing Quotes, Lists, and Other Set-Apart Material

Yet another choice among stops occurs at the outset of a quotation, a list, or other material that is set apart from text. You may precede this material with no stop at all, a comma, or a colon. Your choice should reflect how much of a connection you want between the preceding text and the set-apart material.

Sometimes you want the quoted or listed material to flow smoothly into the sentence, without any introduction, as it would if the numbers or quotation marks were absent. For this effect, do not use any stop, and do not capitalize the initial letter of the quoted or listed material. For example (the transitions are in italics):

> The five factors *are (1) the* maker's intent, (2) . . .
> HomeElderCare's president told us that she wanted to *know* "*whether* the living wills will be valid."
> The court ruled *that* "[*t*]*hese* contracts are enforceable if they do not run contrary to public policy."

In the third sentence, [*t*] shows that *these* had an initial capital letter in the original source, but the writer changed that capitalization to make the quotation fit the rules of this punctuation format.

If you want a medium pause to set apart a quotation from the accompanying text and if the quotation is an independent clause, precede the quote with a comma and a signaling verb (in boldface). For example:

> HomeElderCare's president **said**, "*We* want to know whether the living wills will be valid."
> The court **ruled**, "*These* contracts are enforceable if they do not run contrary to public policy."

Note that each quotation begins with a capital letter.

If you prefer an emphatic break before the set-apart material, use a more formal introduction, followed by a colon. For example:

> The five factors are *as follows: (1) the* maker's intent, (2) . . .
> HomeElderCare's president clearly *expressed her concern*: "*We* want to make sure that the living wills will be valid."

In the second example, note that the set-apart quotation begins with a capital letter.

When a colon is not followed by a quoted sentence, whether to capitalize the first word after the colon depends on what follows the colon. If what follows is a complete sentence, the first word may or may not be capitalized. If what follows is not a complete sentence, the first letter should not be capitalized (unless, e.g., the word is a proper noun).

iv. Other Uses and Misuses of Commas

In addition to the comma usages discussed above, use a comma (1) on either side of the year when it follows the month and the day (in that order), (2) after an introductory phrase or word at the beginning of a sentence, and (3) after all but the last item in a series of three or more items. The first is a *requirement;* the second is a *preference*. Using a comma after items in a series other than the last and second-to-last items is a *requirement;* using a comma after the second-to-last item is a *preference*. For example:

> Interestingly, the client made a second living will on May 15, 1999, when he changed his mind about his do-not-resuscitate preference, his hydration preference, and the person he had named as a proxy in his December 1998 will.

However, if one item in a series contains an internal comma, semicolons (rather than commas) should appear after all but the last item in a series of three or more. For example:

> The client changed his mind regarding his do-not-resuscitate preference; his hydration preference; and the person he had named as a proxy, who subsequently lost the client's trust.

Recall that a clause beginning with *which* must be bounded by commas, but a clause beginning with *that* should not be.

Although a comma, semicolon, or period is required between independent clauses, it is erroneous to place a comma between the subject and verb of the same clause or between a verb and its object, unless some other usage requires the comma. For example:

> Incorrect: The client and his estate-planning attorney, made a second living will.
> Incorrect: The client had decided to amend the provision on hydration, and wrote to his attorney with this instruction.

b. Hyphens

Hyphens are used in three settings: (1) when a word is split between two lines of text (which is not commonly done these days), (2) in words that are hyphenated in the dictionary, and (3) between two or more words that serve as a single adjective and precede the noun. The first two usages are *required*.

The third usage is a reader *preference,* because it removes ambiguity. Usually each word preceding and modifying a noun stands on its own, so that if the other words modifying the noun were taken away, that single modifying word would still carry its intended meaning. For example:

valid testamentary will	valid will
	testamentary will

However, sometimes two or more words preceding a noun need to be tied together to convey the correct meaning. These words (not usually hyphenated on their own) are hyphenated when they occur together before the noun. For example:

do-not-resuscitate order	*not* do order
	not not order
	not resuscitate order

Grammarians disagree about whether to hyphenate when one of the words preceding the noun is an adverb, but the majority rule is not to hyphenate. For example:

very serious error
commonly used form

The adverb (*very, commonly*) could never modify the noun (*error, form*), so the
adverb need not be attached to the adjacent adjective or verb (*serious, used*)
with a hyphen.

Some legal terms almost never are hyphenated, even when they precede a
noun. These terms are very common legal phrases, the names of legal rules and
doctrines, the names of statutes, and foreign terms. For instance:

common law rule
living will statute
unauthorized practice act
prima facie case

Note that a pair of hyphens used to set off a word or phrase from the rest of the
sentence is known as a "dash," not a hyphen.

c. Apostrophes

Apostrophes are *required* in contractions (*can't, won't, don't*). The possessive
pronoun *its* does not contain an apostrophe, but the contraction *it's* does,
because *it's* is the contraction of *it is*. Likewise, the possessive pronoun *whose*
does not contain an apostrophe, but the contraction *who's* does, because it is
the contraction of *who is*.

Apostrophes also are *required* for the possessive form of nouns. Add an
apostrophe and *s* to form the possessive of most singular nouns, plural nouns
not ending in *s* or *z*, and indefinite pronouns. For example:

HomeElderCare's service
women's concerns
everyone's health

If a singular noun ends in *s* or *z*, the majority rule says to form the possessive by
adding an apostrophe and *s* unless the resulting pronunciation is difficult; in
that case, add only an apostrophe. For example:

Dr. Ferris's opinion
Professor Berenz's office
for goodness' sake

The possessive form of a plural noun ending with *s* or *z* is formed by adding an
apostrophe to the noun. For example:

social workers' counseling

In the following passage, the italicized usages are correct, but the boldface
usages are not:

It's disheartening that an *apostrophe's* commercial use is often *its* misuse. Many store and advertising signs misuse apostrophes. For instance, this morning I passed a restaurant called "Tom & **Mavys** Cafe" with a sign that read, "**TACO'S.**" But *who's* to object if the tacos are good? And *whose* sensibilities will be offended?

d. Quotation Marks

Quotation marks appear on either side of quoted text or a new term that is yet undefined. A quote within a quote is bounded by single quotation marks. For example:

> The social worker reported, "The client told me to 'deliver this living will right away.' "

A comma or period at the end of quoted matter always goes inside of the final quotation mark, regardless of whether it was part of the quote. All other punctuation at the end of quoted matter goes outside of the final quotation mark unless it appeared in the original text from which the quote was taken.

Legal style rules governing quotations appear in rule 48 of *ALWD Citation Manual: A Professional System of Citation* and rule 5 of *The Bluebook: A Uniform System of Citation*. These rules are *requirements,* not preferences, and they differ somewhat from style rules outside the legal profession. For example, if the quote is blocked and indented (50 words or more, under *Bluebook* standards), quotation marks are not used to open and close the quotation.

C. WORD USAGE

The following material addresses wording choices that yield text that is precise, concise, and appropriate—all important attributes of good legal writing.

1. Consistent and Distinct Wording Choices

In some fields, elegant variation in writing is prized. However, in legal writing, if you use different words to mean the same thing, the result is usually ambiguity. In the following example, *arrangement, contract,* and *agreement* may or may not all refer to the same thing.

> HomeElderCare's *arrangement* with its clients allows the social workers to furnish services under the *contract* and to bill the clients at the rate in the *agreement.*

Thus, in legal writing, you should always use the same word for a concept, for consistency. And you should use different words for different concepts, so that distinct concepts are perceived as distinct.

2. Nominalization

Some nouns are converted verbs, often formed by the addition of *tion, sion, ment, ence,* and similar suffixes. These nouns are called "nominalizations." Here are some examples:

Verb	*Nominalization*
contend	contention
admit	admission
agree	agreement

Although use of nominalizations is not ungrammatical, readers *prefer* the action of the sentence to be expressed in verbs, not nouns. Also, readers prefer short sentences; nominalizations generally are long words and appear in wordy constructions, such as a verb + noun phrase or a prepositional phrase.

To reduce your use of nominalizations, look for nouns that are made out of verbs (in italics below), and decide whether a straightforward verb would work better. For example:

> In the event of a *refusal* by a client to the *use* of the statutory form, the social worker will make a *referral* to an attorney.

Note that *refusal* appears in a prepositional phrase, and *referral* appears in a noun + verb phrase. Here is a revision:

> If the client refuses to use the statutory form, the social worker will refer the client to an attorney.

3. Unneeded Adverbs

Be alert for adverbs that weaken your text. They violate a *preference* that each word carry some useful meaning. For instance, words like *very, somewhat,* and *rather* often can be deleted with no loss in meaning but a gain in power of the remaining words. For example:

> The living will ~~very~~ accurately represented the wishes of the client.

4. Multiple Negatives

When two or more negative expressions occur in the same sentence, they often slow down the reader and obscure meaning. Thus, readers *prefer* not to see multiple negatives (in italics). For example:

> It is *unlawful* for a social worker to *fail* to use the living will form.

To revise such a sentence, cancel out the pair of negatives, and then assess whether the resulting sentence accurately captures the meaning of the original. For example:

> A social worker must use the living will form.

5. Surplus Words

Readers *prefer* lean text because short sentences are easier to read and understand. Eliminate redundant legal phrases—strings of synonyms where one would do; use only the best word. Examples include *cease and desist, null and void,* and *last will and testament.*[6] Also avoid bulky constructions, typically prepositional phrases such as the following.[7]

Bulky	*Simplified*
at that point in time	then
prior to	before
subsequent to	after
during the time that	during, while
for the period of	for
until such time as	until
by means of	by
by virtue of	by, under
in accordance with	by, under
for the purpose of	to
in order to	to
with a view to	to
by reason of	because of
for the reason that	because
inasmuch as	because
because of the fact that	because
in connection with	with, about, concerning
in relation to	about, concerning
with reference to	about, concerning
in favor of	for
in the event that	if
in the nature of	like
despite the fact that	although, even though
in some instances	sometimes
in many cases	often
in the majority of instances	usually
insofar as _____ is concerned	regarding
there was a situation in which	there
there is no doubt but that	doubtless, no doubt
this is a ____ that	this ____

Similarly, eliminate legalisms that generally add nothing but syllables. Examples are *hereinafter* and *aforementioned.*

---

6. For the historical roots of these redundant phrases, see Richard C. Wydick, *supra* note 3, at 19–20.
7. *See id.* at 9–16, 57–58, 60–61.

6. Precise Word Choices

Some words have several meanings, while other words carry but one meaning. Legal readers *prefer* that, when you have a choice among synonyms, you choose the word with the single meaning, so that the reader will not have to decide which of two or more meanings you intended.

Because, since, and *as* sometimes are used interchangeably, but they are not always synonyms. *Because* shows causation—that something happened by reason of or on account of something else. *Since* can show causation, or it can show a temporal relationship after a particular event in the past. *As* can show a causative relationship, or it can show a concurrent temporal relationship, or it can show sameness. Thus, when you want to show a causative relationship between clauses, you should use *because* rather than *since* or *as*.

Likewise, *although* and *while* sometimes are used interchangeably, but they are not always synonyms. *Although* shows a contrary relationship in the same manner as *even though* or *in spite of the fact that*. *While* can show a contrary relationship in the same manner as *although*, or it can show a concurrent temporal relationship. When you want to show a contrary relationship between clauses, you should use *although*. When you want to show a concurrent temporal relationship, you should use *while*.

Another overlapping pair of conjunctions is *whether* and *if*. *Whether* shows an alternative relationship between two upcoming items. *If* can show a condition (*in the event that*), or it can show an alternative relationship in the same manner as *whether*. Thus, when you want to show an alternative relationship between clauses, you should use *whether* rather than *if*.

Among and *between* are not synonyms. *Between* is used to connect two items; *among* is used to connect three or more items.

7. Gender-Neutral Wording

Formerly, legal writers used masculine pronouns when the gender was not specified. However, during the past two or three decades, the convention has shifted, as more women have entered the legal profession and other positions of influence. Gender-biased wording now carries an implied message that the writer does not care about (or is not aware of) offending women readers, as well as many men who are sensitive to these issues.

Gender-neutral wording is a *preference,* not a requirement. It involves using pronouns carefully so as to avoid implying a particular gender when the gender is unknown. Gender-neutral wording presents your client's message in the most effective light for a wide audience.

The first step in gender-neutral wording is to replace gender-biased words, such as the following:

Former usage	*Replacement*
chairman	chairperson, chair
fireman	firefighter
policeman	police officer
manpower	resources
reasonable man	reasonable person

The second step is to figure out the gender of any known person being discussed and then use the appropriate gender-specific pronoun for that person. In discussing a hypothetical situation, you could generate names for the hypothetical characters and then use the appropriate gender-specific pronouns for those characters. Balance the genders of your hypothetical characters by having nearly equal numbers of male and female characters, and take care to avoid gender stereotypes.

The third step is to omit as many gender-specific pronouns as possible in the following ways:

- Repeat the noun instead of using the pronoun.
- Change the person being discussed from singular to plural, so that *he* or *she* becomes *they.*
- Change the discussion from third person to second person, so that *he* or *she* becomes *you.*
- Change the person being discussed to an indefinite pronoun (*anyone, everybody, no one, nobody, someone, somebody, one*).
- Omit the possessive pronoun; for instance, *his* or *her drafting* becomes *drafting.*
- Replace the pronoun with a noun, so that *he* or *she* becomes *the drafter,* while *his* or *her contract* becomes *the contract.*
- Change the sentence to passive voice and eliminate the actor entirely, so that *he* or *she* disappears.

The fourth step is to reword the remaining pronouns to avoid any implication of gender where the gender is unknown. Exhibit II.7 presents the alternatives with their disadvantages. Weigh the disadvantages in light of the audience and purpose of your document. *He or she* is probably the most commonly chosen alternative.

EXHIBIT II.7

REPLACEMENT PRONOUNS FOR GENDER-NEUTRAL WORDING

Subject	Object	Possessive	Disadvantages
Subject	*Object*	*Possessive*	
he/she	him/her	his/her	too colloquial for formal writing; still has masculine pronoun first
he or she	him or her	his or her	bulky but often workable; favors masculine pronoun by placing it first
she or he	her or him	her or his	bulky and somewhat unexpected by the reader, but often workable; favors feminine pronoun by placing it first
alternating between he or she	alternating between him or her	alternating between his and her	sometimes confusing to reader; may disrupt readability

APPENDIX III.A

CITATION:

ALWD CITATION MANUAL

A. Introduction
B. Citation to Legal Materials
C. Citation to Materials About Your Case
D. *ALWD Citation Manual* as a Style Manual

A. INTRODUCTION

Citation is the practice of providing references to legal and factual materials supporting the assertions made in a legal paper, such as an office memo or appellate brief. Various citation systems exist. Some courts have rules requiring certain citation forms. For many years, several law review staffs have published *The Bluebook: A Uniform System of Citation*. In 2000, the Association of Legal Writing Directors (ALWD) and Professor Darby Dickerson of the Stetson University College of Law published *ALWD Citation Manual: A Professional System of Citation*. This appendix focuses on *ALWD Citation Manual*, currently in its third edition.

You may wonder why a system of citation, especially a uniform system, is necessary or desirable. A system of citation functions much like a system of punctuation and grammar: it facilitates and therefore speeds the processing of information by the reader. Just as we all know, almost without thinking, that a period signifies the end of a sentence and a complete thought, legal readers know what N.W.2d or U.S.C. means. Furthermore, to experienced readers of legal papers, proper citation is a hallmark of the care and professionalism of the writer, and readers may infer that the research and analysis in a paper are only as good as its citations.

For many novices, legal citation is complicated and perplexing, and so are citation manuals, at least at first glance. As you use *ALWD Citation Manual*

EXHIBIT III.A.1

A GUIDE TO *ALWD CITATION MANUAL*

Use the following *access tools* to find the pertinent part, rule, or appendix:

- *fast format and short citation locators (inside front and back covers)*
- *table of contents in front*
- *index in back*

To learn the *basic information* about citing to a specific authority as well as the format if you are citing to a *print source*, peruse the pertinent rule in Part 3:

12. cases
13. constitutions
14. statutes
15. and 16. federal and state legislative materials
17. rules of court, procedure, evidence, and ethics
18. local ordinances
19. and 20. federal and state administrative materials
22. treatises
23. periodicals
24. A.L.R. Annotations
25. dictionaries
26. encyclopedias
27. Restatements

If you are citing to a *primary authority*, consult Appendix 1, which lists primary sources and their abbreviations by jurisdiction (states).

If you are writing to a *specific court*, consult Appendix 2, which provides state court citation rules. For updates to Appendix 2 log onto www.alwd.org.

If you are citing to an *electronic source*, consult Part 4.

To learn about *common matters of detail*, consult the following rules in Part 2:

1. typeface
2. abbreviations and spacing
3. spelling and capitalization
4. numbers
5. pages
6. sections and paragraphs
7. footnotes
8. supplements
11. short forms

If your citation includes a term that can be *abbreviated*, consult the following appendices:

3. general abbreviations
4. court abbreviations
5. periodicals abbreviations

Compare your draft citation to the most analogous citation fast format.
The fast formats are sprinkled throughout Parts 3 and 4.

Consult the following rules in Part 5 as you *insert your citation* into your text:

43. citation placement and use

44. signals

45. order of cited authorities

46. explanatory parentheticals

Consult Part 6 as you incorporate *quotations* into your text.

Compare your work to the *legal memorandum example* in Appendix 6.

to construct a proper citation for a case or other source that you want to cite, you are bound to flip from one part to another. With time, you will develop your own process. In the meantime, Exhibit III.A.1 provides a set of steps that reflects the overall organization of and incorporates the finding tools in *ALWD Citation Manual.*

HOW IMPORTANT IS PROPER CITATION?

Hurlbert v. Gordon,
824 P.2d 1238 (Wash. Ct. App. 1992).

RAP 10.3(a)(4), (5) and RAP 10.3(b) require that reference to the relevant parts of the record must be included for each factual statement contained in the sections of the parties' briefs devoted to the statement of the case and to argument. RAP 10.4(f) provides that references to the record should designate the page and part of the record which supports each factual statement contained in the statement of the case and in the argument.

Although not explicitly stated in RAP 10.3(a)(5), it is implicit in the rule that the citations to legal authority contained in the argument in support of a party's position on appeal should relate to the issues presented for review and should support the proposition for which such authority is cited.

The purpose of these rules is to enable the court and opposing counsel efficiently and expeditiously to review the accuracy of the factual statements made in the briefs and efficiently and expeditiously to review the relevant legal authority.

The record for this appeal was massive, consisting in all of some 6000 pages of clerk's papers, exhibits and verbatim reports of proceedings. Numerous assignments of error were raised. Although the dispositive issue on appeal was of such a nature that the court was not required to address in the decision all of the assignments of error, it was nevertheless necessary for the court and for opposing counsel to track numerous factual statements through the massive record and to review all of the legal authority cited, as to all issues on appeal.

Gateway's attorneys provided this court with a 95-page respondents' brief, special leave having been granted for a lengthy brief because of the number and complexity of the issues on appeal. By Gateway's attorneys' count, there were 413 references made to the record and 187 citations of legal authority. Gateway's brief contained numerous references to clerk's papers which were either non-existent, or difficult if not impossible to find, because of typographical errors in the references. On several occasions the pages cited were irrelevant to the factual statements for which the references were made. Several references were made to 20 or 50 or 100 page documents rather than to specific pages of the record relating to the particular factual statements made.

> Virtually all of the factual statements made in the argument section of the brief were made without reference to the record, in direct violation of RAP 10.3(a)(5) (which is incorporated by references into RAP 10.3(b)), making it necessary to refer back to the statement of facts, many pages earlier in the brief, in order to track (or to attempt to track) the factual statements back to the record. Finally, in several instances case citations contained typographical errors and in numerous other instances cases were cited which did not support the positions for which they were cited.
>
> Pursuant to RAP 10.7, we impose $750 in sanctions upon respondents' attorneys for this appeal, payable to the registry of this court. This type of "laissez-faire" legal briefing falls far below the high standards of professionalism of the firm in question and we do not expect such errors will be repeated. Nevertheless, in this instance, the briefing errors wasted the time of opposing counsel and hampered the work of the court. Accordingly, the violations of the rules will not go unnoticed and unsanctioned.

B. CITATION TO LEGAL MATERIALS

1. Functions of Legal Citations

A citation to a legal source, such as a case or legal periodical, permits the reader to locate the source, should he or she desire to verify its content; assess the authoritativeness of the source; and discern the strength of the source's support for the legal proposition stated in the paper. Proper citation gives credit to the author of the cited material; given the principle that legal writing must rest on thorough research, this bolsters the credibility of the author of the paper.

The citation itself (covered in sections 2 and 3 below) serves the location and authoritativeness functions. The support function is achieved through proper placement of the citation, linking of the citation to the text, use of parentheticals, and sequencing of multiple citations, as covered in the remaining sections.

2. Long Citation Forms for Commonly Cited Sources

The following is a list of illustrative citations, drawn from the HomeElderCare sample office memos. Note that each citation provides information permitting you to ascertain the name of the source; its location, including the page or section number where the specific information appears within the source; the author of the source; and its key date. Key *ALWD Citation Manual* parts, rules, and appendix numbers as well as brief explanations follow. Note that the Minnesota courts did not have citation rules governing the citations below.

Dick Weatherston's Assocd. Mech. Servs. v. Minn. Mut. Life Ins. Co., 100 N.W.2d 819, 824 (Minn. 1960).

- "100 N.W.2d 819" permits the reader to locate the case; "824" directs the reader to a specific page.
- "Minn. 1960" tells the reader that the case was decided in 1960 by the Minnesota Supreme Court. The lack of adverse subsequent history shows that the case remains good law.
- See Section 12 in general, Appendix 3 on case names, and Appendix 1 on which reporter to use.

Minn. Stat. § 481.02 subdiv. 1 (1992).

- The entire citation permits the reader to locate the statute.
- "Minn. Stat." tells the reader it is a statute from Minnesota, and "1992" suggests that it is current law (the memo was written in 1993, Minnesota Statutes is published in even years, and the lack of a supplement cite indicates that there is no updating information).
- Note that 1992 is the date of the source in which the statute appears—not the statute's date of enactment.
- See Section 14 in general, Appendix 3 on subdivisions, and Appendix 1 on which code to use.

E. Allan Farnsworth, *Contracts* § 5.6 (2d ed., Little, Brown & Co. 1990).

- The entire citation helps the reader to locate the treatise, and "§ 5.6" directs the reader to specific pertinent pages.
- The reader can judge the treatise's credibility by its author, fairly recent publication date (again, the memo was written in 1993), and republication in the treatise's second edition (weak treatises tend not to be republished).
- See Section 22.

Howard Orenstein, David Bishop & Leigh D. Mathison, *Minnesota's Living Will . . .*, 46 Bench & B. Minn. 21, 24–25 (Aug. 1989).

- The entire citation permits the reader to locate the article, and "24–25" directs the reader to specific pertinent pages.
- The reader can judge the article's credibility by its author, journal, and date.
- See Section 23 in general and Appendices 3 (dates) and 5 (periodical abbreviations).

3. Short Citation Forms

The citations presented above are complete citations that would appear the first time a source is cited. Fortunately, you need not repeat this long form when you refer to the same source again. Section 11 covers short citation forms, and each section governing a specific source, e.g., Section 12 on cases, also covers short citation forms. Here are short citations for three of the sources cited above:

Weatherston's, 100 N.W.2d at 820.
Minn. Stat. § 481.02 subdiv. 1.
Farnsworth, *Contracts* at § 5.6.

When a source is cited twice (or more) in a row, with no intervening citation to a different source, an even shorter form is used. For example the *id.* short form for the case would be:

Id. at 819.

Id. is used by itself, i.e., without a page or section reference, when the subsequent citation is identical to the immediately preceding one.

4. Placement of Citations Within Text

As discussed in Section 43, citations may be placed within your paper in various ways. In the least intrusive, the citation appears in its own citation sentence immediately following the text it supports; the citation sentence is punctuated as a separate sentence. For example:

> If the unlicensed individual answers difficult or doubtful legal questions, she has committed the unlawful practice of law. *Gardner v. Conway,* 48 N.W.2d 788, 796 (Minn. 1951).

If a citation supports only a portion of the textual sentence, it should be inserted immediately after that portion and punctuated as a clause, with either commas or a comma and a period to set it off. For example:

> The drafting of a testamentary will by a non-lawyer is the unauthorized practice of law, *In re Est. of Peterson,* 42 N.W.2d 59, 63 (Minn. 1950), as is the preparation of complicated tax returns, *Gardner v. Conway,* 48 N.W.2d 788, 796 (Minn. 1951).

In some situations, you may want to refer to a source in your text, so that the reader is more aware of the source itself. For example:

> The Minnesota Supreme Court established the difficult-or-doubtful-question test in *Gardner v. Conway,* 48 N.W.2d 788, 796 (Minn. 1951).

> This case involves two facets of the prohibition on legal practice by non-lawyers found in Minnesota Statutes § 481.02.

In general, citations contain more abbreviations than references in a text sentence.

5. Linking Your Citations and Your Text

You are obligated to provide a citation for every legal proposition you assert—not just for direct quotations. Some propositions will be supported very directly by a legal source, as is true of the examples given above. Other propositions will be supported only indirectly or even contradicted by a source.

Rather than take up space in a text sentence explaining the links between a proposition and a source, you should use signals, covered in Section 44.

The continuum below shows these signals arrayed from the strongest support for a proposition to the strongest contradiction of a proposition:

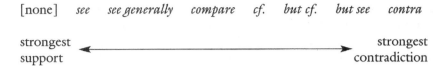

[none]   *see*   *see generally*   *compare*   *cf.*   *but cf.*   *but see*   *contra*

strongest   strongest
support   contradiction

Here are some classic situations in which you would use some of these signals:

- [none] when the citation identifies the source referred to in the text, when the text quotes the source, or when the source directly supports the proposition;
- *see* when the source implicitly supports the proposition;
- *compare* when your proposition is derived from a set of cases with varying outcomes;
- *but see* or *contra* when you are urging a rule other than that stated in an authority of which the reader should be aware.

Accord is used after a citation to a leading source and before a list of other sources that also directly support the proposition. *See also* is used in much the same way, when the listed sources implicitly support the proposition. You may use *e.g.* alone or with other signals, to show that the cited sources are representative of a larger set of similar sources.

You can also use signals, along with textual discussion of sources, for persuasive effect. For example, you can raise an adverse case quickly and in little space through a *but see* or *contra* citation. On the other hand, you might want to provide a full textual discussion of a leading favorable case. The *see, e.g.,* signals permit you to convey to the reader that there is substantial additional authority in support of your proposition.

6. Parentheticals and Other Appended Information

Parenthetical explanations are used in several standard situations. As discussed in Section 46, a parenthetical typically contains a phrase or two (sometimes a quotation) and immediately follows the citation to the source to which it pertains.

In some situations, a citation with a signal may raise questions for the reader. Rule 44.4 encourages the use of parentheticals following signals. For example, a reader may want to know how two cases in a *compare* cite relate to each other:

The court has been inconsistent in its application of the unauthorized practice statute. *Compare Peterson v. Hovland,* 42 N.W.2d 59 (Minn. 1950) (holding that drafting a testamentary will is unauthorized) *with Cardinal v. Merrill Lynch Realty/Burnet, Inc.,* 433 N.W.2d 864 (Minn. 1988) (suggesting that drafting real estate documents is permissible).

Parentheticals also are used to provide information that will help the reader to understand the cited authority. For example, rule 12.11 calls for parenthetical notations when you are citing to a non-majority opinion or to a case decided per curiam or without a written opinion. As another example, rule 14.2(h) provides for parenthetical explanations of the date a statute was enacted or became effective when this information is pertinent.

If a source you are citing has evolved over time, you are obligated to alert the reader. Rule 12.8 lists the various types of subsequent history for cases that must be cited in order for a case citation to be complete. For example, had *Weatherston's* overruled *Buckley, Buckley* would be cited as follows:

> *Buckley v. Humason*, 52 N.W. 385 (Minn. 1892), *overruled, Dick Weatherston's Assocd. Mech. Servs. v. Minn. Mut. Life Ins. Co.*, 100 N.W.2d 819, 822 (Minn. 1960).

Similarly, rule 14.3 requires an indication that a statute has been repealed.

7. Multiple Sources Supporting a Single Point

On occasion, more than one source will support your proposition, and you will provide a string cite. String cites should be used when the reader needs to consult a range of sources to find your legal proposition credible; typical examples are a statute that has been interpreted in a leading case and a statement about a trend in the law. String cites typically support the most critical propositions in a paper. You should not over-use string cites because excessive string citing clutters up text.

To figure out how to order the authorities in a string citation, first determine which signals to use for each, and then follow the list in rule 44.3 (categories of signals). Then turn to rule 45, which specifies the order of citations within a signal; the general principle is that the weightiest source is cited first. Primary authority precedes secondary authority, statutes precede cases, and newer cases precede older cases from the same court. For example, if you were to provide a very full citation to a statement about prohibitions on the unauthorized practice of law, it might read as follows:

> Minnesota prohibits the unauthorized practice of law by a wide variety of non-lawyer professionals. Minn. Stat. § 481.02 (1992); *Gardner v. Conway*, 48 N.W.2d 788 (Minn. 1951) (tax accountant); *In re Est. of Peterson*, 42 N.W.2d 59 (Minn. 1950) (bank cashier).

C. CITATION TO MATERIALS ABOUT YOUR CASE

When writing to a court about your client's case, you are responsible for directing the court to the record—the pleadings, the documents created during discovery before trial, the trial transcript, motions made by the parties and the judge's rulings, and so on. References to the record are governed by rule 29, which generally calls for the document's name (which may be abbreviated), a pinpoint reference, and the date.

D. *ALWD Citation Manual* as a Style Manual

ALWD Citation Manual covers quotations extensively in Part 6. Rules 1, 3, and 4 cover typeface, capitalization, and numbers, respectively.

A POSTSCRIPT ON PLAGIARISM

Iowa Supreme Court Board of Professional Ethics & Conduct v. Lane, **642 N.W.2d 296 (Iowa 2002).**

The following is a summary of the *Lane* case from the Iowa Supreme Court's website:

Following a federal trial, the respondent, William J. Lane, submitted a post-trial brief to the court. The legal portion of the brief was in great part plagiarized from a treatise. Lane later applied to the court for attorney fees, seeking compensation for eighty hours of work spent to prepare the brief at $200 per hour. In total, Lane requested $104,127 in attorney fees plus $13,363.29 in costs for his representation of the plaintiff. He also sought $9000 for time spent preparing his bill. At the ensuing attorney fee hearing, the magistrate judge stated it did not appear that Lane wrote the legal portions of the brief. Lane responded, I borrowed liberally from other sources. Yes, your honor. The judge then ordered Lane to explain or identify these sources within ten days. Lane did not do so, and the judge ultimately reduced the attorney fee award to $20,000. One month later, Lane filed a statement in compliance with the judge's order, but buried the name of the treatise among a list of over 200 sources. The judge later discovered the legal portion of the brief was taken verbatim from a treatise. The Iowa Supreme Court Board of Professional Ethics and Conduct filed a complaint alleging Lane's actions in the federal case and two unrelated bankruptcy matters violated numerous disciplinary rules. Our Grievance Commission found Lane violated several disciplinary rules in the plagiarism case, but concluded the Board did not establish any violations on the bankruptcy matters. The Commission recommended a three-month suspension.

    OPINION HOLDS: I. We agree the Board failed to prove any violations in the bankruptcy cases. II. Lane knowingly presented plagiarized work to the court with the intent to deceive. Lane copied his entire legal argument out of a book and then claimed the brief took him eighty hours to write. The chances are remote that Lane took eighty hours to copy his argument. We find Lane charged an excessive fee by requesting compensation for time he did not spend working on the case, bringing his own integrity into question and the entire legal profession into disrepute. We therefore suspend Lane's license to practice law in Iowa with no possibility of reinstatement for six months. Costs are assessed to Lane.

APPENDIX III.B

CITATION:

THE BLUEBOOK

A. Introduction
B. Citation to Legal Materials
C. Citation to Materials About Your Case
D. *The Bluebook* as a Style Manual

A. INTRODUCTION

Citation is the practice of providing references to legal and factual materials supporting the assertions made in a legal paper, such as an office memo or appellate brief. This appendix focuses on *The Bluebook: A Uniform System of Citation* (18th ed. 2005). *The Bluebook* is the most established and exhaustive text on legal citation, but it is not the only one. Indeed, some courts have their own citation rules.

You may wonder why a "uniform system" is necessary or desirable. A uniform system of citation functions much like a uniform system of punctuation and grammar: it facilitates and therefore speeds the processing of information by the reader. Just as we all know, almost without thinking, that a period signifies the end of a sentence and a complete thought, legal readers know what N.W.2d or U.S.C. means. Furthermore, to experienced readers of legal papers, proper citation is a hallmark of the care and professionalism of the writer, and readers may infer that the research and analysis in a paper are only as good as the citation.

For many newcomers to *The Bluebook*, it is a difficult source to use. Legal citation is inherently complex: many types of authority from many jurisdictions are published in many sources, both print and electronic. In addition, *The Bluebook* is really two citation manuals in one. It began as and continues to

EXHIBIT III.B.1

STRUCTURE OF AND STEPS FOR USING *THE BLUEBOOK*

First, locate the pertinent rule using:	Second, consult the Bluepages near the front, which are aimed at practitioner writing, along with the Bluepages tables:	Third, as needed, read the main rule covering your source in the white pages, and consult the tables augmenting the rule covering your source:	Fourth, consult, as needed, the rules that govern many sources:
• overall table of contents on back cover • detailed table of contents near front cover • index near back cover • quick reference citations inside *back* cover *Note: The quick reference citations inside the front cover are for scholarly writing—not for papers written for clients.*	For example, to cite a case, read Bluepages rule B5 re cases. Check for a jurisdiction-specific citation rule for the state in which your case arises in Bluepages table BT.2.	For example, peruse rule 10 on cases and table 6 on case names. The tables are in the back half in white pages with blue outer margins.	For example, consult Bluepages rule B2 re placing a citation into a paper and B13 re typeface.

The following rules govern citation to the record generated for your case:
- Bluepages rule B10 court and litigation documents
- Bluepages table BT.1 on abbreviations

The Bluebook is also a style manual; see the following rules:
- quotations, including alterations and omissions—Bluepages rule B12 and rule 5
- abbreviations, numerals, and symbols—rule 6
- italicization—rule 7
- capitalization—rule 8
- titles of judges and officials—rule 9

be a citation system for scholarly writing. It now covers, albeit somewhat awkwardly, practitioner work as well.

Exhibit III.B.1 presents both a schematic of *The Bluebook*'s structure and a sequence of steps for using it. It does not encompass all features of *The Bluebook*, but rather focuses on those you are most likely to use early in your career as a legal writer.

HOW IMPORTANT IS PROPER CITATION?

Hurlbert v. Gordon,
824 P.2d 1238 (Wash. Ct. App. 1992).

RAP 10.3(a)(4), (5) and RAP 10.3(b) require that reference to the relevant parts of the record must be included for each factual statement contained in the sections of the parties' briefs devoted to the statement of the case and to argument. RAP 10.4(f) provides that references to the record should designate the page and part of the record which supports each factual statement contained in the statement of the case and in the argument.

Although not explicitly stated in RAP 10.3(a)(5), it is implicit in the rule that the citations to legal authority contained in the argument in support of a party's position on appeal should relate to the issues presented for review and should support the proposition for which such authority is cited.

The purpose of this rules is to enable the court and opposing counsel efficiently and expeditiously to review the accuracy of the factual statements made in the briefs and efficiently and expeditiously to review the relevant legal authority.

The record for this appeal was massive, consisting in all of some 6000 pages of clerk's papers, exhibits and verbatim reports of proceedings. Numerous assignments of error were raised. Although the dispositive issue on appeal was of such a nature that the court was not required to address in the decision all of the assignments of error, it was nevertheless necessary for the court and for opposing counsel to track numerous factual statements through the massive record and to review all of the legal authority cited, as to all issues on appeal.

Gateway's attorneys provided this court with a 95-page respondents' brief, special leave having been granted for a lengthy brief because of the number and complexity of the issues on appeal. By Gateway's attorneys' count, there were 413 references made to the record and 187 citations of legal authority. Gateway's brief contained numerous references to clerk's papers which were either non-existent, or difficult if not impossible to find, because of typographical errors in the references. On several occasions the pages cited were irrelevant to the factual statements for which the references were made. Several references were made to 20 or 50 or 100 page documents rather than to specific pages of the record relating to the particular factual statements made.

Virtually all of the factual statements made in the argument section of the brief were made without reference to the record, in direct violation of RAP 10.3(a)(5) (which is incorporated by references into RAP 10.3(b)), making it necessary to refer back to the statement of facts, many pages earlier in the brief, in order to track (or to attempt to track) the factual statements back to the record. Finally, in several instances case citations contained typographical errors and in numerous other instances cases were cited which did not support the positions for which they were cited.

Pursuant to RAP 10.7, we impose $750 in sanctions upon respondents' attorneys for this appeal, payable to the registry of this court. This type of "laissez-faire" legal briefing falls far below the high standards of professionalism of the firm in question and we do not expect such errors will be repeated. Nevertheless, in this instance, the briefing errors wasted the time of opposing counsel and hampered the work of the court. Accordingly, the violations of the rules will not go unnoticed and unsanctioned.

B. CITATION TO LEGAL MATERIALS

1. Functions of Legal Citations

A citation to a legal source, such as a case or legal periodical, permits the reader to locate the source, should he or she desire to verify its content; assess the authoritativeness of the source; and discern the strength of the source's support for the legal proposition stated in the paper. Proper citation gives credit to the author of the cited material; given the principle that legal writing must rest on thorough research, this bolsters the credibility of the author of the paper.

The citation itself (covered in sections 2 and 3 below) serves the location and authoritativeness functions. The support function is achieved through proper placement of the citation, linking of the citation to the text, use of parentheticals, and sequencing of multiple citations, as covered in the remaining sections.

2. Long Citation Forms for Commonly Cited Sources

The following is a list of illustrative citations, drawn from the HomeElderCare sample office memos. Note that each citation provides information permitting you to ascertain the name of the source; its location, including the page or section number where the specific information appears within the source; the author of the source; and its date. Key *Bluebook* rule and table numbers as well as brief explanations follow.

Dick Weatherston's Assoc'd Mech. Servs. v. Minn. Mut. Life Ins. Co., 100 N.W.2d 819, 824 (Minn. 1960).

- "100 N.W.2d 819" permits the reader to locate the case, and "824" directs the reader to a specific page.
- "Minn. 1960" tells the reader that the case was decided in 1960 by the Minnesota Supreme Court. The lack of adverse subsequent history shows that the case remains good law.
- Note that this citation refers you to a commercial case reporter; in some situations, you would cite to an official reporter as well.
- See especially Bluepages rule B5, rule 10, and tables 1, 6, and BT.2.

Minn. Stat. § 481.02 subdiv. 1 (1992).

- The entire citation permits the reader to locate the statute.
- "Minn. Stat." tells the reader it is a statute from Minnesota, and 1992 suggests that it is current law (the case file was created in 1993, Minnesota Statutes is published in even years, and the lack of a supplement cite indicates there is no updating information).
- Note that 1992 is the publication date of the source in which the statute appears—not the statute's date of enactment.
- See especially Bluepages rule B6, rule 12, and table 1.

E. Allan Farnsworth, *Contracts* § 5.6 (2d ed. 1990).

- The entire citation permits the reader to locate the treatise, and "§ 5.6" directs the reader to specific pertinent pages.
- The reader can judge the treatise's credibility by its author, fairly recent publication date (the case file was created in 1993), and re-publication in the second edition (weak treatises tend not to be re-published).
- See especially Bluepages rule B8 and rule 15.

Howard Orenstein, David Bishop & Leigh D. Mathison, *Minnesota's Living Will . . .*, Bench & B. Minn., Aug. 1989, at 21, 24–25.

- The entire citation permits the reader to locate the article, and "24–25" directs the reader to specific pertinent pages.
- The reader can judge the article's credibility by its authors, journal, and date.
- See especially Bluepages rule B9, rule 16, and table 13.

3. Short Citation Forms

The four citations presented above are complete citations that would appear the first time a source is cited. Fortunately, you need not repeat this long form when you refer to the source again within the same general discussion. The rules governing specific sources also contain sections on short forms;

for example, see Bluepages rule B5.2 (cases) and B6.2 (statutes). Here are short forms for three of the sources cited above:

> *Weatherston's*, 100 N.W.2d at 820.
> § 481.02 subdiv. 3.
> Farnsworth, *supra*, § 5.8.

Note that *supra* is generally not used for cases and statutes.

When a source is cited twice (or more) in a row, with no intervening citation to a different source, an even shorter form is used. For example, the *id.* short form for the case would be:

> *Id.* at 819.

Id. is used by itself, i.e., without a page or section reference, when the subsequent citation is identical to the immediately preceding one.

4. Placement of Citations Within Text

Under Bluepages rule B2, citations may be placed within your text in various ways. In the least intrusive, the citation appears in its own citation sentence immediately following the text it supports; the citation sentence is punctuated as a separate sentence. For example:

> If the unlicensed individual answers difficult or doubtful legal questions, she has committed the unlawful practice of law. *Gardner v. Conway*, 48 N.W.2d 788, 796 (Minn. 1951).

If a citation supports only a portion of the textual sentence, it should be inserted immediately after that portion and punctuated as a clause, with commas or a comma and a period to set it off. For example:

> The drafting of a testamentary will by a non-lawyer is the unauthorized practice of law, *Peterson v. Hovland (In re Peterson's Estate)*, 42 N.W.2d 59, 63 (Minn. 1950), as is the preparation of complicated tax returns, *Gardner v. Conway*, 48 N.W.2d 788, 796 (Minn. 1951).

In some situations, you may want to refer to a source in your text, so that the reader is more aware of the source itself. For example:

> The Minnesota Supreme Court established the difficult-or-doubtful-question test in *Gardner v. Conway*, 48 N.W.2d 788, 796 (Minn. 1951).

> This case involves two prohibited activities by non-lawyers found in section 481.02 subdivision 1.

In general, textual references use fewer abbreviations than citations.

5. Linking Your Citations and Your Text

You are obligated to provide a citation for every legal proposition you assert—not just for direct quotations. Some propositions will be supported very directly by a legal source, as is true of the examples given above. Other propositions will be supported only indirectly by a source or even contradicted by a source.

Rather than take up space in a textual sentence explaining the links between your proposition and your source, you should take advantage of the signals covered in Bluepages rule B4 and rule 1.2. The continuum below shows these signals arrayed from the strongest support for your proposition to the strongest contradiction of your proposition:

[none]   *see*   *see generally*   *compare*   *cf.*   *but cf.*   *but see*   *contra*

strongest
support

strongest
contradiction

Here are classic situations in which you might use some of the more commonly used signals:

- [none] when you cite to a source that is quoted, directly states the proposition, or is identified in the text;
- *see* when the proposition is not directly stated by the source but obviously follows from it;
- *compare* when you have derived a rule from a set of cases with varying outcomes;
- *but see* or *contra* when you are urging the court to adopt one rule found in persuasive precedent and you need to alert the court that there is contrary authority elsewhere.

If you have cited a leading authority and then want to add additional authority, you would use *accord* when the additional authority states or clearly supports the proposition or *see also* when the additional authority less clearly supports the proposition. You can add *e.g.* to show that other un-cited authorities bear the same relationship to your source as the one(s) you have cited.

You also can use signals, along with textual discussion of sources, for persuasive effect. For example, you can raise an adverse case quickly and in little space through a *but see* or *contra* citation. On the other hand, you might want to provide a full textual discussion of a leading favorable case. The *accord* and *see, e.g.*, signals permit you to convey to the reader that there is substantial additional authority in support of your proposition.

6. Parentheticals and Other Appended Information

In some situations, a citation with a signal may raise questions for the reader. For example, the reader may want to know how two cases in a *compare* cite relate to each other. *The Bluebook* provides an economical way of providing this information, which permits you to avoid a textual discussion. Under Bluepages rule B11 and rules 1.5 and 1.6, you would insert a parenthetical explanation, containing a phrase or two explaining the facts and holding of each case, immediately after each case in the *compare* citation. For example:

> The court has been inconsistent in its application of the unauthorized practice statute. *Compare Peterson v. Hovland (In re Peterson's Estate)*, 42 N.W.2d 59 (Minn. 1950) (holding that drafting a testamentary will is unauthorized) *with Cardinal v. Merrill Lynch Realty/Burnet, Inc.*, 433 N.W.2d 864 (Minn. 1988) (suggesting that drafting real estate documents is permissible).

This mechanism is standard with several other signals, such as *cf.* and *see generally.*

More broadly, parentheticals are used when a phrase or two of explanation would further your reader's understanding. For example, if you are referring to a non-majority opinion, you must append a parenthetical indicating this.

Other important information is appended to the citation. In particular, some cases and statutes develop over time. For example, a case from an intermediate appellate court may be affirmed on appeal, or a case from a supreme court may be overruled some years later. A statute may be amended or repealed. Your reader should have this information about the case's or statute's subsequent history. Under Bluepages rule B5.1.5 on cases and rule 12.6 on statutes, this information is appended to the end of the citation, which consists of a phrase signifying what happened and then the location of the pertinent development. If, for example, the *Weatherston's* case had overruled the *Buckley* case, the citation to *Buckley* would read as follows:

> *Buckley v. Humason*, 52 N.W. 385 (Minn. 1892), *overruled by Dick Weatherston's Assoc'd Mech. Servs. v. Minn. Mut. Life Ins. Co.*, 100 N.W.2d 819 (Minn. 1960).

Finally, you may want to note how one source relies on another. For example, you may want to note that a recent case draws key language from an earlier case. Or you may want to note that a periodical article's language has been cited with approval in a case in your jurisdiction. Under rule 1.6, on related authority, you would follow the form in these two examples:

> Newer case (quoting older case).
> Periodical article, *cited with approval in* case.

7. Multiple Sources Supporting a Single Point

On occasion, more than one source will support your proposition, and you will provide a string cite. String cites should be used when the reader needs to consult a range of sources to find your legal proposition credible; typical examples are a statute interpreted in a leading case and a statement about a trend in the law. String cites typically support the most critical propositions in a paper. You should not over-use string cites because excessive string citing clutters up text.

The sources in the string cite may be linked in different ways to the proposition, requiring the use of various signals. Rule 1.3 outlines the order of signals. As to the order of sources following the same signal, see rule 1.4. For example, if you were to provide a very full citation to a statement about prohibitions on the unauthorized practice of law, it might read as follows:

> Minnesota prohibits the unauthorized practice of law by a wide variety of non-lawyer professionals. Minn. Stat. § 481.02 (1992); *Gardner v. Conway*, 48 N.W.2d 788 (Minn. 1951) (tax accountant); *Peterson v. Hovland (In re Peterson's Estate)*, 42 N.W.2d 59 (Minn. 1950) (bank cashier).

C. CITATION TO MATERIALS ABOUT YOUR CASE

When writing to a court about your client's case, you are responsible for directing the court to the record—the pleadings, the documents created during discovery before trial, the trial transcript, motions made by the parties and the judge's rulings, and so on. References to the record appear in parentheses, in either citation sentences or citation clauses as appropriate, under Bluepages rule B10 and table BT.1.

D. *THE BLUEBOOK* AS A STYLE MANUAL

While *The Bluebook* does not purport to be a composition text, it does address certain issues of style and usage. It provides answers to such issues as when to spell out numbers, when to capitalize party designations and court names, and when to indent long quotes. See Exhibit III.B.1 for a list of the style matters covered in *Bluebook* rules.

A POSTSCRIPT ON PLAGIARISM

Iowa Supreme Court Board of Professional Ethics & Conduct v. Lane, **642 N.W.2d 296 (Iowa 2002).**

The following is a summary of the Lane case from the Iowa Supreme Court's Web site:

Following a federal trial, the respondent, William J. Lane, submitted a post-trial brief to the court. The legal portion of the brief was in great part plagiarized from a treatise. Lane later applied to the court for attorney fees, seeking compensation for eighty hours of work spent to prepare the brief at $200 per hour. In total, Lane requested $104,127 in attorney fees plus $13,363.29 in costs for his representation of the plaintiff. He also sought $9000 for time spent preparing his bill. At the ensuing attorney fee hearing, the magistrate judge stated it did not appear that Lane wrote the legal portions of the brief. Lane responded, I borrowed liberally from other sources. Yes, your honor. The judge then ordered Lane to explain or identify these sources within ten days. Lane did not do so, and the judge ultimately reduced the attorney fee award to $20,000. One month later, Lane filed a statement in compliance with the judge's order, but buried the name of the treatise among a list of over 200 sources. The judge later discovered the legal portion of the brief was taken verbatim from a treatise. The Iowa Supreme Court Board of Professional Ethics and Conduct filed a complaint alleging Lane's actions in the federal case and two unrelated bankruptcy matters violated numerous disciplinary rules. Our Grievance Commission found Lane violated several disciplinary rules in the plagiarism case, but concluded the Board did not establish any violations on the bankruptcy matters. The Commission recommended a three-month suspension.

OPINION HOLDS: I. We agree the Board failed to prove any violations in the bankruptcy cases. II. Lane knowingly presented plagiarized work to the court with the intent to deceive. Lane copied his entire legal argument out of a book and then claimed the brief took him eighty hours to write. The chances are remote that Lane took eighty hours to copy his argument. We find Lane charged an excessive fee by requesting compensation for time he did not spend working on the case, bringing his own integrity into question and the entire legal profession into disrepute. We therefore suspend Lane's license to practice law in Iowa with no possibility of reinstatement for six months. Costs are assessed to Lane.

APPENDIX IV

CONTRACT DRAFTING

A. INTRODUCTION

Lawyers engage in two main types of writing: analytical writing and drafting. This book focuses on analytical writing, in which the writer states facts and rules, explains their connection, and posits a legal meaning for the client's situation. By contrast, drafting, in its narrowest sense, entails writing rules—describing situations that may arise and what is to occur as a result. Statutes, court rules, and agency regulations are drafted.

Most lawyers do not draft rules of law, but they do draft transactional documents, such as contracts and wills.[1] This appendix discusses the drafting of contracts,[2] although much of what is said here applies to other drafting contexts as well.

---

1. The term "drafting" also is used to refer to the writing of pleadings, discovery documents, and other litigation papers.
2. *See* Susan L. Brody et al., *Legal Drafting* (1994); Scott J. Burnham, *Drafting and Analyzing Contracts* (2d ed. 1993); Barbara Child, *Drafting Legal Documents: Principles and Practices* (3d ed. 2003); Carl Felsenfeld & Alan Siegel, *Writing Contracts in Plain English* (1981); Thomas R. Haggard, *Legal Drafting: Process, Techniques, and Exercises* (2003); George W. Kuney, *The Elements of Contract Drafting* (2003); Peter Siviglia, *Writing Contracts: A Distinct Discipline* (1996).

It is a privilege to write a contract for a client. In doing so, you give written expression to the client's understanding with the other party to the contract and guide the future conduct of both parties. If you do your job well, their relationship should be harmonious and productive. If you do not do your job well, their relationship may entail inefficiency, conflict, and litigation.

Recall the comparison between a statute and the rules of a game. The same comparison works for a contract. The various provisions tell the two parties what to do as their deal plays out. Some provisions are critical, such as performance and payment. Others deal with contingencies that may not occur but should be anticipated, such as disputes that the parties cannot settle themselves.

The difference between a statute and a contract is the relationship between the governed and the governing. A legislature governs people and organizations. The parties to a contract govern themselves; hence the image of a contract as private law. Thus, when you draft a contract for a client, you should focus to start on learning what the deal is and expect to consult the client from time to time as you go along.

Below are ten tenets by which to draft a contract and its various clauses. Each tenet is stated in general terms and then applied to a fictional contract between HomeElderCare, a geriatric social services agency, and its elderly clients.

B. LAWFULNESS

A well written contract accords with the law. Although they reflect private choices, contracts are highly regulated:

- Some legal rules prohibit certain clauses.
- Other rules require certain clauses.
- Other rules operate more subtly, by discouraging or encouraging certain clauses or providing parameters within which the parties may contract.
- Court opinions construe particular language, so that the parties can predict how a court might view their contract should they incorporate that language.
- Still other legal rules affect the process of contracting, addressing, e.g., capacity to contract, the process of negotiation, or the requirement of a writing.

Some contract rules govern nearly all contracts, others contracts of a particular sort.

A contract is not well written unless it accords with all of the legal rules pertaining to it. Obviously, it must avoid illegality and meet legal require-ments. Less obviously, it should secure the legal position desired by the client, consistent with the deal struck by the parties. For example, if a buyer and seller have discretion as to a particular term and have decided to favor the buyer over the seller on that term, the contract should use language that courts have construed to favor buyers.

Although you, your client, and the other party will not intend that a contract dispute arise and be litigated, it often is useful to think about the contract this way. Ask yourself:

- What could a lawyer for the other party argue based on this language?
- What would I argue on behalf of my client?
- How would a court or arbitrator (or other neutral decision-maker) decide the dispute?

Conforming to the law is a point that is obvious to most clients. However, some clients may want to overreach, that is, include clauses that are contrary to law or so one-sided that they are unlikely to be enforced. A client may intend to obtain an improper advantage from or intimidate an unsophisticated party (the so-called "in terrorem" effect) and gamble that the contract will never come before a court. This situation raises a serious ethical issue for the lawyer as well as the client.

As an example related to the HomeElderCare case, many legal rules would apply to a contract between a geriatric social service agency and its elderly customers. For example, the statute on unauthorized practice of law bars social workers from providing legal services; the contract should not call for them to do so. HomeElderCare should take care to assess each customer's capacity to contract, and the contract should accord with any plain-language requirements applicable to consumer contracts.

A word or two about sample forms: In your legal research, you may well come across sample language in various secondary sources, such as form books. You may get some good ideas from such a source. But you should never adopt the language of a sample form without careful consideration of its suitability for your client's situation. The form may be based on the law of another jurisdiction, it may not be expressed well, and it certainly does not reflect the specific situation of your client.

C. ACCURACY

A well written contract reflects the facts of the client's situation. Although a contract is oriented toward the future, it rests on some present facts—the parties' identities, locations, operations, industry customs—that the contract must state or reflect accurately. Furthermore, the contract must accurately state the parties' agreement. Some contracts include recitals that state the parties' purpose in contracting.

The HomeElderCare contract should, of course, accurately reflect the names of both HomeElderCare and the individual customer. The contract should state the purpose of the contract, i.e., to provide assistance to elderly individuals who seek to reside in their homes. It should correctly specify the services the customer has purchased, the service providers, and the agreed-upon price (or the process by which selection, staffing, and pricing will occur). For example, if some services are priced on an hourly basis and others on a task basis, it is inaccurate to refer only to hourly pricing.

D. BALANCE

A well written contract is fair and realistic. To some extent, the contract's fairness is a product of the parties' negotiations—the contract is fair because they consider it fair. Each party may, of course, consider some clauses one-sided, but presumably the overall agreement is acceptable to both.

Closely related to fairness is realism. A contract may state high aspirations, but ordinarily the aspirations should also be reasonably attainable (or the contract should reflect the inherent riskiness of the deal). In particular, you should guard against unduly high performance standards and very tight time frames.

In most situations, lawyers write not only fully negotiated terms but also undickered terms, that is, terms that the parties have not explicitly discussed. If you are the lawyer primarily responsible for drafting the contract, you may be tempted to write clauses on undickered terms so as to protect your client to the detriment of the other party. However, this strategy often backfires when the other party either resists signing the contract as written or signs the contract but carries mistrust into the contract relationship.

Furthermore, most contracts affect not only the contracting parties but also third parties. As you assess the contract for balance, be sure to consider these third parties' interests, the extent to which they correspond to or diverge from those of your client, and your client's view of how to accommodate those interests.

Most likely, HomeElderCare would provide a form contract with certain spaces, e.g., for services and prices, to be filled in after discussion with a new customer. Through this process, the customer and HomeElderCare presumably would come to a mutually fair agreement as to the sale and purchase of services. Neither HomeElderCare nor the customer should promise more than it can deliver, e.g., a ride to a shopping center on five minutes' notice or a higher fee for the services than a customer's budget permits.

The contract probably would have clauses on undickered terms too, such as a dispute resolution clause. HomeElderCare could favor its interests to the detriment of the customer, e.g., by compelling arbitration and requiring the customer to pay an unreasonable percentage of an arbitrator's fee. HomeElderCare should take care not to do so.

As for the interests of third parties, consider the clause describing the social worker's service as a liaison between the customer and a physician. That clause should at least partially reflect the physician's preferences as to communications among patient, liaison, and physician.

E. COMPREHENSIVENESS

Obviously, a well written contract thoroughly covers intended events. To discern what needs to be covered in the contract's main clauses, consider what the parties intend to have happen during the term of the contract.

Ask yourself as to each such event: who? what? when? where? how? Unless an answer is very obvious, the contract should state all of these dimensions of an intended event. Especially important is the matter of identifying who is to undertake a particular task; few contract provisions should be written in truncated passive voice (lacking the actor).

As to some matters, the law provides default rules, that is, a standard approach that is implied unless the contract provides otherwise. Although a contract need not state a default rule for it to operate, you may want to do so in some situations, so that the parties know what the default rule is. More importantly, if the parties do not want to use the default rule, the contract should state their alternative rule.

Even as you describe intended events, write flexibly enough to cover standard changes in the parties' circumstances, such as changes of address or personnel.

For example, assume that one of the services to be provided in the HomeElderCare contract is grocery shopping. The clause should indicate how the customer will identify needed groceries, how promptly the service provider will buy and deliver the groceries, where the groceries will be bought, how the customer will pay for the groceries, etc. The clause on grocery shopping should be written with some flexibility, e.g., by specifying a category of service provider (in lieu of a specific person) and providing a choice of grocery stores (unless the customer has a very fixed preference that HomeElderCare is willing to honor). The default rule is that payment for a service follows completion of the service, so if HomeElderCare seeks payment in advance, the contract should so provide.

F. FORESIGHT

A well written contract provides for reasonably predictable events other than what the parties intend to occur. Especially when a contract covers a long period of time, calls for several exchanges, or involves circumstances with some risk or volatility, events are unlikely to go exactly as planned. The contract should cover some such situations.

Consider what could happen to derail the intended course of events, both to the advantage and disadvantage of your client. As to each such unintended situation, determine its probability and significance. Plan to cover the most probable and significant events. No contract covers every possible contingency. To write an exhaustive contract would be unduly time-consuming and expensive, and the contract would be too unwieldy for the parties. Furthermore, contract law provides sound default rules for some common situations.

Once you have decided which unintended situations are worth covering, consider your options. To a certain extent, the contract can make some events more or less likely. The contract can create a stick, that is, an adverse consequence when one party fails to meet expectations, such as an adjustment in the price or cancellation of the contract. Another option is a carrot, that is, a favorable consequence when high expectations are met, such as a bonus payment for early delivery. Some situations will be outside the parties' control; then the contract should identify an outcome that is fair to both.

In the HomeElderCare situation, one unintended but very predictable situation is that a customer will die during the term of the contract. HomeElderCare would not be expected to perform services thereafter; hence, this situation would not need to be covered.

Another unintended but very predictable situation is that the customer will not pay for provided services on schedule. This situation merits coverage; options include denial of future services until the account is up-to-date, a penalty on payments that are past due, or a discount on payments that are made early, e.g., when service is provided (as distinct from payment in response to a monthly statement).

G. PRACTICALITY

A well written contract is easily understood as events unfold. Most contracts involve concepts that can be formulated various ways. Consider, for example, the notion of timeliness. One could define timeliness by reference to an abstract and general standard (within a reasonable time), a specific and concrete standard (by 12:00 P.M. on June 26), or a process (as determined by the buyer's general manager).

You should choose a formulation that is as precise and as flexible as the parties need it to be and that will be practical for them to implement during the contract term. Think of your contract as a script, and ask whether the parties will be able to figure out how to act it out as written.

In the HomeElderCare example, consider how to formulate a clause covering the frequency of check-in visits, and assume that the idea to be expressed is *reasonably necessary*. This phrase would be very difficult to implement. A better approach would be to state a formula, e.g., daily for the week following discharge from a hospital, otherwise weekly. Another approach would be to refer to a trusted third party's judgment, such as the customer's physician. Of course, if both parties are willing, the clause could provide for check-ins at a frequency set by the customer.

H. PRECISION

A well written contract says what it means. Choose your words wisely. Each concept should have one word or phrase, and each significant word or phrase should stand for one concept. Choose labels that make sense in terms of common parlance, the language of the pertinent trade, and the language of applicable legal rules.

Definitions: As with statutes, contracts may include definitions. You should establish a definition only when you have created a term without a readily discernible dictionary definition or when you are using a familiar word in a way different from its standard meaning. If a concept appears throughout the contract, its definition should appear in a definitions section, probably at the beginning of the contract;[3] if the concept appears only within a particular part, it should be defined within that part.

Avoid circular and overly complex definitions, especially nested definitions in which one definition incorporates another, which in turn incorporates a third, and so on. Incorporate terms of art from the law or the trade if they are indeed what you mean and are well understood.

Some concepts are amenable to definition via a list. Take care in constructing a list. Be sure to note whether the items listed are exhaustive or illustrative; in the latter situation, be sure you have chosen very representative examples.

In the HomeElderCare contract, the concept of *service provider* most likely would appear in various places throughout the contract and would merit a definition because it is not a commonly used term. One option would be to include a list: employees, independent contractors, volunteers. Another option would be to state the relationship of the service provider to the customer and to HomeElderCare: "an individual selected by HomeElderCare to assist you [the customer] by accomplishing the tasks you have chosen." A concept that could be defined by reference to the law (if it were to appear in the contract at all) is *living will*.

Verbs: Verbs are especially important in contracts because they create legal consequences:

- Most contract provisions state promises by one party to act or not act in a particular way; promises create duties on the part of the promisor and rights on the part of the promisee. They are conveyed by *will* or *must* or *agrees to* as to the promisor's conduct (or *is entitled* as to the promisee).[4]
- Often a duty is conditioned on the occurrence of some other event; this situation is conveyed by *if X occurs, then promisor will do Y.*
- Contrast a privilege, that is, a discretionary authority to act or not act, without creation of a right on the part of the other party. A privilege is conveyed by *may* (or the lack of a privilege by *may not*).

Consider the verbs in the following HomeElderCare clauses:

(1) To request transportation services, you [the customer] may call the HomeElderCare transportation line at any time and answer the questions posed by the recording. (2) If you call to request transportation (a) at least twenty-four hours before the time of pick-up for trips totaling fifty miles or less or (b) at least forty-eight hours before the time of pick-up for trips totaling over fifty miles, (3) HomeElderCare will provide the requested transportation.

---

3. In some settings, in complicated contracts involving many complex definitions, a schedule of definitions at the end may be preferable. *See* Bryan A. Garner, *Legal Writing in Plain English: A Text with Exercises* 97–99 (2001).

4. Another common choice is *shall*. But *shall*, as interpreted by the courts, has many meanings, not only *must*, but also *may, will,* and *is. See* Garner, *supra* note 3, at 105–06.

(4) HomeElderCare may provide the requested transportation with its own van service or arrange for a taxi to transport you.

Clauses 1 and 4 state privileges, clause 2 a condition, and clause 3 a duty.

Ambiguity: To the extent feasible, avoid ambiguity, that is, language that conveys two distinct and inconsistent meanings. Ambiguity typically arises from:

- two passages carrying conflicting implications;
- omission of some information (for example, the actor is missing in a passive-voice sentence);
- awkward construction of a sentence (for example, a modifier is misplaced, a pronoun has two possible antecedents, the import of a negative is unclear); or
- use of an ambiguous word without clarification.

To detect and remove ambiguity, check for the potential troublespots listed above. For example, check the draft for passive voice, and clarify who the actor is, unless the actor is not known or unimportant. As another example, check for plural constructions, and switch to the singular, to avoid the question whether the plural applies to the singular.

Ambiguous words can be quite short. For example, *or* has several meanings: A or B but not both; A or B or both; A, but if not A, then B. The words *from, to,* and *by* can be very ambiguous when used in timing clauses. For example, does "by September 6th" mean before 12:00 A.M. or by 11:59 P.M. of that date?

Consider the following HomeElderCare clause:

Clients may request cleaning services. If you call by 8:00 Monday to request cleaning services for the following week, HomeElderCare will contact a cleaning service for you. Payment for cleaning services must be made at that time.

This passage raises numerous questions:

- May one client acting alone request this service?
- What if the call comes exactly at 8:00?
- Must the client call by 8:00 A.M. or 8:00 P.M.?
- If a client calls on Monday the 1st, will cleaning occur during the week of the 1st or the week of the 8th?
- Has HomeElderCare promised only to make the contact, not to assure that cleaning actually occurs?
- Who must pay the cleaning service?
- At what time—when cleaning occurs or when the contact with the cleaning service occurs?

If the contract also states in another provision that HomeElderCare "will provide [the client] with a monthly statement," the payment issue will be even thornier. Does payment occur at the time of cleaning or via the monthly statement?

HOW IMPORTANT IS PRECISION
IN CONTRACT DRAFTING?

Our law firm represented Merritt, Chapman and Scott Corporation, a general contractor, which had a contract with Farrell Lines to refurbish a Farrell Lines pier on the Hudson River. Part of the job was to replace the corrugated iron siding on the walls of the pier shed. The contract provided that our client was to be paid a dollar amount per square foot of siding. Corrugated siding is put on like shingles on your house. There is an overlap, and a lot of it. But the drafters of the contract, who may or may not have been lawyers, didn't say whether the square feet were to be measured before or after installation. We went to trial with a jury in the United States District Court. The trial took about five days and there were three sets of lawyers: the sheet metal subcontractor was also in the case.

It would have taken no more than an hour for the parties to have agreed on that point in their negotiation, and about two minutes to write the price clause correctly. Instead we had an expensive jury trial. And the worst of it was that the judge was Edward Weinfeld, one of the best judges of our time, and he had to waste a week on this case.

Richard S. Lombard, essay in *Lost Words: The Economic, Ethical, and Professional Effects of Bad Legal Writing* 53, 54–55 (Section of Legal Education & Admissions to the Bar, American Bar Association, 1994).

I. COMPREHENSIBILITY

A well written contract is reasonably easily understood.

Comprehensibility is in part a function of the sequence in which information is presented; it is hard to comprehend a document in which first things are presented second or third. You should employ some logical principle for the sequence of main topics and for the sequence of points within a main topic. Some classic choices are:

- chronological;
- general to specific;
- general rules before exceptions; and
- most to least familiar, important, or commonly used.

To the extent possible, to make your organization readily apparent to the readers of the contract, develop a set of headings and sub-headings that do not overlap and that precisely state the scope of the following material.

For example, one possible organization for the HomeElderCare contract is as follows: preliminary matter (the parties and the purpose of the contract);

definitions; selection of services by the customer; transportation, shopping, cleaning, liaison with physician, etc.; payment; change in service selection; cancellation by the customer; process for resolving disputes; and boilerplate clauses (typically such matters as modification, assignment, dispute resolution, and choice of law).

Comprehensibility is also a function of sentence design. Some contracts are required by law to be written in plain English; many should be. Section 325G.31 of the Minnesota Statutes, for example, calls for consumer contracts to be written "in a clear and coherent manner using words with common and everyday meanings . . . appropriately divided and captioned." Use short simple sentences, framed affirmatively. Avoid the following, which add words, confusion, or both:

- legalese,
- redundant terms (couplets),
- compound prepositional phrases,
- nominalizations,
- passive voice,
- expletives (*it is agreed that*), and
- lapses in parallel structure.

A particularly troublesome legalism is the proviso—*provided that . . .*— typically appended to a lengthy sentence. This phrase has been interpreted to mean *if, except,* and *in addition.* Furthermore, most sentences with provisos are too long and complicated to be readily understood. In general, avoid provisos.

Avoid stating a point twice. Although this practice is common in other forms of legal writing, it can lead to confusion in a contract, which is a very economically written document in which each statement is deemed to have meaning not conveyed elsewhere in the contract.

Do, however, provide links between sentences that address the same topic. Some links are semantic, such as transitional words and repeated references. Other links are structural, such as an introductory phrase or clause followed by a list of related phrases or clauses in parallel structure.

As an example of poor sentence design, consider the following sentence:

In the event that any dispute, controversy, or disagreement arising hereunder shall proceed to litigation, it is the parties' agreement that it shall be the law of the jurisdiction of Minnesota that shall be utilized by the court called upon to adjudicate such dispute, controversy, or disagreement.

This sentence of forty-seven words contains nearly all of the writing problems listed above; its meaning can be conveyed in fewer than ten words.

Also on the topic of sentence design, review the transportation clause stated in Part H. Note that each sentence makes its own discrete point, the points proceed chronologically, there is a semantic link (the phrase "the requested transportation"), and clauses (a) and (b) are written in parallel structure.

J. Aptness

A well written contract has a style and tone that reflects the parties' relationship.

Generally, contract parties want a contract that conveys that the parties have entered voluntarily into a mutually advantageous agreement between equals. The contract should read as though they wrote it for each other, not as though a lawyer wrote it for a judge forced to adjudicate a dispute. This is especially true when a contract has been fully negotiated by the parties.

Some contracts fit into a different paradigm, in which a large company presents a standard form contract to many consumers. Some large companies opt for a legalistic and tough tone; others opt for contracts that are conversational and friendly. In these situations, in choosing a tone, you should consider the contract from the client's perspective, of course. But also consider it from the perspective of the typical consumer (who may well be less sophisticated in the transaction) as well as the perspective of a judge or an arbitrator.

Compare the transportation clause in Part H with the choice-of-law clause in Part I. The two clauses differ in tone. The choice-of-law clause is abstract and technical. The transportation clause is more personal and direct. One obvious and significant difference is their means of referring to the contracting parties: "the parties" in the choice-of-law clause, "HomeElderCare" and "you" in the transportation clause.

K. Aesthetics

A well written contract is easy to peruse. Few people read contracts for fun; rather, they read them to find pertinent information. You may use the following tools to make the contract easy to peruse:

- clear headings and sub-headings, cleanly formatted;
- simple numbering/lettering system;
- tabulation and enumeration for lists of related items;
- fairly short paragraphs and sentences;
- easily readable type and font; and
- plenty of white space.

This appendix employs these principles.

EXERCISES

This series of exercises involves the liability of a seller of liquor to persons who are injured by the acts of an intoxicated buyer of liquor. Most pertain to the following client situation, which you may wish to review from time to time:

One evening in Stamford, Connecticut, Gary Masters visited two bars over the course of four to six hours. He drank three shots of tequila and six bottles of beer at the first. When he arrived at the second bar, the smell of liquor was on his breath. He kept to himself and appeared sullen and withdrawn. He paid for and drank three more shots and six more bottles of beer at the second bar. Shortly after leaving the second bar, he drove his car across the highway into oncoming traffic. He struck a car carrying a child, who was killed. At this point, you do not know Gary Masters' age.

The child's father has brought suit against your client, the second bar, for negligence and for damages under the Connecticut Dram Shop Act, which applies to commercial vendors of liquor.

The materials referred to here are real legal materials from Connecticut on this topic, but they are not necessarily exhaustive or current.

EXERCISES FOR CHAPTER 2

THE STRUCTURE OF LEGAL RULES

Consider the following rules:

Rule #1

"Two conditions [] must coexist before statutory negligence can be actionable. First, the plaintiff must be within the class of persons protected by the statute. Second, the injury must be of the type which the statute was intended to protect." *Wright v. Brown,* 356 A.2d 176, 179 (Conn. 1975).

Rule #2

"Failure to exercise due care is negligence, and whether there is such a failure must depend on the circumstances of a particular case. Generally, in the absence of some rule of conduct specifically prescribed by legislation, the standard of due care is that of the ordinary prudent person under the circumstances." *Burritt v. Plate,* 481 A.2d 425, 427 (Conn. Super. Ct. 1984).

Rule #3

"The inquiry whether, in a particular case, a party conducted himself with ordinary care, always involves the consideration of the difficulties and obstacles to be encountered, his knowledge of their existence, and his means and power to overcome them. And if men of ordinary prudence would regard the ability of the party insufficient for the purpose, without hazard, there is want of ordinary care in making the attempt." *See Fox v. Town of Glastonbury,* 29 Conn. 204, 208–09 (1860).

1. Restate each of the rules in if/then form; use letters or numbers to set off the various elements and legal consequences. Identify the relationships among the elements, e.g., conjunctive, aggregate, a combination. Finally, note whether the consequence is an ultimate practical consequence or intermediate legal consequence.

2. Select one of these rules, and depict it in a flowchart.

3. Write your own rule about the liability of a bar for injuries caused by a customer who consumed liquor at the bar and afterward injured a third party in a car accident. Try to state an ultimate practical consequence in the then-clause. Present your rule in if/then form, and state how the elements are related to each other.

EXERCISES FOR CHAPTER 3

READING CASES

By way of background: The case used in this set of exercises involves a claim that the defendants acted negligently. Negligence is a common law claim involving "a departure from the conduct expectable of a reasonably prudent person under like circumstances." *Black's Law Dictionary* 1032 (6th ed. 1990). Negligence per se arises when the breached duty involves violation of a statute or municipal ordinance. Because *Moore* involves negligence per se, there are several references to Connecticut statutes. (You will learn more about statutes in Chapters 5 and 6). In addition to breach of a duty, to establish negligence, the plaintiff must show that the defendant's acts "proximately caused" the plaintiff's injury, that is, that the defendant's conduct "created the risk of a particular harm and was a substantial factor in causing that harm." *Quinnett v. Newman*, 568 A.2d 786, 790 (Conn. 1990).

1.   Read the following case and the introductory material. Label the case according to the components of the case brief presented in Chapter 3, e.g., facts, issues, reasoning.

510   Conn.   **228 ATLANTIC REPORTER, 2d SERIES**

Milton MOORE, Administrator (ESTATE of
John H. MOORE)

v.

Bradford E. BUNK et al.

Supreme Court of Connecticut.

March 23, 1967.

Action for death of plaintiff's decedent allegedly caused by defendants' furnishing alcoholic liquor to him. The Superior Court, New Haven County at Waterbury, Benjamin M. Leipner, J., sustained demurrers by defendants and plaintiff having failed to plead over rendered judgment for defendants, and plaintiff appealed. The Supreme Court, King, C. J., held that 16-year-old minor who consumes liquor is presumed to have done so voluntarily and minor's consumption of liquor and not the furnishing of the liquor was proximate cause of intoxication and resulting injuries and death.

No error.

1. Intoxicating Liquors ⬅291

The general common-law rule is that proximate cause of intoxication is voluntary consumption, rather than furnishing, of intoxicating liquor.

2. Negligence ⬅56(3)

Common-law rule as to proximate cause applies in any common-law action of negligence, even though that action includes, as specifications of negligence, one or more alleged violations of applicable statutes.

3. Evidence ⬅62

Minor aged 16 or over is presumed to have capacity to decide whether to violate law, and if he consumes intoxicating liquor, he is presumed to have done so voluntarily. C.G.S.A. §§ 30–77, 30–86.

4. Intoxicating Liquors ⬅291

Where 16-year-old voluntarily consumed intoxicating liquor, his consumption rather than any violation of statutes by person furnishing intoxicating liquor to minor was proximate cause of his intoxication and of injuries and death claimed to have resulted therefrom. C.G.S.A. § 30–86.

5. Negligence ⬅121(5)

Negligence, whether common-law or statutory, must be proved to have been proximate cause of injuries complained of if it is to constitute actionable negligence.

6. Pleading ⬅214(5)

Allegations of legal conclusions are not admitted by demurrer.

7. Intoxicating Liquors ⬅306

Pleading ⬅8(3)

Allegations of complaint that defendants' furnishing of liquor to minor decedent was proximate cause of his intoxication, injuries and death were legal conclusions and were ineffective to negate common-law rule that voluntary consumption, rather than furnishing, of liquor was proximate cause of intoxication and resulting injuries and death. C.G.S.A. §§ 30–77, 30–86.

8. Pleading ⬡8(17), 214(5)

Allegation of complaint that defendants, having allowed minor decedent to become intoxicated, neglected and failed to exercise any degree of care or control to prevent his injury and death at time when they were under duty so to do was mere legal conclusion and in absence of allegation of any specific duty or facts giving rise to any duty defendants' demurrers did not admit existence of any such duty. C.G.S.A. §§ 30–77, 30–86.

9. Intoxicating Liquors ⬡291

Any violation by holder of club liquor permit of duty to prevent persons on permit premises from giving or delivering intoxicating liquor to minor decedent was not proximate cause of minor's intoxication or of any injuries resulting from such intoxication. C.G.S.A. §§ 30–77, 30–86.

───────◆───────

Joseph H. Sylvester, Shelton, with whom was David B. Cohen, Derby, for appellant (plaintiff).

Alan H. W. Shiff, New Haven, with whom, on the brief, was Philip R. Shiff, New Haven, for appellees (defendants Bunk et al.).

John H. Cassidy, Jr., Watertown, for appellee (defendant Zalenski).

Thomas J. Hagarty, Hartford, with whom, on the brief, was Joseph T. Sweeney, Hartford, for appellee (defendant Smith).

Before KING, C. J., and ALCORN, HOUSE, THIM and RYAN, JJ.

KING, Chief Justice.

This action was brought by the administrator of the estate of John H. Moore to recover damages for his death. The first count runs against the defendants Bradford

E. Bunk and St. Stanislawa Benefits and Mutual Society, Inc., hereinafter referred to as Society, as permittee and backer, respectively, of Society's club liquor permit. The second count runs against the defendants Joseph Zalenski, George Smith, and George Morey.

The complaint alleges that on July 18, 1964, the decedent, a minor sixteen years of age, while he was on Society's club premises, was given, and consumed, intoxicating liquors in such quantity that he became intoxicated and, as a consequence of that intoxication, so operated a motor vehicle as to cause it to collide with some trees, which resulted in the injuries from which he died.

The second count alleges that Zalenski, Smith, and Morey gave the liquor to the decedent, or permitted him to consume it, and that these acts were violations of General Statutes §§ 30–77 and 30–86 and constituted a proximate cause of his intoxication.

The first count alleges that Society and Bunk rented to the defendant Zalenski, who was not a member of Society, a portion of the club premises, knowing, or chargeable with knowledge, that intoxicating liquors would therein be dispensed to minors. It is further alleged that the decedent's intoxication, injuries, and death were proximately caused by Society and Bunk in that they rented the club premises to a nonmember, failed to obtain the signatures of the guests in a guest book, and failed to seal off the club barroom from the rented portion of the premises, all in violation of regulations of the liquor control commission; in that they allowed minors to loiter on the premises in violation of General Statutes § 30–90; in that they gave intoxicating liquor or allowed it to be given to a minor on the club premises; and in that they knew or should have known that minors were on the premises and were being given intoxicating liquor, but they failed or neglected to prevent such action from taking place.

All defendants demurred to the complaint, and, upon the sustaining of the demurrers, the plaintiff declined to plead over. From the judgment rendered for the defendants, the plaintiff appealed.

The plaintiff's primary claims are based on alleged violations of various general statutes and of regulations of the liquor control commission claimed to have been enacted for the benefit and protection of persons in the general circumstances of this plaintiff's decedent. Although it is not stated with the precision desirable in pleadings, it appears that the plaintiff is claiming that the violations of these statutes and regulations constituted negligence per se.

[1, 2] The crucial allegations of the complaint are that these violations were the proximate cause of the decedent's intoxication. It is, however, the general common-law rule that the proximate cause of intoxication is the voluntary consumption, rather than the furnishing, of intoxicating liquor. Nolan v. Morelli, 154 Conn. 432, 436, 226 A.2d 383. Thus, the furnishing of intoxicating liquor was not the proximate cause of intoxication or of any damage proximately resulting from such intoxication, whether sustained by the intoxicated person himself or by another. The common-law rule as to proximate cause, of course, applies in any common-law action of negligence, even though that action includes, as specifications of negligence, one or more alleged violations of applicable statutes. This would include, of course, General Statutes § 30–86, which prohibits the furnishing of intoxicating liquor to minors, whether gratuitously or by sale.

The complaint alleges that the decedent consumed the liquor furnished, or permitted to be furnished, by the defendants. The voluntariness of that consumption, while not expressly alleged, is in nowise negated, as it must be to avoid the common-law rule.

There remains for consideration the question whether the portion of § 30–86 which

prohibits, with certain exceptions not applicable to the present case, the furnishing of intoxicating liquor to minors, whether gratuitously or by sale, amounts to a legislative declaration that minors are legally incapable of consenting to the consumption of liquor and thus preclude their action in drinking the liquor from being voluntarily within the meaning of the common-law rule.

[3] Although a minor is subject to a legal disability in the management of his property and in his contractual obligations, he nevertheless is permitted to make a will at the age of eighteen (General Statutes § 45–160), and he may be licensed to operate a motor vehicle after he becomes sixteen. General Statutes § 14–36. A minor may be held criminally responsible for his violations of law at age sixteen. General Statutes §§ 17–53, 17–65, 17–72. Under General Statutes § 52–217, in actions for recovery of damages for injury to person or property, a minor under sixteen is entitled to have the trier of fact determine whether his violation of a statutory duty was negligence, while one sixteen years of age or older is subject to the general rule that the violation of an applicable statute is negligence per se. Santor v. Falnis, 151 Conn. 434, 436, 199 A.2d 2; Bevins v. Brewer, 146 Conn. 10, 15, 147 A.2d 189. Thus, a minor aged sixteen or over is presumed to have the capacity to decide whether or not to violate the law. As a sixteen-year-old minor may be held accountable for violating § 14–227a by operating a motor vehicle while he is intoxicated, he may certainly be held accountable for deciding to consume intoxicating liquor in the first place. Furthermore, § 30–89 provides a criminal penalty for any minor who purchases or attempts to purchase intoxicating liquor. Thus, at least in the case of a minor aged sixteen or over, he may be presumed, if he consumes liquor, to have done so voluntarily.

[4, 5] Since here the decedent's consumption of intoxicating liquor was voluntary, his consumption, rather than any

violation, by any of the defendants, of § 30-86 or of other statutes or liquor control commission regulations, was, under the common-law rule, the proximate cause of his intoxication and of the injuries and death claimed to have resulted therefrom. Of course, negligence, whether common-law or statutory, must be proved to have been a proximate cause of the injuries complained of if it is to constitute actionable negligence. Nolan v. Morelli, 154 Conn. 432, 443, 226 A.2d 383.

[6, 7] It is true that the complaint specifically alleges that the giving of liquor to the decedent was a proximate cause of his intoxication, injuries and death. But allegations of legal conclusions are not admitted by demurrer. Rossignol v. Danbury School of Aeronautics, Inc., 154 Conn. —, 227 A.2d 418; McAdam v. Sheldon, 153 Conn. 278, 282, 216 A.2d 193; Barnes v. Viering, 152 Conn. 243, 244, 206 A.2d 112. Consequently, the allegations of proximate cause are ineffective to negate the common-law rule that the voluntary consumption, rather than the furnishing, of the liquor was the proximate cause of the intoxication and the resulting injuries and death.

[8] Finally, we consider briefly certain other allegations of duty appearing in the complaint. As to Zalenski, Smith, and Morey, the complaint alleges that, having allowed the decedent to become intoxicated, they neglected and failed to exercise any degree of care or control to prevent his injury and death at a time when they were under a duty so to do. But the allegation of the existence of such a duty is merely a legal conclusion. Neither any specific duty nor any facts giving rise to any duty are alleged. The demurrers, therefore, did not admit the existence of any such duty. Rossignol v. Danbury School of Aeronautics, Inc., supra; McAdam v. Sheldon, supra; see Nolan v. Morelli, supra.

[9] As to Bunk and Society, the complaint, construed favorably to the plaintiff, alleges a duty to prevent others on the permit premises from giving or delivering intoxicating liquor to the decedent as a minor. But if such a duty exists, as to the minor decedent in the present case, under the common-law rule any violation of that duty was not a proximate cause of intoxication resulting from the decedent's voluntary consumption of that liquor or of any injuries resulting from such intoxication.

There is no error.

In this opinion the other judges concurred.

2.   Read the following three sample briefs of *Moore,* and critique them according to the criteria in Chapter 3. For example: Are all relevant facts presented? Does the issue link facts and law in question form?

Sample #1

Moore v. Bunk, Connecticut Supreme Court 1967

FACTS: 16 year old P drank too much liquor provided by Ds. P drove car, collided with trees, died as result of injuries.

PROCEDURE: P sued; Ds demurred; trial ct sustained demurrers. P appeals demurrer.

ISSUE: Does absence of proximate cause bar lawsuit against liquor seller for death of minor?

HOLDING: Yes, proximate cause bars suit, bcz minor caused own injuries.

REASONING: "It is the general common-law rule that the proximate cause of intoxication is the voluntary consumption, rather than the furnishing, of intoxicating liquor." This rule applies to minors. Minors voluntarily consume liquor, as they make other legal decisions voluntarily.

Sample #2

Moore v. Bunk, Connecticut Supreme Court 1967

FACTS: Minor person drank liquor on premises of one D, where another had liquor permit, & 3 other Ds were there giving liquor to minor. Minor then became drunk, drove, killed himself by running into tree. Two counts were agst permittee, backer, 3 other Ds. Ds won at trial court (they are respondents).

ISSUE: Was it error to sustain demurrers agst P's cause of action?

HOLDING: There is no error. This is neg per se lawsuit, based on violations of liquor laws re minors drinking. There must be proximate cause. Ds did not cause minor to drink.

REASONING: Minors can choose to drink, just as they can choose to make wills, drive, commit crimes. Therefore Ds did not violate statutes. Nor did Ds fail to control minor when they had duty to do so.

Sample #3

Moore v. Bunk, Connecticut Supreme Court 1967

FACTS: Administrator of John H. Moore estate brought action to recover damages for his death. First count against Bradford Bunk & St. Stanislawa Benefits & Mutual Society (Society). Second count against Joseph Zalenski, George Smith, George Morey.

July 18, 1964, Moore became intox'd on Society's premises & then operated motor vehicle so as to cause it to collide with trees, which resulted in injuries, from which he died.

Violations of statutes 30-77, 30-86, 30-90 alleged (renting to non-member, failing to obtain signatures in book, failing to seal off barroom, allowing minors to loiter, etc.).

PROCEDURE: Admin. of estate sued Bunk, Society, Zalenski, Smith, Morey. All Ds demurred. Trial ct sustained demurrers. P did not re-plead. P appeals jmt rendered for Ds.

ISSUE: Is Society neg where minor Moore becomes intox'd after defendants Zalenski etc. give him liquor on Society premises, Moore drives & wrecks car, & therefore dies?

HOLDING: No, defendants aren't neg where minor Moore becomes intox'd after defendants Zalenski etc. give him liquor on Society premises, Moore drives & wrecks car, & therefore dies. Affirmed.

REASONING: Claims are not well pleaded, but basically allege neg per se. There must be proximate cause. There is no proximate cause where furnishing liquor doesn't cause injury, whether sustained by intox'd person or another, whether minor buys or is given liquor. Minors can make many legally binding decisions: will at 18, drive at 16, criminal acts at 16, neg per se at 16, driving while intox'd at 16, buying liquor at?? So their decision to drink & drive should preclude suits agst liquor sellers. This goes for suit agst Zalenski, Smith, Morey for letting Moore drink.

3. Write your own brief of *Moore.*

4. *Moore* does not include concurrences or dissents. Imagine that you are a concurring justice; what outcome would you urge, and what might your reasoning be? What if you dissented? Do you personally agree with the actual decision, or your concurrence, or your dissent?

5. Which state and federal courts would be bound by the decision in *Moore,* and in what circumstances? Which state and federal courts might use the decision as persuasive precedent, and in what circumstances?

EXERCISES FOR CHAPTER 4

FUSING CASES

Consider the following five case briefs:*

Ely v. Murphy, Connecticut Supreme Court 1988

FACTS: Ds hosted high school graduation party involving youth drinking all night. Legal drinking age is 19. No bartenders or security staff; no one monitored drinking. Ds said they took car keys of drunk partygoers. 18 year old guest became very drunk, said keys were in car (& Ds never got keys), left early in morning, drove into another guest, killing him.

PROCEDURE: Among other claims, father of killed guest sued Ds for common law neg in serving liquor. Court granted motion to strike neg count re serving liquor. P appeals.

ISSUE: Is there neg cause of action where social host provides liquor to minor, minor becomes drunk, drives, & fatally injures third party?

HOLDING: Reversed & remanded. Social host may be liable in neg for serving liquor to minor who thereafter becomes drunk & injures third party; proximate cause is not lacking.

REASONING: General rule at common law is: no neg cause of action agst person who by sale or gift serves liquor to person who becomes intox'd & then injures self or another, bcz proximate cause of intox'n is consumption, not furnishing of liquor. Rule assumes knowing & intelligent exercise of choice to drink. But statutes on drinking by minors & public attitudes indicate that minors are incompetent by reason of youth & inexperience to deal with liquor. Thus consumption of liquor by youth is not intervening act necessary to break proximate cause chain. *Moore & Nelson* are overruled. Court also cites persuasive precedent in support of new rule. Proximate cause in minor case is now question of fact.

*   *   *   *   *

Kowal v. Hofher, Connecticut Supreme Court 1980

FACTS: According to complaint: D restaurant owner served liquor to already intox'd person, who then negligently drove into car in which decedent was riding.

PROCEDURE: Admin of estate sued D for neg & reckless conduct. D moved to strike those counts; ct granted motion. P appeals.

ISSUES: Are there (1) neg or (2) reckless conduct causes of action where commercial seller of liquor serves intox'd person who drives into third party's car, killing him?

---

*The cases may be found as follows: *Ely* at 540 A.2d 54; *Kowal* at 436 A.2d 1; *Moore* at 228 A.2d 510; *Nelson* at 365 A.2d 1174; and *Nolan* at 226 A.2d 383.

HOLDING: Affirmed in part, reversed & remanded in part. Where seller of liquor serves intox'd person who then injures third party, (1) there is no neg cause of action, but (2) there may be reckless conduct cause of action.

REASONING: (1) General rule at common law is: no neg cause of action agst person who by sale or gift serves liquor to person who becomes intox'd & then injures self or another, bcz proximate cause of intox'n is consumption, not furnishing of liquor. This rule covers neg claim.

(2) Where, however, conduct is not neg but wanton & reckless, i.e., in reckless disregard of another's safety, one must bear greater responsibility for injuries due to conduct. Causation is expanded in reckless conduct cases. Therefore there may be proximate cause in this case as to recklessness claim. Cites persuasive precedent & Restatement of Torts.

CONCURRENCE WITHOUT OPINION: One justice.

CONCURRENCE/DISSENT: Majority is correct as to reckless conduct; should hold similarly as to neg as well. (One justice.)

DISSENT: Decision affronts court's precedent that there is no tort cause of action on these facts. Difference bet neg & reckless conduct is only theoretical & unwise; in any event, distinction pertains not to causation but to degree of care. Distinguishes majority's persuasive precedent. (One justice.)

* * * * *

Moore v. Bunk, Connecticut Supreme Court 1967

FACTS: According to complaint, Moore (decedent), 16 yrs old, was given & drank liquor on premises of defendant Society. Other defendants are Bunk, liquor permittee of Society, & persons who rented premises & gave liquor to decedent. Society & Bunk engaged in acts violating liquor laws in renting premises knowing liquor would be served to minors, failing to close off bar, allowing minors to loiter, etc. Decedent became intox'd, drove car, collided with trees, died as result of injuries.

PROCEDURE: Admin. of estate sued. All Ds demurred. Trial ct sustained demurrers. P did not replead. P appeals jmt rendered for Ds.

ISSUE: Is there neg cause of action agst commercial seller of liquor that permits serving of liquor to minor in violation of liquor laws, where minor becomes intox'd, drives & wrecks car, & dies as result of wreck?

HOLDING: Affirmed; demurrer upheld. There is no cause of action agst seller of liquor based on injuries sustained by minor who became intox'd on liquor provided by seller, in violation of liquor laws, & thereafter died as result of car accident due to minor/driver's intox'n.

REASONING: General common law rule: proximate cause of intox'n—as well as injury—is voluntary consumption of liquor, not furnishing of liquor. This applies to bar common law neg & neg per se, based on statute re furnishing liquor to minors. Rule does not differ where drinker is minor. Tho statute prohibits furnishing liquor to minor, minor still is legally capable of consenting to consumption. See statutes recognizing minor's legal capacity, especially statutes holding minor accountable for driving while intox'd & for purchasing liquor. Here intox'n was cause of injury, not furnishing of liquor, as to all duties alleged. Complaint fails for lack of proximate cause.

*   *   *   *   *

Nelson v. Steffens, Connecticut Supreme Court 1976

FACTS: D sold liquor to already intox'd minor who then drove with two other boys in car. Car went out of control. One passenger was killed; other injured.

PROCEDURE: Mother of dead/injured boys sued D. D demurred. Ct sustained demurrer. P appeals.

ISSUE: Is there neg cause of action where commercial seller of liquor furnishes liquor to intox'd minor who then drives car so as to injure/kill passengers?

HOLDING: Affirmed. There is no neg cause of action agst commercial seller who furnishes liquor to minor who thereafter injures passengers in car wreck.

REASONING: General rule at common law is: no neg cause of action agst person who by sale or gift serves liquor to person who becomes intox'd & then injures self or another, bcz proximate cause of intox'n is consumption, not furnishing of liquor. This is rule suggested in earlier decisions in Connecticut & majority rule elsewhere. P does not cite any reason not to follow this rule.

CONCURRENCE WITHOUT OPINION: Three justices.

DISSENT: Conduct alleged is neg conduct: failure to conform to duty set by statute (here statute prohibiting service of liquor to minor) or duty to exercise reasonable care. Rule adopted by majority is antiquated. Seller should foresee situation that occurred here, so that minor driver's conduct does not break chain of causation. Proximate cause should be jury judgment.

*   *   *   *   *

Nolan v. Morelli, Connecticut Supreme Court 1967

FACTS: D restaurants served adult liquor. He became intox'd, drove car into tree, was injured & died.

PROCEDURE: Driver's wife sued D for neg (among other claims). Ds demurred, ct sustained demurrer. P appeals.

ISSUE: Is there neg cause of action (common law or neg per se) agst commercial seller of liquor for furnishing liquor to adult who then becomes intox'd & kills self in car wreck?

HOLDING: Affirmed. There is no cause of action agst commercial seller of liquor for furnishing liquor to adult who then killed himself when driving while intox'd.

REASONING: General rule at common law is: no neg cause of action agst person who by sale or gift serves liquor to person who becomes intox'd & then injures self or another, bcz proximate cause of intox'n is consumption, not furnishing of liquor. This rule has been followed by lower court in CT. To provide compensation to intox'd person for overindulgence might encourage, rather than discourage, intox'n. Intox'n is voluntary act that is superseding act bet sale & injury. This reasoning covers both common law neg & neg per se.

*   *   *   *   *

1. Construct a hierarchical array of these five cases.

2. Construct a timeline of the cases.

3. Create a features chart for the five cases.

4. Is it workable to fuse a single rule emanating from all five of the cases? Explain.

5. Fuse the cases to derive one or more rules, as appropriate, by use of textual fusion.

6. State your fused rule (or one of them if you derived more than one) in if/then form, and identify the relationship among the elements and the type of consequence.

7. Are you certain about the rule you have developed from these cases, or are there uncertain aspects? If so, what is uncertain?

8. Does your fused rule express your sense of what the law should be? Why, or why not? (You may want to compare the fused rule to the rule you created in response to question 3 for Chapter 2.)

Exercises for Chapter 5

Reading Statutes

Consider the following Connecticut statute, reprinted from West's Connecticut General Statutes Annotated (1990).

§ 30-102. Dram shop act; liquor seller liable for damage by intoxicated person

If any person, by himself or his agent, sells any alcoholic liquor to an intoxicated person, and such purchaser, in consequence of such intoxication, thereafter injures the person or property of another, such seller shall pay just damages to the person injured, up to the amount of twenty thousand dollars, or to persons injured in consequence of such intoxication up to an aggregate amount of fifty thousand dollars, to be recovered in an action under this section, provided the aggrieved person or persons shall give written notice to such seller within sixty days of the occurrence of such injury to person or property of his or their intention to bring an action under this section. In computing such sixty-day period, the time between the death or incapacity of any aggrieved person and the appointment of an executor, administrator, conservator or guardian of his estate shall be excluded, except that the time so excluded shall not exceed one hundred twenty days. Such notice shall specify the time, the date and the person to whom such sale was made, the name and address of the person injured or whose property was damaged, and the time, date and place where the injury to person or property occurred. No action under the provisions of this section shall be brought but within one year from the date of the act or omission complained of.

(1949 Rev., § 4307; 1955, Supp. § 2172d; 1957, P.A. 306; 1959, P.A. 631, § 1, eff. July 1, 1959; 1961, P.A. 432; 1974, P.A. 74–144, § 1, eff. May 8, 1974; 1986, P.A. 86–338, § 7, eff. Oct. 1, 1986; 1987, P.A. 87–227, § 11.)

1. Determine whether any language is *not* pertinent to your client's situation (stated at p. 487), and cross out that language.

2. Label the portions of the statute that are pertinent to your situation according to the statutory components presented in Chapter 5, e.g., definitions, general rule, exceptions, consequences.

3. Read the following three sample briefs. Then critique each brief according to the criteria in Chapter 5. For example: Is the statutory language presented accurately? Is all pertinent information presented? Do the parts of the brief fit together well?

Sample #1

TITLE: Dram Shop Act

DEFINITIONS: None

SCOPE: None

GENERAL RULES: Illegal for any person:

> to sell alcohol to intoxicated person
> where purchaser injures another person.

EXCEPTIONS: Injured person does not:

> give notice within 60 days of intent to sue
> and sue within one year.

CONSEQUENCES/ENFORCEMENT: Just damages paid in action brought by injured person.

Sample #2

IF   any person sells alcoholic liquor to intoxicated person who as consequence injures another person or property

THEN   seller pays $20,000–$50,000 to injured persons.

IF   aggrieved person(s) does not give written notice to seller within 60 days (or up to 120 days in case of death) of injury of intent to bring action—which includes information re sale, injured person, injury

THEN   seller is not liable.

IF   suit is not brought within one year of injury

THEN   seller is not liable.

Sample #3

GENERAL RULE: If any person by himself or agent sells any alcoholic liquor to an intoxicated person, and the purchaser in consequence of intoxication thereafter injures person or property of another, seller pays just damages.

EXCEPTIONS: None.

CONSEQUENCES/ENFORCEMENT: Damages are $20,000 to person injured, up to aggregate of $50,000 to persons injured.

Aggrieved person(s) shall give written notice to seller within 60 days of occurrence of injury to person or property of intention to sue within this statute; time between death or incapacity of injured person and appointment of executor, administrator, conservator, guardian is excluded up to 120 days; notice must include time/date/person to whom sale occurred; name/address of injured person/property; time/date/place of injury to person/property.

No action unless within one year of date of act or omission complained of.

4. Write your own if/then brief of section 30-102 in a traditional paragraph, then also in quasi-outline or flowchart form.

5. Does the statutory rule express your sense of what the law should be? Why or why not? (You may want to compare the statutory rule to the rule you created in response to question 3 for Chapter 2.)

EXERCISES FOR CHAPTER 6

INTERPRETING STATUTES

Return to your own brief of the statute presented in the exercise for Chapter 5, or read the sample brief set out below. Recall the client situation at page 487.

> IF   any person or his/her agent (seller)
> sells
> alcoholic liquor
> to intoxicated person (purchaser)
>
> and purchaser
> in consequence of intoxication
> injures person/property of third party
>
> and third party
> gives written notice of intent to sue
> stating time and date of sale, purchaser;
>   name and address of third party;
>   time, date, place of injury
> to seller
> within 60 days of injury
>   (excluding time [up to 120 days] between death or incapacity of third party
>   and appointment of executor)
> and suit is brought within one year of act/omission
>
> THEN   seller pays to third party just damages
>   up to $20,000 per person, $50,000 aggregate.

1. Do you see any ambiguities in this rule as it relates to your client's situation? If so, what is ambiguous? If you were a court deciding the case, how would you resolve the ambiguity?

2. Read the following points about the statute.[1] Rank the points by how authoritative they are. Review Exhibit 6.1; remember that the authoritativeness of a case is fixed by factors such as jurisdiction and currency. Explain your rankings.

   A. A 1985 case decided by the Connecticut Supreme Court holds that a person may be found to be intoxicated when the following symptoms are manifest to an observer: the person's walk or conversation is abnormal, judgment is disturbed, or will power is temporarily suspended.

---

1. The points listed above are drawn directly or indirectly from the following cases: *Sanders v. Officers Club of Connecticut Inc.*, 493 A.2d 184 (Conn. 1985); *Kowal v. Hofher*, 436 A.2d 1 (Conn. 1980); *Nelson v. Steffens*, 365 A.2d 1174 (Conn. 1976); *Nolan v. Morelli*, 226 A.2d 383 (Conn. 1967); *Pierce v. Albanese*, 129 A.2d 606 (Conn. 1957); *Kelehear v. Larcon, Inc.*, 577 A.2d 746 (Conn. Ct. App. 1990).

B. The prior version of the statute required that the plaintiff establish a causal connection between the provision of the liquor by the defendant and the injury suffered by the plaintiff.

C. According to a 1957 decision by the Connecticut Supreme Court, the legislature was concerned about the danger to public health, safety, and morals from liquor sales and, more specifically, about drunk driving.

D. Under the state's criminal code, "intoxication" is "a substantial disturbance of mental or physical capacities resulting from the introduction of substances into the body."

E. Several decisions by the Connecticut Supreme Court indicate that the Dram Shop Act does not alter one's ability to sue under the common law or the common law cause of action but rather provides a statutory claim for limited damages in specified circumstances.

F. In 1957, the Connecticut Supreme Court upheld the statute against the argument that it was unconstitutional in providing a penalty against the seller even though there was no causal connection between the sale and the injury. The court noted that the statute was a proper exercise of the legislature's broad power to regulate liquor.

G. At the time the statute was passed, a state commerce law deemed the dispensing of food or drink in a restaurant or tavern a "service" rather than a "sale."

H. The Connecticut Supreme Court held in 1957 that a jury could properly infer that two individuals who drank two beers in a bar were sold the beers at the bar; there need not be direct proof of the sale (such as the bartender's testimony).

I. In various cases, the Connecticut Supreme Court has identified three elements of a dram shop case: (1) a sale of intoxicating liquor; (2) to an intoxicated person; (3) who, in consequence of such intoxication, causes injury to the person or property of another.

J. In a 1967 decision by the Connecticut Supreme Court, the court ruled that the Dram Shop Act does not provide recovery where the intoxicated buyer is the injured party.

K. In a 1990 case decided by the Appellate Court of Connecticut, the court accepted the seller's evidence that the buyer was shut off when he became obnoxious, found that evidence that the buyer was seen with a beer can thereafter would not establish a sale, and yet ruled that the jury could find an illegal sale based on sales before the buyer was shut off.

3. To which phrase of the statute does each point pertain? Has your understanding of any portion of the statute changed as a result of any of these points?

4. How might you use canons of construction to enable you to interpret the statute?

5. As you consider the client situation (stated at p. 487), is there any ambiguity remaining in the statute once these points are used to interpret the statute? If so, what remains ambiguous?

6. Does the statute as interpreted express your sense of what the law should be? Why or why not? (You may want to compare the statutory rule as you interpret it to the rule you created in response to question 3 for Chapter 2.)

Exercises for Chapter 7

Reading Commentary

Read the following pages from 4 Fowler V. Harper, Fleming James, Jr. & Oscar S. Gray, *The Law of Torts* § 20.5 (2d ed. 1986 & Supp. 2002). Note: Pages 510-12 are from the 1986 main volume; pages 513-15 are from the 2002 supplement.

1. If you read this material for the primary purpose of better understanding the law of proximate cause as it now stands, what can you learn from this material? Draw a bracket beside the key passage(s).

2. If you looked to this material for critique of the law of proximate cause, what can you learn from this material? Draw a bracket beside the key passage(s).

3. If you read this material as you were researching the liability of a liquor seller in Connecticut, which specific references to primary authority would be of particular interest to you? Why? Draw an asterisk beside them.

4. What would you take into account as you assess how authoritative this material is?

§20.5   LEGAL CAUSE

Much of what has been said about the scope of common law duties is applicable also to duties imposed by statutes. Here, however, the emphasis is on the statutory purpose in determining the interests protected by the duty and the evils sought to be prevented by legislative proscription of conduct, rather than on what a reasonable person in defendant's place would foresee.[19] Because the statutory purpose doctrine was probably clearly and expressly articulated at an earlier time than its counterpart, the limitation on the scope of common law duties, there has been perhaps slightly less urge to obfuscate the former inquiry by pursuing it in terms of proximate cause, but this is done all too often even today. Thus where plaintiff's playmate pushed him under a middle car of defendant's train which was passing at a speed in violation of a local ordinance, the court admitted that the defendant was guilty of negligence per se but found that the "intervening, independent, sole, proximate cause" of the injury was the other boy's push.[20] And where defendant has parked his unlocked car on the street, with the key in the ignition switch in violation of an ordinance, and the car is stolen by a person who, while driving it, causes some damage, the owner has been held not liable on the ground that the

---

[19]See Morris, Duty, Negligence and Causation, 101 U. Pa. L. Rev. 189, 203 (1952) (complaining that "the judicially invented statutory purpose doctrine can produce highly restrictive and somewhat irrational limitations on civil liability"); C. Morris and C. R. Morris, Morris on Torts 167-172 (2d ed. 1980).

[20]Lineberry v. North Carolina Ry. Co., 187 N.C. 786, 123 S.E. 1 (1924). Cf. Daggett v. Keshner, 284 A.D. 733, 134 N.Y.S.2d 524 (1954), criticized in Note, 40 Cornell L.Q. 810 (1955). Green suggested that courts often use the "proximate cause" doctrine "to get rid of the compulsion of the statute." See Green, Proximate Cause in Texas Negligence Law, 28 Tex. L. Rev. 621, 634-635, 764, 771 (1950), and Green, Proximate Cause in Connecticut Negligence Law, 24 Conn. B.J. 24, 28-30 (1950). Cf. James, Statutory Standards and Negligence in Accident Cases, 11 La. L. Rev. 95, 121 (1950).

LEGAL CAUSE   §20.5

proximate cause of the injury was the action of the thief and not the negligence of the owner.[21]

[21]See, e.g., Wannebo v. Gates, 227 Minn. 194, 34 N.W.2d 695 (1948), and Note, 14 Mo. L. Rev. 128 (1949), which make the error pointed out in the text. See annot., 45 A.L.R.3d 787 (1970). Perhaps the leading case *contra* is Ross v. Hartman, 139 F.2d 14 (D.C. Cir. 1943), *cert. denied,* 321 U.S. 790 (1944). See also Note, 34 Iowa L. Rev. 376 (1949), which treats this problem and properly distinguishes the issues of cause and of duty. Variant results in these cases persist but most cases deny recovery. Some do so on the ground that the act of the thief or intermeddler breaks the chain of causation. Cf. State of West Virginia v. Fidelity & Casualty Co. of N.Y., 263 F. Supp. 88 (S.D. W.Va. 1967); Hersh v. Miller, 169 Neb. 517, 99 N.W.2d 878 (1959); Ross v. Nutt, 177 Ohio St. 113, 203 N.E.2d 118 (1964) (because unforeseeable); Nolan v. Bacon, 216 A.2d 126 (R.I. 1966) (same). Others, more accurately it is believed, seek the answer by examining the statutory purpose. Ney v. Yellow Cab Co., 2 Ill. 2d 74, 117 N.E.2d 74, 51 A.L.R.2d 624 (1954) (safety found to be a purpose); Kacena v. Geo. W. Bowers Co., 63 Ill. App. 2d 27, 211 N.E. 563 (1965) (same); Zegarelli v. Colp, 91 Misc. 2d 430, 398 N.Y.S.2d 103 (1977) (same). See also Vining v. Avis Rent-a-Car Systems, Inc., 354 So. 2d 54 (Fla. 1977); Davis v. Thornton, 384 Mich. 138, 180 N.W.2d 11 (1970); Zinck v. Whalen, 120 N.J. Super. 432, 294 A.2d 727 (App. Div. 1972); see §17.6 note 40 *supra;* Restatement (Second) of Torts §281, Comment *i*, §286, and Comments and Illuss. (1965); id., Appendix 346-363 (Reporter's Notes and court citation) (1966). (Note that the motorist's liability insurance may not include coverage of liability for harm caused by unauthorized use of the car in which the key is left. Cf., e.g., Owen v. Wagner, 426 So. 2d 1262 (Fla. App. 1983).)

The key-in-ignition problem too is treated in Petition of Kinsman Transit Co., 338 F.2d 708, 717-718 (2nd Cir. 1964).

The same error as is discussed in the text has appeared in cases absolving a defendant who illegally served alcohol to a visibly intoxicated adult, or to a minor, from liability to the foreseeable victim of the drunk driving of the person so illegally served, on the specious ground that it was the drinking of the alcohol and not its illegal service that caused the accident, e.g., Nelson v. Steffens, 170 Conn. 356, 365 A.2d 1174 (1976). See able analysis *contra* in Vesely v. Sager, 5 Cal. 3d 153, 95 Cal. Rptr. 623, 486 P.2d 151 (1971). (Unfortunately the *Vesely* opinion has apparently been nullified in California, at least in some applications, by a remarkable 1978 statute which stated "the intent of the Legislature to abrogate the holdings in cases such as Vesely v. Sager . . . and to reinstate the prior judicial interpretation of this section as it relates to proximate cause for injuries incurred as a result of furnishing alcoholic beverages to an intoxicated person, namely that the furnishing of alcoholic beverages is not the proximate cause of injuries resulting from intoxication, but rather the consumption of alcoholic beverages is the proximate cause of injuries inflicted upon another by an intoxicated person." Cal. Civ. Code §1714(b) (West 1985). See also Cal. Bus. & Prof. Code §25602(b), (c)

§20.5   LEGAL CAUSE

(West Supp. 1985).). Cf., also rejecting the older no-cause doctrine, Corrigan
v. United States, 595 F. Supp. 1047 (E.D. Va. 1984); Buchanan v. Merger
Enterprises, Inc., 463 So. 2d 121, 126 (Ala. 1984); Nazareno v. Urie, 638 P.2d
671 (Alaska 1981); Ontiveros v. Borak, 136 Ariz. 500, 667 P.2d 200 (1983);
Lewis v. Wolf, 122 Ariz. 567, 596 P.2d 705 (App. 1979) (including useful
compendium of citations to more enlightened opinions, at 596 P.2d 707-708);
Elder v. Fisher, 247 Ind. 598, 217 N.E.2d 847 (1966); Ono v. Applegate, 62
Haw. 131, 612 P.2d 533 (1980); Clark v. Mincks, 364 N.W.2d 226 (Iowa 1985);
Rappaport v. Nichols, 31 N.J. 188, 156 A.2d 1 (1959); Brookins v. The Round
Table, Inc., 624 S.W.2d 547, 549 (Tenn. 1981); Sorensen v. Jarvis, 119 Wis.
2d 627, 350 N.W.2d 108 (1984); McClellan v. Tottenhoff, 666 P.2d 408 (Wyo.
1983); §§17.5 note 21 and 17.6 note 12 *supra.*

    Cf. K-Mart Enterprises of Florida, Inc. v. Keller, 439 So. 2d 283 (Fla. App.
1983) (retailer who unlawfully sold firearm to purchaser who was subject of
felony information and also unlawful user of marijuana, who entrusted gun to
his brother, subject to liability to police officer who was shot in head by the
purchaser's brother).

144

§20.5   LEGAL CAUSE

§20.5 n.21, p.144.   After carryover paragraph of notes, add the following:

Cf., also rejecting older notion that the supplying of alcohol is not a cause of the harm caused by the person intoxicated by it, Jackson v. Cadillac Cowboy, Inc., 337 Ark. 24, 986 S.W.2d 410 (1999); Largo Corp. v. Crespin, 727 P.2d 1098 (Colo. 1986); Ely v. Murphy, 207 Conn. 88, 540 A.2d 54 (1988) (in case of alcohol furnished to and consumed by minors); Craig v. Driscoll, 64 Conn. App. 699, 713, 781 A.2d 440, 449 (2001) ("We reject the . . . argument that providing alcoholic beverages to an already intoxicated [adult] person or a person known . . . to be an alcoholic cannot be the proximate cause of subsequent injuries caused by the drunken person"; liability to closely related bystanders who foreseeably suffer serious emotional injury from sight of victim soon after the accident, cf. §18.4 *supra*); Grayson Fraternal Order of Eagles v. Claywell, 736 S.W.2d 328, 333-334 (Ky. 1987); McGuiggan v. New England Tel. & Tel. Co., 398 Mass. 152, 496 N.E.2d 141 (1986); Brigance v. Velvet Dove Rest., Inc., 725 P.2d 300 (Okla. 1986). Compare Samson v. Smith, 560 A.2d 1024 (Del. 1989) (adhering to older view); Charles v. Seigfried, 165 Ill. 2d 482, 209 Ill. Dec. 226, 651 N.E.2d 154 (1995) (similar).

South Dakota has enacted legislation similar to California's to the effect that the furnishing of alcohol is not a proximate cause of injury resulting from a drunk's intoxication. S.D. Codified Laws Ann. §35-11-1 (1986); cf. id. §35-11-2 (further immunizing social hosts from liability).

In 1986 the Iowa legislature also passed a law similar to the California post-*Vesely* legislation, explicitly providing that "the holding of Clark v. Mincks . . . is abrogated in favor of prior judicial interpretation finding the consumption of alcoholic beverages . . . rather than the serving . . . as the proximate cause of injury inflicted upon another by an intoxicated person." Iowa Code §123.49 para. 1b (1987).

In 1986 an attempt was made in the Tennessee legislature to repudiate *Brookins* and reinstate the older rule on causation. It was partly successful; a provision like the California post-*Vesely* legislation was enacted. A partial exception to this provision was also enacted. The exception permits liability in two cases, if a 12-member jury finds "beyond a reasonable doubt" that harm was caused by the serving of "alcoholic beverage or beer" to a known minor (under the age of 21), or to someone already obviously intoxicated. Tenn. Code Ann. §§57-10-101, 57-10-102 (1989).

A curiosity may be noted in connection with the view of some courts and legislatures that the illegal provider of alcoholic beverages should not be subject to liability in negligence for harm caused by the drunk, on the theory that it was not the serving of the drink, but only its consumption, that was the proximate cause of the harmful conduct. Under certain dram shop statutes that provide a civil remedy against the supplier for harm caused by those who were furnished alcohol illegally, cf. §17.5 note 15 *supra,* it is not necessary to show that the harm was caused by the intoxication; it is instead sufficient to show that the harm was caused by the intoxicated person, who had been served illegally by the defendant. Cf., e.g., Sanders v. Officers Club of Connecticut, 196 Conn. 341, 493 A.2d 184 (1985) (under Connecticut dram shop statute, which prohibits sale to an intoxicated person, seller's liability to the injured party depends on proof that injury was caused by the first person's intoxication, not by the prohibited sale); Thorp v. Casey's Gen. Stores, Inc., 446 N.W.2d 457 (Iowa 1989); Meshefski v. Shirnan, 385 N.W.2d 474 (N.D. 1986) (citing, inter alia, annot., 64 A.L.R.2d 705, 722 (1959)). Cf. Attala Golf and Country Club, Inc. v. Harris, 601 So. 2d 965, 970 (Ala. 1992); Slager v. HWA Corp., 435 N.W.2d 349, 352 (Iowa 1989) (in Iowa "an injured party . . . does not have to show a causal relationship between the intoxication and the injuries" but "the legislature [has] made proximate cause an affirmative defense.").

Cf. O'Toole v. Carlsbad Shell Serv. Station, 202 Cal. App. 3d 151, 247 Cal. Rptr. 663 (1988) (potential liability for negligent entrustment of automobile to drunk driver through sale of gasoline) and Blake v. Moore, 162 Cal. App. 3d 700, 208 Cal. Rptr. 703 (1984) (negligent entrustment of automobile to drunk driver, by the supplier of the drinks) for examples of the partial survival of the reasoning of *Vesely* in California jurisprudence notwithstanding the post-*Vesely* legislation; compare Knighten v. Sam's Parking Valet, 202 Cal. App. 3d 69, 253 Cal. Rptr. 365 (1988).

See also, on "key in ignition" issue, note 39 *infra*.

EXERCISES FOR CHAPTER 8

APPLYING A RULE TO FACTS: DEDUCTIVE REASONING

1. Read the following rules, drawn from the case law presented in the exercises for Chapter 4. (Other rules could be drawn from the same cases.)

IF   A. commercial seller of liquor
     B. *negligently* furnishes liquor to
     C. adult
     D. who then injures
         1. self or
         2. other

THEN   no proximate cause;
       therefore no cause of action
       for negligence against seller.

IF   A. commercial seller of liquor
     B. *recklessly* furnishes liquor to
     C. intoxicated person
     D. who then injures
         1. self or
         2. other

THEN   potential cause of action
       for recklessness against seller.

Identify which of the six classic journalist questions—who, what, when, where, why, and how—each element involves. Apply both rules to your client's facts (stated at p. 487). Assume Masters is thirty-six years old. If you need additional facts, make appropriate assumption(s) and proceed. Use the syllogism or column chart presented in Chapter 8, or develop your own depiction. State your conclusion.

2. Read the following if/then statute brief, used in the exercises for Chapter 6.

IF   A. any person or his/her agent (seller)
         sells
         alcoholic liquor
         to intoxicated person (purchaser)
     B. and purchaser
         in consequence of intoxication
         injures person/property of third party
     C. and third party gives proper notice . . .
     D. and suit is brought within one year of act/omission

THEN   seller pays to third party just damages
       up to $20,000 per person, $50,000 aggregate.

Assume that elements C and D would be met; focus on elements A and B. Identify which of the classic journalist questions—who, what, when, where, why, and how—each element involves. Apply that rule to your client's facts. If you need additional facts, make appropriate assumption(s) and proceed. Use the syllogism or column chart presented in Chapter 8, or develop your own depiction. State your conclusion.

3.   Compare the results of your answers to questions 1 and 2. Are they similar or different? How so?

4.   If you were the court deciding the case, what result would you prefer? Why?

5.   Now assume that in your client's situation, the intoxicated driver injured only himself. Assume further that the applicable rule is that stated in question 2; again assume elements C and D would be met. Recast the rule in negative form. Apply the recast rule to your client's facts. Use the syllogism or column chart presented in Chapter 8, or develop your own depiction. State your conclusion.

Exercises for Chapter 9

Applying a Rule to Facts: Reasoning by Example and Policy Analysis

1.   Read the case briefs presented in the exercises for Chapter 4, in light of your client's situation (stated at p. 487). Select a case you would emphasize in analyzing your client's situation if Mr. Masters is thirty-six years old, and explain why you chose that case. Use a Venn diagram, checkerboard chart, or other technique to compare that case to your client's situation. If you need additional facts, make appropriate assumption(s), and proceed. Indicate whether your client's situation is analogous to or distinguishable from the case you choose.

2.   Now select a case (briefed in the exercises to Chapter 4) that you would emphasize in analyzing your client's situation if Gary Masters is sixteen years old, and explain why you chose that case. Use a Venn diagram, checkerboard chart, or other technique to compare that case to your client's situation. If you need additional facts, make appropriate assumption(s), and proceed. Indicate whether your client's situation is analogous to or distinguishable from the case you choose.

3.   Perform a stakeholder analysis to determine the underlying policy or policies of the statute presented in Chapter 5's exercises. Determine the stakeholders, their interests, and their desired outcomes. State the policy or policies served by the statute. You may use a hub-and-spokes diagram or other technique.

4.   How would a rule read if it favored only the liquor seller's interest? How would a rule read if it favored only the injured third party's interest?

5.   Apply the statutory policy (or policies) you developed in your answer to question 3 to the Masters situation.

Exercises for Chapter 10

Rule-Driven Writing: The IRAC Template

Review your work on the exercises to this point. If you have not done all of them, review the following material:

- the client situation, at page 487;
- the case briefs, at pages 499-501;
- the statutory brief and material regarding the statute, at pages 503 and 507-08.

Assume that you do not know the age of Gary Masters.

1. Read the following paragraph, and label the sentences I, R, A, and C. (Citations are omitted.)

 The second statutory element is that the individual was intoxicated when he was served by the defendant commercial seller.

 Witnesses will testify that he had trouble walking and was using foul language when he entered Joe's and for a while thereafter.

 This was no doubt because Mr. Masters had consumed three shots of tequila and six beers at the first bar, before being served at Joe's.

 This case is thus reminiscent of a 1990 Connecticut Court of Appeals case where the bar was held liable under the statute for serving beer to an obnoxious individual.

Therefore, this element is met.

 Furthermore, the facts meet the definition of a 1985 Connecticut Supreme Court decision indicating that someone is intoxicated when an observer perceives that the drinker's walk or conversation is abnormal, judgment is disturbed, and will power is temporarily suspended.

Mr. Masters' ability to play pool well while at Joe's is not significant in light of the other aspects of his behavior.

Does the paragraph follow IRAC well? How so, or how not? How might you improve the paragraph?

2. Select an element of one of the rules that applies to the facts in a straightforward way. Write an IRAC paragraph on that element. You need not include proper citations but should provide simple references to the law. Label your sentences I, R, A, or C.

3. Select an element of one of the rules as to which the law is clear, but both sides have sound arguments on the facts. Write an IRAC paragraph on that element. You need not include proper citations but should provide simple references to the law. Label your sentences I, R, A, or C.

4. Select an element of one of the rules to which several authorities pertain. Write the I and R components of an IRAC discussion of that element. Indicate where you would apply the rule, e.g., after the entire R or after portions of the R. You need not include proper citations but should provide simple references to the law.

Exercises for Chapter 12

The Office Memo: The Discussion

Review your work on the exercises to this point. If you have not done all of them, review the following material:

- the client situation, at page 487;
- the case briefs, at pages 499-501;
- the statutory brief and material regarding the statute, at pages 503 and 507-08.

Assume that you do not know the age of Gary Masters.

1. Prepare an outline, a boxchart, or other sketch of the discussion of a memo on the case. Explain how you chose your sequence of topics. Did you use any of the standard legal conventions set out in part C of Chapter 12?

2. Do any topics appear twice? How would you handle any such topics?

3. Does the analysis of this problem involve any branchpoints? If so, state the type of branchpoint(s)—ambiguous or unsettled rules, unknown or disputed facts, unclear application of law to facts, interlocking rules. Select one branchpoint, and diagram the branches.

4. Write the first sentence of each IRAC; show how each one connects to the others.

Exercises for Chapter 13

The Office Memo: Issues, Short Answers, and Conclusion

1. Read the following sample issues and short answers, which draw on the statutory brief and material at pages 507-08. Critique each pair according to the criteria developed in Chapter 13.

Sample #1

ISSUE: Is our client liable under the Connecticut Dram Shop Act to the child killed by Gary Masters?

SHORT ANSWER: Our client clearly is liable under the Dram Shop Act.

Sample #2

ISSUE: Under the Connecticut Dram Shop Act, is a bar liable to a child killed when a drunk driver drives across oncoming traffic and into the car carrying the child after the driver consumed three shots of tequila and six beers at the bar and, prior to that, also consumed three shots of tequila and six beers at a different bar?

SHORT ANSWER: The bar is most likely liable under these facts because the driver was intoxicated.

Sample #3

ISSUE: When is a bar liable under the Connecticut Dram Shop Act to a third party injured by a drunk driver?

SHORT ANSWER: A bar is liable under the Dram Shop Act when the bar serves liquor to an intoxicated person who, as a consequence of intoxication, injures another.

2. Write your own issue and short answer for an office memo discussing the client situation on the assumption that Mr. Masters is thirty-six years old. Base your draft on the following case law rule:

> IF A. commercial seller of liquor
>   B. negligently furnishes liquor to
>   C. adult
>   D. who then injures
>   1. self or
>   2. other
> THEN no proximate cause; therefore no cause of action for negligence against seller.

3.   Frame a draft conclusion for an office memo regarding the client situation at page 487, analyzed under the rule stated in question 2 above as well as the following rule:

> IF   any person or his/her agent (seller)
>   sells
>   alcoholic liquor
>   to intoxicated person (purchaser)
>   and purchaser
>   in consequence of intoxication
>   injures person/property of third party
>
> THEN   seller pays to third party just damages
>   up to $20,000 per person, $50,000 aggregate.

First, write a sentence or two summarizing your answers to the legal issues. Then sketch out your recommendations to your client in full sentences, a decision tree, or form of your own making.

4.   In advising your client, the bar, would you factor in non-legal considerations? Why or why not?

Exercises for Chapter 14

The Office Memo: The Facts

Note: These exercises involve a different situation from the Masters situation, although it is governed by the same legal authorities.

Read the following facts. Assume your client is Jody Harrison, who is considering a suit against Hillside Country Club.

Taken from police report:
1. A car driven by Marsha Lewis (age 26) crashed going around a bend on Highway 56 near the Simpson farm at about 3:30 p.m.
2. The car was going approximately 80 m.p.h.
3. Weather and road conditions were fine.
4. There was no oncoming traffic.
5. Both Lewis and passenger Jody Harrison (age 24) were severely injured and taken to the county hospital by ambulance.
6. Both Lewis and Harrison smelled of alcohol.
7. A search of the car revealed no valid driver's license for Lewis.

Statement of Marsha Lewis:
8. My car spun out near the Simpson farm when it hit a wet spot in the road.
9. The car's speed was approximately 40 m.p.h.
10. Jody was hurt so badly because she wasn't wearing her seat belt.
11. Jody and I each drank about four beers during the early afternoon, over two hours, stopping at 3:00 p.m.
12. We drank them at Hillside Country Club after finishing a round of golf; we also ate lunch.
13. One bartender, Mark Johnson, served us the first two beers; a second, Gary Martinez, served us the second two.
14. We were never drunk, neither of us (maybe tipsy).

Statement of Gary Martinez:
15. I served both Harrison and Lewis two beers between 2:30 and 3:15 p.m. along with an order of nachos.
16. They were eating, but not drinking, when I arrived on shift.
17. Harrison was becoming loud and boisterous, so I told her I had decided not to serve her more if she was driving, which she said she was not.
18. Shortly after, Lewis and Harrison left angrily.
19. Lewis showed no signs of being inebriated.

Statement of Andrew Harrison (Jody's husband):
20. Doctors say Jody has suffered long-term memory loss and diminished concentration, although her abdominal injuries have healed.
21. Our marriage is showing signs of strain due to Jody's disability and reduced earning capacity.

22. Jody and Marsha often drank, Marsha heavily, after golf on Saturdays, so Jody generally drove.
23. Marsha drove that Saturday because our car was being fixed.

Laboratory report:
24. Lewis's blood alcohol level was .10.
25. Harrison's blood alcohol level was .12.

1. Construct a factual matrix chart to weave the facts together.

2. Use a timeline to weave the facts together.

3. Did you discern discrepancies in these facts? Identify two, and explain how you would deal with each.

4. Assume the following three rules of law apply:

IF   A. commercial seller of liquor
     B. negligently furnishes liquor to
     C. adult
     D. who then injures
        1. self or
        2. other

THEN   no proximate cause; therefore no cause of action for negligence against seller.

IF   A. commercial seller of liquor
     B. recklessly furnishes liquor to
     C. intoxicated person
     D. who then injures third party

THEN   there may be proximate cause and cause of action for recklessness.

IF   any person or his/her agent (seller)
     sells
     alcoholic liquor
     to intoxicated person (purchaser)
     and purchaser
     in consequence of intoxication
     injures person/property of third party

THEN   seller pays to third party just damages
       up to $20,000 per person, $50,000 aggregate.

In light of these rules, list the relevant, background, and residual facts from each source. Which facts would you exclude from your fact statement? Why?

5. Write an introductory paragraph to set the stage for the rest of the fact statement.

6. By what principle(s) would you organize the remaining facts? List your main topics.

7. Critique the following sentence according to the criteria in Chapter 14; then revise it. After drinking heavily and annoying the bartender, Lewis and Harrison left Hillside.

8. Are there additional facts you would like to know? If so, what are they?

Exercises for Chapter 15

Advisory Writing: The Function and Format of the Advice Letter

For the following exercises, refer to the client situation stated at page 487, the statute presented at page 503, and the material regarding the statute at pages 507-08.

1. Read the following sample introduction; then critique it according to the principles set forth in Chapter 15.

> Dear Client:
>   This letter presents our analysis of the facts you recounted last Friday in light of the pertinent statute. That statute provides for liability on the part of any person ("seller") who sells alcoholic liquor to an intoxicated person ("purchaser") where that purchaser then injures a third party ("victim"), the victim's injury/death being a consequence of the purchaser's intoxication. On the assumption that the procedural requirements of the statute are met, such liability most probably follows in your situation. The victim's recovery would be capped at $20,000.
>   This letter is current as of the date of this writing and is based on the following facts as you have recounted them to this office.

2. Assume that your client is *the bar,* a regular client. Rewrite the introduction presented above.

3. Now assume that your client, a first-time client, is *the father of the killed child.* Rewrite the introduction presented above.

4. Write a paragraph for the explanation component on the issue of whether Mr. Masters was "intoxicated" within the meaning of that term in the Connecticut Dram Shop Act. Assume that *the bar* is your client. Would this paragraph differ at all if *the father* were your client? If so, how so?

5. Assume that you have concluded that your client, *the bar,* probably would be ordered to pay $20,000 under the Dram Shop Act if the procedural requirements were met by the claimant. Assume further that the claimant sent a notice to the bar, but it was three days late. Write your advice section, beginning with a summary of your legal analysis.

6. If *the bar* were your client, which model of lawyering—hired gun, godfather, guru, or friend—would you employ? Are there more facts you would want to know before making this choice? Explain.

7. If *the father* were your client, which model of lawyering—hired gun, godfather, guru, or friend—would you employ? Are there more facts you would want to know before making this choice? Explain.

EXERCISES FOR CHAPTER 16

PERSUASIVE WRITING: THE FUNCTION AND FORMAT OF THE DEMAND LETTER

For the following exercises, refer to the client situation stated at page 487, the cases presented in the exercises for Chapter 4 at pages 499-501, and the two common law rules presented in question 1 for the Chapter 8 exercises at page 517. Assume that you represent the father of the killed child.

1. Critique the following opening paragraph according to the principles set forth in Chapter 16:

> Dear Bar Owner:
>   I am writing to alert you to the potential claim for a substantial remedy by the next of kin of Daniel Edwards, who died at the hands of Gary Masters, to whom your bar served alcohol well past the point of intoxication. You may find it wise to hire an attorney to represent you in this manner.

2. How would you organize your statement of your client's situation? Would you proceed chronologically or by some other approach?

3. Write out your client's legal position. Would you quote or cite the statute?

4. How would you frame your demand to make it appealing to the opponent? For example, would you note goals shared by your client and the opponent or offer various ways to meet the demand?

5. What figure would you state for a monetary recovery? (Assume that your client supports the approach you favor.) Assume that the highest recovery in Connecticut for a killed child, albeit in a hunting accident, is $300,000.

6. What non-monetary remedy might you seek? (Assume that your client supports the approach you favor.)

Exercises for Chapter 17

Advocacy Writing in the Pre-Trial and Trial Setting: The Function and Format of the Motion Practice Memorandum

Note: These exercises involve a different situation from the Masters situation, although it is governed by the same legal authorities.

The following is the factual record for the case of *Harrison v. Hillside Country Club:*

Taken from police report:
1. A car driven by Marsha Lewis (age 26) crashed going around a bend on Highway 56 near the Simpson farm at about 3:30 p.m.
2. The car was going approximately 80 m.p.h.
3. Weather and road conditions were fine.
4. There was no oncoming traffic.
5. Both Lewis and passenger Jody Harrison (age 24) were severely injured and taken to the county hospital by ambulance.
6. Both Lewis and Harrison smelled of alcohol.
7. A search of the car revealed no valid driver's license for Lewis.

Deposition of Marsha Lewis:
8. My car spun out near the Simpson farm when it hit a wet spot in the road.
9. The car's speed was approximately 40 m.p.h.
10. Jody was hurt so badly because she wasn't wearing her seat belt.
11. Jody and I each drank about four beers during the early afternoon, over two hours, stopping at 3:00 p.m.
12. We drank them at Hillside Country Club after finishing a round of golf; we also ate lunch.
13. One bartender, Mark Johnson, served us the first two beers; a second, Gary Martinez, served us the second two.
14. We were never drunk, neither of us (maybe tipsy).

Deposition of Gary Martinez:
15. I served both Harrison and Lewis two beers between 2:30 and 3:15 p.m. along with an order of nachos.
16. They were eating, but not drinking, when I arrived on shift.
17. Harrison was becoming loud and boisterous, so I told her I had decided not to serve her more if she was driving, which she said she was not.
18. Shortly after, Lewis and Harrison left angrily.
19. Lewis showed no signs of being inebriated.

Deposition of Andrew Harrison (Jody's husband):
20. Doctors say Jody has suffered long-term memory loss and diminished concentration, although her abdominal injuries have healed.

21. Our marriage is showing signs of strain due to Jody's disability and reduced earning capacity.

22. Jody and Marsha often drank, Marsha heavily, after golf on Saturdays, so Jody generally drove.

23. Marsha drove that Saturday because our car was being fixed.

Laboratory report:

24. Lewis's blood alcohol level was .10.

25. Harrison's blood alcohol level was .12.

Ms. Harrison has sued the club on three counts: two counts under Connecticut common law, one for negligence and a second for recklessness (derived from the cases briefed at pages 499-501 and presented in question 1 for Chapter 8 at page 517), and a third count under the Connecticut Dram Shop Act (presented at page 503 with supporting materials at 507-08).

The club is moving for summary judgment on the common law counts (not the Dram Shop count). Assume that Connecticut law requires the movant to establish (1) that there is no genuine issue of material fact and (2) that the movant is entitled to judgment as a matter of law.

1. Assume that the Connecticut trial courts operate on a block system. As counsel for Defendant *Hillside,* would you bring this motion? Why or why not?

2. Assume that the Connecticut trial courts operate on a block system. As counsel for Plaintiff *Ms. Harrison,* would you defend against the motion? Why or why not?

3. If you did not have to follow a particular format, and you represented *Hillside,* which of the following components would you present first: introduction or summary, issues, or facts? Explain your choice.

4. If you did not have to follow a particular format, and you represented *Ms. Harrison,* which of the following components would you present first: introduction or summary, issues, or facts? Explain your choice.

5. Read the following sample issues. First, analyze their content by marking each as follows: straight underline for substantive law, squiggly underline for procedural law, and no underline for the facts. Second, indicate for each sample whether you were inclined to answer "yes" or "no" or neither. Third, critique each sample according to the criteria presented in Chapter 17.

Sample #1

A. Are there genuine issues of material fact precluding summary judgment on the common law claim?

B. Is Defendant entitled to judgment as a matter of law on the common law claim?

Sample #2

Is a commercial seller of alcoholic beverages liable under the common law where an adult purchased and consumed beverages at the seller's establishment and then injured the Plaintiff by driving recklessly?

Sample #3

Is a country club entitled to summary judgment under the common law where the plaintiff was injured by the reckless driving of a patron, that patron drank several beers at the club over the course of several hours and ate food as well, the plaintiff also ate and drank at the club, the plaintiff but not the patron appeared drunk to the club's bartenders, and the patron's blood alcohol level was .10?

Sample #4

Where a club served an adult golfer and friend four drinks over two hours and also served the golfer food, the golfer did not become loud or obnoxious (although her friend did), the golfer and her friend left, the golfer then drove recklessly and crashed, and the friend was injured:

   A. are there genuine issues of material fact, and
   B. is the club entitled to judgment as a matter of law where the law permits recovery in cases where a commercial seller of liquor acts recklessly, but not negligently?

6. Write an introduction or summary on behalf of *Hillside*.

7. Write an introduction or summary on behalf of *Ms. Harrison*.

8. (a) Review the list of facts stated above. If you represented *Hillside*, which facts would you include in your fact statement? List them by number. Are any of them residual facts you would not have included in an office memorandum? Explain.

   (b) Draft the opening paragraph of your fact statement.

   (c) Which organization would you use for the body of your fact statement: topical, chronological, perceptual, or a combination? Why?

   (d) Draft the closing paragraph of your fact statement; assume that you have not included a procedure component.

9. (a) Review the list of facts stated above. If you represented *Ms. Harrison*, which facts would you include in your fact statement? List them by number. Are any of them residual facts you would not have included in an office memorandum? Explain.

   (b) Draft the opening paragraph of your fact statement.

   (c) Which organization would you use for your fact statement: topical, chronological, perceptual, or a combination? Why?

(d) Draft the closing paragraph of your fact statement; assume that you have not included a procedure component.

10.   Assume that you represent *Hillside*. Use an outline or quasi-outline, boxchart, schematic (see Exhibit 17.5), or other device to show how you would combine the substantive and procedural law with the facts in your argument section.

11.   Assume that you represent *Ms. Harrison*. Use an outline or quasi-outline, boxchart, schematic (see Exhibit 17.5), or other device to show how you would combine the substantive and procedural law with the facts in your argument section.

12.   Read the following sample point headings. First, analyze their content by marking each as follows: straight underline for substantive law, squiggly underline for procedural law, and no underline for the facts. Then critique each according to the criteria presented in Chapter 17.

Sample #1

The club is not liable because it did not act recklessly when it served a patron several drinks over a period of two hours and the patron showed no signs of intoxication.

Sample #2

A.   There is no genuine issue of material fact because the testimony of all witnesses on the relevant facts is in accord.
B.   The club is entitled to judgment as a matter of law, where the law affords recovery only when a liquor seller acts recklessly, because the club acted at most negligently in serving several drinks during an afternoon to a patron who was not intoxicated in the eyes of anyone present.

Sample #3

Summary judgment is not appropriate where there is a genuine issue of material fact and the moving party is not entitled to judgment as a matter of law.

A.   There are fact issues because the testimony of some parties conflict.
B.   Defendant is not entitled to judgment as a matter of law because the law does afford a cause of action for recklessness.

Sample #4

The club is liable because it did act recklessly when it served an apparently drunk patron several drinks over two hours.

    A.   Entitlement to judgment as a matter of law
    B.   Genuine issues of material fact

13.   Write improved point headings on behalf of *Hillside*.

14.   Write improved point headings on behalf of *Ms. Harrison*.

EXERCISES FOR CHAPTER 18

FUNDAMENTALS OF ADVOCACY

Read the factual record in the introductory material for the Chapter 17 exercises, as well as the legal materials referred to there. Continue with the same facts and assumptions. Again, Hillside is moving for summary judgment only on the common law counts.

1. (a) Identify and explain a conflict in the record as to an important fact.

    (b) How would you handle that fact if you represented *Hillside?*

    (c) How would you handle that fact if you represented *Ms. Harrison?*

2. (a) Review the procedural rule on summary judgment. What type of rule is it: conjunctive, disjunctive, aggregate, or balancing?

    (b) Review the substantive rules on liability of liquor sellers, as developed in the common law. What type of rules are they: conjunctive, disjunctive, aggregate, or balancing?

    (c) As *Hillside's* counsel, what must or may you do to succeed in your motion?

    (d) As *Ms. Harrison's* counsel, what must or may you do to successfully defend against the motion?

3. (a) If you represented *Hillside,* would any of your potential arguments be alternatives to each other? If so, explain.

    (b) If you represented *Ms. Harrison,* would any of your potential arguments be alternatives to each other? If so, explain.

4. List in a T-chart the main assertions Hillside is likely to make and the probable responses of Ms. Harrison. Identify the points of clash by drawing an X between the clashing assertions.

5. (a) If you represented *Hillside,* would you consider your case to be strong on facts, law, or policy (or some combination)? What is its overall weakness? Explain.

    (b) Identify a case that you would emphasize. Why did you choose that case, and how would you emphasize it?

    (c) Is there an unfavorable case you deem yourself ethically bound to raise even if opposing counsel does not? Explain. How would you handle that case?

    (d) Would you seek to emphasize or de-emphasize the procedural rule? Explain.

    (e) Which facts would you emphasize? Why? How would you emphasize those facts?

    (f) Which facts would you de-emphasize? Why? How would you de-emphasize those facts?

    (g) Is there any policy you would seek to emphasize? Explain.

    (h) Is there any policy you would seek to de-emphasize? Explain.

(i) Based on this analysis, develop your theory of the case. Write it into a pie chart, or state it in a brief sentence, or both.

6.   (a) If you represented *Ms. Harrison,* would you consider your case to be strong on facts, law, or policy (or some combination)? What is its overall weakness? Explain.

(b) Identify a case that you would emphasize. Why did you choose that case, and how would you emphasize it?

(c) Is there an unfavorable case you deem yourself ethically bound to raise even if opposing counsel does not? Explain. How would you handle that case?

(d) Would you seek to emphasize or de-emphasize the procedural rule? Explain.

(e) Which facts would you emphasize? Why? How would you emphasize those facts?

(f) Which facts would you de-emphasize? Why? How would you de-emphasize those facts?

(g) Is there any policy you would seek to emphasize? Explain.

(h) Is there any policy you would seek to de-emphasize? Explain.

(i) Based on your analysis above, develop your theory of the case. Write it into a pie chart, or state it in a brief sentence, or both.

EXERCISES FOR CHAPTER 19

ADVOCACY WRITING IN THE APPELLATE SETTING: THE FUNCTION AND FORMAT OF THE APPELLATE BRIEF

Read the case briefs at pages 499-501 and the statute at page 503. This material forms the law pertinent to the following case:

> The plaintiff, Phillip E. Quinnett, as administrator of the estate of his five year old son, Benjamin L. Quinnett, brought this action seeking damages for the wrongful death of his son.

> The jury might reasonably have found that on December 1, 1983, at approximately 5:15 p.m., Gary Mastrobattisto [then thirty-six years old] stopped at Gindee's bar in New Haven, an establishment operated by the defendants Virginia Newman and Gindee's Corporation, where he remained for two to three hours. During that time, Mastrobattisto consumed three shots of tequila and six twelve-ounce bottles of beer. He thereafter drove to Pickles bar in Branford, an establishment operated by the defendants Brett Kerr and Pacarrie, Inc. (defendants), where he remained for an additional two to three hours. While there, Mastrobattisto drank three more shots of tequila and six more twelve-ounce bottles of beer. Shortly after leaving Pickles bar, Mastrobattisto drove his vehicle across the highway into the lane for oncoming traffic and struck the car carrying the plaintiff's decedent, causing the injuries that thereafter led to his death.

> The suit involving Gindee's bar was resolved by stipulated judgment. The case involving Pickles bar was thereafter submitted to the jury solely on the issue[] of wanton and reckless misconduct. The trial court, J. Flanagan, J., directed the jury to render a verdict for the defendants on the remaining count of the complaint, concluding that, as a matter of law, there is no cause of action based upon negligence . . . in selling alcohol to an adult who thereafter injures another by reason of his intoxication. The jury returned a verdict in favor of the defendants on the recklessness count and as directed by the court on the remaining count[]. The trial court denied the plaintiff's motion to set aside the verdicts . . . and thereafter rendered judgment for the defendants.*

Assume that the Connecticut Appellate Court affirmed, Mr. Quinnett has appealed to the Connecticut Supreme Court, and that court has granted review. Also assume that the following procedural law and standards of review apply:

> In reviewing a trial court decision to direct a verdict for the defendant, the appeals court considers the evidence in the light most favorable to the plaintiff and then determines whether the jury reasonably and legally could have reached a conclusion other than in the defendant's favor.

---

*The citation to this material appears *infra*.

A jury verdict is entitled to acceptance unless the reviewing court can say as a matter of law that the jury's conclusions were such that reasoning minds could not reasonably have reached them.

The trial court has broad discretion in deciding a motion to set aside the verdict on the grounds it is contrary to law and the evidence; that decision will not be disturbed in the absence of clear abuse.

1. If Mr. Quinnett were to appeal his losses on both counts, would the appeal fall within the scope of appellate review? Explain your answer by applying the following rules:

(1) final judgment rule
(2) rule prohibiting new facts on appeal
(3) rule prohibiting new theories on appeal
(4) reversible error rule

2. Assume that the Connecticut Supreme Court uses the factors stated in Chapter 19 in deciding whether to grant discretionary review. Why should it grant review in this case?

3. What legal points must Mr. Quinnett show to win on appeal as to each claim (negligence and recklessness)? Your statement should reflect the standard of review, the procedural law, and the substantive law. Which issue (if either) is he more likely to win? Why?

For the remaining questions, assume that you represent either Mr. Quinnett, the appellant, or Pickles bar, the respondent. (Or answer these questions twice, once for each side.) If you have not yet read Chapter 20, you should think of your answers here as works-in-progress. You may want to return to these exercises to refine your answers once you have read that chapter.

4. (a) Here are two neutral, broad ways of phrasing the issues that could be raised on appeal:

Does a cause of action in negligence exist against a commercial vendor who sells intoxicating liquor to an adult who thereafter, as a consequence of his intoxication, injures another?

On the facts of this case, could the jury reasonably find that the commercial vendor did not act recklessly?

Rephrase the two issues so as to subtly suggest an answer favoring your client. You may introduce sub-issues. Underline the procedural law or standard of review, draw a dotted underline under the substantive law, draw a squiggly line under policy, and leave the facts without an underline.

(b) State the trial court's holding on each issue, from your client's perspective.

5. Write a paragraph setting forth the nature of the case and its relevant procedural history.

6. (a) The facts stated above are presented as a court would phrase them, dispassionately, in a straight chronological order. Would you exclude any of the stated facts? Explain.

(b) On the assumption that the record contained the information you needed, would you include any of the following facts? Why or why not?

    (1) the physical or emotional effects of the loss suffered by Mr. Quinnett
    (2) the events prompting Mr. Mastrobattisto to drink that day
    (3) the condition of his car or of the road
    (4) the economic state of the Pickles bar

(c) List three ways you would alter the presentation of the facts stated above, other than adding or deleting facts.

(d) Write the first sentence of the body of your fact statement.

7.   Sketch out the main topics to be covered in your argument. (See Exhibit 19.6 for one example.) Be sure to include the substantive and procedural law – including the standard of review, policy, and facts, and to convey the relationships among them.

8.   Write a set of point headings for your argument. You may write more than one major heading; you may use minor headings as well. Underline the procedural law or standard of review, draw a dotted underline under the substantive law, draw a squiggly line under policy, and leave the facts without an underline.

9.   Write a summary for your argument. Aim for one paragraph, three to five sentences long. Circle up to ten words you hope your reader will remember best from your summary and from the argument.

Exercises for Chapter 20

Advanced Advocacy

Read the case briefs at pages 499-501, the statute at page 503, and the fact situation at 543.

Consider the following two grounds for appeal in this case: first, that the jury erred in its verdict on the recklessness count; second, that the trial court erred in directing a verdict on the negligence count.

1. Assess the two grounds for appeal from the perspectives of both Mr. Quinnett and Pickles bar. For both recklessness and negligence, consider which side has the stronger case as to the following dimensions of the topic:

   (1) the substantive law
   (2) the procedural rule and standard of review
   (3) the facts
   (4) public policy

For questions 2 through 10 below, assume that you represent either Mr. Quinnett, the Appellant, or Pickles bar, the Respondent. (Or answer these questions twice, once for each side.)

2. Develop a theory of your case linking its legal, policy, and factual dimensions. Remember that the legal dimension is both substantive and procedural. Draw a pie chart, write out your theory, or both.

3. In light of the strengths and weaknesses of your client's case, allocate percentages of the argument to the two main topics and within each topic to the law, policy, and facts.

4. In which order would you present your main arguments? Explain why you chose that sequence.

5. Write the topic sentences for the paragraphs in your argument on the negligence cause of action. Draw a star by the assertions you deem the strongest for your client, and write a question mark by the least convincing assertions. Did you use the sandwich, running-start, or momentum sequences? Explain.

6. Below are sentences that could appear in a discussion of the recklessness cause of action. Re-order them as you would present them to state your client's position most effectively. As appropriate, after each sentence, write a transition to the next sentence. Then write in your introductory and concluding sentences.

   — A jury verdict is to be accepted unless, as a matter of law, reasoning minds could not reasonably have reached the jury's conclusion.
   — When a liquor seller recklessly serves an intoxicated person who then injures a third party, the seller may be liable to the third party.

—   One who acts recklessly must bear great responsibility for his actions, great enough to overshadow the responsibility of the drunk driver.

—   Gary Mastrobattisto drank three shots of tequila and six twelve-ounce bottles of beer over two to three hours at Gindee's bar.

—   Afterward, he drove to Pickles bar, where he stayed for two to three hours.

—   While at Pickles bar, Mastrobattisto drank three more shots of tequila and six more twelve-ounce bottles of beer.

—   Shortly after leaving Pickles bar, Mastrobattisto drove into oncoming traffic and struck the car carrying Benjamin Quinnett.

Does your sequence follow IRAC? Explain.

7.   Re-read the second paragraph of the case description at page 543. Rewrite it so as to favor your client, without changing its content, by use of the syntax and semantic strategies discussed in Chapter 20. (You may re-order the material if you wish.) In the margin, identify your strategies, such as passive voice and vivid language.

8.   Write a sentence or two using one or more of the following rhetorical devices: juxtaposition, allusion, aphorism, anaphora, epistrophe, alliteration, rhetorical question.

9.   Identify a point on which both sides concur and that favors your opponent. Write out your statement of the point and the surrounding material. What type of concession did you present, e.g., confession and avoidance, assuming arguendo? How did you minimize the concession?

10.   Identify an assertion of your opponent that you might choose to state explicitly and rebut. Write out that passage. How did you minimize the statement of the opponent's assertion and maximize your rebuttal?

Assume for the remaining questions that you are a member of the Connecticut Supreme Court.

11.   How would you respond to the following sentences if they appeared in the parties' briefs? If you believe any sentence needs editing, write in your changes.

(1)   Moments after leaving Pickles, Mastrobattisto slaughtered an innocent and unsuspecting child.

(2)   This Court's opinion in *Kowal* disregards the legitimate interests of the driving public in favor of the interests of commercial establishments that place drunk drivers on our state's roads.

(3)   Counsel for Appellant has shown little regard for the principle of stare decisis in her argument on the negligence cause of action.

(4)   How many more children must die before the rule of *Nolan v. Morelli* is overruled?

(5)   Appellant's counsel would have us believe that it is law-abiding establishments, such as the restaurant sued in this case, that cause the regrettable injuries in cases of this sort. But, as this Court knows, it is clear that the culprits are the Gary Mastrobattistos of this world, who are unable to control their deadly impulses.

12. If you were to rule in favor of Mr. Quinnett on the negligence cause of action and thereby change the law, how would you construct your opinion? More specifically, what would you say as to the following:

    (1) current case law
    (2) persuasive precedent
    (3) the equities of the new rule
    (4) the fairness of applying the new rule to the present case
    (5) the limits of the new rule (situations falling within and outside its scope)
    (6) the public policies favoring the new rule

13. If you were to rule in favor of Pickles bar and thereby adhere to current law, how would you construct your opinion? More specifically what would you say as to the following:

    (1) current case law
    (2) persuasive precedent
    (3) the equities of the current rule
    (4) the fairness of applying the proposed rule to the present case
    (5) the limits of the proposed rule (situations falling within and outside its scope)
    (6) the public policies favoring the current rule

Exercises for Chapter 21

Oral Advocacy

Read the case briefs at pages 499-501, the statute at page 503, and the fact situation at 543.

For the following questions, assume that you represent either Mr. Quinnett, the Appellant, or Pickles bar, the Respondent. (Or answer these questions twice, once for each side.)

1.   Write out the introduction to your oral argument before the Connecticut Supreme Court. Include your theory of the case and a roadmap, summarizing the issues or arguments to be discussed.

2.   List the key facts in the order in which you would state them. Then talk through those facts, and time yourself. How long does it take you to state these facts?

3.   Write out and recite the procedural posture of the case. Time yourself. How long does it take you to state the procedural posture?

4.   Prepare an outline of your planned argument. Try to note your assertions concisely, rather than write out lengthy sentences, and be sure to include transitions. Assume you have thirty minutes to argue; allocate fifteen minutes to the assertions you have identified. Mark stars next to the most important material to convey.

5.   Write out the conclusion to your oral argument.

6.   Select the three sources you deem the most likely to be discussed extensively in an oral argument. Write out index cards for each of these three sources, with the name of the source and its most important points.

7.   Write out questions you might be asked, and sketch out your answers. Try to pose and answer at least one question in each of the following categories:

   (1)   question about the facts
   (2)   question about the law
   (3)   question about public policy
   (4)   question about a hypothetical situation
   (5)   question seeking concession
   (6)   question about your opponent's argument

POSTSCRIPT

In *Quinnett v. Newman*, 568 A.2d 786 (Conn. 1990), the Connecticut Supreme Court noted its longstanding rule that there is no proximate cause in a negligence case involving an adult drinker and a commercial seller, as well as the "limited exception" of *Ely v. Murphy*, 540 A.2d 54 (1988), that there is proximate cause when the drinker is a minor and the provider is a social host. *Quinnett*, 568 A.2d at 787. In *Quinnett*, the court declined to expand the *Ely* exception. Instead the court noted that the legislature had provided a remedy for cases such as this (unlike the situation in *Ely*) in the Dram Shop Act, Connecticut General Statutes section 30-102 (1990), albeit with a limitation on the amount of recovery. *Quinnett*, 568 A.2d at 788. The majority also found no error in the trial court's denial of Mr. Quinnett's motion to set aside the jury verdicts, *id*. at 787, and declined to recognize a claim for public nuisance, *id*. at 788–89.

Chief Justice Peters and Justice Hull dissented. *Id*. at 789–91. "The continued existence of the present law is a blot on the social conscience and will, sooner or later, be corrected by this court. Why not now?" *Id*. at 791 (Hull, J., dissenting).

In February of 2003, the Connecticut Supreme Court decided *Craig v. Driscoll*, 813 A.2d 1003 (2003), stating:

> We conclude that sensible reform is appropriate in this area. The issue of whether to recognize a common-law cause of action in negligence is a matter of policy for the court to determine based on the changing attitudes and needs of society. In making such a determination, we are mindful that the law of torts involves the allocation of losses arising out of human conduct, and its purpose is to adjust these losses by affording compensation for injuries sustained by one person as a result of the conduct of another. It seems self-evident that the serving of alcoholic beverages to an obviously intoxicated person by one who knows or reasonably should know that such intoxicated person intends to operate a motor vehicle creates a reasonably foreseeable risk of injury to those on the roadways. Simply put, one who serves alcoholic beverages under such circumstances fails to exercise reasonable care and therefore may be held liable for negligence.

Id. at 1020-21 (citations and footnotes omitted.)

In June of 2003, in Public Act 03-91, the Connecticut General Assembly increased the amount recoverable under the Dram Shop Act to $250,000 and added the following final sentence: "Such injured person shall have no cause of action against such seller for negligence in the sale of alcoholic liquor to a person twenty-one years of age or older."

TABLE OF AUTHORITIES

Note: The following table includes sources on legal reasoning and writing; it does not include authorities pertaining to the HomeElderCare case or the torts exercises. Nor does it include the sources of the chapter-opening quotes.

INDEX